Records of the
Colonial Office, Dominions Office, Commonwealth Relations Office and Commonwealth Office

SOURCES FOR COLONIAL STUDIES IN THE
PUBLIC RECORD OFFICE

Volume 1

Records of the
Colonial Office, Dominions Office, Commonwealth Relations Office and Commonwealth Office

ANNE THURSTON

A revised and expanded version of
Public Record Office Handbook No 3:
Records of the Colonial and Dominions Offices
by R B Pugh

LONDON: HMSO

© *Crown copyright 1995*
Applications for reproduction should be made to HMSO

ISBN 0 11 440246 9

British Library Cataloguing in Publication Data

A CIP catalogue record for this book
is available from the British Library

Printed on acid-free Archival Sovereign Wove

HMSO publications are available from:

HMSO Publications Centre
(Mail, fax and telephone orders only)
PO Box 276, London SW8 5DT
Telephone orders 0171 873 9090
General enquiries 0171 873 0011
(queuing system in operation for both numbers)
Fax orders 0171 873 8200

HMSO Bookshops
49 High Holborn, London WC1V 6HB
(counter service only)
0171 873 0011   Fax 0171 873 1326
68–69 Bull Street, Birmingham B4 6AD
0121 236 9696   Fax 0121 236 9699
33 Wine Street, Bristol BS1 2BQ
0117 9264306   Fax 0117 9294515
9–21 Princess Street, Manchester M60 8AS
0161 834 7201   Fax 0161 833 0634
16 Arthur Street, Belfast BT1 4GD
01232 238451   Fax 01232 235401
71 Lothian Road, Edinburgh EH3 9AZ
0131 228 4181   Fax 0131 229 2734

HMSO's Accredited Agents
(see Yellow Pages)

and through good booksellers

Printed in the United Kingdom for HMSO
Dd 294242   C5   1/95

Contents

		page
PREFACE		xi
LIST OF ABBREVIATIONS		xiii

Chapter 1	*Constitutional arrangements for the Oversea Empire, 1600 to 1968*	1
1.1	Central control of colonial affairs before 1696	1
1.2	The Board of Trade and the secretaries of state in partnership, 1696 to 1782	3
1.3	Colonial affairs under the Home Office, 1782 to 1801	4
1.4	The War and Colonial Department, 1801 to 1854	4
1.5	The Colonial Office, 1854 to 1925	5
1.6	The Colonial, Dominions, Commonwealth Relations and successor Offices, 1925 to 1968	6

Chapter 2	*Internal organization of the Colonial Office, 1795 to 1966*	10
2.1	Office structure, 1795 to 1925	10
2.2	The joint establishment, 1925 to 1947	11
2.3	Reorganization of the Colonial Office, 1925 to 1939	12
2.3.1	Review of office operations	12
2.3.2	Advisory staff	13
2.3.3	Advisory committees	14
2.3.4	Geographical and subject departments	14
2.3.5	Unification of the Colonial Service	15
2.4	Impact of the Second World War on the Colonial Office	16
2.4.1	Geographical and subject departments	16
2.4.2	Advisers and advisory committees	17
2.4.3	Regional organization during the war	17
2.5	Post-war Colonial Office organization	18
2.5.1	The need for reorganization	18
2.5.2	Organizational inquiries	19
2.5.3	Advisers and advisory committees	19
2.5.4	Subject and geographical departments	20

Chapter 3	*Organization of the Dominions, Commonwealth Relations and Commonwealth Offices, 1925 to 1968*	23
3.1	Developments in the Dominions Office, 1925 to 1947	23
3.1.1	Separation from the Colonial Office	23
3.1.2	The Imperial Conference of 1926	23
3.1.3	Extension of the high commissioner system	24
3.1.4	Intra-imperial economic and scientific services	26
3.2	The impact of the Second World War on the Dominions Office	27
3.3	The Commonwealth Relations and Commonwealth Offices, 1947 to 1968	27
3.3.1	Merger with the India Office	27
3.3.2	Relations with the new Commonwealth	28
Chapter 4	*Records of the Colonial Office and its Predecessors, 1660 to 1966*	30
4.1	1660 to 1782	30
4.2	1782 to 1801	32
4.3	1801 to 1925	33
4.3.1	Registration before 1849	33
4.3.2	Registration of in-letters, 1849 to 1925	34
4.3.3	Copying and registration of out-letters	36
4.3.4	The form of original correspondence	36
4.3.5	Circulating and minuting papers	38
4.3.6	Make-up of the records	39
4.3.7	Reorganization of the records	39
4.3.8	Other record series	40
4.4	1926 to 1950	41
4.4.1	Introduction of the file system	41
4.4.2	Arrangement of files and registers	42
4.4.3	Reorganization of the registry and sub-registries	43
4.4.4	Introduction of subject registration numbers	44
4.4.5	Registration of military and economic papers	44
4.4.6	Geographical and subject registration	45
4.5	1948 to 1966	45
4.5.1	The impact of the Colonial Office and Treasury investigations on registration	45
4.5.2	Introduction of the subject code classification scheme	46
4.5.3	Registration by geographical or subject departments	47
4.5.4	Registration by region	47

4.6	Circular despatches and memoranda, savingrams and telegrams	48
4.7	Secret and semi-official communications	49
4.8	Confidential print and other printed records	51
4.9	Acts, sessional papers, gazettes, blue books and newspapers	52
4.10	Related colonial records	53
4.10.1	Records of chartered companies	53
4.10.2	Records withdrawn from Colonial Office record classes	53
4.10.3	Private office papers and private collections	53
4.10.4	Domestic records of oversea governments	54

Chapter 5 *Records of the Dominions Office, Commonwealth Relations Office and Successor Offices, 1922 to 1968* — 56

5.1	1922 to 1930	56
5.1.1	Transition to the file system	56
5.1.2	Introduction of the single dominions correspondence series	56
5.1.3	Communication with dominions governments	57
5.2	1930 to 1936	57
5.3	1936 to 1946	58
5.4	1947 to 1951	59
5.5	1951 to 1967	59
5.6	1967 to 1968	60
5.7	Secret correspondence	60
5.8	Confidential print	60
5.9	Department of Technical Co-operation and Overseas Development Administration records	61
5.10	Central African Office records	61

Chapter 6 *General Information about the records and their use* — 62

6.1	Custody and selection of the records	62
6.2	Access	64
6.3	Means of reference	65
6.3.1	Arrangement of the finding aids	65
6.3.2	Supplementary finding aids	65
6.3.3	Reference by other means	66
6.3.4	Understanding registry codes and procedures	67
6.4	Photographs, posters and maps	67
6.4.1	Photographs and posters	67
6.4.2	Maps	67

Chapter 7		Lists of Ministers and Senior Officials responsible for Colonial, Dominions and Commonwealth Affairs, 1768 to 1968	69
	7.1	Secretaries of state who administered the affairs of the colonies between 1768 and 1794	70
	7.2	Secretaries of state for the Colonial and War Departments from 1794 to 1854	70
	7.3	Secretaries of state for the colonies and Colonial Office ministers	70
	7.4	Colonial Office officials	72
	7.5	Secretaries of state for dominions affairs and Dominions Office ministers	86
	7.6	Dominions Office officials	86
	7.7	Secretaries of state for Commonwealth relations and Commonwealth Relations Office ministers	88
	7.8	Commonwealth Relations Office officials	89
	7.9	Secretaries of state for Commonwealth affairs and Commonwealth Office ministers	93
	7.10	Commonwealth Office officials	93
	7.11	Overseas Development Administration ministers and officials	95
Chapter 8		Colonial Office Advisers, 1926 to 1965	96
Chapter 9		Standing Advisory Bodies to the Colonial, Dominions, Commonwealth Relations and Successor Offices	108
	9.1	Chronological list	109
	9.2	Alphabetical list	110
Chapter 10		Official and Non-Official Organizations, Institutions, etc, Associated with the Colonial, Dominions, Commonwealth Relations and Successor Offices	128
	10.1	Chronological list	128
	10.2	Alphabetical list	130
Chapter 11		Colonial Office Geographical Departments and their Records	159
	11.1	Line chart of geographical department development	160
	11.2	List of geographical record classes with historical notes	162
	11.3	Alphabetical list of territories showing the geographical departments responsible for their affairs, 1861 to 1965	287
	11.4	Breakdown of geographical department business, 1861 to 1965	293

Chapter 12	*Colonial Office Subject Departments and their Records*	310
12.1	Line chart of subject department development	313
12.2	List of subject department record classes with historical notes, 1934 to 1965	310
12.3	Breakdown of subject department business, 1934 to 1966	321
Chapter 13	*Colonial Office Internal Services and other Departments and their Records*	345
Chapter 14	*Dominions Office and Commonwealth Relations Office Departments and their Records*	351
14.1	Breakdown of Dominions Office departmental business	352
14.2	Breakdown of Commonwealth Relations Office departmental business	354
Chapter 15	*Registry Codes*	399
15.1	Abbreviations used in the registration of in-letters, 1849 to 1925	399
15.2	Allocation of Colonial Office file numbers, 1927 to 1951	400
15.2.1	File registration numbers, 1927 to 1934	400
15.2.2	Subject file registration numbers, 1935 to 1951	406
15.3	Colonial Office Economic Original Correspondence (CO 852) file registration numbers, 1935 to 1951	407
15.3.1	CO 852: breakdown by principal subjects	407
15.3.2	CO 852: box location list	415
15.4	Departmental filing codes	415
15.4.1	Colonial Office, 1951 to 1965	415
15.4.2	Commonwealth Relations Office, 1951 to 1966	416
15.4.3	Foreign Office, Commonwealth Office, Diplomatic Service Administration Office (political and functional departments), 1967 to 1968	418
Chapter 16	*Illustrations of Colonial Office Registry Procedures*	421
16.1	Action taken on a letter received from the Treasury in 1901	421
16.2	Action recorded in 1939 on the question of raising a further loan for Tanganyika	423

Preface

This guide is published as a companion volume in the British Documents on the End of Empire Project and as a Public Record Office handbook. It supersedes R B Pugh's earlier work, *The Records of the Colonial and Dominions Offices*, London 1964. Pugh's volume, incorporated here in a revised form, was produced when records were open only to the early part of the twentieth century, and it concentrates on record practices up to about 1925.

From 1925 the structure of the bureaucracy for handling colonial and dominions affairs grew in complexity. Following the passage of the Public Records Act 1967, which reduced the closure period of public records from fifty to thirty years, the need for an update has become increasingly pressing. In the late 1970s Dr (now Professor) J M Lee held a grant from the Nuffield Foundation, and with his research assistant, Ms Jasmina Ljuhar, extended the information about the Colonial and Dominions/Commonwealth Relations Offices to about 1950.

My own work, in which I have been greatly assisted by Ms Lucy Hannan, has been funded by the Economic and Social Research Council. I have sought, in chapters 1–6, to draw together and amplify (for the twentieth century), the work by Pugh and Lee and to extend the coverage to 1968. Chapters 7–16 have been added to facilitate the use of the records and have been cross-referenced to the text. Chapter 11.2 was originally prepared for Pugh's volume by Dr R F Hunnisett of the Public Record Office and was extended substantially in the early 1980s by R Mellor, a former Foreign Office official who later worked for the Public Record Office. The version which appears here has been rearranged, expanded and internally cross-referenced. Chapter 16.1 has been taken directly from Pugh's volume.

Perhaps partly because of the lack of a comprehensive guide, these records have tended to be an under-utilized source, for the study not only of individual territories and regions but of larger policy issues. It is hoped that the additions provided here will enhance the use of the records, opening them as a resource for undergraduate students and making them more accessible to postgraduate students and overseas governments wishing to trace relevant records in the Public Record Office. A second part to the guide is planned to extend researchers' awareness of available sources through an examination of the involvement of other departments of state in colonial affairs and the relevant records they produced, particularly in the period following the Second World War.

I would like to thank the staff of the Public Record Office and of the Records Branch of the Library and Records Department of the Foreign and Commonwealth Office who have so generously provided information toward the preparation of this guide.

Anne Thurston

List of abbreviations

ANZAM	Australia, New Zealand and Malaya
ANZUS	Australian, New Zealand and US Defence Pact, Pacific Security Treaty
BB&S	Basutoland, Bechuanaland Protectorate and Swaziland
BBC	British Broadcasting Corporation
BIS	British Information Service
CAO	Central African Office
CDC	Commonwealth Development Corporation
CDFC	Commonwealth Development Finance Company
CD&W	Colonial Development and Welfare
CELU	Commonwealth Education Liaison Unit
CENTO	Central Treaty Organization
CHBE	Cambridge History of the British Empire
CICT	International Film and Television Council (Conseil international du cinema et de la television)
CO	Colonial Office
COI	Central Office of Information
COS	Chiefs of Staff Secretariat
CRO	Commonwealth Relations Office
CTB	Commonwealth Telecommunications Board
CTCA	Commission for Technical Co-operation in Africa
DAC	Development Assistance Committee
DO	Dominions Office
DTC	Department of Technical Co-operation
EACSO	East African Common Services Organization
ECA	Economic Commission for Africa
ECAFE	Economic Commission for Asia and the Far East
ECE	Economic Commission for Europe
ECLA	Economic Commission for Latin America

ECOSOC	Economic and Social Council (UNO)
ECSC	European Coal and Steel Community
EDC	European Defence Community
EEC	European Economic Community
EFTA	European Free Trade Association
ELDO	European Launcher Development Organization
EPC	European Political Community
ESRO	European Space Research Organization
EURATOM	European Atomic Energy Community
FAMA	Foundation for Mutual Assistance in Africa (South of the Sahara)
FAO	Food and Agriculture Organization
FBI	Federation of British Industry
FO	Foreign Office
GATT	General Agreement on Tariffs and Trade
HMOCS	His/Her Majesty's Overseas Civil Service
IBRD	International Bank for Reconstruction and Development
ICAO	International Civil Aviation Organization
ICTA	Imperial College of Tropical Agriculture
IDA	International Development Association
IDC	Imperial Defence College
IFC	International Finance Corporation
ILO	International Labour Organization
IMF	International Monetary Fund
ITA	Independent Television Authority
ITU	International Telecommunications Union
KAR	King's African Rifles
LPS	Lord Privy Seal
NATO	North Atlantic Treaty Organization
O&M	Organization and Methods Division (Treasury)
OAU	Organization of African Unity
ODM	Office of Defence Mobilization (USA)
OECD	Organization for Economic Co-operation and Development

OEEC	Organization for European Economic Co-operation
PRO	Public Record Office
RAF	Royal Air Force
SCAAP	Special Commonwealth African Assistance Plan
SEATO	South-East Asia Treaty Organization
SUNFED	Special United Nations Fund for Economic Development
TCS	Technical Co-operation Scheme
UAR	United Arab Republic
UKHC	United Kingdom High Commission
UN	United Nations
UNESCO	United Nations Educational, Scientific and Cultural Organization
UNICEF	United Nations International Children's Emergency Fund
UNO	United Nations Organization
UNRRA	United Nations Relief and Rehabilitation Administration
UPU	Universal Postal Union
VSO	Voluntary Service Overseas
WAFF	West Africa Frontier Force
WEU	Western European Union
WHO	World Health Organization
WMO	World Meteorological Organization

CHAPTER 1

Constitutional arrangements for the Oversea Empire, 1600 to 1968

1.1 Central control of colonial affairs before 1696

When Britain first began to plant colonies, royal authority was exerted through and with the advice of the Privy Council. It was only by slow degrees that the management of colonial affairs was brought under a single control, and, until it was, the council, its committees and parallel conciliar bodies met the need. Many short-term experiments, not all of them successful, were made before a relatively satisfactory system evolved. In the early seventeenth century plantations were regarded mainly as sources of raw materials and there was therefore a close association between trade and plantations which sometimes resulted in a single body to advise on both subjects.

The first special conciliar body convened to advise on plantations questions was the Commission of Trade in 1625.[1] It was strictly subordinate to the council, to which it reported and through which its recommendations were effected by order in council. Typical of many seventeenth-century bodies set up to advise the council on particular issues, it was dissolved when it had done so. There was no permanent committee of the council to deal with all plantations affairs until 1634, though there were several temporary bodies concerned with particular territories, the first of which was the commission on Virginia of 1631. These committees or commissions were not always wholly, or even partly, composed of privy councillors but included outside experts. Varied as their constitutions might be, the bodies were all advisory except the Commission for Foreign Plantations (1634 to 1641) which could make laws, remove governors, and hear and determine colonial complaints. Soon after the outbreak of the Civil War it was replaced by a parliamentary commission of eighteen which lasted until 1649.

The Council of State, which temporarily superseded the Privy Council, was the main organ of colonial government from its establishment in 1649 until December 1652. Its standing Committee on Trade and Foreign Affairs was extended to cover the plantations. An active committee, it worked through sub-committees and outside referees. When it came to an end in 1653 the welfare of the plantations lay largely in the hands of the Protector's Council and the Council of State, working either through ad hoc committees or standing council committees not specially concerned with the plantations. Until the summer of 1657 the Trade and Navigation Committee, subordinate to the Council of State, also handled some plantations questions of commercial import. A large body drawn from all parts of the realm, it was composed of official and mercantile elements. From 1656 to 1660 a standing committee on Jamaica and the West Indies, which eventually embraced America as well, dealt with a number of particular questions. It was composed of army officers and London merchants.

During the Interregnum, control of the plantations was exercised without a consistent plan. There were, however, certain common features. There was no single responsible minister or dominating figure; trade questions were associated with the pure administration of the plantations; outside experts were employed as referees either in conjunction with councillors of state or alone, and the council had overriding authority. It employed specialist bodies in a predominantly advisory role.

After the Restoration, plantation affairs began to attract greater governmental interest owing to the belief that colonial trade had an important contribution to make to the national revenue. Out of this grew the administrative system that was to prevail until 1782. In 1660 a Council of Trade and a Council of Foreign Plantations were established. Each was composed largely of merchants and sea captains who were not privy councillors but had expertise in the areas of the councils' work. Each council had its own officers and operated through sub-committees. A Privy Council committee, the Committee for Foreign Plantations, superintended the work. The specialist councils broke down in 1665 and the Privy Council resumed control, which it exercised until 1668. It then formed itself into four committees through which all draft orders in council affecting the plantations had to pass.

In 1670 a specialist council, the Colonial Council, was once again established. Three outstanding features made it important: it was small, its members were paid, and it acted under carefully drawn instructions. It was more competent, active and efficient than any of its successors. Two of its functions were later to play a prominent part in the work of the Colonial Office and its forerunners: the review of colonial laws and the preparation of instructions for colonial governors. In 1672 the parallel Council for Trade, also set up in 1670, was fused with the Colonial Council and the two became a joint Council for Trade and Plantations. The instructions for the new council were revised and formed the groundwork for all the councils or committees that succeeded it.

However, while the council did secure more effective control over the colonies, so far as that could be done by corresponding with colonial governors, it was composed largely of persons who were not the king's ministers and lacked the power to carry through its policies. It was dismissed in December 1674, and the Privy Council Committee once again assumed responsibility. The old council's defects were partially remedied in 1675 by commissioning a special Privy Council committee, the Lords of Trade and Plantations, which exercised uninterrupted authority for twenty-one years. This committee enjoyed real power because it was largely composed of the chief ministers of state.

During the seventeenth century the various conciliar bodies described above had deprived the secretaries of state of the opportunity to exert much influence on colonial affairs. From 1675, however, they were always lords of trade, and occasionally, for example during Sir Leoline Jenkins's term of office (1680–1684), they took a personal interest in colonial work. The southern secretary bore the main responsibility but there was no rigidity. The secretaries were the channel for conveying the king's will to the Lords of Trade and to colonial governors, but they did not acquire a monopoly of correspondence with the governors either at this time or later.

1.2 The Board of Trade and the secretaries of state in partnership, 1696 to 1782[2]

The Privy Council committee of 1675 ended with the revolution of 1688 and was replaced by a new one which the king's secretaries continued fitfully to attend. This body fell from favour during the French war, and Parliament demanded the establishment of a statutory Council of Trade. William III, anxious to safeguard the prerogative, countered in 1696 by abolishing the committee and appointing instead a body called 'the Lords Commissioners for promoting the Trade of our Kingdom, and for inspecting and improving our Plantations in America and elsewhere', usually abbreviated as the Board of Trade.

Nominally a large body comprising all the leading ministers, its effective core was a group of eight paid commissioners, one of whom was named president. The board was to advise the Crown on plantations questions, trade, and the poor law, but in practice the first activity occupied most of its energies. Until 1749 it was mainly concerned with the American colonies, but after the insolvency of the Royal African Company of England African trade problems began to occupy more of its time.

Originally the board had no executive functions. It was required to investigate the administration of justice, examine governors' instructions, consider candidates for colonial appointments, scrutinize colonial legislation with a view to allowance or disallowance, and hear complaints against the conduct of governors. Successive secretaries, in the end exclusively the southern secretaries, leant upon the board increasingly for advice. It was subordinate to the secretaries, but the secretaries were dependent upon it for effective action in many fields of colonial affairs.

In the ensuing eighty years sometimes one partner was prominent, sometimes the other. Between 1714 and 1748 the Board of Trade was less active. Correspondence declined and meetings were fewer and less well attended. For part of this period, between 1739 and 1748, Britain was at war, and the strategic and political aspects of colonial affairs necessarily preponderated over the economic; the secretary was more deeply implicated than normally. In 1748, however, the young and energetic Earl of Halifax was made president of the board. He tried to enlarge his authority through the conversion of his presidential post into a third secretaryship of state, but this was refused. On his resignation in 1761 the board continued to conduct correspondence with governors, but it was deprived of its power to recommend appointments to colonial offices.

These measures depressed the standard of the presidential office, and the board was forced to concede more of its authority to the secretary of state. During the period when relations between Britain and the North American colonies were growing increasingly strained and causing daily anxiety, there was a lack of unity in central control and a domestic struggle for power between the secretaries of state and the Board of Trade. Under the new secretary in 1766 it was at once apparent that there was no place for an independent board, and correspondence between governors and the board was henceforth forbidden; the lords of trade acted only when moved to do so by the secretary. This arrangement was equally transient, for in 1768 a third secretaryship of state was created to which the colonial functions of the southern secretary were transferred. The board's commission was revised and its paid membership reduced to seven; the colonial secretary became president. The board, diminished in status, became an adjunct of the new secretary's department. These arrangements lasted until 1779 when the presidency of the board was again separated from the secretaryship.

1.3 Colonial affairs under the Home Office, 1782 to 1801[3]
With the loss of the American colonies, the Board of Trade and colonial secretaryship were abolished by act of parliament in 1782 (22 Geo III), and until 1801 colonial affairs were in the hands of the home secretary. A small Plantations Bureau was set up in the Home Office but lasted only until 1786, when the Board of Trade, which had been revived in 1784, was established on a permanent footing as adviser to the government on trade and colonial questions. The new board, however, never obtained any powers of direct access to the colonies. Except in the matter of reviewing colonial legislation its authority in colonial questions quickly declined and hardly continued after 1801.

1.4 The War and Colonial Department, 1801 to 1854[4]
In 1794 a third secretary of state was again appointed, with responsibility for managing the war with France; in 1801 after the Treaty of Amiens his responsibilities temporarily declined, and the administration of the colonies was transferred to him. From 1801 therefore the third secretary became a secretary of state for war and the colonies. When hostilities were resumed in 1803, responsibility for the colonies was not withdrawn, but the war effort occupied most of the secretary of state's attention and the colonies were largely neglected for several years. After 1812, however, when Lord Bathurst and Henry Goulburn became respectively secretary of state and parliamentary under-secretary, military affairs were no longer predominant in the office's work. Accordingly, when the war ended in 1815 and the military work declined sharply, the office was able to survive as a mainly colonial department.

The American War of Independence had deprived Britain of a significant proportion of its colonial possessions, although it retained the West Indian colonies, the East India Company's possessions, Gibraltar, St Helena and parts of what is now Canada, so that by the end of the Napoleonic Wars there was the nucleus of a new empire. The conquered territories included Ceylon, the Cape of Good Hope, Mauritius, the Seychelles, the Ionian Islands, Malta, Heligoland, three provinces of Dutch Guiana, and the three West Indian islands of St Lucia, Tobago and Trinidad. In addition, Britain had acquired possession of New South Wales, Van Diemen's Land, Norfolk Island and Sierra Leone. New forms of government were devised for these new colonies.

In 1825 the office acquired a second under-secretary to handle the business of half the colonies. The office holder was a member of parliament, and over the subsequent ten years the practice of distinguishing between the parliamentary and the permanent under-secretary developed. With the appointment of Sir James Stephen in 1836 the office was established as the permanent head of business of the whole department. Stephen was one of the greatest civil servants of the nineteenth century and his influence on the department's work and on its records was profound.

In the decade following the Napoleonic Wars the department began to take steps to consolidate its control of colonial affairs. There were other authorities in competition. Not only did the Board of Trade continue to be involved, but the Treasury,

Customs, Post Office, and Boards of Ordnance and Admiralty, plus the Board of Control dealing with the East India Company and its territories, maintained their own offices in the colonies from time to time and were apt to send instructions at variance with those the governors received from the Colonial Department, as it was now commonly called. These influences gradually declined, but it was not until 1861 that the Board of Trade ceased to scrutinize non-commercial legislation, or until 1869 that the Post Office relinquished the last vestiges of its patronage.

On the outbreak of the Crimean War in 1854 colonial and military affairs were divided and a separate Colonial Office, headed by a secretary of state for the colonies, was established. This development relieved colonial ministers of certain burdens, but the functions of the Colonial Department had already corresponded with its name for years.

1.5 The Colonial Office, 1854 to 1925

By the time the Colonial Office was formally established, political events were already changing the nature of colonial affairs. Convict settlements established in the antipodes from 1788 were fostered by an influx of ordinary settlers in the 1840s after transportation began to wane. Meanwhile, with the abolition of the slave trade and later of slavery, followed by the decision to remove the protective tariff on West Indian sugar, the West Indies became less important, although as humanitarian issues both slavery and the slave trade continued to concern the British government.

Increasingly, the Colonial Office was dealing with a widening range of problems. By the 1870s the constant threat, and eventual outbreak of war in South Africa had raised colonial questions to Cabinet level, while the growth of autonomy in British North America, the Australian colonies and New Zealand introduced the Colonial Office to diplomatic responsibilities. The nature of the office's work continued to expand as new territories were acquired, not only in West Africa but also in Asia with Britain's growing interests in Hong Kong (1842) and Sarawak (1841), and following the transfer of responsibility for the Straits Settlements (Singapore, Penang and Malacca) from the government of India to the Colonial Office in 1867.

This trend continued in the 1870s and 1880s, when the 'scramble for Africa' resulted in Britain's acquisition of many new territories to add to her existing possessions in West Africa (Sierra Leone, the Gambia, and the Gold Coast) and in southern Africa. This period also saw colonial questions become an important theme in European international relations.

The new colonies were at first administered as protectorates by the consular service. Their transfer followed a precedent set in 1880 when Cyprus, acquired as a protectorate in 1878, passed out of the Foreign Office's sphere and became the responsibility of the Colonial Office. Eventually only the Anglo–Egyptian Sudan remained under the Foreign Office. Administratively, the two major developments in this period were the establishment of Crown Colony government, and progressive steps towards responsible government in the colonies of settlement.

These rapid changes naturally left their mark on the office, adding greatly to its labours and swelling the bulk of its records. In addition, the nineteenth century ended with a colonial war in South Africa in which, almost for the first time, the office found itself in the forefront of public attention.

In 1907, in pursuance of a decision of the Imperial Conference, the office was split in two.[5] A new division, under a separate assistant under-secretary, was formed to deal with dominions affairs and the Imperial Conference. The Dominions Division also dealt with certain territories thought to possess special affinities with the dominions: the Western Pacific High Commission territories, Fiji, Northern and Southern Rhodesia, Basutoland, the Bechuanaland Protectorate, and Swaziland. The last three were the dependent areas forming the residuary responsibilities of the high commissioner in and for South Africa after the formation of the Union. Nauru was administered with the Western Pacific High Commission territories until 1921, and then by Australia. Tristan da Cunha came under the Dominions Division from 1921.

Responsibility for the dependencies lay with a Crown Colonies Division which was to remain the core of Colonial Office operations over the next five decades, for in the twentieth century Britain fought no more colonial wars and acquired, in absolute possession, no more dependencies. However, after the First World War certain parts of the former German and Turkish empires were 'mandated' to her. The ex-German colonies comprised Tanganyika and parts of the Cameroons and Togoland; the ex-Turkish territories were Palestine and Iraq.

The creation of the Dominions Division acknowledged the special status of the self-governing parts of the empire, and thereafter the role of the Colonial Office in relation to the dominions declined. Although it attempted to resist the reduction of its position, the First World War accentuated the situation. The Foreign Office handled an increasing number of matters which would normally have fallen to the Colonial Office, and the Committee of Imperial Defence came to play the dominant role in shaping defence policy. With the creation of the Cabinet Office in 1916 the Colonial Office lost even the function of providing the secretariat and machinery for Imperial Conferences. The Imperial War Conferences of 1917 and 1918 were serviced by the Cabinet secretary, Sir Maurice Hankey, rather than by the Colonial Office, and he retained his role when the first post-war conference was held in 1921. The Colonial Office provided support staff, but the Cabinet secretariat maintained its key co-ordinating role. By the 1920s it was too late for the Colonial Office to regain the initiative.

1.6 The Colonial, Dominions, Commonwealth Relations and successor Offices, 1925 to 1968

In 1925 a separate Dominions Office, with its own secretary of state and under-secretaries, was created as a new department of state to deal with the 'autonomous communities within the British Empire'. However, the Colonial and Dominions Offices continued to share a common establishment, and until 1930, and for two short periods thereafter, the same minister cared for colonial and dominions affairs. At other times it was comparatively easy to arrange for one minister to supervise both departments in the absence of the other.

Under the new arrangement the Colonial Office administered the dependent territories, including those allotted to Britain under the League of Nations mandate system, while the Dominions Office was responsible for the conduct of diplomatic relations between Britain and the dominions. In addition to matters relating to Canada, Australia, New Zealand and South Africa, the office had responsibility for Southern Rhodesia and the South Africa High Commission Territories of Basutoland, Bechuanaland Protectorate and Swaziland, and for relations with the Irish Free

State (later known successively as Eire and the Republic of Ireland). The Western Pacific High Commission territories, Fiji and Tristan da Cunha remained the responsibility of the Colonial Office.

The title of the Dominions Office was changed to Commonwealth Relations Office in July 1947, and the secretary of state for dominions affairs became the secretary of state for commonwealth relations. The following month responsibility for relations with India and Pakistan, which then became independent and joined the Commonwealth, was transferred to the Commonwealth Relations Office, and the India Office was abolished. The staff of the India Office was transferred to the new department, as was the staff of the Burma Office when it was abolished the following year. Burma, however, did not become a member of the Commonwealth, and business connected with Burma was transferred to the Foreign Office. Ceylon became a fully self-governing member of the Commonwealth in 1948.

The termination of the mandates in the Middle East at the end of the Second World War, and the rapid transfer of power to self-governing territories between 1957 and the mid 1960s, led to a marked reduction in Colonial Office responsibilities. Most of the former colonial territories became members of the Commonwealth, and relations with them became the concern of the Commonwealth Relations Office.

On the formation of the Federation of Rhodesia and Nyasaland in 1953 the Commonwealth Relations Office became responsible for relations with the federal government as well as continuing to deal with the government of Southern Rhodesia. The governments of Northern Rhodesia and Nyasaland remained the concern of the Colonial Office. In March 1962 relations with the federation and the individual territories passed to a new Central African Office, a department of state created to supervise the dismantling of the federation. Initially under the control of the then home secretary, R A Butler, it was transferred to the newly designated secretary of state for Commonwealth relations and for the colonies in October 1963. The federation was dissolved at the end of 1963, and in April 1964 the Central African Office was absorbed into the Commonwealth Relations Office. See under Federation of Rhodesia and Nyasaland in chapter 11.2.

As the Commonwealth Relations Office continued to assume functions from the Colonial Office, it became increasingly obvious that the offices could not indefinitely carry out separate functions.[6] As early as 1954 there was a Commons debate about the possibility of a merger, and the idea continued to be discussed thereafter. The 1959–1960 Select Committee on Estimates strongly favoured amalgamation, and the issue was debated again in the Commons in 1960.

The creation of the Department of Technical Co-operation in July 1961 was the first step in this direction. In July 1961 overseas aid work and related staff of the Foreign Office, Colonial Office, Commonwealth Relations Office and Ministry of Labour were brought together under the new department. It also took over responsibilities from several colonial research councils and committees formerly subordinate to the Colonial Office, and had concurrent powers with the Colonial Office for the Colonial Development and Welfare Acts. It was headed by the secretary for technical co-operation who had the status of minister of state and was not statutorily responsible to any other minister but operated within the framework of general overseas policies.

In October 1964 the department became the Ministry of Overseas Development under a minister of overseas development. At the same time it acquired from the

Colonial Office, Commonwealth Relations Office, Foreign Office and Treasury responsibilities in the field of technical assistance and development. It also took over responsibility for liaison with the United Nations and its specialized agencies from the Board of Trade, the Department of Education and Science, and the Ministry of Agriculture, Fisheries and Food. The ministry's Science and Technology Department, part of the Natural Resources and Personnel Services Division, became responsible for research bodies such as the Tropical Products Institute and the Anti-Locust Research Centre, which are described in chapter 10.

After the loss of many of its functions to the Department of Technical Co-operation, the Colonial Office remained a viable department of state but declined further in importance. In July 1962 ministerial responsibilites for colonial affairs were added to the duties of the secretary of state for Commonwealth relations. Amalgamation was discussed over the next three years, but the departments continued to be separate establishments, physically and administratively distinct; where a matter was of common interest, the officers conferred at departmental level and decided which should take the lead. In October 1964 the Labour government again appointed separate secretaries of state for the colonies and for Commonwealth relations, with one minister common to both.

By 1965 there was a high degree of liaison between the Commonwealth Relations Office and the Foreign Office. In January, as part of a scheme to unite responsibility for all external affairs within one department, a common Diplomatic Service and Diplomatic Service Administration Office was established jointly between the two. In June the creation of the Commonwealth Secretariat relieved the Commonwealth Relations Office of its responsibility for overall management of the Commonwealth.

In August 1966 the Commonwealth Relations Office and the Colonial Office merged to form a single Commonwealth Office under a secretary of state for Commonwealth affairs. What remained of the Colonial Office became the Dependent Territories Division, and the post of secretary of state for the colonies disappeared a few months later. The scheme was completed in October 1968 by the merger of the Commonwealth Office and the Foreign Office in a single Foreign and Commonwealth Office.

Notes

1   For administrative developments up to 1696 see C M Andrews, *British Committees, Commissions and Councils of Trade and Plantations, 1622–1675*, John Hopkins University Studies in History and Political Science, Series XXVI (1908); G L Beer, *The Old Colonial System, 1660–1754*, Part I (1912).

2   Of the many sources for this period particular mention may be made of C M Andrews, *Guide to the Materials for American History, to 1783, in the Public Record Office of Great Britain, I, the State Papers* (1912); A H Basye, *The Lords Commissioners of Trade and Plantations* (1925); and M M Spector, *The American Department of the British Government* (1940).

3   For information on this period see *Cambridge History of the British Empire*, II (1940), pp 143–145.

4   For the period from 1801 to 1925 see *Cambridge History of the British Empire*, III (1959), pp 711–768, and the sources therein cited at pp 905–907. Also D Murray Young, *The Colonial Office in the Early Nineteenth Century* (1961). For the period after 1925 see Sir C Jeffries, *The Colonial Empire and its Civil Service* (1938) and *The Colonial Office* (1956); Sir Cosmo Parkinson, *The Colonial Office from Within, 1909–1945* (1947); K E Robinson, *The Dilemmas of Trusteeship* (1965); and J M Lee and M Petter, *The Colonial Office, War and Development Policy* (1982).

5   The Imperial Conference is described in chapter 10.

6   The merger of the two offices and the eventual merger with the Foreign Office are discussed in detail in J Garner, *The Commonwealth Office, 1925–1968* (1978) and in J A Cross, *Whitehall and the Commonwealth: British Departmental Organization for Commonwealth Relations, 1900–1966* (1967).

CHAPTER 2

Internal organization of the Colonial Office, 1795 to 1966

2.1 Office structure, 1795 to 1925

From at least 1822 the work of the Colonial Office was organized by branches or departments, each with its complement of clerks. At first these departments were exclusively geographical and other arrangements, described below, were made for handling questions of common concern to several colonies or to none in particular. The office started off with four geographical departments, and, with the possible exception of a short period in the 1840s, the number remained constant until the early 1870s. In 1828 these departments were: Eastern (New South Wales, Van Diemen's Land, Ceylon, Mauritius), North American (including Bermuda), Mediterranean and African, and West Indies.[1] In 1843 it was proposed to create a fifth miscellaneous department by removing particular colonies from each of the existing four, but if this department ever materialized it cannot have lasted long, for by 1849 the geographical departments again numbered four.[2]

In 1867 there was an important regrouping. The Eastern Department lost all Australian and New Zealand business to the North American Department, henceforth the North American and Australian (or Australasian) Department, which managed the affairs of the leading responsible government colonies. In 1871 the department was reconstituted on even more logical lines, for it lost Western Australia and Bermuda, which did not enjoy responsible government, and received in exchange British Columbia, which did. These measures were the first step towards creating the Dominions Office. Between 1889 and 1896 the four departments were numbered 1 to 4 respectively. From this period until 1906 the departments underwent a rapid series of changes to accommodate the acquisition of new territories in Africa.

In 1904 a special section of military liaison officers, seconded from the War Office and concerned with the West Africa Frontier Force, was established; in 1907 responsibilities for the King's African Rifles in East and Central Africa were added. A special branch was established in 1912 to deal with medical work in tropical Africa.

As a result of the acquisition by mandate of the ex-Turkish territories, a new Middle East Department was set up in 1921 with its own assistant under-secretary. This arrangement did not include British relations with Egypt, which were the responsibility of the Foreign Office, nor at first the administration of Aden, since the Treasury insisted that the Indian government should retain financial responsibility. By 1926 the Middle East Department had become a division, but was not subdivided into departments. It was balanced by the Colonies and Protectorates Division which by then consisted of nine departments.

Not all the work of the office was or could be fitted into a territorial framework, for quite a number of matters affected the colonies collectively. Moreover, there was the military work, so long as it lasted, and the management of the common services of the office, including the library and registry. These functions were at first discharged partly by the chief clerk and partly by specially appointed officers who existed at various periods, such as the librarian, the registrar, and the clerk for the parliamentary papers.

The chief clerk, appointed in 1795, was the most senior of the clerks, and between 1843 and 1849 his office achieved departmental status. Thereafter, the chief clerk continued to exist as an office holder, but several new departments, General (1870), Accounts/Financial (1874), and Emigration (1878) gradually took over many of his responsibilities, as described in chapter 13.1.

The development of the geographical departments is set out in detail in chapter 11, and that of the internal services and other departments in chapter 13.

2.2 The joint establishment, 1925 to 1947

When the Dominions Office was separated from the Colonial Office in 1925 a close relationship remained. They continued to use the Downing Street wing of the Whitehall public offices and some of the smaller buildings which housed its overspill until 1947. Largely for the benefit of outsiders, a separation was made on the ground floor between enquiries for each office, but the allocation of other rooms in the building was haphazard, dictated by the needs of the moment. The staff met regularly at tea-clubs or in the corridor.

The offices were linked by a common administrative establishment and by common services manned by clerical staff, such as the Accounts Branch, the Telegraph Section, the Library, the Printing Unit and the Revision of Records Branch. Neither office employed officers of the executive grade before 1947. In this situation the Whitley Council, which brought together the 'official' and 'staff' sides of both offices under the chairmanship of the permanent under-secretary, acquired increased significance.[3] It became a Colonial Office convention for questions of organization and registration to be handled in the first instance by a sub-committee of the Whitley Council, while its staffing committee met annually to review the clerical staff complement in both offices before the preparation of the annual estimates.[4]

Each office had its own registry run by clerical staff. Incoming letters and telegrams addressed to either office went from the Central Opening Section or the Telegraph Section to the appropriate registry, and then to the sub-registry where the papers of the relevant group of administrative departments were handled. Clerical sections also existed in the administrative departments, the greatest concentration of staff being in those departments handling large volumes of routine correspondence, such as the Colonial Office General Department, the Personnel Division, or, after the Second World War, the economic departments.

In addition to the published annual volume of *The Colonial Office and Dominions Office List*, the two offices issued news and notes for internal circulation through the 'Colonial Office and Dominions Office Bulletin'. This symbol of joint establishment was suspended in June 1932. The Colonial Office revived its own bulletin in July 1935, but it was discontinued in November 1937 when the office began to print the staff distribution in work lists and charts on a regular basis. The bulletins are in the record class Establishment Miscellanea (CO 878). The equivalent source of Dominions Office work allocations has been largely destroyed, and there is no parallel to the Colonial Office class.

While the heart of the joint establishment was the common services provided by the clerical staff, the offices were linked by the provision that all staff in the administrative class below assistant under-secretary were in theory interchangeable. In practice, as the offices became increasingly specialized, the value of interchangeability was reduced, but there was still some movement between the Dominions Office and the Colonial Office and, by the 1940s, the colonial services.

The key figure of the joint establishment until 1947 was the establishment officer, who was responsible for the recruitment, promotion and posting of all staff (see 2.3.5). He also supervised office procedures and registry practice. When the joint establishment broke up in 1947 and the Dominions Office became the Commonwealth Relations Office, a separate establishment officer was appointed.

There were also attempts to associate the offices by linking the dominions with colonial territories. Canada took an intermittent interest in the Caribbean, while Australia and New Zealand accepted responsibilities in the South Pacific, although taking a different view of colonial questions from Britain's. South Africa's northward ambitions were a constant source of embarrassment to the Colonial Office, and there was considerable opposition to the Union extending its influence in tropical Africa. Several meetings were held between the offices in early 1943 to involve the dominions with the idea of developing a Commonwealth Charter for the colonial peoples, but they were inconclusive.[5]

2.3 Reorganization of the Colonial Office, 1925 to 1939

2.3.1 Review of office operations

The separation of the Dominions Office from the Colonial Office was one of a number of measures marking recognition of the distinction between the constitutional position of colonies and dominions. It opened the way for a reorganization of the Colonial Office to fit it for a wider role in colonial development. A succession of measures followed, many of them initiated by L S Amery, secretary of state for the colonies between 1924 and 1929, and worked out by a series of committees.

One of the first steps taken was the appointment of a committee chaired by the permanent under-secretary, Sir Samuel Wilson, to examine ways of more effectively co-ordinating the geographical departments' work to meet the needs of the colonies as a whole and to improve the provision of technical advice. The committee, which met in 1928 and 1929, called for a rapid increase in subject specialization, particularly in social and economic fields, and its three reports put forward specific proposals for the appointment of specialist advisers, the improvement of administrative control over the colonies, and interchange of staff between the Colonial Office and the colonies.[6]

Another committee was appointed to review the work of the special private secretary Major R D Furse who, with a small staff, administered the colonial service posts within the secretary of state's patronage and had already conducted a survey of the staffing needs of the agricultural, veterinary, and medical services, and the provisions needed for scientific research.[7] Its recommendations led to the establishment of the Personnel Division. A further committee, set up in 1929 and chaired by Lord Lovatt, recommended that an agricultural service, and possibly a veterinary research service, should be created.

These initiatives set in motion a major reorganization of Colonial Office machinery which continued through the next decade; all of the recommendations were, partially at least, implemented. In practice there was little in the way of a systematic plan. However, in retrospect it is possible to discern a pattern in which the need to secure greater co-ordination in colonial policy and to improve the level of technical advice resulted in the growth of three distinct but interlocking elements: advisers, advisory committees, and subject departments to complement geographical departments. They emerged haphazardly depending on circumstances, with no assurance that the development of one in a particular field would be followed by the other two.

2.3.2 Advisory staff

The appointment of specialist advisers received immediate attention. Although the office had not employed permanent technical or scientific staff, apart from a legal adviser appointed in 1866, an advisory network had developed from the late nineteenth century to solve technical problems. It included specialist committees, ad hoc and permanent, and bureaux, bodies separate from the office such as the Imperial Institute, the Bureau of Hygiene and Tropical Diseases, and the Imperial Agricultural Bureau. There were also long established contacts with experts in such places as the Royal Botanic Gardens and the London and Liverpool Schools of Tropical Medicine. This system was no longer adequate. As a first step toward improving it, Amery began appointing technical advisers, in large measure in response to the then current discussion of empire products and marketing. The advisers are listed in chapter 8.

The number of advisory staff began to grow toward the end of the 1930s but was not systematically expanded until after the Second World War. Advisers were much less tied to routine procedures than were departmental staff, and at least until the end of the war the rationale for their functions was much less clearly articulated or understood. There were no hard and fast rules about the allocation of advisers' work between subject and geographical departments, and they used their discretion to act as a bridge between the two, although they were not empowered to authorize action. Suggestions for the appointment of advisers in various fields were frequently made, and the existence of a suitable candidate was sometimes the determining factor. It was axiomatic that whoever was appointed should command the confidence of both the office and the branch of the Colonial Service involved.

Before the war advisers were sometimes financed, if only in part, by sources outside the Colonial Office parliamentary vote and therefore beyond Treasury control. However, assistant advisers began to be appointed in the late 1930s, and as their numbers increased in the major fields of social policy there was a tendency for the whole advisory system to be regulated within the normal procedures of departmental funding.

The advisers were involved with identifying regional differences across the empire, and were able to take a broader regional approach to technical co-operation and the management of the unified services than were the officers in the geographical departments. They examined regionalization in terms of common services and technical programmes for a number of contiguous colonies, or as the first step towards a closer union between colonies considering federation.

Customarily the advisers corresponded directly with their opposite professional numbers on technical matters, but not about staff and policy. They minuted on departmental files, and their own activities were discussed by senior administrative staff on establishment files. However, with the exception of the legal adviser's files, which were registered from 1949 when the Legal Department was created with executive powers, the advisers' own office papers were regarded as private and can only be found in a systematic form in a private collection such as the Orde Browne papers in Rhodes House Library. The private papers of Sir Christopher Cox, the only officially appointed education adviser, have been deposited in the Public Record Office (CO 1045) and are a major source for the history of education policy.[8]

Lord Hailey's position in the Colonial Office was a special case outside the normal pattern of advisory posts. His authority stemmed from his experiences in India, and from his *African Survey* which provoked much discussion on social policy when it appeared in 1938. At the beginning of the war he was commissioned to undertake another African journey (January–June 1940) to study 'native administration' and make recommendations on constitutional development. Most of his communications within the office were by letter. Occasionally he minuted on files, but less so than the other advisers. He was chairman of the office Committee on Post-War Reconstruction in the Colonies (later the Committee on Post-War Problems) between May 1941 and November 1942, and of the Research Committee established in 1942. His appointment as a constitutional adviser was discussed but did not materialize.[9]

2.3.3 Advisory committees
The use of advisory committees was also greatly expanded as a result of the reorganization, with at least five new ones established between 1927 and 1930. The standing advisory committees are listed in chapter 9. While some committees were essentially technical in nature, others assisted in policy formulation. They were generally chaired by the parliamentary under-secretary with the appropriate assistant under-secretary as vice-chairman; usually the head of the relevant department sat as a member with one of the officers as secretary. Committee members, appointed by the secretary of state, included the highest authorities in Britain on a wide range of scientific and social subjects. The secretary of state was not obliged to refer any matters to these advisory committees nor to accept their advice, but their views were given due weight in the office. Large committees set up sub-committees whenever a subject merited special treatment.

Some of the advisory committees were associated with disbursements from special funds. Notably the Colonial Development Act 1929 provided for an advisory committee to recommend expenditure of development funds. Moreover, some advisory committees had their own source of income. For instance, the Discovery Committee, which sponsored research in the Falkland Islands dependencies, administered a fund to finance exploration, while the Advisory Committee on Education in the Colonies had a Phelps-Stokes Fund grant which supported a part-time secretary.[10]

2.3.4 Geographical and subject departments
Although Amery rejected the idea of comprehensive reorganization along subject lines, the General Department was split in two in 1928 as a first step toward a

division of duties by subject. One side dealt mainly with personnel questions, the other with subjects in which specialist advisers were thought desirable, notably communications, defence, economic development, finance, international relations, labour, and health. A separate Personnel Division was set up in 1930 and is described in chapter 13.

The Economic Department, established in 1934, and the Social Services Department, set up in 1939, had their origins in the increasing office tendency to deal with broad economic and social questions across territorial lines, a pattern which was to grow during and after the Second World War. However, the division of responsibilities between subject and geographical departments was not always clear. Some argued that as the office's role was fundamentally political only the geographical departments should exercise executive authority, and the subject departments should provide supporting staff to advisers and advisory committees. However, this view did not prevail, and the subject departments assumed executive functions of their own. Most topics required interdepartmental consultation, and no department could override another without reference to higher authority. The growth of subject departments and their records is described in chapter 12.

2.3.5 Unification of the Colonial Service

The other significant aspect of the new look at the Colonial Office was the reorganization of the Colonial Service. In 1930 the interdepartmental Colonial Services Committee, chaired by the permanent secretary of the Treasury, Sir Warren Fisher, recommended that the colonial services be unified by designating posts in each territorial administration to be filled by candidates from a common pool, so that any member in a technical field could be considered when a vacancy occurred.[11] A detailed unification scheme was then applied, first to the administrative service, established in 1932, and then to the professional and technical services. The legal service was set up in 1933, medical in 1934, forestry in 1935, veterinary and agriculture in 1935, police in 1936, and customs, geological, postal, and survey in 1938. As the services developed, regular conferences and training courses were held regionally or in Britain, and the Tropical African Service courses at Oxford and Cambridge Universities, approved in 1925 and expanded in 1933 to include Malayan civil servants, also promoted unification.[12]

The mechanics of unification were achieved by the Personnel Division which incorporated Furse and his staff as the Appointments Department and an enlarged staff to deal with promotions, pensions, transfers, conditions of employment and office establishment matters. It was assisted by a Colonial Services Appointments Board, appointed by the secretary of state on the nomination of the Civil Service commissioners.

There was also an attempt to promote closer contact between Colonial Office staff and the colonial services. It was frequently argued that the two should be fused, and the Warren Fisher Committee considered the possibility of staffing the Colonial Office entirely with experienced colonial service officers. This never happened, but the home and field services began to work together more closely under Amery's administration. From 1926 junior administrative staff were required to serve a period with a colonial government to qualify for promotion, and one of the assistant under-secretary posts was opened to governors on secondment. Sir Henry Moore, governor of Sierra Leone, was the first governor to serve in this capacity before becoming governor of Kenya. The convention was continued with Sir Alan Burns in 1940, in between terms as governor of British Honduras and of the Gold Coast, and with Sir William Battershill, from 1941 to 1949, between terms as governor of Cyprus and of Tanganyika.

Amery also encouraged the secondment of colonial service officers, known as beachcombers, to the Colonial Office, normally for a period of two years. With Treasury pressure to increase such recruitment, this became an established feature in the Colonial Office even before a circular despatch of 1935 put it on a regular footing.[13] However, as some governors objected to local knowledge being readily available at the centre, beachcombers did not normally serve in the geographical department supervising the territory from which they were drawn.

2.4 Impact of the Second World War on the Colonial Office

2.4.1 Geographical and subject departments

The war manifestly transformed the context of Colonial Office work. With the need to mobilize the empire's resources to support the allies, the office gave most of its energies to administering emergency controls, defining war aims, and planning for reconstruction. This led to a new concept of what could be achieved from the centre. It also resulted in a greater belief in the potential of planning for economic growth, particularly for production and supply, and a growing emphasis on regionalism. The geographical and subject departments were involved in intensive activity, as demonstrated by the increase in the number of despatches and telegrams sent and received from 7,600 in 1937 to 40,000 in 1944.[14] However, the primary impact of this increased activity was on the subject side of the office.[15]

Initially the war reduced the capability of the geographical departments and the Personnel Department. Between April 1939 and December 1942 the number of administrative officers on the geographical side dropped from 75 to 53, and in Personnel from 83 to 53. The subject departments, on the other hand, expanded, and in the same period the number of administrative officers increased from 66 to 170.[16] As they intensified their work on production and supply questions and began to provide broad subject management across different regions, their interests tended to conflict with those of the geographical departments. Soon after the outbreak of war the permanent under-secretary issued instructions on consultation between the two and suggested that the geographical departments should arrange to see duplicates of despatches sent by the subject departments.[17]

New subject departments were established during the war, including Defence, Public Relations, French Relations, Prisoners of War and Civil Internees, Welfare and Students, and Communications, as described in chapter 12.2. The Military Section, which had previously dealt with the West Africa Frontier Force and the King's African Rifles, now became part of the Defence Department and was expanded to handle all work in connection with the African colonial forces and local forces of all other dependencies.

Even more important than the proliferation of new subject departments was the growth of the Economic Department as a result of the demands of war production and supply, and of the need to formulate plans for post-war reconstruction. By the end of the war the economic departments (Finance, Supplies, Production, Marketing, and Research), massively outpaced the Social Services Department. The shift in basic responsibility for colonial development to the economic side reflected and encouraged the new emphasis on long-range economic planning as opposed to the pre-war emphasis on social welfare, and it paved the way for the revised Colonial Development and Welfare Act of 1945.

2.4.2 Advisers and advisory committees

A variety of new advisory posts, listed in chapter 8, were created during the war, particularly as a result of the discussions on post-war reconstruction beginning in 1942. The discussions stressed the importance of the advisory service and urged its expansion, while pointing out the danger that its advice might conflict with the office's executive departments. This led to a more careful consideration of the advisers' role. Their constitutional and legal position was considered at the end of 1942, and a directive issued in April 1943 emphasized that their function was to use their special knowledge to assist the secretary of state, and to advise the administrative officers. In addition, an attempt was made to institutionalize regular meetings between the advisers and the official staff.[18]

The advisory committee system was also expanded, as set out in chapter 9, again particularly following discussions on post-war reconstruction in 1943. By 1945 it was a convention to distinguish between advisory committees which handled policy and those dealing with research. Research committees generally appointed their own secretaries who could then act as figures in their own professions.

2.4.3 Regional organization during the war

The wartime supply and production arrangements, instituted to mobilize imperial resources, particularly raw materials, stimulated a new degree of regional co-operation.[19] To a large extent co-ordination was achieved through the existing regional governors' conferences in East, Central and West Africa. In addition, the prime minister appointed a number of special Cabinet ministers to reside in regions important to the war effort including West Africa, the Middle East and the Far East. Ministers resident were also appointed to the allied headquarters in North West Africa, and to Washington to handle supply questions. The governors' conferences and regional ministers' posts are described in the relevant regional entries in chapter 11.2.

These arrangements were underpinned by the creation of marketing boards to regulate the sale of colonial products. By 1940 the Colonial Office was deeply involved in the problem of securing export markets for colonial producers cut off from their regular customers, and in 1941 it set up a committee to examine alternative uses of raw materials. The West Africa Produce Control Board and the Colonial Products Research Council, set up in 1942, provided marketing and research precedents which the economic departments followed.[20]

Reconstruction planning for the eastern territories involved close interdepartmental effort. A centre for post-war planning, the Malayan Planning Unit, was set up in the War Office Directorate of Civil Aviation in July 1943 and was in constant contact with the Colonial Office Eastern Department.[21] In July 1944 the Colonial Office set up a new department, hived off from the Eastern Department, to concentrate on reconstruction questions for the eastern territories. The department's correspondence is in CO 865. Between November 1943 and 1945 the office also produced a special series of circular memoranda on major reconstruction questions to keep the colonial services in touch with current policy decisions.[22]

Regional thinking led to a number of special new appointments.[23] In 1941 a Colonial Office adviser was posted to Delhi as chairman of the Eastern Group Supply Council, while another was sent to Washington to take charge of Colonial Office business in the British Colonial Supply Mission. The next year an adviser was posted to Dakar as head of the Allies' Economic Mission in West Africa, and a fourth adviser was sent to Accra to join the resident minister's staff.

More important than these essentially wartime expedients was the appointment as comptroller for colonial development and welfare in the West Indies of Sir Frank Stockdale, who had been the office's principal adviser on tropical agriculture. He was appointed to the post in 1940 to follow up the West India Royal Commission's recommendations and initiate implementation of the Colonial Development and Welfare Act 1940.[24] His office in Barbados, described in chapter 11.2, provided a body of experts who undertook regular reviews of the region's needs and framed development schemes in collaboration with colonial governments. When Stockdale was appointed to the new post of development planning adviser in 1944 it was a major step in the development of post-war reconstruction.

The trend toward regional thinking became a regular feature of colonial policy after the war. Regional co-operation was regularly encouraged to facilitate shared knowledge and experience and achieve economy by the unified control of technical services.

2.5 Post-war Colonial Office organization

2.5.1 The need for reorganization

The end of the war brought a gradual reorientation of Colonial Office activities and a new set of demands. Work connected with military operations, wartime trade, shipping controls, and the organization of colonial economies on a war footing declined, and efforts were redirected toward expanding development activities and strengthening economic and social services. Moreover, the post-war economic crisis, the emphasis on constitutional evolution toward self-government, and the growing international interest in the colonies increased the complexity of administrative work and necessitated wider consultation in Whitehall and beyond, with the office participating in an increasing number of high level interdepartmental committees. Whereas twenty years earlier the greater part of the office's correspondence had been with colonial governments, now it was with outside departments and organizations. As the office assumed an increasingly directive role in initiating development, the subject departments were expanded and rearranged, advisory staff increased, and central technical services strengthened.

This post-war expansion compounded existing strains in the office structure. Whereas in 1928 there had been four advisers, by the end of the war there were eleven, with a number of assistant advisers; the handful of advisory committees had become many, and the seven geographical departments and one subject department had become eight geographical and eighteen subject departments.[25] This had led to a fundamental problem of division of responsibility between the geographical and subject departments, for with the balance of work weighted on the subject side, the geographical departments increasingly felt that apart from political questions they were left with only routine work, and that their primary functions were undermined. Moreover, rapid personnel changes contributed to delay, discords, duplication of effort and overlap of functions.

These organizational problems were exacerbated by the physical dispersal of staff, which had resulted, even before the war, in an increasing number of outhoused services. During the war the staff had grown from 400 to over 800, and various office buildings had been acquired to accommodate it.[26] It was decided that the Colonial Office should give up its Downing Street offices and move to a separate headquarters building which could accommodate all its departments and divisions under one roof. At the end of the war Church House was leased from the Church of England as a temporary measure. This building, and later Sanctuary Buildings opposite in Great Smith Street, was to house the greater part of the Colonial Office from 1947 onwards. Plans for a new building continued to be discussed until the mid 1950s, when they were abandoned.

2.5.2 Organizational inquiries

The need for a full scale inquiry into the organization of the Colonial Office was recognized by its own officials and by outside observers. Late in 1947, at a time when the convertibility crisis had resulted in a major reorganization of economic planning across the government, the office sought assistance from the Treasury Organization and Methods Unit.[27] The Cabinet, determined to apply economic development to the African and other colonies, decided to review and strengthen Colonial Office machinery.[28] Though delayed by the dissolution of the joint establishment with the Dominions Office and the Colonial Office's move to Church House, the O & M inquiry got under way in November 1947, while a Colonial Office Organization Committee under Sir Thomas Lloyd, under-secretary of state for the colonies, was appointed in April 1948.[29] Both looked closely at the relationship between geographical and subject departments, and where to place overruling authority.

The Organization Committee's June 1949 'Lloyd Report' stressed that subject departments should deal with matters of general interest and geographical departments with matters relating to specific territories, allowing discretion in dealing with issues of a primarily specialist or technical nature. Both types of department were to retain executive authority, but a subject department could not authorize a charge on colonial government funds without the consent of the geographical department concerned. A limited number of functions were to be transferred from subject to geographical departments, but essentially the respective spheres of the departments were considered correct.

The committee's discussions prompted various organizational changes. Notably a new post of minister of state for colonial affairs was created, responsibilities at the top of the office were reallocated, the Economic Division was strengthened and reorganized, and registries and registry practices were overhauled as described in chapter 4.5.1–3.

2.5.3 Advisers and advisory committees

With the new emphasis on economic development, the number of advisers and assistant advisers was systematically expanded after the war, as described in chapter 8, to create a comprehensive pool of technical expertise. Seven new advisory posts were created between 1947 and 1949 and others were established during the 1950s, the last new post being established as late as 1961 shortly before nearly all the advisers were transferred to the Department of Technical Co-operation. Moreover, an increasing number of outside specialists was drawn in to advise, including the chief medical officer, the head of the African Studies Branch, the principal of the Colonial Products Advisory Bureau, and the directors of research institutes. For a brief period from 1948, four economic liaison officers and a director of economic investigations were appointed to travel in respective regions of the empire monitoring such matters as supplies and hard currencies.[30] These posts were discontinued after 1951.

The number of advisory committees also increased rapidly after the war due to the complexity and range of problems which the office had to address, and the need to extend the field of consultation and the supply of specialist advice. By 1948 most of the pre-war committees had been reconstituted, and a dozen new committees had been added reflecting expanding areas of Colonial Office interest. Sub-committees were set up to consider particular problems where necessary.

The committees were usually concerned with particular subjects and were, with few exceptions, the responsibility of a subject department. About half of the subjects they covered were ones for which the office had a principal adviser, and in most other cases advisers were associated with the work of the committee. Their membership included Colonial Office officials and outside members representing other government departments, organizations with colonial interests, educational or scientific organizations, etc. No limits were placed on the size of the committees, which usually ranged from less than a dozen to just over two dozen members. Members tended to serve for a term of three years.

Matters to be placed before a committee were normally determined by the head of the relevant department, in consultation with the appropriate adviser. Usually they concerned more than one territory, and some involved prolonged research and discussion. Research committees were mainly concerned with schemes to be financed wholly or in part from UK funds under the Colonial Development and Welfare Acts.

2.5.4 Subject and geographical departments

In 1947 the Africa Division expanded its scope considerably. While Malaya was by far the more important dollar-earner, Africa was seen as the most promising field for large-scale new development, and it was hoped that African farmers could be encouraged to move from hand-cultivation to mechanization and expansion of exports. The office took a much greater initiative in policy-making than ever before, but at the same time it attempted to include a broad range of opinion in development planning for Africa. The African Governors' Conference in London in 1947 was intended to open up policy discussions, and the same year the first summer school for officers serving in Africa was held in Cambridge to discuss local government policy. Various administrative topics were discussed at successive summer schools. The African Studies Branch was established in 1948 to carry out social research in relation to administrative problems and is described in chapter 11.2 under Africa.

Responsibilities of the other geographical departments remained relatively constant until the 1950s when, with the rapid transfer of power to independent governments, they began to decline rapidly. In its last year, the office was reduced to greatly diminished geographical departments responsible for the remaining dependent territories.

The subject departments, largely responsible for technical development, did not experience the same contraction until the early 1960s. Although few new departments were created after the war, there were many changes involving renaming, amalgamation and reallocation of duties, as set out in chapter 12. The economic departments, which by 1949 accounted for one-third of the administrative establishment of the Colonial Office and oversaw colonial economic planning, were the most affected.

The transfer of technical assistance work to the Department of Technical Co-operation in 1961 marked the end of the Colonial Office's independent status. This transfer included the Communication Department, Social Service Department 'A', part of Social Service Department 'B', part of Economic Department 'A', part of the Finance Department, the Research Department, part of the Production and Marketing Department, the Students Branch, the African Studies Branch, some work from the Information Department, the Directorate of Overseas Surveys, the Anti-Locust Research Centre, and the Overseas Services Resettlement Bureau. Most of the advisory staff and the whole of the Overseas Service Division were also transferred.

Over the next several years there was an overlap of functions between the Colonial Office and the DTC. For instance, within the DTC the Communications Department looked after such subjects as air services, agreements, shipping, other forms of transport, and telecommunications, all of which still closely concerned the Colonial Office. Consequently the department liaised with the Colonial Office geographical departments and was effectively regarded as a Colonial Office department. It was transferred back to the Colonial Office in 1964. Similarly, although the Overseas Division had become part of the DTC, the Colonial Office was still responsible for transferring, promoting and disciplining its members; the division continued to make recommendations and submit advice directly to the Colonial Office through the geographical departments.

The transfer of ministerial responsibility for colonial affairs to the secretary of state for Commonwealth relations in July 1962 further reduced Colonial Office autonomy. However, the office continued to exist as a separate establishment, and where a matter was of common interest the officers conferred at the departmental level and decided which would take the lead. A separate secretary of state for colonial affairs was appointed again in October 1964, but the merger with the Commonwealth Relations Office in August 1966 brought the remaining geographical responsibilities under the Dependent Territories Division in the new Commonwealth Office.

Notes

1 D Young, *The Colonial Office in the Early Nineteenth Century* (1956), pp 54–55.

2 CO 878/2, no 17.

3 CO 878/21/1045.

4 For instance CO 866/30/1167.

5 CO 323/1831/4433, part 2.

6   CO 885/30, Colonial Office Organization Committee: Interim and Final Reports, 1928 (Conf Print Misc no 391).

7   K E Robinson, *The Dilemmas of Trusteeship* (1965), pp 40, 62–63.

8   At the time of writing, Sir Christopher's papers have not been arranged, but may be seen with prior notice.

9   See R D Pearce, 'Lord Hailey and Colonial Office Thought on African Policy', *The Turning Point in Africa: 1938–1948* (1982).

10   J S Lewis, *Phelps–Stokes Reports on Education in Africa* (1962), p 10.

11   CO 866/6/99086; CO 885/33, Report of the Administrative Service Sub-Committee of the Colonial Service Committee, 1931 (Conf Print Misc no 426).

12   Robinson, *op cit*, p 42.

13   CO 866/12/28553.

14   Sir John Shuckburgh, 'Official History of the Colonial Office During the Second World War', vol IV, part 6, p 209. The history was originally written for the Cabinet Office series edited by Sir Keith Hancock and can now be consulted at the Public Record Office (CAB 102/140–141) or at the library of the Institute of Commonwealth Studies.

15   J M Lee and M Petter develop this theme in *The Colonial Office, War and Development Policy* (1982), pp 59–65.

16   *ibid*, p 63.

17   CO 866/16/1015.

18   CO 866/30/1619. See also Lee and Petter, *op cit*, p 178.

19   *ibid*, chapter 3, 'The Mobilisation of Resources'.

20   CO 852/346/10; CO 852/482/12. See also Colonial Products Research Council in chapter 9.

21   CO 825/43/55104.

22   CO 323/1842/6657.

23   CO 878/27.

24   CO 866/39/1362.

25   Sir Cosmo Parkinson, *The Colonial Office from Within, 1909–1945* (1947), p 56.

26   Lee and Petter, *op cit*, p 62.

27   CO 866/32/1293.

28   CAB 21/1690.

29   CO 885/118, Report of the Colonial Office Organization Committee (Conf Print Misc no 516); the files on the committee are in CO 866/49 and 50. See also T 222/181–183 and 525–526.

30   CO 866/59/1902/3.

CHAPTER 3

Organization of the Dominions, Commonwealth Relations and Commonwealth Offices, 1925 to 1968

3.1 Developments in the Dominions Office, 1925 to 1947[1]

3.1.1 Separation from the Colonial Office
The growing strength and sense of nationhood of the dominions after the First World War led to an increasing dissatisfaction with the Colonial Office as the forum for the conduct of business between the imperial and dominions governments. Work related to both the colonies and the dominions had become more complex, and suffered from their business being handled by one office. There were mutual advantages to a continued association between the dominions and Britain, but the form and machinery required for its articulation were open to question.

When L S Amery was appointed secretary of state for the colonies in November 1924 it was on condition that a new department of state be created for the dominions. Upon the establishment of an independent Dominions Office in June 1925, Amery took up the post of secretary of state for the dominions concurrently with that of secretary of state for the colonies and was responsible for the reorganization of both offices.[2] The original establishment, consisting of one permanent under-secretary, one assistant under-secretary, two assistant secretaries, one acting assistant secretary and four principals, was gradually expanded as set out in chapter 7. The office's work was initially undertaken by three departments, A to C, as it had been under the Colonial Office, and was organized partly on a subject and partly on a geographical basis. Its subsequent development is described in chapter 14.

By 1925 Amery was already working on proposals to change the machinery for dealing with the dominions, now sometimes referred to collectively as the Commonwealth, to be raised at the Imperial Conference in October 1926. An interdepartmental Cabinet committee had been appointed in February 1925 to report on the organization for the conference.[3] It established the goal of extending the high commission system, whereby the dominions were represented in London by high commissioners, throughout the Commonwealth.

3.1.2 The Imperial Conference of 1926
The conference resulted in a number of significant decisions on the status of dominions, and on the conduct of relations between Britain and the dominions. Much of the work was handled by the Inter-Imperial Relations Committee consisting

of prime ministers and heads of delegations, presided over by Lord Balfour. Its report, adopted unanimously by the conference, came to be known as the Balfour Declaration.[4] This defined the position and mutual relations of Great Britain and the dominions in the following terms:

> 'They are in autonomous Communities within the British Empire, equal in status, in no way subordinate one to another in any aspect of their domestic or external affairs, though united by a common allegiance in the Crown and freely associated as members of the British Commonwealth of Nations.'

The report went on to declare that in practice 'existing administrative, legislative and judicial forms are admittedly not wholly in accord' with the position set out in the declaration. This opened the way to an extensive review and to changes in organizations.

In addition, the report examined the position of the governors-general, who represented the monarch but served also as representatives of the British government. It recommended that they should continue to represent the sovereign, but that the channel of communication with the dominion governments should be through high commissioners as representatives of the British Government.

Resolutions of this conference and those of the Imperial Conference of 1930 were given effect by the Statute of Westminster of 1931.

3.1.3 Extension of the high commissioner system

After 1926 the Dominions Office organized itself to act as the channel of communication between the British Government and the dominion governments, which now formed a looser, more dispersed, yet arguably stronger Commonwealth. Broadly speaking, its functions were diplomatic and political, in common with the Foreign Office, as opposed to those of the Colonial and India Offices which were directive and regulatory. It advised ministers on aspects of British policy likely to affect members of the Commonwealth, co-ordinated British departmental views on Commonwealth countries' policies, and advised the Cabinet on relevant policy matters. The office also provided information on matters of common concern, promoted co-operation between the UK and the dominions in trade, commerce and other affairs, and facilitated consultation between dominion governments on foreign and defence policy matters.

The period between the 1926 Imperial Conference and the Second World War was characterized by attempts to establish effective liaison arrangements between Britain and the dominions by gradually linking up and multiplying channels of overseas communication. At the time the office was created there was a well-established pattern of dominions representation in London but no regular system of British representation in the dominions.

In the later part of the nineteenth century the self-governing territories had appointed agents-general in London who performed services for them on the lines of the Crown Agents on behalf of the dependencies. Gradually the agents-general were replaced by high commissioners. The high commissioners were not representatives of the sovereign but of the government. They could not therefore be accredited to the head of state in the normal manner of the diplomatic corps, at least not while the British monarch was the ruler of the dominions as well as the United Kingdom.

Canada established a high commissioner's office in London in 1880. New Zealand, Australia and South Africa followed suit in 1909, 1910 and 1912 respectively, and

Ireland and Southern Rhodesia in 1924 and 1925. In the period following the war the dominions made increasing use of their representatives.

The British counterpart of colonial or dominions agents-general had been trade commissioners. In 1908 there were four trade commissioners in the dominions. They were transferred to the Department of Overseas Trade when it was set up in 1917. The department had close ties with the Dominions Office until 1946, when it was absorbed into the Board of Trade.

Britain's only precedent for diplomatic representation in the dominions was in Australia where the trade commissioner's commercial post had recently been combined with that of liaison officer; a representative for migration had also been appointed to Australia in 1925.

In 1927 a Cabinet committee, chaired by Lord Balfour, was set up to consider appointing British officials to the dominions.[5] At first the majority of the Cabinet rejected the idea for fear that it would encourage dominions separatism. The Treasury opposed the recommendations on the grounds of expenditure, and the Foreign Office considered that its representatives should cover the whole world. However, when the United States appointed its own ambassador to Ottawa in 1928 Britain agreed to follow suit and a high commissioner's office was opened in Ottawa the same year.

In the years that followed, a network of high commissioners representing Britain and the dominions was developed piecemeal. In 1930 Britain appointed a high commissioner in South Africa. Initially neither Australia nor New Zealand wished to formalize its relationship with Britain in this way and instead asked for a more informal liaison. Australia had already, in 1924, appointed a liaison officer in London who had direct access to the Cabinet secretary and the Committee of Imperial Defence. Britain reciprocated by asking its trade commissioner to combine his commercial post with that of liaison officer. Meanwhile a Foreign Office official was seconded to the Prime Minister's Office in New Zealand. British high commissions were later established in Australia in 1936 and in New Zealand in 1939. No high commissioner was appointed to the Irish Free State as it was thought that such an appointment would obscure the essentially subordinate nature of that state embodied in the Anglo–Irish Treaty of 1921. However, a special representative was accredited to the government at the beginning of Second World War. There were no comparable forms of liaison with Newfoundland in the period before Newfoundland relinquished dominion status in 1933 (see chapter 11.2).

The post of British high commissioner in Pretoria was anomalous in Commonwealth relationships to the extent that it was combined with the office of high commissioner for the three dependent territories outside the Union – Basutoland, Bechuanaland and Swaziland. These territories were administered by the Dominions Office rather than the Colonial Office but qualified for aid under the Colonial Development Acts and received some technical advice from the colonial services.

The extension of the high commissioner system between the other members of the Commonwealth began in 1938 with South Africa's appointment of an accredited representative in Ottawa. After the outbreak of war in September 1939 the Canadian prime minister appointed high commissioners in Australia, New Zealand and South Africa; Australia appointed a high commissioner in Ottawa in 1940.

The result was a corps of high commissioners in the important capital cities of the Commonwealth linking the governments. The high commissioners had direct access to ministers and departmental heads and to confidential information and documents not granted to foreign representatives, so that messages moved easily between the British government and the dominions. The system strengthened the empire structure and provided a unifying factor as the Commonwealth grew. The high commissioners' weekly meetings with the secretary of state for the dominions enabled them to play a leading part when day to day contact was necessary during a diplomatic crisis, such as the German move into the Rhineland in 1935.[6]

Nevertheless, the high commissioners were frequently by-passed by direct communications between prime ministers, who were reluctant to jeopardize their control over foreign policy by relying upon high commissioners in London who might be vulnerable to influence from Whitehall, while Britain treated the high commissioners as a source of information on dominions attitudes and favoured recipients of information, rather than as an integral part of the consultations for foreign policy formulation.

3.1.4 Intra-imperial economic and scientific services

The Dominions Office, as the focal point for intra-imperial service, co-ordinated the exchange of economic information and co-operation in research.[7] Trade was the primary concern until overtaken by defence matters in the Second World War. Senior staff kept in touch with the dominions by making tours, but unlike the Colonial Office the Dominions Office had no specialist advisers. Instead it established specialist institutes as agencies to serve the empire as a whole. Committees were set up at the Imperial Conferences as well as standing committees, which are described in chapters 9 and 10. Of these the Imperial Economic Committee, the Imperial Communications Advisory Committee and the Imperial Shipping Committee were the most significant, while the Empire Marketing Board was another important Dominions Office initiative in intra-imperial trade.

The Imperial Conference of 1930 paid particular attention to the subject of intra-imperial trade through its Committee on Economic Co-operation. This committee met again at the Imperial Economic Conference in Ottawa in July 1932 to examine the promotion of trade and economic co-operation. At that time a new set of trade agreements was negotiated including special provisions relating to the non-self-governing colonies, protectorates and mandated territories. Under these 'Ottawa Agreements', Britain imposed substantial restrictions on foreign imports and guaranteed either free entry or a preference to most Commonwealth products in return for a preferential rate for her exports.

The Dominions Office had limited departmental autonomy in economic affairs. After the Ottawa Conference it set up a department charged solely with economic matters, but it had to defer to the Treasury, the Board of Trade and other departments, while currency and finance questions were handled by the Bank of England. Moreover, between the wars financial relations between London and the dominions capitals tended to be the realm of the City of London, which met the dominions' requirements for development capital.

The Dominions Office was also continuously concerned with securing more effective means of maritime transport, postal services, and telegram and telephone communications. Air services developed as a significant form of transport during the 1930s and the dominions were encouraged to expand them on a co-operative basis.

The most significant achievement was the inauguration of an Empire Air Mail Service in 1937.

3.2 The impact of the Second World War on the Dominions Office

The war widened the scope of Commonwealth consultation and co-operation. The high commissioners in London met on a daily basis with the secretary of state for the dominions to hear Foreign Office telegrams and military reports, at times joined by the foreign secretary. They also met the prime minister at intervals. The system was somewhat inhibited by the fact that while the dominions secretary usually attended War Cabinet meetings, he was not a member, except between February 1942 and September 1943.[8] Nevertheless the dominions' vital support for Britain's war effort brought them closer to the centre of power.

As strategic plans evolved, economic relations were monitored centrally. The Dominions Office became involved in such matters as exchange control within the sterling area; supply and procurement of munitions, hardware, raw materials and foodstuffs; and financing purchases on a vast scale. War production in Canada, and to a lesser extent Australia, rose dramatically, and the dominions assumed a new importance in world trade.

The Dominions Office in turn began to play a different role in Whitehall.[9] It remained continuously in contact with the Prime Minister's Office and developed a close relationship with the Ministry of Defence and the Military Secretariat at the War Cabinet Office. It was also involved with the new wartime departments (the Ministries of Economic Warfare, War Transport, Supply, Production, Food, and Information). Particularly toward the end of the war when post-war planning questions were to the fore, it co-operated effectively with the Treasury and the Board of Trade.

As the dominions could now make their voices heard in international debate, the major British departments of state often derived value from associating the Dominions Office in their discussions. The similar nature of Dominions Office and Foreign Office functions was increasingly accepted, and they too began to co-operate more closely, particularly as the Foreign Office was responsible for relations with two major allies and the Dominions Office for four.

Moreover, the war altered the relative status of the Dominions Office and the Colonial Office. The Dominions Office had been the smaller, weaker partner, but as its position was elevated this relationship began to be reversed. Moreover, the accelerated time scale which emerged during the war for transforming dependent into self-governing territories blurred the line between the two offices.

3.3 The Commonwealth Relations and Commonwealth Offices, 1947 to 1968

3.3.1 Merger with the India Office

With the creation of the Commonwealth Relations Office out of the Dominions Office in August 1947, the India Office was abolished and its staff transferred to the CRO. Initially the two offices continued to exist more or less side by side, the old

Dominions Office as Department A and the old India Office as Department B, each with its own permanent under-secretary and sub-officials. The integration of senior India Office officials into the existing CRO hierarchy was not easy, especially as the staff of the former was nearly five times larger, but in January 1949 the office was unified under one permanent under-secretary.[10] A major reorganization that year reduced its twenty departments to seventeen arranged on a functional basis in several divisions as had been the tradition in the Dominions Office. This pattern continued until the early 1960s when more weight was given to the division of work by region. See chapter 7 for a description of the staff structure of the CRO and chapter 14.2 for a breakdown of departmental business.

The merger with the India Office intensified the widening gap between the Colonial and Commonwealth Relations Offices, although the Colonial Office, with its responsibility for the vast dependent empire, remained the more important department. Its move to Church House in the summer of 1947 left the Downing Street building to the new CRO, along with the old India Office wing. This marked the end of the joint establishment and many other aspects of close relations between the Colonial Office and the CRO, and it underscored the coming of age of the CRO. Only the library remained as it had always been, a service common to both departments.

3.3.2 Relations with the new Commonwealth

The responsibilities of the CRO increased sharply after the war also as dependencies in the colonial empire became independent and, with few exceptions, became members of the Commonwealth. Here the growth of the CRO was the obverse of the reduction of the Colonial Office. Nevertheless responsibility for new Commonwealth countries was absorbed into an office which retained a functional rather than a geographical basis of organization.

The CRO also came to provide the administrative support for meetings of Commonwealth prime ministers. In 1944 Commonwealth prime ministers' meetings were initiated as gatherings to be held about every two years, though by the 1960s they were held on average once a year. These meetings were conducted on a more informal basis than pre-war imperial conferences. Nevertheless the Cabinet secretary continued to act as secretary, with the CRO servicing the meetings until, in June 1965, the Commonwealth Secretariat was set up by the Commonwealth heads of government to assume this responsibility.

As the 1950s progressed Whitehall's involvement with Europe increased and its interest in the Commonwealth and the dependent empire declined, but the status of the CRO continued to grow as it gained in size and experience. The increased importance of the inter-departmental committee system enhanced the position of the Cabinet Office and in turn of the CRO, with which it maintained a close relationship. The high degree of liaison with the Foreign Office grew. There was also continuous collaboration with the Treasury about the state of the British economy and the strength of sterling, and with the service departments on defence matters.[11]

The reversal of roles between the Colonial and Commonwealth Relations Offices was completed in August 1966 with their merger to form the Commonwealth Office, followed two years later by the merger with the Foreign Office to create the Foreign and Commonwealth Office in October 1968.

Notes

1 The many sources for this period include J Garner, *The Commonwealth Office, 1925–1968* (1978); F M G Willson, *The Organization of British Central Government*, 2nd ed, (1968); J A Cross, *Whitehall and the Commonwealth: British Departmental Organisation for Commonwealth Relations, 1900–1966* (1967); H Duncan Hall, *A History of the British Commonwealth of Nations* (1971).

2 Garner, *op cit*, pp 3–14.

3 Hall, *op cit*, pp 580–584.

4 Cmd 2768, *Summary of the proceedings of the Imperial Conference*, 1926 (1926, xi, 545); Cmd 2769, *Appendices to the Summary of the proceedings of the Imperial Conference*, 1926 (1926, xi, 607).

5 CAB 27/347, Representation in the Dominions of HM Government in Great Britain Committee.

6 Cross, *op cit*, p 56.

7 The machinery of intra-imperial co-operation was reviewed by the Skeleton Committee which reported in 1933, Cmd 4335, *Report of the Imperial Committee on Economic Consultation and Co-operation* (1932–33, xi, 415).

8 Cross, *op cit*, p 57.

9 Garner, *op cit*, pp 173–175; Lee and Petter, *op cit*, pp 152–153.

10 *ibid*, pp 287–295.

11 *ibid*, pp 369–373. See also Cmnd 2276, *Report of the Committee on Representational Services Overseas*, 1964, (1963–4, xi, 1).

CHAPTER 4

Records of the Colonial Office and its Predecessors, 1660 to 1966

4.1   1660 to 1782

There are no known records of the advisory bodies on plantations affairs that sat before the Restoration. However, an apparently incomplete copy of the journal of the Council of Foreign Plantations of 1660–1664 survives (CO 1/14) and two records of the contemporary Council of Trade (CO 388/1, CO 389/1). Entry books of patents and of petitions and reports are said to have existed. The councils of 1670 and 1672 kept a number of records known as 'the rough books' comprising a register of commissions and instructions, 'A Journal', 'Orders of Council of Foreign Plantations' (1670 and 1672), 'Petitions, References and Reports', 'Addresses and Advices', 'Letters and Answers', 'Miscellanies', 'Barbados', 'Leeward Islands', 'Jamaica', 'Virginia' and 'Letters from the Council' (1672), but these are not in the Public Record Office.[1]

Thereafter more complete records are available, but there are complexities in their arrangement. Due to the preoccupation of the Board of Trade with plantations business in its early years, described in chapter 1.1–2, its records, which passed to the State Paper Office as records of the secretary of state, were later combined with the records of the Colonial Office. The reorganization of Colonial Office records in the nineteenth century and again in 1908–1910, described in chapter 4.3.7, has compounded the situation, and it is now difficult to reconstruct the original arrangement of the papers of the secretaries of state and the Board of Trade. The former contain a higher proportion of important papers than the latter because governors addressed despatches on military and political topics to the secretary of state. However, by the early eighteenth century some governors were reluctant to trouble the secretaries with lengthy communications or with questions of administration or commerce, or matters of minor importance. The despatches to the secretaries at that time are therefore apt to be briefer and the board's records generally bulkier. Nevertheless, the distinction between what was fit for the secretary of state and what was fit for the board was blurred in practice and governors sometimes wrote to both on the same day in substantially the same terms.

The dual channel of communications was unified between 1766 and 1768, and the secretaries' papers contain numerous Board of Trade in-letters evidently sent to them by the board in original and never returned. Beginning in 1765 there is a series of entry books containing in-letters and out-letters alike, the former being copied on the left-hand pages and the latter on the right (eg CO 5/1374). These letter books divide into two series in 1768 (eg CO 5/1372 in, and 1375 out) and continue until 1782, when the practice of copying in-letters was abandoned. There is also a series of précis books which abstract correspondence with governors and military commanders.

The Privy Council Committee of 1675 (the Lords of Trade and Plantations) kept records in a business-like fashion, the lack of proper records having been accounted a defect of the preceding bodies. A well-kept journal (CO 391) and new series of entry books were begun, and the original papers were arranged in a greater number of series. The Lords of Trade also collected records kept by the proprietors of properties after those territories had become royal colonies. The continuity of these series has been obscured by the work of later record keepers but has now been reconstructed on paper.

In 1696 the committee's papers were transferred to the offices of the new Board of Trade where some of them were destroyed by fire in January 1698. The board introduced no radical change in the paper-keeping arrangements. The journal was continued, and although new entry books were started they were on the old model. However, the new board's methods showed greater care, and indexing and cross-referencing were more thorough. By 1703 the system of registration was more regular, and in that year a series of small 'calendars' was started (eg CO 326/11). At first they were small square books, with abstracts of papers relating only to one colony, but from 1759 they were larger, each containing all the documents received in a given year, arranged by colonies or subjects. The abstracts usually correspond with the dockets on the original papers. The 'calendars' also include abstracts of out-letters.

Bundles of papers were bound into volumes from time to time in this period, but there is no correlation between volumes and bundles. Some volumes contain several bundles and sometimes a bundle is split between two volumes. The papers were arranged in forty-three groups, most of which took the names of individual colonies.

Other groups were called 'Miscellanies', 'Naval Office Lists', 'Plantations General', 'Properties', 'Custom House Accounts' and 'Book of Maps'. 'Plantations General' includes papers about the colonies in general or about a plurality of colonies. Where a paper, although relating to two or more colonies, was too important to warrant this classification it was placed in the section to which it more particularly belonged, and a slip was inserted in the other section or sections directing the reader to it. 'Properties' at its greatest extent included Rhode Island, Connecticut, Maryland, Pennsylvania, New Jersey, and the Bahamas. These were proprietary or corporate colonies, the patrimony of individuals. As they became royal colonies, they were classified separately. 'Trade', uniting the old divisions called 'Trade Foreign', 'Trade Domestic', and 'Trade and Fishery' in 1717, contains a number of papers not concerned in any way with the colonies.

The 'Naval Office Lists' were kept by the naval officers, who, under the governors, enforced the acts of trade by giving bonds and examining ships' cargoes and papers. These lists begin for the West Indian colonies in about 1680. At their fullest they show vessels entered and cleared at the various colonial ports, the time of clearing, name and place, masters' names, when and where built, kind of vessel, tonnage, armament, complement, when and where registered, owner's name, character of the cargo, where bound, when and where bond was given, and consignor and consignee of the cargo.

Despatches to the Board of Trade from the colonies, normally sent in duplicate, frequently contained voluminous enclosures, including extracts from proceedings in council or assembly, records of trials at law, commissions, warrants, petitions, proclamations or addresses, printed broadsides and extracts from newspapers. The bulkier of the enclosures were separated from their covering despatches and bound in separate series. Enclosures are also apt to be missing from their places because they were sent in original to other authorities. If these other authorities were secretaries of state, the enclosures may sometimes be found among their in-letters. The in-letters consist not only of despatches from overseas but of letters from various public authorities at home and from private persons.

The board made abstracts of governors' despatches and arranged them in alphabetical order, either on the back of the documents or on slips. Until about 1745–1750 the despatches were often marked to show the portions corresponding to the abstracts and were lettered alphabetically. No doubt these abstracts were read to the board in preference to the originals and they must have been a useful aid to making up the journal.

The in-letters are paralleled by several separate series of entry books, grouped on the same plan and also marked alphabetically. They contain chiefly despatches and letters, reports and representations[2], governors' commissions and instructions, and abstracts and drafts of letters. Before 1700 they contain copies of in-letters as well as of out-letters, but this practice was steadily abandoned thereafter and eventually even the habit of noting the titles of in-letters was dropped.

The board's memorials to the king in council, Parliament and the like were copied in these entry books. Commissions and royal instructions to governors were also entered, in full where they were new or significant, or by reference to some other preceding or parallel instrument with notes of variation. In addition to entering the full texts of outgoing communications, the board collected and bound up the drafts, which are now arranged with the other entry books.

The Board of Trade also accumulated acts and proceedings of colonial councils or legislatures. The acts are broadly of two sorts: acts printed in the colonies or in England, and manuscript copies attested and certified by the secretaries and governors and sealed with the colony's seal. As soon as a manuscript act reached England it was referred to the law officers or to the board's own legal advisers who reported on it. It then went with the board's comments to the Privy Council, where it was referred to a council committee, who reported back to the full council. The council's final decision was usually endorsed upon the act. A register was kept of acts received (CO 5/273–282).

See chapter 11.2 under colonies general and individual territories for further information about the records for this and subsequent periods.

4.2   1782 to 1801

After 1782 the journals and papers of the revived Board of Trade are grouped with other records of the modern board in the BT record classes. Otherwise the system is not at first dissimilar. In-letters are arranged colony by colony as are some of the out-letter books. The series of acts and proceedings continue for those colonies with legislative institutions. The association of the colonies with home affairs during the period 1782–1801 resulted, however, in the entry of letters concerning the colonies between the Home Office and other departments of state in what are now Home Office entry books (eg HO 29).

The précis books started in the 1760s also continue and are carried on for a time by the War and Colonial Department. They do not readily reveal their purpose, but they are not registers. They relate to most if not all of the colonies, the Barbary States (CO 173/5), theatres of war like Egypt, the Mediterranean (CO 173/3–4) and the Iberian peninsula, and potential theatres like the Channel Islands. They cover the period 1789 to 1814, but for some years some colonies are not represented. They are to be found in the class called Colonies General, Entry Books, Series I (CO 324) and among the records of particular colonies. In many instances in-letters and out-letters are digested in the same books, the out-letters on the left side and the in-letters on the right, with the substance of each in-letter and the action taken shown.

4.3 1801 to 1925

4.3.1 Registration before 1849

The creation of the War and Colonial Department in 1801 did not result in any immediate change in the records. The first important innovation in the form of the records came with the inception of registration. The earliest compilation in any way resembling a register dates from 1810. It is the first of a series of volumes (CO 326/77–83) particularizing the despatches and letters received and sent, with the date and subject. The papers are not numbered and the volumes are in a fair hand, suggesting that they are merely shelf-lists or catalogues of papers preserved. Moreover, as the entries appear to be confined to military affairs and the European colonies, the registers probably relate to the war rather than to the colonial side of the department's work. There is a somewhat similar list of letters received from the Commissioners of Eastern Inquiry (CO 326/84, 1821–1831). In 1818 it was laid down that governors' official despatches should be numbered each year in a single annual series.

With the appointment of a registrar in 1822 the first series of modern registers begins. In 1825 the registrar was formally placed on the establishment and the post of deputy registrar was added. The registers they created particularize the despatches received, with date and subject, and from January 1823 each communication is also numbered and the number inscribed on the communication itself. The registers were kept colony by colony and by groups of colonies, doubtless corresponding with the departmental structure of the office.

In 1823 letters from departments and individuals at home are entered in separate registers from those used for despatches. All the domestic correspondence for 1823 and 1824 appears to be lumped together, but in 1825 it is segregated by groups of colonies with a 'despatches' and a 'domestic' register for each group. From 1824 to 1831 there are distinct registers for semi-official letters to the permanent under-secretary. The practice of registering letters from potential emigrants had ceased by the mid-1830s. For a reason still unexplained some registers for the period 1830–1832 are duplicated. There are no registers of out-letters as such, but most of the entry books of out-letters are indexed.

In 1833 the post of registrar was fused with that of chief clerk, and later in the same year the deputy registrar's post was also removed leaving no responsible officer. The work of compiling the rough, or preparatory, register was then distributed among the junior clerks of the office's four departments who were in practice also responsible for the collection and custody of recent papers. From 1841 the rough registers which these clerks kept were copied out by a temporary officer. The process

D

of registration was thus fragmented and not uniform and was condemned by secretaries of state from 1846 and by the Trevelyan–Northcote Committee of 1848–1849.[3]

4.3.2 Registration of in-letters, 1849 to 1925

The strictures of the Trevelyan–Northcote Committee were effective, and in 1849–1850 a registrar was reappointed and a central registry established. The system of registration then evolved was remarkably thorough and effective. Though much altered in detail, it was essentially consistent for about seventy years. Its novel features were the opening in 1849 of a general or daily register of in-letters, and the replacement in 1849–1850 of the departmental registers by a much larger number of colony and subject registers. Generally there was one set of registers for each colony. The subject registers were few at first but in time grew more numerous.

Each incoming communication was stamped with a receipt date (as had been done since at least 1827), inscribed with a running number from an annual series common to the whole office, and entered in a daily register. This register showed, under the registration date, the number, date, and place of origin of the communication, the colony or equivalent classification, the substance, and the department of the office to which the paper was assigned for action. An enlarged index to the public offices and miscellaneous sections of the correspondence accompanied, and was eventually embodied in, the daily register. In 1873, so far as despatches were concerned, the system was modified in two directions. First the subject matter was omitted. Second, when several despatches arrived from the same source their dates were also omitted; the numerical boundaries of the daily numbers were given and their distribution to the departments noted in general terms.

After it had passed through the daily register, each communication was next entered in the appropriate colony register. This register was cut according to the correspondent; for instance governors' despatches were entered in one cutting, letters from the Foreign Office in another, letters from private individuals whose names began with a particular letter in a third. The cutting called Parliament was used mainly for parliamentary questions. Papers originating in the Colonial Office, such as minutes, despatches or out-letters, or registered press-extracts, were entered under the Colonial Office cutting. The separate registration of these papers began in 1873. After 1868 the cutting devoted to individuals became, at least in principle, an index to the names of individuals mentioned in the despatches. It is not complete as an index, although in 1870 the registrar claimed that it was, but it may sometimes help in searching, and in some cases provides an index of subjects.

The pages of the register were divided into columns: (a) registration number and date, taken from the daily register; (b) sender; (c) date of the communication; (d) number of the despatch or a statement that it had been sent by telegram (after 1928 number of the telegram); (e) subject with a short extract; (f) former and other papers; (g) how disposed of. Communications from the more distant oversea territories composed towards the end of a year are apt to be registered in the ensuing year. However, when the despatches were bound up they were grouped by the date of issue rather than the date of registration, so that some original correspondence classes, eg Victoria (CO 309), begin a year before the corresponding registers.

The references in column (f) should enable searchers to set a particular paper in its context. If the paper is the reply to some other communication they will be able to find the communication that provoked the reply. If they want to see what happened next, they will be able to follow the correspondence forward. The references consist of the registration number, as shown in the daily register, together with code letters which are given in chapter 15.1.

To take an example, 'Admy 32305' in the Jamaica colony register (CO 351/19) for 1906 means: the preceding (or subsequent) paper in this sequence has been classed with the letters to and from the Admiralty for this year forming part of the Jamaica class. If it has been preserved it will be found there, and if not a brief indication of its content will be found in the Admiralty cutting of this register under the number 32305. If the connected paper belongs to a different year and/or a different class, the entry in this column is a little more complicated to interpret. Thus 'Gov 36634/03 Ceylon', in the same register means see the Ceylon register for 1903 for a description of the contents.

The final column (g) is, so far as the interpretation of the code symbols is concerned, similar to (f). Three points, however, need explanation. First, the use of the abbreviation 'cons', for consideration, shows that an answer was desired. Second, the column often contains a multiplicity of entries, showing that a variety of authorities or persons needed to be consulted or informed about the substance of the incoming communication. Third, this column often contains the letters 'LF', which stood originally for 'lithographed form' and is described below, or '3 pn' which means 'third personal note'.

For the most part colony registers bear the name of the territory concerned. For example, registers relating to Gibraltar are called Gibraltar Register of Correspondence (CO 342) and are a key to Gibraltar Original Correspondence (CO 91). There are, however, some colony registers relating to a number of territories, notably those for the South Africa High Commission (CO 545 and DO 1), the Western Pacific High Commission (CO 492), and the Federated Malay States (CO 717). In these cases there are no separate classes of original correspondence, but there are classes of printed documents for each territory covered. These and other exceptional colony registration arrangements are covered in chapter 11.2.

The 'subject' registers are complementary to the colony registers which refer to them in the 'how disposed of' column. Where such a cross-reference is inserted, the 'former and other papers' column is left blank. Subject registers can be divided roughly into two classes, those with a geographical title but which cover a broader area than a single colony, and those where there is no kind of geographical grouping. The first might seem to be of the same nature as the colony registers referring to a number of territories mentioned above, but those concern the activities of only one officer who administered the affairs of several territories, whereas the 'subject' registers with a geographical title concern the activities of a number of distinct officers serving in broadly the same region. Consequently they are treated here as subject registers and used in the same way.

At first 'subject' registers were few and were virtually confined to domestic correspondence. When the new system of registration began in 1849–1850 only four series were created: British North America General (CO 328), British North America Emigration (CO 327), West Indies General (CO 375) and Emigration (CO 428). However, the number expanded considerably during the latter part of the nineteenth century and the early twentieth century. The inception of CO 622 coincides with changes under the Exchequer and Audit Act 1866. The introduction of CO 581 and CO 641 marks the first attempt to register military papers separately.

In 1866 a set of registers was started for letters not subjected to the full processes of registration. This register of 'unregistered' correspondence (CO 652) takes a different form from other registers, recording name of correspondent, date, colony, subject, and how disposed of. It also contains lists of insane correspondents, and directions for dealing with certain types of application and enquiry by transfer to other departments. The same series contains registers of correspondence filed. A register of governors' schedules acknowledging the receipt of despatches ceased in 1892.

4.3.3 Copying and registration of out-letters

Once registration was complete, a paper was sent forward for action in one of the departments or branches of the office. Where, as usually happened, action resulted in the despatch of a communication, it was copied in an entry book of out-letters. The series of out-letter books was not affected by the changes of 1849 to 1850 and there continues to be, in principle, one out-letter book for each colony or 'subject'. Each book is indexed.

After 1870 the practice of copying all out-going communications declined, and printed commissions were pasted into books instead of being copied. From 1872 the entering of out-going correspondence was abandoned as inaccurate, and by the end of the year manuscript commissions, instructions, patents and warrants were no longer entered. The indexes to out-letters were maintained until 1926 and form separate series called registers of out-letters, in principle one for each colony or subject. Some volumes for 1872 (eg CO 379/1) are both entry book and out-letter index. Until 1907 the office referred to these as indexes to registers. The arrangements for entering general correspondence are described in chapter 11.2 under colonies general.

A daily register of out-letters (CO 668) was started in 1901 and ceased in 1926. The registers have been transferred to the Public Record Office to 1910, but the rest have not survived. The volumes are cut according to destination and show, under each destination, all the communications leaving the office in the year in question. The cuttings are similar to, if not the same as, those in the registers of in-letters, eg 'Admiralty', 'Agents, Other', 'Miscellaneous Offices'. They give the registration number, date and classification.

4.3.4 The form of original correspondence

In the early days of the Colonial Office the term original correspondence implied in-letters alone. Later, however, minutes and drafts of out-letters were kept with the in-letters and the original correspondence comes to tell a much greater part of the story.

Before leaving the registry, incoming letters were inscribed with the series name, eg 'Jamaica', and registration number. They then circulated and were minuted upon as described below. At first minutes were written on the backs, margins or 'turn ups', a practice prevailing as early as the 1820s. Gradually extra blank sheets were attached. In 1868 printed minute sheets were introduced, modelled upon those used in the Treasury and already in use in the War Office and the Board of Trade. In 1872 they became more elaborate, in imitation of those used in the Board of Trade, and were divided into panels. At the top were panels for the colony or 'subject' classification, registration number and date of receipt. Below were further panels for the place and date of origin, a précis of the letter, and the number of the last preceding paper. Still lower were panels for the minutes themselves and for particulars of the action eventually taken. In 1884 a panel was added for details about subsequent papers.

By 1909 'ladders' were in use for circulating papers, and in 1921 they began to be printed on minute sheets. These ladders were oblong panels, ruled horizontally into smaller panels, like the spaces separating the rungs of a ladder. Here the names or titles of the secretary of state, junior ministers and senior officials were printed, and spaces were also left blank in which the names of other officials, or of branches of the office, might be inserted.

The draft of a reply to an in-letter was attached to it, and to the minute sheet, and was put away with it when the action was finished. Such drafts are encountered from the early 1830s. By that time it was customary to stamp them with a ladder headed with the word 'minute', below which were the names and ranks of the various officers through whose hands the draft should pass. The date inserted in ink against the word 'minute' was that of the last minute on the paper itself. As the draft was passed on, each person handling it dated it. It became the practice for the person who decided that the draft should be issued as a letter without going to higher authority to write against his name the expression 'for sig' or 'fs'. The former was in use by at least 1866. Printed drafting paper had come in by 1872. Its form was modified in 1880.

In the course of time, drafts began to be inscribed with references to letters received in reply, or with directions for further action such as the preparation and despatch of copies to other persons or authorities than the addressee. Until entry books were abandoned in 1872, drafts were inscribed with the word 'entered' as soon as they had been copied. After 1872 they were inscribed 'indexed' as soon as they had been posted into the registers of out-letters.

After 1872 the draft normally furnishes the only lasting verbatim text of an outward communication. It is true that from an unascertained date, perhaps from the introduction of typewriters in the 1890s, flimsies were temporarily preserved with the drafts, but most were removed at 'weeding'.

The 'further action' panel was particularly useful as a place for the inscription of directions about the use of 'LFs', the lithographed forms, already mentioned. These forms, some of which were in the first person and others in the third, bore stereotyped expressions, such as an acknowledgement of the receipt of a communication or a request that the recipient himself answer a communication transferred to him. They were in use by 1858 and amounted to a hundred different types in 1870, when the whole corpus was revised. In 1900 it was ruled that all 'LFs' to officers administering government departments should be in the first person and all to government departments in the third.

Before a paper was put away the final action resulting was noted on it. This practice seems to have begun in 1834. Originally these inscriptions, noted on the in-letter itself, merely show the date of the out-letter issued in reply. Later they are made upon the minute sheet and include more exact particulars. Thus, in the form ultimately evolved, every paper should show at a glance what outward communications it provoked, with a reference to any further communication to which that reply may have led. All the registry inscriptions on a paper, whether entered on receipt or when action was completed, should tally with the corresponding entries in the colony or subject register.

4.3.5 Circulating and minuting papers

The system of minuting and circulating incoming communications was devised by Sir James Stephen during his period as permanent under-secretary (1836–1847). Before his day many important matters had been debated in private correspondence, which only doubtfully expressed an official view. Minutes had been used previously, and were sufficiently valued that their preservation was required, but they were short and simple except for exchanges between the secretary of state when absent in the country for his three months' long vacations and the under-secretaries left behind in London. Moreover, the method of conducting business favoured had been oral discussion, both within the office and with other departments. By the 1830s it was felt that this system of conferences wasted time and resulted in an inadequate record of views and decisions, a problem compounded by the fact that ministers spent much time in their country houses and clerks did not always keep fixed hours. Stephen introduced a full system of minuting which was gradually elaborated and grew in importance.

The procedure was as follows. Once incoming letters had been registered they were delivered to the senior clerk of the appropriate department, who minuted them and usually proposed the form of an answer or the practical course of dealing with the subject. When the correspondence had been prolonged or complicated and required an explanation or analysis, he or his assistants prepared a statement of the relevant facts which he attached to the letter. The papers, attached to a docket, then passed up the ladder, with each official minuting his observations, until they reached the secretary of state himself, who recorded his decision upon them. The papers were returned through the same channel to the senior clerk who, having checked that the instructions were not at variance with facts, regulations, or precedents, executed them with the help of his assistants. Drafts were sometimes also prepared by the permanent under-secretary and assistant under-secretary.

Initially all drafts received the sanction of the parliamentary under-secretary and of the secretary of state, but later an officer who felt in a position to take action could stop the passage of a draft up the ladder by writing the traditional phrase 'at once' at the end of the minutes. Many papers circulated called for no reply and were simply put away after they were read. Instructions for doing so had been conveyed since early in the century by the words 'put by'.

This system of circulating papers had three outstanding features. Within the office every public document was exposed to public view so that public issues were not settled by private communication. Second, everyone handling such a document was normally required to make some comment on the method of dealing with it and to give reasons for his views. Third, policy was settled by general instructions, and the conversion of those instructions into an outgoing communication was a subsequent and subordinate activity.

Gradually the system was subject to small changes. For example, papers were sent to the most junior rather than the most senior officer of a department, they moved forward with a prepared draft reply rather than an outline of an answer, fewer and fewer papers reached ministerial level, and the number of people handling papers tended to decline. Yet despite devices to simplify or accelerate business, the system retained many of its original features throughout the life of the Colonial Office.

A study of the Colonial Office system of minuting exposes not only the process of administration but the reasons for the action taken. The minutes, which are sometimes quite extensive, reveal the main formulators of office policy and how their minds were working, or at least the opinions they wished their colleagues to attribute to them. In this respect Colonial Office records are far richer than most departmental records of the nineteenth century. The lists of senior officials in chapter 7 may be used to identify the authors of initialled minutes.

4.3.6 Make-up of the records

From the early nineteenth century until 1926 the original correspondence, when no longer current, was assembled by colonies and 'subjects' and bound. When, as was usual, the papers for one year were too numerous to bind into a single volume, the despatches were placed together in one or more volumes and followed by separate volumes devoted to other categories of letters. Typical classifications for these other categories were 'Public Offices' (the major government departments), 'Miscellaneous Offices' (eg lesser government departments, Agents General, the West India Committee or the Hudson's Bay Company), and 'Miscellaneous' (individuals). At other times the titles 'Miscellaneous Government Offices' and 'Miscellaneous Institutions and Individuals' were used.

The appropriateness of the practice of binding papers in volumes was questioned by the Trevelyan–Northcote Committee (1848–1849) to no avail.[4] In 1873 it was decided to store the papers in 'book-shaped boxes' where they might stay for the first ten to twelve years of their lives. Then they could be transferred to cheaper boxes and the 'book-boxes' released for newer papers. Nevertheless binding was later resumed for papers which had gone through a review process, described in chapter 6.1, which continued until well into the twentieth century.

4.3.7 Reorganization of the records

A calendar of colonial state papers was begun in 1859, and as part of the process the early papers were rearranged in strictly chronological order regardless of their administrative origin. The project in its earliest form was a calendar to the end of 1688, and for this reason the class Colonies General (CO 1) virtually ends in that year.

Early in the twentieth century, after the Colonial Office had begun transferring increasing quantities of records to the Public Record Office, the PRO undertook a large scale reorganization of the records, which went on for a number of years from 1907, with the aim of arranging them topographically as far as possible. For each territory most or all of the following classes were established: original correspondence; registers; entry books, commissions and petitions; acts; sessional papers (mainly legislative and executive council proceedings and administrative reports of the various departments of colonial governments); government gazettes; and miscellanea (blue books of statistics, newspapers, etc). A few general classes were also constructed. See chapter 4.9 for more information about the non-correspondence categories of records.

During the reorganization existing bundles or volumes of Colonial Office records were split up and distributed among other bundles, with the result that the administrative process by which the records evolved up to 1782 was obscured. For instance, the original correspondence classes were subdivided between the Board of Trade and secretary of state correspondence, but the classes of entry books and acts were not. Moreover, existing references were changed. The Public Record Office published no key to the new references it assigned, but this was partially remedied by private efforts. The keys thus produced are described in chapter 6.3.2.

The problems were not altogether confined to the period up to 1782, for the same principles guided the arrangement of later records. Thus the records of the various commissions of inquiry that sat from 1819 have been mixed with Colonial Office domestic records. To take another example, the Newfoundland Original Correspondence (CO 194) is an amalgam of the pre-1782 Board of Trade correspondence and the correspondence of the southern secretary of state (to 1768), the third secretary of state (1768–1782), the home secretary (1782–1801), the secretary of state for war and the colonies (1801–1854), and the secretary of state for the colonies (1854–1925).

Moreover, an attempt was made to divide the records for the period 1801 to 1854, when the War Department and the colonies were under one secretary of state, into two distinct record groups corresponding to the two separate departments which emerged. This could not, however, be readily achieved, and as a result there are War Department records in the CO classes and records on colonial affairs in the WO classes.

4.3.8 Other record series

Various documents of a miscellaneous kind never formed part of any series within the Colonial Office, or were held back when the bulk of some particular set of original correspondence was forwarded to the Public Record Office. This has resulted in the creation of the artificial class called Supplementary Correspondence (CO 537), which includes papers which were never part of a properly organized series as well as papers formerly secret that have been desecretized. The secret correspondence is described in chapter 4.7. The class called Colonies General Miscellanea (CO 325) is somewhat akin. There is no distinct set of registers for either, but many communications within them have been registered in secret or 'subject' registers.

Another category of records outside the normal pattern is the analytical and chronological indexes to governors' correspondence, and to that between the Colonial Office and other British government departments, compiled by the library staff in the nineteenth century (CO 714). The chronological indexes are lists of the contents of each volume prepared in duplicate; one copy was placed in the volume and one pasted into a book. These are less useful than the registers, but can help where a reader has only a vague idea of the date of a certain event or is searching a particular subject or individual over a number of years. For many colonies they run from 1815 to 1870 when they were abandoned.

Two further categories of Colonial Office records do not form part of the registered papers series or of the printed documents or returns transmitted from the colonies. These are the Colonial Statistical Tables (CO 442), a set of United Kingdom Command Papers issued between 1833 and 1913, and four classes of printed reports of Prize Court cases (CO 836–CO 839) from 1914 to 1921.

4.4 1926 to 1950

4.4.1 Introduction of the file system

The reorganization of the Colonial Office in the second half of the 1920s was accompanied by important changes in the registration system. While these changes resulted largely from the increasing bulk of correspondence and its enlarged ephemeral element, they were at least partly due to the growing tendency to deal with the work by subject rather than by territory. By the 1920s the trend of office discussions was toward a subject approach to its functions.

The first major change was the move toward a subject file system. Until the twentieth century each document arriving in the Colonial Office was registered separately, first in the central registry and then in the relevant sub-registry, and kept under a separate docket sheet. The transition to subject files can be traced from the system of registration which evolved for the Tropical African Service personal files and was first sanctioned in 1908 for European officers serving in West Africa. The rapidly growing service created an increasing amount of minor correspondence not requiring separate registration.

These communications were sent to the branch registry where they were placed in jackets with distinctive numbers from a tropical African series and were marked with the officer's name, appointment, and territory. Subsequent communications received, with the drafts of those sent, were arranged in the relevant jacket in the order of receipt and despatch on the right side, with all minutes written on continuous sheets on the left side. In 1919 this 'split file' or 'jacket' system was extended to all the sub-registries dealing with the colonies[5], and by the mid 1920s it had been extended to all officers overseas, except those under the dominions sub-registry, and to Accounts Department papers. At first the only record kept of these filed letters seems to have been a numerical list written on loose sheets. From 1909 to 1912 they were entered in a book of non-registered letters covering West and East Africa, the West Africa Frontier Force and the King's African Rifles and forming part of the series Registers of 'Unregistered' Correspondence (CO 652). Later, inward and outward correspondence was briefly recorded in loose-leaf personal-file registers in the respective branch or sub-registries and only when a communication about an officer was sent to a governor was it entered in the main registers.

At the same time the office sanctioned the broader use of the 'waiting bundle' practice developed in the dominions sub-registry for papers registered 'dominions' and 'war trade'. 'Dominions' papers were kept according to a list of settled subjects. Under this system, when further correspondence developed from a paper subsequent papers were attached to it, but each was registered separately. When the subject was considered dead, the papers were split up and returned to their series.

In June 1925 a Colonial Office Registration Committee reported that a single-paper unit system and a file system prevailed in the office in roughly equal proportions.[6] The committee, while well aware of the likely future effect of the office's growing emphasis on a subject approach, proposed no far-sweeping changes, as it felt that this would result in confusion. However, it did recommend that the file system be extended to all suitable cases. Thus single paper unit files remained in use for certain types of correspondence, while the use of subject files increased rapidly.

During 1926 there was a major transition to subject file registration or the 'Home Office system'. This causes difficulties in using the 1926 records and requires explanation. At the beginning of the year incoming papers received numbers in the normal running sequence. When further correspondence was received on a given subject the subsequent papers were not entered in the daily register and did not receive unique numbers but were entered direct in the appropriate colony or subject register. The registry entry for the new paper was cross-referenced to the earlier paper and marked with its number, while the entry for the original paper was marked with a red 'F' to signify that it now represented a file. The correspondence was then transferred to a file jacket varying in form only slightly from the single letter docket. As 1926 progressed, more and more correspondence was placed on files. Single papers which did not develop into files were later bound.

The difficulties of tracing papers for 1926 through both volumes and boxes of files have been compounded by the review procedure, which is described in chapter 6.1. Where papers and files were destroyed the registers should have been marked 'destroyed under statute'. However, readers should be aware that this practice was not infallible, particularly for the complex registers of 1926, and that cross-references from papers to files were not marked 'destroyed'.

Subject file registration was extended to all correspondence other than personal files from 1 January 1927; thereafter every communication received was registered to a file. Files were frequently divided into sub-files so as to include several cases similar in nature but having no direct relation. The communications were sub-numbered consecutively and any portion of the file could be temporarily removed for separate action. However, action necessary as a result of a question raised was taken on the main file. Parliamentary questions were attached to separate jackets marked 'parliamentary question' and bearing the title of the subject file to which the question related with its number and the next sub-number.

4.4.2 Arrangement of files and registers

Subject files were arranged in the split file pattern evolved for the Tropical African Service. The file jacket, with standard printed panels, showed the reference number and the previous and subsequent files, and it recorded file movements within the office. For a short period correspondence continued to be filed with the earliest communication first and subsequent items following, but the pattern was soon reversed, with the earliest letter placed at the back of the file. The minute sheets listed the item number and date of each piece of correspondence in and out in consecutive order, followed by the officers' minutes. From March 1926 the minutes no longer began on the docket but on the first page following it.

The registers were adjusted in line with the changes in filing practice and from 1927 they were no longer arranged in cuts. As each new file was opened and given a number, a file register sheet was prepared upon which a précis of all correspondence subsequently placed on the file was recorded, thus ending the necessity to trace correspondence through a number of connections in different parts of the register and enhancing office efficiency. The sheets were arranged in numerical order and were bound at the end of each year. A list of file titles and their reference numbers was normally added at the front of the bound register.

From 1926 the files were closed annually and boxed, and a new file was opened with the first letter of the new year relating to the subject. If a file started late the previous year it might continue through the second year. Files containing replies to circulars, or to despatches treated as circulars, continued until replies were complete. During the Second World War files were allowed to run on over two or three years to save paper. When this happened, a continuation sheet was inserted in the next year's register and the numbering of the items on the file and register sheets continued consecutively. From 1941 onwards the files were boxed in three-yearly sets.

Several new 'subject' file series were opened in 1927: East Africa (CO 822), Eastern (CO 825), and Military (CO 820). The first two series exemplify the way in which problems common to a region were beginning to be treated collectively. The latter was a continuation of the series for the West Africa Frontier Force (CO 445) and the King's African Rifles (CO 534), the two military forces which were covered by the Military Section of the Colonial Office and the only forces for which there are separate correspondence series. The records in the military series relate primarily to the organization and operations of these forces, while questions on defence strategy and military policy tended to be registered 'general' (CO 323); some material on local defence schemes was filed in the country series (see also 4.4.5).

4.4.3 Reorganization of the registry and sub-registries

The 1925 Registration Committee recommended other changes involving the organization of the Colonial Office registry itself. For some time the registry had been divided into sub or branch registries, each handling the papers of a group of administrative departments. The number had been growing since 1896, and in 1925 there were six, not including the dominions sub-registry. The General Department, the Honours and Ceremonies sections, and the Accounts Branch performed registry work in their respective branches. The committee saw advantages of economy and interchangeability of staff in centralizing registration, and wanted to amalgamate the six sub-registries. This was not possible because of accommodation restrictions, but the six sub-registries were reorganized as two in 1925. Sub-registry 'X' now covered the West African, East African, and Mediterranean Departments, and the Military Section, while sub-registry 'C' dealt with the Far Eastern, Middle East, West Indian, and General Departments. The dominions sub-registry remained separate and became the Dominions Office registry in 1926. There continued to be two sub-registries throughout the 1920s, but during the 1930s the number expanded as the office grew and more departments were created. By 1939 there were again six sub-registries: general, economic, non-African, African, military, and personnel, each under a higher clerical officer who reported to the chief registrar. A despatch section handled all the incoming mail and recorded precedents.

Incoming correspondence continued to be entered in a daily register (CO 382), but in 1926, the last year for which daily registers have survived, three series of numbers rather than one running number were used, each corresponding to a sub-registry. The correspondence handled by sub-registry 'C' was registered in the volume now bearing the reference CO 382/80, that registered by sub-registry 'X' is in CO 382/81 and that registered by the dominions sub-registry is in CO 382/82. Distinct letters were prefixed to the numbers of each series and each sub-registry used a different coloured docket jacket. Outgoing despatches were also numbered in series by destination, but this practice ceased at the end of 1926 when the Colonial Office stopped keeping daily registers of out-letters (CO 668).

While the registry used the daily registers to identify individual papers, a card index system started in 1909 was now the means of tracing files. After the 1925 reorganization of the sub-registries each kept a subject index of file titles and the subjects of incoming papers. It has not proved possible to make these card indexes available to researchers.

4.4.4 Introduction of subject registration numbers

These changes were accompanied by another major innovation – the introduction of standardized blocks of subject file numbers in 1927. Separate blocks of numbers were allocated to each registry or other branch concerned at the beginning of the year, with the letter 'X' or 'C' to distinguish the sub-registry and the year to form part of the reference, thus X/12345/26. Various numerations were tried. The registers for 1927 and 1928 were arranged in single numerical sequences without apparent segregation of subjects, but from 1929 onwards there were attempts to allocate blocks of numbers by subject or by appropriate sections of the Colonial Office, and this principle governed the allocation of file numbers until the registry system changed in 1951/1952.

Until 1935 the blocks used were intermittent. Especially in the early years staff were inclined to deal less systematically with categories than the system required. They also tended to allocate too few file numbers one year, which meant that a category might have to be given additional numbers away from the main sequence allocated in the next year, thus displacing numerically the main sequence of the succeeding category. Moreover, certain functions were passed from one section to the next and appeared under different categories in different years. From 1933 onwards the general series was allocated its own regular sub-divisions, although the numbers did not necessarily correspond from year to year.

In 1935 new blocks of numbers were allotted to each registry and were intended to last for a five-year period. In fact, they remained in use throughout the war, and many continued until 1951/1952. From 1938 onwards this structure became increasingly unwieldy, and the exigencies of war put far greater demands on some categories than previously, causing irregularities in the numerical allocations within the larger blocks. Nevertheless, the overall stability of the numbering system frequently makes it possible to trace a subject through a succession of years by means of its file number. A table of the blocks of numbers allocated is found in chapter 15.2 and can be used to trace the Colonial Office department handling a file indicated in a cross-reference, and hence the record class in which it may now be found.

4.4.5 Registration of military and economic papers

The registration of military and economic papers needs further explanation. Military records were assigned registry blocks in the normal manner, and from 1935 the block 34001–35000 was used. In 1939 military registration was extended to cover the whole of British colonial Africa, except South Africa, and the following year the military liaison staff in the Colonial Office was expanded and attached to the newly formed Defence Department. Registration was then broadened to cover military matters relating to local forces in all dependencies, although many of the papers on military organization and operations were now filed in a new defence series (CO 968), or handled in the War Office itself. Naturally enough, much of the business relating to defence in the colonies passed to the War Office and is reflected in its records.[7]

Two registration blocks were allocated in 1939 to cater for the expanded scope of responsibilites. The first, 34001–35000, was essentially for the African forces, although after 1946 it was increasingly adulterated by files relating to military questions for the rest of the empire. The second covered military questions throughout the empire and from 1940 it was sub-divided: 36001–36500 was used for broad military questions including some on Africa, while 36501–37000 covered military questions excluding Africa. From 1946 less important material was filed in the military series, and more important papers in the defence series. A high proportion of the military papers, until the series ended in 1952, were on decorations and pensions.

In the same period, economic registration was affected by the steadily growing emphasis on economic matters, particularly during the war, and by the numerous reorganizations of departmental responsibilities. These resulted in a proliferation of responsibilities from the original Economic Department, created in 1934, to a group of new economic departments which were drawn together as the Economic Division in 1949. They are described in chapter 12.2. A chart in chapter 15.3.1 provides a breakdown of the numbers used for economic subjects between 1934 and 1952 when the registration system was changed.

4.4.6 Geographical and subject registration
A final change resulting from office reorganization was the reversal of the relative proportions of material filed by territory and by subject between 1925 and the late 1940s. Registration by subject grew steadily after the establishment of the Economic Department and of the Social Services Department in 1939. It increased dramatically during the war, particularly in the spheres of economic policy and raw material control, and by 1945 the number of files registered by subject exceeded the geographical. This trend continued after the war as the subject departments expanded.[8]

The boundaries between geographical and subject departmental responsibilites were not always clearly defined, and officers tended to take responsibility for action on each other's papers by mutual agreement. However, this did not affect registration unless there were a permanent change in departmental responsibilities; when this occurred the Establishment Department issued an establishment notice (CO 878).

4.5 1948 to 1966

4.5.1 The impact of the Colonial Office and Treasury investigations on registration
The post-war organizational problems in the Colonial Office described in chapter 2.5.1 had implications for registry practices. With the wartime growth of the subject departments and advisory staff, there were, from early in the war onwards, many suggestions about how to organize the clerical officers around the administrative staff, and how to reform the registries. Essentially the office was too centralized for its increasingly complex work and the old registry system was becoming unworkable. The administrative staff, attempting to cope with numerous changes in responsibilities and an inexperienced registry staff, resorted to a number of devices to short circuit the normal degree of centralization. Increasingly they approached colonies and other departments direct, often through a specific person. A large amount of

unofficial correspondence resulted, but the proportion is difficult to estimate.

The Treasury O & M Division investigation and the Colonial Office Organization Committee described in chapter 2.5.2 looked carefully at the registration of papers, and most of the changes in registration which followed arose from their discussions.[9] Some changes began almost immediately. For instance, in 1948 the practice of including a summary of the subject matter of incoming letters and despatches on minute sheets was discontinued and entries were confined to a single line in red ink.

In the same year it was decided that the sub-registries should be reorganized. Although the chief registrar and deputy registrar retained general oversight and co-ordinated common registry practice, the sub-registries ceased to form a common service and were integrated with the departments they served, some serving more than one department. By the end of the year the new system was operating in several subject departments. Members of the decentralized registry staff assisted the departments by taking initial action or minuting on certain assigned file series, providing simple initial drafting and undertaking specific tasks devolved by the departments' principals.

By 1949 the Treasury O & M Division had completed surveys of Colonial Office procedures, including record keeping, and had discussed proposals for improvements with the Colonial Office Establishment Department. These proposals, with a few modifications, resulted, in 1951, in the introduction of a new classification scheme which was to last until the closure of the office.[10] Under the reorganized system there was a correspondence series for each department.

To avoid disrupting the day to day work in the registries during the transition period, the new system was introduced in one or two registries at a time, beginning with the East African and the Central African and Aden sub-registries in June. Until late 1952, when the Economic Section was the last to introduce the system, there were two registration systems running in the office. From the end of 1951 sub-registries were known as sections. The term registry now referred to the work of all the staff of the sections as a whole.

4.5.2 Introduction of the subject code classification scheme

Under the new system, departmental files were grouped into well-defined themes using a standard alphabetical list of subject headings prepared by the Treasury O & M Division and maintained by the chief registrar. Most papers required more than one heading to describe their content, and the combination of headings describing a group of papers constituted a theme. The files within a theme constituted a file series. One theme, for instance, consisted of the subject headings 'malaria', 'colonial development and welfare scheme' and 'Jamaica'. The title of a file in this series was 'Application for assistance under Colonial Development and Welfare Scheme for control of malaria in Jamaica'. To avoid large series, themes were chosen to be capable of only fairly narrow interpretation.

The file reference number had three elements. First, prefix letters symbolized the department, as set out in the list in chapter 15.4.1. In the example above, the West Indies Department was represented by 'WIS'. Next, the subject headings used were related to numbers. In the example, 'malaria' was represented as 17, and 'development and welfare scheme, Jamaica' as 9. The sections did not use standardized numbers, except that the subject department sections used 1 to 54 as common territorial numbers. Where there were more than two subjects they avoided unwieldy theme numbers by allocating either one number to the whole theme or one number to one heading and another to the rest. The number of the most important subject came first, bringing files in the same series together in the register. The last element in the number, designating the file itself, was allocated in sequence, starting at 01. Thus the full reference for the example was WIS 17/9/01. Bulky files were split into parts A, B and C.

Each section kept a subject index to its own files, and the registrar's office kept a central subject index of file series in all sections. To ensure continuity of indexing, new numbers were allocated to all subjects in January 1953. These remained constant, with the exception of the Finance and Honours Department sections for which new numbers were introduced in 1961, until the Colonial Office was merged with the Commonwealth Relations Office in 1966.

Unit or 'case' files, opened when a number of requests or enquiries were made on a given subject, were classified on similar lines. Each unit file series had a theme within which there was a file for each 'case'. Thus the Legal Department series 'naturalization certificates' contained unit files on individuals applying for certificates. The reference number had three elements: a prefix denoting the department, a letter denoting the series and a number indicating the file, for instance LEG/B50. This system continued until 1966.

A three year file cycle was introduced at this time whereby files on subjects that were likely to be of continuing importance were closed after three years and new ones opened. However, less used files tended to be allowed to run on for longer. Colonial Office files are not, therefore, opened annually.

4.5.3 Registration by geographical or subject departments

The long-standing question of whether papers should be registered geographically or by subject was examined by the Colonial Office Organization Committee, and the principles set out in its 1949 report were applied throughout the 1950s. Questions affecting a single territory or a region were generally handled by the geographical department concerned, while questions covering a wider colonial field were handled by subject departments.

However, with the transfer of most of the subject departments from the Colonial Office to the Department of Technical Co-operation in 1961, these guidelines were no longer appropriate and created complications. Some matters, notably political questions and public revenue and expenditure, clearly remained the responsibility of the secretary of state for the colonies. In these cases DTC papers were usually registered on Colonial Office geographical department files. If a subject registered with the DTC as a technical issue later became political, communications were still prepared in the DTC but were sent to the appropriate geographical department for authorization, and copies were registered on the relevant Colonial Office files.

4.5.4 Registration by region

From the 1930s onward there had been an increasing tendency to register geographical files regionally rather than territorially. By the beginning of the war there were series for most regions, and during and after the war regional series by degrees replaced the old country classes. The process was completed in 1951 with the final abolition of country series. Up to 1951 the regional series were: Africa (CO 847), East Africa (CO 822), West Africa (CO 554), Middle East (CO 732), Western Pacific

(CO 225), Eastern (CO 285), Mediterranean (CO 926), and West Indies (CO 318).

After 1951 most of the old regional series disappeared (Africa, General, Middle East, Western Pacific, West Indies, and Eastern). The East and West Africa and Mediterranean series continued, and new series, corresponding with the existing departments, were created for Central Africa and Aden (CO 1015), South-East Asia (CO 1022), Far East (CO 1030), Hong Kong and Pacific (CO 1023), West Indies (CO 1031), and General (CO 1032). As Colonial Office responsibilities contracted during the 1950s and 1960s, some of these series ceased and new ones were created. These can be established by consulting chapters 11.1, 11.4 and 15.4.1. A number of special series relating to specific regions were also created during and after the war, including the West Indies US Bases (CO 972), Development and Welfare in the West Indies (CO 1042), Far Eastern Reconstruction (CO 865), Malayan Union and Singapore (CO 991), Fiji: South Pacific Office (CO 1009), and African Studies Branch (CO 955).

4.6 Circular despatches and memoranda, savingrams and telegrams

By at least 1794 it had become customary to send circular despatches to the colonies on subjects concerning all or a group of them. A separate collection of such despatches from 1808 to 1929 is in CO 854, but it is not certain that it is complete. Minutes connected with the drafting of such documents and the papers leading up to them are found elsewhere. It may help in tracing them to know that in 1850 circulars were drafted in the North American and Miscellaneous Division, and in April 1868 this became the responsibility of the Chief Clerk's Department, its natural successor. In 1870 circulars, like other communications, became the concern of geographical departments, although there were circumstances when they were handled generally, for instance when their aim was to elicit information for another government department. To help fix internal responsibility it was decided the same year that all circulars should be lettered either 'G' (general) or 'D' (departmental). Circulars in the volumes for 1881 and 1900 (CO 854/22 and 36) provide references to the registered papers on which the drafts were prepared. A Register of Replies to Circular Despatches (CO 862) was started in 1862 and shows the disposition of replies.

The use of circular despatches continued throughout the office's existence. They were bound together in annual volumes in two series 'confidential and secret' and the rest. The section clerk and departmental officer, where necessary, decided whether it would be more convenient to have all replies on one file, to register them in geographical groups, or to have a separate file for each reply. After 1943 it proved convenient in certain circumstances to communicate with colonial governments by means of a short despatch which varied to meet the territory's circumstances, covering a circular memorandum. Circular memoranda were prepared by the departments concerned in the same manner as circular despatches. Circular telegrams were also used.

In November 1939 saving telegrams, or savingrams, as developed in the Foreign Office, were introduced as another economical method of communicating with the territories.[11] Such messages were written in condensed telegraphic form, thus saving time and labour in drafting and copying correspondence. They could be sent in plain language, code or cypher, according to the nature of their contents and method of transmission. Codes and cypher were normally used only for communications of a confidential or secret character and then in the same way as in telegrams. Savingrams were used where there was not sufficient urgency to necessitate telegrams and they were sent in the same way as despatches. During the height of the war most went by the Air Ministry Microgram Service, but after the war they again went by normal post. There were also circular savingrams.

Like telegrams, which were numbered in series for each territory from 1928 regardless of security classification, savingrams were numbered in a distinct series and filed as ordinary despatches. However, from 1952 savingrams were numbered with the despatches in a single annual outgoing series for each territory.

Circular communications (despatches, memoranda, telegrams and savingrams) are preserved in CO 854, and the replies are in CO 862. The index to these series in CO 949 provides a useful means of tracing file numbers on given subjects, particularly on cross-territorial questions. There is correspondence about the circular despatches in CO 323.

4.7 Secret and semi-official communications

In 1818, when governors' despatches began to be numbered, despatches not immediately connected with the series of official correspondence, or which concerned private matters, were registered in the normal way but kept apart from the main series with copies of the replies and marked 'separate or private'. At the time, private correspondence with the colonies and inter-departmentally was common, particularly by the under-secretaries. The phrases 'private', 'secret', 'confidential' and 'private and confidential' are all found in the 1820s. These labels were not used with the precision that became customary later on. 'Secret' letters, however, seem at this time to have been those intended for the secretary of state or an under-secretary alone. 'Private' was used to indicate that the communication should be withheld from Parliament.

The practice of non-public correspondence with the overseas territories was discouraged from 1823, and the correspondence is not separately preserved for many years thereafter. Nothing, however, could prevent ministers and governors from writing private letters to one another, especially in an age when the two groups were so often related by blood or marriage. Indeed Lord Carnarvon, when secretary of state (1866–1867, 1874–1878), encouraged it. Ministers took such private correspondence away with them when they went out of office.

Later in the century new classifications were introduced. In 1864 only two gradings were recognized officially: numbered 'public' despatches and 'private and confidential' despatches. The latter were used when governors found it necessary to address the secretary of state in a more reserved manner than a public despatch would permit. In 1867 the second of these gradings was changed to 'confidential', and in 1871 three gradings were introduced: 'numbered', 'secret' and 'confidential'. The first were public despatches, the second might be shown secretly by a governor to his executive council and made public if he thought it necessary, the third could only be published with the secretary of state's approval. In 1888 the second and third categories were reversed so that a 'secret' document assumed its present position as a more private document than a 'confidential' one.

The multiplication of gradings was encouraged by the regular nineteenth-century practice of laying papers before Parliament, and the parallel obligation in the

E

colonies for governors to make known the contents of communications from London. Communications were worded in a form suited to the circumstances of public exposure, and the contents of the public despatches are at times startlingly unlike those of the non-public ones.

Secret registers were kept from 1865 (CO 694). What precisely was entered in them is difficult to pinpoint, for the meaning of the words secret and confidential continued to vary from time to time. However, something is known of the procedure for dealing with secret and confidential documents for 1888, the year in which the former meanings of the two words were reversed. Any paper that reached the registry in an envelope marked confidential was taken unopened to a private secretary, who decided whether it was to be registered in the open registry or secretly in the department to which it related. Similarly, if the registrar found that the contents of an envelope not marked confidential were of a secret character, he took it to the permanent under-secretary or to an assistant under-secretary for a decision. Secret papers were locked up in the respective departments. In the geographical departments higher division clerks looked after such papers, but in the general department, where the greater number were kept, two lower division clerks had access to them.

The total number of secret papers was small and originally they were registered under a separate numeration. This practice was abandoned in 1899 and thereafter secret papers were included in the sequence of the year but were still kept separately (CO 537). Their numbers were entered in red in the daily registers and in the relevant country or 'subject' registers, with the letter 'S' added, and also in the secret registers, which were divided into general and geographical department series. Top secret documents were entered in secret registers only.

With the introduction of files in 1926, secret files were numbered in the normal registry blocks for the relevant territory, region, or subject. From 1935 they were sub-numbered in the same series as existing open files on the same subject, and the open and closed files were cross-referenced in the card index. If no open file existed the registry officer recorded the subject in the card index, and any file opened subsequently took a sub-number from the secret file. Dummy sheets were placed on the registers when it was necessary to indicate that the sensitivity of the file warranted its registration elsewhere. After files were introduced, the secret registers were divided simply as African and non-African, but during the Second World War the non-African secret registers were discontinued. Separate territorial secret registers were opened, and the general secret registers lost some of their subjects to separate subject secret registers. Secret registers were discontinued in the 1950s, but top secret papers continued to be registered in a separate registry. The secret registers are closed for fifty years or longer.

In 1934 a joint Dominions and Colonial Office committee considered the general principles of desecretization and opened the majority of papers to 1919. Subsequently an ad hoc desecretization committee, comprising a deputy under-secretary of state, the establishment officer, and the officer in charge of the revision of records, was called to consider specific papers and files. Upon desecretization the markings denoting secret were crossed out in the registers.

Declassified files for the period 1925 to about 1945 were amalgamated with the relevant original correspondence series. However, this practice led to problems and the separate secret series was resuscitated. Post-1946 declassified secret files are thus found in CO 537 along with the pre-1926 desecretized papers. With the reorganization of the registry system in 1951–1953 separate secret registers came to an end, although a few departments appear to have continued them for a few years. Thereafter, secret and top secret files have been listed in the relevant departmental class and CO 537 comes to an end. 'Ts' in the file number column of the departmental lists indicates that the file was top secret, which is a significant distinction as there may be another file with the same number but a different security classification. The class often provides an excellent starting point for tracing office policy on key issues.

4.8 Confidential print and other printed records

During the nineteenth century an ever-increasing amount of Colonial Office correspondence was printed for Parliament, far more than in the twentieth century. Such papers were often first printed confidentially and subsequently edited for parliamentary use. Confidential prints may originally have been mainly Cabinet memoranda, which today would be duplicated. From the early 1860s, however, regular series of confidential print began, each bearing its own set of reference numbers. The date appearing on an early print is not necessarily the date of first printing; many documents must have been printed retrospectively. In or about 1864 the practice began of stamping the words 'Printed for Parliament' or 'Printed Confidentially' (or the equivalent) against appropriate entries in the colony and 'subject' registers, and this provides a means of gauging the extent of printing. Precise references to the prints are inserted in the registers from 1871, and from 1876 in the case of parliamentary and confidential print respectively.

From 1864 elaborate registers (CO 600) were kept of documents sent to the printer by what was eventually to be called the Printing Department. Documents printed by the Colonial Office were of two sorts: those printed as single papers owing to their bulk or on account of urgency or some similar cause, and those printed in 'slip' form and later combined into collective volumes of continuous correspondence. The former were entered in the registers called 'printed papers', which began in 1864. These volumes show the dates of receipt of the print in the Printing Branch, the despatch to the printer, the name of the printer, the date of return from the printer, the number of copies made and the disposal of the paper in the Colonial Office. Where one print is incorporated in another the fact is stated. Papers printed as 'slips' were, from 1875, entered in a separate set of registers which show the registered number of the paper containing the document, the printer's name, the dates of despatch and return, and the number of copies made (CO 600/14–18, 21–24).

Volumes of confidential print which grouped together the main correspondence, memoranda and other documents on a particular subject had a great practical administrative advantage. They enabled an official, particularly one new to it, to master a subject quickly and made it unnecessary for him to collect a mass of separate original papers. With the introduction of the file system and consequent grouping of papers on the same subject within the covers of one jacket, the need for the extensive printing of the nineteenth century was reduced. The practice of producing confidential print for internal use in the office, or in some cases for circulation to the Cabinet, continued but became more selective after the First World War. Printing was reduced further during the Second World War, but its regular use was revived after 1955 as the African territories began to approach independence.

Reference to the confidential print is through printed lists and class lists. A bound volume in the reference room at PRO, Kew contains 'A List of Papers Printed for the Use of the Colonial Office, with an Index to Titles' (confidential print misc 141) for the period to September 1920, and a continuation of the list to June 1934 (misc 380). There are also copies of these lists in the Confidential Print Catalogues Series (CO 601/4–6). An annotated version of misc 141 to 1916 has been published as *PRO Handbooks no 8* which gives PRO reference numbers.

After 1934, details of the confidential print series are given in the class lists: Africa (CO 879), Eastern (CO 882), Mediterranean (CO 883), West Indian (CO 884), Western Pacific (CO (934), Middle East (CO 935), and Miscellaneous (CO 885). The Miscellaneous Print series includes papers on the colonial services as well as some committee papers, notably of the Colonial Advisory Medical Committee.

4.9 Acts, sessional papers, gazettes, blue books and newspapers

In 1817 governors were instructed to forward annual details about the civil and military offices in their colonies, with the emoluments of those offices and names of their incumbents. In 1822 they were required to submit various types of statistical data entered in blank books with twenty-two printed headings supplied from London. By 1837 all colonies that had printing presses were printing their own standard quarterly returns of revenue and expenditure, known as blue books from the colour of their binding. Contemporaries held that the early returns were very imperfect, especially in the case of responsible government colonies, but they were eventually improved in response to pressure from Whitehall. In some of the dominions they evolved on different lines from those originally laid down. For instance, the Canadian Blue Books (CO 47, DO 30) consist from 1925 of the *Commercial Intelligence Journal* which contains articles on commercial topics as well as statistical material.

Colonial regulations issued in 1837 required the half-yearly transmission to London of proceedings of the several houses of assembly and of privy and legislative councils, lists of members of executive and legislative councils, copies of acts passed, new compilations or corrected editions of laws, 'reports of progress in geographical and topographical knowledge', government gazettes, and 'generally such books or pamphlets issuing from the colonial press as may be useful.'

Acts, ordinances and proclamations (the terminology varied with constitutional arrangements in each territory), sessional papers (mainly proceedings of legislative and executive bodies, and administrative reports)[12], and government gazettes had always formed a constituent part of the records relating to each dominion or colony. However, the 1837 regulations systematized formerly haphazard arrangements for their transmission. Act registers, which had long been kept departmentally, were continued in this period (CO 383).

Presumably it was in pursuance of the 1837 regulations that colonial newspapers began to be accumulated, and several early specimens are preserved in the records. A circular despatch of 1870 enjoined each governor to send two newspapers in addition to the official gazette. The result was that in 1872 one hundred and twenty-six daily and weekly newspapers were being received, and by 1904 the office received twenty-six thousand issues annually. Up to 1891 the older issues were periodically sent to the British Museum. The relatively small number of copies that remained in the office became part of the miscellanea classes for individual territories. Subsequently the office did not retain newspapers permanently.

The various categories of printed records continued to accumulate in the Colonial Office throughout its existence, and the relevant classes for each territory and region are listed in chapter 11.2. Some were temporarily suspended during the Second World War, and blue books were discontinued during the 1940s.

4.10 Related colonial records

4.10.1 Records of chartered companies

From time to time colonial functions which would normally have been the concern of the Colonial Office and the local colonial government were entrusted to chartered companies; the records of some of these companies are in the Public Record Office. Records of the Company of Royal Adventurers of England trading with Africa, the Royal African Company of England, and the Company of Merchants trading to Africa are in T 70 with a few papers of 1744–1745 in PRO 22/78, and of 1783–1784 in PRO 30/29/3/8 and BT 6. Microfilm copies of the records of the Hudson's Bay Company are in BH 1. Records of the West New Jersey Society are in TS 12, of the New Zealand Company in CO 208, and of the British North Borneo Company in CO 874. See also 4.10.4.

4.10.2 Records withdrawn from Colonial Office record classes

In 1836 the Foreign Office took over responsibility for relations with the consuls on the Barbary Coast, which had been entrusted to the War and Colonial Department in 1804, and the records were transferred at the same time. They are now part of the Foreign Office records. The attempt to divide the papers of the War and Colonial Department is discussed in chapter 4.3.7.

In 1908 the secretary of state for the colonies assented to a rule enabling the master of the rolls to transmit to colonial governments Colonial Office records not of sufficient value to justify their preservation in London. A portion of the New Zealand Company's records was then sent to New Zealand in accordance with a schedule of February 1909 made under this rule. Under the same schedule duplicate despatches from several colonial governments were sent to the territories from which they had originally come. These duplicates, of which there is still a residue in the Public Record Office (CO 412), formed part of the earliest transfer of Colonial Office records. Some duplicates of the papers of the commissioners of Eastern Inquiry were similarly disposed of under a schedule of February 1910. Since 1958 this rule has been replaced by the provisions of the Public Records Act which authorize the disposal of duplicate material in a similar manner.

4.10.3 Private office papers and private collections

Various private office papers of the Colonial Office are in CO 967, and of the Dominions Office in DO 121.

Much of the non-public correspondence created in the Colonial Office and taken away by ministers is now in private custody or in libraries, but a few collections have reached the Public Record Office. Some private correspondence and letter books of Earl Bathurst, secretary of state 1812–1827, and of R W Hay, permanent under-secretary of state 1825–1836, are in CO 323/142–175 and CO 324/73–94 respectively.

Private letter books of R J Wilmot Horton, under-secretary of state 1821–1828, concerning North America and the West Indies, are in CO 324/95–100, and of William Huskisson, secretary of state 1827–1828, in CO 324/101–102. Private correspondence of Lord Stanley (later Earl of Derby) when secretary of state, concerning Canada 1842–1845, is in CO 537/140–143. The Colonial Office classes also contain the private correspondence of one colonial governor, Matthew, Lord Aylmer, governor of Lower Canada covering the period 1830–1837. See also CO 959, Various Private Collections.

The papers of four other secretaries of state for the colonies have been deposited in the Public Record Office. These are the Russell Papers (PRO 30/22), the Cardwell Papers (PRO 30/48), the Carnarvon Papers (PRO 30/6) and the Granville Papers (PRO 30/29).

Material relating to colonial affairs will also be found in the following classes: Amherst Papers (WO 34), Brownrigg Papers (WO 133), Buller Papers (WO 132), Chartwell Trust Papers (PRO 31/19), Codrington Papers (PRO 30/29), Anglo–American Committee of Inquiry on Palestine, 1946 – 'Crick Papers' (PRO 30/78), Kitchener Papers (PRO 30/57), Lowry Cole Papers (PRO 30/43), Milner Papers (PRO 30/30), Murray Papers (WO 80), General Sir Charles Napier Papers (PRO 30/64), Northcote Papers (PRO 30/56), Roberts Papers (WO 105), Shaftesbury Papers (PRO 30/24), Harry Smith Papers (WO 135). The papers of C R Attlee as secretary of state for the dominions are in CAB 118.

4.10.4   Domestic records of oversea governments

The domestic records of oversea governments do not form part of the Colonial and Dominions Office records and are kept by those governments themselves in their own national archives. These governments possess, in principle, the original despatches of which London holds the copies, and the copies of despatches preserved in London in original.

There are, however, a few cases where some of the records of an oversea government have been sent to London and become part of the Public Record Office holdings. When Tangier was abandoned in 1684, the court books of its municipal assemblies under English rule, local notarial and testamentary records and similar material were sent to London and are in CO 279/34–49. The surrender of the protectorate over the Ionian Islands to Greece in 1864 resulted in the despatch of the records of the local government to the Public Record Office (CO 136/300–1433). Some fifty volumes of records of the government of Ceylon (1800–1805) are in CO 55/11–60. The records of the superintendent of convicts in New South Wales, formerly in CO 207, were returned to the government of New South Wales in 1973. Microfilm copies are retained in the same class.

Records of the Colony of Sierra Leone which were found to be decaying and which did not duplicate material already held by the Colonial Office were transferred to the Public Record Office in 1891. They include three volumes of governors' despatches to the under-secretaries of state (1826–1835) in CO 268/9–11, seventeen volumes of council minutes (1792–1827) in CO 270/1–18, three volumes of council letterbooks (1834–1866) in CO 298/12–14, and one volume of letters to the court of directors (1794–1798) in CO 298/5.

Other less significant examples can also be cited. These include, for instance, a volume of papers from the office of the chief secretary to the government of

Heligoland (CO 122/1), and the records of the officer at arms of the Order of St Michael and St George at Malta (CO 745/3).

In addition, the Colonial Office classes include some documents formerly in the custody of a foreign power. These are part of the records of the Dutch West India Company relating to the administration of Essequibo, Demerara and Berbice (1686 to 1792) which are in the class British Guiana Miscellanea (CO 116). They were surrendered to the United Kingdom government by the government of the Netherlands in 1819, on the ground that they were needed for the effective administration of the territories. The remainder of the records are in the Rijksarchief at The Hague.

Still other records are or have been held temporarily by the British government for security or other reasons but have never been transferred to the Public Record Office.

Notes

1   The location of the surviving records was worked out by C S S Higham. See *The Colonial Entry Books, A Brief Guide to the Colonial Records in the Public Record Office Before 1906 (Helps for Students of History, No 45)*, 11–16. One of the records is now in the Library of Congress.

2   A list of the more important of these memorials prepared not only by this board but by preceding advisory bodies is in the American Historical Association Report for 1913, p 319.

3   *Report from the Select Committee on Miscellaneous Expenditure*, pp 161, 529 (1847–48, xviii(1)); *Reports of Committee of Enquiry into Public Offices and papers connected therewith*, p 47, HC (1854, XXVII).

4   *Reports of Committee of Enquiry into Public Offices*, p 60.

5   CO 885/26, Registering and Filing of Official Papers, memorandum by Mr Drayson, 1919 (Conf Print Misc no 343).

6   CO 885/28, Report of the Colonial Office Registration Committee, 1925 (Conf Print Misc no 374).

7   The major War Office classes for East and West Africa for this period are: WO 276, East African Command Papers; WO 173, War Diaries for West Africa; WO 169, War Diaries Middle East Forces; WO 106, Directorate of Military Operations and Intelligence. See *PRO Handbooks no 15, The Second World War, A Guide to Documents in the Public Record Office*, (2nd edn, 1993) for further references.

8   See J M Lee and M Petter, *The Colonial Office, War and Development Policy* (1982), p 64, for a graph of the relative increase in file creation.

9   T 222/181–183 and 525–526; CO 866/49 and 50.

10   CO 878/30, Establishment Notice 22 of 1951.

11   CO 866/36/1407; CO 878/26, Establishment Notice 194 of 1939.

12   There is a list of the proceedings of councils and legislatures in the Report of the American Historical Association for 1908.

CHAPTER 5

Records of the Dominions Office, Commonwealth Relations Office and Successor Offices, 1922 to 1968

5.1 1922 to 1930

5.1.1 Transition to the file system

By the early 1920s, a group of clerical officers in the dominions sub-registry had evolved their own style of paper keeping for communications to and from self-governing countries, and their own filing conventions. During the First World War they had introduced subject classifications resulting in the three series Trade, War, and Prisoners of War (CO 687, CO 616, and CO 693). Moreover, they had created the 'waiting-bundle system', described above in chapter 4.4.1, with bundles lettered and numbered in red ink in the top right corner of the docket or jacket, and also in the register.

By 1925 the registry had also developed a single subject file which combined the advantages of the file and the single paper. When, on the receipt of a communication, it was judged that further correspondence would accumulate but that the subject would probably not grow complex, a subject file was created. The first communication was registered as usual, and later communications were attached to it. Each was briefly docketed and entered in the dominions register in the appropriate cutting and the proper chronological order. The registered number in each case was that of the first paper, to which the letter 'F' was added to indicate that it was a file, and was attached to that paper. Although this system anticipated the use of subject files, papers continued to be registered individually until the end of 1929, and once a subject was no longer active the bundles were split up and bound in the appropriate annual volumes by country and subject.

5.1.2 Introduction of the single dominions correspondence series

A major change in registration took place during the 1920s. Until then there were separate country classifications for papers relating to Australia, Canada, New Zealand, South Africa and Newfoundland (CO 418, CO 42, CO 209, CO 551, and CO 194 respectively). Thereafter nearly all in and out-letters were amalgamated in a single 'Dominions' series, CO 532 and, from 1925, DO 35. DO 35 continues uninterrupted until at least 1963 and is succeeded by a range of country and subject classes. See chapter 14 for an annual breakdown of the subjects covered.

Country registers ceased in 1922 and the main registers of dominions in-letters (CO 708 and, from 1926, DO 3) were expanded to include cuts for the dominions and their states (alongside the existing cuts for government offices and for individuals). Daily registers of dominions in-letters continued in a simplified form, but only one volume, 1926 to 1929, has been transferred to the PRO and has been placed at the end of the Colonial Office Daily Registers (CO 382/82).

Dominions out-letters were numbered in sub-series for each overseas destination. The registers of out-letters (CO 709 and, from 1926, DO 4) ceased in 1929 and were replaced by indexes of out-letters, which have not yet been transferred to the PRO.

The Dominions Division prepared its own index to the dominions series between 1922 and the adoption of subject files in 1930. These indexes, known as 'dominions notebooks', in three volumes, contain an alphabetically classified list of subjects with entries in yearly blocks under each subject. They have not yet been transferred to the Public Record Office.

Several other series were maintained for a few years but were then absorbed into the main series. The Irish Free State correspondence (CO 739) became part of the main series in 1924, while the South Africa High Commission correspondence (CO 417 and, from 1926, DO 9) and the Southern Rhodesia correspondence (CO 767 and, from 1926, DO 63) were included from 1930. The Dominions Office honours correspondence was kept as a separate Dominions Office series from 1927 (DO 36) but was absorbed into the main dominions class in 1930. Similarly, the Imperial Service Order papers formed a dominions series in 1927 (DO 81) but were included in the main series in 1930. Papers on the Order of St Michael and St George (CO 447) remained only a Colonial Office series. The records of the Oversea Settlement Committee continued to be kept separately from the main dominions series.

5.1.3 Communication with dominions governments

The appointment of high commissioners following the Balfour Declaration of 1926 altered the pattern of dominions correspondence. Until then the Colonial Office corresponded with the dominions through the governors-general in Australia, New Zealand, Canada, and South Africa, the governors of Southern Rhodesia, Newfoundland, and the Australian states, and the High Commissioner for the southern African territories. It also corresponded with the agents-general and dominions high commissioners in London.

Once high commissioners had been posted to the dominions, they replaced the sovereign's representatives as the main channel of communication, and received copies of all despatches to the dominions governments. The governors-general and governors remained responsible for correspondence concerning the monarch personally, and for honours and ceremonial matters. Whereas the records of the governors-general and governors form a permanent part of the records of the government concerned, the records of the high commissioners, as diplomatic representatives, have been regularly transferred to the PRO and are available as DO classes.

5.2 1930 to 1936

With the rapid growth of correspondence after 1926 it was necessary to revise the office's registry procedures and an office committee was appointed in October 1929 to make recommendations.[1] It condemned the 'waiting-bundle system' and the practice of giving each paper a new number in annual series. Instead, it recommended the 'Home Office system', already in use in the Colonial Office, of keeping papers on the same subject together on files.

The new system was introduced in January 1930, and while files were not universally adopted immediately, the office's records took on a new structure and arrangement. Registration was now essentially by subject, still within the one dominions series (DO 35), and each of the office's departments was allotted a block of subject file numbers. Department A was allocated 4001–6000, B 6001–8000, C 8001–10000, D 10001–12000, and Honours 12000–14000. As each new file was opened it took the next consecutive number from the departmental block. The files were boxed by registration number.

Register sheets, like those used in the Colonial Office, were introduced and were bound in annual volumes (DO 3). In a few cases a group of numbers relating to correspondence with a distinctive subject content was removed from its sequence to make a consolidated register, as for instance, 'Aviation' 8000–9790 or the 'South Africa High Commission Territories', 10041–21511. Newfoundland correspondence was registered distinctively as N1000–N1121. From 1930 the Dominions Office registry maintained a card index, which is available at Kew to 1936, recording file reference numbers and précis of the correspondence. The subject headings used are listed at the beginning of the DO 3 class list.

Dominions Office file jackets, printed with standard panels reproducing the information in the correspondence register, were similar to Colonial Office jackets but somewhat different in format. By 1931 the ladders used for circulating papers were twofold, one for circulation and one for the officer taking action. In 1933 printed panels headed 'further action' and 'printing' (instructions about confidential print) were added to the left-hand bottom corner of the jacket. Minutes commenced on the jacket front and carried over inside.

5.3   1936 to 1946

It had been hoped that blocks of numbers could be maintained for each department's work, but by 1936 it was clear that this system was unsuitable for the fluid character of Commonwealth relationships. Dominions Office subjects were frequently transferred from one assistant secretary to another, or involved a number of assistant secretaries, and a registry system tied to assistant secretary departments could not keep pace. Nor were the blocks large enough.

Consequently, in January 1937, an amended form of registration was introduced which followed subjects rather than departments. Number blocks were replaced by subject classifications symbolized by letters, which are listed at the beginning of the DO 3 class list. For instance, aviation papers were prefixed 'A' and international trade questions 'T'. Within these broad classifications specific subjects were allotted consecutive numbers, and aspects of subjects were given sub-numbers, for instance A10/3. The Dominions Office also made extensive use of single instance sub-files, to a far greater extent than did the Colonial Office, to indicate allied sub-divisions of the original subject. The office continued to create both unit papers and subject files, but files were no longer marked 'F', which was now a letter classification indicating foreign. Rather, the registers were inscribed with the word 'file' in red ink. The registers themselves (DO 3) were bound by their letter prefixes.

Files were much more widely used during the Second World War, and a number of new subject classifications, distinguished by the prefix 'W', were introduced to deal with wartime aspects of subject groups. For example, 'WF' became 'Constitutional, War Aspects of'. At the same time some entirely new classification group letters were introduced. In 1943 numbers were reallocated to the letter prefixes at a higher level than those used the previous year.

The dearth of trained clerks to staff the registry and the shortage of paper led to the abandoning of the correspondence registers (DO 3) in 1943. The card index served as a substitute until 1946 but as there was no subject précis or record of the action taken it is of limited value. It is, therefore, harder to trace papers during this period.

5.4   1947 to 1951

Normal registry procedure was restored in 1947 and correspondence registers were resumed, although they have not yet been transferred to the PRO. The 'A'–'Z' alphabetical classification of 1937 was readopted with a fresh number allocation within each letter prefix. The new numbers were linked with the preceding ones in the 'previous file' panel of the register. The use of files was now extended to all incoming correspondence, and unit files were abandoned. By this time the layout of the file jacket and minutes nearly replicated the Colonial Office files except that the jacket included a panel for printing instructions.

5.5   1951 to 1967

At the beginning of 1951, following a Treasury O & M team registry investigation, the CRO adopted a registry system recommended by the Treasury and similar to that adopted in the Colonial Office in the same period. Like that of the Colonial Office, it was to last fundamentally until the introduction of a common system with the Foreign Office at the beginning of 1967.

Under the new system departments were allocated two or three letter prefixes which are listed in chapter 15.4.2, and their files were classified under one, two, or more headings drawn from a standard list of subjects prepared by the Treasury O & M Division. The numbers allocated to the subjects constituted the file series, and within the series files took consecutive piece numbers. All departments used the numbers 1 to 9 for the Commonwealth countries, but otherwise every department numbered its own series.

Following the passage of the Public Records Act 1958, the Public Record Office urged departments to submit files to a first review not later than five years after the creation of the last paper on the file. To achieve this the Commonwealth Relations Office decided that it would be more practical and convenient to run files in more closely controlled cycles of three year periods, and a new series was begun on 1 January 1964. Existing files were closed, and new files were opened with reference numbers distinguished from the 1952 to 1963 series by the addition of the figure '2' to the departmental prefix, viz 2ADM, 2CON, 2DEF. This system of registration lasted until the end of 1966.

5.6   1967 to 1968

On 1 January 1967 the Foreign Office, Commonwealth Office, and Diplomatic Service Administration Office adopted a new common registration system in preparation for their merger in 1968. Under the new system different filing guides were used for the various categories of departments (political, functional, technical, and administrative) and provided a framework of broad subject groups into which the correspondence of those departments could be fitted. Where the number of files to be opened on a particular group was likely to be excessive over the whole file cycle, it was possible to arrange for planned sub-grouping.

The file number was formed using the departmental designation followed by the group number, an oblique stroke, and the file serial number beginning at 1. For instance, TE 1/5 represents the fifth file in group 1 of the West and General Africa (Economic) Registry. Case file references consisted of the departmental designation, the sub-divisional letter, the group number followed by the letter 'C', and the case file serial number. For instance, ENS 22C/15 represents the fifteenth file in the case file series of group 22 of the Soviet section of the Eastern European and Soviet registry.

Over the next twenty months many of the departments in the three offices were joined, causing complexities in the 1967/1968 file cycle. When the offices were finally merged, all files were closed, and a completely new set of files with new subject filing codes was begun on 17 October 1968.

5.7   Secret correspondence

From the time the Dominions Office was established, classified papers, unless top secret, were recorded in the main dominions registers (CO 708 and DO 3) and in secret registers, which have not yet been transferred to the PRO. A joint Dominions Office and Colonial Office committee considered the general principles of desecretization in 1934 and opened the majority of the papers to 1919, as noted in chapter 4.7, and subsequently an ad hoc Desecretization Committee considered specific papers. The papers desecretized for the period 1926 to 1929 are in DO 117. Thereafter desecretized files and papers have been replaced in the main correspondence series (DO 35), and the markings denoting secret have been crossed out in the registers.

5.8   Confidential print

The Dominions Office continued the Colonial Office practice of regularly printing correspondence for departmental use. Printing was selective, and in general the rule was that only correspondence dealing with major constitutional, political, or economic developments of lasting importance to the Commonwealth should be printed. This increased the number of copies available in the department and met the overseas high commissioners' need for references on important matters. The Commonwealth Relations Office series began in 1947 and continued until the merger with the Foreign Office in 1968. The print is in CO 886 and, from 1926, DO 114. There are separate series of prints on Australia (CO 881 and DO 115) until 1936, and on South Africa (CO 808, CO 879 and DO 116) until 1944.

A list of dominions papers printed between 1920 and 1929 is kept in the reference room at Kew and there is a copy at DO 114/14; thereafter the prints are individually described in the DO 114 class list.

5.9 Department of Technical Co-operation and Overseas Development Administration records

With the transfer of large areas of Colonial Office responsibilities to the Department of Technical Co-operation in July 1961 the two offices were closely connected, and they continued to use the same registration system. Personal files relating to the work of the Overseas Service Division were handed over to the DTC, while subject files remained with the Colonial Office. The DTC created its own files on technical issues, and there was constant communication between the two offices on many issues as described in chapter 4.5.3. Responsibility for the Communications Department was handed back to the Colonial Office in January 1966, together with the files created since 1961.

The records of the DTC are in the OD record classes: records created or inherited by the Department of Technical Co-operation, and of successive overseas development bodies. These classes also include the records of the Overseas Territories Tax Office, the Commonwealth Teacher Training Bursary Scheme, and the Directorate of Overseas Surveys. The records of the research institutes for which the DTC and the ODA were responsible are in the AY classes.

5.10 Central African Office records

The Central African Office, which was established on 19 March 1963 to look after relations with the Central African Federation and the territories of Northern and Southern Rhodesia and Nyasaland, maintained its own filing system following the Colonial Office pattern. The files were prefixed CAO and ran for the period 1962/1964. When the federation ceased to exist on 1 January 1964, responsibility for the three territories was taken over by the CRO. It is likely that the CAO files will form part of the DO (Dominions Office and Commonwealth Relations Office) classes.

Notes
1   CO 885/30, Organization of the Colonial and Dominions Offices; Papers, 1928–1932 (Conf Print Misc no 392).

CHAPTER 6

General information about the records and their use

6.1 Custody and selection of the records

In 1839, the earliest year for which there is detailed information about the custody of Colonial Office records, the older papers were in the charge of the librarian who was largely occupied as a record keeper. Some of the purely military papers had been sent to the State Paper Office at the end of the Napoleonic Wars, but the colonial papers were retained on the grounds that they were needed for frequent and immediate reference.

The office was in general very ill-housed until the Downing Street wing was available in 1876. In 1839 the building was acknowledged to be shaky and the records were intentionally packed in the basement to help to stabilize it. As the basements had to be pumped dry each day it is remarkable that the records should have survived in such relatively good condition. The library staff not only looked after them and bound them but compiled indexes to them as described in chapter 4.3.8.

The library ceased to be so concerned with the records when elimination and transfer to the Public Record Office began. In 1860 the Colonial Office sent some duplicate colonial despatches and minutes of assemblies and councils to the Public Record Office. This first transfer was looked upon as a special arrangement, a means of discarding some documents of minor importance. However, a year later the Colonial Office began sending larger quantities of records, and by 1869 the main files had been transferred up to 1850. The Colonial Office was well satisfied with the arrangements and the librarian noted in 1862 that all the volumes deposited 'can be obtained at a moment's notice'.[1]

In April 1880 the Treasury brought to the notice of all departments the provisions of the Public Record Office Act of 1877 as to the disposal of 'valueless' documents. Previously the Colonial Office had not destroyed any of its records but had bound up together the ephemeral and the important, and there was a good deal of doubt about the advisability of destruction at all. It was decided that papers that had already been bound, ie all those up to 1873, should not be touched, and instructions were given to bind no more for the present. The act required each department to prepare an inventory or schedule of valueless documents, but the Colonial Office was slow to do so.

By 1902 little had been done and the situation was becoming urgent owing to the strain on office accommodation. An office committee was formed to review the situation and made the following recommendations in its 1903 report: only post-1874 unbound papers in the office should be 'weeded'; 'weeding' should take place ten years from date of closure except for a few specific categories of papers; the originals of papers printed for Parliament or confidentially should be destroyed, although minutes upon them, if of importance, should be preserved; where the original of a print was destroyed a docket sheet giving the reference was to be inserted in its place and the reference noted in the register; documents printed in or for a colony should be detached from the papers and placed in the library; the register entries of destroyed papers should be stamped 'destroyed' or 'partly destroyed'; after 'weeding', papers should be arranged in register order and bound; a separate branch of the registry charged with the elimination of valueless documents should be formed.[2] These findings were adopted, a schedule was laid before Parliament in February 1904, and the work of 'weeding', binding and transfer proceeded. This first destruction schedule provided the basis for the selection of papers and files for the next fifty years. It was amended in 1924 and comprehensively revised for the Colonial Office and the Dominions Office in 1936, when a joint schedule was made. The 1936 schedule increased the period of preservation for various classes of documents from ten to twenty years, and it specifically required the preservation of all politically and historically important papers and those containing decisions on points of principle. The power to destroy scheduled documents before the scheduled period was granted under a defence regulation in 1941 and confirmed in the revised schedule of 1947.

Several special schedules dealt with particular record series. The first, laid in 1929, concerned the Overseas Settlement Department and resulted in the complete destruction of the Emigrants' Information Office records. A second, laid in 1934, covered the Empire Marketing Board records (CO 758 – CO 760 and CO 868). The last, laid in 1948, dealt with the records of the British Colonial Supply Mission in Washington DC.

Until the end of the joint establishment in 1947, records revision was undertaken jointly by the Colonial Office and the Dominions Office. The process was supervised by the Revision of Records Committee, which was considered part of the Whitley Council after 1923. Like the Desecretization Committee, it was called into being whenever decisions were required.

The first Commonwealth Relations Office schedule, framed in January 1949, provided for the review of Commonwealth Relations Office documents and those of the United Kingdom high commissioners and representatives abroad. India Office records were outside its scope as they came under the custody of a separate India Office Library and Records Department where they remain still. The department now forms part of the Oriental and India Office Collections of the British Library.

By the late 1940s the review of records in the Colonial Office and the Commonwealth Relations Office was governed by the underlying principle of minimum destruction revolving around two separate selection processes. The first, approximately ten years after the papers' creation, disposed of the obviously minor ephemeral and duplicated material. During the second, in a further fifteen years, every paper or file was considered on its merit and those which had outlived administrative or historical usefulness were destroyed. In 1950 the Colonial Office took the unusual step of placing records administration in the care of the librarian, while in the CRO it came under the Communications Department.

The procedures for reviewing records in British government departments were considered by the Committee on Departmental Records (the Grigg Committee) in 1954, and this led to the passage of the Public Records Act in 1958.[3] The old parliamentary schedules now ceased to have force and the departments instituted arrangements for selection based on the committee's recommendations. This required a departmental review five years after the records were created and a second review twenty years later by the departmental record officer in liaison with a Public Record Office inspecting officer.

6.2 Access

Historians were already consulting Colonial Office records in the 1820s, and in 1858 the office library was being visited by 'gentlemen who have the permission of the heads of the office to consult it for reference, particularly to Colonial Statutes'.[4] In 1868, after transfer to the Public Record Office had begun, the 'open' date was 1702 for North American correspondence and 1760 for other records. In 1872 the North American correspondence was also opened to 1760. In 1908 the office adopted the principles laid down by an interdepartmental committee which sought to impose a uniform date upon all departments and to abolish the former system of special permits. Colonial Office records were then opened to 1837 with few reservations. This was the year also chosen by the Foreign Office, and thereafter the Colonial Office and the Dominions Office kept pace with Foreign Office practice.

In 1948 the 'open' date was fixed at 1902 for all registered papers and for the proceedings of executive councils; access to legislative council proceedings and other official publications was unrestricted. With the passage of the Public Records Act 1958, public records were normally open to inspection fifty years from their date of creation, which was taken as the latest paper on the file or assembly of papers. The Public Records Act 1967 reduced the closure period to thirty years.

Files created on a three-year cycle are closed until thirty years from the completion of the cycle, the 1957 to 1959 block being opened in 1990 and so on. Files which were allowed to run over the three year period are opened with the main block for the period in which they were created unless subject to extended closure.

The Foreign and Commonwealth Office can, with the Lord Chancellor's permission, retain documents which are more than thirty years old, or prescribe a longer or shorter closure period for whole classes or for particular items. Files or volumes which have been closed for more than thirty years contain documents with material falling into one or more or the following categories: personal information which would cause distress to or endanger living persons or their immediate descendants, information obtained under a pledge of confidence, confidential commercial correspondence, and exceptionally sensitive papers the disclosure of which would be contrary to public interest whether on security or other grounds.

When records have been placed under extended closure the FCO decides how this is to be indicated. The list may give the title of the file and the period of closure, or may indicate the reference number and closure period but not the title. If all records listed on one page of a class list are closed the entire page is withheld and replaced by a note indicating the piece numbers it covers and when that page will be made available.

GENERAL INFORMATION ABOUT THE RECORDS

6.3 Means of reference

6.3.1 Arrangement of the finding aids

The regularly updated *Public Record Office Current Guide* provides an overview of all the record holdings and is the starting point for locating individual items. Part 1, division 800, gives an account of the departments which had some primary responsibility for overseas affairs. It describes their history, function and organization with cross-references to the classes of records they created.

Part 2 summarizes the record classes and is arranged by lettercodes and class numbers in alphanumeric order. Each class entry includes the title, covering dates and number of pieces. If the content is not implicit from the title, a general description indicates the contents of the class, with a note on any variations in the thirty-year rule and where necessary cross-references to other classes. Part 3 is an index to parts 1 and 2.

The records are described more specifically in class lists, now normally prepared by the transferring department with PRO advice. In order to locate the relevant class list, the reader will need to determine how the subject was handled; chapters 11–14 of this guide should assist.

Until fairly recently many lists of Colonial Office original correspondence classes for the period after the introduction of the file system in 1926 (see chapter 4.4) indicated only box and departmental file numbers. These lists are gradually being revised to include full file titles and new piece numbers, but in many cases readers must still requisition the departmental registers to obtain the file titles and numbers and then relate them to the skeletal list. The register sheet should carry a pencilled tick where the files have been preserved and be stamped 'DUS' where they have been destroyed under statute, but there are cases where this has not been done. If selection has resulted in gaps in a series, the registers can be used as sources in their own right, since register sheets summarize the contents of the papers on the original file. However, there are several classes for which the registers have not been transferred for the post-Second World War years and full lists have not yet been prepared. Users then need to work their way through the contents of whole boxes or rely on continuity of file registers obtained from references of other years. No registers have been transferred post 1951 as the records for this period are fully listed.

6.3.2 Supplementary finding aids

The calendaring of colonial state papers mentioned in chapter 4.3.7 is an ongoing project started in 1859; it currently covers the period up to 1739. The earlier papers have not been completely calendared but the omissions do not seem numerous or important. A calendar of East Indies papers begun at the same time includes state papers held in the Public Record Office and the British Library, and records of the India Office. A separate transcript of the Board of Trade journals (abstracts of which had previously been included in the colonial calendars) was begun in 1920 and eventually covered the period 1704 to 1782. The whole series has now been published.

The reorganization of early colonial records by the Public Record Office, also described in chapter 4.3.7, resulted immediately in the need for keys to obsolete references. By 1912 keys had been published to early colonial and Board of Trade records, including correspondence, entry books, acts and miscellanea.[5] The keys were later extended to include government gazettes, state papers domestic, Home Office records, naval lists, colonial newspapers, sessional papers, etc. A full copy of the keys, in three volumes, is available in the Reference Room at Kew under the title 'Colonial Office Key'.

There is a note on how to use the main class of Dominions Office correspondence (DO 35) at the beginning of the class list; a more detailed explanation of its use between 1937 and 1942 is available. Lists of Dominions Office subject headings used between 1930 and 1936 and of registration letter prefixes used between 1937 to 1952 are found at the beginning of the DO 3 class list.

The Dominions Office card index described in chapter 5.2 is available in the Reference Room for the years 1930–1936 with a note on its use. The Colonial Office card index, covering the work of the central and the sub-registries, survives but is incomplete and unwieldy and requires a considerable amount of work before it can be made useful. It is not at present available to readers. The PRO has, therefore, put its emphasis on completing the listing of CO classes.

A typescript index to CO/DO record classes is kept with the Colonial Office class lists. It covers country and subject classes with supplementary sections on Colonial Office records relating to Malaysia and newspapers in Colonial Office records.

Colonial records in the PRO and elsewhere are described in several printed guides including: M D Wainwright and N Matthews, *A Guide to Western Manuscripts and Documents in the British Isles relating to South and South East Asia* (London, 1965) and *A Guide to Manuscripts and Documents in the British Isles Relating to Africa* (London, 1971); P Walne, ed, *A Guide to Manuscript Sources for the History of Latin America and the Caribbean in the British Isles* (London, 1973); P Mander Jones, ed, *Manuscripts in the British Isles relating to Australia, New Zealand and the Pacific* (Canberra, 1972); P Jones, *Britain and Palestine 1914–1948: Archival Sources for the History of the British Mandate* (Oxford, 1979); and Alice Prochaska, *Irish History from 1700: A Guide to the Sources in the Public Record Office* (British Records Association, Archives and the User 6, 1986). Some space is devoted to Canada, Bermuda and the Caribbean in C M Andrews, *Guide to the Materials for American History, to 1783, in the Public Record Office of Great Britain* (Washington DC, 1912) and in C O Paullin and F L Paxson, *Guide to the Materials in London Archives for the History of the United States since 1783* (Washington DC, 1914).

6.3.3 Reference by other means

From 1862 onwards the annual *Colonial Office List* (from 1926 the *Dominions Office and Colonial Office List*) is the principal source of information on the organization and functions of these departments. Unfortunately its publication was suspended in 1940, and it was not produced during the war when both the Colonial Office and the Dominions Office underwent major organizational changes. When it was resumed in 1946 it did not cover the Dominions Office. The Commonwealth Relations Office published its own list between 1951 and 1965, and *Commonwealth Office Yearbooks* were published in 1966 and 1967. Thereafter the Foreign and Commonwealth Office has produced *Yearbooks of the Commonwealth*.

The Colonial Office establishment correspondence (CO 866) and establishment notices (CO 878) also provide a useful record of changes in departmental procedures. The notices normally carry the relevant establishment file numbers and after 1948

GENERAL INFORMATION ABOUT THE RECORDS

the file numbers are given in the index to the notices (CO 878/28). The corresponding Dominions Office/Commonwealth Relations Office establishment records do not survive.

Various other printed sources contribute to an overview of procedural and policy changes. In addition to the standard categories of printed records for each territory, which are described in chapters 4.9 and 11.2, HMSO published a consolidated annual report on colonial territories between 1937 and 1961. White Papers on colonial affairs laid before the two houses of the British Parliament are to be found in the published series of House of Commons and House of Lords sessional papers, which are available in the Public Record Office under the class references ZHC 1 and ZHL 1. Annual territorial reports were printed as sessional papers to 1917. White Papers on colonial subjects and allied publications, including the numbered series which ran from 1924 to 1966, are described in the HMSO sectional lists. See list 34 *The Colonial Office*.

6.3.4 Understanding registry codes and procedures

The allocation of registry codes and file registration numbers is explained in chapter 15. Chapter 16 provides illustrations of Colonial Office registry procedures.

6.4 Photographs, posters and maps

6.4.1 Photographs and posters

The PRO has a continuing project to note the existence and whereabouts of photographs found in the course of its work. Although new editions are produced periodically, it must be stressed that the catalogue is compiled on an ad hoc basis, and it by no means represents a complete picture of the PRO's holdings of photographs. Some photographs have been extracted from their original documents in the interests of conservation and these have been allocated references beginning with the letter code CN. CN 3 comprises photographs removed from Colonial Office classes.

There are other classes consisting wholly of photographs which are not included in the catalogue. These include the Central Office of Information British Empire Collection of Photographs (INF 10), which relates entirely to the former Colonial and Dominions Office territories. It comprises 8000 photographs showing the geography and way of life of colonial territories and Commonwealth countries from the post-Second World War period up to the 1960s.

The Empire Marketing Board posters in the class CO 956 illustrate production and marketing schemes throughout the empire between 1926 and 1939.

6.4.2 Maps

Maps present a more formidable problem. Of the vast number of maps in the Public Record Office, probably numbering several millions, the overwhelming majority are on registered files or in bundles and volumes of correspondence. The aim is gradually to identify them and either extract them from the files and catalogue them in full, or describe them in summary form, but leave them *in situ*, as appropriate. From 1980 transferring departments have been asked to indicate the existence of maps in their class lists, but otherwise there is no ready means of knowing which documents contain maps, and only a very small proportion have been located. Readers are therefore cautioned that the means of reference described below are only a jumping-off point and that they should by no means infer that if a map is not described there, it is not in the PRO.

The main Colonial Office map series is being transferred to the PRO in several stages. Material to 1910 is described in a printed indexed catalogue: *Maps and Plans: Series One* (CO 700). A second deposit of more than 1,100 maps covering the period to 1940 is in CO 1047. The remaining material is being transferred as CO 1054. The residue, not selected for permanent preservation in the Public Record Office, has been deposited in the library of the Royal Geographical Society. No Dominions Office map class has yet been transferred.

A published catalogue, *Maps and Plans in the Public Record Office*, describing roughly 25,000 items, is available in three volumes, two of which, *America and the West Indies* (1974) and *Africa* (1983) include maps of the former empire. A fourth volume on Europe will include maps of the former colonial territories of Gibraltar, Cyprus, Malta, the Ionian Islands and Heligoland. This catalogue includes maps located in files as well as the maps in CO 700 and other major map classes, notably FO 925, Foreign Office Maps and Plans, an especially important source of boundary maps. The *America* and *Africa* volumes do not include unamended printed maps that seem to correspond to maps in the British Library *Catalogue of Printed Maps, Charts and Plans* (1967), so it is worth referring back to CO 700 and FO 925, which do cover them. The *Europe* volume will describe such printed material.

A card index in the Map Room describes in full material located after the catalogue's publication and covers regions outside its scope. It is hoped in due course to produce a computerized catalogue based on the cards, which will ultimately include the published catalogue. The summary calendar of unextracted maps provides a means of reference to some of the maps which have, since 1985, been discovered within original files and volumes, and which are not otherwise served by finding aids.

Notes

1 CO 323/263, PRO to CO, 25 January 1862.

2 CO 885/8, Valueless Colonial Office Documents; Report of the Committee and Schedule, 1903 (Conf Print Misc No 155).

3 Cmnd 163, HC (1953–1954) XI, Report of the Committee on Departmental Records.

4 CO 878/2, no 107.

5. C M Andrews, *Guide to the Materials for American History, to 1783, in the Public Record Office of Great Britain*, Carnegie Institute of Washington, 1912, Appendix B, pp 279–307. C S S Higham subsequently published, *The Colonial Entry Books, A Brief Guide to the Colonial Records in the Public Record Office Before 1696*, in the Historical Association series *Helps for Students of History*, No 45.

CHAPTER 7

Lists of Ministers and Senior Officials responsible for Colonial, Dominions and Commonwealth Affairs, 1768 to 1968

This section comprises chronological lists of ministers and senior officials from secretaries of state down to assistant secretaries. It can be used to trace the source of minutes initialled on files, but it may be necessary to search the lists at several levels to locate an individual. It should also assist, in conjunction with chapters 11, 12, and 13, in understanding office organization. The names of principals are not included but can be found in the printed lists indicated below.

The lists provided here are arranged by the date of appointment, except those for the assistant under-secretaries in the Colonial and Commonwealth Offices (who tended to be heads of divisions) and assistant secretaries (heads of departments) in all offices. The lists are arranged annually.

The details have been taken from the *Colonial Office List, Commonwealth Relations Office List* and the *Commonwealth Office Yearbook*. Names appear in the form given in these publications. The lists were not published during the Second World War, and the *Commonwealth Relations Office List* did not appear until 1953, causing gaps in the information. It was the practice to issue these lists in the year printed on the spine, but in fact they were normally prepared during the previous year. For consistency the dates here reflect the dates on the spines, but readers may need to check the previous or sometimes the subsequent year to locate a given individual. Where there is uncertainty, reference should be made to the record of officers' service in the printed lists to confirm the date of appointment. Information about Colonial Office assistant under-secretaries and assistant secretaries for the years 1941–1945 has been added from a list prepared by Professor J M Lee.

Contents:

7.1 Secretaries of state who administered the affairs of the colonies between 1768 and 1794
7.2 Secretaries of state for the Colonial and War Departments from 1794 to 1854
7.3 Secretaries of state for the colonies and Colonial Office ministers
7.4 Colonial Office officials
7.5 Secretaries of state for dominions affairs and Dominions Office ministers
7.6 Dominions Office officials
7.7 Secretaries of state for Commonwealth relations and Commonwealth Relations Office ministers
7.8 Commonwealth Relations Office officials

7.9 Secretaries of state for Commonwealth affairs and Commonwealth Office ministers
7.10 Commonwealth Office officials
7.11 Overseas Development Administration ministers and officials

7.1 Secretaries of state who administered the affairs of the colonies between 1768 and 1794

1768 Feb	Wills Hill, Earl of Hillsborough	1782 July	Thomas Townshend
1772 Aug	William, Earl of Dartmouth	1783 Apr	Frederick Lord North
1776 Jan	Lord George Sackville Germaine	1783 Dec	Thomas Lord Sydney
1782 Mar	Welbore Ellis	1789 June	William Wyndham Grenville
1782 Apr	Marquess of Lansdowne and Earl of Shelburne	1791 June	Henry Dundas
		1794 Aug	William Henry, Duke of Portland

7.2 Secretaries of state for the Colonial and War Departments from 1794 to 1854

1794	Rt Hon Henry Dundas	1833	Rt Hon E G Stanley
1801	Lord Hobart	1834	Rt Hon Thomas Spring Rice, Earl of Aberdeen
1804	Earl Camden		
1805	Viscount Castlereagh	1835	Rt Hon Chas Grant
1806	Rt Hon W Windham	1839	Marquess of Normanby, Lord John Russell
1807	Viscount Castlereagh		
1809	Earl of Liverpool	1841	Lord Stanley
1812	Earl Bathurst	1845	Rt Hon W E Gladstone
1827	Rt Hon F J Robinson (Viscount Goderich), Rt Hon W Huskisson	1846	Earl Grey
		1852	Rt Hon Sir John S Pakington
1828	Rt Hon Sir George Murray	1852	Duke of Newcastle
1830	Viscount Goderich		

7.3 Secretaries of state for the colonies and Colonial Office ministers

Secretaries of state for the colonies

1854 June	Rt Hon Sir G Grey	1868 Dec	Earl Granville
1855 Feb	Rt Hon Sidney Herbert	1870 July	Earl of Kimberley
1855 Mar	Lord John Russell	1874 Feb	Earl of Carnarvon
1855 July	Rt Hon Sir William Molesworth	1878 Feb	Rt Hon Sir Michael E Hicks-Beach
1855 Nov	Rt Hon Henry Labouchere		
1858 Feb	Lord Stanley	1880 Apr	Earl of Kimberley
1858 May	Rt Hon Sir Edward Bulwer Lytton	1882 Dec	Earl of Derby
		1885 June	Rt Hon F A Stanley
1859 June	Duke of Newcastle	1886 Feb	Earl Granville
1864 Apr	Rt Hon Edward Cardwell	1886 Aug	Rt Hon Edward Stanhope
1866 July	Earl of Carnarvon	1887 Jan	Rt Hon Sir Henry Thurstan Holland
1867 Mar	Duke of Buckingham and Chandos		
		1892 Aug	Marquess of Ripon

LISTS OF MINISTERS AND SENIOR OFFICIALS

1895 June	Rt Hon Joseph Chamberlain	1936 May	Rt Hon W G A Ormsby-Gore
1903 Oct	Rt Hon Alfred Lyttelton	1938 May	Rt Hon Malcolm MacDonald
1905 Dec	Rt Hon Earl of Elgin and Kincardine	1940 May	Rt Hon Lord Lloyd
		1941 Feb	Rt Hon Lord Moyne
1908 Apr	Earl of Crewe	1942 Feb	Rt Hon Viscount Cranborne
1910 Nov	Rt Hon Lewis Harcourt	1942 Nov	Rt Hon O F G Stanley
1915 May	Rt Hon A Bonar Law	1945 Aug	Rt Hon G H Hall
1916 Dec	Rt Hon W H Long	1946 Oct	Rt Hon A Creech Jones
1919 Jan	Viscount Milner	1950 Mar	Rt Hon James Griffiths
1921 Feb	Rt Hon Winston Churchill	1951 Oct	Rt Hon Oliver Lyttelton
1922 Oct	Duke of Devonshire	1954 July	Rt Hon Alan T Lennox-Boyd
1924 Jan	Rt Hon J H Thomas	1959 Oct	Rt Hon Iain Macleod
1924 Nov	Rt Hon L S Amery	1961 Oct	Rt Hon Reginald Maudling
1929 June	Rt Hon Lord Passfield	1962 July	Rt Hon Duncan Sandys
1931 Aug	Rt Hon J H Thomas	1964 Oct	Rt Hon Anthony Greenwood
1931 Nov	Rt Hon Sir Philip Cunliffe-Lister	1965 Dec	Rt Hon The Earl of Longford
1935 June	Rt Hon Malcolm MacDonald	1966 Apr	Rt Hon Frederick Lee
1935 Nov	Rt Hon J H Thomas		

Ministers of state for colonial affairs

1948 Jan	Rt Hon The Earl of Listowel	1962 Apr	Most Hon The Marquess of Lansdowne
1950 Mar	Rt Hon John Dugdale		
1951 Nov	Rt Hon Alan T Lennox-Boyd	1963 Oct	Most Hon The Marquess of Lansdowne and His Grace the Duke of Devonshire (joint ministers of state for commonwealth relations and for the colonies)
1952 May	Rt Hon Henry Hopkinson		
1955 Dec	Hon John H Hare		
1956 Oct	Rt Hon John Maclay		
1957 Jan	Rt Hon The Earl of Perth		

Parliamentary under-secretaries of state for the colonies

1830	Viscount Howick	1868	Rt Hon W Monsell
1833	Sir John Shaw Lefevre	1871	E H Knatchbull-Hugessen
1834	Rt Hon W E Gladstone	1874	J Lowther
1835	Sir George Grey	1878	Earl Cadogan
1839	Rt Hon Henry Labouchere	1880	Rt Hon Sir M E Grant Duff
1839	R V Smith	1881	L H Courtney
1841	G W Hope	1882	Rt Hon Evelyn Ashley
1845	Lord Lyttelton	1885	Earl of Dunraven
1846	B Hawes	1886	Rt Hon Sir G Osborne Morgan
1851	F Peel	1886	Earl of Dunraven
1852 Feb	Rt Hon Earl of Desart	1887	Earl of Onslow
1852 Dec	F Peel	1888	Baron Henry de Worms
1855	J Ball	1892	S C Buxton
1857	C S Fortescue	1895	Earl of Selborne
1858	Earl of Carnarvon	1900	Earl of Onslow
1859	C S Fortescue	1903	Duke of Marlborough
1865	W E Forster	1905	Winston L S Churchill
1866	Rt Hon Sir C B Adderley	1908	Col J E B Seely

1911 Mar	Rt Hon Lord Lucas	1940	Rt Hon G H Hall
1911 Oct	Rt Hon Lord Emmott	1942	Rt Hon Harold Macmillan
1914	Rt Hon Lord Islington	1943	Duke of Devonshire
1915	Sir Arthur Steel-Maitland	1945	Rt Hon A Creech Jones
1917	W A S Hewins	1946	I Thomas
1919	Rt Hon Lt-Col L S Amery	1947 Oct	D R Rees-Williams
1921	Hon E F L Wood	1950 Mar	T F Cook
1922	Hon W G A Ormsby-Gore	1951 Nov	Rt Hon The Earl of Munster
1924 Jan	Lord Arnold	1954 Oct	Lord Lloyd
1924 Nov	Rt Hon W G A Ormsby-Gore	1957 Jan	J D Profumo
1929 June	W Lunn	1958 Dec	Rt Hon Julian Amery
1929 Dec	Dr T Drummond Shiels	1960 Oct	Hon Hugh Fraser
1931	Sir Robert Hamilton	1962 July	N Fisher
1932	Earl of Plymouth	1964 Oct	Mrs Eirene White
1936	Rt Hon Earl De La Warr	1966 Apr	J Stonehouse
1937	Marquess of Dufferin and Ava		

Parliamentary under-secretaries of state for Commonwealth relations and for the colonies

1963 Oct	N Fisher, J Tilney, R Hornby	1965 Oct	Lord Beswick
1964 Oct	Lord Taylor		

7.4 Colonial Office officials

Permanent under-secretaries of state for the colonies

1825	R W Hay	1916	Sir George V Fiddes
1836	Sir James Stephen	1921	Sir James E Masterton-Smith
1847	H Merivale	1925	Brig-Gen Sir Samuel H Wilson
1860	Sir Frederic Rogers	1933	Sir John Maffey
1871	Hon Sir Robert G Wyndham Herbert	1937 July	Sir A C Parkinson
		1940 Feb	Sir George Gater
1892	Hon Sir Robert H Meade	1940 May	Sir A C Parkinson
1897	Sir Edward Wingfield	1942 Apr	Sir George Gater
1900	Sir Montague F Ommanney	1947 Feb	Sir Thomas Lloyd
1907	Sir Francis J S Hopwood	1956 Aug	Sir John Macpherson
1911	Sir John Anderson	1959 Aug	Sir Hilton Poynton

Deputy under-secretaries of state for the colonies

1931 Aug	Sir John Shuckburgh	1956 July	Sir John Martin; Sir Hilton Poynton (joint)
1942 Mar	Sir William Battershill		
1945 Apr	Sir Arthur Dawe	1959 Aug	Sir William Gorell Barnes; Sir John Martin (joint)
1947 Apr	Sir Sydney Caine; Sir Charles Jeffries (joint)		
		1965 Jan	A N Galsworthy
1948 Aug	Sir Hilton Poynton; Sir Charles Jeffries (joint)		

Assistant under-secretaries of state for the colonies

This list includes deputy under-secretaries where they had direct responsibilities for departments.

1927–1928
Sir Gilbert Grindle: General, West Indian, Far Eastern, Ceylon and Mauritius
Sir John Shuckburgh: Middle East
Sir Charles Strachey: Gold Coast and Mediterranean, Nigeria, East Africa, Tanganyika and Somaliland, West Africa Frontier Force (WAFF), King's African Rifles (KAR)

1929–1930
Sir Cecil Bottomley: West Africa, East Africa, Tanganyika and Somaliland, WAFF, KAR
Sir Gilbert Grindle: General, West Indian, Far Eastern
Sir John Shuckburgh: Middle East, Ceylon and Mediterranean

1931
Sir Cecil Bottomley: as above
Sir Gilbert Grindle: as above
Sir John Shuckburgh: as above
G J Tomlinson: Personnel

1932
Sir Cecil Bottomley: as above
A C Parkinson: Middle East (including Aden and Cyprus)
Sir John Shuckburgh: General, West Indian, Eastern, Pacific and Mediterranean
G J Tomlinson: Personnel

1933–1937
Sir John Shuckburgh: General, Eastern, Pacific and Mediterranean (excluding Cyprus)
Sir Cecil Bottomley: West Africa, East Africa, Tanganyika and Somaliland, WAFF, KAR
A C Parkinson: Middle East, West Indian (including Cyprus)
G J Tomlinson: Personnel

1938
Sir Cecil Bottomley: West Africa, East Africa, Tanganyika and Somaliland, WAFF, KAR
Sir Henry Moore: Economic, West Indies, Eastern
Sir George Tomlinson: Personnel

1939
A J Dawe: West Africa, East Africa, Tanganyika and Somaliland, WAFF, KAR
Sir Henry Moore: as above
Sir George Tomlinson: as above

1940
Sir Alan Burns: West Indies, Eastern
G L Clauson: Economic
A J Dawe: as above
C J Jeffries: Personnel

1941
W D Battershill: West Indies, Eastern
G L Clauson: as above
A J Dawe: as above
Sir John Shuckburgh (deputy under-secretary): General, Defence, Pacific and Mediterranean, Colonial Development and Social Services, Middle East
Sir George Tomlinson: as above

1942
Sir William Battershill (deputy under-secretary): Middle East, West Indies, Pacific and Mediterranean
G L Clauson: Economic
A J Dawe: West Africa, East Africa, Tanganyika
G E Gent: General, Defence, Eastern, Public Relations
C J Jeffries: Colonial Service, Colonial Development and Social Services

1943
Sir William Battershill (deputy under-secretary): Middle East, Mediterranean
G L Clauson: Economic
G H Creasy: Supplies, Production

A J Dawe: West Africa, East Africa, Central Africa
G E Gent: Defence, Eastern, Ceylon and Pacific, Communications, Prisoners of War
C J Jeffries: Colonial Service, Welfare
T I Lloyd: General, Social Services, West Indies, Public Relations

1944
S Caine: Supplies, Production, Economic and Finance
G H Creasy: West Africa, East Africa, Central Africa
A J Dawe: Middle East, Mediterranean
G E Gent: Defence and General, Eastern, Far Eastern Commerce, Prisoners of War
C J Jeffries: Colonial Service, General, Ceylon and Pacific
T I Lloyd: Social Services, West Indies, Public Relations, Communications

1945
S Caine: Supplies, Production, Economic and Finance, Research
G H Creasy: as above
G E Gent: as above
C J Jeffries: Colonial Service, General, Ceylon and Pacific
T I Lloyd: as above
J M Martin: Middle East, Mediterranean

1946
S Caine: Supplies, Production, Economic and Finance, Research
G H Creasy: as above
G E Gent: as above
C J Jeffries: as above
T I Lloyd: as above
J M Martin: Middle East, Mediterranean

1947
Sir Gerard Clauson: Commercial Relations and Supplies, Communications, Marketing
C G Eastwood: Finance, Research, Production

C J Jeffries: Colonial Service, Ceylon and Pacific
T I Lloyd: Eastern, Prisoners of War
J M Martin: Middle East, Mediterranean, Public Relations
A H Poynton: Social Services, Welfare, International Relations
G F Seel: West Africa, East and Central Africa, General

1948
Sir Gerard Clauson: Commercial Relations and Supplies, Communications, Production and Marketing
A B Cohen: Africa
C G Eastwood: Production and Marketing (except papers going to Sir Gerard Clauson)
W L Gorell Barnes: Finance, Economic Intelligence and Planning, Research
J M Martin: Middle East, Mediterranean
A H Poynton: International Relations, Social Services, Welfare
G F Seel: Eastern, General, West Indies

1949
Sir Gerard Clauson: Communications, Economic Relations, Production and Marketing
A B Cohen: as above
C G Eastwood: as above
W L Gorell Barnes: Economic General, Finance, Statistics, Supplies
J M Martin: International Relations, Mediterranean, Social Services
J J Paskin: Eastern, Hong Kong and Pacific
G F Seel: Defence and General, West Indian

1950
Sir Gerard Clauson: as above
A B Cohen: as above
C G Eastwood: as above
W L Gorell Barnes: as above
J M Martin: as above
J J Paskin: Hong Kong and Pacific, South-East Asia
G F Seel: as above
J B Williams: Colonial Service, Welfare

LISTS OF MINISTERS AND SENIOR OFFICIALS

1951
Sir Gerard Clauson: as above
A B Cohen: as above
C G Eastwood: as above
W L Gorell Barnes: as above
S E Luke: Defence and General, West Indian
J M Martin: as above
J J Paskin: as above
J B Williams: as above

1952
C G Eastwood: Production and Marketing, Research
W L Gorell Barnes: Africa
S E Luke: as above
Sir John Martin: International Relations, Mediterranean, Social Services
E Melville: Economic General, Finance, Statistics, Supplies
W B Monson: Communications, Economic Relations
J J Paskin: as above
J B Williams: Colonial Service, Students

1953
C Y Carstairs: Information, Communications
W L Gorell Barnes: as above
Sir John Martin: as above
E Melville: as above
W B Monson: Production and Marketing, Research
J J Paskin: as above
P Rogers: Defence and General, West Indian
A R Thomas: Colonial Service, Students, Coronation

1954
H T Bourdillon: International Relations, Mediterranean, Social Services
C Y Carstairs: Defence and General, Information, Communications
W L Gorell Barnes: as above
Sir John Martin: Hong Kong and Pacific, South-East Asia
E Melville: Economic General, Finance, Statistics, Supplies, Commercial Treaties
W B Monson: as above
P Rogers: West Indian

A R Thomas: Colonial Service, Students

1955
H T Bourdillon: International Relations, Social Services
C Y Carstairs: as above
C G Eastwood: West African
W L Gorell Barnes: Central African and Aden, East African
Sir John Martin: Pacific, Mediterranean, Far Eastern
E Melville: Economic General, Finance, Statistics, Commercial Relations and Supplies
W B Monson: as above
P Rogers: as above
A R Thomas: Overseas Service, Students

1956
H T Bourdillon: International Relations, Social Services, General
C Y Carstairs: Defence, Information, Communications, Intelligence and Security, Police
C G Eastwood: as above
W L Gorell Barnes: African Studies, Central African and Aden, East African
Sir John Martin: as above
E Melville: Economic General, Finance, Statistics
W B Monson: as above
P Rogers: as above
A R Thomas: as above

1957
H T Bourdillon: as above
C Y Carstairs: as above
C G Eastwood: as above
A N Galsworthy: Economic General, Finance, Statistics
W L Gorell Barnes: as above
E Melville: Far Eastern, Mediterranean
W B Monson: as above
P Rogers: West Indian, Pacific
A R Thomas: as above

1958
H T Bourdillon: as above

C Y Carstairs: as above
C G Eastwood: West African, St Helena,
   Ascension and Tristan da Cunha
W L Gorell Barnes: as above
A N Galsworthy: as above
E Melville: as above
W B Monson: as above
P Rogers: West Indian, Pacific, Falkland
   Islands and Antarctic
A R Thomas: as above

1959
H T Bourdillon: as above
C Y Carstairs: as above
C G Eastwood: as above
A N Galsworthy: as above
W L Gorell Barnes: as above
E Melville: as above
W B Monson: as above
P Rogers: as above
A R Thomas: Overseas Service (director of
   recruitment), Students

1960
H T Bourdillon: Deputy UK Commissioner,
   Singapore
C Y Carstairs: Defence, Information,
   Communications, Intelligence, Police and
   Security, Social Services
C G Eastwood: West African, St Helena,
   Ascension and Tristan da Cunha,
   International Relations, Gulf of Aden and
   General
A N Galsworthy: Economic General 'A',
   Finance, Statistics
E Melville: as above
W B Monson: African Studies, Central
   African, East African
P Rogers: as above
T Smith: Production and Marketing,
   Research, Economic General 'B'
A R Thomas: West Indian, Pacific and Indian
   Ocean, Falkland Islands and Antarctic

1961
H T Bourdillon: as above
C Y Carstairs: as above

C G Eastwood: West African, St Helena,
   Ascension and Tristan da Cunha,
   International Relations, General
A N Galsworthy: as above
E Melville: as above
W B Monson: as above
P Rogers: as above
T Smith: as above
A R Thomas: as above

1962
C Y Carstairs: Defence, Intelligence and
   Security, Information, International
   Relations and General, Social Services
C G Eastwood: Aden, Far Eastern,
   Mediterranean, Gambia, St Helena,
   Ascension and Tristan da Cunha
A N Galsworthy: Economic General (part),
   Economists Branch, Finance
W B Monson: Central African, East African,
   Southern African
T Smith: Economic General (part), Economic
   Relations
A R Thomas: as above

1963
C G Eastwood: Mediterranean and Atlantic,
   International Relations and General,
   Social Services, Aden Affairs
A N Galsworthy: as above
W B Monson: East African, Southern Africa
T Smith: as above
A R Thomas: as above
W I Wallace: Defence, Intelligence and
   Security, Information, Far Eastern

1964
C G Eastwood: Defence, Intelligence and
   Security, Information, International
   Relations and General, Mediterranean and
   Atlantic
A N Galsworthy: Economic General (part),
   Economists Branch, Finance, Social
   Services
W B Monson: Aden, Southern Africa
T Smith: Economic General (part), Economic
   Relations, Pacific and Indian Ocean
W I Wallace: Hong Kong, West Indies

LISTS OF MINISTERS AND SENIOR OFFICIALS

1965
C G Eastwood: Defence, Intelligence and Security, Information, International Relations and General, Atlantic
J E Marnham: Aden, Southern Africa
T Smith: Economic General, Pacific and Indian Ocean
W I Wallace: as above

1966
C G Eastwood: Defence, Intelligence and Security, Information, International Relations and General, Atlantic, Constitutional Planning
J E Marnham: as above
T Smith: Economic General, Pacific and Indian Ocean, Communications
W I Wallace: as above

Assistant secretaries of state
1926
W C Bottomley: East Africa
H R Cowell: Ceylon and Mauritius
E R Darnley: West Indies
W D Ellis: Far Eastern
A R Fiddian: Gold Coast and Mediterranean
J F Green: Tanganyika and Somaliland
A J Harding: Nigeria
O G Williams: General
H W Young: Middle East

1927
W C Bottomley: East Africa
H R Cowell: Ceylon and Mauritius
E R Darnley: West Indies
W D Ellis: Far Eastern
A R Fiddian: Gold Coast and Mediterranean
J E Flood: Nigeria
J F Green: Tanganyika and Somaliland
A J Harding: Middle East
O G Williams: General

1928
H R Cowell: Ceylon and Mauritius
E R Darnley: West Indies
W D Ellis: Far Eastern
A R Fiddian: Gold Coast and Mediterranean
J E Flood: Nigeria
J F Green: Tanganyika and Somaliland
A J Harding: Middle East
A C Parkinson: East Africa
O G Williams: General

1929
H R Cowell: Ceylon and Mauritius
E R Darnley: West Indies
W D Ellis: Far Eastern

A R Fiddian: Gold Coast and Mediterranean
J E Flood: Nigeria
J F Green: Tanganyika and Somaliland
A J Harding: Middle East
A C Parkinson: East Africa
O G Williams: General

1930
H R Cowell: Ceylon and Mauritius
E R Darnley: West Indies
W D Ellis: Far Eastern
A R Fiddian: General
J E Flood: West Africa
J F Green: Tanganyika and Somaliland
A C Parkinson: East Africa
O G Williams: Middle East

1931
H R Cowell: Ceylon and Mediterranean
E R Darnley: West Indies
W D Ellis: Far Eastern
A R Fiddian: West Africa
J E Flood: Middle East
R D Furse: Personnel (Recruitment and Training)
J F Green: Tanganyika and Somaliland
C J Jeffries: Personnel (Colonial Service)
A C Parkinson: East Africa
R V Vernon: General

1932
H T Allen: East Africa
H Beckett: West Indies
H R Cowell: Eastern
E R Darnley: Pacific and Mediterranean
A R Fiddian: West Africa

J E Flood: Middle East
R D Furse: Personnel (Recruitment and
   Training)
J F Green: Tanganyika and Somaliland
C J Jeffries: Personnel (Colonial Service)
R V Vernon: General

1933
H T Allen: East Africa
H Beckett: West Indies
J A Calder: Tanganyika and Somaliland
H R Cowell: Eastern
A R Fiddian: West Africa
J E Flood: Pacific and Mediterranean
R D Furse: Personnel (Recruitment and
   Training)
C J Jeffries: Personnel (Colonial Service)
R V Vernon: General
O G Williams: Middle East

1934
H T Allen: Pacific and Mediterranean
H Beckett: West Indies
H R Cowell: Eastern
J A Calder: Tanganyika
A R Fiddian: West Africa
J E Flood: East Africa
R D Furse: Personnel (Recruitment and
   Training)
C J Jeffries: Personnel (Colonial Service)
R V Vernon: General
O G Williams: Middle East

1935
H T Allen: Pacific and Mediterranean
H Beckett: West Indies
J A Calder: Tanganyika and Somaliland
G L Clauson: General (Economic)
H R Cowell: Eastern
A R Fiddian: West Africa
J E Flood: East Africa
R D Furse: Personnel (Recruitment and
   Training)
C J Jeffries: Personnel (Colonial Service)
R V Vernon: General
O G Williams: Middle East

1936–1937
J Beckett: West Indies
J A Calder: Tanganyika and Somaliland
G L Clauson: General (Economic)
H R Cowell: Eastern
A J Dawe: Pacific and Mediterranean
H F Downie: West Africa
J E Flood: East Africa
R D Furse: Personnel (Recruitment and
   Training)
C J Jeffries: Personnel (Colonial Service)
R V Vernon: General
O G Williams: Middle East

1938
A B Acheson: Pacific and Mediterranean
H Beckett: West Indies
E B Boyd: Tanganyika and Somaliland
J A Calder: General
G L Clauson: General (Economic)
H R Cowell: Eastern
A J Dawe: East Africa
H F Downie: Middle East
R D Furse: Personnel (Recruitment and
   Training)
C J Jeffries: Personnel (Colonial Service)
O G Williams: West Africa

1939
A B Acheson: Pacific and Mediterranean
E B Boyd: General
H Beckett: West Indies
J A Calder: Economic
G L Clauson: Social Services
G H Creasy: Tanganyika and Somaliland
H F Downie: Middle East
L B Freeston: East Africa
R D Furse: Personnel (Recruitment and
   Training)
G E Gent: Eastern
C J Jeffries: Personnel (Colonial Service)
O G Williams: West Africa

1940
A B Acheson: Pacific and Mediterranean
H Beckett: West Indian
E B Boyd: Tanganyika and Somaliland
S Caine: Economic

LISTS OF MINISTERS AND SENIOR OFFICIALS

J A Calder: General
G H Creasy: Colonial Development and Social Services
H F Downie: Middle East
R D Furse: Personnel (Recruitment and Training)
G E Gent: Eastern
T I Lloyd: Personnel (Colonial Service)
G F Seel: East Africa
O G Williams: West Africa

1941
A B Acheson: Pacific and Mediterranean
H Beckett (Oct): East Africa
H Beckett (Oct): Tanganyika
E B Boyd (Oct): Middle East
S Caine: Economic
J A Calder: Defence
H F Downie (Oct): West Indies
R D Furse: Appointments
G E Gent (K W Blaxter, Acting): Eastern
F J Howard: Establishments
T I Lloyd: Colonial Service
J J Paskin (Mar): Colonial Development and Social Services
J B Sidebotham (Oct): General
O G Williams: West Africa

1942
A B Acheson: Pacific and Mediterranean
H Beckett (July): West Indies
H Beckett/G F Seel: East Africa
K W Blaxter (July): Colonial Development and Social Services
E B Boyd: Middle East
S Caine (Mar): Financial Adviser
G H Creasy: Economic
R D Furse: Appointments
F J Howard: Establishments
T I Lloyd: Defence
J J Paskin (July): Eastern
N J Sabine (Nov): Public Relations
G F Seel (July): Tanganyika
G F Seel/S E Luke (Nov): Colonial Service
J B Sidebotham: General
O G Williams: West Africa

1943
A B Acheson: Pacific and Mediterranean
H Beckett: West Indies
W J Bigg (July): Communications
K W Blaxter: Colonial Development and Social Services
K W Blaxter (Apr): Social Services
E B Boyd: Middle East
S Caine: Financial Adviser
C Y Carstairs (Apr): Production
A B Cohen (Apr): Central Africa
A B Cohen: Tanganyika
A K Cole (Apr): Prisoners of War
G H Creasy: Economic (Supplies and Food)
C G Eastwood: General
R D Furse: Appointments
J L Keith: Welfare
S E Luke: Colonial Service
A H Poynton: Defence
J J Paskin: Eastern
S Robinson: Establishments
N J Sabine: Public Relations
G F Seel: East Africa
J B Sidebotham (Apr): Ceylon and Pacific
J B Williams (Apr): Supplies
O G Williams: West Africa

1944
A B Acheson: General
A B Acheson: Mediterranean
H Beckett: West Indies
W J Bigg: Communications
K W Blaxter: Social Services
A B Cohen: Central Africa
A K Cole: Prisoners of War
C G Eastwood: Middle East
R D Furse (Feb): Appointments (A)
J L Keith: Welfare
S E Luke (Sept): Colonial Service (A)
N L Mayle (July): Far Eastern Commerce
W B Monson (July): Production
A F Newbolt (Feb): Appointments (C)
J J Paskin: Eastern
F J Pedler: Economic and Finance
A H Poynton: Defence and General
S Robinson: Establishments
N J Sabine: Public Relations
G F Seel: East Africa

J B Sidebotham: Ceylon and Pacific
R A Whittle (Sept): Colonial Service (B)
J B Williams: Supplies
O G Williams: West Africa

1945
A B Acheson: General
A B Acheson: Mediterranean
H Beckett: West Indies
W J Bigg: Communications
K W Blaxter: Social Services
C Y Carstairs (June): Research
A B Cohen: East and Central Africa
A K Cole: Prisoners of War
T W Davis (June): Commercial Relations and Supplies
C G Eastwood: Middle East
R D Furse: Appointments (A)
J L Keith: Welfare
S E Luke: Colonial Service
N L Mayle: Far Eastern Commerce
W B Monson: Production
J J Paskin: Eastern
F J Pedler (Feb): Appointments (C)
A H Poynton: Defence
S Robinson: Establishments
N J Sabine: Public Relations
G F Seel: Colonial Service (A)
J B Sidebotham: Ceylon and Pacific
R A Whittle: Colonial Service (B)
J B Williams (Feb): Economic and Finance
O G Williams: West Africa

1946
A B Acheson/E R Edmonds: General
H Beckett: West Indies
W J Bigg: Communications
K W Blaxter: Social Services
A B Cohen: East and Central Africa
A K Cole: Prisoners of War
T W Davis: Commercial Relations and Supplies
J L Keith: Welfare
S E Luke: Mediterranean
N L Mayle: Eastern (B)
E Melville (May): Marketing
W B Monson: Production
A F Newbolt: Appointments (A)

J J Paskin: Eastern (A)
F J Pedler: Appointments (B)
A H Poynton/J S Bennett (July): International Relations
K E Robinson (Nov): West Africa
N J Sabine: Public Relations
J B Sidebotham: Ceylon and Pacific
T Smith: Middle East
A R Thomas: Colonial Service (A)
R A Whittle: Colonial Service (B)
J B Williams: Finance

1947
no information

1948
A B Acheson: General
J S Bennett: Mediterranean
H Beckett: West Indies
W J Bigg: Communications
K W Blackburne: Information
K W Blaxter: Social Services (A)
H T Bourdillon: Eastern (A)
H R Butters: Finance
T W Davis: Commercial Relations and Supplies
E R Edmonds: Colonial Service (A)
A N Galsworthy: International Relations
A D Garson: Appointments (B)
C A Grossmith: Social Services (B)
J G Hibbert: Research
J L Keith: Welfare
N L Mayle: Eastern (B)
E Melville: Production and Marketing (A)
A F Newbolt: Appointments (A)
P Rogers: Establishments
J B Sidebotham: Pacific
T Smith: Middle East
R A Whittle: Colonial Service (B)
vacant: West Africa
vacant: Marketing

1949
H Beckett: West Indies (A)
J S Bennett: Mediterranean
W J Bigg: Communications
K W Blackburne: Information
K W Blaxter: Colonial Service (D)

H T Bourdillon (Apr): Finance
M H Dorman: Social Services (A)
E R Edmonds: Colonial Service (C)
A Emanuel: Economic General
A N Galsworthy: International Relations
L H Gorsuch: West Africa
C A Grossmith: Social Services (B)
J G Hibbert: Research
J D Higham: Eastern
R S Hudson (Aug): African Studies
J L Keith: Welfare (Students)
C E Lambert: Central Africa
J E Marnham: West Indies (B)
N L Mayle: Production and Marketing (B)
E Melville: Economic Relations
A F Newbolt: Colonial Service (A)
P Rogers: Establishments and Organization
J B Sidebotham: Hong Kong and Pacific
T Smith (June): Defence and General
J H Wallace: East Africa (and Aden)
R A Whittle: Colonial Service (D)
T B Williamson: Production and Marketing (A)

1950
H Beckett: West Indies (A)
J S Bennett: Mediterranean
W J Bigg: Communications
K W Blackburne: Information
K W Blaxter: Colonial Service (B)
H T Bourdillon: Finance
M H Dorman (Mar): Social Services (A)
E R Edmonds: Colonial Service (E)
A Emanuel: Economic General
A N Galsworthy: International Relations (A)
A D Garson: Colonial Service (C)
L H Gorsuch: West Africa
C A Grossmith: Social Services (B)
J G Hibbert: Research
J D Higham (Oct): South-East Asia
R S Hudson (July): African Studies
J L Keith: Welfare
C E Lambert: Central Africa and Aden
J E Marnham (Feb): West Indies (B)
W A Mathieson (Mar): Economic Relations
N L Mayle: Production and Marketing (B)
E Melville: Economic Relations
W A Morris: Supplies

A F Newbolt: Colonial Service (A)
P Rogers: Establishments and Organization
J B Sidebotham: Hong Kong and Pacific
J H Wallace: East Africa
W I Wallace (Nov): International Relations (B)
R A Whittle: Colonial Service (D)
T B Williamson (Feb): Production and Marketing (A)
vacant: Defence and General

1951
H Beckett: West Indies (A)
J S Bennett: Mediterranean
W J Bigg: Communications
K W Blaxter: Colonial Service (B)
H T Bourdillon: Finance
C Y Carstairs: Information
E R Edmonds: Colonial Service (E)
A Emanuel: Economic General
A N Galsworthy: International Relations (A)
A D Garson: Colonial Service (C)
H A Harding: Production and Marketing (B)
J G Hibbert: Research
J D Higham: South-East Asia
R S Hudson: African Studies
J L Keith: Welfare
C E Lambert: Central African and Aden
J E Marnham: Economic Relations (A)
N L Mayle (May): West Indies (B)
W A Morris: Economic Relations (B)
W A Morris: Supplies
A F Newbolt: Colonial Service (A)
P Rogers (Feb): East Africa
J B Sidebotham: Hong Kong and Pacific
T Smith: Defence and General
A R Thomas: Establishment and Organization
W I Wallace: International Relations (B)
N D Watson (Nov): Social Services (B)
F D Webber: Social Services (A)
R A Whittle: Colonial Service (D)
T B Williamson: Production and Marketing (A)

1952
J S Bennett: Mediterranean
W J Bigg: Communications
K W Blaxter: Colonial Service (B)

H T Bourdillon: Finance
C Y Carstairs: Information
E R Edmonds: Colonial Service (E)
A Emanuel: Economic General
A D Garson: Colonial Service (C)
B O Gidden: International Relations (A)
H A Harding: Production and Marketing (B)
J G Hibbert: Research
J D Higham: South-East Asia
R S Hudson: African Studies Branch
J L Keith: Students
F Kennedy: Supplies
C E Lambert: Central African and Aden
J E Marnham (Jan): Economic Relations (A)
N L Mayle: West Indian (B)
W A Morris: Economic Relations (B)
A F Newbolt: Colonial Service (A)
P Rogers: East African
J B Sidebotham: Hong Kong and Pacific
T Smith: Defence and General
S J Southgate: Production and Marketing (A)
A R Thomas: Establishment and Organization
W I Wallace (Nov): West Indian (A)
N D Watson: Social Services (B)
F D Webber: Social Services (A)
R A Whittle: Colonial Service (D)
T B Williamson: West African

1953
W J Bigg: Communications
K W Blaxter: Colonial Service (B)
H T Bourdillon: Finance
E R Edmonds: Colonial Service (E)
A Emanuel: Economic General
S H Evans: Information
A D Garson: Colonial Service (C)
B O Gidden: International Relations
H A Harding: Production and Marketing (B)
R S Hudson: African Studies Branch
J L Keith: Students
F Kennedy: Supplies
C E Lambert: Research
A M Mackintosh: South-East Asia
J E Marnham: Central African and Aden
N L Mayle: West Indian (B)
W A Morris: Mediterranean
A F Newbolt: Colonial Service (A)
J B Sidebotham: Hong Kong and Pacific

T Smith: Defence and General
S J Southgate: Production and Marketing (A)
J K Thompson: Social Services (A)
W I Wallace: West Indian (A)
N D Watson: Social Services (B)
F D Webber: Establishment and Organization
R A Whittle: Colonial Service (D)
T B Williamson: West African
Appointment pending: East Africa

1954
J S Bennett: Defence and General
W J Bigg: Communications
K W Blaxter: Colonial Service (B)
E B David: East African
E R Edmonds: Colonial Service (E)
A Emanuel: Economic General
S H Evans: Information
A D Garson: Colonial Service (C)
A N Galsworthy: Finance
H A Harding: Production and Marketing (B)
R S Hudson: African Studies Branch
J L Keith: Students
F Kennedy: Supplies
C E Lambert: Research
A M Mackintosh: South-East Asia
J E Marnham: Central African and Aden
W A Mathieson: International Relations
N L Mayle: West Indian (B)
W A Morris: Mediterranean
J B Sidebotham: Hong Kong and Pacific
J K Thompson: Social Services (A)
J W Vernon: Production and Marketing (A)
R J Vile: West African (B)
W I Wallace: West Indian (A)
N D Watson: Social Services (B)
F D Webber: Establishment and Organization
R A Whittle: Colonial Service (D)
T B Williamson: West African (A)

1955
J S Bennett: Defence and General
W J Bigg: Communications
K W Blaxter: Overseas Service (A)
E R Edmonds: Overseas Service (D)
A Emanuel: Economic General
S H Evans: Information
A N Galsworthy: Finance

LISTS OF MINISTERS AND SENIOR OFFICIALS

A D Garson: Overseas Service (B)
H P Hall: Pacific
H A Harding: Production and Marketing (B)
R S Hudson: African Studies Branch
J L Keith: Students
F Kennedy: Commercial Relations and Supplies
C E Lambert: Research
A M Mackintosh: Far Eastern
J E Marnham: International Relations
W A Mathieson: East African
N L Mayle: West Indian (B)
W A Morris: Mediterranean
W D Sweaney: Central African and Aden
J K Thompson: Social Services (A)
J W Vernon: Production and Marketing (A)
R J Vile: West African (B)
W I Wallace: West Indian (A)
N D Watson: Social Services (B)
F D Webber: Establishment and Organization
R A Whittle: Overseas Service (C)
T B Williamson: West African (A)

1956
J S Bennett: Defence
W J Bigg: Communications
E R Edmonds: Overseas Service Division (D)
A Emanuel: Economic General
S H Evans: Information
A N Galsworthy: Finance
A D Garson: Overseas Service Division (B)
H P Hall: Pacific
H A Harding: Overseas Service Division (A)
R S Hudson: African Studies Branch
J B Johnston: Far Eastern
J L Keith: Students
F Kennedy: West Indian (B)
J M Kisch: Production and Marketing (B)
C E Lambert: Research
J E Marnham: International Relations
W A Mathieson: East African
J C Morgan: Central African and Aden
O H Morris: Social Services (B)
W A Morris: Mediterranean
P A Robertson: Police
W D Sweaney: Overseas Service Division (C)
J K Thompson: Social Services (A)
J W Vernon: Production and Marketing (A)

R J Vile: West African (B)
W I Wallace: West Indian (A)
N D Watson: Intelligence and Security
I B Watt: General
F D Webber: Establishment and Organization
T B Williamson: West African (A)

1957
J S Bennett: West African (B)
W J Bigg: Communications
A Campbell: Defence
E R Edmonds: Overseas Service (D)
A Emanuel: Economic General
A D Garson: Overseas Service (B)
H P Hall: Pacific
H A Harding: Overseas Service (A)
R S Hudson: African Studies Branch
J B Johnston: Far Eastern
F Kennedy: West Indian (B)
J M Kisch: Production and Marketing (B)
C E Lambert: Research
J E Marnham: International Relations
W A Mathieson: East African
J C Morgan: Central African
O H Morris: Social Services (B)
W A Morris: Mediterranean
P A Robertson: Police
B G Stone: Students Branch
W D Sweaney: Overseas Service (C)
J K Thompson: Social Services (A)
J W Vernon: Production and Marketing (A)
R J Vile: Finance
W I Wallace: West Indian (A)
F D Webber: Establishment and Organization
N D Watson: Intelligence and Security
I B Watt: General
T B Williamson: West African (A)
vacant: Information

1958
J S Bennett: Social Services (B)
A Campbell: Defence
E R Edmonds: Overseas Service Division (D)
A Emanuel: West African
A D Garson: Overseas Service Division (B)
H P Hall: Pacific
H A Harding: Overseas Service Division (A)
J D Higham: Mediterranean

R S Hudson: African Studies Branch
T C Jerrom: International Relations
F Kennedy: West Indian (B)
J M Kisch: Production and Marketing (B)
C E Lambert: Research
J E Marnham: West Indian (A)
W A Mathieson: East African
J C Morgan: Central African and Aden
O H Morris: Information
W A Morris: Production and Marketing (A)
A H Sheffield: Communications
B G Stone: Students Branch
W D Sweaney: Overseas Service Division (C)
J K Thompson: Social Services (A)
J W Vernon: Economic General (B)
R J Vile: Finance
W I Wallace: Far Eastern
N D Watson: Intelligence and Security
N D Watson (acting): Police
I B Watt: General
F D Webber: Establishment and Organization
T B Williamson: Economic General (A)

1959
J S Bennett: Social Services (B)
A Campbell: Defence
E R Edmonds: Overseas Service Division (D)
A Emanuel: West African
A D Garson: Overseas Service Division (B)
B O Gidden: Establishment and Organization
H P Hall: Pacific and Indian Ocean
H A Harding: Overseas Service Division (A)
J D Higham: Mediterranean (A)
R S Hudson: African Studies Branch
T C Jerrom: International Relations
F Kennedy: West Indian (B)
J M Kisch: Production and Marketing (B)
C E Lambert: Research
J E Marnham: West Indian (A)
N L Mayle: Mediterranean (B)
J C Morgan: Central African and Aden
O H Morris: Information
W A Morris: Production and Marketing (A)
A H Sheffield: Communications
B G Stone: Students Branch
W D Sweaney: Overseas Service Division (C)
J W Vernon: Economic General (B)
R J Vile: Finance

W I Wallace: Far Eastern
N D Watson: Intelligence, Police and Security
I B Watt: General
F D Webber: East African
T B Williamson: Economic General (A)
vacant: Social Services (A)

1960
J S Bennett: Social Services (B)
E R Edmonds: Overseas Service Division (D)
A Emanuel: West African
A D Garson: Overseas Service Division (B)
B O Gidden: Establishment and Organization
H P Hall: Pacific and Indian Ocean
H A Harding: Finance
J D Higham/J O Moreton: Mediterranean
R S Hudson: African Studies Branch
T C Jerrom: International Relations
J M Kisch: Production and Marketing (B)
C E Lambert: Research
A M Mackintosh: West Indian (B)
J E Marnham: West Indian (A)
O H Morris: Information
W A Morris: Production and Marketing (A)
A H Sheffield: Communications
D M Smith: Social Services (A)
M G Smith: Overseas Service Division (A)
B G Stone: Students Branch
W D Sweaney: Overseas Service Division (C)
J W Vernon: Economic General (B)
R J Vile: Defence
R J Vile: Intelligence, Police and Security (Acting)
W I Wallace: Far Eastern
N D Watson: Central African
I B Watt: Gulf of Aden and General
F D Webber: East African
T B Williamson: Economic General (A)

1961
J N Armitage-Smith: Intelligence, Police and Security
J S Bennett: Social Services (B)
E R Edmonds: Overseas Service Division (D)
A Emanuel: West African
A D Garson: Overseas Service Division (B)
B O Gidden: Establishment and Organization
H P Hall: Pacific and Indian Ocean

LISTS OF MINISTERS AND SENIOR OFFICIALS

H A Harding: Finance
J D Higham: Mediterranean
R S Hudson: African Branch Studies
T C Jerrom: International Relations
J M Kisch: Production and Marketing (B)
A M Mackintosh: West Indian (B)
W A Mathieson: Research
O H Morris: Information
W A Morris: Production and Marketing (A)
A H Sheffield: Communications
D M Smith: Social Services (A)
M G Smith: Overseas Service Division (A)
B G Stone: Students Branch
W D Sweaney: Overseas Service Division
J W Vernon: Economic General (B)
R J Vile: Defence
W I Wallace: Far Eastern
N D Watson: Central African
I B Watt: Aden and General
F D Webber/J C Morgan: East African (A) and (B)
D Williams: West Indian (A)
T B Williamson: Economic General (A)

1962
J N Armitage-Smith: Defence, Intelligence and Security
J S Bennett: Social Services
B O Gidden: Establishment and Organization
J D Higham: Finance
T C Jerrom: International Relations and General
J M Kisch: Mediterranean
J E Marnham: Pacific and Indian Ocean
J C Morgan: East African (B)
O H Morris: Information
W A Morris: Economic General
R W Piper: West Indian (B)
E L Sykes: Southern Africa
J W Vernon: Economic Relations
W I Wallace: Far Eastern
N D Watson: Central African
F D Webber: East African
D Williams: West Indian (A)

1963
J N Armitage-Smith: Defence, Intelligance and Security
J S Bennett: Economic General
A Campbell: Southern African
B O Gidden: Establishment and Organization
J D Higham: Far Eastern
T C Jerrom: International Relations and General
J M Kisch: Mediterranean and Atlantic
D J Kirkness: Finance
J E Marnham: Pacific and Indian Ocean
P R Noakes: Information
R W Piper: West Indian (B)
C S Roberts: Aden and Social Services
J W Vernon: Economic Relations
F D Webber: East African
D Williams: West Indian (A)

1964
J S Bennett: Economic General and Social Services
A Campbell: Southern African
B O Gidden: Establishment and Organization
J D Higham: Defence, Intelligence and Hong Kong
T C Jerrom: International Relations and General
D J Kirkness: Finance
J M Kisch: Mediterranean and Atlantic
J E Marnham: Pacific and Indian Ocean
P R Noakes: Information
R W Piper: West Indian (B)
C S Roberts: Aden
J W Vernon: Economic Relations
D Williams: West Indian (A)

1965
J S Bennett: Atlantic
A Campbell: Southern African
A J Fairclough: Pacific and Indian Ocean
H P Hall: Establishment and Organization
J D Higham: Defence, Intelligence and Hong Kong
G W Jamieson: Economic General
T C Jerrom: International Relations and General
D J Kirkness: Finance
P R Noakes: Information
R W Piper: West Indian (B)

C S Roberts: Aden
D Williams: West Indian (A)

1966
J S Bennett: Atlantic
R M Blaikley: Defence and Intelligence
W S Carter: Hong Kong and West Indian (C)
K C Christofas: Economic
A J Fairclough: Pacific and Indian Ocean

H P Hall: Establishment and Organization
T C Jerrom: International and General
D J Kirkness: Finance
P R Noakes: Information
R W Piper: West Indian (B)
C S Roberts: Aden
J W Stacpoole: Constitutional Planning
S P Whitley: Communications
D Williams: West Indian (A)

7.5 Secretaries of state for dominions affairs and Dominions Office ministers

Secretaries of state for dominions affairs

1925	L S Amery	1940 May	Thomas Walker Hobart Inskip, 1st Viscount Caldecote
1929	Sidney Webb, 1st Baron Passfield		
1930	J H Thomas	1940	Robert Arthur James Gascoyne-Cecil, Viscount Cranborne
1935	M MacDonald		
1938 May	Edward Montague Cavendish Stanley, Lord Stanley	1942	C R Attlee
		1942	Robert Arthur James Gascoyne-Cecil, Viscount Cranborne
1938 Nov	M MacDonald		
1939 Feb	Sir Thomas Inskip	1945	Christopher Addison, 1st Viscount Addison
1939 Sep	R A Eden		

Parliamentary under-secretaries of state for dominions affairs

1925	George Villiers, 6th Earl of Clarendon	1935 Nov	D Hacking
		1936	Edward Cavendish, Marquess of Hartington
1927	Simon Frazer, 14th Baron Lovat		
1929 Jan	I Windsor-Clive	1940	G Shakespeare
1929 June	A Ponsonby	1942	P V Emrys-Evans
1929 Dec	W Lunn	1945	J Parker
1931	M MacDonald	1946	A G Bottomley
1935 June	Edward Montague Cavendish Stanley, Lord Stanley		

7.6 Dominions Office officials

Permanent under-secretaries of state for dominions affairs

1925	Sir Charles Davis	1940 Feb	Sir Cosmo Parkinson
1930	Sir Edward Harding	1940 May	Sir Eric Machtig
1939 Oct	Sir Eric Machtig		

Deputy under-secretaries of state for dominions affairs

1939	Sir Eric Machtig	1940	Sir John Stephenson

LISTS OF MINISTERS AND SENIOR OFFICIALS

Assistant under-secretaries of state for dominions affairs

1925–1930	E J Harding	1939–1942	P Liesching
1930–1939	Sir Harry Batterbee	1940–1947	Sir Charles Dixon
1936–1939	E G S Machtig	1942–1946	P A Clutterbuck
1939–194	J E Stephenson	1946–1947	C G Syers

Assistant secretaries of state for dominions affairs

1926–1927
H F Batterbee
A C Parkinson
G G Whiskard

1928
H F Batterbee
G G Whiskard
R A Wiseman

1929
H F Batterbee
C W Dixon (acting)
G G Whiskard
R A Wiseman

1930–1932
C W Dixon
E G Machtig (acting)
H N Tait
R A Wiseman

1933–1935
E T Crutchley
C W Dixon
E G Machtig
H N Tait
R A Wiseman

1936
C W Dixon
D F Plant
J E Stephenson (acting)
H N Tait
R A Wiseman

1937
W Bankes Amery
D F Plant
J E Stephenson
H N Tait
R A Wiseman

1938
W Bankes Amery
C W Dixon
J E Stephenson
H N Tait
R A Wiseman

1939
W Bankes Amery
C W Dixon
W C Hankinson
P Liesching
H N Tait
R A Wiseman

1940
M E Antrobus
N E Archer
W Bankes Amery
C W Dixon
W C Hankinson
S L Holmes
C R Price
H N Tait
R A Wiseman

7.7 Secretaries of state for Commonwealth relations and Commonwealth Relations Office ministers

Secretaries of state for Commonwealth relations

1947 July	Christopher Addison, 1st Viscount Addison	1952 Dec	Philip Cunliffe-Lister, 1st Viscount Swinton
1947 Oct	P J Noel-Baker	1955 Apr	Alexander Frederick Douglas-Home, 14th Earl of Home
1950	P C Gordon Walker		
1951 Oct	General Sir Hastings Lionel Ismay, 1st Baron Ismay	1960 July	D Sandys (secretary of state for Commonwealth relations and the colonies from July 1961)
1952 Mar	Robert Arthur James Gascoyne-Cecil, 5th Marquess of Salisbury		
		1964 Oct	A G Bottomley

Ministers of state for Commonwealth relations

1947 Aug	A Henderson	1963 Oct	George John Charles Mercer Petty-Fitzmaurice, 8th Marquess of Lansdowne (minister of state for Commonwealth relations and for the colonies)
1959 Oct	C J Alport		
1962	Andrew Robert Buxton Cavendish, 11th Duke of Devonshire		
		1964 Oct	C Hughes

Parliamentary under-secretaries of state for Commonwealth relations

1947 July	A G Bottomley	1962 July	J D Tilney (parliamentary under-secretary of state for Commonwealth relations and for the colonies, from October 1963)
1947 Oct	P C Gordon Walker		
1950 Mar	Angus William Eden Holden, 3rd Baron Holden of Oakworth House		
1950 July	David Rees Rees-Williams, 1st Baron Ogmore	1963 Oct	N Fisher (parliamentary under-secretary of state for Commonwealth relations and for the colonies)
1951 June	Colonel Sir George Charles Patrick Bingham, 6th Earl of Lucan	1963 Oct	R Hornby (parliamentary under-secretary of state for Commonwealth relations and for the colonies)
1951 Nov	J G Foster		
1954 Oct	A D Dodds-Parker		
1955 Dec	Commander A H P Noble	1964 Oct	Lord Taylor (parliamentary under-secretary of state for Commonwealth relations and for the colonies)
1956 Nov	Lord John Adrian Hope		
1957 Jan	C J Alport		
1959 Oct	R H Thompson		
1960 Oct	Andrew Robert Buxton Cavendish, 11th Duke of Devonshire	1965 Oct	Lord Beswick (parliamentary under-secretary of state for Commonwealth relations and for the colonies)
1961 Feb	B Braine		

7.8 Commonwealth Relations Office officials

Permanent under-secretaries of state for Commonwealth relations

1947 July	Sir Eric Machtig	1955 Feb	Sir Gilbert Laithwaite
1947 Aug	Sir Archibald Carter	1959 Sep	Sir Alexander Clutterbuck
1949 Jan	Sir Percivale Liesching	1962 Jan	Sir Saville Garner

Deputy under-secretaries of state for Commonwealth relations

1947 July	Sir John Stephenson	1952 Aug	A C B Symon
1947 Aug	Sir William Croft	1953 Apr	Sir Saville Garner
1948 Jan	Sir Gilbert Laithwaite	1956 Oct	H J Lintott
1948 June	C G Syers	1958 Dec	H A F Rumbold
1949 Jan	Sir Cecil Syers	1961 July	N Pritchard
1950 Dec	J J S Garner	1962 Jan	Sir Arthur Snelling
1951 Aug	Sir Stephen Holmes	1963 Sep	Sir Neil Pritchard

Assistant under-secretaries of state for Commonwealth relations

1947–1948	Sir Charles Dixon	1955–1959	A W Snelling
1947–1948	C G L Syers	1956	G E B Shannon
1948	N E Archer	1957–1958	J M C James
1948	J J S Garner	1958–1960	W A W Clark
1947–1948	Sir Paul Patrick	1958–1960	N E Coster
1947–1948	G H Baxter	1959–1962	C M Walker
1949	Sir Paul Patrick	1959–1960	D W S Hunt
1949–1955	G H Baxter	1961	R H Belcher
1949–1950	J J S Garner	1960	G W St J Chadwick
1949	N E Archer	1960–1961	N Pritchard
1949–1959	W A B Hamilton	1961–1962	M R Metcalf
1949	W J Garnett	1961	G P Hampshire
1949–1952	A C B Symon	1962	W A B Hamilton
1949–1954	R R Sedgewick	1962	L B Walsh Atkins
1950–1954	N Pritchard	1962	C S Pickard
1953–1954	A C B Symon	1963	N D Watson
1954–1956	W A W Clark	1964	E L Sykes
1954–1956	A F Morley	1964	M R Metcalf
1954–1958	H A F Rumbold	1964	Sir Arthur Clark
1955–1957	I M R Maclennan		

Assistant secretaries of state for Commonwealth relations

1953

M E Antrobus: General
W H Bishop: Far Eastern
W A W Clark: Central African and Territories
D M Cleary: Western and United Nations
C G Costley-White: Political Affairs
Hon F E H T Cumming-Bruce: Establishment
H E Davies: Development
R W Fowler: South Asian
J P Gibson: Communications
D W S Hunt: Overseas Finance
C Iddon: Services
A H Joyce: Information
M R Metcalf: Commodities
A F Morley: Constitutional
Sir G Scoones: Defence
L B Walsh Atkins: Trade

1954
no information

1955
M E Antrobus: Protocol
R H Belcher: Trade
D M Cleary: Western and United Nations
B Cockram: Information
C G Costley-White: Communications
G E Crombie: Far Eastern
Hon F E Cumming-Bruce: Commodities
B R Curson: Defence
R W Fowler: Central African and Territories
J P Gibson: General
F A Harrison: Constitutional
C Iddon: Services
G Kimber: South-East Asian and Middle East
M R Metcalf: Establishment
J Thomson: Development
vacant: Overseas Finance

1956
B Cockram: Information
C G Costley-White: Communications
D J Crawley: Economic Policy
B R Curson: Economic Relations I
R W Fowler: Central African and Territories
J P Gibson: General
G P Hampshire: Colombo Plan
F A Harrison: Constitutional
R C Hunt: Far Eastern
R L Jasper: Western and United Nations
G Kimber: Defence
C S Pickard: South Asian and Middle East
J Thomson: Economic Relations II
C M Walker: Establishment
vacant: Protocol

1957
M E Allen: Defence
B Cockram: Information and Cultural Relations
C G Costley-White: Communications
D J Crawley: Economic Policy
B R Curson: Colombo Plan
H E Davies: Economic Relations I
J P Gibson: Migration and General
W G Head: Protocol and Nationality
D W S Hunt: Central African and Territories
R L Jasper: Western and United Nations
C S Pickard: South Asian and Middle East
G W St J Chadwick: Far Eastern
J Thomson: Economic Relations II
C M Walker: Establishment
L B Walsh Atkins: Constitutional

1958
M E Allen: Ghana
H G Bass: Western and United Nations
B Cockram: Information and Cultural Relations
N E Costar: Middle East
C G Costley-White: Communications
D J Crawley: Economic Policy
B R Curson: Colombo Plan
H E Davies: Economic Relations I
Sir Charles Dixon (temporary): Constitutional
J P Gibson: Migration and General
D W S Hunt: Central African and Territories
R L Jasper: Economic Relations II
J B Johnston: Defence
C S Pickard: South Asia and Far Eastern
G W St J Chadwick: Malaya
C M Walker: Establishment
vacant: Protocol and Nationality

1959
M E Allen: Ghana
H G Bass: United Nations
B Cockram: Information and Cultural Relations
C G Costley-White: Communications
G E Crombie: Economic Relations I
G Davey: Colombo Plan
J P Gibson: Migration and General
D W S Hunt: Middle East
J J Hunt: Economic Relations II
J B Johnston: Defence and Western
E N Larmour: Malaya
M J Moynihan: Economic Policy
G W St J Chadwick: Constitutional
D A Scott: Central African and Territories
H A Twist: South Asia and Far Eastern
L B Walsh Atkins: Establishment

LISTS OF MINISTERS AND SENIOR OFFICIALS

1960
R H Belcher: United Nations
J R Bottomley: Economic Policy
D M Cleary: Migration and General
B Cockram: Information and Cultural Relations
C G Costley-White: Communications
F A Harrison: Middle East
J J Hunt: Economic Relations II
T W Keeble: Defence and Western
E N Larmour: Establishment
M J Moynihan: Colombo Plan
M J Moynihan: Economic Relations I
G W St J Chadwick: Constitutional
D A Scott: Central Africa
W J Smith: Malaya
E L Sykes: Southern Africa
H A Twist: South Asia and Far Eastern
vacant: Ghana

1961
G D Anderson: Technical Assistance
J R Bottomley: Economic Policy
D M Cleary: General
D L Cole: Administration
C G Costley-White: Communications
B J Greenhill: Nigeria
G P Hampshire: Western and Middle East
F A Harrison: Central Africa
J T Hughes: Information Services
R C Hunt: Economic Relations II
G Kimber: United Nations
E N Larmour: Personnel
V C Martin: South Asia
J O Moreton: West and General Africa
R C Ormerod: Far East and Pacific
P Pares: Education
C R Price: Defence
T A Scott: News
H Smedley: Information Policy
W J Smith: Economic Relations I
E L Sykes: Southern Africa
L J Wakely: Constitutional

1962
D M Cleary: General
D L Cole: Personnel
C G Costley-White: Communications
T L Crosthwait: South Asia
H E Davies: Economic Relations I
K A East: West and General Africa
J S Gandee: Administration
J T Hughes: Information Services
R C Hunt: Economic Relations II
G Kimber: United Nations
E G Le Tocq: Central Africa
V C Martin: Nigeria
R C Ormerod: Far East and Pacific
P Pares: Cultural Relations
C S Pickard: Economic Policy
C R Price: Defence
A W Redpath: Western and Middle East
T A Scott: News
H Smedley: Information Policy
L J Wakely: Constitutional

1963
H G Bass: United Nations
J R Bottomley: Common Market
D L Cole: Personnel
C G Costley-White: Communications
T L Crosthwait: Economic Relations II
H E Davies: Economic Policy
K A East: East and General Africa
J S Ellis: Information Services
E J Emery: South-East Asia
J S Gandee: Administration
A A Golds: Far East and Pacific
J T Hughes: Information Policy
V C Martin: West Africa
J C Morgan: Nationality and General
P Pares: Cultural Relations
C R Price: Defence
A H Reed: Economic Relations I
H Smedley: News
E L Sykes: West Indies
Vacant: Africa Economic
Vacant: Constitutional
Vacant: Western and Middle East

1964
N Aspin: East Africa
A J Brown: Information Policy
C G Costley-White: Communications
T L Crosthwait: Economic Relations II
H E Davies: Financial Policy

J M Dutton: Constitutional
K A East: Personnel
J S Ellis: Information Services
E J Emery: South Asia
J D Fraser: Defence Supplies
J S Gandee: Administration
A A Golds: Far East and Pacific
J T Hughes: Cultural Relations
T W Keeble: Commercial Policy
W G Lamarque: Africa Economic
V C Martin: West Africa
C R Price: Defence
A H Reed: Economic Relations I
J D Shaw: United Nations and General Africa
H Smedley: News
Miss L E Storar: Nationality and General
E L Sykes: West Indies
Vacant: Western and Middle East

1965
N Aspin: East Africa Political
H G Bass: Southern Rhodesia
D M Cleary: Atlantic
C G Costley-White: Communications
B R Curson: Information Policy
J M Dutton: Constitutional and Protocol
J S Ellis: Information Services
J D Fraser: Defence Supplies
A A Golds: Far East and Pacific
F A Harrison: West and General African
J D Hennings: Financial Policy and West Africa Economic
J T Hughes: Cultural Relations
T W Keeble: Commercial Policy
J M Kisch: Malta
W G Lamarque: East Africa Economic
V C Martin: South Asia
J M McNeill: Defence
J C Morgan: Mediterranean
K J Neale: Malawi and Central Africa Economic
A H Reed: Western Economic

J D Shaw: United Nations, Western and Middle East
W S Smele: News
Miss L E Storar: Nationality and General
H A Twist: Asia Economic
S P Whitley: Zambia

1966
N Aspin: East Africa Political
A J Brown: Far East and Pacific
D M Cleary: Atlantic
C G Costley-White: Political Affairs
B R Curson: Joint Information Administration
C E Diggines: Mediterranean
J S Ellis: Information Services
F G Gallagher: Western Economic
B J Greenhill: Africa and General Africa Political
J D Hennings: Development Policy and West and East Africa Economic
J T Hughes: Cultural Relations
R L Jasper: Nationality and Consular
T W Keeble: Economic General
V C Martin: South Asia
R W Mason: Joint Research
A L Mayall: Joint Protocol
J M McNeill: Defence
K J Neale: Rhodesia
A H Reed: Irish Trade Negotiations Unit
F B Richards: Joint Information Policy and Guidance
W S Smele: News
H S Stanley: Joint Malaysia/Indonesia
Miss L E Storar: General and Migration
H A Twist: Asia Economic
R Walker: Commonwealth Policy and Planning
I Watt: United Nations, Western and Middle East
S P Whitley: Malawi and Zambia

7.9 Secretaries of state for Commonwealth affairs and Commonwealth Office ministers

Secretaries of state for Commonwealth affairs
1966 Aug Rt Hon A G Bottomley
1966 Aug Rt Hon H Bowden
1967 Aug Rt Hon George Thomson

Ministers of state for Commonwealth affairs
1966 Aug J Hart
1967 Jan G Thomas
1967 July Lord Shepherd

Parliamentary under-secretaries of state for Commonwealth affairs
1966 Aug Lord Beswick
1967 July William Whitlock

7.10 Commonwealth Office officials

Permanent under-secretaries of state for Commonwealth Affairs
1966 Aug Sir Saville Garner
1967 Nov Sir Morrice James

Deputy under-secretaries of state for Commonwealth affairs
1966 Aug Sir Arthur Snelling
1966 Aug Sir Neil Pritchard
1966 Aug A N Galsworthy
1966 Aug Sir Morrice James
1967 Oct Sir Leslie Monson

Assistant under-secretaries of state for Commonwealth affairs
1967
Sir Arthur Clark: Joint Information Policy and Guidance, Joint Information Administration, Joint Information Services, Cultural Relations, News
H P Hall: Associated States, Hong Kong and West Indian C, West Indian A and Swaziland, West Indian B, International and General, Dependent Territories and Constitutions
W A Hamilton: General and Migration, Aviation and Telecommunications, Consular, Nationality and Treaty
Sir John Johnston: Asia Economic (shared department), South Asia, Atlantic, Far East and Pacific (Ceylon and the Maldives only)
Sir Leslie Monson: East Africa (shared department), Zambia, Rhodesia Economic, Rhodesia Political
J O Moreton: Asia, Far East and Pacific (except Ceylon and the Maldives), Middle East, Western and United Nations
E G Norris: East Africa, West and General Africa
E G Norris: Aid
G E Shannon: Economic General, Western Economic
T Smith: Pacific and Indian, Gibraltar and South Atlantic
L B Walsh Atkins: Commonwealth Policy and Planning, Defence, Political Affairs

1968
J R Bottomley
P L Carter
H P Hall
R C Hunt
Sir John Johnston
J O Moreton
J C Morgan
E G Norris
J V Rob
G E Shannon

Assistant secretaries of state for Commonwealth affairs

1967
H G Bass: Consular (FO/CO)
J S Bennett: Gibraltar and South Atlantic
R M Blaikley: Aviation and Telecommunications
W S Carter: Hong Kong and West Indian (C)
K C Christofas: Aid
D M Cleary: Atlantic
R A Clinton-Thomas: Rhodesia Economic
N D Clive: Information (FO/CO) Research
C G Costley-White: Political Affairs
B R Curson: Joint Information Administration
C E Diggines: Middle East, Western and United Nations
A A Duff: South Asia
A J Fairclough: Pacific and Indian Ocean
J F Ford: Joint Research
F G Gallagher: Western Economic
B H Heddy: General and Migration
T C Jerrom: International and General
G S Littlejohn Cook: Joint Information Policy and Guidance
D MacFarlane: National and Treaty (FO/CO)
V C Martin: Cultural Relations
A L Mayall: Protocol and Conference (FO/CO)
J M McNeill: Defence
F S Miles: West and General Africa
K J Neale: Rhodesia Political
P R Noakes (Acting): News
R W Piper: West Indian (B)
A H Reed: Far East and Pacific
T R Sewell: Associated States
T R Sewell: West Indian (A) and Swaziland
M Scott: East Africa
J W Stacpoole: Dependent Territories Division
C J Treadwell: Joint Information Services
R Walker: Commonwealth Policy and Planning
J F Wearing: Economic General
G S Whitehead: Asia Economic
J R Williams: Zambia

1968
J S Bennett: Gibraltar and South Atlantic
R M Blaikley: Aviation and Telecommunications
W S Carter: Hong Kong
K C Christofas: Commonwealth Financial Policy
R A Clinton-Thomas: Rhodesia Economic
D D Condon: News
C G Costley-White: Political Affairs
A A Duff: South Asia
R H Edmonds: Middle East, Western and United Nations
R S Faber: Rhodesia Political
A J Fairclough: Pacific and Indian Ocean
F G Gallagher: Common Market
B H Heddy: General and Migration
D G Holland (chief economic adviser): Economists
T C Jerrom: International and General
E G Le Tocq: Atlantic
V C Martin: Cultural Relations
Major-General J M McNeill: Defence
W Peters: Zambia and Malawi
R W Piper, T C Jerrom: West Indian B
A H Reed: Far East and Pacific
M Scott: East and Southern Africa
T R Sewell: Associated States
T R Sewell: West Indian A and Swaziland
J W Stacpoole: Dependent Territories Constitutions
D C Tebbitt: West and General Africa
R Walker: Commonwealth Policy and Planning
G S Whitehead: Commonwealth Trade

7.11 Overseas Development Administration ministers and officials

Ministers of overseas development
1964 Oct   Rt Hon Barbara Ann Castle
1965 Dec   Rt Hon Anthony Greenwood
1966 Aug   Rt Hon Arthur George Bottomley
1967 Aug   Rt Hon Reginald Prentice

Parliamentary secretaries of overseas development
1964 Oct   A E Oram

Permanent secretaries of overseas development
1964 Oct   Sir Andrew Cohen

Deputy permanent secretaries of overseas development
1964 Oct   Sir Alan Dudley
1966 Apr   G M Wilson

CHAPTER 8

Colonial Office Advisers, 1926 to 1965

With few exceptions the Colonial Office did not employ permanent technical or scientific staff before Leopold Amery's tenure as secretary of state (1924–1929). The first post created, legal adviser to the secretary of state, took its origin from the reorganization of the office in 1866–1867. It was held by one of the assistant under-secretaries until 1912, when a separate legal adviser was appointed. A post of medical adviser was created at the turn of the century, but it remained vacant for many years until it was revived in 1926. An unpaid personal adviser to the secretary of state on business questions (Sir James Stevenson) was appointed in 1921.

Experts were appointed as advisers to the secretary of state in a growing number of fields from 1926 onwards. Their number expanded gradually during the 1930s and rapidly after the Second World War. The principal advisers were provided with one or more specialist assistants, and the post of legal adviser was exceptional in its accumulation of assistant posts, the first being appointed in 1898 and the numbers growing steadily thereafter. While the legal adviser had executive authority to approve drafts and grant permissions in the same manner as other administrative staff, the other advisers did not take executive action in the name of the secretary of state but gave their opinion in their own right.

A number of special advisers were appointed during the war. These included an adviser on food supplies, Dr Clyde (November 1942); on demography, R B Kuczynski (January 1944); on civil aviation, B H Cross (in February 1944); on development planning, Sir Frank Stockdale (November 1944); and on engineering appointments, G N Loggin (March 1945).

The advisers minuted on departmental files, but with the exception of the legal adviser's files, which were registered from 1949, their office papers were regarded as private. See chapters 2.3.2, 2.4.2 and 2.5.3.

The list that follows has been taken from the *Colonial Office List*, which was not published during the Second World War. It was the practice to issue these lists in the year printed on the spine, but in fact they were normally prepared during the previous year. For consistency the dates here reflect the dates on the spines, but readers should be aware that they may need to check the previous or sometimes the subsequent year to locate a given individual. Names appear here in the form given in the lists.

1926
Legal Adviser: Sir John S Risley
Assistant Legal Advisers: H G Bushe, A Ehrhardt (*temporary*)

1927
Legal Adviser: Sir John S Risley
Assistant Legal Advisers: H G Bushe, A Ehrhardt (*temporary*)
Chief Medical Adviser: A T Stanton

1928
Legal Adviser: Sir John S Risley
Assistant Legal Advisers: H G Bushe, A Ehrhardt (*temporary*)
Chief Medical Adviser: A T Stanton
Economic and Financial Adviser: Sir G Schuster

1929
Legal Adviser: Sir John S Risley
Assistant Legal Advisers: H G Bushe, A Ehrhardt (*temporary*)
Chief Medical Adviser: A T Stanton
Financial Adviser: vacant
Assistant Agricultural Adviser: F A Stockdale

1930
Legal Adviser: Sir John S Risley
Assistant Legal Advisers: H G Bushe, J B Thomson
Chief Medical Adviser: A T Stanton
Financial Adviser: Sir John Campbell (February)
Assistant Agricultural Adviser: F A Stockdale

1931
Legal Adviser: Sir John S Risley
Assistant Legal Advisers: H G Bushe, H H Duncan
Chief Medical Adviser: A T Stanton
Financial Adviser: Sir John Campbell
Agricultural Adviser: F A Stockdale
Fisheries Adviser: J O Borley
Adviser on Animal Health: R E Montgomery

1932
Legal Adviser: H G Bushe
Assistant Legal Advisers: H H Duncan, K O Roberts-Wray
Chief Medical Adviser: A T Stanton
Financial Adviser: Sir John Campbell
Agricultural Adviser: F A Stockdale
Fisheries Adviser: J O Borley
Adviser on Animal Health: R E Montgomery

1933
Legal Adviser: H G Bushe
Assistant Legal Advisers: H H Duncan, K O Roberts-Wray
Chief Medical Adviser: A T Stanton
Financial Adviser: Sir John Campbell
Agricultural Adviser: F A Stockdale
Fisheries Adviser: J O Borley

1934
Legal Adviser: H G Bushe
Assistant Legal Advisers: H H Duncan, K O Roberts-Wray
Chief Medical Adviser: A T Stanton
Assistant Medical Adviser: A J O'Brien
Financial Adviser: Sir John Campbell
Agricultural Adviser: F A Stockdale
Fisheries Adviser: J O Borley

1935
Legal Adviser: H G Bushe
Assistant Legal Advisers: H H Duncan, K O Roberts-Wray
Legal Assistant: W L Dale
Chief Medical Adviser: Sir Thomas Stanton
Assistant Medical Adviser: A J O'Brien
Financial Adviser: Sir John Campbell
Agricultural Adviser: F A Stockdale
Fisheries Adviser: J O Borley

1936
Legal Adviser: Sir Grattan Bushe
Assistant Legal Advisers: H H Duncan, K O Roberts-Wray
Legal Assistant: W L Dale
Chief Medical Adviser: Sir Thomas Stanton
Assistant Medical Adviser: A J O'Brien
Financial Adviser: Sir John Campbell
Agricultural Adviser: F A Stockdale
Fisheries Adviser: J O Borley

1937
Legal Adviser: Sir Grattan Bushe
Assistant Legal Advisers: H H Duncan, K O Roberts-Wray
Legal Assistant: W L Dale
Chief Medical Adviser: Sir Thomas Stanton
Assistant Medical Adviser: A J O'Brien
Financial Adviser: Sir John Campbell

Agricultural Adviser: Sir Frank Stockdale
Fisheries Adviser: J O Borley

1938
Legal Adviser: Sir Grattan Bushe
Assistant Legal Advisers: H H Duncan, K O Roberts-Wray, W L Dale
Chief Medical Adviser: A J O'Brien
Assistant Medical Adviser: A G Smart
Financial Adviser: Sir John Campbell
Agricultural Adviser: Sir Frank Stockdale
Fisheries Adviser: Dr H A Tempany

1939
Legal Adviser: Sir Grattan Bushe
Assistant Legal Advisers: H H Duncan, K O Roberts-Wray, W L Dale
Chief Medical Adviser: A J O'Brien
Assistant Medical Adviser: A G Smart
Financial Adviser: Sir John Campbell
Agricultural Adviser: Sir Frank Stockdale
Assistant Agricultural Adviser: Dr H A Tempany
Labour Adviser: Maj G St J Orde Browne

1940
Legal Adviser: Sir Grattan Bushe
Assistant Legal Advisers: H H Duncan, K O Roberts-Wray, W L Dale
Chief Medical Adviser: Vacant
Assistant Medical Adviser: A G Smart
Financial Adviser: Sir John Campbell
Agricultural Adviser: Dr H A Tempany
Labour Adviser: Maj G St J Orde Browne
Educational Adviser: C W Cox
Hon Business Adviser: C Figg
Adviser on Animal Health: J Smith

1941
Legal Adviser: Sir Grattan Bushe
Assistant Legal Advisers: H H Duncan, K O Roberts-Wray, W L Dale
Economic and Financial Adviser: Sir John Campbell
Medical Adviser: A G Smart
Assistant Medical Adviser: W E Glover
Agricultural Adviser: Dr H A Tempany
Assistant Agricultural Adviser: vacant

Labour Adviser: Maj G St J Orde Browne
Educational Adviser: C W Cox
Business Adviser: C Figg
Adviser on Animal Health: J Smith

1942
no information available

1943
Legal Adviser: Sir Kenneth Poyser
Assistant Legal Advisers: H H Duncan, K O Roberts-Wray, W L Dale
Financial Adviser: S Caine
Medical Adviser: A G Smart
Assistant Medical Adviser: W H Kauntze
Agricultural Adviser: Dr H A Tempany
Labour Adviser: Maj G St J Orde Browne
Educational Adviser: C W Cox
Assistant Educational Adviser: T R Rowell
Business Adviser: C Figg
Adviser on Animal Health: J Smith
Adviser on Wartime Food Supplies: Dr W M Clyde

1944
Legal Adviser: Sir Kenneth Poyser
Assistant Legal Advisers: H H Duncan, K O Roberts-Wray, W L Dale
Additional Assistant to Legal Adviser: Rt Hon Sir Sidney Abrahams
Financial Adviser: S Caine
Medical Adviser: A G Smart
Assistant Medical Adviser: W H Kauntze
Agricultural Adviser: Dr H A Tempany
Labour Adviser: Maj G St J Orde Browne
Educational Adviser: C W Cox
Assistant Educational Adviser: T R Rowell
Business Adviser: C Figg
Adviser on Animal Health: J Smith
Adviser on Wartime Food Supplies: W M Clyde

1945
Legal Adviser: H H Duncan
Assistant Legal Advisers: K O Roberts-Wray, W L Dale
Additional Assistants to Legal Adviser: The Rt Hon Sir Sidney Abrahams, Sir Alison

Russell, W G W Hastings
Medical Adviser: W H Kauntze
Assistant Medical Advisers: W H Hart, A W M Rae
Agricultural Adviser: Dr H A Tempany
Assistant Agricultural Adviser: G M Roddan
Forestry Adviser: W A Robertson
Labour Adviser: Maj G St J Orde Browne
Educational Adviser: C W Cox
Assistant Educational Adviser: G A J Bieneman
Business Adviser: Sir Clifford Figg
Adviser on Animal Health: J Smith
Adviser on Wartime Food Supplies: Dr W M Clyde
Air Transport Adviser: B C H Cross

1946
Legal Adviser: K O Roberts-Wray
Assistant Legal Adviser: W L Dale
Legal Assistants (permanent): J C McPetrie, J A Peck
Legal Assistants (temporary): Rt Hon Sir Sidney Abrahams, Sir Alison Russell, C R Stuart, Sir A Henry Webb
Medical Adviser: W H Kauntze
Deputy Medical Adviser: A M Wilson Rae
Assistant Medical Adviser: J M Cruikshank
Chief Nursing Officer: Miss F N Udell
Forestry Adviser (part-time): W A Robertson
Agricultural Adviser: F Clay
Development Planning Adviser: Sir Frank Stockdale
Assistants to Agricultural Adviser: H W Jack, G M Roddan
Labour Adviser: Maj G St J Orde Browne
Educational Adviser: C W Cox
Deputy Educational Adviser: W E Ward
Assistant Educational Advisers: R S Foster, L McDowall Robison
Demographic Statistical Work in Colonies: Prof R B Kuczynski
Chief Statistician: G P Lamb
Adviser on Animal Health (part-time): J Smith
Staff Officer to Colonial Forces: I-Lt-Col J D Chalmers

1947
No information available

1948
Agricultural Adviser: G F Clay
Deputy Agricultural Adviser: G W Nye
Assistant Agricultural Adviser: L Lord
Adviser on Animal Health: J Smith
Adviser on Co-operation: B J Surridge
Ceremonial and Reception Secretary: Rear Adm Sir Arthur Bromley
Educational Adviser: C W Cox
Deputy Educational Adviser: W E Ward
Assistant Educational Advisers: L McDowall Robison, T H Baldwin, Miss F H Gwilliam
Fisheries Adviser: C F Hickling
Forestry Adviser: W A Robertson
Adviser on Inland Transport: A J Bunning
Labour Adviser: E W Barltrop
Assistant Labour Adviser: Miss S A Ogilvie
Legal Adviser: K O Roberts-Wray
Deputy Legal Advisers: W L Dale, J A Peck
Senior Legal Assistant (permanent): J C McPetrie
Legal Assistant (permanent): A B McNulty
Legal Assistants (temporary): The Rt Hon Sir Sidney Abrahams, Sir Alison Russell
Medical Adviser: vacant
Deputy Medical Adviser: A M Rae
Assistant Medical Advisers: J M Cruikshank, R S Hennessey
Chief Nursing Officer: Miss F N Udell
Adviser on Social Welfare: W H Chinn
Surveys Adviser and Director of Colonial (Geodetic and Topographical) Surveys: Brig M Hotine
Geological Adviser and Director of Colonial Geological Surveys: F Dixey
Principal Geologist, Directorate of Colonial Geological Surveys: E S Willbourn

1949
Head of African Studies Branch: R S Hudson
Agricultural Adviser: G F Clay
Deputy Agricultural Adviser: G W Nye
Assistant Agricultural Adviser: L Lord
Adviser on Animal Health: R J Simmons
Adviser on Co-operation: B J Surridge

Educational Adviser: C W Cox
Deputy Educational Adviser: W E Ward
Assistant Educational Advisers: L McDowall Robison, T H Baldwin, Miss F H Gwilliam
Fisheries Adviser: C F Hickling
Forestry Adviser: W A Robertson
Adviser on Inland Transport: A J Bunning
Labour Adviser: E W Barltrop
Assistant Labour Advisers: E Parry, Miss S A Ogilvie
Legal Adviser: Sir Kenneth Roberts-Wray
Deputy Legal Adviser: W L Dale
Senior Legal Assistants: J A Peck, J C McPetrie
Legal Assistant (permanent): A B McNulty
Legal Assistants (temporary): The Rt Hon Sir Sidney Abrahams, S C Meyer, J H De Comarmond
Chief Medical Officer: E D Pridie
Deputy Medical Adviser: A M Rae
Principal Medical Officers: J C Buchanan, T A Austin
Chief Nursing Officer: Miss F N Udell
Police Adviser: W C Johnson
Assistant to Police Adviser: Sir George Abbiss
Adviser on Social Welfare: W H Chinn
Adviser on Training Courses for the Colonial Service: Maj Sir Ralph Furse
Surveys Adviser and Director of Colonial (Geodetic and Topographical) Surveys: Brig M Hotine
Geological Adviser and Director of Colonial Geological Surveys: F Dixey

1950
Head of African Studies Branch: R S Hudson
Agricultural Adviser: G F Clay
Deputy Agricultural Adviser: G W Nye
Assistant Agricultural Adviser: L Lord
Adviser on Animal Health: R J Simmons
Assistant Adviser on Animal Health: W A Allan
Adviser on Co-operation: B J Surridge
Educational Adviser: Sir Christopher Cox
Deputy Educational Adviser: W E Ward
Assistant Educational Advisers: L McDowall Robison, T H Baldwin, Miss F H Gwilliam
Fisheries Adviser: C F Hickling
Forestry Adviser: W A Robertson
Adviser on Inland Transport: A J Bunning
Labour Adviser: E W Barltrop
Assistant Labour Advisers: E Parry, Miss S A Ogilvie
Legal Adviser: Sir Kenneth Roberts-Wray
Deputy Legal Adviser: W L Dale
Senior Legal Assistants: J A Peck, J C McPetrie
Legal Assistants (permanent): A B McNulty, A R Rushford
Legal Assistants (temporary): The Rt Hon Sir Sidney Abrahams, J H DeComarmond
Chief Medical Officer: E D Pridie
Deputy Medical Adviser: A M Rae
Principal Medical Officers: J C Buchanan, T A Austin
Chief Nursing Officer: Miss F N Udell
Police Adviser: W C Johnson
Assistant to Police Adviser: Sir George Abbiss
Adviser on Social Welfare: W H Chinn
Adviser on Training Courses for the Colonial Service: Maj Sir Ralph Furse
Surveys Adviser and Director of Colonial (Geodetic and Topographical) Surveys: Brig M Hotine
Geological Adviser and Director of Colonial Geological Surveys: F Dixey

1951
Head of African Studies Branch: R S Hudson
Agricultural Adviser: G F Clay
Deputy Agricultural Adviser: G W Nye
Assistant Agricultural Adviser: L Lord
Adviser on Animal Health: R J Simmons
Assistant Adviser on Animal Health: W A Allan
Adviser on Co-operation: B J Surridge
Economic Liaison Officer: J L Leyden
Educational Adviser: Sir Christopher Cox
Deputy Educational Adviser: W E Ward
Assistant Educational Advisers: L McDowall Robison, T H Baldwin, Miss F H Gwilliam
Assistant Educational Adviser: F J Harlow
Fisheries Adviser: C F Hickling
Forestry Adviser: F S Collier
Adviser on Inland Transport: A J Bunning
Labour Adviser: E W Barltrop

COLONIAL OFFICE ADVISERS

Assistant Labour Advisers: E Parry, Miss S A Ogilvie
Legal Adviser: Sir Kenneth Roberts-Wray
Deputy Legal Adviser: W L Dale
Senior Legal Assistants: J A Peck, J C McPetrie
Senior Legal Assistant (temporary): The Rt Hon Sir Sidney Abrahams
Legal Assistant (permanent): A R Rushford
Legal Assistants (temporary): D G Gordon-Smith, J E Hopkinson
Chief Medical Officer: E D Pridie
Deputy Chief Medical Officer: A M Rae
Principal Medical Officers: J C Buchanan, T A Austin
Chief Nursing Officer: Miss F N Udell
Inspector-General of Colonial Police: W C Johnson
Deputy to Inspector-General of Colonial Police: R E Foulger
Adviser on Social Welfare: W H Chinn
Telecommunications Liaison Officer: J L Creighton
Surveys Adviser and Director of Colonial (Geodetic and Topographical) Surveys: Brig M Hotine
Geological Adviser and Director of Colonial Geological Surveys: F Dixey

1952
Head of African Studies Branch: R S Hudson
Agricultural Adviser: Sir Geoffrey Clay
Deputy Agricultural Adviser: G W Nye
Assistant Agricultural Adviser: L Lord
Secretary for Colonial Agricultural Research: G A Herklots
Adviser on Animal Health: R J Simmons
Assistant Adviser on Animal Health: W A Allan
Ceremonial and Reception Secretary: Rear Adm Sir Arthur Bromley
Head of Commercial Treaties Branch: Lt-Col G Darby
Adviser on Co-operation: B J Surridge
Economic Liaison Officer: J L Leyden
Educational Adviser: Sir Christopher Cox
Deputy Educational Adviser: W E Ward

Assistant Educational Advisers: L McDowall Robison, T H Baldwin, Miss F H Gwilliam, F J Harlow
Fisheries Adviser: C F Hickling
Forestry Adviser: F S Collier
Hon Adviser on Information Services: G Huxley
Adviser on Overseas Information Services: W H Ingrams
Labour Adviser: E W Barltrop
Assistant Labour Advisers: E Parry, Miss S A Ogilvie
Legal Adviser: Sir Kenneth Roberts-Wray
Deputy Legal Advisers: W L Dale (seconded to Libya), Sir Leslie Gibson
Principal Assistant Legal Adviser: J A Peck
Senior Legal Assistants: J C McPetrie, The Rt Hon Sir Sidney Abrahams
Chief Medical Officer: E D Pridie
Deputy Chief Medical Officer: A M Rae
Principal Medical Officers: J C Buchanan, T A Rankine
Director of Colonial Medical Research: R Lewthwaite
Chief Nursing Officer: Miss F N Udell
Inspector-General of Colonial Police: W A Muller
Assistant to Inspector-General of Colonial Police: Sir George Abbiss
Director of Colonial Products Research: Sir John Simonsen
Security Officer for Overseas Duties: Maj Gen D Dunlop
Adviser on Social Welfare: W H Chinn
Surveys Adviser and Director of Colonial (Geodetic and Topographical) Surveys: Brig M Hotine
Geological Adviser and Director of Colonial Geological Surveys: F Dixey
Chief Statistician: W F Searle

1953
Head of African Studies Branch: R S Hudson
Agricultural Adviser: Sir Geoffrey Clay
Deputy Agricultural Adviser: G W Nye
Secretary for Colonial Agricultural Research: G A Herklots
Adviser on Animal Health: R J Simmons

Head of Commercial Treaties Branch: Lt-Col G Darby
Adviser on Co-operation: B J Surridge
Educational Adviser: Sir Christopher Cox
Deputy Educational Adviser: W E Ward
Assistant Educational Advisers: L McDowall Robison, T H Baldwin, Miss F H Gwilliam, F J Harlow
Fisheries Adviser: C F Hickling
Forestry Adviser: F S Collier
Adviser on Overseas Information Services: W H Ingrams
Labour Adviser: E W Barltrop
Legal Adviser: Sir Kenneth Roberts-Wray
Chief Medical Officer: Sir Eric Pridie
Deputy Chief Medical Officer: A M Rae
Director of Colonial Medical Research: R Lewthwaite
Chief Nursing Officer: Miss F N Udell
Inspector-General of Colonial Police: W A Muller
Adviser on Social Welfare: W H Chinn
Surveys Adviser and Director of Colonial (Geodetic and Topographical) Surveys: Brig M Hotine
Geological Adviser and Director of Colonial Geological Surveys: F Dixey
Adviser on Drainage and Irrigation: G Lacey
Engineering Adviser: R W Foxlee
Colonial Building Research Liaison Officer and Housing Adviser: G A Atkinson

1954
Head of African Studies Branch: R S Hudson
Agricultural Adviser: Sir Geoffrey Clay
Deputy Agricultural Adviser: G W Nye
Assistant Agricultural Adviser: L Lord
Secretary for Colonial Agricultural Research: D Rhind
Adviser on Animal Health: R J Simmons
Adviser on Co-operation: B J Surridge
Educational Adviser: Sir Christopher Cox
Deputy Educational Adviser: W E Ward
Assistant Educational Advisers: L McDowall Robison, T H Baldwin, Miss F H Gwilliam, F J Harlow
Fisheries Adviser: C F Hickling
Forestry Adviser: F S Collier

Labour Adviser: E W Barltrop
Assistant Labour Advisers: E Parry, Miss S A Ogilvie
Legal Adviser: Sir Kenneth Roberts-Wray
Deputy Legal Adviser: W L Dale
Assistant Legal Advisers: J A Peck, J C McPetrie
Chief Medical Officer: Sir Eric Pridie
Deputy Chief Medical Officer: A M Rae
Principal Medical Officer: J C Buchanan
Director of Colonial Medical Research: R Lewthwaite
Chief Nursing Officer: Miss F N Udell
Inspector-General of Colonial Police: W A Muller
Deputy Inspector-General of Colonial Police: I H Stourton
Chief Security Officer: Maj-Gen D Dunlop
Adviser on Social Welfare: W H Chinn
Surveys Adviser and Director of Colonial (Geodetic and Topographical) Surveys: Brig M Hotine
Geological Adviser and Director of Colonial Geological Surveys: F Dixey
Adviser on Drainage and Irrigation: G Lacey
Engineering Adviser: R W Foxlee
Colonial Building Research Liaison Officer and Housing Adviser: G A Atkinson
Colonial Road Research Liaison Officer: F H Williams
Colonial Pest Infestation Liaison Officer: D W Hall

1955
Agricultural Adviser: Sir Geoffrey Clay
Deputy Agricultural Adviser: G W Nye
Assistant Agricultural Adviser: L Lord
Secretary for Colonial Agricultural Research: D Rhind
Adviser on Animal Health: R J Simmons
Adviser on Co-operation: B J Surridge
Educational Adviser: Sir Christopher Cox
Deputy Educational Adviser: W E Ward
Assistant Educational Advisers: L McDowall Robison, T H Baldwin, Miss F H Gwilliam, F J Harlow
Fisheries Adviser: C F Hickling
Forestry Adviser: F S Collier

COLONIAL OFFICE ADVISERS

Labour Adviser: E W Barltrop
Deputy Labour Adviser: E Parry
Assistant Labour Adviser: Miss S A Ogilvie
Legal Adviser: Sir Kenneth Roberts-Wray
Assistant Legal Advisers: J A Peck, J C McPetrie
Assistant Legal Adviser: Sir Ralph Hone
Chief Medical Officer: Sir Eric Pridie
Deputy Chief Medical Officer: A M Rae
Principal Medical Officer: J C Buchanan
Director of Colonial Medical Research: R Lewthwaite
Chief Nursing Officer: Miss F N Udell
Inspector-General of Colonial Police: W A Muller
Deputy Inspector-General of Colonial Police: I H Stourton
Chief Security Officer: Maj-Gen D Dunlop
Adviser on Social Welfare: W H Chinn
Surveys Adviser and Director of Colonial (Geodetic and Topographical) Surveys: Brig M Hotine
Geological Adviser and Director of Colonial Geological Surveys: F Dixey
Engineering Advice: R W Taylor

1956

Agricultural Adviser: Sir Geoffrey Clay
Deputy Agricultural Adviser: G W Nye
Assistant Agricultural Adviser: L Lord
Secretary for Colonial Agricultural Research: D Rhind
Adviser on Animal Health: R S Marshall
Adviser on Co-operation: B J Surridge
Educational Adviser: Sir Christopher Cox
Deputy Educational Advisers: A Astley (Acting), H Houghton (designate)
Assistant Educational Advisers: W E Ward, T H Baldwin, Miss F H Gwilliam, F J Harlow
Fisheries Adviser: C F Hickling
Forestry Adviser: F S Collier
Labour Adviser: E W Barltrop
Deputy Labour Adviser: E Parry
Assistant Labour Adviser: Miss S A Ogilvie
Legal Adviser: Sir Kenneth Roberts-Wray
Assistant Legal Advisers: J A Peck, J C McPetrie, Sir Ralph Hone

Chief Medical Officer: Sir Eric Pridie
Deputy Chief Medical Officer: A M Rae
Principal Medical Officer: J C Buchanan
Director of Colonial Medical Research: R Lewthwaite
Chief Nursing Officer: Miss F N Udell
Inspector-General of Colonial Police: W A Muller
Deputy Inspectors-General of Colonial Police: I H Stourton, G R Gribble, J W Deegan
Chief Security Officer: Maj-Gen D Dunlop
Adviser on Social Welfare: W H Chinn
Surveys Adviser and Director of Colonial (Geodetic and Topographical) Surveys: Brig M Hotine
Geological Adviser and Director of Colonial Geological Surveys: F Dixey
Engineering Advice: R W Taylor

1957

Agricultural Adviser: G W Nye
Deputy Agricultural Adviser: G M Roddan
Assistant Agricultural Adviser: L Lord
Secretary for Colonial Agricultural Research: D Rhind
Adviser on Animal Health: R S Marshall
Adviser on Co-operation: B J Surridge
Educational Adviser: Sir Christopher Cox
Deputy Educational Adviser: H Houghton
Woman Educational Adviser: Miss F H Gwilliam
Assistant Educational Advisers: T H Baldwin, J C Jones
Fisheries Adviser: C F Hickling
Forestry Adviser: F S Collier
Labour Adviser: E W Barltrop
Deputy Labour Adviser: E Parry
Assistant Labour Adviser: Miss S A Ogilvie
Legal Adviser: Sir Kenneth Roberts-Wray
Assistant Legal Advisers: J A Peck, J C McPetrie, Sir Ralph Hone
Chief Medical Officer: Sir Eric Pridie
Deputy Chief Medical Officer: A M Rae
Principal Medical Officer: J C Buchanan
Director of Colonial Medical Research: R Lewthwaite
Chief Nursing Officer: Miss F N Udell

Inspector-General of Colonial Police: I H Stourton
Deputy Inspector-General of Colonial Police: J W Deegan
Chief Security Officer: Maj-Gen D Dunlop
Adviser on Social Welfare: W H Chinn
Surveys Adviser and Director of Colonial (Geodetic and Topographical) Surveys: Brig M Hotine
Geological Adviser and Director of Colonial Geological Surveys: F Dixey
Engineering Advice: R W Taylor
African Studies, Head of Branch: R S Hudson
African Studies, Land Tenure Specialist: S R Simpson
Colonial Building Research Liaison Officer and Housing Adviser: G A Atkinson
Adviser on Drainage and Irrigation: G Lacey
Adviser on Engineering Appointments: Sir Hubert Walker
Adviser on Film Production: W Sellers
Parliamentary Liaison: Sir William McLean
Colonial Liaison Officer, National Institute of Agricultural Engineering: J E Mayne
Colonial Pest Infestation Liaison Officer: D W Hall
Colonial Section Road Research Laboratory, Head: R S Millard
Security Intelligence Advisers: A M MacDonald, G R Gribble
Consultant on Tuberculosis: F R Heaf
Military Staff Officer: Maj A E Majendie

1958
Agricultural Adviser: G W Nye
Deputy Agricultural Adviser: G M Roddan
Secretary for Colonial Agricultural Research: D Rhind
Adviser on Animal Health: R S Marshall
Adviser on Co-operation: B J Surridge
Educational Adviser: Sir Christopher Cox
Deputy Educational Adviser: H Houghton
Woman Educational Adviser: Miss F H Gwilliam
Assistant Educational Advisers: T H Baldwin, J C Jones
Fisheries Adviser: C F Hickling
Forestry Adviser: F S Swabey

Labour Adviser: G Foggon
Deputy Labour Adviser: E Parry
Assistant Labour Adviser: Miss S A Ogilvie
Legal Adviser: Sir Kenneth Roberts-Wray
Assistant Legal Advisers: J A Peck, J C McPetrie, Sir Ralph Hone
Chief Medical Officer: A M Rae
Deputy Chief Medical Officer: J C Buchanan
Director of Colonial Medical Research: R Lewthwaite
Chief Nursing Officer: Miss F N Udell
Inspector-General of Colonial Police: I H Stourton
Deputy Inspectors-General of Colonial Police: J W Deegan, N G Morris
Chief Security Officer: Maj-Gen D Dunlop
Adviser on Social Welfare: W H Chinn
Surveys Adviser and Director of Colonial (Geodetic and Topographical) Surveys: Brig M Hotine
Geological Adviser and Director of Colonial Geological Surveys: F Dixey
Engineering Advice: R W Taylor
African Studies, Head of Branch: R S Hudson
African Studies, Land Tenure Specialist: S R Simpson
Colonial Building Research Liaison Officer and Housing Adviser: G A Atkinson
Adviser on Drainage and Irrigation: H A Morrice
Adviser on Engineering Appointments: T L Bowring
Adviser on Film Production: W Sellers
Parliamentary Liaison: Sir William McLean
Colonial Liaison Officer, National Institute of Agricultural Engineering: vacant
Colonial Pest Infestation Liaison Officer: D W Hall
Colonial Section Road Research Laboratory, Head: R S Millard
Security Intelligence Advisers: G R Gribble, J A Harrison
Military Staff Officer: Maj A E Majendie
Adviser on Tropical Soils: H Greene

1959
Agricultural Adviser: G W Nye
Deputy Agricultural Adviser: G M Roddan

Secretary for Colonial Agricultural Research: D Rhind
Adviser on Animal Health: R S Marshall
Adviser on Co-operation: B J Surridge
Educational Adviser: Sir Christopher Cox
Deputy Educational Adviser: H Houghton
Woman Educational Adviser: Miss F H Gwilliam
Assistant Educational Advisers: T H Baldwin, J C Jones
Fisheries Adviser: C F Hickling
Flora and Fauna Advice: E B Worthington
Forestry Adviser: F S Swabey
Labour Adviser: G Foggon
Deputy Labour Adviser: E Parry
Assistant Labour Adviser: Miss S A Ogilvie
Legal Adviser: Sir Kenneth Roberts-Wray
Assistant Legal Advisers: J A Peck, J C McPetrie, Sir Ralph Hone
Chief Medical Officer: A M Rae
Deputy Chief Medical Officer: J C Buchanan
Director of Colonial Medical Research: R Lewthwaite
Chief Nursing Officer: Miss F N Udell
Inspector-General of Colonial Police: I H Stourton
Deputy Inspectors-General of Colonial Police: J W Deegan, N G Morris
Chief Security Officer: Maj-Gen D Dunlop
Adviser on Social Welfare: W H Chinn
Surveys Adviser and Director of Colonial (Geodetic and Topographical) Surveys: Brig M Hotine
Geological Adviser and Director of Colonial Geological Surveys: F Dixey
Engineering Advice: Sir Reginald Taylor
African Studies, Head of Branch: R S Hudson
African Studies, Land Tenure Specialist: S R Simpson
African Studies, Research Officer: L Branney
Head of Tropical Building Section and Housing Adviser: G A Atkinson
Adviser on Drainage and Irrigation: H A Morrice
Adviser on Engineering Appointments: T L Bowring
Adviser on Film Production: W Sellers
Parliamentary Liaison: Sir William McLean

Colonial Pest Infestation Liaison Officer: D W Hall
Tropical Section, Road Research Laboratory, Head: R S Millard
Tropical Section, Road Research Laboratory, Deputy to Head: F H Williams
Security Intelligence Advisers: J A Harrison, G R Gribble
Military Staff Officer: Maj A E Majendie
Adviser on Tropical Soils: H Greene

1960
Agricultural Adviser: Sir Geoffrey Nye
Deputy Agricultural Adviser: G M Roddan
Secretary for Colonial Agricultural Research: D Rhind
Adviser on Animal Health: R S Marshall
Adviser on Co-operation: B J Surridge
Educational Adviser: Sir Christopher Cox
Deputy Educational Adviser: H Houghton
Woman Educational Adviser: Miss F H Gwilliam
Adviser on Technical Education: J C Jones
Assistant Educational Adviser: T H Baldwin
Fisheries Adviser: C F Hickling
Flora and Fauna Advice: E B Worthington
Forestry Adviser: F S Swabey
Labour Adviser: G Foggon
Deputy Labour Adviser: E Parry
Assistant Labour Adviser: Miss S A Ogilvie
Legal Adviser: Sir Kenneth Roberts-Wray
Assistant Legal Advisers: J A Peck, J C McPetrie, Sir Ralph Hone
Chief Medical Officer: A M Rae
Deputy Chief Medical Officer: J C Buchanan
Director of Colonial Medical Research: R Lewthwaite
Chief Nursing Officer: Miss F N Udell
Inspector-General of Colonial Police: I H Stourton
Deputy Inspectors-General of Colonial Police: J W Deegan, N G Morris
Adviser on Prison Administration in the Overseas Dependent Territories: O V Garrat
Chief Security Officer: Maj-Gen D Dunlop
Adviser on Social Welfare: W H Chinn

Surveys Adviser and Director of Colonial (Geodetic and Topographical) Surveys: Brig M Hotine
Deputy Director of Overseas (Geodetic and Topographical) Surveys: Lt-Col G J Humphries
Deputy Director of Overseas (Geodetic and Topographical) Surveys: W D Wiggins
Geological Adviser and Director of Overseas Geological Surveys: K A Davies
The Principal, Mineral Resources Division, Overseas Geological Surveys: E H Beard
Engineering Advice: Sir Reginald Taylor
African Studies, Head of Branch: R S Hudson
African Studies, Land Tenure Specialist: S R Simpson
African Studies, Research Officer: L Branney
Head of Tropical Building Section and Housing Adviser: G A Atkinson
Adviser on Drainage and Irrigation: vacant
Adviser on Engineering Appointments: T L Bowring
Adviser on Film Production: W Sellers
Parliamentary Liaison: Sir William McLean
Colonial Pest Infestation Liaison Officer: D W Hall
Tropical Section, Road Research Laboratory, Head: R S Millard
Tropical Section, Road Research Laboratory, Deputy to Head: F H Williams
Security Intelligence Advisers: J A Harrison, G R Gribble
Military Staff Officer: Maj A E Maynard
Adviser on Tropical Soils: H Greene

1961
Agricultural Adviser: Sir Geoffrey Nye
Deputy Agricultural Adviser: G M Roddan
Secretary for Colonial Agricultural Research: D Rhind
Adviser on Animal Health: R S Marshall
Adviser on Co-operation: B J Surridge
Educational Adviser: Sir Christopher Cox
Deputy Educational Adviser: H Houghton
Woman Educational Adviser: Miss F H Gwilliam
Adviser on Technical Education: J C Jones
Assistant Educational Adviser: T H Baldwin

Fisheries Adviser: C F Hickling
Flora and Fauna Advice: E B Worthington
Forestry Adviser: F S Swabey
Labour Adviser: G Foggon
Deputy Labour Adviser: E Parry
Assistant Labour Adviser: Miss S A Ogilvie
Legal Adviser: J C McPetrie
Assistant Legal Advisers: J A Peck, A R Rushford, Sir Ralph Hone
Chief Medical Officer: J C Buchanan
Deputy Chief Medical Officer: J M Liston
Adviser on Colonial Medical Research: R Lewthwaite
Chief Nursing Officer: Miss F N Udell
Inspector-General of Colonial Police: Sir Ivo Stourton
Deputy Inspector-General of Colonial Police: N G Morris
Adviser on Prison Administration in the Overseas Dependent Territories: O V Garrat
Chief Security Officer: Maj-Gen D Dunlop
Adviser on Social Welfare: W H Chinn
Surveys Adviser and Director of Colonial (Geodetic and Topographical) Surveys: Brig M Hotine
Geological Adviser and Director of Overseas Geological Surveys: K A Davies
Engineering Advice: Sir James Farquharson
African Studies, Head of Branch: R S Hudson
African Studies, Land Tenure Specialist: S R Simpson
African Studies, Research Officer: L Branney
Head of Tropical Building Section and Housing Adviser: G A Atkinson
Adviser on Land Drainage and Irrigation: D S Ferguson
Adviser on Engineering Appointments: T L Bowring
Adviser on Film Production: W Sellers
Adviser on Television: Cdr J C Proud
Parliamentary Liaison: Sir William McLean
Tropical Liaison Officer: D W Hall
Tropical Section, Road Research Laboratory, Head: R S Millard
Tropical Section, Road Research Laboratory, Deputy to Head: F H Williams

Security Intelligence Advisers: J P Morton, G R Gribble
Military Staff Officer: Maj W A Maynard
Adviser on Tropical Soils: H Greene

1962
Legal Adviser: J C McPetrie
Assistant Legal Advisers: J A Peck, A R Rushford
Inspector-General of Colonial Police: Sir Ivo Stourton
Deputy Inspector-General of Colonial Police: N G Morris
Chief Security Officer: Maj-Gen D Dunlop
Parliamentary Liaison: Sir William McLean
Military Staff Officer: Lt Col W M Adler

1963
Legal Adviser: J C McPetrie
Assistant Legal Advisers: J A Peck, A R Rushford
Inspector-General of Colonial Police: Sir Ivo Stourton
Deputy Inspector-General of Colonial Police: N G Morris
Chief Security Officer: Maj-Gen D Dunlop
Parliamentary Liaison: Sir William McLean
Military Staff Officer: Lt Col W M Adler

1964
Legal Adviser: J C McPetrie
Assistant Legal Advisers: J A Peck, A R Rushford
Inspector-General of Colonial Police: Sir Ivo Stourton
Deputy Inspector-General of Colonial Police: J W Deegan
Chief Security Officer: Maj-Gen D Dunlop
Parliamentary Liaison: Sir William McLean
Military Staff Officer: Lt Col W M Adler

1965
Legal Adviser: J C McPetrie
Assistant Legal Advisers: J A Peck, A R Rushford
Inspector-General of Colonial Police: Sir Ivo Stourton
Deputy Inspector-General of Colonial Police: J W Deegan
Chief Security Officer: Maj-Gen D Dunlop
Parliamentary Liaison: Sir William McLean
Military Staff Officer: Lt Col W M Adler

1966
Legal Adviser: J C McPetrie
Assistant Legal Advisers: A R Rushford, D G Gordon-Smith
Inspector-General of Colonial Police: Sir Ivo Stourton
Deputy Inspector-General of Colonial Police: J W Deegan
Chief Security Officer: Maj-Gen D Dunlop
Parliamentary Liaison: Sir William McLean
Military Staff Officer: Lt Col W M Adler

CHAPTER 9

Standing Advisory Bodies to the Colonial, Dominions, Commonwealth Relations and Successor Offices

The standing advisory bodies are listed here in order of their date of creation (9.1) and in alphabetical order of the first significant words (9.2). Entries in the alphabetical list consist, where possible, of the title and covering dates of the body, the location of its records (if they are kept as a distinct entity), its terms of reference or functions, an indication of the periods when it was chaired by the secretary of state or an under-secretary, details of the transfer of its functions, and cross-references to related bodies.

The information has been taken from the *Dominions Office and Colonial Office List*, *Commonwealth Relations Office List* and *Commonwealth Office Yearbook*, which contain further details. No lists were issued during the Second World War and the *Commonwealth Relations Office List* did not appear until 1953, causing gaps in the information. In some cases it has been difficult to determine precisely when an advisory body was constituted or disbanded, which may have led to some discrepancies. No information is provided about the advisory bodies after 1967; where they continued to exist the closure date has been left open. The list provided here is not necessarily exhaustive.

If no specific class has been allocated to the advisory body's records, they will usually be found in the original correspondence classes. The records of early committees tend to be mainly in the Colonies General class (CO 323). There are also some minutes and papers of advisory bodies in the class Miscellaneous Confidential Print (CO 885). After the establishment of the subject departments readers should refer to the correspondence of the subject department concerned with the area of the advisory body's responsibility; see chapter 12.3, which provides a breakdown of subject department business. There is a particularly large number of papers of advisory bodies in the correspondence of the Economic Department/Division (CO 852), the Social Services Department (CO 859), and the Research Department (CO 927). The papers of committees established under the Dominions, Commonwealth Relations or Commonwealth Offices are in DO 35. The papers of committees set up by the Department of Technical Co-operation or the Overseas Development Administration are in the OD classes.

9.1 Chronological list

- 1905 Colonial Survey Committee
- 1907 Colonial Veterinary Committee
- 1909 Advisory Medical and Sanitary Committee for Tropical Africa
  Entomological Research Committee
- 1918 Government Emigration Committee
- 1919 Colonial Research Committee
  Oversea Settlement Committee
- 1920 Imperial Shipping Committee
- 1922 Irish Distress Committee
- 1923 Advisory Committee on Native Education in the British Tropical African Dependencies
  Committee for Research in the Dependencies of the Falkland Islands
- 1924 African Liquor Traffic Control Committee
- 1925 Imperial Economic Committee
- 1927 Colonial Advisory Medical Research Committee
- 1928 Oversea Mechanical Transport Council and Oversea Transport Directing Committee
  Advisory Committee on Education in the Colonies
- 1929 Colonial Advisory Council of Agriculture and Animal Health
  Colonial Development Advisory Committee
  Imperial Communications Advisory Committee
- 1930 Colonial Office Currency Committee
- 1931 Colonial Labour Committee
- 1932 Standing Financial Committee
- 1935 Empire Forestry Conference and Standing Committee on Empire Forestry
- 1936 Committee on Nutrition in the Colonial Empire
- 1937 Colonial Penal Administration Committee
- 1941 Central Welfare Co-ordinating Committee
  Colonial Products Research Council
- 1942 Advisory Committee on the Welfare of Colonial Peoples in the United Kingdom
  Colonial Labour Advisory Committee
- 1943 Colonial Advisory Council of Agriculture, Animal Health and Forestry
  Colonial Economic Advisory Committee
  Colonial Fisheries Advisory Committee
  Colonial Social Welfare Advisory Committee
  Committee on the Training of Nurses for the Colonies
  Venereal Disease Sub-Committee of the Colonial Advisory Medical Committee
- 1944 Colonial Housing Research Group
  Colonial Social Science Research Council
  Colonial Universities Grants Advisory Committee
  Office Committee on Co-operation in the Colonies
  Tsetse Fly and Trypanosomiasis Committee
- 1945 Colonial Agricultural, Animal Health and Forestry Research Committee
  Colonial Land Tenure Advisory Panel
  Colonial Medical Research Committee
  Commonwealth Air Transport Council
- 1946 British Commonwealth Scientific Committee
  Colonial Economic and Development Council
  Colonial Native Law Advisory Panel
  Commonwealth Advisory Aeronautical Research Council
- 1947 Advisory Committee on Co-operation in the Colonies
  Colonial Economic Research Committee
  Colonial Insecticides Committee
  Colonial Primary Products Committee
  Committee of the Commonwealth Collections of Micro-Organisms

1948	Commonwealth Committee on Mineral Resources and Geology		Advisory Panel Oversea Migration Board
	Commonwealth Liaison Committee	1955	Committee on Colonial Road Research
	Working Party on the Employment in the United Kingdom of Surplus Colonial Labour	1957	Council for Technical Education and Training for Overseas Countries
1949	Advisory Committee on Colonial Geology and Mineral Resources	1958	Commonwealth Economic Consultative Council
	Committee on Mass Education (Community Development)	1959	Commonwealth Education Liaison Committee
	Commonwealth Telecommunications Board	1960	Commonwealth Committee on Mineral Processing
	Colonial Local Government Advisory Panel		Commonwealth Consultative Space Research Committee
1950	Advisory Committee on Colonial Colleges of Arts, Science and Technology		Commonwealth Council of Mining and Metallurgical Institutions
	Commonwealth Committee on Fuel Research		Tropical Medicine Research Board
		1961	Advisory Committee on Agriculture, Animal Health, Forestry and Fisheries
1951	Colonial Agricultural Machinery Advisory Committee	1962	Advisory Committee on Co-operatives
	Consultative Committee on the Welfare of Colonial Students in the United Kingdom		Committee for University Secondment
			Tropical Pesticides Research Committee
1952	Advisory Committee on the Treatment of Offenders in the Colonies	1963	Medical Advisory Committee
		1964	Consultative Panel on Education
1953	Advisory Committee on Social Development in the Colonies	1965	Consultative Panel for Social Development
	Colonial Housing and Town Planning	1967	Overseas Pest Control Committee

9.2 Alphabetical list

The letters qv are used to direct the reader's attention to other parts of the chapter.

Advisory Committee on Agriculture, Animal Health, Forestry and Fisheries, 1961–1964

Constituted by the secretary for technical co-operation, it covered general problems in the fields of agriculture, animal health and fisheries, including problems relating to research. It advised on methods of providing technical assistance from the UK in terms of the supply of personnel and expert advice, provision of training facilities, and UK links with overseas research.

See also Colonial Veterinary Committee, 1907–1919; Colonial Advisory Council of Agriculture and Animal Health, 1929–1943; Colonial Advisory Council of Agriculture, Animal Health and Forestry, 1943–1961; Colonial Agricultural, Animal Health and Forestry Research Committee, 1945–1961.

Advisory Committee on Colonial Colleges of Arts, Science and Technology (CO 995), 1950–1957
Advised on the development of colleges, including the expenditure of colonial development and welfare funds. It was primarily concerned with Fourah Bay College, Sierra Leone; the Kumasi College of Technology, Ghana; the Nigerian College of Arts, Science and Technology; the Royal Technical College, Kenya; and the Singapore Polytechnic. To allow the services of the committee to continue to be available to Kumasi College and similar institutions in the newly independent territories, as well as to colleges in the colonies, the advisory committee was reconstituted on 1 July 1957 as the Council for Overseas Colleges of Arts, Science and Technology. It advised on questions of professional, technical and commercial education, and when requested nominated representatives to visit colleges and to serve on governing councils. The council's secretariat carried out a lot of work on behalf of the colleges, the most important being the recruitment of staff. In 1962 its functions were taken over by the Council for Technical Education and Training for Overseas Countries (qv).

See also Council for Technical Education and Training for Overseas Countries, 1957–1962. In chapter 10 see Inter-University Council for Higher Education Overseas, 1946–1966.

Advisory Committee on Colonial Geology and Mineral Resources, see Advisory Committee on Overseas Geology and Mineral Resources

Advisory Committee on Co-operation in the Colonies, 1947–1961
Consisted of people with practical experience of co-operative movements in the UK and elsewhere. It co-ordinated general policy, advised on the means of promoting co-operative societies, and developed connections between societies in the UK and the colonies. It was chaired by the parliamentary under-secretary of state 1947–1950, 1952–1957, and by the minister of state 1950–1951, 1957–1961.

Advisory Committee on Co-operatives, 1962–1966
Constituted by the secretary for technical co-operation and reconstituted by the minister of overseas development to advise on problems arising from providing British technical assistance for the promotion of co-operative societies of all kinds in developing countries. It assisted in developing training facilities, reported on training, and provided personnel and expert advice.

Advisory Committee on Education in the Colonies (CO 987), 1923–1961
Constituted as the Advisory Committee on Native Education in the British Tropical African Dependencies, 1923–1928, it advised on and attempted to promote education in the dependencies and was chaired by the parliamentary under-secretary of state. Renamed the Advisory Committee on Education in the Colonies in 1929, it was chaired by the parliamentary under-secretary of state, 1929–1947, 1950–1951, 1957–1961, and by the minister of state 1948–1950, 1952–1956. There were a number of sub-committees including Higher Education, and Recruitment and Training of Women in the Education Service. A note (Memorandum 113) kept in the Reference Room at Kew provides further information on the committee's papers.

See also Commonwealth Education Liaison Committee, 1959–1967, and Consultative Panel on Education, 1964–1967. In chapter 10 see Council for Education in the Commonwealth, 1964–.

Advisory Committee on Native Education in the British Tropical African Dependencies, see Advisory Committee on Education in the Colonies

Advisory Committee on Overseas Geology and Mineral Resources (CO 1001), 1949–1962
Constituted as the Advisory Committee on Colonial Geology and Mineral Resources, 1949–1957, to advise on matters relating to the geological surveys of the colonial empire and the investigation of its mineral resources.
See also Commonwealth Committee on Mineral Resources and Geology, 1948–. In chapter 10 see Overseas Geological Surveys, 1947–1960.

Advisory Committee on Social Development in the Colonies, 1953–1961
Constituted to replace the Colonial Social Welfare Advisory Committee (qv), and the Committee on Mass Education (Community Development) (qv). It advised on the provision of social welfare services, promotion of community development, co-operation with voluntary agencies, and training of social workers and community development staff. It was chaired by the minister of state, 1953–1957, and by the parliamentary under-secretary of state, 1958–1961.
See also Central Welfare Co-ordinating Committee, 1941–1943, and Consultative Panel for Social Development, 1965–1967.

Advisory Committee on the Treatment of Offenders in the Colonies (CO 912), 1952–1961
Formerly the Colonial Penal Administration Committee (qv), 1937–1943, and the Colonial Social Welfare Advisory Committee Penal (later Treatment of Offenders) Sub-committee, 1943–1952, it advised on matters relating to the treatment of offenders.

Advisory Committee on the Welfare of Colonial Peoples in the United Kingdom, 1942–1950
Appointed to deal with all questions concerning the welfare of colonial people in the UK. It was chaired by the parliamentary under-secretary of state, 1942–1947, and by the minister of state, 1948–1950.
See also Advisory Committee on Social Development in the Colonies.

Advisory Medical and Sanitary Committee for Tropical Africa, see Colonial Advisory Medical and Sanitary Committee

African Liquor Traffic Control Committee, 1924–194?
Appointed to consider and advise upon applications for approved brands of liquor admitted into the West African colonies and protectorates, and questions about their retention on the schedule.

British Commonwealth Forestry Conference and the Standing Committee on British Commonwealth Forestry, 1935–
The Empire Forestry Conference and the Standing Committee on Empire Forestry became the Commonwealth Forestry Conference and the Standing Committee on British Commonwealth Forestry in 1950. The conference usually met quinquennially to discuss questions of forest policy in the Commonwealth and wider technical aspects of forestry. The preparatory work for the conferences and the necessary steps taken to effect resolutions were carried out by the Standing Committee on British Commonwealth Forestry.

In chapter 10 see Commonwealth Forestry Association, 1921–1966; Commonwealth Forestry Institute, University of Oxford, 1924–; Colonial Forest Resources Development Department, 1935–1940.

British Commonwealth Scientific Committee, 1946–
Set up as a standing committee for the British Commonwealth Scientific Official Conference, it was originally constituted with executive heads of government organizations for scientific, industrial, and agricultural research in Commonwealth countries. In its permanent capacity, from 1958, it retained the same basis of membership and the same general functions. Its terms of reference were to follow up recommendations and decisions of conferences and initiate any further action, to consider the best means of ensuring fullest possible collaboration between civil government scientific organizations of the Commonwealth, and to offer advice on the organization of research and development of research laboratories to any particular country which requested it. The name was changed to Commonwealth Scientific Committee in 1966.

The Commonwealth Scientific Liaison Offices (London) (see chapter 10) supplied the secretariat for the committee and acted under its aegis, as did the Commonwealth Committee on Mineral Resources and Geology (qv), the Committee of the Commonwealth Collections of Micro-Organisms (qv) and the Commonwealth Committee on Mineral Processing (qv).

Central Welfare Co-ordinating Committee, 1941–1943
Appointed following a request by Lord Hailey that agencies used in social welfare work should be reviewed at the territorial level and better co-ordinated. The committee reviewed the development of specific programmes and provided a forum for advisers to raise questions of mutual interest.

Colonial Advisory Council of Agriculture and Animal Health (AY 3, CO 996), 1929–1943
Constituted in accordance with the recommendations of the Committee on the Organization of a Colonial Agriculture Service and of the Colonial Veterinary Services Committee, it was concerned with the supply and training of field officers for the colonial agricultural services, establishment of research stations, collection and distribution of scientific information in the fields of agriculture and veterinary science not covered by other agencies, and the general progress of agriculture, food production and animal husbandry in the empire.

See also Colonial Advisory Council of Agriculture, Animal Health and Forestry.

Colonial Advisory Council of Agriculture, Animal Health and Forestry (CO 996), 1943–1961
In 1943 the functions of the Colonial Advisory Council of Agriculture and Animal Health (qv) were enlarged to include forestry and its title changed. Its functions and terms were to keep under review the general condition of agriculture, animal health and forestry and to maintain contact with the work of the colonial departments concerned; to advise on general and particular aspects of policy and development in those fields; to bring attention to any problems on which research or investigation was required; and to visit colonial territories or to make arrangements for the visit of experts. It was chaired by the parliamentary under-secretary of state, 1929–1950, 1955–1956, and by the minister of state 1950–1954, 1957–1961.

A Soil Sub-Committee was set up in 1944 to investigate soil use in the colonies. It commissioned a survey as a basis for a soil conference to discuss soil genesis, morphology and fertility. See CO 996/12.

See also Colonial Veterinary Committee, 1907–1919; Colonial Agricultural, Animal Health and Forestry Research Committee, 1945–1961; Colonial Agricultural Machinery Advisory Committee, 1951–1959; Advisory Committee on Agriculture, Animal Health, Forestry and Fisheries, 1961–1964. In chapter 10 see Colonial Forest Resources Development Department, 1935–1940.

Colonial Advisory Medical Committee (CO 885, CO 994), 1931–1960
Previously the Colonial Advisory Medical and Sanitary Committee (qv) the committee also took over the functions of an early Colonial Medical Research Committee, 1927–1930, which had advised on various aspects of medical research in colonial interests, including research into tropical diseases. The committee was further reconstituted in 1952 to provide a forum for discussion on general medical and health problems affecting the territories, with a panel of specialist advisers. It was chaired by the parliamentary under-secretary of state, 1937–1946, 1950–1951, 1958–1961, and by the minister of state for colonial affairs, 1948–1950, 1952–1957. It was succeeded by the Tropical Medicine Research Board (qv) in 1960.

See also Colonial Advisory Medical and Sanitary Committee, 1922–1931; Venereal Disease Sub-committee, 1943–1948; Colonial Medical Research Committee, 1945–1960; Medical Advisory Committee, 1963–1966. In chapter 10 see Commonwealth Medical Advisory Bureau, 1965–.

Colonial Advisory Medical and Sanitary Committee, 1922–1931
Constituted when the Advisory Medical and Sanitary Committee for Tropical Africa, 1909–1922, was extended to cover all dependencies. Both committees advised on medical and sanitary questions, and a sub-committee advised on the selection of candidates for medical appointments in the colonies. In 1931 the committee took over the functions of the original Colonial Medical Research Committee, which was dissolved in 1930, and its title was changed to Colonial Advisory Medical Committee (qv).

See also Colonial Advisory Medical Committee, 1931–1960; Colonial Medical Research Committee, 1945–1960; Tropical Medicine Research Board, 1945–1966.

Colonial Agricultural, Animal Health and Forestry Research Committee (CO 908), 1945–1961
Appointed to examine, initiate and assist research in the areas of its coverage; to review the publication and dissemination of technical and scientific information required for such research; to make results available, and to promote developments and improvements. It also advised on the recruitment, training and terms of employment of governmental scientific personnel. It had three sub-committees on soil research, cocoa research and stored products research.

See also Colonial Advisory Council of Agriculture and Animal Health, 1929–1943; Colonial Advisory Council of Agriculture, Animal Health and Forestry, 1943–1961; Advisory Committee on Agriculture, Animal Health, Forestry and Fisheries, 1961–1964.

Colonial Agricultural Machinery Advisory Committee, 1951–1959
Appointed to review the development of mechanization of agriculture, to stimulate trials of existing types of agricultural machinery, and to encourage the manufacture of new types.

Colonial Development Advisory Committee (CO 970), 1929–1940
Appointed with the approval of the Treasury in accordance with the Colonial Development Act 1929. It examined applications for assistance from the Colonial Development Fund and sought to aid schemes that developed agriculture and industry and therefore promoted commerce. The Colonial Development and Welfare Act of 1940 envisaged a similar committee, but in wartime conditions advice was provided instead through an office committee.

Colonial Economic Advisory Committee (CO 990), 1943–1946
Advised on solutions to the many and complex economic problems in the administration and development of the colonies. It worked largely through sub-committees.

Colonial Economic and Development Council (CO 999), 1946–1951
Appointed to advise on the framing and subsequent review of plans for economic and social development in the colonial empire and on questions of general economic and financial policy. It was chaired by the parliamentary under-secretary of state, 1947–1950, and by the minister of state, 1950–1951.

Colonial Economic Research Committee (CO 898), 1947–1962
Appointed to advise on matters relating to economic research and statistics. Conducted surveys and research in conjunction with colonial governments on such topics as the distribution of industry in Jamaica, manpower problems in Tanganyika, and the socio-agricultural implications of rice farming in Sierra Leone. It also co-ordinated regional institutes for economic research, such as the West African Institute of Social and Economic Research. See CO 852/1355/13.

Colonial Fisheries Advisory Committee (CO 910), 1943–1961
Appointed to advise on problems concerning marine and freshwater fisheries. It was chaired by the parliamentary under-secretary of state, 1943–1950, 1955–1957, and by the minister of state, 1950–1955, 1957–1961.

Colonial Housing Research Group (CO 1005), 1944–
Appointed to advise on the collection and dissemination of information regarding the physical structure of existing and desirable types of housing in the colonies, and in particular regarding building materials.

Colonial Housing and Town Planning Advisory Panel, 1953–1961
Advised, collectively or individually, on matters referred in the field of colonial housing and town planning. Usually chaired by a senior official.
See also Colonial Housing Research Group.

Colonial Insecticides Committee/Colonial Insecticides, Fungicides and Herbicides Committee, see Colonial Pesticides Research Committee

Colonial Labour Advisory Committee (CO 888), 1942–1961
Replacing the Colonial Labour Committee (qv), 1931–1942, it was established partly for wartime purposes, but its creation had already been called for by the Trades Union Congress and recommended by the Royal Commission on the West Indies. It advised on questions concerning the employment of labour in the colonial dependencies and could co-opt anyone with necessary special knowledge. The committee achieved very little during the war years when the need for secrecy prevented its members from obtaining information they required, nor was it in a position to contribute significantly to post-war planning. However, in the years following the war it was enlarged and operated on a far more effective basis. The committee was chaired by the parliamentary under-secretary of state, 1942–1947, 1950–1951, 1958–1961, and by the minister of state, 1948–1950, 1952–1957.

Colonial Labour Committee (CO 888), 1931–1942
Set up to review, and where necessary to formulate, the general principles on which colonial labour legislation should be based and its application. Initially it was an interdepartmental committee, including representatives from the Ministry of Labour and the Factories Division of the Home Office, but after the collapse of the Labour Government in 1931 it ceased to meet frequently and was mainly used to counter Parliamentary questions.

Colonial Land Tenure Advisory Panel (CO 993), 1945–1953
Constituted as a result of a suggestion by the Committee on Native Land Tenure in Africa, chaired by Lord Hailey, to advise on problems of land tenure in the colonies.

Colonial Local Government Advisory Panel (CO 915), 1949–1961
Advised on local government questions, training for local government posts, and the provision of technical aid.

Colonial Medical Research Committee (CO 913), 1945–1960
Created in 1945 by the secretary of state for the colonies jointly with the Medical Research Council to advise on all matters affecting medical research in and for the colonies regardless of the source of funds, but with particular reference to the employment of funds provided for research under the Colonial Development and Welfare Act 1940. From 1953 this included promoting work through home

universities and research organizations. It was succeeded by the Tropical Medicine Research Board (qv) in 1960.

Its sub-committees initiated and co-ordinated research into potential cures and methods of control of such diseases as malaria, typhus and helminthiasis (worm-related diseases). Regional councils were also set up, such as the East Africa Council for Medical Research, the Standing Advisory Committee for Medical Research in the British Caribbean Territories, and the West African Council for Medical Research, which included experts from within the region. The Personnel Sub-Committee vetted skilled and specialized personnel before attaching them to specific projects.

See also Colonial Advisory Medical and Sanitary Committee, 1922–1931; Colonial Advisory Medical Committee, 1931–1960; Venereal Disease Sub-Committee, 1943–1948; Medical Advisory Committee, 1963–1966. In chapter 10 see Commonwealth Medical Advisory Bureau, 1965–.

Colonial Native Law Advisory Panel (CO 1003), 1946–1961
Advised on questions relating to investigations of African law and native courts, supplied colonial governments with information on the problems of native law everywhere, advised on the provision and training of personnel for investigations, and acted as a clearing house for questions relating to African courts and native law.

Colonial Office Currency Committee, 1930–194?
Appointed to advise on currency questions in the empire. It consisted of official and banking representatives.

Colonial Penal Administration Committee, 1937–1943
Advised on penal administration in the empire. It was chaired by the parliamentary under-secretary of state, 1940 to 1943. It then became a sub-committee of the Colonial Social Welfare and Advisory Committee (qv), 1943–1953.

See also Advisory Committee on the Treatment of Offenders in the Colonies, 1952–1961.

Colonial Pesticides Research Committee (CO 911), 1947–1961
Constituted initially as the Colonial Insecticides Committee, it became the Colonial Insecticides, Fungicides and Herbicides Committee in 1949. In 1956 it became the Colonial Pesticides Research Committee with essentially the same functions. It advised on problems concerning the use of insecticides, fungicides and herbicides (including arboricides and defoliants); it examined, advised, initiated research, and carried out experimental field work; it co-ordinated agricultural, medical and veterinary interests in the use of such chemicals, etc, and it ensured that the latest information was available.

See also Tropical Pesticides Research Committee, 1962–1966, and Overseas Pest Control Committee, 1967–. In chapter 10 see Tropical Pesticides Research Headquarters and Information Unit, 1963–.

Colonial Primary Products Committee (CO 1002), 1947–1949
The committee embraced the Colonial Office as sponsors, the Ministry of Food, Board of Trade and the Treasury. It was responsible for reviewing, commodity by commodity, the possibility of increasing colonial production, with regard to both the

interests of the dependent territories and of the world, and the desirability of increasing foreign exchange resources.

Colonial Products Research Council (CO 899, AY 3), 1941–1954
Constituted in early 1943 following the recommendation on the Committee of Alternative Uses for Colonial Products, which was set up in 1941. It reviewed colonial production and advised on raw materials for manufacture of intermediate and other products required by industry. It also supervised and initiated research and could call into consultation experts in science, industry and other related fields. It was accommodated at the Imperial Institute. In 1954 it was replaced by a Colonial Products Council, which, in addition to performing the duties of its predecessor, oversaw the work of the Colonial Products Laboratory. In 1959 it was dissolved and replaced by the Tropical Products Institute Steering Committee.

In chapter 10 see Colonial Products Advisory Bureau (Plant and Animal), 1949–1954.

Colonial Research Committee, see Overseas Research Council

Colonial Research Council, see Overseas Research Council

Colonial Social Science Research Council (CO 901), 1944–1961
Advised on matters relating to research in the social sciences in or for the benefit of the colonial territories, including the distribution of funds made available under the Colonial Development and Welfare Acts. It reviewed the organization of research, examined research projects, submitted published results and initiated new programmes not otherwise covered. Standing committees on anthropology and sociology, history and administration, law (including land tenure), linguistics, and the training of research personnel were set up in 1949.

Colonial Social Welfare Advisory Committee (CO 997), 1943–1953
Advised on problems affecting the social welfare of urban and rural communities in the colonies, the training of social workers, and other allied matters. Its functions were transferred to the Advisory Committee on Social Development in the Colonies (qv) in 1953. It was chaired by the parliamentary under-secretary of state, 1943–1947, 1950–1951, and by the minister of state, 1948–1950, 1951–1953.

See also Advisory Committee on the Treatment of Offenders in the Colonies, 1952–1961, and Consultative Panel for Social Development, 1965–.

Colonial Survey and Geophysical Committee, 1905–1948
Constituted as the Colonial Survey Committee, 1905–1934, to advise on matters affecting the surveying of colonies and protectorates, especially those in tropical Africa, it was renamed in 1935. It considered geophysical, meteorological and astronomical questions, as well as survey and geological questions. It was constituted as far as possible on an ex officio basis.

See also Commonwealth Committee on Mineral Resources and Geology, 1948–. In chapter 10 see Directorate of Overseas Surveys, 1946–.

Colonial Universities Grants Advisory Committee (CO 1004), 1944–1965
Constituted, in accordance with a recommendation of the Commission on Higher Education in the Colonies, as a sub-committee of the Advisory Committee on Education in the Colonies (qv). It advised on expenditure of both UK funds for developing higher education in the colonies and funds available from other sources. It was guided on academic aspects by the opinion of the Inter-University Council for Higher Education Overseas. A summary of its work between 1946 and 1954 can be found in Cmd 9515, *Inter-University Council For Higher Education Overseas* (1955–56, xiv, 843).

Colonial Veterinary Committee, 1907–1919
Established with the co-operation of the Board of Agriculture and Fisheries to collect information on tropical diseases affecting livestock, and to advise on the best method of investigation into the veterinary aspect of tropical diseases.
 See also Colonial Agricultural, Animal Health and Forestry Research Committee, 1945–1961.

Committee for Research in the Dependencies of the Falkland Islands, see Falkland Islands Dependencies Scientific Committee

Committee for University Secondment, 1962–1966
The committee was set up to advise the secretary for technical co-operation (later the minister of overseas development) on the expenditure of Commonwealth education funds and other public money to help staff universities in developing countries and to secure the continuing co-operation of British universities. The committee was serviced jointly by the Ministry of Overseas Development and the British Council and worked closely with the Inter-University Council for Higher Education Overseas and other agencies concerned with recruitment for universities overseas.

Committee of the Commonwealth Collections of Micro-Organisms, 1947–
Established following a recommendation of the British Commonwealth Scientific Official Conference in 1946, with the function of fostering the maintenance and extension of existing culture collections and increasing the general availability and use of cultures where necessary. The central administration took the form of a permanent committee, with each member country represented; secretariat services were provided by the Commonwealth Scientific Liaison Offices (London) (see chapter 10).

Committee on Colonial Road Research, 1955–
Established to advise on matters of road research for the benefit of the colonies. The committee also exercised a general oversight over the work of the Tropical Road Research Section which, as the Colonial Road Research Section, was established in 1955 at the Road Research Laboratory to deal with road problems peculiar to tropical and rapidly developing territories.

Committee on Mass Education (Community Development) (CO 1000), 1949–1953
Following recognition by the Colonial Office Summer Conference, 1948, that mass education and community development covered a far wider field than those for

which colonial departments of education were responsible, it was decided that the mass education sub-committee should be replaced by a more representative new committee. It considered matters of policy and new programmes, encouraged progress and innovation, and advised on the provision of training for specialist staff. It maintained close association with the Advisory Committee on Education in the Colonies (qv) and acted as a fundamental education sub-committee of the national co-operating body which advised the government on relations with UNESCO.

See also the Advisory Committee on Social Development in the Colonies, 1953–1961.

Committee on Nutrition in the Colonial Empire, 1936–194?
Appointed to survey the state of knowledge regarding nutrition in the empire and to advise on appropriate measures to apply and increase such knowledge. Prior to September 1939 it functioned as a Committee of the Economic Advisory Council of the Cabinet, but it then became a Colonial Office committee. It was chaired by the parliamentary under-secretary of state for the colonies, 1940–?.

In chapter 10 see London School of Hygiene and Tropical Medicine, Department of Human Nutrition, 1961–.

Committee on the Training of Nurses for the Colonies (CO 998), 1943–1945
Appointed on the basis of the Colonial Advisory Medical Committee's recommendation that nurses' training for work in the colonies was inappropriate and should receive attention.

Commonwealth Advisory Aeronautical Research Council, 1946–
Appointed to encourage and co-ordinate aeronautical research throughout the Commonwealth and to ensure complementary research programmes. Its membership was composed of appointed delegates. Its functions were strictly advisory, and its appointed delegates were responsible for fostering the aims and recommendations of the council in their own countries.

Commonwealth Air Transport Council, 1945–
Established following a recommendation approved at the Commonwealth Air Conversations held in Canada in October 1944, to keep under review the progress and development of Commonwealth civil air communications and to advise on civil aviation matters referred to it by Commonwealth governments. It also served as a forum for exchange of views and information between Commonwealth countries on civil air transport matters. The Southern Africa Air Transport Council and the South Pacific Air Transport Council were ancillary to the Council and performed similar functions on a regional basis.

Commonwealth Committee on Fuel Research, 1950–1964
Established following a recommendation of the British Commonwealth Scientific Official Conference (1946) that a specialist conference should be held. The committee was subsequently appointed to facilitate liaison and collaboration in the field of fuel research, and to call future specialist conferences. Subjects discussed were facilities for fuel research, educational and training facilities, and methods of

collaboration and liaison. Membership was open to member countries of the British Commonwealth Scientific Committee (qv).

Commonwealth Committee on Mineral Processing, 1960–
Established after a report from the Standing Committee for the British Commonwealth Scientific Conference (1952) paid particular attention to research on utilization and beneficiation of low grade ores. The committee promoted collaboration and interchange of information within the Commonwealth through the circulation of research programmes, unpublished reports, and details of staff and specialized equipment at mineral processing research establishments in member countries. It also encouraged the interchange of staff among the various Commonwealth organizations active in the field of mineral processing and it published annual reports.

See also Commonwealth Council of Mining and Metallurgical Institutions, 1960–.

Commonwealth Committee on Mineral Resources and Geology, 1948–
Established following the recommendation of a committee for the British Commonwealth scientific official conference (1946) that a Commonwealth organization be established to promote collaboration and the exchange of information in the field of mineral resources and geology. After a specialist conference (1948), permanent machinery was set up; a Commonwealth geological liaison office was established in 1950 under a serving officer of the Commonwealth geological survey. The officer acted as secretary to the committee and carried out duties for all member countries.

See also Advisory Committee on Overseas Geology and Mineral Resources, 1949–1962.

Commonwealth Communications Council, 1929–1949
Constituted as the Imperial Communications Advisory Committee, 1929–1944, in accordance with the recommendations of the Imperial Wireless and Cable Conference, 1928, to advise on telegraphic communications. Its purpose was to co-ordinate the telegraphic services (wireless and cable) connecting the various parts of the empire, and to consider any questions of policy regarding the institution of new services, discontinuance of existing services, alteration in rates, or distribution of traffic between alternative routes. The committee was composed of members from the UK, Canada, Commonwealth of Australia, New Zealand, Union of South Africa, Irish Free State, India and the colonies and protectorates.

Commonwealth Consultative Space Research Committee, 1960–
Founded after the Commonwealth representatives decided, at a meeting held by the British National Committee on Space Research, to form their own permanent scientific committee to further Commonwealth co-operation in this field. It was concerned with rocket and satellite vehicles employed to carry out scientific experiments within and beyond the earth's atmosphere, and it investigated problems relating to the earth's environment in the solar system. The committee was of a consultative nature, and its function was to consider and initiate proposals, to work out details of co-operative enterprises and to serve as a centre for the exchange of information.

Commonwealth Council of Mining and Metallurgical Institutions, 1960–
Founded to convene successive mining and metallurgical congresses within the Commonwealth as a means of promoting development of mineral resources and fostering a high level of technical efficiency and professional status. It served as an organ of inter-communication and co-operation between constituent bodies, and for the promotion and protection of their common interests.

See also Advisory Committee on Overseas Geology and Mineral Resources, 1949–1962, and Commonwealth Committee on Mineral Processing, 1960–.

Commonwealth Economic Committee, 1925–1954
Set up as the Imperial Economic Committee following proposals of the Imperial Economic Conference of 1923, it was the first permanent body composed of representatives of Commonwealth governments. Its functions, enlarged from time to time as a result of imperial conferences, included investigating marketing methods and production for export, preparing surveys and intelligence of any area of Commonwealth trade and marketing, facilitating conferences among those engaged in particular industries in the Commonwealth, and investigating economic questions referred by Commonwealth governments. It became the Commonwealth Economic Committee in 1946 and operated until it was absorbed by the Commonwealth Secretariat.

Commonwealth Economic Consultative Council, 1958–
Established to co-ordinate the existing economic consultative machinery of the Commonwealth following a proposal of the Commonwealth Trade and Economic Conference, Montreal, 1958, the council consisted of the finance and economic ministers of the Commonwealth countries, who met when circumstances demanded. It incorporated various channels and bodies through which economic consultation took place, and set up any further bodies as necessary. It met at the level of finance ministers each year before the meetings of the International Monetary Fund and the International Bank for Reconstruction and Development. The council had no permanent headquarters and met by arrangement in any Commonwealth country. Its meetings were serviced by the Commonwealth Secretariat.

Commonwealth Education Liaison Committee, 1959–1967
Appointed as a result of a recommendation by the Commonwealth Education Conference, it provided a forum for consideration at policy level of various schemes of educational assistance agreed upon at the conference. It was established on a permanent basis by the second Commonwealth Education Conference, 1962. Its functions supplemented normal bilateral arrangements between member governments and it sought to develop and improve Commonwealth co-operation in education. The Commonwealth Education Liaison Unit, which served as the secretariat of the committee, was integrated with the Commonwealth Secretariat in 1967 to form its Education Division.

See also Advisory Committee on Education in the Colonies, 1923–1961, and Consultative Panel on Education, 1964–.

Commonwealth Liaison Committee, 1948–
Established to supplement the existing inter-governmental channels for keeping Commonwealth countries fully informed on matters connected with the European Recovery Programme. Its functions were expanded in 1949 to cover discussion of financial and economic problems of general concern to all Commonwealth countries. In 1955 it took over the remaining functions of the former Sterling Area Statistical Committee. The Commonwealth Liaison Committee did not formulate policy but provided for an exchange of information on economic matters. An exception to this was in 1964 when Commonwealth prime ministers agreed the committee should consider proposals about Commonwealth development projects, administrative training, higher education, the Commonwealth Medical Conference, the Commonwealth Parliamentary Association, the Commonwealth Foundation, and satellite communications. Later these were pursued through other channels. All Commonwealth governments were members of the committee.

Commonwealth Scientific Committee, see British Commonwealth Scientific Committee

Commonwealth Shipping Committee, 1920–1963
Appointed following a resolution of the Imperial War Conference, 1918, as the Imperial Shipping Committee, 1920–1948. Its functions were to enquire into complaints regarding ocean freights, facilities and conditions in inter-imperial trade or questions referred to it by any nominating authorities and report the conclusions to the governments concerned; to survey facilities for maritime transport on necessary trade routes; and to make recommendations for improvements and co-ordination taking into account facilities for air transport.
　See also Commonwealth Air Transport Council, 1945–.

Commonwealth Telecommunications Board, 1949–
Established following a recommendation of the Commonwealth Telecommunications Conference, 1945, and under the terms of the Commonwealth Telegraphs Agreement, 1948; a new agreement was reached in 1963. Each member government (UK, Canada, Australia, New Zealand, South Africa, India and Southern Rhodesia) was required to appoint a department, body or public corporation to operate as a national body and maintain external telecommunications services. The board made recommendations to partner governments and their national bodies on matters relating to external telecommunications systems and, with the agreement of partner governments, prescribed matters relating to the special financial arrangements operating between the national bodies. It also acted as an advisory body to the partner governments. On·the inauguration of the board, the Commonwealth Communications Council, set up in 1944 to succeed the Imperial Communications Advisory Committee, was dissolved.

Consultative Committee on the Welfare of Colonial Students in the United Kingdom, 1951–1960
Advised on problems concerning the welfare of colonial students in the UK. It included representatives of the overseas students unions and of UK political parties, the London University adviser to overseas students, and representatives of the British

Council and the Colonial Office. It was chaired by the parliamentary under-secretary of state, 1952–1960.

Consultative Panel for Social Development, 1965–1967
Constituted by the minister of overseas development, the panel acted as consultants on aspects of social development of importance to countries that requested British technical co-operation or any other similar aid. It was specially concerned with advisory services, training facilities and staff. The panel had working groups on adult literacy, adult education, social development training and youth services to which additional members were co-opted. It was chaired by the parliamentary secretary of the Ministry of Overseas Development, 1965–.

See also Advisory Committee on Social Development in the Colonies, 1953–1961.

Consultative Panel on Education, 1964–1967
Originally constituted by the secretary for technical co-operation, it was taken over by the minister of overseas development in October 1964. It advised the minister on educational assistance for overseas countries with special reference to aspects not already dealt with by other agencies. The panel had working groups on teacher training, research and planning, and books, to which additional members were co-opted.

See also Advisory Committee on Education in the Colonies, 1923–1961, and Commonwealth Education Liaison Committee, 1959–.

Council for Overseas Colleges of Arts, Science and Technology, see Advisory Committee on Colonial Colleges of Arts, Science and Technology

Council for Technical Education and Training for Overseas Countries, 1957–1962
Set up by the secretary for technical co-operation to give advice and expert assistance on promoting technical and commercial education and training in the UK and developing countries. It promoted contacts, recruited staff for overseas service, and facilitated the training and education in the UK of trainees and others from developing countries.

See also Advisory Committee on Colonial Colleges of Arts, Science and Technology, 1950–1957.

Discovery Committee, see Falkland Islands Dependencies Scientific Committee

Empire Forestry Conference and Standing Committee on Empire Forestry, see British Commonwealth Forestry Conference and the Standing Committee on British Commonwealth Forestry

Entomological Research Committee, 1909–1913
Appointed to further the study of economic entomology by examining the relationship between biting flies and disease (human and animal) and between insects and economic plants. It was divided into sub-committees, with special reference to the colonies and protectorates of tropical Africa: insects in relation to the diseases of human beings and animals, insects in relation to plants, publications, and financial matters. It received an annual grant from imperial funds and contributions from

Southern Nigeria, Gold Coast, Sierra Leone and the Gambia. In 1910 it was given a private donation to provide scholarships for study abroad. Its work was extended to the West Indies in 1912.

See also Commonwealth Institute of Entomology, 1913–1948, in chapter 10.

Falkland Islands Dependencies Scientific Committee, 1923–1956
Appointed originally as the Committee for Research in the Dependencies of the Falkland Islands, 1923–1930, it controlled investigations, mainly connected with whaling, recommended by the Inter-Departmental Committee on Research and Development in the Dependencies of the Falkland Islands. Ships were acquired and specially constructed, and a marine biological station was established at South Georgia in 1925. The committee was renamed the Discovery Committee, 1931–1948, which was chaired by the under-secretary of state, 1935–1948. In 1947 a Scientific Sub-Committee was formed. In 1948 it became the Falkland Islands Dependencies Scientific Committee, which advised on scientific matters connected with the Falkland Islands Dependencies Survey (see chapter 10).

In chapter 10 see Royal Society National Committee on Antarctic Research, 1962–.

Government Emigration Committee, 1918–194?
The committee is described under Emigration Departments/Overseas Settlement Department in chapter 13.1.

Imperial Communications Advisory Committee, see Commonwealth Communications Council

Imperial Economic Committee, see Commonwealth Economic Committee

Imperial Shipping Committee, see Commonwealth Shipping Committee

Irish Distress/Grants Committee (CO 762, CO 905/21), 1922–1926
The Irish Distress Committee was replaced a year after its formation by the Irish Grants Committee. It was charged with recommending what grants or loans should be made to refugees from Ireland and what advances should be made under the Criminal and Malicious Injuries Acts of the Irish Free State.

Medical Advisory Committee, 1963–1966
Set up by the secretary for technical co-operation following a report on medical aid to developing countries, the committee was responsible to the minister of overseas development from 1964. It consisted of prominent members of various branches of the medical profession of Britain, of the dental, nursing and auxiliary services, and of government organizations concerned with technical assistance in medicine. It reviewed the technical assistance provided by the ministry in medical fields, provided assistance through sub-committees and panels, made recommendations and advised. Permanent panels were established to consider technical assistance problems in the following areas: medical education, recruitment of medical staff, visitors and consultants, nursing services, preventive medicine, ancillary medical services and equipment, dental services and associations between British and overseas medical practitioners.

See also Colonial Advisory Medical Committee, 1931–1960.

Office Committee on Co-operation in the Colonies (CO 1004), 1944–
Established to determine how the colonies should be advised on co-operation, and what changes in organization within the Colonial Office should be made to enable the subject to be dealt with adequately.

Oversea Mechanical Transport Council and Oversea Transport Directing Committee, 1928–1934
Appointed to investigate questions relating to the use of mechanical transport in less developed countries. The council, which supervised the work of the directing committee, was composed of representatives of the Empire Marketing Board and the contributing countries. The directing committee was composed of technical experts under a non-technical chairman.

Oversea Migration Board, 1953–1965
Appointed to consider and advise upon specific proposals for schemes of emigration from the UK to other Commonwealth countries and upon related matters. Chaired by the parliamentary under-secretary of state for Commonwealth relations, 1957–1965, and by the minister of state for Commonwealth relations, 1966.

Oversea Settlement Committee, 1919–1935
The committee is described under Emigration Departments/Overseas Settlement Department in chapter 13.1. It was chaired by the parliamentary under-secretary for the colonies, 1919–1921, 1922–1923, and the parliamentary under-secretary of state for dominions affairs, 1926, 1935–1939.

See also Oversea Migration Board, 1953–1965. In chapter 13 see under Emigration Departments/Overseas Settlement Department.

Overseas Pest Control Committee, 1967–
Appointed to advise the minister of overseas development of the needs of the developing countries and of the research activities directed through the ministry towards the control of tropical pests. In particular it reviewed the scientific programmes of the Anti-Locust Research Centre, the Tropical Stored Products Centre, the Tropical Pesticides Research Unit, the Tropical Pesticides Research Headquarters and Information Unit, and the Termite Research Unit in the light of the resources available.

See also Colonial Pesticides Research Committee, 1947–1961, and Tropical Pesticides Research Committee, 1962–1966. See chapter 10 for further information on the institutions mentioned above.

Overseas Research Council (CO 900), 1919–1964
The Colonial Research Committee was first appointed in 1919 to administer a parliamentary grant for the assistance of poorer colonies in undertaking research work on matters of economic importance. It was wound down in 1932 but reactivated between 1942 and 1947 to continue this function, to advise on the expenditure of money under the Colonial Development and Welfare Act 1940, and to co-ordinate the wide range of research in colonial studies.

The Colonial Research Council was established in 1948 to replace the committee and to advise on general questions relating to research policy in the empire or for its benefit. It also co-ordinated the work of the various committees which advised the secretary of state on special aspects of research and it advised on research matters not falling within the province of those committees. It was chaired by the parliamentary under-secretary of state for the colonies 1948–1950, 1952–1957. In 1959 the council was dissolved and replaced by a new Overseas Research Council, working under and advising the Privy Council Committee on Overseas Research. The latter council was dissolved in 1964, as its work was duplicated by the Department of Technical Co-operation and its advisory bodies.

Standing Financial Committee, 1932–194?
Formed to consider any general financial questions affecting the colonies as a whole. It was chaired by the permanent under-secretary of state for the colonies, 1937–194?.

Tropical Medicine Research Board, 1960–
The board replaced the Colonial Medical Research Committee (qv), and advised the minister of overseas development, through the Medical Research Council, on all medical research financed through ministry funds. It also advised the Medical Research Council on all medical research in or for tropical/sub-tropical countries financed from its own budgets.
    See also Colonial Advisory Medical Committee, 1931–1960, and Medical Advisory Committee, 1963–1966.

Tropical Pesticides Research Committee, 1962–1966
Constituted following the disbandment of the Colonial Research Council (qv), it advised the minister of overseas development on any problems concerning pesticides use and research.
    See also Colonial Pesticides Research Committee, 1947–1961, and Overseas Pest Control Committee, 1967–. In chapter 10 see Tropical Pesticides Research Headquarters and Information Unit, 1963–.

Trypanosomiasis Panel (CO 902), 1944–
The Tsetse Fly and Trypanosomiasis Committee, 1944–1961, was appointed to consider and advise on the co-ordination of action, including research, directed against human and animal trypanosomiasis and, in particular, against the tsetse fly as the chief vector. It became the Trypanosomiasis Panel following the establishment of the Department of Technical Co-operation in 1961.

Tsetse Fly and Trypanosomiasis Committee, see Trypanosomiasis Panel

Venereal Disease Sub-Committee of the Colonial Advisory Medical Committee, 1943–1948
Appointed to advise on the problems of venereal disease in the colonies.
    See also Colonial Advisory Medical Committee, 1931–1960.

Working Party on the Employment in the United Kingdom of Surplus Colonial Labour (CO 1006), 1948–
Constituted following suggestions from colonies that the shortage of manpower in the UK might be matched with employment in overseas territories, the working party enquired into the number and quality of recruits available from the colonies and the openings available in the UK.

CHAPTER 10

Official and Non-Official Organizations, Institutions, etc, Associated with the Colonial, Dominions, Commonwealth Relations and Successor Offices

This chapter covers British-based bodies connected with imperial and Commonwealth affairs. In some cases the Colonial or other Offices were directly responsible for the bodies, in others they were represented on them, in still others the involvement was indirect. The associated bodies are listed here in order of their date of creation (10.1) and in alphabetical order (10.2). The entries in the alphabetical list consist of the title and covering dates of the body, its terms of reference or functions, details of the transfer of its functions, and cross-references to related bodies. In the few cases where the archives of these bodies are in the Public Record Office the references are given.

The information provided has been drawn from the *Dominions Office and Colonial Office List*, *Commonwealth Relations Office List* and *Commonwealth Office Yearbook*, which contain further details. No lists were issued during the Second World War, and the *Commonwealth Relations Office List* did not appear until 1953, causing gaps in the information. In some cases it has been difficult to determine precisely when the bodies were constituted or disbanded, which may have led to some discrepancies. No information is provided about the associated bodies after 1967; where they continued to exist the closure date has been left open. Some of the bodies still exist today, but the information is provided in past tense as it refers to their constitution and functions during the colonial period.

For information about other relevant bodies see Chris Cook, *Sources in British Political History, 1900–1951, Volume 1: A Guide to the Archives of Selected Organizations and Societies* (1975).

10.1 Chronological list

1750	West India Committee	1855	Emigrants Commission
1759	Royal Botanic Gardens, Kew	1866	East India Association
1823	Royal Asiatic Society	1868	Royal Colonial Institute
1833	Joint Agents General for the Crown Colonies	1870	Colonial Government Emigration Agencies at Calcutta
1840	Colonial Land and Emigration Commission	1886	Emigrants Information Office
		1887	Imperial Conference
		1888	Ceylon Association in London
1853	Mauritius Chamber of Agriculture	1893	Imperial Institute of the United

OFFICIAL AND NON-OFFICIAL ORGANIZATIONS, INSTITUTIONS, ETC. 129

      Kingdom, the Colonies and India
1894 Society of Comparative Legislation and International Law
1896 Overseas Nursing Association
1898 Incorporated Liverpool School of Tropical Medicine
1899 London School of Tropical Medicine
1900 Corona Club
1901 League of the Empire
      Royal African Society
      Royal Central Asian Society
      Visual Instruction Committee
1902 Pacific Cable Board
1903 Straits Settlements Association
1908 Bureau of Hygiene and Tropical Diseases
      West Indian Club Ltd
1910 Australian-British Trade Association
      Overseas Club and Patriotic League
      Royal Overseas League
1911 Empire Parliamentary Association
      British Imperial Council of Commerce
      Overseas Audit Department
1912 West African Currency Board
1913 Imperial Bureau of Entomology
      Universities Bureau of the British Empire
1915 British Empire Union Ltd
1916 British Empire Producers Organization
      School of Oriental Studies
1919 Women's Migration and Overseas Appointments Society
1920 British Association of Malaya
      Imperial Bureau of Mycology
      East African Currency Board
      Royal Institute of International Affairs
      Southern Africa Settlement Association
      Uganda Railway Publicity Office
1921 British Empire Ex-Services League
      Empire Forestry Association
      Empire Cotton Growing Association
      Imperial College of Tropical Agriculture
1922 Standing Conference for the Co-ordination of Scientific Research
1923 Joint Africa Board
1924 British Leprosy Relief Association
      Imperial Forestry Institute
      Sarawak Association
1925 British Commonwealth League
      New Zealand Society
1926 Empire Industries Association
      Empire Marketing Board
      International African Institute
      Palestine Currency Board
1927 Imperial Defence College
1929 Anti-Locust Research Centre
      Imperial Agricultural Bureau
      London School of Hygiene and Tropical Medicine
1934 British Council
      Women's Council
1935 Colonial Forest Resources Development Department
      Oversea Settlement Board
1937 Colonial Empire Marketing Board
      Women's Corona Society
1939 Colonial Film Unit
1940 Children's Overseas Reception Board
1941 Colonial Supply Liaison
1942 Colonial Income Tax Office
      Overseas Territories Income Tax Office
1945 Road Research Board
1946 Conference of Engineering Institutions of the British Commonwealth
      Directorate of Overseas Surveys
      Inter-University Council for Higher Education Overseas
1947 Colonial Geological Surveys
      Institute of Commonwealth Studies, Oxford University
1948 Colonial Development Corporation
      Commonwealth Scientific Liaison Offices (London)
      Overseas Division, Building Research Station
      Overseas Food Corporation
1949 Colonial Products Advisory Bureau (Plant and Animal)
      Community Development Clearing House
      Conservative Overseas Bureau
      Institute of Commonwealth Studies,

J

University of London
Institute of Rural Life at Home and Overseas
Termite Research Unit
1950 British Caribbean Currency Board
1951 Falkland Islands Dependencies Scientific Bureau
Pakistan Society
1952 Applied Nutrition Unit
Library Association, Advisory Committee on Library Services in the Colonies
1953 Commonwealth Development Finance Company
Conservative Commonwealth and Overseas Council
1954 British Academy Archaeological and Historical Advisory Committee for Overseas Co-operation
Commonwealth Migration Council Ltd
Queen Elizabeth House, Oxford
1956 West Africa Committee
1957 Overseas Services Resettlement Bureau
Royal Agricultural Society of the Commonwealth
Tropical Products Institute
1958 British Caribbean Association
British Institute of International and Comparative Law
Oversea Service
Voluntary Service Overseas
1959 Commonwealth Education Liaison Unit
Commonwealth Scholarship Commission in the United Kingdom
Falkland Islands Dependencies Survey
1960 Board of Commissioners of Currency, Malaya and British Borneo
British Institute of History and Archaeology

National Council for the Supply of Teachers Overseas
Overseas Development Institute Ltd
1961 British Antarctic Survey
British-Nigeria Association
London School of Hygiene and Tropical Medicine, Department of Human Nutrition
1962 Anglo-Sierra Leonean Society
British Society for International Health Education
Joint Commonwealth Societies Council
Office of the Trade Representative for Seychelles
Royal Society National Committee on Antarctic Research
1963 African Studies Association
Overseas Students Advisory Bureau
Tropical Pesticides Research Headquarters and Information Unit
1964 Commission in the United Kingdom of the Eastern Caribbean Governments
Commonwealth League for Economic Co-operation
Council of Commonwealth Municipalities
Council for Education in the Commonwealth
Uganda Britain Society
1965 Commonwealth Medical Advisory Bureau
Overseas Service College
Women Speakers for the Commonwealth
1966 Royal Society for India, Pakistan and Ceylon
1967 Conservative Parliamentary Commonwealth Affairs Committee
Malaysia-Singapore Commercial Association Inc

10.2 Alphabetical list

The letters qv are used to direct the reader's attention to other parts of this list.

African Studies Association, 1963–
Founded to advance academic studies related to Africa by providing facilities for the interchange of information and ideas. It produced a bulletin and organized interdisciplinary conferences and symposia. Its members mostly held teaching posts or research appointments in universities or other higher education institutions in the UK.

Anglo-Sierra Leonean Society, 1962–
Formed to foster friendship and contact between the UK and Sierra Leone and to assist in the encouragement of cultural, literary and social relations between the two countries. The Society issued bulletins and held film shows and lectures.

Anti-Locust Research Centre (AY 11, AY 20), 1929–
Specialist research into locust problems was started at the Imperial Bureau of Entomology (qv) in 1929 under the auspices of the Committee of Civil Research (later absorbed by the Economic Advisory Council). The Anti-Locust Research Centre, as the office came to be known, conducted and fostered research on locusts and grasshoppers, promoted technical co-operation in this field by assisting overseas governments and organizations, provided research and training facilities for visiting scientists and students, and advised the government on locust and grasshopper problems.

From 1939 the Locust Sub-Committee of the Cabinet Committee of Civil Research and its successors, the Committee on Locust Control of the Economic Advisory Council and the Interdepartmental Committee on Locust Control (set up in 1942), instituted research through the centre at the Imperial Bureau. In 1945 the centre became a separate body under the administration and control of the Colonial Office, with a grant from the Colonial Development and Welfare Fund. From 1946 it was guided in its scientific work by the Advisory Committee on Anti-Locust Research, and for a time the interdepartmental Committee on Locust Control remained in existence to co-ordinate the work with interested departments of state. Control of the centre passed to the Department of Technical Co-operation in 1961, and to the Ministry of Overseas Development in 1965.

The papers of Sir Boris Uvarov, who directed the centre from 1929 until his retirement in 1959, are in AY 20.

In chapter 9 see Overseas Pest Control Committee, 1967–.

Applied Nutrition Unit, 1952–1961
Established as a joint undertaking of the London School of Hygiene and Tropical Medicine and the Colonial Office, it was financed in part by colonial development and welfare funds. Its main functions were to study and exchange information on colonial nutrition and food technology, to provide advice and assistance in field work and investigations, and to assist in arrangements for training colonial personnel in nutrition work. Contact between the unit and the colonial territories for the exchange of technical information was maintained by nutrition liaison officers appointed for each territory.

See also London School of Hygiene and Tropical Medicine, Department of Human Nutrition, 1961–.

Association of British Malaya, see British Association of Malaya

Association of Commonwealth Universities, 1913–
Founded as the Universities Bureau of the British Empire, 1913–1948, it became the Association of Universities of the British Commonwealth, 1948–1963. It then received a royal charter under its present name. A voluntary organization, financed by subscriptions of its member institutions, it provided liaison between the administrations of the various universities in Britain and other Commonwealth countries, and it organized periodic conferences. It also provided the secretariat of the committee of vice-chancellors and principals of the universities of the UK, and acted as London agent for overseas member institutions. In addition, it dealt with the selection of candidates for scholarships, and provided information concerning the universities.

See also Inter-University Council for Higher Education Overseas, 1946–1966.

Australian-British Trade Association, 1910–
Founded to promote trade between Britain and Australia, it gave assistance in matters concerning exports, including specialist services on tariff matters, promotion, and public relations. Its head office was in Canberra, Australia.

Board of Commissioners of Currency, Malaya and British Borneo, 1960–1963
Constituted as a result of a new currency agreement between the governments of the Federation of Malaya, the states of Singapore and Brunei and the colonies of Sarawak and North Borneo, the Board had sole right to issue currency notes and coin in those territories and to manage the currency fund.

British Academy Archaeological and Historical Advisory Committee for Overseas Co-operation, 1954–
Set up by invitation of the secretary of state for the colonies, it acted as a consultative committee to advise on matters relating to the archaeology and history of the colonial territories. In 1961 the committee was transferred to the Department of Technical Co-operation.

British Antarctic Survey, 1961–
The survey was under the Colonial Office until 1961 when it was established as an independent body responsible for the administration and control of British antarctic activities and for publication of the scientific results.

See also Falkland Islands Dependencies Survey, 1959–1961, and Royal Society National Committee on Antarctic Research, 1962–1966. In chapter 9 see Falkland Islands Dependencies Scientific Committee, 1923–1956.

British Association of Malaya, 1920–1963
Founded as a successor to the Straits Settlements Association (qv), 1903–1919, it was concerned with all matters of public interest affecting Singapore, the Federation of Malaya, Sarawak, and North Borneo. It provided a link between past and present residents in these territories, involved itself in the welfare of Malayan students in the UK, and published the monthly magazines *Malayan Bulletin* and *Malaya*.

British Caribbean Association, 1958–
Formed with the intention of strengthening friendship and understanding between the peoples of the Caribbean and Britain and improving race relations generally, its membership included a large number of members of Parliament drawn from the main political parties. It held meetings regularly, made recommendations for constructive action, maintained contact with the ministries and local authorities concerned, and published a newsletter.
See also West India Committee, 1750–, and West Indian Club Ltd, 1908–1966.

British Caribbean Currency Board, 1950–1965
The board was appointed by the secretary of state to provide for and control the supply of a uniform currency to the eastern group of British Caribbean colonies. In 1964 the board was reconstituted to act for new currency authorities, and it ceased to issue currency when the new authorities were established.

British Commonwealth Ex-Services League, 1921–
Founded as the British Empire Ex-Services League to link together the ex-service organizations of the Commonwealth, it maintained contact with them and provided a support system for Commonwealth ex-servicemen. It acted as the overseas agent of a number of ex-service charitable organizations in Britain, gave advice and guidance on pension and other technical matters, and provided a Commonwealth ex-services information service through a quarterly Bulletin.

British Commonwealth League, see Commonwealth Countries League

British Commonwealth Union Ltd, 1915–
Established as the British Empire Union, 1915–1960, it was founded to secure a closer union commercially, politically, socially and otherwise, both between Britain and the overseas countries of the Commonwealth, and between the Commonwealth and other friendly states. Through pamphlets it provided the general public with information concerning specific problems in Britain and the Commonwealth.

British Council (BW Classes), 1934–
Founded to promote a wider knowledge of Britain and the English language abroad and to develop closer cultural relations between Britain and other countries. After the Second World War it placed more emphasis on education, with increasing importance placed on English language teaching. The council gave overseas assistance through experts, graduates and trained teachers, and by providing books, teaching materials, film, television, etc. It awarded scholarships and bursaries for study in Britain, and assisted overseas students with accommodation. It worked to improve and provide libraries, either by itself or in association with others, particularly in Africa. In dependent territories, the council worked in close collaboration with territorial governments, carrying on educational activities which did not fall within the official sphere.

British Empire Ex-Services League, see British Commonwealth Ex-Services League

British Empire Producers Organization, see Commonwealth Producers Organization

British Empire Union Ltd, see British Commonwealth Union Ltd

British Imperial Council of Commerce, see Federation of Commonwealth Chambers of Commerce

British Institute of History and Archaeology, 1960–
Supported by grants from the British Academy and the Kenya Government, its object was to promote research into the history and archaeology of East Africa. The institute was based in Nairobi, with the director responsible to a governing council in London. Research work was carried out by its staff and research students, and results were published in the institute's annual journal *Azania*. Although autonomous, the institute had a formal association with the University of East Africa.

British Institute of International and Comparative Law, 1958–
Founded when the Grotius Society and the Society of Comparative Legislation and International Law were amalgamated to provide a centre for study in London. It was an independent body which initially received support from foundations and was partly financed by subscriptions of its international membership. The institute was particularly concerned with all aspects of law in the Commonwealth and published *The International and Comparative Law Quarterly*. It also prepared surveys on legal topics, organized lectures and conferences, and awarded fellowships to lawyers in the Commonwealth for advanced study in public international law in Britain.

British Leprosy Relief Association, 1924–
Founded as a Christian medical organization to co-ordinate and spearhead the work of various missions and other bodies throughout the territories, it later financed and encouraged leprosy research. Results were published through its quarterly *Leprosy Review*, a worldwide circular. It advised governments and missions on anti-leprosy work, including training of ancillary staff, and it financed the provision of specialist staff. In 1965 it established a pilot leprosy control project in Malawi. The association supported all bodies engaged in approved anti-leprosy work in the Commonwealth.

British-Nigeria Association, 1961–
Founded as a non-political organization with the aim of promoting friendship and mutual understanding between Britain and Nigeria. The association organized regular social and cultural activities, lectures and film shows, and provided hospitality for Nigerian visitors and students.

British Society for International Health Education, 1962–
Founded to provide assistance for health education overseas, especially in developing countries, it arranged training courses overseas and offered fellowships for post-graduate training in health education. It operated predominantly in Africa, and it was supported by voluntary donations, charitable grants, etc.

Bureau of Hygiene and Tropical Diseases, 1908–
The bureau was a centre for the collection and general distribution of information regarding hygiene and tropical diseases. It was financed by proceeds of the sale of its publications, and by contributions from the British government, and other govern-

ments and institutions. It published the *Tropical Diseases Bulletin* and *Abstracts on Hygiene*. The bureau was under the general control and direction of an honorary managing committee.

See also London School of Hygiene and Tropical Medicine, 1929–.

Ceylon Association in London, 1888–
The association had its origin in the proposal of the Planters Association of Ceylon to establish a branch in London. It liaised with public bodies in Ceylon to protect and further the general interests of the colony.

Children's Overseas Reception Board (DO131), 1940–1946
Set up to manage the evacuation to the dominions of children whose lives were endangered by enemy action.

Colonial Building Liaison Section, Building Research Station, see Overseas Division, Building Research Station

Colonial Development Corporation, see Commonwealth Development Corporation

Colonial Empire Marketing Board (CO 868), 1937–194?
Set up by the secretary of state for the colonies in 1937 to help the colonies develop their own sources of wealth and sell more goods to better advantage by means of a service of marketing officers and an organized system of publicity, including participation in exhibitions and research. The board included representatives from the Colonial Office, Parliament, the Department of Overseas Trade and the business world. It started work in 1938, presented its first report in 1939, but did not survive the Second World War.

See also Empire Marketing Board, 1926–1933.

Colonial Film Unit (INF 6), 1939–1955
Established during the war under the auspices of the Ministry of Information to make films, mainly about British and colonial war efforts, for colonial audiences. The control and direction of the unit were transferred to the Colonial Office Information Department in 1950. The unit developed film production in the colonies (particularly educational films for rural areas), provided film stock and equipment, offered advisory and instructional services, provided editing and distribution services, and published a quarterly magazine *Colonial Cinema*. The activities of the unit were financed under the Colonial Development and Welfare Act 1940.

Colonial Forest Resources Development Department, 1935–1940
Set up to promote the marketing of colonial forest products.

See also Commonwealth Forestry Association, 1921–; Commonwealth Forestry Institute, University of Oxford, 1924–. In chapter 9 see British Commonwealth Forestry Conference, and the Standing Committee on British Commonwealth Forestry, 1935–.

Colonial Geological Surveys, see Overseas Geological Surveys

Colonial Government Emigration Agencies at Calcutta, 1870–1920
Established to provide for the recruitment and despatch of Indians to work as field labourers. There were also government agencies in Calcutta and Madras representing the colonies of British Guiana, Trinidad, Jamaica and Fiji. Officers in charge were members of the Colonial Civil Service and staff were recruited locally.

Colonial Income Tax Office, see Overseas Territories Income Tax Office

Colonial Land and Emigration Commission, 1840–1855
The commission is described under Emigration Departments/Overseas Settlement Department in chapter 13.1.

Colonial Products Advisory Bureau (Plant and Animal), 1949–1954
Established when the secretary of state for the colonies assumed responsibility for the Plant and Animal Products Department of the Imperial Institute. The bureau dealt with investigations and inquiries relating to all plant and animal products, such as foodstuffs, oilseeds, drugs, hides and skins, insecticides, etc. There were advisory committees on various products.

See also Commonwealth Institute, 1925–1957. In chapter 9 see Colonial Products Research Council, 1941–1954.

Colonial Supply Liaison, 1941–1946
Established in Washington DC to handle problems arising out of the United States Lend-Lease Act of 1941. It was renamed the British Colonial Supply Mission in 1942, and until it came to an end in 1946 it arranged for the supply of certain commodities to the colonies from the United States, Canada and elsewhere.

Commission in the United Kingdom of the Eastern Caribbean Governments, 1964–
Following the dissolution of the Federation of the West Indies, the governments of Antigua, Barbados, Dominica, Grenada, Montserrat, St Kitts (St Christopher), St Lucia and St Vincent established their own office in London. The office was mainly concerned with the welfare of students and migrants, and the promotion of trade and tourism.

Commonwealth Agricultural Bureau, 1929–
Set up as the Imperial Agricultural Bureau to administer eight bureaux organized as clearing houses of information on research in specialized fields of agricultural science, it was financed by a common fund provided by the governments of the dominions and colonies and governed by an executive council. Several more institutes were subsequently established under the organization's control. Set up as imperial bureaux, they later became Commonwealth bureaux. They comprised: Institute of Entomology (qv), Mycological Institute (qv), Parasite Service (later Institute of Biological Control), Institute of Entomology (Trinidad), Bureau of Animal Breeding and Genetics, Bureau of Animal Health, Bureau of Animal Nutrition, Bureau of Dairy Science (later Bureau of Dairy Science and Technology), Forestry Bureau, Bureau of Helminthology, Bureau of Horticulture and Plantation Crops, Bureau of Plant Breeding and Genetics, Bureau of Soil Science (later Bureau of Soils), Bureau of Agricultural Economics.

Commonwealth Countries League, 1925–
Formerly the British Commonwealth League, it was founded to co-ordinate the work of the Overseas Committee of the International Alliance of Women for Suffrage and Equal Citizenship and the British Dominions Women's Citizens Union. The League had no party affiliation and aimed to secure equality of liberty, status and opportunity between women and men in the Commonwealth. It had affiliations throughout the Commonwealth and carried out its work by means of conferences and social gatherings.

Commonwealth Development Corporation, 1948–
The Colonial Development Corporation was established as a public corporation to assist colonial territories in developing their economies. The acts setting out its functions were consolidated in the Overseas Resources Development Act 1959 and it was renamed following the passage of the Commonwealth Development Act in 1963, which restored its full power of operation in all Commonwealth countries which had achieved independence since 1948. It undertook projects for the promotion or expansion of a wide range of enterprises specified in the act, which included agriculture, forestry, fisheries, mining, industrial enterprises, gas, electricity and water undertakings, transport, housing, hotels and engineering. It was able to act as managing agent and render advisory services.

Commonwealth Development Finance Company, 1953–
Established as a result of the Commonwealth Economic Conference of 1953, its objects were to assist in the provision of financial assistance for development projects in the Commonwealth, particularly those designed to increase Commonwealth resources and strengthen the sterling area's balance of payments; co-operate with other organizations in the United Kingdom and overseas working in the same field and with overseas capital markets; and to co-operate with the International Bank for Reconstruction and Development. The company did not normally take a direct part in development programmes but aimed to invest in cases where the project helped to strengthen the sterling area and where other forms of capital provision were inappropriate and finance was insufficient.

Commonwealth Education Liaison Unit, 1959–
Formed on the recommendation of the Commonwealth Education Conference, it worked under the general direction of the Commonwealth Education Liaison Committee to supplement normal bilateral contacts between Commonwealth countries on educational matters. It received information from governments on the progress of educational schemes arising from the conference other than the Commonwealth Scholarship and Fellowship Plan and reported on them periodically to all member countries. The unit acted generally as a centre of reference on Commonwealth educational co-operation.
See also Commonwealth Scholarship Commission in the UK, 1959–.

Commonwealth Forestry Association, 1921–1966
Constituted by royal charter as the Empire Forestry Association, it sought to foster public interest in forestry, secure general recognition of the dependence of timber supply on forest management, collect and circulate information relating to forestry

and commercial utilization, form a centre for those engaged in forestry, and provide a means of communication between all concerned. The association was managed by a governing council with representatives of the colonial territories.

See also Commonwealth Forestry Institute, University of Oxford, 1924–; Colonial Forest Resources Development Department, 1935–1940. In chapter 9 see British Commonwealth Forestry Conference and the Standing Committee on British Commonwealth Forestry, 1935–.

Commonwealth Forestry Institute, University of Oxford, 1924–
Founded as a result of a resolution of the British Empire Forestry Conference, 1923, it was financed jointly by Oxford University and by colonial and Commonwealth governments; it was originally called the Imperial Forestry Institute. It provided undergraduate and postgraduate training, undertook research on biological, silvicultural, management and economic problems in forestry, including work on diseases and pests and their control. It carried out anatomical examination and identification of timbers, identification of trees and the compilation of forest floras, plant lists, etc. Much of the work had a tropical basis. The institute developed one of the most complete forestry libraries in the world.

See also Commonwealth Forestry Association, 1921–1966.

Commonwealth Industries Association Ltd, 1926–
Founded in 1926 as the Empire Industries Association to promote imperial co-operation and the protection of home industries. It had links with the old Tariff Reform League and aimed to include, or be associated with, all other organizations in any way concerned with the development of imperial preference, including the British Empire Producers' Association (qv), the Federation of British Industries, and the National Union of Manufacturers. It merged with the British Empire League in 1947 and changed its name to the Commonwealth and Empire Industries Association in 1958 and to the Commonwealth Industries Association in 1960. In 1965 it merged with the Commonwealth Fellowship and the Commonwealth Union of Trade, and in 1967 it became a company limited by guarantee. Its affairs were managed by a council elected by the members, and it maintained close contact with both houses of Parliament through a parliamentary committee.

The association aimed to: strengthen the Commonwealth by means of mutual preferential trade, capital investment, migration, and technical and scientific co-operation; maintain free enterprise; strengthen the Sterling Area; ensure a continuing market for Commonwealth foods, foodstuffs and raw materials, etc, and generally promote and protect all aspects of Commonwealth trading in industry and agriculture. It issued a *Monthly Bulletin*, and lecturers and speakers regularly addressed audiences. The association depended entirely on voluntary funds.

Commonwealth Institute (PRO 36/76), 1893–
The Imperial Institute of the United Kingdom, the Colonies and India was erected at South Kensington as the National Memorial of the Jubilee of Queen Victoria, by whom it was opened. In 1902 it ceased to act as an independent institution and was placed under the care of the Colonial Office and the Board of Trade, but it was transferred to the Department of Overseas Trade in 1923 and amalgamated with the Imperial Mineral Resources Bureau. It was renamed the Imperial Institute. In 1949 it

was transferred to the control of the minister of education, and in 1953 it became an independent grant-aided organization, although the minister of education retained responsibility to parliament for its activities. It became the Commonwealth Institute in 1958, and in 1962 it moved to a new building specifically designed for its purposes.

The object of the institute was to foster commercial and industrial development, and to utilize the natural resources of the overseas empire/Commonwealth by means of chemical and technical investigations and by disseminating information concerning production and potential economic uses. It established exhibitions illustrating natural resources and cultural life, etc, and offered public lectures and information services, including a cinema and a library. It was supported by Britain and the dominions and housed other organizations including the executive council of the Imperial Agricultural Bureau (qv) and the secretariat of the Imperial Economic Committee (see chapter 9).

Commonwealth Institute of Entomology, 1913–1948
Established as the Imperial Bureau of Entomology and known as the Imperial Institute of Entomology from 1930, it sought to further the study of economic entomology particularly in the tropical African colonies and protectorates, and to encourage and co-ordinate entomological work in relation to human and animal diseases and to agriculture. It acted as a centre for the collection, co-ordination and dissemination of all relevant information. It had an extensive library and published a quarterly journal, *The Bulletin of Entomological Research*, and a monthly journal, *The Review of Applied Entomology*. The institute received financial contributions from the UK and overseas governments.

See also Commonwealth Agricultural Bureau, 1929–.

Commonwealth League for Economic Co-operation, 1964–1965
The league was an all-party organization formed with the object of fostering economic co-operation between members of the Commonwealth and of disseminating knowledge about economic and other affairs throughout the Commonwealth.

Commonwealth Medical Advisory Bureau, 1965–
Maintained by the British Medical Association to advise and assist doctors visiting the UK. The medical director was assisted by an advisory committee which included representatives of Commonwealth high commissioners in London and of related societies and medical organizations. Enquiries mainly concerned postgraduate medical education.

Commonwealth Migration Council Ltd, 1954–
Founded shortly after the Second World War, it became a company limited by guarantee in 1954. Its purpose was to increase the flow of British migrants to Canada, Australia and New Zealand, and to strengthen Commonwealth ties by expanding trade and economic development. It supplied speakers and lecturers, promoted public meetings and discussions, held conferences, ran a student scheme, and published a newsletter of statistical and economic data. The executive included a strong parliamentary element in order to promote parliamentary interest in its aims and objects. The council also monitored the press and supplied material to press, radio and television sources.

Commonwealth Mycological Institute, 1920–
Formerly known as the Imperial Bureau of Mycology, 1920–1931, and later the Imperial Mycological Institute, 1931–1948, the institute was founded as a result of a proposal by the Imperial War Conference in 1918 that a central organization should encourage and co-ordinate work through the empire on plant diseases caused by fungi. Initially under the control of an honorary committee of management, it was placed under the Executive Council of the Commonwealth Agricultural Bureau in 1933. It received contributions from the UK and overseas governments and issued various publications, including a monthly *Review of Applied Mycology*. Its primary function was to assist economic mycologists overseas by the accumulation and distribution of information on all matters connected with plant diseases and the identification of specimens.

See also Commonwealth Agricultural Bureau, 1929–.

Commonwealth Parliamentary Association, 1911–
Formerly the Empire Parliamentary Association, 1911–1949, it was founded at the coronation of George V to facilitate the exchange of visits and information between those engaged in the parliamentary government of the countries of the empire, and so bring about closer understanding between parliamentary governments within the empire on an all-party basis. It began with six branches in Britain and the dominions and expanded as the number of self-governing nations of the Commonwealth grew. There were also auxiliary, affiliated and subsidiary branches in countries at different stages of responsible government. The name was changed to 'Commonwealth' after a general council was set up in 1949 to co-ordinate the work of all branches, a function previously carried out by the UK branch. The association provided hospitality, information, meetings and conferences, annual discussions, parliamentary privileges for visiting members, and quarterly publications. It had a close relationship with the British-American Parliamentary Group at Westminster. Eleven plenary conferences were held between 1948 and 1965, and they were annual thereafter.

Commonwealth Producers Organization, 1916–
Originally established as the British Empire Producers Organization, it was designed to promote the interests of Commonwealth primary producers and develop reciprocal trade with the Commonwealth. It had special links with Australia, New Zealand, the West Indies, Africa and Cyprus.

Commonwealth Scholarship Commission in the United Kingdom, 1959–
Constituted by an act of Parliament to administer the Commonwealth Scholarship and Fellowship Plan drawn up at the first Commonwealth Education Conference, held at Oxford in 1959. The commission had responsibility for selecting the recipients of Commonwealth scholarships, Commonwealth visiting professorships and Commonwealth medical awards offered by the British government, as well as other related educational work. It was assisted by the British Council (qv) in relation to the personal welfare, stipends and travel of award holders. The Association of Commonwealth Universities (qv) provided the secretariat for the commission.

See also Commonwealth Education Liaison Unit, 1959–.

Commonwealth Scientific Liaison Offices (London), 1948–
Formed as a result of a recommendation by the British Commonwealth Scientific Official Conference that Commonwealth scientific liaison offices in London should occupy a joint headquarters but continue as autonomous units. The liaison offices dealt with scientific enquiries to and from their home countries, kept in touch with scientific developments in Britain and stimulated the exchange of scientific information. They acted as scientific advisers to their high commissioners and represented their countries on Commonwealth and international committees and conferences. The London headquarters dealt with matters of common concern and controlled the activities of a common services section which provided secretariat services for the British Commonwealth Scientific Committee (see chapter 9). It formed a useful channel through which recommendations of that committee could be implemented.

Community Development Clearing House, 1949–1964
Set up as a unit within the Department of Education in Tropical Areas at the University of London Institute of Education at the request of the Colonial Office. It was originally intended to provide information for, and contact between, personnel engaged in community development, social welfare and allied fields in British territories, but its scope was enlarged to cover social developments of all kinds outside education throughout the world. In addition to acting as an information, advice and meeting centre, it had a reference collection of documents, books, official records, manuscripts, etc, from all parts of the world covering a great variety of issues. It published a quarterly journal, *The Community Development Bulletin*, including a French language edition.

Conference of Engineering Institutions of the British Commonwealth, 1946–
Established through the initiative of the councils of the Institute of Civil Engineers, the Institution of Mechanical Engineers and the Institution of Electrical Engineers, who proposed that bonds between the engineering institutions of the Commonwealth should be consolidated and be made more permanent. The conference met every four years. It was essentially an advisory body, whose meetings provided an opportunity for the exchange of views and the development of contacts.

Conservative Commonwealth and Overseas Council, 1953–
Largely a non-parliamentary body, it sought to contribute to the spread of detailed knowledge on problems of the Commonwealth and of remaining dependencies. It was in close touch with the Parliamentary Commonwealth Affairs Committee and with party spokesmen through working groups. Its purpose was, in particular, to stimulate thought on essential Commonwealth and related matters beyond the press of immediate issues, and to suggest courses of action consistent with enlightened British policy and contemporary Conservative outlook. The views expressed in its publications were unofficial.

Conservative Overseas Bureau, 1949–1958
Founded as the department of the Conservative Party responsible for relations with overseas countries. Its supervisory committee was representative of all sectors of the party organization. It dealt with enquiries, inter-party relations and overseas parties' requests for policy and organizational information. It serviced the Conservative

Commonwealth and Overseas Council and the Foreign Affairs Forum for Parliamentary Candidates, and it assisted overseas students. It also issued a monthly *Commonwealth, European and Overseas Review* and maintained working liaison with diplomatic missions in London and with voluntary bodies. The bureau arranged for UK citizens abroad to enrol in the party and assisted party members travelling overseas.

Conservative Parliamentary Commonwealth Affairs Committee, 1967–
Membership of the committee and sub-committees was open to all Conservative MPs and Conservative peers. The sub-committees covered East and Central Africa, West Africa, the Mediterranean, the West Indies, Far East smaller territories, and economic development.

Corona Club, 1900–1966
Founded by Joseph Chamberlain to provide an opportunity for officers on leave from the colonies to meet each other and other members. A dinner was held annually under the presidency of the secretary of state for the colonies. The club was open to all past and present members of the government service in the dependent territories, of the Colonial Office, and of the office of the Crown Agents for Oversea Governments and Administrations.

See also Women's Corona Society, 1937–.

Cotton Research Corporation, 1921–
Established as the Empire Cotton Growing Association, 1921–1966, it had a small headquarters in London that carried out research on cotton growing in co-operation with the ministries of agriculture in many overseas countries. It was financed by income from the original capital grant by the British government and by annual contributions from overseas countries. Some assignments were later taken in partnership with the Ministry of Overseas Development. The main object of the research and allied work was to assist cotton growing countries to increase yields and improve quality.

Council for Education in the Commonwealth, 1964–
Set up to increase public awareness of the problems of education in the Commonwealth. It was non-party and drew members from all parts of the Commonwealth. It held regular monthly discussion meetings at the House of Commons when parliament was in session where members heard eminent educationalists from overseas and Britain and could participate. The council established various working parties and presented recommendations to the ministers concerned. It raised subjects for mutual discussion through its personal and official contacts, and welcomed suggestions for educational activities or subjects for research.

In chapter 9 see Advisory Committee on Education in the Colonies, 1923–1961.

Council of Commonwealth Municipalities, 1964–
The council was an all-party organization formed to foster co-operation between local government individuals and authorities in the Commonwealth and to disseminate information concerning Commonwealth affairs throughout the world.

Crown Agents for Oversea Governments and Administrations (CAOG Classes), 1833–
Most of the colonial agents, who under a variety of forms had represented the individual colonies in Britain since the middle of the eighteenth century, were united in 1833 under the title of 'Joint Agents General for the Crown Colonies'. The agents, however, continued to specialize individually in the affairs of different colonies until 1858, when they were more closely welded and the word 'joint' dropped from their title. In 1863 the agents were given control of their staff and were made wholly responsible for their own actions under the general guidance of the Colonial Office; they became known as the Crown Agents for the Colonies. In 1878–1880 the agents were radically reorganized; self-governing colonies, which had already begun to appoint their own agents general (some of them the precursors of high commissioners), were urged to take over the responsibilities that the Crown Agents had hitherto borne for them. By 1881 the Crown Agents were dealing with Crown colony work only. Later they also acted, by special arrangement, for governments and organizations outside the Commonwealth entirely. In the twentieth century, their office, which came to be known as that of the Crown Agents for Oversea Governments and Administrations in 1953, relieved the Colonial Office of much detailed work. They helped to recruit technical staff, arranged the floating of colonial loans, purchased stores and equipment, negotiated engineering contracts, and paid the salaries of officers resident in Britain.

Directorate of Overseas Surveys, 1946–
The Directorate of Colonial (Geodetic and Topographic) Surveys, 1946–1957, was approved following a recommendation of the Colonial Survey and Geophysical Committee, 1935–1948. It was renamed in 1958. It was set up to undertake geodetic surveys and topographical mapping within the empire and to publish any work accomplished. The director was also adviser to the secretary of state for the colonies on all matters relating to geodetic and topographical surveying. In 1961 the directorate became part of the new Department of Technical Co-operation, and in 1964 it joined the Ministry of Overseas Development. It was expanded to include specialists in fields of geomorphology, geology, ecology, climatology, hydrology, tropical agriculture, etc, who undertook field investigations at the request of overseas governments. Its maps, produced by modern air survey methods, were used for planning development schemes. The directorate provided practical training in cartographic and photogrammetric techniques for technical officers from overseas government departments, and it sent experts to take up temporary appointments with overseas governments and international organizations.
In chapter 9 see Colonial Survey and Geophysical Committee, 1905–1948.

East African Currency Board, 1920–1963
The board was appointed by the secretary of state for the colonies to provide for and control the supply of currency to the East African territories. Its headquarters was in Nairobi.

East India Association, 1866–1965
Founded to promote friendship and understanding between the peoples of Great Britain, India, Pakistan and Burma. An unofficial body with no affiliation with any political party, it sought to provide an open platform for the consideration of current

problems relating to India, Pakistan and Burma. Contact was promoted by social gatherings, hospitality to students from these countries and the annual publication of *Asian Review*.

Emigrants Commission, 1855–1886
The commission is described under under Emigration Departments/Overseas Settlement Department in chapter 13.1.

Emigrants Information Office, 1886–1935
The office is described under Emigration Departments/Overseas Settlement Department in chapter 13.1.

Empire Cotton Growing Association, see Cotton Research Corporation

Empire Forestry Association, see Commonwealth Forestry Association

Empire Industries Association, see Commonwealth Industries Association

Empire Marketing Board (CO 758 – CO 760, CO 956), 1926–1933
Established by the secretary of state for the dominions to promote the marketing of empire products in Britain and generally to foster inter-imperial trade, it carried out its functions with the aid of committees dealing especially with such aspects of the subject as research, publicity and marketing. The board included representatives from Britain, the dominions, India, and the colonies and protectorates. It was dissolved owing to a lack of overseas interest. The records of the board contain a considerable amount of material on both the dependent empire and the self-governing dominions.
See also Colonial Empire Marketing Board, 1937–194?.

Empire Parliamentary Association, see Commonwealth Parliamentary Association

Falkland Islands Dependencies Scientific Bureau, 1951–1959
The bureau dealt with scientific reports, maps, photographs, specimens, etc, from the Antarctic. It also edited scientific papers, lectures and broadcasting material concerning the dependencies.

Falkland Islands Dependencies Survey, 1959–1961
The London office recruited personnel and ordered stores for the Antarctic bases.
See also Falkland Islands Dependencies Scientific Bureau, 1951–1959; British Antarctic Survey, 1961–; Royal Society National Committee on Antarctic Research, 1962–1966. In chapter 9 see Falkland Islands Dependencies Scientific Committee, 1923–1956.

Federation of Commonwealth Chambers of Commerce, 1911–
The Federation evolved from the British Imperial Council of Commerce. It sought to establish a permanent link between business communities in the empire. With the introduction of a new constitution in 1961 it became a federation of representative committees. Their membership, drawn from the chambers of commerce, was

representative of leading business opinion in each country, and they enabled rapid expression of authoritative national views on matters affecting Commonwealth trade. The federation aimed to promote world as well as Commonwealth trade and to guide public opinion through the dissemination of information. It organized a congress every two years to provide a forum for debating economic and social affairs. Smaller ad hoc conferences gave consideration to special matters, and reports were widely circulated and submitted to governments.

Imperial Agricultural Bureau, see Commonwealth Agricultural Bureau

Imperial Bureau/Institute of Entomology, see Commonwealth Institute of Entomology

Imperial Bureau of Mycology/Imperial Mycological Institute, see Commonwealth Mycological Institute

Imperial College of Tropical Agriculture, see University of the West Indies, Faculty of Agriculture

Imperial Conference, 1887–1937
The Colonial Conference, 1887–1907, was reconstituted as the Imperial Conference in 1907. It was held every four years to discuss questions of common interest between the British government and the self-governing dominions overseas, with the UK prime minister as ex-officio president. Discussions were conducted by no more than two representatives from each government, and each government had only one vote. A permanent secretarial staff, under the secretary of state for the colonies, obtained information for the use of the conference, attended to its resolutions and conducted correspondence. Matters of immediate importance were attended to by subsidiary conferences.

Imperial Defence College, 1927–
Established on the recommendation of the Committee of Imperial Defence, it trained selected members of the armed forces and civil services of the UK and overseas Commonwealth countries in broad aspects of policy and strategy, including threats to world peace. The college was financed from public funds and nominal fees for Commonwealth students.

Imperial Forestry Institute, see Commonwealth Forestry Institute, University of Oxford

Imperial Institute of the United Kingdom, the Colonies and India, see Commonwealth Institute

Imperial Mineral Resources Bureau, see Commonwealth Institute

Incorporated Liverpool School of Tropical Medicine, 1898–
Founded by a prominent ship owner, John Holt, the school's objects were to train

medical practitioners proceeding to the tropics, to conduct original research into tropical diseases and to deal with clinical tropical medicine. It held courses of instruction in tropical medicine, bacteriology, parasitology, tropical hygiene, etc, and it provided facilities for research.

Institute of Commonwealth Studies, Oxford University, 1947–

The Institute of Colonial, later Commonwealth, Studies, was established as a result of post-war plans for training colonial service officers in Oxford and the increasing interest in comparative overseas studies. It was a teaching centre for administrative and foreign service officers from developing countries (later by agreement with the Ministry of Overseas Development) and for postgraduate students of the university. The institute also undertook research and bibliographical work in topics relating to the Commonwealth, with special emphasis on the history, politics and economics of the tropical Commonwealth.

See also Queen Elizabeth House, Oxford, 1954–.

Institute of Commonwealth Studies, University of London, 1949–

Established to promote advanced study of the Commonwealth, with interests primarily in social sciences and recent history. It encouraged collaboration at the postgraduate level between workers employing different techniques of research in the study of Commonwealth problems, and it provided a meeting place for postgraduate students and members of the academic staffs of universities and research institutions in the UK and the Commonwealth. The library placed particular emphasis on primary material relating to government, economic and social development, race relations, and demography.

Institute of Rural Life at Home and Overseas, 1949–

Established to encourage wider study and understanding of the countryside and to foster the acceptance of Christian values by those engaged in administration, agriculture, education and social development in rural areas throughout the world. Its programme included an annual conference and lectures in London designed to interest non-members in colonial affairs (particularly in the rural context) and to be of use to government servants, missionaries and overseas visitors.

International African Institute, 1926–

Founded for the purpose of providing an international centre for the promotion of research and the dissemination of information relating to the cultures, languages and social institutions of African peoples. The institute carried out extensive research, particularly into problems of the impact of Western civilization on African societies, and it organized seminars and meetings on various aspects of African social studies. Financial support for research projects and publications was received from the British, French and Belgian governments, African governments, UNESCO and others. The institute published monographs on African ethnology, sociology and linguistics and a quarterly review concerned with African studies.

Inter-University Council for Higher Education Overseas (BW 90), 1946–1966

Constituted by universities in the UK and the colonial territories, on the recommendation of the Asquith Commission on Higher Education in the Colonies, it was initially known as the Inter-University Council for Higher Education in the Colonies, 1946–1954. The council consisted of one representative of each of the participating universities, co-opted members, and the educational adviser to the Colonial Office (later the Ministry of Overseas Development). Its general purpose was to encourage co-operation between UK and overseas universities and to assist in the development of higher education. It provided common services and regular advice on academic questions. Funds were made available to colonial universities on the advice of the Colonial Universities Grants Advisory Committee (see chapter 9).

See also Association of Commonwealth Universities, 1913–. In chapter 9 see Advisory Committee on Colonial Colleges of Arts, Science and Technology, 1950–1957.

Joint Africa Board, 1923–
Set up as the Joint East Africa Board by a small group of London businessmen and members of parliament, its scope was later enlarged and its name changed to the Joint East and Central African Board. Its object was to promote British agricultural, commercial and industrial interests and it sought to provide a channel of unofficial communication between authorities and individuals in the UK and Africa. Financed by subscriptions, it provided information and advice and material for debates in Parliament. In 1965 the name was changed to the Joint Africa Board to reflect interests in central Africa and southern Africa.

Joint Agents General for the Crown Colonies, see Crown Agents for Oversea Governments and Administrations

Joint Commonwealth Societies Council, 1962–
Established with the support of the secretary of state for Commonwealth relations to co-ordinate the activities of recognized societies, with the object of avoiding overlapping and duplication of effort and to promote mutual understanding and personal friendship between peoples of the Commonwealth. Representatives of the Commonwealth Office, the Commonwealth Institute and the British Council attended meetings.

League for the Exchange of Commonwealth Teachers, 1901–
Founded as the League of the Empire, it later became the League of the British Commonwealth and Empire and in 1963 it was renamed the League for the Exchange of Commonwealth Teachers. Its object was to promote friendly and educational intercourse between the participating countries through a scheme for the interchange of teachers. The work was entirely non-political and non-sectarian. The league was governed by a council comprising representatives of Commonwealth teachers' associations. It administered the Scheme for the Interchange of Teachers on behalf of the British government, which financed the cost of living and travel grants for teachers from Britain and subsidised the league's administration.

See also National Council for the Supply of Teachers Overseas, 1960–1967.

League of the Empire, see League for the Exchange of Commonwealth Teachers

Library Association, Advisory Committee on Library Services in the Colonies, 1952–1956
Appointed by the secretary of state for the colonies, the committee considered all aspects of library services in the colonies and made recommendations to the Colonial Office and other appropriate bodies, such as the National Co-operating Body for Libraries and the United Kingdom National Commission for UNESCO. It also considered and advised on matters affecting library services in the colonies referred to it by the Colonial Office and the National Co-operating Body for Libraries.

London School of Hygiene and Tropical Medicine, 1929–
The school was formed by the union of the London School of Tropical Medicine, which had been actively engaged in teaching and research since 1899, and the University of London teaching departments for the diploma in public health. In 1934 the Ross Institute of Tropical Hygiene was incorporated with the school. The school provided a variety of diploma and non-diploma courses and offered scholarships and research funds.

See also Bureau of Hygiene and Tropical Diseases, 1908–.

London School of Hygiene and Tropical Medicine, Department of Human Nutrition, 1961–
The department received a small proportion of its funds from colonial territories. Its main functions were to teach nutrition, mainly to postgraduate students, collect and exchange information on nutrition and food technology and provide assistance in field work and investigations.

See also Applied Nutrition Unit, 1952–1961. In chapter 9 see Committee on Nutrition in the Colonial Empire, 1936–194?.

London School of Tropical Medicine, see London School of Hygiene and Tropical Medicine

Malaysia-Singapore Commercial Association Inc, 1967–
Founded to protect UK commercial and economic interests in Malaysia and Singapore. Its membership represented a cross-section of British firms and enterprises.

Mauritius Chamber of Agriculture, 1853–
A private association of millers, planters and others connected with sugar and other agricultural industries. Its objects were to promote the welfare and progress and safeguard the economic interests of the Mauritius agricultural community. It was responsible for formulating the broad policy of the sugar industry and for implementing Mauritius's contractual obligations under the Commonwealth and International Sugar Agreements. It was administered by a bureau of five members elected at the annual general meeting.

National Council for the Supply of Teachers Overseas, 1960–1967
Established under the minister of education, it was transferred to the minister of overseas development in 1965. The council brought together representatives of teachers' organizations, local education authorities, recruiting bodies and interested

government departments in all matters concerning the recruitment of teachers for service in posts overseas.

See also League for the Exchange of Commonwealth Teachers, 1901–.

New Zealand Society, 1925–
Designed to promote the interests of New Zealand in the UK and to provide New Zealanders and others interested in New Zealand with opportunities and activities of mutual interest.

Office of the Trade Representative for Seychelles, 1962–1966
The office promoted investment and established industries, emigration of workers, immigration for retirement, exports and marketing, imports, holiday and business visits, tourism and publicity.

Oversea Service, 1958–1965
Incorporated as a non-profit making company, its objective was to educate persons leaving for overseas appointments or residence on the culture and conditions of the country concerned so as to render them fit representatives of Western Christian civilization. It provided short introductory courses and study conferences. The board of governors included nominees of the British Council of Churches, the Conference of British Missionary Societies and the UK government as well as elected members. Funding included contributions from the UK and colonial governments.

Oversea Settlement Board, 1935–194?, see under Emigration Departments/Overseas Settlement Department in chapter 13.1.

Overseas Audit Department, 1911–
Originally constituted as the Colonial Audit Department, 1911–1954, the department audited the accounts of most colonies and protectorates on behalf of the secretary of state. A director-general supervised the Overseas Audit Service and was assisted in London by an establishment connected with the Colonial Office. Officers were also appointed in independent territories at the request of the governments concerned.

Overseas Club and Patriotic League, 1910–1922
The Overseas Club, founded in 1910, and the Patriotic League of Britons Overseas, founded in 1914, were amalgamated to enable British residents in foreign countries to contribute towards the defence of the empire. In 1919 they were amalgamated with the League of the Empire (qv).

Overseas Development Institute Ltd, 1960–
Founded to promote the economic development of the countries of Africa, Asia and South America and their relations with the industrially developed areas of the world. Funds were received from the Ford Foundation, British industry and commerce, and the Nuffield Foundation. The institute was non-profit making. Its policies were determined by an independent and non-governmental council. Its main function was to provide a centre for work on development problems (although it did not provide technical aid or financial help); it directed studies of its own, encouraged work on development topics, acted as a forum, disseminated information and kept the

urgency of the problems before the public and the responsible authorities. It held meetings at which officials, businessmen, politicians and scholars could meet others with first hand experience of development problems. The results of its work and surveys were usually published.

Overseas Division, Building Research Station, 1948–
The Colonial Building Liaison Section of the Department of Scientific and Industrial Research (later Ministry of Technology) was established in 1948 at the Building Research Station. Financed by colonial development and welfare funds, it was expanded in 1953 to deal with planning and housing matters in the colonies. It was renamed the Tropical Division in 1958. In 1966, to reflect the expanded field of work, it became the Overseas Division. Its main functions were to collect from and supply to overseas territories and countries information on building, housing and planning matters and to disseminate information on relevant developments in the UK; to assist with the solution of specific technical problems and answer enquiries; to advise the secretary of state for the colonies and later the minister of overseas development on building, housing and planning matters. Information was disseminated through papers, lectures and articles.

Overseas Food Corporation, 1948–1955
Established under the provisions of the Overseas Resources Development Act 1948, the corporation worked to secure the investigation, formulation and implementation of projects for the production or processing of foodstuffs or other agricultural products and for marketing them in the East African territories. Responsibility for the corporation was transferred from the minister of food to the secretary of state for the colonies in 1951; it was transferred to the Tanganyika Agricultural Corporation in 1955.

Overseas Geological Surveys, 1947–1960
Originally appointed as the Colonial Geological Surveys, 1947–1957, to direct a systematic geological survey of the empire. The director acted as adviser to the secretary of state for the colonies on all matters relating to geology and was assisted by an advisory committee which included representatives of the major geological, mining, and related research organizations and of the universities. The Mineral Resources Division carried out laboratory investigations related to rock, ore, minerals, etc, primarily from the colonial territories, with the object of finding new sources of raw materials and promoting the development of mining. It maintained close contact with trade and industry and provided an intelligence service on the scientific, technical and commercial aspects of overseas mineral industries and colonial mining law. The division published the *Overseas Geology and Mineral Resources* quarterly and an annual Statistical Summary of the Mineral Industry.

In chapter 9 see Advisory Committee on Overseas Geology and Mineral Resources, 1949–1962.

Overseas Nursing Association, 1896–
At the request of the Colonial Office and later the Ministry of Overseas Development, the association recommended nurses and other officers for appointment to the service of overseas governments. It also undertook recruitment for various related

services for private European nursing homes, mainly in the colonies.

Overseas Service College, 1965–
Established at Farnham Castle, the Overseas Service College provided short introductory courses for men and women going overseas. It was financially assisted by contributions from trusts and business firms.

Overseas Services Resettlement Bureau, 1957–
Set up to assist in resettling officers of Her Majesty's Overseas Civil Service who retired early as a result of the granting of self-government or independence. The bureau helped find employment in the UK or overseas by establishing contact with employers in commerce, industry, government and quasi-government organizations covering administrative, professional and technical fields.

Overseas Students Advisory Bureau, 1963–
Constituted as a charitable trust, the bureau placed overseas students on full-time and sandwich courses at colleges and universities in the UK and in practical training vacancies with industry and commerce. Its work was encouraged by the Ministry of Overseas Development and the Inner London Education Authority.

Overseas Territories Income Tax Office (OD 1), 1942–
Established as the Colonial Income Tax Office at the request of the colonies to act as agent in the UK, under colonial tax legislation, for income tax commissioners in various territories. It dealt with the assessment and collection of income tax payable by companies and pensioners resident in the UK and with general enquiries. It worked in close liaison with the Crown Agents for Oversea Governments and Administrations. The Colonial Office was responsible for the recruitment of the office's senior staff, and the official representative reported annually to the secretary of state for the colonies. However, the office was financed by the colonial territories it served. In 1957 the name was changed and in 1961 responsibility for the office was transferred to the Department of Technical Co-operation.

Pacific Cable Board, 1902–1928
The Pacific Cable was owned and worked by all interested governments, and the management was vested in the board.

Pakistan Society, 1951–
Established to increase knowledge of the arts, languages, literature, music, history, religion, etc of Pakistan. Membership was open to all nationalities. There were frequent lectures, and the society's bulletin was published twice a year.

Palestine Currency Board, 1926–1952
Appointed by the secretary of state for the colonies to provide for and control the supply of currency to Palestine. After British withdrawal, agencies were maintained at Amman and in London by the Ottoman Bank and Barclays Bank.

Queen Elizabeth House, Oxford, 1954–
Constituted by royal charter, it was a corporate body administered by a governing

body whose president was appointed by the UK government; other appointments were made jointly by the University of Oxford and the government. Its purposes were to facilitate and encourage political, economic, legal, administrative, social, cultural and other studies affecting the peoples of the Commonwealth; to provide a centre to which people of authority or influence might resort for study and the exchange of information; and to help such people to obtain access to the academic resources of institutions in the University of Oxford and elsewhere.

See also Institute of Commonwealth Studies, Oxford University, 1947–.

Road Research Board, 1945–
In 1933 the Road Research Organization took over responsibility for the direction and supervision of road research from the Ministry of Transport; it became the Road Research Board in 1945. The existing experimental station became the road research laboratory. It was divided into several branches, one of which was developed in the late 1940s to deal with road and transport problems in overseas territories and resulted in the appointment of a colonial liaison officer in 1950. The post was later abolished following the establishment of a Colonial Road Research Section in 1955, subsequently renamed the Tropical Section, financed by the Colonial Office and later by the Ministry of Overseas Development. Its functions were to undertake research, road planning, and construction in developing countries, and to improve methods; to assist with specific technical problems and answer enquiries; to train highway engineers and transport planners, and to advise on applications for road development projects. In 1965 responsibility for road research was returned to the Ministry of Transport.

Royal African Society, 1901–
Founded in memory of Mary Kingsley, it sought to foster interest in Africa, particularly in territories within the British empire, and it provided a centre for the study of African affairs. The society published a periodical, *African Affairs*, and held lectures, meetings and social functions. It provided access to a reference library and reading room, later part of the Royal Commonwealth Society. It was non-political, and, while seeking to maintain a scientific outlook, it aimed specifically at keeping human interest to the forefront.

Royal Agricultural Society of the Commonwealth, 1957–
Established at a meeting of representatives of royal agricultural societies held at the English Royal Show in 1957. The object was to encourage and arrange the interchange of knowledge and experience in the practice and science of agriculture, including improving crop production, livestock breeding and the efficiency of agricultural implements and machinery; it also encouraged the exchange and settlement of young farmers within the Commonwealth. Its first conference was held at Sydney in 1963, the second at Cambridge in 1965 and the third at Toronto in 1967. Printed reports were prepared for member societies and others interested.

Royal Asiatic Society, 1823–
Founded to promote the study of art, archaeology, history, sociology, languages, literature, science and customs of the East. It published a bi-annual journal and administered various trust funds for the publication of translations from oriental

languages and of original monographs. It had a lending library for members and research students and organized regular lectures in London.

Royal Botanic Gardens, Kew, 1759–
Initially the Botanic Garden of Augusta, Dowager Princess of Wales, Kew became famed for its unrivalled variety of plants collected throughout the world; in 1841 control was assumed by the state. In addition to housing a collection of living plants, it was an institution for their study, identification and classification. From 1856 there was a steady compilation of flora of different parts of the Commonwealth. A special interest was taken in plants of economic use, and Kew played a notable part in distributing useful plants to colonial territories and Commonwealth countries. The director of the gardens held the title of botanic adviser to the secretary of state for the colonies from 1902.

Royal Central Asian Society, 1901–
Founded to encourage interest in the contemporary life of central, western and south-east Asia. It provided a centre for contact, development and information. Its quarterly journal included reports of the society's lectures, discussions and papers, and a full review of books.

Royal Colonial Institute, see Royal Commonwealth Society

Royal Commonwealth Society, 1868–
Founded in 1868 as the Royal Colonial Institute, it became the Royal Empire Society in 1928 and the Royal Commonwealth Society in 1958. It had both a social and cultural function, with extensive social and residential amenities and programmes of film shows, lectures, study conferences, seminars and meetings. The society's Commonwealth Library contained extensive collections of important periodicals, transactions of learned societies, gazettes and other official publications of Commonwealth governments. It also contained valuable works and documents including accounts of voyages and explorations, and it issued bibliographies of literature on Commonwealth subjects. The Information Bureau provided up-to-date information on living conditions overseas, including health, housing, education, recreation, taxation, etc, and offered a loan service of visual ideas for schools and exhibitions. It published the bi-monthly *Commonwealth Journal*. The society had branches nationally and internationally.

Royal Institute of International Affairs, 1920–
Founded as an unofficial non-partisan organization as a result of a meeting by members of British, Dominions and United States delegations to the peace conference in Paris in 1919. The body received a royal charter in 1926. The objects of the institute were the advancement of international politics, economics and jurisprudence; the provision of information by lectures, publications, etc, and the encouragement of similar activities within the Commonwealth. It published a *Survey of International Affairs*, a wide range of books and quarterly and monthly journals, and maintained an extensive library and press archives. It organized private meetings, discussions and study groups on current problems, and Commonwealth conferences were held at intervals in different Commonwealth countries.

Royal Overseas League, 1910–
Founded to promote friendship between peoples of the Commonwealth and to maintain traditions through individual service. It had residential club facilities and a travel and theatre bureau and sponsored a variety of Commonwealth projects.

Royal Society for India, Pakistan and Ceylon, 1966–
Formed by amalgamation of the East India Association (qv) and the Royal India, Pakistan and Ceylon Society, its aim was to advance the study of arts, languages, literature, history, religions, etc, and to make more accessible to the general public a knowledge of all problems and conditions affecting these countries. It held meetings and lectures, read papers, held discussions, and produced, published and circulated periodicals and literature.

Royal Society National Committee on Antarctic Research, 1962–1966
The Society took over the commitments of the Falkland Islands Dependencies Scientific Committee (see chapter 9). Its terms of reference were to advise the high commissioner of the British Antarctic Territory, through the director of the British Antarctic Survey, on scientific aspects of the survey's work, on scientific aspects of any other proposals or activities arising from the British occupation of the territory, and on the use of scientific specimens and data that the survey accumulated.

See also Falklands Islands Dependencies Scientific Bureau, 1951–1959; Falkland Islands Dependencies Survey, 1959–1961; British Antarctic Survey, 1961–. In chapter 9 see Falkland Islands Dependencies Scientific Committee, 1923–1956.

Sarawak Association, 1924–
Founded for those who had been connected with Sarawak by official or business relations or who had lived in Sarawak for not less than one year. It encouraged members to keep in touch with each other, acquainted them with information relating to Sarawak, arranged social functions and generally furthered the interests of Sarawak.

School of Oriental Studies (later School of Oriental and African Studies), 1916–
Established to further research in and to extend the study and knowledge of the languages of eastern and, later of African peoples, ancient and modern, and the literature, history, religion, law, customs and art of those peoples. Courses were provided for first and higher degrees of the University of London, and instruction also given to members of government departments, overseas representatives for British industrial and commercial firms and for members of their technical and executive staffs. In addition, short basic orientation or advanced courses on the various regions of Asia and Africa were arranged for government staff and business executives.

Society of Comparative Legislation and International Law, 1894–1954
Founded as the Society of Comparative Legislation, 1894–1952, to promote a knowledge of the course of legislation in different countries. The society developed and maintained a close interest in all aspects of law, other than purely domestic. It published a quarterly journal *The International and Comparative Law Quarterly*.

Southern Africa Settlement Association, 1920–1960
The object of the association was to introduce suitable people to establish themselves in southern Africa. It was a voluntary organization and offered a free advisory service on all matters relating to settlement in southern Africa to people proceeding to assured employment, seeking employment in trades or professions, with fixed incomes, wishing to settle in southern Africa, or possessing sufficient capital to engage in farming.

Standing Conference for the Co-ordination of Scientific Research, 1922–1932
Consisted of representatives of the Development Commission, Medical Research Council, Department of Scientific and Industrial Research and the Biological Secretary of the Royal Society. They were primarily concerned with co-ordinating borderline research questions in the fields of agricultural, fishery, medical, and industrial research.

Straits Settlements Association, 1903–1919
The association was composed mainly of those who had lived in the Straits and all who were connected by direct professional or commercial ties, but it included anyone interested. All members were British subjects. The association provided a centre for discussion of any questions affecting the colony and furthered its interest where possible or necessary. It was succeeded by the British Association of Malaya (qv), 1920–1963.

Termite Research Unit, 1949–
Set up by the Colonial Office and financed as a colonial development and welfare research scheme, its work was later financed by the Ministry of Overseas Development. It aimed to study termites in the field, in particular their biology in relation to agriculture and forestry, and to undertake taxonomic work. Its headquarters were moved from East Africa to the British Museum (Natural History) in 1953. Field studies were continued in West Africa, 1956–1960, and British Honduras, 1960–1963. Overseas tours had covered much of the Caribbean, Africa south of the Sahara, India, Malaysia and Australia. The unit functioned as an information centre, dealing especially with problems of identification and control. It was guided in its scientific work by the Overseas Pest Control Committee (see chapter 9).
See also Tropical Pesticides Research Headquarters and Information Unit, 1963–.

Tropical Pesticides Research Headquarters and Information Unit, 1963–
Housed at the Tropical Products Institute, the unit comprised a small research section and an information service which advised on pest control matters in agriculture and public health and published a quarterly journal *Pest Articles and News Summaries*. It also undertook studies in the economics of pest control and co-ordinated research on fundamental problems in the field financed by the Ministry of Overseas Development in universities, research organizations, etc. It had close functional links with the FAO and WHO. The Overseas Pest Control Committee guided its work (see chapter 9).
See also Termite Research Unit, 1949–. In chapter 9 see Colonial Pesticides

Research Committee, 1947–1961; Tropical Pesticides Research Committee, 1962–1966; Overseas Pest Control Committee, 1967–.

Tropical Products Institute (AY 3, AY 4, AY 12–AY 15, AY 19), 1957–
In 1949 the Plant and Animal Products Department of the Imperial Institute was transferred to the control of the Colonial Office as the Colonial Products Advisory Bureau (Plant and Animal) (qv). In 1953 the bureau and the Colonial Products Research Council (see chapter 9) were brought together under one director, the bureau being renamed the Colonial Products Laboratory and placed under the oversight of the council, which at the same time was renamed the Colonial Products Council. In 1957 the laboratory was moved from the Imperial Institute to Grays Inn Road and received its present title. In 1959 control passed to the Department of Scientific and Industrial Research, and the Colonial Products Council was replaced by a Tropical Products Institute Steering Committee, set up by the Council for Scientific and Industrial Research; the word 'steering' was subsequently dropped from its title. Financial responsibility for the institute was assumed by the Department of Technical Co-operation in 1963 and by the Ministry of Overseas Development in 1964. Administrative control remained with the Department of Scientific and Industrial Research until 1965 when full responsibility was taken over by the Ministry of Overseas Development. At the same time the Tropical Products Institute Committee was replaced by a Tropical Products Institute Advisory Committee.

The institute's aim was to improve the economic viability of underdeveloped tropical territories, especially those in the Commonwealth. It worked to improve the technology of existing industries, and to introduce new industries as a result of research into new uses for tropical plant and animal products; undertook scientific investigations, mainly concerned with the properties and composition of such products; promoted the improvement of methods of production, marketing, quality, control of insect pests, etc; and provided an advisory service. It published a quarterly journal, *Tropical Science*. The implementation of its development projects was the concern of the Colonial Development Corporation (qv), established in 1948 and renamed the Commonwealth Development Corporation in 1963.

Uganda Britain Society, 1964–
Founded as a non-political organization with the object of promoting friendship and mutual understanding. It organized social functions and cultural activities and formed a meeting point for Britons who had lived in Uganda.

Uganda Railway Publicity Office, 1920
Established for the purpose of exhibiting and distributing literature, advertising, and supplying information in reply to any inquiries concerning the Uganda Railway project.

Universities Bureau of the British Empire, see Association of Commonwealth Universities

University of the West Indies, Faculty of Agriculture, 1921–
Established as the Imperial College of Tropical Agriculture in 1921, as the outcome

of recommendations made in the report of the Tropical Agricultural College Committee in 1919. Its main objectives were to provide instruction and to conduct research in tropical agriculture. It was the recognized centre in the Commonwealth for postgraduate training in tropical agriculture and the agricultural sciences for officers serving in the colonial agricultural services. Agriculture was taught at undergraduate and postgraduate levels. In 1960 the Imperial College of Tropical Agriculture became the faculty of agriculture of the University College of the West Indies; University College became a full university in 1962.

Visual Instruction Committee, 1901–1919
Appointed to provide, through illustrated lectures, popular knowledge of the geography, social life and economic possibilities of the component parts of the empire. All lectures were prepared with a special view to use in schools.

Voluntary Service Overseas, 1958–
Founded as an independent voluntary organization to provide temporary auxiliaries to help with educational and social service projects in developing countries and, at the same time, to give selected young people from Britain the opportunity of working alongside local people under challenging conditions overseas. Its council included members of parliament, headmasters, businessmen and officials from voluntary organizations. Volunteers were sent overseas at the request of overseas governments, Christian councils or other agencies, to help in social welfare work, schools, universities, youth clubs, hospitals, or rural development. VSO arranged and paid for travel to and from the overseas country while the host country supplied the other costs. VSO relied heavily on fundraising but was also subsidised by the British government.

West Africa Committee, 1956–
Established as an independent organization, its objects were to facilitate effective contribution towards the economic development of the West African countries of Ghana, Nigeria, Sierra Leone and the Gambia by companies and firms from other countries to the mutual economic advantage of both. The committee had members representing trading concerns, banking, industrialists, mining, plantations, etc. Membership was not limited to British concerns but had to be predominantly expatriate in character.

West African Currency Board, 1912–1965
The board was appointed by the secretary of state for the colonies to provide for and control the supply of currency to the British West African colonies and protectorates. Following the independence of Ghana and Nigeria, the board's currency became legal tender only in the Gambia and Sierra Leone.

West India Committee, 1750–
Established about 1750 and incorporated by royal charter in 1904, it was an association of British subjects interested in the West Indies, the Bahamas, British Guiana and British Honduras. Its object was to promote the interests of the agricultural and manufacturing industries of those territories, further their trade and advance the general welfare of their peoples.

See also West Indian Club Ltd, 1908–1966.

West Indian Club Ltd, 1908–1966
The object of the club was to further the interests of the West Indies and British Guiana by providing headquarters for concerted action in social matters.
See also West India Committee, 1750–.

Women's Corona Society, 1937–
Established as the Women's Corona Club, 1937–1953, members were originally connected with the overseas public service and public services in colonial territories. However, it became an open, voluntary and non-political association of women of all races. It acted as a link between members throughout the Commonwealth and provided service, hospitality and information. A variety of social occasions was held, as well as briefing sessions, conferences, lectures and films.
See also Corona Club, 1900–1966.

Women's Council, 1934–
Non-political and non-sectarian, it developed out of the Women's Advisory Council on Indian Affairs and grew between the 1940s and 1960s to include members from many Middle East and Asian countries. It aimed to promote knowledge of and co-operation between women in these countries through meetings, talks, informal hospitality and conferences. It published an annual *Bulletin* and was formally linked to many organizations in Britain.

Women's Migration and Overseas Appointments Society, 1919–1963
Established as the Society for the Overseas Settlement of British Women, it took over the responsibilities and assets, under government auspices, of the British Women's Emigration Association, the Colonial Intelligence League and the South African Colonization Society. During the existence of the Overseas Settlement Department of the Dominions Office it acted as the department's women's branch. The governing body was an executive committee elected by the members and a wide range of women's organizations was represented on an advisory council. The London Office gave advice on living conditions in Commonwealth countries, supplied information about employment prospects overseas for skilled and professional women, selected suitable applicants for vacancies and assisted women settlers with immigration regulations and travel arrangements. The society worked in close co-operation with the Commonwealth Relations Office and the Ministry of Labour.

Women Speakers for the Commonwealth, 1965–
The panel included women from all parts of the Commonwealth who spoke at various functions and engagements, offering accurate and up-to-date information about the countries they had lived in. It maintained contact with other Commonwealth organizations such as the Royal Commonwealth Society (qv) and the English-Speaking Union.

CHAPTER 11

Colonial Office Geographical Departments and their Records

Under the War and Colonial Department responsibility for the overseas territories was organized by departments covering broad geographical regions. In 1822 there were four: West Indian, North American, Eastern, and Mediterranean and African. These departments stayed essentially the same under the Colonial Office until 1867 when there was an important regrouping (see chapter 2.1). Thereafter there were splits, mergers and reallocations of geographical department responsibility as the number of territories the office supervised expanded and departmental responsibilities were reorganized. In 1907 the Dominions Division took over responsibility for the older self-governing colonies and related territories, and in 1925 a separate Dominions Office was established to handle their affairs.

In the late 1920s the Colonial Office underwent a major reorganization to facilitate a broader approach to development planning. This led to the creation of subject departments, and as they expanded in number and importance the geographical departments handled a decreasing proportion of business. After the Second World War subject department records were the more substantial. The geographical departments continued to have overall responsibility for each colony's affairs and to deal with anything particularly affecting a geographical area, especially political questions.

In addition to the creation of subject departments, the practice developed of filing geographical departments' papers by region, rather than by territory. Gradually, the old territorial file series were replaced by regional series, and this is reflected in the Public Record Office classes into which these records have been placed. The process was completed in 1951 with the final abolition of the country series. After 1951 there is a class for each regional department. Class numbers have not yet been allocated for records post 1959, but forthcoming classes can be determined by using the line chart in chapter 11.1, the breakdown of business in 11.4, and the list of Colonial Office departmental filing codes in 15.4.1. After independence, records about the former territories can be found in the records of the Commonwealth Relations Office in DO 35. See chapter 14.

Contents:

11.1 Line chart of geographical department development

11.2 List of geographical record classes with historical notes

11.3 Alphabetical list of territories showing the geographical departments responsible for their affairs, 1861 to 1965

11.4 Breakdown of geographical department business, 1861 to 1965

11.1 Line chart of geographical department development

11.2 List of geographical record classes with historical notes

This list describes the development of administrative responsibility for each of the territories supervised by the Colonial, Dominions and Commonwealth Relations Offices, and sets out the relevant record classes. It is arranged in broad regional divisions, and usually the first entry covers records relating to the whole region. It is always advisable to check the regional as well as the territorial entry. Regional entries include confidential print, which is arranged in regional classes; there is only one confidential print class for Africa (CO 879).

Territorial entries follow, arranged in alphabetical order under the names used during the colonial period but with cross-references from the modern period. The brief historical notes account for the acquisition of the territory by, or its association with, Britain, the emergence of parliamentary institutions, the grant of responsible government or severance of connection with Britain, and the date of the territory's adherence, in most cases, to the Commonwealth.

There are generally several principal record classes for each territory. In addition to original correspondence, these comprise entry books, letter books, registers, acts, miscellanea, and sessional papers. The miscellanea classes include nineteenth-century newspapers, shipping returns and blue books of statistics (discontinued during the 1940s). The sessional papers classes include legislative and executive council minutes and annual departmental reports, all of which except executive council minutes are normally open without restriction. There are also some annual territorial reports, but as a rule these are retained in the Foreign and Commonwealth Office Library.

The Colonies General Supplementary Original Correspondence (CO 537), noted under most territories, is composed mainly of secret despatches and telegrams withheld from the original correspondence classes and now declassified. Between 1926 and about 1945, and after about 1953, it has been integrated in the relevant correspondence classes. See chapter 4.7.

The letters qv are used to direct the reader's attention to other parts of this chapter.

Contents:
GENERAL:
    Colonies, Dominions

AFRICA:
    Africa

AFRICA: CENTRAL AND SOUTHERN:
    Central Africa, Amatongaland, Basutoland, Bechuanaland Protectorate, British Bechuanaland, British Central Africa Protectorate, British South Africa Company, Cape Colony or Cape of Good Hope, Federation of Rhodesia and Nyasaland, Griqualand West, Lesotho, Malawi, Namibia, Natal, North-Eastern Rhodesia, Northern Rhodesia, Nyasaland, Orange Free State, Orange River Colony, Rhodesia, South Africa, South Africa High Commission, Southern Rhodesia, South West Africa, Swaziland, Transkeian Territories, Transvaal, Transvaal and Orange River Colony, Union of South Africa, Zambia, Zimbabwe, Zululand

COLONIAL OFFICE GEOGRAPHICAL DEPARTMENTS

AFRICA: EAST:
East Africa, East Africa High Commission, East Africa Protectorate, Kenya, King's African Rifles, Somaliland, Sudan, Tanganyika, Tanzania, Uganda, Zanzibar

AFRICA: NORTH:
Tangier

AFRICA: WEST:
West Africa, Ashanti, British Cameroons, Fernando Po, Gambia, Ghana, Gold Coast, Gold Coast Northern Territories, Lagos, Niger Coast Protectorate, Nigeria, Northern Nigeria, Protectorate of Southern Nigeria, Senegambia, Sierra Leone, Southern Nigeria, Togoland, West Africa Frontier Force

ASIA:
Far East/South-East Asia, British Malaya, Brunei, Ceylon, Christmas Island, Cocos Islands, Federated Malay States, Federation of Malaya, Hong Kong, India, Jelebu, Johore, Kedah and Perlis, Keeling Islands, Kelantan, Labuan, Malacca, Malayan Union, Malaysia, Negri Sembilan, Sungei Ujong and Jelebu, North Borneo, Pahang, Pakistan, Penang, Perak, Perlis, Sabah, Sarawak, Selangor, Singapore, Sri Lanka, Straits Settlements, Sungei Ujong, Trengganu, Unfederated Malay States, Wei-Hai-Wei

ATLANTIC:
Ascension, Bermuda, Falkland Islands and Dependencies, St Helena and Dependencies, Tristan da Cunha

AUSTRALIA AND NEW ZEALAND:
Australia General, Australia and New Zealand, Auckland Islands, Commonwealth of Australia, New South Wales, New Zealand, New Zealand Company, Norfolk Island, North Australia, Northern Territory, Queensland, South Australia, Tasmania, Victoria, Western Australia

CARIBBEAN AND WEST INDIES:
West Indies, America and West Indies, Antigua and Montserrat, Bahamas, Barbados, Bay Islands, Belize, Bermuda, British Guiana, British Honduras, British Virgin Islands, Caicos Islands, Cayman Islands, Curaçao, Dominica, Federation of the West Indies, Grenada, Grenadines, Guadeloupe, Guyana, Havana, Jamaica, Leeward Islands, Martinique, Montserrat, Nevis, St Christopher, St Croix, St Eustatius, St Kitts, St Lucia, St Thomas, St Vincent, Santo Domingo, Surinam, Tobago, Trinidad, Turks and Caicos Islands, Windward Islands

EUROPE:
Heligoland, Ireland, Irish Free State

INDIAN OCEAN:
British Indian Ocean Territory, Mauritius, Seychelles, Zanzibar

MEDITERRANEAN:
Mediterranean, Corsica, Cyprus, Gibraltar, Ionian Islands, Malta, Minorca

MIDDLE EAST:
Middle East, Aden, Aden Protectorate, Protectorate of South Arabia, Arabia, Iraq, Jordan, Kuria Muria Islands, Palestine, South Yemen, Transjordan

L

North America:
British North America, Alberta, America and West Indies, British Columbia, Canada, Cape Breton, Hudson's Bay, Manitoba, New Brunswick, Newfoundland, North-West Territories, Nova Scotia and Cape Breton, Ontario, Prince Edward Island, Quebec, Saskatchewan, Vancouver Island

Western Pacific:
Western Pacific High Commission, British New Guinea (Papua), British Solomon Islands Protectorate, Fiji, Gilbert and Ellice Islands, Kiribati, Nauru, New Guinea (former German territory), New Hebrides, Papua New Guinea, Solomon Islands, Tonga, Tuvalu, Vanuatu, Western Samoa

GENERAL

Colonies General

Broadly speaking these are documents that concern more than one colony or no colony in particular. Most of the correspondence covered in this section constitutes the records of the Colonial Office General Department under its various titles. See under Chief Clerk's and General Departments in chapter 13.1 for an account of the history of the departments up to 1930, and under General Departments/Division in chapter 12.2 for an account of the evolution of the General Department after 1930. The Emigration and Overseas Settlement Departments and their records are described in chapter 13.1. See also chapter 4.

In addition to the records of the General Department, the Colonies General Original Correspondence class (CO 323) includes law officers' reports on colonial acts, applications for passports and for colonial appointments, and circular despatches. It also includes records of the Board of Trade from 1625 to 1782 (see chapters 1.1–2 and 4.1) and of the War and Colonial Department from 1801 to 1854 (see chapters 1.5 and 4.3). The earlier part of CO 323 includes the series of Board of Trade papers called 'Plantations General'. Other Board of Trade records relating to colonial affairs are in CO 288 – CO 391. The board's original correspondence has also been mixed with that of the secretaries of state in various Colonial Office country classes, particularly America and the West Indies Original Correspondence (CO 5). Conversely, colonial records are to be found in the papers of the Board of Trade and the War Office, and reference should be made to the appropriate sections of the Public Record Office *Current Guide*.

CO 324 contains commissions, instructions, petitions, grants, orders in council, and law officers' opinions; CO 381 is similar but is arranged by colonies. CO 325 includes historical sketches and tracts on the colonies, returns of colonial appointments, and registers of applications for them, statistical returns and précis.

The methods of registering 'general' or 'miscellaneous' papers varied from time to time in the nineteenth century as a result of changes in the organization of the general business of the office, and between 1851 and 1870 it may be necessary to consult several sets of registers. Up to 1854 the chief clerk dealt with both military and 'general' papers. The military papers appear to have been mainly registered in a volume called Military: Chief Clerk's Department (CO 324/155), which ran from 1851 to 1854. Probably it should have been transferred to the War Office in 1854, but it was not. The non-military papers appear to have been registered at first in British North America General Registers (CO 328) and from 1852 in Colonies General: Register of Correspondence (CO 378/1–2).

In 1860 the General Miscellaneous registers (CO 378) were re-entitled Colonies General and seem to cover most of the general correspondence from that time on. Nevertheless, the General Miscellaneous registers continued for certain purposes and now form CO 432. Entries were comparatively few and the series was abolished in 1870. In addition, a set of Chief Clerk's registers was started in 1860 and ran to 1867. It is in the class Entry Books Series I (CO 324/157, 161, 164 and 168).

Whether registered 'General', 'Miscellaneous' or 'Chief Clerk', the papers should, with the exception of five categories, be sought in Colonies General: Original Correspondence (CO 323). During the period 1860 to 1870 when the varieties of registers are most abundant, the class branches into three, corresponding to the three sets of registers, which should assist in searching. The excepted categories are the military correspondence for 1851 to 1854 (see above), the correspondence class called Governors' Pensions Original Correspondence (CO 449), the class called Patronage Original Correspondence (CO 429), two volumes (CO 878/16 and 18) in the class called Establishment Miscellanea, and the Colonies General Supplementary Original Correspondence (CO 537). For details about the Governors' Pensions and Patronage classes see under Personnel Divisions in chapter 13.1.

The entry books of general correspondence are also somewhat complicated in the nineteenth century, but follow the pattern of the registers. A set called General Miscellaneous, reserved for domestic categories, begins in 1851 and in 1860 is converted into a set called Colonies General which runs to 1870. It consists of CO 324/151–152, 154, 165, 169 and 171.

In 1860 a new set called Miscellaneous Letters begins, and in 1861 another set called Miscellaneous Despatches. These seem to have been used for correspondence about the office establishment and colonial subjects affecting only one or two colonies. The first (CO 324/158, 162–163, 167, 170 and 173) runs to 1870, the second (CO 324/160, 166, 172 and 175) to 1872. Until 1870 correspondence with other government departments out of which circulars arose was entered in the Colonies General Book, while letters enclosing the replies were entered in the Miscellaneous Book. It was then arranged that there should be only two sets of general or miscellaneous entry books, one for despatches and the other for domestic letters. In addition, a set of Chief Clerk's Miscellaneous Entry Books (CO 324/153, 156 and 174) was kept at this time, mainly for letters about the payments of charges on commissions and stamps on warrants; it was also terminated in 1870. The first surviving volume begins in 1856 but as this is lettered Volume 3 on the spine it may be supposed that the series began earlier.

The Emigration and Overseas Settlement Departments of the Colonial Office and their records are described in chapter 13.1.

Colonies General: Original Correspondence (CO 323) 1689 to 1952, 1931 volumes, files

Duplicates of Correspondence (CO 412) 1603 to 1863, 247 bundles

General Department: Original Correspondence (CO 1032) 1949–1960, 209 files

General Registers (CO 326) 1623 to 1849, 358 volumes

Colonies General: Register of Correspondence (CO 378) 1852 to 1952, 218 volumes

Colonies General: Register of Out-letters (CO 379) 1871 to 1925, 24 volumes

Colonies General: Register of General Miscellaneous Correspondence (CO 432) 1860 to 1870, 2 volumes

Colonies General: Register of 'Unregistered' Correspondence (CO 652) 1886 to 1927, 4 volumes

Register of Daily Correspondence (CO 382) 1849 to 1929, 82 volumes

Register of Daily Correspondence, Out-letters (CO 668) 1901 to 1910, 9 volumes

Colonies General: Entry Books, Series I (CO 324) 1662 to 1872, 176 volumes

Colonies General: Entry Books Series II (CO 381) 1740 to 1872, 93 volumes

Index to Correspondence (CO 714) 1795 to 1874, 171 volumes

Colonies General: Supplementary Original Correspondence (CO 537) 1759 to 1955, 7862 volumes, files

Colonies General: Register of Secret Correspondence (CO 694) 1865 to 1938, 42 volumes

Colonies General: Secret Entry Books and Registers of Out-letters (CO 570) 1870 to 1895, 2 volumes

Colonies General: Draft Letters Patent, Commissions, Royal Instructions, Warrants, etc (CO 380) 1764 to 1925, 215 volumes

Colonies General: Miscellanea (CO 325) 1744 to 1909, 54 volumes

Colonies General: Original Letters Patent, Warrants, etc (CO 816) 1834 to 1882, 7 documents

Chief Clerk: Original Correspondence (CO 523) 1843 to 1931, 92 volumes

Chief Clerk: Registers of Correspondence (CO 863) 1902 to 1931, 8 volumes

Chief Clerk: Registers of Out-letters (CO 864) 1902 to 1933, 4 volumes

Colonies General: Circular Despatches (CO 854) 1808 to 1956, 198 volumes

Colonies General: Indexes to Circular Despatches (CO 949) 1808 to 1956, 13 volumes

Colonies General: Registers of Replies to Circular Despatches (CO 862) 1862 to 1931, 25 volumes

See also:

Board of Trade: Entry Books (CO 389) 1660 to 1803, 59 volumes

Board of Trade: Original Correspondence (CO 388) 1654 to 1792, 95 volumes, etc

Board of Trade: Minutes (CO 391) 1675 to 1782, 120 volumes

Board of Trade: Miscellanea (CO 390) 1654 to 1799, 15 volumes, etc

Colonial Statistical Tables Command Papers (CO 442) 1833 to 1912, 63 volumes

Confidential Print Catalogues (CO 601) [1642] to 1934, 6 volumes

Coronation: Original Correspondence (CO 1021)

Honours: Register of Correspondence (CO 728) 1859 to 1940, 21 volumes

Honours: Original Correspondence (CO 448) 1858 to 1952, 139 volumes, files

Honours: Register of Out-letters (CO 729) 1872 to 1934, 4 volumes

Imperial Service Order (Dominions): Original Correspondence (DO 81) 1927 to 1929, 1 volume

Imperial Service Order: Original Correspondence (CO 524) 1902 to 1932, 14 volumes

Imperial Service Order: Register of Correspondence (CO 834) 1902 to 1926, 2 volumes

Imperial Service Order: Register of Out-letters (CO 835) 1902 to 1926, 2 volumes

Precedence: Original Correspondence (CO 851) 1873 to 1887, 31 files

Printing Registers (CO 600) 1864 to 1914, 26 volumes

Private Office Papers (CO 967) 1873 to 1956, 278 files

Prize Court: Original Correspondence (CO 969) 1939 to 1951, 314 files

Prize Court: Overseas Appeals (CO 837) 1914 to 1919, 2 volumes

Prize Court: Naval Appeals (CO 836) 1916 to 1921, 2 volumes

Prize Court: Naval Prize Tribunal (CO 839) 1918 to 1921, 1 volume

Prize Court: Registers of Correspondence (CO 988) 1941 to 1951, 12 volumes

Prize Court: United Kingdom Appeals (CO 838) 1914 to 1921, 13 volumes

Register of Acts (CO 383) 1781 to 1892, 93 volumes

Dominions General
In 1907 the Colonial Office was divided into two divisions, a Crown Colonies Division and a Dominions Division, in pursuance of a decision of the Imperial Conference. The former dealt with the dependencies, while the Dominions Division was concerned with dominions affairs and imperial conferences. It also dealt with certain dependencies thought to have a special affinity with the dominions: the South Africa High Commission territories, Northern and Southern Rhodesia, the Western Pacific High Commission territories, and Fiji. Nauru was administered with the Western Pacific High Commission territories until 1921 and thereafter by Australia. Tristan da Cunha came under the Dominions Division from 1921. In 1925 the Dominions Division became independent of the Colonial Office as the Dominions Office. It

continued to have responsibility for questions relating to the South Africa High Commission territories and Southern Rhodesia.

From the creation of the Dominions Division until 1922, correspondence about individual dominions was registered in separate country series. The Dominions Register of Correspondence (CO 708) covered papers relating to all or several of the dominions. In 1922 when the old series of 'colony' registers were closed, CO 708 continued as the sole register for papers handled in the Dominions Division. This series continues in DO 3. From 1922 most of the original correspondence about the dominions is in CO 532 which continues in DO 35 and runs until at least 1963 but probably 1966.

The records of the Overseas Settlement Department, created under the Colonial Office and later part of the Dominions Office, are described in chapter 13.1.

Dominions: Original Correspondence (CO 532) 1907 to 1925, 335 volumes

Dominions Office and Commonwealth Relations Office: Original Correspondence (DO 35) 1926 to 1961, 7158 volumes, files

Dominions: Supplementary Original Correspondence (DO 117) 1926 to 1929, 189 files

Dominions: Register of Correspondence (CO 708) 1907 to 1926, 37 volumes

Dominions: Register of Correspondence (DO 3) 1927 to 1942, 184 volumes

Register of Daily Correspondence (CO 382) 1849 to 1929, 82 volumes

Dominions: Register of Out-letters (CO 709) 1907 to 1926, 12 volumes

Dominions: Register of Out-letters (DO 4) 1927 to 1929, 3 volumes

Agreements, Treaties and Miscellaneous Documents (DO 118) 1856 to 1965, 477 volumes, maps, photographs, etc

Children's Overseas Reception Board (DO 131) 1940 to 1959, 113 files

Confidential Print: Dominions (CO 886) 1907 to 1925, 11 volumes

Confidential Print: Dominions (DO 114) 1924 to 1951, 119 volumes

Dominions (War of 1914 to 1918): Original Correspondence (CO 616) 1914 to 1919, 82 volumes

Dominions (War of 1914 to 1918): Register of Correspondence (CO 752) 1914 to 1919, 8 volumes

Dominions (War of 1914 to 1918): Register of Out-letters (CO 753) 1914 to 1919, 5 volumes

Dominions (War of 1914 to 1918): Trade Original Correspondence (CO 687) 1916 to 1919, 68 volumes

Dominions (War of 1914 to 1918): Trade Register of Correspondence (CO 756) 1916 to 1919, 4 volumes

Dominions (War of 1914 to 1918): Trade Register of Out-letters (CO 757) 1916 to 1919, 4 volumes

Dominions (War of 1914 to 1918): Prisoners Original Correspondence (CO 693) 1917 to 1919, 10 volumes

Dominions (War of 1914 to 1918): Prisoners Register of Correspondence (CO 754) 1917 to 1919, 2 volumes

Dominions (War of 1914 to 1918): Prisoners Register of Out-letters (CO 755) 1917 to 1919, 2 volumes

Colonial Empire Marketing Board: Original Correspondence (CO 868) 1938 to 1939, 7 boxes

Empire Marketing Board: Original Correspondence (CO 758) 1922 to 1934, 107 boxes

Empire Marketing Board: Posters (CO 956) 1926 to 1939, 734 posters, maps

Empire Marketing Board: Card Index (CO 759) 1922 to 1934, 134 packets

Empire Marketing Board: Minutes and Papers (CO 760) 1926 to 1933, 39 volumes

Overseas Settlement: Original Correspondence (CO 721) 1918 to 1925, 118 volumes

Overseas Settlement: Original Correspondence (DO 57) 1926 to 1936, 189 boxes

Overseas Settlement: Register of Correspondence (CO 791) 1918 to 1936, 10 volumes

Overseas Settlement: Register of Correspondence (DO 5) 1927 to 1936, 12 volumes

Overseas Settlement: Daily Register of Correspondence (CO 792) 1919 to 1927, 4 volumes

Overseas Settlement: Daily Register of Correspondence (DO 6) 1928 to 1929, 3 volumes

See also:

Colonies General: Supplementary Original Correspondence (CO 537) 1759 to 1955, 7862 volumes, files

AFRICA

Africa
The records listed below deal with questions common to the African dependencies. From the 1920s the African departments of the Colonial Office were under one assistant under-secretary, and a general African series (CO 847) began in 1932. In 1947 the Africa Division set up the African Studies Branch, a small specialist section closely associated with but not part of the African departments, to collect and disseminate information on administrative and social questions arising in connec-

tion with the African territories. It produced the *Journal of African Administration*, organized periodical summer conferences on African administration, and provided a secretariat for the Land, Law, and Local Government Panels. There are some early papers on the work of the branch in CO 847. The branch was transferred to the Department of Technical Co-operation in 1961.

Africa: Exploration, etc (CO 2) 1794 to 1843, 25 volumes

Africa: Exploration, Entry Books (CO 392) 1825 to 1844, 4 volumes

Africa: Original Correspondence (CO 847) 1932 to 1960, 74 files

Africa: Registers of Correspondence (CO 917) 1932 to 1951, 9 volumes

African Studies Branch: Original Correspondence (CO 955) 1950 to 1959, 86 files

Confidential Print: Africa (CO 879) 1848 to 1961, 190 volumes

See also:

Colonies General: Supplementary Original Correspondence (CO 537) 1759 to 1955, 7862 volumes, files

General Registers (CO 326) 1623 to 1849, 358 volumes

Hailey Papers (CO 1018) 1946 to 1955, 88 files

AFRICA: CENTRAL AND SOUTHERN

Central Africa

Before 1950 papers relating to the region as a whole, or to more than one of the territories, were filed under the individual territories. For a brief period in 1950 and 1951 papers on subjects common to Northern Rhodesia (qv) and Nyasaland (qv) or on the Central African Council and Rhodesia Railways were registered in CO 952. Territorial series cease in 1951 and CO 1015 continues for the whole region. Later it includes files on Somaliland (qv), Aden (qv) and Bechuanaland (qv) as well as on the Central African territories and the Central African Federation. The earliest files in this class overlap in subject matter with those in CO 952 and sometimes continue from them, so the two classes should be seen in conjunction.

The Central African Governors' Conference was placed on a permanent footing with its own secretariat in 1940. This led to the creation in 1944 of the Standing Central African Council to promote close contact and co-ordinate policy and action between the governments of Southern Rhodesia, Northern Rhodesia and Nyasaland on matters of common interest. Standing committees were established on such subjects as trypanosomiasis, civil aviation, industrial problems, African housing, and distribution of goods. The council was replaced in 1950 by the Standing Advisory Rhodesia-Nyasaland Inter-territorial Conference, but with the coming into force of the constitution of the Federation of Rhodesia and Nyasaland (qv) in September 1953 it was rapidly wound up.

Central Africa: Original Correspondence (CO 952) 1950 to 1951, 16 files

Central Africa: Register of Correspondence (CO 1014) 1950, 1 volume

Central Africa and Aden: Original Correspondence (CO 1015) 1950 to 1961, 2146 files

Amatongaland
Amatongaland was declared a British Protectorate in 1895. In 1897 it was incorporated into Zululand which was annexed to Natal (qv) in the same year.

Amatongaland: Proclamations (CO 4) 1896 to 1897, 1 volume

Basutoland (Lesotho)
The Basotho as a nation came into prominence in 1818 when their various clans, scattered by the raids of the Zulu and Matabele, grouped together to avert further attacks. The new nation then went through a period of struggle with the emigrant Boers and lost a portion of their land as a result. The Basotho had repeatedly sought the protection of the British government during this period.

Finally, on 12 March 1868, the British high commissioner for South Africa issued a proclamation declaring the Basotho to be British subjects and their territory to be British territory. In 1871 Basutoland was annexed to Cape Colony and the governor assumed legislative powers. As a result of unrest in the territory the administration was handed over to the imperial government in 1884. A resident commissioner was then appointed under the direction of the high commissioner for South Africa.

Before the introduction of constitutional reforms in 1960 Basutoland was governed using the existing system of hereditary chiefs owing allegiance to a paramount chief. The 1960 constitution provided for an advisory executive council and a legislative body known as the Basutoland National Council, which was partly elected. A conference held in London in 1964 agreed a new constitution which gave Basutoland a national assembly elected by universal adult suffrage and a senate composed of chiefs and nominated members. Following further constitutional talks in 1965 and 1966, Basutoland became an independent state within the Commonwealth on 4 October 1966 under the name of Lesotho.

See also under South Africa, South Africa High Commission. See Dominions General under GENERAL.

Basutoland: Sessional Papers (CO 646) 1903 to 1921, 3 volumes

Basutoland (Lesotho): Sessional Papers (DO 92) 1921 to 1965, 50 volumes, files

Basutoland: Miscellanea (CO 566) 1903 to 1925, 23 volumes

Basutoland: Miscellanea (DO 25) 1926 to 1946, 18 volumes

See also:

Dominions: Original Correspondence (CO 532), 1907 to 1925, 335 volumes

Dominions Office and Commonwealth Relations Office: Original Correspondence (DO 35) 1926 to 1961, 7158 volumes, files

Basutoland and Lesotho; Bechuanaland Protectorate and Botswana; and Swaziland: Government Gazettes (DO 145) 1961 to 1975, 56 volumes

Basutoland, Bechuanaland Protectorate and Swaziland Acts: (DO 150) 1961 to 1966, 10 volumes

Bechuanaland Protectorate (Botswana)

Northern Bechuanaland was treated as part of British Bechuanaland (qv) until 1895, since when it was administered as a separate territory by a resident commissioner under the high commissioner for South Africa. Up to 1960 the constitutional position of the protectorate was governed largely by orders in council and proclamations issued by the high commissioner. The tribal administrations and courts were formally recognized and their powers defined by various proclamations through the years.

In 1960 a new constitution was introduced providing for an advisory executive council, a partly elective legislative council, partly elective advisory African council and a judicature with a high court. On 27 September 1963 the territory was made independent of High Commission rule, the resident commissioner becoming Her Majesty's commissioner and being directly responsible to the secretary of state for the colonies. A revised constitution, which came into effect on 3 March 1965, established internal self-government based on universal adult suffrage and a ministerial form of government. Sir Seretse Khama, of the Bamangwato tribe, became the first prime minister of Bechuanaland and subsequently the first president of the Republic of Botswana, as it became, on 30 September 1966.

See also under British Bechuanaland, South Africa, South Africa High Commission. See Dominions General under GENERAL.

Bechuanaland Protectorate: Sessional Papers (DO 102) 1921 to 1965, 41 volumes, files

Bechuanaland Protectorate: Miscellanea (CO 567) 1896 to 1925, 19 volumes

Bechuanaland Protectorate: Miscellanea (DO 26) 1926 to 1947, 22 volumes

See also:

Dominions: Original Correspondence (CO 532) 1907 to 1925, 335 volumes

Dominions Office and Commonwealth Relations Office: Original Correspondence (DO 35) 1926 to 1961, 7158 volumes, files

Private Office Papers (DO 121) 1911 to 1955, 224 files

Basutoland and Lesotho; Bechuanaland Protectorate and Botswana; and Swaziland: Government Gazettes (DO 145) 1961 to 1975, 56 volumes

Basutoland, Bechuanaland Protectorate and Swaziland: Acts (DO 150) 1961 to 1966, 10 volumes

British Bechuanaland

The Bakswana people of Bechuanaland, like the related people of Basutoland, were directly affected in the first half of the nineteenth century by the expansion of the Zulus under Chaka, and especially by the Matabele. In their drive northwards, the Matabele met the stoutest resistance from the Bamangwato tribe of the Bakswana, under Chief Sekgoma. His son Khama III, who came to power in 1872, also successfully withstood the Matabele and brought stability and order to the territory. Meanwhile embittered relations between the Boers from the Transvaal and other Bakswana tribes prompted the local chiefs to appeal for assistance to the Cape authorities. In 1884 the British government responded by appointing a deputy commissioner to the Bakswana people. In 1885, with the concurrence of Chief Khama and other principal chiefs, the whole of Bechuanaland was placed under British protection. The southern part of the country was constituted a Crown colony, called British Bechuanaland. In 1895 it was annexed to Cape Colony.

See also under Bechuanaland Protectorate.

British Bechuanaland: Government Gazettes (CO 451) 1887 to 1895, 1 volume

British Central Africa Protectorate see Nyasaland

British South Africa Company

In 1889 the British South Africa Company was granted a royal charter to develop and administer the Rhodesias (qv). This charter was abrogated in 1923 and in the following year the company surrendered the last of its administrative rights, for which it was paid compensation. The two classes listed here are continued by the classes CO 671 and CO 815 under Southern Rhodesia, while the company's government gazettes for North-Eastern and Northern Rhodesia will be found in CO 669 and CO 670 under those heads. The class CO 468 under Rhodesia consists of the company's reports on the administration of Rhodesia. Some correspondence relating to the company will be found in CO 417 under South Africa High Commission (qv).

British South Africa Company: Ordinances (CO 3) 1891 to 1899, 1 volume

British South Africa Company: Government Gazettes (CO 455) 1894 to 1923, 8 volumes

Cape Colony or Cape of Good Hope

The Portuguese reached the Cape of Good Hope in 1486 and it was annexed by English sailors in 1620, but James I repudiated the annexation. The Dutch East India Company took possession of the territory in 1652. Britain occupied it in 1795, restored it to the Batavian Republic in 1803 under the terms of the Treaty of Amiens, recaptured it in 1806 and finally received it by cession in 1814. In 1910 it became a province of the Union of South Africa (qv).

From 1806 the Cape was administered by a governor aided by executive officers; in 1825 an advisory council was set up, which was replaced by nominated executive and legislative councils in 1834; in 1853 representative government was introduced with an appointed executive council and an elected legislative council and house of assembly; in 1872 responsible government was established and this constitution continued unchanged until 1910.

After the close of the Napoleonic Wars the government appointed several commissions of inquiry into the colonies. An inquiry into Cape Colony was carried out during 1823–1826, the records of which are held mainly in CO 414, with some commissioners' reports in CO 48.

For records before 1807 see War Office correspondence in WO 1. For records after 1910 see under Union of South Africa. From 1922 see Dominions General under GENERAL.

Cape of Good Hope (Cape Colony): Original Correspondence (CO 48) 1807 to 1910, 606 volumes

Cape of Good Hope (Cape Colony): Register of Correspondence (CO 336) 1850 to 1910, 17 volumes

Cape of Good Hope (Cape Colony): Register of Out-letters (CO 462) 1872 to 1910, 7 volumes

Cape of Good Hope (Cape Colony): Entry Books (CO 49) 1795 to 1872, 62 volumes

Cape of Good Hope (Cape Colony): Acts (CO 50) 1825 to 1910, 11 volumes

Cape of Good Hope (Cape Colony): Sessional Papers (CO 51) 1825 to 1925, 418 volumes

Cape of Good Hope: Sessional Papers (DO 31) 1926 to 1961, 45 volumes

Cape of Good Hope (Cape Colony): Government Gazettes (CO 52) 1823 to 1925, 120 volumes

Cape of Good Hope: Government Gazettes (DO 32) 1926 to 1961, 68 volumes

Cape of Good Hope (Cape Colony): Miscellanea (CO 53) 1799 to 1909, 147 volumes

Commissioners of Eastern Inquiry, Cape of Good Hope (Cape Colony) (CO 414) 1805 to 1830, 15 volumes, etc

High Commissioner for South Africa, and High Commissioner for Basutoland, the Bechuanaland Protectorate and Swaziland, and UK High Commissioner in the Union of South Africa: Correspondence (DO 119) 1843 to 1956, 1175 volumes, files, papers

Governor of Cape Colony and High Commission for South Africa including Territories: Registers of Correspondence (DO 120) see *Current Guide* Part 1: 803/5/1

See also:

General Registers (CO 326) 1623 to 1849, 358 volumes

Index to Correspondence (CO 714) 1795 to 1874, 171 volumes

Colonies General: Supplementary Original Correspondence (CO 537) 1759 to 1955, 7862 volumes, files

Federation of Rhodesia and Nyasaland

The possibility of establishing some form of closer political association between Northern Rhodesia (qv), Southern Rhodesia (qv) and Nyasaland (qv) had been considered over many years. A conference of officials in 1951 recommended that this association should take the form of a federation under which the federal government should have specified powers to deal mainly with matters common to all three territories, leaving residual matters with the territorial governments. The proposals were examined over two years, and in January 1953 a conference of ministers produced a draft scheme setting out the details of a federal constitution. This was approved by the legislative councils of Northern Rhodesia and Nyasaland, and by a referendum in Southern Rhodesia. Following an order in council setting out the constitution, the Federation of Rhodesia and Nyasaland came into being on 3 September 1953. The Commonwealth Relations Office became responsible for relations with the federal government, while the governments of Northern Rhodesia and Nyasaland remained the concern of the Colonial Office.

A commission appointed in 1959 under Viscount Monckton to advise the governments concerned on the federation, recommended 'prompt and far-reaching reform of the federal structure'. A constitutional review conference accordingly met in December 1960 but did not reach any decisions.

In March 1962 the British government formed the Central African Office, which took over responsibility from the Commonwealth Relations Office and the Colonial Office for the conduct of British relations with the federation and with its constituent territories. It was placed under the first secretary of state, R A Butler, then secretary of state for the Home Department, until October 1963, and then under the newly designated secretary of state for Commonwealth relations and the colonies.

In the face of growing opposition, from 1961, to the federation in Nyasaland and in Northern Rhodesia, the British government accepted that these territories could not be kept in the existing federation against their will. A conference was, in consequence, held at the Victoria Falls from 28 June to 3 July 1963 to arrange for the orderly dissolution of the federation. It came formally to an end on 31 December 1963. The Central African Office was absorbed by the Commonwealth Relations Office in April 1964.

See also under Central Africa.

Federation of Rhodesia and Nyasaland: Acts (DO 129) 1954 to 1963, 10 volumes

Federation of Rhodesia and Nyasaland: Sessional Papers (DO 123) 1953 to 1963, 28 volumes

Federation of Rhodesia and Nyasaland: Government Gazettes (DO 125) 1953 to 1963, 27 volumes

Commission on the Constitution of Rhodesia and Nyasaland, the Monckton Commission (CO 960) 1960, 50 files

See also:

Private Office Papers (DO 121) 1911 to 1955, 224 files

Dominions Office and Commonwealth Relations Office: Original Correspondence (DO 35) 1926 to 1961, 7158 volumes, files

Griqualand West

The territory was surrendered to Great Britain in 1871.

In 1872 the governor of the Cape of Good Hope was made governor of Griqualand West, which was then given a nominated executive council and a partly elective legislative council. These were abolished in 1880 when the territory was annexed to the colony of the Cape of Good Hope (qv).

Griqualand West: Original Correspondence (CO 107) 1875 to 1880, 9 volumes

Griqualand West: Register of Correspondence (CO 344) 1875 to 1880, 22 volumes

Griqualand West: Register of Out-letters (CO 522) 1876 to 1880, 1 volume

Griqualand West: Sessional Papers (CO 108) 1873 to 1880, 3 volumes

Griqualand West: Government Gazettes (CO 109) 1876 to 1880, 1 volume

Griqualand West: Miscellanea (CO 461) 1873, 1 volume

King's African Rifles see under AFRICA: EAST

Lesotho see Basutoland

Malawi see Nyasaland

Namibia see South West Africa

Natal

British settlers arrived in Natal in 1824. In 1844 it was annexed to Cape Colony (qv), under which it was given a lieutenant-governor and executive council in 1845 and an official legislative council for advisory purposes in 1847. In 1856 it was separated from the Cape and given a partly elective legislative council with an executive council. The lieutenant-governor was made supreme in Natal, although elsewhere he was subordinate to the governor of the Cape as high commissioner for South Africa. Natal received responsible government in 1893, an elective legislative assembly being added to the legislative council. In 1910 it became a province of the Union of South Africa (qv).

Natal: Original Correspondence (CO 179) 1846 to 1910, 256 volumes

Natal: Register of Correspondence (CO 357) 1849 to 1910, 15 volumes

Natal: Register of Out-letters (CO 480) 1872 to 1910, 6 volumes

Natal: Entry Books (CO 405) 1852 to 1872, 7 volumes

Natal: Acts (CO 180) 1848 to 1910, 12 volumes

Natal: Sessional Papers (CO 181) 1846 to 1924, 73 volumes

Natal: Sessional Papers (DO 39) 1925 to 1960, 34 volumes

Natal: Government Gazettes (CO 182) 1858 to 1925, 59 volumes

Natal: Government Gazettes (DO 40) 1926 to 1961, 48 volumes

Natal: Miscellanea (CO 183) 1850 to 1908, 58 volumes

See also:

General Registers (CO 326) 1623 to 1849, 358 volumes

Index to Correspondence (CO 714) 1795 to 1874, 171 volumes

North-Eastern Rhodesia
For the history of the territory see Rhodesia.

North-Eastern Rhodesia: Government Gazettes (CO 669) 1903 to 1911, 1 volume

Northern Rhodesia (Zambia)
Barotseland and North-Western Rhodesia were separated from North-Eastern Rhodesia (qv) in 1895 and jointly received a British resident, who became the administrator in 1900. In 1899 North-Western Rhodesia was placed under the high commissioner for South Africa (qv). In 1911 North-Western and North-Eastern Rhodesia were united to form Northern Rhodesia under a single administrator and a resident commissioner reporting to the high commissioner for South Africa. In 1918 a partly elective advisory council was established. In 1924 the British South Africa Company (qv) surrendered the administration of the territory to the Crown, and a governor was appointed with an executive council and a partly elective legislative council. The high commissioner in Cape Town ceased to have any jurisdiction in Northern Rhodesia from that date.

After a series of conferences in 1951, 1952 and 1953 on the closer political association of Northern Rhodesia, Southern Rhodesia (qv) and Nyasaland (qv), a draft constitution for a federal form of government was approved by all parties and the Federation of Rhodesia and Nyasaland (qv) came into existence on 3 September 1953. It was dissolved on 31 December 1963.

Meanwhile, in the territorial government of Northern Rhodesia constitutional changes in 1953, 1959 and 1962 led to an elected majority in the legislative council and an unofficial majority in the executive council. A new constitution giving the country internal self-government came into effect in January 1964, and on 24 October 1964 Northern Rhodesia, under the name of the Republic of Zambia, became fully independent and a member of the Commonwealth.

See also under British South Africa Company, Rhodesia, Federation of Rhodesia and Nyasaland, and Central Africa.

Northern Rhodesia: Original Correspondence (CO 795) 1924 to 1951, 170 volumes, files

Northern Rhodesia: Register of Correspondence (CO 796) 1924 to 1951, 23 volumes

Northern Rhodesia: Register of Out-letters (CO 797) 1924 to 1926, 1 volume

Northern Rhodesia: Proclamations (CO 743) 1911 to 1964, 16 volumes

Northern Rhodesia and Zambia: Sessional Papers (CO 799) 1923 to 1965, 50 volumes, files

Northern Rhodesia and Zambia: Government Gazettes and Acts (CO 670) 1911 to 1970, 56 volumes

Northern Rhodesia: Miscellanea (CO 798) 1924 to 1948, 25 volumes

See also:

Dominions: Original Correspondence (CO 532) 1907 to 1925, 335 volumes

Dominions Office and Commonwealth Relations Office: Original Correspondence (DO 35) 1926 to 1961, 7158 volumes, files

Union of South Africa: Miscellanea (CO 553), 1910 to 1925, 20 volumes

Colonies General: Supplementary Original Correspondence (CO 537), 1759 to 1955, 7862 volumes, files

Nyasaland (Malawi)

British interest in Nyasaland may be said to have begun with the visit of David Livingstone to Lake Nyasa in 1859. It was sustained by the missionary work of the Universities Mission to Central Africa (Anglican) from 1861, the Free Church of Scotland from 1875 and the established Church of Scotland from 1876. In 1883 a British consul was appointed; and in 1889 Nyasaland was proclaimed a British protectorate, the area of which was extended in 1891 and named the British Central Africa Protectorate in 1893. Until 1904 the protectorate was under a commissioner and a consul general, but the latter office was abolished in that year when responsibility for the protectorate was transferred from the Foreign Office to the Colonial Office. In 1907 the name Nyasaland Protectorate was resumed, the commissioner became governor, and nominated executive and legislative councils were established.

The possibility of associating Nyasaland with one or more of its neighbours was considered at various times over the years. As a result of a series of conferences in 1951, 1952 and 1953 a federal form of government for Nyasaland, Southern Rhodesia (qv), and Northern Rhodesia (qv) was approved by all governments concerned and the Federation of Rhodesia and Nyasaland (qv) came into existence on 3 September 1953. The federation was dissolved on 31 December 1963.

Meanwhile, constitutional advance in Nyasaland had continued. The elective element in the legislative council had been increased and the franchise widened in 1959. In 1961 a new constitution was introduced and in 1963 full internal self-government was achieved. On 6 July 1964 Nyasaland became an independent state within the Commonwealth under the name of Malawi. On 6 July 1966 Malawi became a republic.

See also under Central Africa and Federation of Rhodesia and Nyasaland and under King's African Rifles. Readers should also refer to FO 2 and other Foreign Office records which are described in the PRO handbook *The Records of the Foreign Office, 1782–1939*.

Nyasaland: Original Correspondence (CO 525) 1904 to 1951, 221 volumes, files

Nyasaland: Register of Correspondence (CO 703) 1904 to 1951, 28 volumes

Nyasaland: Register of Out-letters (CO 704) 1904 to 1926, 5 volumes

Nyasaland: Acts (CO 625) 1901 to 1964, 14 volumes

Nyasaland (Malawi): Sessional Papers (CO 626) 1907 to 1965, 43 volumes

Nyasaland (Malawi): Government Gazettes (CO 541) 1894 to 1975, 65 volumes

Nyasaland: Miscellanea (CO 452) 1897 to 1941, 45 volumes

See also:

Colonies General: Supplementary Original Correspondence (CO 537) 1759 to 1955, 7862 volumes, files

Orange Free State

The territory between the Orange and Vaal Rivers was settled by Boers from the Cape during the Great Trek of 1836–1837 and became a republic in 1842. In 1848 it was declared to be under British sovereignty and a British resident was appointed, but in 1854 the Orange Free State was recognized as independent. In 1899 it allied itself with the South African Republic and in 1900 was annexed to Britain under the name of the Orange River Colony. In 1910 it became a province of the Union of South Africa (qv) and resumed its former name of Orange Free State.

From 1854 until 1900 it had an elected president and an executive council which was responsible to an elective Volksraad. In 1902 the Orange River Colony was given a governor and nominated executive and legislative councils. Responsible government was granted in 1907, when an elective legislative assembly was added to the nominated legislative council. This constitution survived until 1910.

See also under Orange River Colony, and Transvaal and Orange River Colony.

Orange Free State: Sessional Papers (CO 661) 1911 to 1924, 9 volumes

Orange Free State: Sessional Papers (DO 55) 1925 to 1962, 29 volumes

Orange Free State: Government Gazettes (CO 662) 1911 to 1925, 10 volumes

Orange Free State: Government Gazettes (DO 56) 1926 to 1961, 47 volumes

Orange River Colony

For history and further records see under Orange Free State. The registers for 1901 to 1902 will be found under Transvaal and Orange River Colony.

See also under South Africa.

Orange River Colony: Original Correspondence (CO 224) 1853 to 1910, 33 volumes

Orange River Colony: Register of Correspondence (CO 663) 1903 to 1910, 3 volumes

Orange River Colony: Register of Out-letters (CO 664) 1903 to 1910, 2 volumes

Orange River Colony: Acts (CO 596) 1902 to 1910, 5 volumes

Orange River Colony: Sessional Papers (CO 599) 1902 to 1910, 19 volumes

Orange River Colony: Government Gazettes (CO 597) 1900 to 1910, 13 volumes

Orange River Colony: Miscellanea (CO 598) 1905 to 1906, 1 volume

Rhodesia

Rhodesia was first explored by the Portuguese in the eighteenth century and visited by David Livingstone in 1855. In 1889 the British South Africa Company (qv) was granted a royal charter to develop and administer Northern and Southern Rhodesia, and in 1890 Northern Rhodesia (qv) was declared a British protectorate. From 1890 to 1895 Northern Rhodesia and Nyasaland (qv) were under the commissioner for Nyasaland. In 1895 North-Eastern and North-Western Rhodesia were separated, and North-Eastern Rhodesia (qv) was again placed under the commissioner for Nyasaland. In 1910 North-Eastern Rhodesia was placed under the high commissioner for South Africa (qv), but the company's administrator retained executive powers. In 1911 North-Eastern and North-Western Rhodesia were united to form Northern Rhodesia (qv).

The following class of records consists of British South Africa Company reports on the administration of Rhodesia:

Rhodesia: Sessional Papers (CO 468) 1889 to 1902, 3 volumes

South Africa

In 1889, there was a customs union between Cape Colony (qv) and the Orange Free State (qv), joined in 1898 by Natal. It was renewed and joined by Transvaal (qv), Southern Rhodesia (qv), Basutoland (qv) and Bechuanaland (qv) in 1903. In the same year, an Intercolonial Council representative of the Transvaal and the Orange River Colony (the former Orange Free State) was set up to oversee the financial administration of the railways and the constabulary, as well as other expenditure common to the two territories. CO 549 consists of the printed and duplicated minutes of the Executive and Public Sessions and Railway Committees with papers laid before them. The Board of Control for Railways was a financial body. The tour of South Africa by Joseph Chamberlain, secretary of state for the colonies, provided a stimulus for these developments towards complete union. As union approached, the Intercolonial Council was dissolved in 1908.

See also under Union of South Africa.

South Africa: Customs Union (CO 547) 1906 to 1909, 4 volumes

South African Constabulary: Original Correspondence (CO 526) 1902 to 1908, 8 volumes

South African Constabulary: Register of Correspondence (CO 639) 1902 to 1908, 2 volumes

South African Constabulary: Register of Out-letters (CO 640) 1902 to 1908, 2 volumes

South Africa: Intercolonial Council Original Correspondence (CO 527) 1904 to 1908, 16 volumes

South Africa: Intercolonial Council Register of Correspondence (CO 634) 1904 to 1908, 2 volumes

South Africa: Intercolonial Council Register of Out-letters (CO 635) 1904 to 1908, 2 volumes

South Africa: Intercolonial Council, Transvaal and Orange River Colony (CO 549) 1903 to 1908, 11 volumes

South Africa: Railways Original Correspondence (CO 528) 1902 to1903, 7 volumes

South Africa: Railways Register of Correspondence (CO 636) 1903, 1 volume

South Africa: Railways Register of Out-letters (CO 637) 1903, 1 volume

South Africa: Secretary of State's Tour Original Correspondence (CO 529) 1902 to 1903, 1 volume

South Africa: Secretary of State's Tour Register of Correspondence (CO 638) 1902 to 1903, 1 volume

South Africa High Commission
The High Commission in southern Africa dates from 1845 when the governor of the Cape Colony was appointed as the high commissioner for relations with the territories in Southern Africa not administrated by Britain. The office of high commissioner was held by the governor of the Cape until 1901 when the position remained with Milner on his move from the governorship of the Cape to that of the Transvaal. It was reorganized in 1878 under the title of high commissioner in and for South Africa. The incumbent was then formally charged with conducting relations with the South African Republic (the Transvaal) and the Orange Free State, when these states were independent, and with the African states and tribes, as they then were, that lay in southern Africa outside Cape Colony and Natal. At various times the high commissioner was responsible for British Bechuanaland, Pondoland, Basuto-

land, the Bechuanaland Protectorate, and Swaziland as well as relations with the British South Africa Company, which managed the whole of Rhodesia between 1900 and 1923/1924, and with the adjacent Portuguese and German territories. Gradually some of the responsibilities were terminated. The Transvaal, the Orange Free State and the associated areas went in 1900; Southern Rhodesia in 1923 and Northern Rhodesia in 1924. In the end the high commissioner had responsibility only for Basutoland (now Lesotho), the Bechuanaland Protectorate (now Botswana) and Swaziland, which, until they attained their independence separately, came to be known as the High Commission Territories. When the Union of South Africa became a republic in May 1961 responsibility for the High Commission Territories was transferred to the Colonial Office.

The records listed below relate mainly to the High Commission Territories of Basutoland (qv), Bechuanaland Protectorate (qv) and Swaziland (qv) but also contain material on other territories for the periods when the high commissioner had wider responsibilities. For the period when the high commissioner was the sole channel of communication, there are no separate classes of original correspondence for these territories. Colonial Office correspondence with the Cape on High Commission business is held with Cape Colony Original Correspondence (CO 48) down to 1883. The archives of the High Commission itself are held in DO 119. However, certain records from the high commissioner's office were deposited with the Central African Archives in 1949 and are now in the National Archives of Zimbabwe.

South Africa: Original Correspondence (CO 417) 1884 to 1925, 716 volumes

South Africa High Commission: Original Correspondence (DO 9) 1926 to 1929, 15 volumes

South Africa: Register of Correspondence (CO 545) 1884 to 1927, 27 volumes

South Africa High Commission: Register of Correspondence (DO 1) 1928 to 1929, 1 volume

South Africa: Register of Out-letters (CO 546) 1884 to 1928, 15 volumes

South Africa High Commission: Register of Out-letters (DO 2) 1929, 1 volume

South Africa: Proclamations (CO 550) 1906 to 1923, 7 volumes

South Africa High Commission: Proclamations (DO 10) 1924 to 1961, 33 volumes

South Africa: Government Gazettes (CO 548) 1901 to 1922, 3 volumes

South Africa High Commission: Government Gazettes (DO 91) 1923 to 1960, 8 volumes

South Africa High Commission: Agreements and Treaties (DO 141) 1881 to 1920, 17 files

See also:

Colonies General: Supplementary Original Correspondence (CO 537) 1759 to 1955, 7862 volumes, files

Dominions: Original Correspondence (CO 532) 1907 to 1925, 335 volumes

Dominions Office and Commonwealth Relations Office: Original Correspondence (DO 35) 1926 to 1961, 7158 volumes, files

High Commissioner for South Africa, and High Commissioner for Basutoland, the Bechuanaland Protectorate and Swaziland, and UK High Commissioner in the Union of South Africa: Correspondence (DO 119) 1843 to 1956, 1175 volumes, files, papers

Governor of Cape Colony and High Commission for South Africa including Territories: Registers of Correspondence (DO 120)

See *Current Guide* Part 1: 803/5/1

Southern Rhodesia (Zimbabwe)

In 1888 Southern Rhodesia was declared to be under British protection and in 1889 the British South Africa Company (qv) was granted a royal charter to develop and administer the territory. In 1891 an administrator, nominated by the company, was appointed. His position was reinforced in 1896 by a resident commissioner appointed by the government. In 1898 the resident commissioner was given an executive council and a partly elective legislative council, but Southern Rhodesia was placed under the supervision of the high commissioner for South Africa (qv). In 1923 the territory was annexed to the crown and was granted responsible government with a governor-general, executive council, nominated legislative council and elective legislative assembly. The British government's reserved powers, as far as internal affairs were concerned, fell away in time, with the important exception concerning any differential legislation affecting African interests.

After a series of conferences in 1951 to 1953, Southern Rhodesia joined with Northern Rhodesia (qv) and Nyasaland (qv) to form the Federation of Rhodesia and Nyasaland (qv) on 3 September 1953. The federation had its main seat of government in Salisbury, Southern Rhodesia.

A new constitution for the territorial government of Southern Rhodesia had come into force in November 1962, but with the dissolution of the federation on 31 December 1963 Southern Rhodesia reverted to its status of a self-governing colony. Discussions on independence were held in London in 1964 and in 1965 but proved inconclusive.

On 11 November 1965 the Southern Rhodesia government made a unilateral and unconstitutional declaration of independence and in March 1970, equally illegally, declared the country a republic. No country in the world recognized Southern Rhodesia's self-asserted status and sanctions were invoked by the United Nations. However, constitutional talks between the white minority government, the British government, and the nationalist groups in the African National Council continued until 1975. They failed to agree proposals for a settlement that met all the requirements laid down by the British government for the grant of legal independence. A new government of Zimbabwe Rhodesia (as it was named) took office on 1 June 1979, but guerrilla activity by the main nationalist groups continued to increase throughout the country.

Against this background the Commonwealth Heads of Government met in Lusaka (Zambia) in August 1979, and as a result of agreement reached there a constitutional conference was held at Lancaster House in London in September–December 1979 with the African leaders concerned. The Lancaster House agreements were signed on 21 December 1979 and Southern Rhodesia became independent as Zimbabwe on 18 April 1980.

For Government Gazettes and Ordinances earlier than those listed below, see CO 455 and CO 3, which are listed under the British South Africa Company.

See also under Rhodesia, Federation of Rhodesia and Nyasaland, South Africa High Commission, Central Africa. See Dominions General under GENERAL.

Southern Rhodesia: Original Correspondence (CO 767) 1923 to 1925, 5 volumes

Southern Rhodesia: Original Correspondence (DO 63) 1926 to 1929, 6 volumes

Southern Rhodesia: Register of Correspondence (CO 800) 1923 to 1926, 1 volume

Southern Rhodesia: Register of Correspondence (DO 7) 1927 to 1929, 1 volume

Southern Rhodesia: Register of Out-letters (CO 801) 1923 to 1926, 1 volume

Southern Rhodesia: Register of Out-letters (DO 8) 1927 to 1929, 1 volume

Southern Rhodesia: Acts (CO 671) 1901 to 1925, 4 volumes

Southern Rhodesia: Acts (DO 88) 1926 to 1966, 26 volumes

Southern Rhodesia: Sessional Papers (CO 603) 1896 to 1925, 30 volumes

Southern Rhodesia: Sessional Papers (DO 64) 1926 to 1966, 102 volumes

Southern Rhodesia: Government Gazettes (CO 815) 1923 to 1925, 1 volume

Southern Rhodesia: Government Gazettes (DO 65) 1926 to 1975, 109 volumes

Miscellaneous Seals (DO 122), [1952] to [1965], 2 seals in boxes

High Commission and Consular Archives, Southern Rhodesia and Federation of Rhodesia and Nyasaland: Correspondence (DO 154) 1946 to 1958, 12 files

See also:

Dominions: Original Correspondence (CO 532) 1907 to 1925, 335 volumes

Dominions Office and Commonwealth Relations Office: Original Correspondence (DO 35) 1926 to 1961, 7158 volumes, files

Union of South Africa: Miscellanea (CO 553) 1910 to 1925, 20 volumes

South Africa: Original Correspondence (CO 417) 1884 to 1925, 716 volumes

Colonies General: Supplementary Original Correspondence (CO 537) 1759 to 1955, 7862 volumes, files

South West Africa (Namibia)

A German protectorate from 1880 to 1915, South West Africa was surrendered to forces from the Union of South Africa in 1915. Under the terms of the Treaty of Versailles it was declared a mandate and entrusted to South Africa with full powers of administration and legislation. Towards the end of the Second World War, the Union government advised the conference of the United Nations at San Francisco of its intention to incorporate South West Africa in the Union. This was challenged by the UN General Assembly, and South Africa did not formally annex the territory. The International Court of Justice ruled in 1971 that South Africa's presence was illegal. Constitutional talks begun in 1975 broke down, however, and in 1977 the five Western members of the UN Security Council drew up a plan for a peaceful settlement, which was implemented in 1989 following a series of talks between Cuba, Angola, South Africa and the USA. Elections to a National Assembly were held the same year, and independence was declared on 21 March 1990 when Namibia joined the Commonwealth.

Since 1931 Walvis Bay has been administered as part of South West Africa. It was proclaimed British territory in 1878 and annexed to Cape Colony (qv) in 1884. Although claimed by Namibia it remains under South African sovereignty.

See also under Union of South Africa. From 1922 see Dominions General under GENERAL.

South West Africa: Government Gazettes (CO 738) 1915 to 1925, 2 volumes

South West Africa: Government Gazettes (DO 78) 1926 to 1968, 56 volumes

South West Africa: Sessional Papers (DO 110) 1931 to 1946, 1 volume

Swaziland

From 1894 until 1899 Swaziland was administered by the government of the South African Republic. In 1902 a British special commissioner was appointed and in 1903 Swaziland was put under the high commissioner for South Africa, in whom legislative authority was vested and who thereafter administered through a resident commissioner. In 1921 an elective European advisory council was established to advise on affairs concerning Europeans. In 1964 a new post of Her Majesty's commissioner was created in place of the post of resident commissioner, and in the same year a new constitution provided for a nominated executive council and a partly elective legislative council. However, the traditional Swazi political system was largely retained, with the Swazi paramount chief being advised by two councils. In 1967 a new constitution, designed to take the country to independence, brought in many changes. Swaziland became a protected state and the paramount chief was recognized as king and head of state. A parliament was established comprising a house of assembly, with an elected majority, and a senate, which was partly elective. Swaziland became a fully independent state within the Commonwealth on 6 September 1968.

CO 609 is a volume of certified copies and duplicates of proclamations of the governor of the Transvaal relating to Swaziland from 1904 to 1906.

See also under South Africa High Commission, South Africa. See Dominions General under GENERAL.

Swaziland: Proclamations (CO 609) 1904 to 1906, 1 volume

Swaziland: Sessional Papers (DO 93) 1921 to 1965, 48 volumes

Swaziland: Miscellanea (CO 608) 1906 to 1924, 17 volumes

Swaziland: Miscellanea (DO 67) 1925 to 1947, 18 volumes

See also:

Dominions: Original Correspondence (CO 532) 1907 to 1925, 335 volumes

Dominions Office and Commonwealth Relations Office: Original Correspondence (DO 35) 1926 to 1961, 7158 volumes, files

Basutoland and Lesotho; Bechuanaland Protectorate and Botswana; and Swaziland: Government Gazettes (DO 145) 1961 to 1975, 56 volumes

Basutoland, Bechuanaland Protectorate and Swaziland: Acts (DO 150) 1961 to 1966, 10 volumes

Colonies General: Supplementary Original Correspondence (CO 537) 1759 to 1955, 7862 volumes, files

Transkeian Territories

From 1858 to 1865 the Transkeian Territories were neutral under the protection of Cape Colony, which then abandoned them. From 1879 to 1894 they were annexed to Cape Colony, and legislative authority was vested in the governor of the Cape in council. In 1894 the Transkeian Territories General Council was established, which was extended to all the territories by 1903 and given considerable powers of local government.

Transkeian Territories: Sessional Papers (DO 101) 1931 to 1963, 9 volumes

Transvaal

The Transvaal was occupied by Boers from the Cape in 1837 during the Great Trek. In 1852 it was recognized as independent, but consisted of several communities until they were united and formed into the South African Republic in 1858. In 1877 it was annexed to Britain, but its independence was restored in 1881 under British suzerainty. In 1899 it allied with the Orange Free State, in 1900 it was annexed to Britain and in 1910 it became an original province of the Union of South Africa (qv).

The constitution of 1858 provided for an elective president, an executive council and an elective legislature, the Volksraad. There was a British resident from 1881 to 1884. In 1890 the Volksraad was made into two elective chambers, but the old constitution came to an end in 1899. In 1902 the Transvaal and the Orange River Colony were given a common governor, but the Transvaal received its own lieutenant-governor, executive council and nominated legislative council. In 1906 an elective legislative assembly was added and responsible government was introduced and continued until 1910.

The records in CO 610 are the minutes of the Town Council of Johannesburg, and those in CO 611 the minutes of the Town Council and Municipal Commission of Pretoria. The Green Books (CO 477) are official publications of the South African Republic.

The registers for 1901 to 1902 will be found under Transvaal and Orange River Colony. For other records from 1881 see under South Africa High Commission and South Africa, and after 1910 under Union of South Africa.

Transvaal: Original Correspondence (CO 291) 1877 to 1910, 145 volumes

Transvaal: Register of Correspondence (CO 510) 1877 to 1910, 10 volumes

Transvaal: Register of Out-letters (CO 511) 1877 to 1910, 5 volumes

Transvaal: Acts (CO 292) 1880 to 1910, 7 volumes

Transvaal: Sessional Papers (CO 293) 1880 to 1925, 70 volumes

Transvaal: Sessional Papers (DO 72) 1925 to 1960, 40 volumes

Transvaal: Government Gazettes (CO 294) 1869 to 1925, 58 volumes

Transvaal: Government Gazettes (DO 73) 1926 to 1964, 56 volumes

Transvaal: Miscellanea (CO 476) 1878 to 1909, 6 volumes

Transvaal: Green Books (CO 477) 1884 to 1899, 3 volumes

Transvaal: Municipality of Johannesburg (CO 610) 1901 to 1906, 7 volumes

Transvaal: Municipality of Pretoria (CO 611) 1902 to 1903, 4 volumes

Transvaal and Orange River Colony

From 1903 to 1910 papers about these territories are registered in two separate series: Orange River Colony (qv) and Transvaal (qv). The original correspondence for 1901 to 1910 will also be found in two separate series under those two headings. For correspondence and registers before 1901 see South Africa High Commission.

Transvaal and Orange River Colony: Register of Correspondence (CO 679) 1901 to 1902, 2 volumes

Transvaal and Orange River Colony: Register of Out-letters (CO 680) 1901 to 1902, 1 volume

Union of South Africa

In 1910 Cape Colony (qv), Natal (qv), the Orange River Colony (qv) and the Transvaal (qv) were joined together in the Union of South Africa. The Union was given a unitary constitution with an executive consisting of the governor-general and executive council and a legislature consisting of the governor-general, a partly elective senate and an elective house af assembly. The four constituent colonies, henceforth provinces, were each given an administrator, executive committee and an elective provincial council for provincial matters. For original correspondence from 1922 and confidential print after 1944 see Dominions General under DOMINIONS.

The Union of South Africa withdrew from the Commonwealth on 1 December 1961 and the secretary of state for Commonwealth relations ceased to be responsible for the conduct of relations between Britain and the new Republic of South Africa from that date, when responsibility passed to the Foreign Office.

Union of South Africa: Original Correspondence (CO 551) 1910 to 1922, 157 volumes

Union of South Africa: Register of Correspondence (CO 705) 1910 to 1922, 9 volumes

Union of South Africa: Register of Out-letters (CO 748) 1910 to 1922, 5 volumes

Union of South Africa: Acts (CO 632) 1910 to 1925, 9 volumes

Union of South Africa: Acts (DO 77) 1926 to 1931, 2 volumes

Union of South Africa: Sessional Papers (CO 633) 1910 to 1925, 191 volumes

Union of South Africa: Sessional Papers (DO 11) 1926 to 1960, 262 volumes

Union of South Africa: Government Gazettes (CO 552) 1910 to 1925, 57 volumes

Union of South Africa: Government Gazettes (DO 12) 1926 to 1978, 343 volumes

Union of South Africa: Miscellanea (CO 553) 1910 to 1925, 20 volumes

Union of South Africa: Miscellanea (DO 13) 1926 to 1950, 26 volumes

Confidential Print: Dominions (South African) (DO 116) 1913 to 1944, 8 volumes

See also:

Colonies General: Supplementary Original Correspondence (CO 537) 1759 to 1955, 7862 volumes, files

Dominions: Original Correspondence (CO 532) 1907 to 1925, 335 volumes

Dominions Office and Commonwealth Relations Office: Original Correspondence (DO 35) 1926 to 1961, 7158 volumes, files

Dominions: Supplementary Original Correspondence (DO 117) 1926 to 1929, 189 files

Zambia see Northern Rhodesia

Zimbabwe see Southern Rhodesia

Zululand

Zululand first came under British influence in 1879, after long conflicts with the Boers and the Natal government. A British resident was then appointed as adviser to the thirteen Zulu chiefs holding office. In 1887 Zululand was declared British territory. The office of resident commissioner was continued under the governor of Natal, in whom legislative authority was vested. In 1897 Zululand was annexed to Natal (qv).

Zululand: Original Correspondence (CO 427) 1887 to 1897, 28 volumes

Zululand: Register of Correspondence (CO 619) 1887 to 1897, 2 volumes

Zululand: Register of Out-letters (CO 620) 1887 to 1897, 1 volume

Zululand: Acts (CO 322) 1887 to 1897, 1 volume

Zululand: Miscellanea (CO 472) 1889 to 1896, 8 volumes

AFRICA: EAST

East Africa
Records in these classes deal with matters relating to the region as a whole and especially to the question of the 'closer union' and the administration of the common services of the four territories of Kenya, Tanganyika, Zanzibar and Uganda. From 1951 the territorial classes disappear and CO 822 becomes the main geographical class for the whole region.

The Governors' Conference was a permanent feature in the political life of the region from 1926, and its proceedings are in CO 962. After 1943 there are also Governors' Conference records in CO 822. The conference was strengthened and extended during the Second World War. In 1940 it was reconstructed with a permanent post of deputy chairman with special responsibility for maintaining contact with the military authorities and co-ordinating supplies through a Civil Supplies Board. The board itself liaised closely with the East African War Supplies Board, which purchased East African products for the military authorities and later formed part of the East African Production and Supply Council. The East Africa High Commission (qv) was established in January 1948 to replace the Governors' Conference.

East Africa: Original Correspondence (CO 822) 1927 to 1958, 1201 volumes, files

East Africa: Register of Correspondence (CO 869) 1927 to 1951, 22 volumes

East Africa Conference of Governors (CO 962) 1926 to 1943, 16 volumes

East Africa Royal Commission (1953–1955) (CO 892) 1953–1955, 17 files

East Africa Economic and Fiscal Commission (1960) (CO 893) 8 files

East African Common Services Organization and East African Community: Government Gazettes (CO 1050) see *Current Guide* Part 1: 802/9/3

See also:

Colonies General: Supplementary Original Correspondence (CO 537) 1759 to 1955, 7862 volumes, files

East Africa High Commission
The High Commission, consisting of the governors of Kenya, Tanganyika and Uganda, was established in January 1948 to replace the Governors' Conference (see East Africa). It was charged with the administration of various East African common

services. From the start it was a more extensive and complex organization than the regional bodies in West or Central Africa. It administered a large number of inter-territorial services such as the East African Posts and Telegraphs, the East African Inter-Territorial Languages Committee, the Lake Victoria Fisheries Board, the East African Literature Bureau and the East African Veterinary Research Organization.

In addition, a central legislative assembly was set up consisting of the principal executive officers of the High Commission, together with a number of nominated and unofficial members drawn in the main from the legislatures of the three territories. The High Commission legislated with the advice and consent of the assembly for matters within its sphere of responsibility. Its legislation had effect throughout the East African territories.

In 1961 the High Commission was replaced by the East African Common Services Organization which was independent of the British government.

East Africa High Commission: Gazettes (CO 921) 1948 to 1966, 16 volumes

East Africa High Commission: Acts (CO 924) 1948 to 1963, 5 volumes

East Africa High Commission: Sessional Papers (CO 942) 1948 to 1965, 23 volumes, files

East Africa Protectorate see Kenya

Kenya

Kenya was formerly the East Africa Protectorate. The protectorate was proclaimed in 1890, and the territory was administered by the Imperial British East Africa Company from 1891. In 1895 it was put under the control of the Foreign Office, which appointed a commissioner. In 1905 control of the territory was transferred from the Foreign Office to the Colonial Office, and in 1906 a governor was appointed and nominated executive and legislative councils were established. In 1920 part of the mainland territories of the sultan of Zanzibar became the Protectorate of Kenya and the remaining territory became Kenya Colony. The governor of the colony and the two councils were given authority over both colony and protectorate, and the legislative council was made partly elective. Constitutional amendments were made in 1923 and again in 1944, on the question of communal representation on the legislative council. Further major changes were made in 1951 raising the number of seats to be filled from each community.

Between October 1952 and January 1960 a state of emergency existed which was known officially as the Mau Mau rebellion. In 1954 a new constitution was introduced. It provided for a council of ministers with representatives from all sections of the community exercising collective responsibility. The 1954 constitution, however, proved unworkable and a new constitution was introduced in 1958. It increased the number of African elected members in the legislative council and set up a council of state: further constitutional amendments followed in 1960. Full internal self-government was established in early 1962, and Kenya became an independent member of the Commonwealth on 12 December 1963.

COLONIAL OFFICE GEOGRAPHICAL DEPARTMENTS

Readers should also refer to FO 2, FO 84 and other Foreign Office records which are described in the PRO handbook *The Records of the Foreign Office, 1782–1939*.

East Africa and Uganda Protectorate: Original Correspondence (CO 519) 1904 to 1905, 1 volume

Kenya: Original Correspondence (CO 533) 1905 to 1951, 764 volumes, files

Kenya: Register of Correspondence (CO 628) 1904 to 1951, 44 volumes

Kenya: Register of Out-letters (CO 629) 1904 to 1925, 9 volumes

Kenya: Acts (CO 630) 1901 to 1963, 30 volumes

The Stamp Mission: Transfer of Land in Kenya (OD 2) 1964 to 1965, 13 files, volumes

Kenya: Sessional Papers (CO 544) 1903 to 1965, 111 volumes

East Africa and Uganda Protectorates: Government Gazettes (CO 457) 1899 to 1907, 7 volumes

Kenya: Government Gazettes (CO 542) 1908 to 1975, 103 volumes

Kenya: Miscellanea (CO 543) 1901 to 1946, 35 volumes

Kenya: Coastal Strip Commission (1961) (CO 894) 1961, 14 files

Kenya: Constituencies Delimitation Commission (1962) (CO 895) 1962, 7 files, volumes, maps

Kenya: Northern Frontier District Commission (1962) (CO 896) 1962, 5 files

Kenya: Regional Boundaries Commission (1962) (CO 897) 1962, 9 files, maps

Kenya: Land Transfer (DO 143)

See also:

Colonies General: Supplementary Original Correspondence (CO 537) 1759 to 1955, 7862 volumes, files

King's African Rifles

In 1902 the armed forces of the East African dependencies (Uganda, the East Africa Protectorate, Somaliland and the British Central Africa Protectorate) were reorganized as one regiment, the King's African Rifles. In 1927 the administration of the unit was brought together with that of the West Africa Frontier Force (qv) to form the military branch of the Colonial Office. Thus papers were then registered and kept together.

King's African Rifles: Original Correspondence (CO 534) 1905 to 1926, 63 volumes

King's African Rifles: Register of Correspondence (CO 623) 1905 to 1926, 8 volumes

King's African Rifles: Register of Out-letters (CO 624) 1905 to 1926, 7 volumes

See also:

Military: Original Correspondence (CO 820) 1927 to 1951, 77 volumes, files

Military: Register of Correspondence (CO 871) 1927 to 1952, 25 volumes

Somaliland

The Egyptians claimed Somaliland in 1875; when they withdrew in 1884 it became a British protectorate. It was administered by the resident at Aden as a dependency of the Government of India until 1898, when it was transferred to the control of the Foreign Office. In 1905 control was transferred to the Colonial Office. In 1940 it was occupied by the Italians, but they were driven out by the British in 1941.

From 1898 Somaliland was under an administrator and from 1914 either a governor or a commissioner. It was under British military administration from 1941 to 1948.

In 1960 British Somaliland became independent and joined with its neighbour, the former Italian colony and United Nations trust territory, to form an enlarged and independent Somalia.

Records about Somaliland after 1951 are found in the class: Central Africa and Aden (CO 1015) and after 1959 in the class: East Africa (CO 822). Readers should also refer to the Public Record Office *Current Guide* for the relevant Foreign Office and War Office records and to the PRO handbook *The Records of the Foreign Office, 1782–1939*.

Somaliland: Original Correspondence (CO 535) 1905 to 1951, 152 volumes

Somaliland: Register of Correspondence (CO 713) 1905 to 1951, 18 volumes

Somaliland: Register of Out-letters (CO 769) 1905 to 1926, 2 volumes

Somaliland: Acts (CO 673) 1900 to 1960, 6 volumes

Somaliland: Sessional Papers (CO 830) 1925 to 1961, 26 volumes, files

Somaliland: Government Gazettes (CO 922) 1941 to 1960, 8 volumes

Somaliland: Miscellanea (CO 607) 1901 to 1938, 38 volumes

See also:

Colonies General: Supplementary Original Correspondence (CO 537) 1759 to 1955, 7862 volumes, files

Sudan

The Sudan was conquered by the khedive of Egypt in 1821/1822. From 1869 many British administrators were employed there. Between 1881 and 1885 the Sudan gradually won its independence, but by 1898 it had been reconquered by Britain. In 1899 an Anglo-Egyptian condominium was established, whereby the Sudan was to be autonomous under a governor-general appointed by the khedive on the recommendation of Britain. Britain's relations with the Sudan have been the concern of the

Foreign Office. The presence of the following records among the Colonial Office records is at present unexplained.

Sudan: Government Gazettes (CO 675) 1907 to 1917, 2 volumes

Tanganyika

Tanganyika was under German control from 1884 until it was captured by British and Belgian forces in 1916 to 1917. It was placed under British civil administration in 1917 and assigned by mandate to Britain in 1919. Ruanda-Urundi, also formerly part of German East Africa, was assigned to Belgium. The administration of Tanganyika continued to be carried out under the terms of the mandate until its transfer to the trusteeship system under the United Nations.

Before 1920 there was a British administrator. A governor was first appointed in 1920 and was given an executive council. A nominated legislative council was established in 1926. The non-official element in the legislative council and African and Asian membership was increased over the years. From 1948 onwards the executive council, which had assisted the governor only in an advisory capacity, was remodelled, giving individual members 'ministerial' responsibility for some government departments. In 1957 they were designated as ministers, and assistant ministers were appointed in the legislative council to speak for their departments. Following the first general election in 1958 and 1959 a council of ministers was established with elected representatives taking ministerial office. The second general election, held in 1960, brought in elected majorities in both the executive and legislative spheres. Among other changes was the abolition of the executive council and the introduction of the post of chief minister. On 1 May 1961 Tanganyika attained internal self-government, and on 9 December 1961 it became a fully independent member of the Commonwealth. On 9 December 1962 Tanganyika became a republic. On 26 April 1964 Tanganyika joined with Zanzibar (qv) to form the United Republic of Tanganyika and Zanzibar, which became the United Republic of Tanzania on 29 October 1964.

See also under East Africa and Zanzibar.

Tanganyika: Original Correspondence (CO 691) 1916 to 1951, 217 volumes, files

Tanganyika: Register of Correspondence (CO 746) 1916 to 1951, 29 volumes

Tanganyika: Register of Out-letters (CO 747) 1916 to 1926, 6 volumes

Tanganyika: Acts (CO 735) 1919 to 1961, 15 volumes

Tanganyika: Sessional Papers (CO 736) 1918 to 1963, 62 volumes

Tanzania: Sessional Papers (DO 147) 1964 to 1965, 2 volumes

Tanganyika: Government Gazettes (CO 737) 1919 to 1964, 72 volumes

Tanzania: Goverment Gazettes (DO 146) 1964 to 1975, 29 volumes

Tanganyika: Miscellanea (CO 726) 1921 to 1948, 30 volumes

See also:

Colonies General: Supplementary Original Correspondence (CO 537) 1759 to 1955, 7862 volumes, files

Tanzania see Tanganyika and Zanzibar

Uganda

Uganda was claimed by Germany in 1885 but was assigned to the British East African Company in 1890. A protectorate over Buganda was declared in 1890 and over the rest of present-day Uganda when the Crown took over the administration in 1896. Construction of the Ugandan Railway, considered for some years previously, was started in 1896. In 1903 responsibility for the railway's administration was transferred from the Foreign Office to the government of the East Africa Protectorate (see Kenya). In 1905 control of the administration of Uganda was transferred from the Foreign Office to the Colonial Office. From 1893 there was a British commissioner, replaced in 1905 by a governor, and in 1920 an executive council and a nominated legislative council were established. In 1953 the legislative council was expanded and in 1955 a ministerial system of government was introduced. In 1960 the legislative council was made mainly elective and the governor's executive council was converted into a council of ministers. A commission under Lord Munster was appointed to consider the relationship of the Kingdoms of Buganda, Ankole, Bunyoro, and Toro to the central government. Following a constitutional conference in London, Uganda attained internal self-government in March 1962. The new constitution provided for a single chamber legislature, the national assembly. Buganda's relationship with Uganda was defined at that time as a federal one. Following a further conference in London, Uganda became an independent sovereign state and a member of the Commonwealth on 9 October 1962. As a result of a constitutional amendment, the British monarch ceased to be head of state of Uganda in 1963. Uganda was formally proclaimed a republic on 8 September 1967.

Besides the correspondence in class CO 614 (see below) there are 39 volumes of papers relating to the Uganda Railway in CO 537, which are registered in CO 615, as well as some unregistered papers about the railway. The correspondence in CO 519 is registered in the Kenya registers (CO 628).

Readers should also refer to FO 2 and other Foreign Office records which are described in the PRO handbook *The Records of the Foreign Office*, 1782–1939.

East Africa and Uganda Protectorate: Original Correspondence (CO 519) 1904 to 1905, 1 volume

Uganda: Original Correspondence (CO 536) 1905 to 1951, 22 volumes, files

Uganda: Register of Correspondence (CO 682) 1905 to 1951, 26 volumes

Uganda: Register of Out-letters (CO 683) 1905 to 1926, 5 volumes

Uganda: Acts (CO 684) 1901 to 1960, 12 volumes

Uganda: Sessional Papers (CO 685) 1907 to 1965, 63 volumes

East Africa and Uganda Protectorates: Government Gazettes (CO 457) 1899 to 1907, 7 volumes

Uganda: Government Gazettes (CO 612) 1908 to 1973, 74 volumes

Uganda: Miscellanea (CO 613) 1901 to 1945, 45 volumes

Uganda Railway: Construction (CO 614) 1895 to 1904, 14 volumes

Uganda Railway: Register of Correspondence (CO 615) 1895 to 1905, 7 volumes

See also:

Colonies General: Supplementary Original Correspondence (CO 537) 1759 to 1955, 7862 volumes, files

Zanzibar

The first British consul was posted to Zanzibar in 1840. Germany claimed administrative responsibility in 1885, but British administration continued and by 1890 Zanzibar was exchanged with Germany for Heligoland and was declared a British protected state. A regular government under a British minister was set up in 1891, and from 1906 the British ruled more directly. Control was transferred from the Foreign Office to the Colonial Office in 1913 with effect from 1914. The government was then vested in a British resident, who was subject to the governor of the British East Africa Protectorate as high commissioner, and a nominated advisory protectorate council, with the sultan as president, was established. In 1925 the office of high commissioner was abolished, the British resident becoming directly responsible to the Colonial Office, and in 1926 the protectorate council was replaced by an executive council and a nominated legislative council. By 1960 a degree of responsible government was achieved. Elected ministers, one of whom was chief minister, formed the majority in the executive council, and in the legislative council there was a large elected majority. In 1962 universal adult suffrage was introduced and the legislative council further expanded. On 24 June 1963 internal self-government was introduced and Zanzibar attained full sovereign independence under the sultan as head of state on 10 December 1963. On 12 January 1964 Zanzibar was proclaimed a people's republic. Zanzibar joined with Tanganyika to form the single sovereign state of the United Republic of Tanganyika and Zanzibar on 26 April 1964. The name Tanzania was adopted by the United Republic on 29 October 1964.

The mainland territories of the former Sultanate of Zanzibar were handed over to the British East African Association in 1887 and in 1920 became the Protectorate of Kenya (qv).

See also under Tanganyika and East Africa. Readers should also refer to FO 2, FO 54, FO 84 and FO 107 which are described in the PRO handbook *The Records of the Foreign Office, 1782–1939*.

Zanzibar: Original Correspondence (CO 618) 1913 to 1951, 88 volumes, files

Zanzibar: Register of Correspondence (CO 772) 1913 to 1950, 13 volumes

Zanzibar: Register of Out-letters (CO 805) 1913 to 1926, 2 volumes

Zanzibar: Acts (CO 842) 1926 to 1962, 11 volumes

Zanzibar: Sessional Papers (CO 688) 1909 to 1963, 46 volumes

Zanzibar: Government Gazettes (CO 689) 1913 to 1965, 67 volumes

Zanzibar: Miscellanea (CO 690) 1913 to 1947, 35 volumes

See also:

Colonies General: Supplementary Original Correspondence (CO 537) 1759 to 1955, 7862 volumes, files

AFRICA: NORTH

Tangier (Tanger)
Tangier was ceded by Portugal to England in 1661 as part of the dowry of Catherine of Braganza, Charles II's Portuguese wife, but Charles evacuated it in 1683 to 1684. From 1661 to 1684 it was under a British governor, who had legislative authority and was at the head of a military administration until 1668, when a charter of incorporation established an elective council, headed by a mayor and aldermen. The following records include entry books and local records sent to London when Tangier was abandoned in 1684, including the court books of its municipal assemblies under English rule, local notarial documents, and similar material.

Tangier: Original Correspondence, etc (CO 279) 1661 to 1735, 49 volumes, etc

AFRICA: WEST

West Africa
Records relating to West Africa in general or to more than one colony in the region were, from 1911, registered separately and are found in the class CO 554 which also includes papers on the West African Inter-Territorial Conference. From 1951 the territorial classes disappear and CO 554 becomes the main geographical class for the whole region.

The West African Governors' Conference, inaugurated in 1939 to facilitate meetings between the four West African governors, set up a permanent office organization in 1940 and a supply centre in 1941. The system was superseded in 1942 after the region had become an important staging post in the airlift of supplies to the armies in the western desert, by the creation of a new post of Cabinet minister resident in West Africa. It was his job to secure the effective co-operation of the territories in the prosecution of the war. He stimulated the production of war requirements and brought the French and Belgian territories into consultation for strategic and economic purposes. He relied on the assistance of the economic adviser for West Africa appointed by the West African governments. The resident minister's office was linked to the Cabinet through its Africa Committee, and the Colonial Office provided his London secretariat. When the office was abolished in 1945, the co-ordinating agency for West Africa became the secretariat of the West African Council in Accra.

With the end of hostilities in 1945 the West African War Council was reconstituted as the West African Council, chaired by the secretary of state, with the four governors as members. In 1951 it was replaced by the West African Inter-Territorial Council, which became a conference in 1953, with the governor of Nigeria as permanent president. It was serviced by a secretariat and its concern with inter-territorial collaboration on research and on economic, social, technical, military and other matters resulted in the establishment of a number of inter-territorial research institutes.

West Africa: Original Correspondence (CO 554) 1911 to 1963, 2131 volumes, files

West Africa: Register of Correspondence (CO 555) 1911 to 1951, 25 volumes

West African Currency Board (CO 984) 1880 to 1974, 58 files, volumes

See also:

Colonies General: Supplementary Original Correspondence (CO 537) 1759 to 1955, 7862 volumes, files

Ashanti

Ashanti was annexed to the Gold Coast (qv) in 1901. In 1906 the boundaries were readjusted. The Ashanti Confederacy was restored in 1935. Administration was through a chief commissioner.

Ashanti: Acts (CO 834) 1920 to 1934, 2 volumes

British Cameroons

The Cameroons, German since 1888, were conquered by British and French troops in 1916. In 1919 they were divided between Britain and France. The two parts were placed under British and French mandates by the League of Nations in 1922, later the trusteeship system of the United Nations, and the British Cameroons were administered as part of Nigeria (qv). The Cameroons ceased to be part of Nigeria when Nigeria became independent in October 1960, but a plebiscite was held in February 1961 to decide whether the Cameroons should join Nigeria or the Cameroon Republic. Northern Cameroons voted to become part of Nigeria and formally joined the federation on 1 June 1961. The Southern Cameroons opted to join the Republic of Cameroon and did so on 1 October 1961.

See also under West Africa.

Cameroons: Original Correspondence (CO 649) 1915 to 1926, 31 volumes

Cameroons: Register of Correspondence (CO 750) 1915 to 1926, 5 volumes

Cameroons: Register of Out-letters (CO 751) 1915 to 1926, 4 volumes

After 1926 see:

Nigeria: Original Correspondence (CO 583) 1912 to 1951, 318 volumes, files

Nigeria: Registers of Correspondence (CO 763) 1912 to 1951, 43 volumes

Cameroons see British Cameroons

Colony and Protectorate of Southern Nigeria see Southern Nigeria

Fernando Po

Fernando Po, under Spanish administration until 1778, was entrusted to Britain from 1827 to 1834 as a naval base for action against the slave trade. The last British superintendent continued as Spanish governor until his death in 1854. For records concerning Fernando Po before 1828 and after 1842 see under Sierra Leone.

Fernando Po: Original Correspondence, Entry Books, etc (CO 82) 1818 to 1844, 12 volumes

Gambia (The Gambia)

In 1651 an English colony was established on St Andrew's Island and in 1661 it was taken over by the African Company and renamed James Island. Thereafter it frequently changed hands until ceded to Britain by France in 1783. On the dissolution of the African Company, Gambia was placed under the administration of Sierra Leone (qv) in 1821. In 1843 Gambia became a separate colony, from 1866 to 1888 it was part of the West African Settlements administered from Freetown, and in 1888 it again became a separate colony. The Gambia Protectorate area first came under British administration in 1894.

From 1816 to 1822 a military commandant administered Gambia, assisted by a board of merchants called 'The Settlement Court', and from 1822 to 1829 the commandant governed alone. In 1829 a lieutenant-governor was appointed, while in 1843 Gambia was given an administrator and nominated executive and legislative councils. It retained its own legislative council from 1866 to 1888, when the 1843 constitution was resumed at its second separation. The title of administrator was changed to that of governor in 1901. By 1902 only Bathurst (Banjul) and its environs were governed as a Crown colony; the remainder of the territory, the protectorate, was administered through the existing traditional chiefdoms. Constitutional development, involving both the colony and the protectorate, gathered pace after the Second World War with the widening of the franchise and the formation of political parties. New constitutions were introduced in 1946, 1954 and 1959. In 1960 the legislative council was replaced by a house of representatives, and further constitutional changes in 1962 and 1963 brought full internal self-government. The Gambia became an independent state within the Commonwealth in February 1965 and a republic on 24 April 1970.

The Gambia's relationship with Senegal has always been an important factor in political and economic policy. In February 1982 the Senegambia Confederation was formally instituted based on certain joint institutions and integration of policies, but each country remained sovereign and independent.

For records before 1828 see the classes listed under Sierra Leone. See also under West Africa.

Gambia: Original Correspondence (CO 87) 1828 to 1951, 270 volumes

Gambia: Registers of Correspondence (CO 341) 1849 to 1949, 22 volumes

Gambia: Register of Out-letters (CO 481) 1872 to 1926, 8 volumes

Gambia: Entry Books (CO 401) 1827 to 1872, 16 volumes

Gambia: Acts (CO 88) 1843 to 1966, 18 volumes

Gambia: Sessional Papers (CO 89) 1843 to 1965, 46 volumes, files

Gambia: Government Gazettes (CO 460) 1883 to 1974, 46 volumes

Gambia: Miscellanea (CO 90) 1822 to 1945, 119 volumes

See also:

General Registers (CO 326) 1623 to 1849, 358 volumes

Index to Correspondence (CO 714) 1795 to 1874, 171 volumes

Colonies General: Supplementary Original Correspondence (CO 537) 1759 to 1955, 7862 volumes, files

Ghana see Gold Coast

Gold Coast (Ghana)

The Gold Coast was occupied from 1600 by the English, Danes, Dutch, Germans, and Portuguese, but by 1750 only British, Dutch, and Danish settlements remained. From 1664 the British settlements were under the control of the African Company and its successor, the Royal African Company, until the abolition of the latter in 1821, when the British government took them over. They were placed under the control of the government of Sierra Leone (qv) and from 1828 to 1843 their government was entrusted to a committee of London merchants. Sierra Leone then resumed control until 1850. The British Gold Coast possessions then became separate until they were again put under Sierra Leone in 1866. In 1874 the Gold Coast and Lagos (qv) became the Gold Coast Colony, but Lagos was separated in 1886. The last Danish and Dutch settlements were ceded to Britain in 1850 and 1871 respectively. In 1896 treaties of trade and protection were concluded with several tribes north of Ashanti and a protectorate over the area now known as the Northern Territories was established in 1898. Ashanti (qv) was annexed to the Gold Coast in

1901. In 1922 a part of the adjoining German territory of Togoland (qv) was placed under British administration by a League of Nations mandate and from that time was administered as part of the Gold Coast.

Nominated executive and legislative councils were first set up in 1850 under a governor. From 1866 to 1874 the governor was replaced by an administrator, the executive council was abolished and the legislative council reduced in size, but in 1874 the 1850 councils were re-established under a governor-in-chief. In 1925 the legislative council became partly elective. The next major advance was the Burns constitution of 1946 which established a legislative council, with a majority of African members, which represented Ashanti as well as the colony. Disturbances in the south in 1948 led to a court of enquiry (the Watson Commission) being set up to report on general conditions in the country. An all-African committee appointed as a result of the enquiry recommended several detailed constitutional changes which were generally accepted. Internal self-government was attained by 1954 and on 6 March 1957 the Gold Coast became an independent state within the Commonwealth under the name of Ghana. A republican constitution was adopted on 29 June 1960.

For original correspondence before 1843 see under Sierra Leone and West Africa.

Gold Coast: Original Correspondence (CO 96) 1753 to 1951, 830 volumes, files

Gold Coast: Register of Correspondence (CO 343) 1849 to 1951, 56 volumes

Gold Coast: Register of Out-letters (CO 482) 1872 to 1926, 22 volumes

Gold Coast: Entry Books (CO 402) 1843 to 1872, 13 volumes

High Commission and Consular Archives, Ghana (Gold Coast): Correspondence (DO 153) 1955 to 1958, 1 file

Gold Coast: Acts (CO 97) 1852 to 1957, 20 volumes

Gold Coast: Sessional Papers (CO 98) 1829 to 1956, 102 volumes

Ghana: Sessional Papers (DO 138) 1956 to 1965, 14 volumes

Gold Coast: Government Gazettes (CO 99) 1872 to 1957, 103 volumes

Ghana: Government Gazettes (DO 132) 1957 to 1975, 75 volumes

Gold Coast: Miscellanea (CO 100) 1845 to 1946, 96 volumes

Commission of inquiry into disturbances in the Gold Coast (Watson Commission, 1948) (CO 964) 1948, 32 files

See also:

General Registers (CO 326) 1623 to 1849, 358 volumes

Index to Correspondence (CO 714) 1795 to 1874, 171 volumes

Colonies General: Supplementary Original Correspondence (CO 537) 1759 to 1955, 7862 volumes, files

Gold Coast, Northern Territories

The territories north of Ashanti (qv) were formed into a separate district in 1896, recognized as a protectorate and placed under a commissioner. In 1901 the protectorate was put under the control of the government of the Gold Coast (qv) to be administered by a chief commissioner. The records form part of the Gold Coast correspondence.

From 1923 the northern section of the British sphere of Togoland (qv) was administered as part of the Northern Territories.

Gold Coast, Northern Territories: Acts (CO 849) 1920 to 1933, 1 volume

Lagos

A British consul was appointed to Lagos in 1852 and in 1861 Lagos was ceded to Britain by its king. In 1862 it became a colony with a governor and nominated executive and legislative councils. In 1866 it became part of the West African Settlements, subject to the governor-in-chief at Sierra Leone (qv), but with a lieutenant-governor and its own nominated legislative council. From 1874 to 1886 it was part of the Gold Coast Colony (qv) under an administrator until 1883 and then a lieutenant-governor, but retaining the legislative council. It became a separate crown colony again in 1886 with a governor and nominated executive and legislative councils. In the same year Lagos Protectorate was established out of other bordering territories. In 1906 the colony and protectorate amalgamated with the Protectorate of Southern Nigeria to form the Colony and Protectorate of Southern Nigeria (qv).

Lagos correspondence for 1883 to 1886 is registered in the Gold Coast registers (CO 343)

Lagos: Original Correspondence (CO 147) 1861 to 1906, 179 volumes

Lagos: Register of Correspondence (CO 421) 1861 to 1906, 10 volumes

Lagos: Register of Out-letters (CO 843) 1872 to 1906, 8 volumes

Lagos: Entry Books (CO 420) 1861 to 1901, 6 volumes

Lagos: Acts (CO 148) 1862 to 1905, 3 volumes

Lagos: Sessional Papers (CO 149) 1872 to 1906, 7 volumes

Lagos: Government Gazettes (CO 150) 1881 to 1906, 12 volumes

Lagos: Miscellanea (CO 151) 1862 to 1905, 43 volumes

Niger Coast Protectorate

Although the Nigerian coast had been visited by Europeans from 1472, British influence was paramount there from 1713. From 1849 British consuls, responsible to the Foreign Office, were appointed for the eastern part of the coast, a development which was formally recognized in 1872. The Oil Rivers Protectorate was established over that part of the coast in 1885, and in 1891 a commissioner and consul-general replaced the consul at Old Calabar. In 1893 the protectorate was extended and named the Niger Coast Protectorate. In 1899 responsibility was transferred from the Foreign Office to the Colonial Office, and in 1900 the protectorate was united with the southern portion of the territories of the Royal Niger Company to form the Protectorate of Southern Nigeria (qv).

The correspondence in CO 444 is registered in the Southern Nigeria Registers (CO 589). Readers should also refer to FO 2 and other Foreign Office classes which are described in the PRO handbook *The Records of the Foreign Office, 1782–1939*.

Niger Coast Protectorate: Original Correspondence (CO 444) 1899, 4 volumes

Niger Coast Protectorate: Miscellanea (CO 464) 1896 to 1900, 4 volumes

Nigeria

The Colony and Protectorate of Nigeria was formed in 1914 by the amalgamation of the Colony and Protectorate of Southern Nigeria (qv) with Northern Nigeria (qv). A nominated advisory Nigerian council was added to the executive council at Lagos (qv) under a governor. In 1922 the Nigerian council was replaced by a partly elective legislative council for Southern Nigeria, but the governor retained legislative powers for the north. In 1947 a partly elective legislative council was established for the whole of Nigeria and at the same time houses of assembly were set up in Eastern, Western and Northern Nigeria (qv) with a house of chiefs in the northern region and later also in the western region. This introduction of the principle of regionalization was developed in successive constitutions. In 1951 a new constitution established a council of ministers, with equal representation from the regions, and a house of representatives, whose members were elected by each regional house of assembly. The 1954 constitution gave increased responsibilities to Nigerian ministers at the centre but carried regionalization a step further by declaring Nigeria a federation. In August 1957 the first federal prime minister was appointed. On 1 October 1960 the Federation of Nigeria became an independent state within the Commonwealth, and on 1 October 1963 the Federal Republic of Nigeria was inaugurated.

Railways began to be constructed in the territories which were later to form Nigeria in 1896, and the railway departments of Southern and Northern Nigeria were united at the beginning of 1913.

After 1922 the British Cameroons (qv) were administered as part of Nigeria. They ceased to be part of Nigeria when Nigeria became independent in 1960. In a plebiscite held in February 1961, the Northern Cameroons voted to become part of Nigeria again and formally joined the federation on 1 June 1961. The Southern Cameroons opted to join the Republic of Cameroon of which they became part on 1 October 1961.

See also under West Africa, Niger Coast Protectorate, Protectorate of Southern Nigeria.

Nigeria: Original Correspondence (CO 583) 1912 to 1951, 318 volumes, files

Nigeria: Registers of Correspondence (CO 763) 1912 to 1951, 43 volumes

Nigeria: Registers of Out-letters (CO 764) 1912 to 1926, 8 volumes

Nigeria: Acts (CO 656) 1914 to 1960, 26 volumes

Nigeria: Sessional Papers (CO 657) 1912 to 1966, 157 volumes

Nigeria: Government Gazettes (CO 658) 1914 to 1976, 273 volumes

Nigeria: Miscellanea (CO 660) 1913 to 1945, 35 volumes

Nigeria Railway (CO 741) 1912 to 1922, 2 volumes

Nigeria: Customs and Trade Journal (CO 659) 1911 to 1916, 3 volumes

Commission on Minority Groups in Nigeria (Willink Commission) (CO 957) 1957 to 1958, 41 files

Nigeria: Council of Ministers: Papers (CO 1039) 1952 to 1959, 123 files

See also:

Colonies General: Supplementary Original Correspondence (CO 537) 1759 to 1955, 7862 volumes, files

Niger And West Africa Frontier Force see West Africa Frontier Force

Northern Nigeria

The Royal Niger Company gradually extended its administration into this area after 1886. Legislative power was vested in the governor and council of the company in London. In 1899 its charter was surrendered to the Crown, and in 1900 Northern Nigeria was proclaimed a protectorate under a high commissioner, in whom legislative authority was vested. In 1908 the high commissioner was replaced by a governor. In 1914 Northern Nigeria was amalgamated with Southern Nigeria (qv) to form the Colony and Protectorate of Nigeria (qv).

Northern Nigeria: Original Correspondence (CO 446) 1898 to 1913, 114 volumes

Northern Nigeria: Register of Correspondence (CO 584) 1898 to 1913, 7 volumes

Northern Nigeria: Register of Out-letters (CO 585) 1898 to 1913, 6 volumes

Northern Nigeria: Acts (CO 587) 1900 to 1913, 3 volumes

Northern Nigeria: Government Gazettes (CO 586) 1900 to 1913, 4 volumes

Northern Nigeria: Miscellanea (CO 465) 1900 to 1913, 14 volumes

Various Private Collections (CO 959) 1869 to 1955, 6 pieces

Protectorate of Southern Nigeria see Southern Nigeria

Senegambia see Gambia

Sierra Leone

A British trading station was established on the coast of Sierra Leone in 1672. In 1788 part of the Sierra Leone was sold and ceded to newly-arrived British settlers, and additional territory was ceded to the colony from time to time by local chiefs. From 1791 Sierra Leone was colonized by the Sierra Leone Company, which also administered it until 1808, when it became a colony. From 1821 until 1843 Gambia (qv), and from 1821 until 1850 the Gold Coast (qv), were under the administration of Sierra Leone. In 1866 the government of the West Afrcan Settlements was re-established, the governor of Sierra Leone becoming governor-in-chief of Sierra Leone, Gambia, the Gold Coast and Lagos with headquarters in Sierra Leone; each territory retained its own legislative council. In 1874 Lagos (qv) and the Gold Coast were separated, as was Gambia in 1888, leaving Sierra Leone a single colony again. In 1896 the hinterland was declared a protectorate.

From 1792 Sierra Leone had a governor and a nominated advisory council, as well as a constitution, which was retained in 1808. In 1853 separate executive and legislative councils were established, and in 1924 the legislative council was made partly elective. In 1951 the number of elected members in the legislative council was increased. In 1953 a ministerial system was introduced and the title of chief minister accorded to the leader of the majority party in the council. Under a new constitution which came into force in 1956, the legislative council became the house of representatives and was enlarged. The constitution was altered in 1958 by the exclusion of all ex officio members from the executive council and the house of representatives, and the chief minister was appointed prime minister. On 27 April 1961 Sierra Leone became a fully independent member state of the Commonwealth and on 19 April 1971 assumed the status of a republic.

The original correspondence of Sierra Leone includes Fernando Po (qv) before 1828 and after 1842; Goree, Cape Coast Castle, and Gambia (qv) before 1828; and the Gold Coast (qv) before 1843. Original correspondence with the Sierra Leone Company, 1800 to 1807, is in the War Office class WO 1, In-letters.

See also under West Africa.

Sierra Leone: Original Correspondence (CO 267) 1664 to 1951, 702 volumes, files

Sierra Leone: Register of Correspondence (CO 368) 1849 to 1951, 42 volumes

Sierra Leone: Register of Out-letters (CO 484) 1872 to 1926, 13 volumes

Sierra Leone: Entry Books (CO 268) 1672 to 1872, 57 volumes

Sierra Leone: Acts (CO 269) 1801 to 1961, 21 volumes

Sierra Leone: Sessional Papers (CO 270) 1776 to 1965, 104 volumes

Sierra Leone: Government Gazettes (CO 271) 1817 to 1975, 114 volumes

Sierra Leone: Board of Education (CO 672) 1899 to 1900, 1 volume

Sierra Leone: Miscellanea (CO 272) 1819 to 1943, 120 volumes

See also:

General Registers (CO 326) 1623 to 1849, 358 volumes

Index to Correspondence (CO 714) 1795 to 1874, 171 volumes

Colonies General: Supplementary Original Correspondence (CO 537) 1759 to 1955, 7862 volumes, files

Southern Nigeria

In 1886 the Royal Niger Company was established and was empowered to administer the Niger delta area; thereafter it gradually extended its jurisdiction northwards. In 1899 its charter was surrendered to the Crown and in 1900 the southern portion of its territories was united with the Niger Coast Protectorate (qv) to form the Protectorate of Southern Nigeria under a high commissioner. In 1906 this territory was combined with Lagos (qv) to form the Colony and Protectorate of Southern Nigeria under a governor, an executive council, and a nominated legislative council. In 1914 it was amalgamated with Northern Nigeria (qv) to form the Colony and Protectorate of Nigeria (qv).

Southern Nigeria Protectorate: Original Correspondence (CO 520) 1900 to 1913, 131 volumes

Southern Nigeria Protectorate: Register of Correspondence (CO 589) 1899 to 1913, 8 volumes

Southern Nigeria Protectorate: Register of Out-letters (CO 590) 1899 to 1913, 6 volumes

Southern Nigeria Protectorate: Acts (CO 588) 1900 to 1913, 4 volumes

Southern Nigeria Protectorate: Sessional Papers (CO 592) 1906 to 1913, 16 volumes

Southern Nigeria Protectorate: Government Gazettes (CO 591) 1900 to 1913, 12 volumes

Southern Nigeria Protectorate: Miscellanea (CO 473) 1900 to 1913, 16 volumes

The Gambia see Gambia

Togoland

Togoland was generally regarded as being under British suzerainty until 1885 and 1886 when the British and the French formally recognized German influence. After capture by British colonial and French troops in 1914, the territory was divided provisionally into British and French spheres. In 1922 the council of the League of Nations confirmed its approval of this arrangement and both parts became mandated territories. From 1923 the northern section of the British sphere was administered as part of the Northern Territories of the Gold Coast (qv) and the southern section as part of the Eastern Province of the Gold Coast Colony (qv). The governor of the Gold Coast Colony was empowered to legislate for both sections of the British sphere.

Togoland: Original Correspondence (CO 724) 1920 to 1926, 4 volumes

Togoland: Register of Correspondence (CO 803) 1920 to 1926, 1 volume

Togoland: Register of Out-letters (CO 804) 1920 to 1926, 1 volume

After 1926 see Gold Coast correspondence classes

West Africa Frontier Force

The Niger and West Africa Frontier Force, known from 1900 as the West Africa Frontier Force and from 1918 as the Royal West Africa Frontier Force, was raised locally in 1897 to protect the frontiers of the British protectorates in West Africa in the face of French aggression. It was paid by the imperial government, and officered by the British Army. From 1927 the administration of the unit was brought together with that of the King's African Rifles to form the Military Branch of the Colonial Office. Their papers were then registered and kept together.

Niger and West Africa Frontier Force: Original Correspondence (CO 445) 1898 to 1926, 69 volumes

Niger and West Africa Frontier Force: Register of Correspondence (CO 581) 1898 to 1899, 1 volume

West Africa Frontier Force: Register of Correspondence (CO 641) 1900 to 1926, 10 volumes

Niger and West Africa Frontier Force: Register of Out-letters (CO 582) 1898 to 1899, 1 volume

West Africa Frontier Force: Register of Out-letters (CO 642) 1900 to 1926, 10 volumes

See also:

Military: Original Correspondence (CO 820) 1927 to 1951, 77 volumes and files

Military: Register of Correspondence (CO 871) 1927 to 1952, 25 volumes

Accounts Branch: Miscellanea (CO 701) 1794 to 1913, 28 volumes

Colonies General: Supplementary Original Correspondence (CO 537) 1759 to 1955, 7862 volumes, files

ASIA

Far East/South-East Asia

The earliest correspondence for the region is in CO 77, East Indies Original Correspondence, 1570 to 1856. The other records listed here relate largely to the South-East Asia territories generally or to more than one territory. In certain periods they also cover Hong Kong, Ceylon, Wei-Hai-Wei, Mauritius, Seychelles, Fiji, and the Western Pacific High Commission territories. From 1951 the territorial classes disappear and CO 1022 and CO 1030 become the main correspondence classes for the whole region.

The appointment in December 1941 of a minister of state for the Far East with headquarters at Singapore lasted only until the fall of Singapore in January 1942.

After the Second World War, policy in South-East Asia included the appointment, in May 1946, of a governor-general, Malcolm MacDonald, who was responsible for co-ordinating policy and administering an area which included the Malayan Union (qv), Singapore (qv), and Brunei (qv), and which, on the conclusion of negotiations with the rajah of Sarawak and the British North Borneo Company, was extended to the new colonies of Sarawak (qv) and North Borneo (qv). The governor-general had co-ordinating, but no direct administrative, functions, and power to convene conferences of governors. In respect of Brunei he acted as the channel of communication between the secretary of state and the resident. In defence matters, he was chairman of the British Defence Co-ordination Committee, Far East, on which sat the commanders-in-chief of the services and the special commissioner (see below). On this committee the governor-general represented the interests of the territories in his area of authority and of Hong Kong.

In 1946 a special commissioner, Lord Killearn, under the secretary of state for foreign affairs, assumed responsibility for advising the UK government on general problems affecting the conduct of foreign affairs in a region including Burma, Siam, Indo-China, and the Netherlands East Indies. He had the special duty of improving the production and distribution of food supplies in the area.

The two posts were combined in May 1948 and Malcolm MacDonald became the commissioner-general for the United Kingdom in South-East Asia, with headquarters in Singapore. He had the same responsibilities towards the Federation of Malaya and the colonies of Singapore, Sarawak and North Borneo as he had as governor-general. His direct administrative responsibilities towards Brunei lapsed when, in May 1948, the governor of Sarawak was appointed high commissioner for Brunei; his other responsibilities in respect of Brunei continued. MacDonald was responsible to the secretary of state for foreign affairs for duties previously performed by the special commissioner.

The commissioner-general's organization consisted of a colonial side, headed by an assistant commissioner-general (colonial affairs) and a foreign side, headed by a deputy commissioner-general (foreign affairs). He was also assisted by an economic adviser. The staff on the colonial side were seconded from the colonial service and were paid for by the Malayan and Borneo governments, which also contributed towards the cost of services shared by the colonial and foreign sides of the organization.

After MacDonald was succeeded in September 1955 by Sir Robert Scott, the commissioner-general's organization was recognized as a United Kingdom office and was staffed in the main by United Kingdom-based officers and paid for by UK funds. Officers seconded from the Malayan or Borneo governments were, however, paid by those governments. The commissioner-general was now officially responsible to the prime minister in carrying out duties previously performed by the special commissioner, and not, as before, to the secretary of state for foreign affairs, although in practice he still reported to the Foreign Office. The commissioner-general's direct responsibilities declined during the 1950s but he continued to advise the government on British South-East Asian policy.

The commissioner-general's files from at least 1950 have been transferred to the Public Record Office and are in the Foreign Office class Registered Files: Commissioner-General for South-East Asia (FO 1091).

East Indies: Original Correspondence, Entry Books, etc (CO 77) 1570 to 1856, 66 volumes

Eastern: Original Correspondence (CO 825) 1927 to 1951, 90 files

Eastern: Register of Correspondence (CO 872) 1927 to 1951, 12 volumes

South-East Asia Department: Original Correspondence (CO 1022) 1950 to 1956, 494 files

Far East Department: Original Correspondence (CO 1030) 1948 to 1967, 906 files

Far Eastern Reconstruction: Original Correspondence (CO 865) 1942 to 1945, 86 files

Far Eastern Reconstruction: Registers of Correspondence (CO 975) 1942 to 1944, 1 volume

Far Eastern Economic and Supplies Committee: Minutes and Papers (CO 1008) 1944 to 1945, 2 folders

Confidential Print: Eastern (CO 882) 1847 to 1952, 32 volumes

See also:

Colonies General: Supplementary Original Correspondence (CO 537) 1759 to 1955, 7862 volumes, files

British Malaya
By British Malaya is meant the area comprising the settlements of Singapore (qv), Penang (qv), Labuan (qv), Christmas Island and the Dindings (see Straits Settlements), the Federated Malay States and the states of Johore (qv), Kedah and Perlis (qv), Kelantan (qv) and Trengganu (qv). The records in class CO 740 are the annual returns of imports and exports.

British Malaya: Miscellanea (CO 740) 1921 to 1937, 15 volumes

Brunei
The Sultanate of Brunei included Sarawak (qv), Labuan (qv) and North Borneo (qv) until their cession to Britain. Brunei itself was placed under British protection by the sultan by a treaty of 1888. From 1906 the sultan acted on the advice of a British resident, who represented the British government under the governor of the Straits Settlements (qv), and a nominated advisory council. Brunei was occupied by the Japanese from 1941 to 1945. From 1946 the governor-general for South-East Asia acted as the channel of communication between the secretary of state and the resident. These responsibilities lapsed in 1948 when the governor of Sarawak was

appointed high commissioner for Brunei, a post which continued until 1959. Under a new agreement signed in 1959 with the sultan, the British government continued to be responsible for the defence and external affairs of the state. The agreement provided for administrative separation from Sarawak and the appointment of a high commissioner, resident in Brunei. In 1963 Brunei rejected the option open to the state to join the other Borneo territories in the new federation of Malaysia (qv). In 1971 under an amending agreement to the 1959 agreement, Brunei ceased to be a protected state though the external affairs of the state rested with Britain and consultation over defence matters was agreed. The sultan and the British government signed a new treaty on 7 January 1979 under which Brunei became a fully sovereign independent state at the end of 1983.

See also under Far East/South-East Asia.

Brunei: Original Correspondence (CO 943) 1946 to 1951, 2 boxes, files

Brunei: Sessional Papers (CO 824) 1906 to 1965, 6 volumes

Brunei: Government Gazettes (CO 985) 1951 to 1975, 25 volumes

See also:

Federated Malay States: Original Correspondence (CO 717) 1920 to 1951, 210 volumes, files

Borneo Territories: Original Correspondence (CO 954) 1946 to 1951, 8 boxes of files

North Borneo, Brunei and Sarawak: Registers of Correspondence (CO 992) 1942 to 1951, 6 volumes

Colonies General: Supplementary Original Correspondence (CO 537) 1759 to 1955, 7862 volumes, files

Ceylon (Sri Lanka)

Great Britain took possession of Dutch settlements in Ceylon in 1796 and annexed them to the presidency of Madras. In 1802 Ceylon became a separate colony. In 1815 the Kandyan kingdom of the interior was overcome and the whole island came under British rule. A governor was first appointed in 1798 and a council of government was set up in 1801. This was replaced in 1833 by an executive council and a nominated legislative council. The latter became partly elective in 1910. In 1931 a new constitution was established providing for a mainly elective state council with legislative powers and seven executive committees composed of groups of the elected members of the legislature.

Following a declaration made by the British government in 1943 on the grant of responsible government after the war, a new constitution based on the recommendations of the commission was approved in May 1946. After further constitutional discussions Ceylon became a fully self-governing member of the Commonwealth on 4 February 1948. On 22 May 1972 Ceylon adopted a new constitution as the Republic of Sri Lanka within the Commonwealth.

From 1887 until 1948 Ceylon included the British protected state of Maldive Islands, the British representative being the governor of Ceylon. The Maldive Islands remained a British protected state until 26 July 1965 when they became fully independent as the Republic of Maldives.

After the end of the Napoleonic Wars the British government appointed several commissions of inquiry to the colonies especially to those territories recently acquired. The so-called Commissioners of Eastern Inquiry visited Ceylon between 1828 and 1830 and the records of the commissioners are held in CO 416 and in CO 54/111. The records also include some fifty volumes of the domestic records of the government of Ceylon from 1800 to 1805 which were sent to London (CO 55/11–60).

See also under Far East/South-East Asia and WESTERN PACIFIC.

Ceylon: Original Correspondence (CO 54) 1798 to 1949, 1004 volumes

Ceylon: Register of Correspondence (CO 337) 1849 to 1948, 46 volumes

Ceylon: Register of Out-letters (CO 488) 1872 to 1926, 17 volumes

Ceylon: Entry Books (CO 55) 1794 to 1872, 121 volumes

Ceylon: Acts (CO 56) 1835 to 1947, 24 volumes

Ceylon: Sessional Papers (CO 57) 1831 to 1946, 283 volumes

Ceylon: Sessional Papers (DO 109) 1947 to 1965, 121 volumes

Ceylon: Government Gazettes (CO 58) 1813 to 1946, 314 volumes

Ceylon and Sri Lanka: Government Gazettes (DO 104) 1947 to 1975, 230 volumes

Ceylon: Miscellanea (CO 59) 1795 to 1945, 161 volumes

Ceylon: Miscellanea (DO 111) 1946 to 1949, 1 volume

Commissioners of Eastern Inquiry, Ceylon (CO 416) 1829 to 1830, 32 volumes

Special Commission on the Constitution of Ceylon (CO 1041)

See also:

General Registers (CO 326) 1623 to 1849, 358 volumes

Index to Correspondence (CO 714) 1795 to 1874, 171 volumes

Colonies General: Supplementary Original Correspondence (CO 537) 1759 to 1955, 7862 volumes, files

Christmas Island see Straits Settlements

Cocos Islands see Straits Settlements

Federated Malay States
In 1895 a treaty of federation was signed by the rulers of the four states of Negri Sembilan (qv), Pahang (qv), Perak (qv) and Selangor (qv). The federation was at first executive and judicial only, under a resident-general responsible to the high

commissioner for the Federated States, a post held by the governor of the Straits Settlements (qv). In 1909 a nominated federal council was set up for legislative purposes. In 1911 the resident-general's title was changed to chief secretary to the government. From 1942 to 1945 the states were under Japanese occupation. After the British military administration of 1945 to 1946 (see WO 203) the federation was not revived and in 1946 all four states joined the short-lived Malayan Union (qv) and in 1948 the new Federation of Malaya (qv).

As the high commissioner of the Federated Malay States was the channel of communication with the Colonial Office there are no separate classes of original correspondence for the individual states, although there are classes of printed documents. Until 1920 correspondence for the federated states is found under Straits Settlements, but thereafter is in a separate class (CO 717) which also includes correspondence relating to the unfederated Malay states, the Malayan Union and the Federation of Malaya.

See also under individual states and Far East/South-East Asia.

Federated Malay States: Original Correspondence (CO 717) 1920 to 1951, 210 volumes, files

Federated Malay States: Register of Correspondence (CO 786) 1919 to 1951, 19 volumes

Federated Malay States: Register of Out-letters (CO 787) 1920 to 1926, 3 volumes

Federated Malay States: Acts (CO 828) 1925 to 1948, 5 volumes

Federated Malay States: Sessional Papers (CO 576) 1896 to 1948, 79 volumes

Federated Malay States: Government Gazettes (CO 574) 1909 to 1948, 96 volumes

Federated Malay States: Miscellanea (CO 575) 1904 to 1949, 38 volumes

Federation of Malaya

Under the Federation of Malaya Agreement, 1948, between the British Crown and the rulers of nine Malay states the Federation of Malaya was constituted on 1 February 1948. It comprised the Malay states of Johore (qv), Pahang (qv), Negri Sembilan (qv), Selangor (qv), Perak (qv), Kedah and Perlis (qv), Kelantan (qv) and Trengganu (qv) and the two British settlements of Penang (qv) and Malacca (qv).

The agreement was from time to time amended providing for an executive council presided over by the high commissioner and a legislative council with a majority of elected members. Because of an outbreak of communist terrorism in 1948, the first federal elections based on universal adult suffrage were not held until 1955. Elections were also held in each state and settlement for the state and settlement councils. A new constitution based on the recommendations of an independent constitutional commission was adopted at a conference held in London in May 1957, and the Federation of Malaya (qv) became an independent member of the Commonwealth on 31 August 1957. In 1963 the federation joined Malaysia (qv), the new grouping of states in the region.

See also under Federated Malay States, Malayan Union and Far East/South-East Asia.

Federation of Malaya: Acts (CO 923) 1948 to 1957, 9 volumes

Federation of Malaya: Sessional Papers (CO 941) 1946 to 1965, 87 volumes, files

Federation of Malaya (Malaysia): Government Gazettes (CO 930) 1948 to 1980, 181 volumes

Federation of Malaya Constitutional Commission (1956) (CO 889) 1956, 9 volumes, etc

Hong Kong

Hong Kong became a British colony in 1841 and was formally ceded by China in 1842. The Kowloon peninsula was ceded to Britain in 1860 and the New Territories were leased to her for ninety-nine years in 1898. From 1941 to 1945 Hong Kong was occupied by the Japanese.

In 1843 Hong Kong was given its charter as a Crown colony with administration by a governor assisted by an executive council and a legislative council with official and unofficial members. A partially elective urban council was added in 1935. Unofficial majorities were created in the executive council by 1966 and in the legislative council by 1976.

In a joint declaration initialled in December 1984 and ratified in May 1985, Great Britain and China agreed to restore sovereignty over Hong Kong to China on 1 July 1997. Thereafter a special administrative region (SAR) will be established under the direct authority of the Chinese central government. However, the social and economic systems in the SAR will remain unchanged for 50 years.

See also under Far East/South-East Asia.

Hong Kong: Original Correspondence (CO 129) 1841 to 1951, 629 volumes, files

Hong Kong: Register of Correspondence (CO 349) 1849 to 1952, 43 volumes

Hong Kong: Register of Out-letters (CO 489) 1872 to 1926, 15 volumes

Hong Kong: Entry Books (CO 403) 1843 to 1872, 21 volumes

Hong Kong: Acts (CO 130) 1844 to 1965, 24 volumes

Hong Kong: Sessional Papers (CO 131) 1844 to 1966, 178 volumes, files

Hong Kong: Government Gazettes (CO 132) 1846 to 1990, 714 volumes

Hong Kong: Miscellanea (CO 133) 1844 to 1940, 111 volumes

See also:

General Registers (CO 326) 1623 to 1849, 358 volumes

Index to Correspondence (CO 714) 1795 to 1874, 171 volumes

Colonies General: Supplementary Original Correspondence (CO 537) 1759 to 1955, 7862 volumes, files

Hong Kong and Pacific Department: Original Correspondence (CO 1023) 1946 to 1955, 242 files

India

The records of the British administration in India are held separately in the Oriental and India Office Collections, a division of the British Library.

India: Registered Files (DO 142)

India: Sessional Papers (DO 148) 1960 to 1965, 22 volumes

India: Government Gazettes (DO 105) 1948 to 1979, 469 volumes

High Commission and Consular Archives, India: Correspondence (DO 133) 1946 to 1954, 147 files

India: Miscellanea (DO 112) 1946 to 1950, 5 volumes

India Office Library (DO 144)

Indian Records Section: Registered Files (R Series) (DO 184) 1936 to 1966, 31 files

Jelebu see Negri Sembilan

Johore

Johore became a British protected state in 1885 and agreed to receive a British agent, with consular functions, in 1895. A written constitution was introduced that year which provided for a council of ministers (Malay), an executive council of Malay and British officials, and a legislative council of state with nominated members. A British adviser was appointed in 1910 and a British general adviser in 1914. The advisers were responsible to the governor of the Straits Settlements (qv) under which head correspondence concerning Johore will be found.

Between 1941 and 1945 Johore was occupied by the Japanese and from 1945 to 1946 was under British military administration. Relevant material for this period is in the War Office record class WO 203. In 1946 Johore with the other Malay States joined the Malayan Union which, however, was soon abandoned. In its place the Federation of Malaya (qv) was created in 1948 consisting of the same territories as the Malayan Union. In 1963 the federation, independent since 1957, joined with other territories in the region to form Malaysia (qv).

See also Unfederated Malay States.

Johore: Sessional Papers (CO 715) 1910 to 1940, 6 volumes

Johore: Government Gazettes (CO 653) 1911 to 1979, 66 volumes

Kedah and Perlis

Kedah was under Portuguese rule from 1654 until 1711. Penang, to the south of Kedah State, was brought under British East India Company rule in 1786 and Province Wellesley in 1800. In 1821 the Siamese took possession of Kedah, but in 1843 they allowed its sultan to resume government. A Siamese adviser was sent to Kedah in 1905, but he was replaced by a British adviser in 1909 when Kedah became a British protected state.

Perlis was subject to Kedah until the Siamese occupation of 1821. It became an independant state under a rajah in 1841. In 1909 it became a British protected state and a British adviser replaced the Siamese adviser.

After 1909 the sultan of Kedah and the rajah of Perlis were both assisted by nominated state councils, including the British advisers. Both states were under Japanese occupation from 1942 to 1945, and under British military administration from 1945 to 1946 when they joined the Malayan Union. Kedah and Perlis became part of the Federation of Malaya (qv) in 1948, which in turn merged with other independent territories in 1963 to form Malaysia (qv).

For correspondence relating to both states see under Straits Settlements. See also Unfederated Malay States.

Kedah and Perlis: Sessional Papers (CO 716) 1905 to 1940, 4 volumes

Kedah and Perlis: Government Gazettes (CO 819) 1925 to 1979, 38 volumes

Perlis: Government Gazettes (CO 931) 1948 to 1977, 10 volumes

Keeling Islands see Straits Settlements

Kelantan

Formerly under Siamese suzerainty, Kelantan received a British adviser in 1903 by agreement with Siam. In 1909 it formally became a British protected state, and an advisory state council was established. It was under Japanese occupation from 1942 to 1945 and British military administration from 1945 to 1946, when it joined the Malayan Union. For subsequent developments and for other relevant records see as in Johore above.

See also Unfederated Malay States.

Kelantan: Sessional Papers (CO 827) 1909 to 1940, 2 volumes

Kelantan: Government Gazettes (CO 928) 1948 to 1979, 21 volumes

Labuan

Labuan was ceded to Britain in 1846 by the sultan of Brunei (qv). It was given a nominated legislative council under a governor in 1848 and was a separate colony until 1890, when administration was entrusted to the British North Borneo Company. Its Borneo representative became governor of Labuan with legislative powers, and the legislative council was abolished. In 1906 the governor of the Straits Settlements was appointed governor of Labuan, which was annexed to the Straits Settlements (qv) in 1907 as part of Singapore. It was constituted as a separate settlement in 1912. It was under Japanese occupation during WWII until their surrender in 1945 and in 1946 it was united with North Borneo (qv).

The Labuan registers of correspondence (CO 352) and registers of out-letters (CO 487) also cover British North Borneo correspondence to 1914.

Labuan: Original Correspondence (CO 144) 1844 to 1906, 81 volumes

Labuan: Register of Correspondence (CO 352) 1849 to 1914, 7 volumes

Labuan: Register of Out-letters (CO 487) 1871 to 1914, 4 volumes

Labuan: Entry Books (CO 404) 1847 to 1872, 5 volumes

Labuan: Acts (CO 145) 1849 to 1906, 9 volumes

Labuan: Sessional Papers (CO 434) 1849 to 1889, 1 volume

Labuan: Government Gazettes (CO 573) 1890 to 1906, 1 volume

Labuan: Miscellanea (CO 146) 1848 to 1906, 60 volumes

See also:

Index to Correspondence (CO 714) 1795 to 1874, 171 volumes

Malacca (Melaka)
Occupied by the Portuguese from 1511 and then by the Dutch from 1641, Malacca was ceded to Britain in 1824. It became part of the Straits Settlements (qv) in 1826. When the Straits Settlements administration was dissolved in 1946 Malacca was incorporated in the short-lived Malayan Union and then in the Federation of Malaya (qv) in 1948.

Malacca: Sessional Papers (CO 944) 1946 to 1950, 2 volumes

Malacca: Government Gazettes (CO 929) 1948 to 1979, 18 volumes

Malayan Union
In January 1946 the British government set out proposals in a white paper for a Malayan Union which would unite Malaya, including the four Federated Malay States, the five unfederated Malay states and the settlements of Penang and Malacca, but excluding Singapore, Labuan, Christmas Island and the Cocos (Keeling) Islands, under a governor with a strong unitary government. Because of strong opposition throughout the country the Malayan Union, established on 1 April 1946, was soon abandoned. In its place the Federation of Malaya (qv), consisting of the same territories as the Malayan Union, was established on 1 February 1948.

Correspondence will be found in the original correspondence classes relating to the Federated Malay States (CO 717) and Singapore (CO 953). See also under Far East/South-East Asia.

Malayan Union and Singapore: Registers of Correspondence (CO 991) 1946 to 1951, 8 volumes

Malaysia
The idea of political association between the Federation of Malaya (qv), Singapore (qv) and the British territories in Borneo (the colonies of North Borneo (qv) and

Sarawak (qv) and the Protected State of Brunei (qv)) had been mooted for some years. Following talks in London in 1961 between the British and Malayan prime ministers, a joint Anglo-Malayan Commission, under the chairmanship of Lord Cobbold, was set up to ascertain the wishes of the people of North Borneo and Sarawak, to seek the views of the Sultan of Brunei, and to make recommendations. The commission's report concluded that a substantial majority of people in both territories were in principle in favour of the creation of Malaysia. The necessary detailed constitutional arrangements were then set in hand. It did not prove possible for the Malayan and Brunei governments to reach agreement over the accession of Brunei to Malaysia. In London on 9 July 1963, Britain, the Federation of Malaya (qv), North Borneo, Sarawak and Singapore signed the Malaysia Agreement. In accordance with the agreement, Britain relinquished sovereignty over the colonies of North Borneo and Sarawak and the state of Singapore. These territories then joined the existing states of the Federation of Malaya as the states of Sabah, Sarawak and Singapore to form the federation thereafter called Malaysia, which came into being on 16 September 1963. Malaysia automatically became a member of the Commonwealth. On 9 August 1965 Singapore separated from Malaysia and became an independent sovereign state within the Commonwealth.

Correspondence relating to the setting up of the federation will be found in the correspondence classes of the Federated Malay States (CO 717) and Singapore (CO 953). See also under Malayan Union and Far East/South-East Asia.

Commission of Enquiry in North Borneo and Sarawak Regarding Malaysian Federation (Cobbold Commission, 1962) (CO 947) 1962, 61 pieces

Maldive Islands see under Ceylon

Negri Sembilan, Sungei Ujong and Jelebu

Negri Sembilan, the 'Nine States', was formerly part of the kingdom of Malacca (qv). A confederation known as 'the old Negri Sembilan', which did not include Sungei Ujong and Jelebu, was established in 1889 and received a British resident. Sungei Ujong and Jelebu had received British residents in 1874 and 1883 respectively. They both joined the modern Negri Sembilan which was constituted in 1895 and had a single resident. In the same year this new federation was included in the Federated Malay States (qv). In 1898 the Negri Sembilan federation was made a unitary state and supreme authority was vested in the yam tuan of Sri Menati who presided over the state council. The state was under Japanese occupation from 1942 to 1945. After the British military administration of 1945 to 1946 it joined the Malayan Union (qv) in 1946 and the Federation of Malaya (qv) in 1948 as a separate state.

See also under Sungei Ujong and Federated Malay States.

Negri Sembilan, Sungei Ujong and Jelebu: Sessional Papers (CO 435) 1888 to 1929, 4 volumes

Negri Sembilan, Sungei Ujong and Jelebu: Government Gazettes (CO 463) 1896 to 1980, 26 volumes

North Borneo (Sabah)

British North Borneo was part of the Sultanate of Brunei until ceded to a British syndicate in 1878. In 1882 the British North Borneo Company assumed charge of the territory under a charter of 1881 and continued to govern it until it fell to the Japanese in 1942. When liberated in 1945 it was placed under military administration. Under the company, North Borneo was administered by a governor and civil service appointed by the Court of Directors in London; from 1883 there was a nominated advisory council, superseded in 1912 by a nominated legislative council. In 1946 North Borneo became a Crown colony, to which Labuan was joined, under a governor with an advisory council. During the post-war period matters common to North Borneo, Sarawak (qv) and Brunei (qv) were dealt with by the UK commissioner for South-East Asia, appointed to ensure co-ordination of policy in the area under British control. These records are in CO 954 and CO 992. The British North Borneo Company, the last of the chartered companies to administer British territory, wound up its affairs in 1952 and transferred its surviving records to the Public Record Office (see below).

Following the findings of the Cobbold Commission (CO 947) into the possible political association with Malaya, the colony of North Borneo became the state of Sabah in July 1963 on joining Sarawak, and Singapore (qv) and the Federation of Malaya to form the independent federation thereafter called Malaysia (qv).

For other records before 1907 see under Labuan. Borneo original correspondence for 1907 to 1914 is registered under Labuan (CO 532) as are the out-letters (CO 487). See also under Far East/South-East Asia.

British North Borneo: Original Correspondence (CO 531) 1907 to 1951, 50 volumes

British North Borneo: Register of Correspondence (CO 777) 1915 to 1941, 4 volumes

British North Borneo: Register of Out-letters (CO 778) 1915 to 1926, 1 volume

British North Borneo: Acts (CO 986) 1951 to 1963, 6 volumes

British North Borneo (Sabah): Sessional Papers (CO 648) 1908 to 1965, 43 volumes, files

British North Borneo and Sabah: Government Gazettes (CO 855) 1883 to 1980, 108 volumes

British North Borneo: Miscellanea (CO 966) 1907 to 1941, 1 volume

See also:

Borneo Territories: Original Correspondence (CO 954) 1946 to 1951, 8 boxes of files

North Borneo, Brunei and Sarawak: Register of Correspondence (CO 992) 1942 to 1951, 6 volumes

British North Borneo Company Papers (CO 874) 1865 to 1952, 1114 files, volumes

Commission of Enquiry in North Borneo and Sarawak Regarding Malaysian Federation (Cobbold Commission, 1962) (CO 947) 1962, 61 pieces

Colonies General: Supplementary Original Correspondence (CO 537) 1759 to 1955, 7862 volumes, files

Pahang

Once a vassal state of Malacca (qv) and then part of the Johore (qv) sultanate, Pahang was recognized as independent in 1882. In 1888 it came under British protection and received a British resident. In 1895 it was included in the Federated Malay States (qv). It was under Japanese occupation from 1942 to 1945. After the British military occupation of 1945 to 1946 it joined the Malayan Union (qv) in 1946 and the Federation of Malaya (qv) in 1948 as a separate state.

While Pahang was one of the Federated States, supreme authority was vested in the sultan, who presided over the state council.

See also Federated Malay States.

Pahang: Sessional Papers (CO 437) 1888 to 1939, 5 volumes

Pahang: Government Gazettes (CO 466) 1897 to 1977, 25 volumes

Pakistan

The records of the British administration in India are held separately in the Oriental and India Office Collections, a division of the British Library.

Pakistan: Government Gazettes (DO 106) 1948 to 1972, 107 volumes

High Commission and Consular Archives Pakistan: Correspondence (DO 134) 1948 to 1958, 26 files

Pakistan: Sessional Papers (DO 149) 1961 to 1965, 3 volumes

Penang

Penang consists of the island of Penang and Province Wellesley on the mainland of Peninsula Malaysia. It was one of the Straits Settlements (qv) which were incorporated in the Federation of Malaya (qv), formed in 1948, which became part of Malaysia (qv) in 1963.

Penang: Government Gazettes (CO 933) 1948 to 1977, 27 volumes

Perak

Perak was placed under British protection and received a British resident in 1874. In 1895 it was included in the Federated Malay States (qv). It was under Japanese occupation from 1942 to 1945. After the British military occupation of 1945 to 1946 it joined the Malayan Union (qv) in 1946 as a separate state.

While Perak was one of the Federated States, supreme authority was vested in the sultan, who presided over the state council.

See also Federated Malay States.

Perak: Sessional Papers (CO 438) 1888 to 1939, 5 volumes

Perak: Government Gazettes (CO 467) 1888 to 1980, 56 volumes

Perlis
For details see under Kedah and Perlis.

Kedah and Perlis: Sessional Papers (CO 716) 1905 to 1940, 4 volumes

Perlis: Government Gazettes (CO 931) 1948 to 1977, 10 volumes

Sabah (North Borneo) see under North Borneo

Sarawak
Sarawak was a province of the Sultanate of Brunei (qv) until 1839, when James Brooke put down a revolt and in return was made rajah in 1841. It was recognized as an independent state by Britain in 1864 and was granted British protection in 1888. It was under Japanese occupation from 1941 until 1945 and became a British colony in 1946.

In 1855 the rajah established two nominated representative councils – the supreme council, for legislative and administrative purposes, and an advisory general council. A new constitution in 1941 substituted two new nominated councils – the executive supreme council and the legislative council. After British military administration in 1945 to 1946 (see WO 203) and the cession of Sarawak to the Crown, a new constitution in 1946 restored the two councils as in 1941 but under a governor instead of a rajah. During the post-war period matters common to Sarawak, Brunei and North Borneo (qv) were dealt with by the UK commissioner for South-East Asia appointed to ensure co-ordination of policy in the area under British control. These records are in CO 954 and CO 992. See under Far East/South-East Asia.

A new constitution came into force in 1957 which provided for an elected majority in the legislature and for half the members of the supreme council to be elected. Further constitutional changes in 1962 and 1963 gave a large measure of self-government. Following the findings of the Cobbold Commission into possible political association, Sarawak and North Borneo (Sabah) joined Singapore (qv) and the Federation of Malaya (qv) on 16 September 1963 to form the independent federation thereafter called Malaysia (qv). A Malaysia Act, providing for the relinquishment of sovereignty, was passed by the British parliament in July 1963.

For other records before 1946 see classes listed under British North Borneo.

Sarawak: Original Correspondence (CO 938) 1946 to 1951, 12 files

Sarawak: Acts (CO 1020) 1958 to 1963, 4 volumes

Sarawak: Sessional Papers (CO 802) 1900 to 1965, 24 volumes

Sarawak: Government Gazettes (CO 604) 1903 to 1980, 115 volumes

The Rajah of Sarawak Fund: Papers (CO 1040)

See also:

Borneo Territories: Original Correspondence (CO 954) 1946 to 1951, 8 boxes of files

North Borneo, Brunei and Sarawak: Registers of Correspondence (CO 992) 1942 to 1951, 6 volumes

Commission of Enquiry in North Borneo and Sarawak Regarding Malaysian Federation (Cobbold Commission, 1962) (CO 947) 1962, 61 pieces

Selangor

Previously part of Perak (qv), Selangor became independent early in the eighteenth century but was forced to acknowledge Dutch suzerainty in 1782. In 1874 it was placed under British protection and received a British resident. In 1895 it was included in the Federated Malay States (qv). It was under Japanese occupation from 1942 to 1945. After the British military administration of 1945 to 1946 it joined the short-lived Malayan Union (qv) as a separate state and in 1948 it became part of the new Federation of Malaya (qv). In 1963 the Federation of Malaya joined with Sabah (qv), Sarawak (qv) and Singapore (qv) to form Malaysia (qv).

While Selangor was one of the Federated States (qv), supreme authority was vested in the sultan, who presided over the state council.

Selangor: Sessional Papers (CO 439) 1888 to 1941, 5 volumes

Selangor: Government Gazettes (CO 469) 1890 to 1975, 41 volumes

Singapore

Singapore was an integral part of the Straits Settlements (qv) from 1826 until 1946, when the latter was dissolved. On 27 March 1946, Singapore, the Cocos (Keeling) Islands and Christmas Island were united to form the separate colony of Singapore. At the same time Labuan (qv), which had been united with Singapore, was detached and became part of the colony of British North Borneo (qv). The Cocos (Keeling) Islands and Christmas Island were later transferred to Australia in 1955 and 1958 respectively.

After the end of the war with Japan, a short period of military administration (see WO 203) was followed by the restoration of civil government. A provisional advisory council was created pending the establishment of fully representative executive and legislative councils. A partly elected legislative council met in April 1948. A new constitution in 1955 introduced a large measure of internal self-government. A council of ministers was formed, responsible collectively to a legislative assembly with an elected majority. A speaker replaced the governor to preside over the assembly, and a chief minister was appointed. A new constitution conferring full internal self-government and the title State of Singapore was introduced in 1959. Singapore became a member state when Malaysia (qv) was formed on 16 September 1963. On 9 August 1965 Singapore separated from Malaysia and became an independent sovereign state within the Commonwealth.

Some 1946 correspondence relating to the then new colony of Singapore will be found in the original correspondence classes of the Straits Settlements (CO 273) and of the Federated Malay States (qv) (CO 717).

Singapore: Original Correspondence (CO 953) 1936 to 1951, 10 files

Singapore: Registers of Correspondence (CO 1010) 1046 to 1951, 5 volumes

Malayan Union and Singapore: Registers of Correspondence (CO 991) 1946 to 1951, 8 volumes

Singapore: Acts (CO 925) 1946 to 1959, 12 volumes

Singapore: Sessional Papers (CO 940) 1946 to 1965, 175 volumes, files

Singapore: Government Gazettes (CO 932) 1945 to 1970, 123 volumes

Singapore: Miscellanea (CO 939) 1946, 1 volume

Sri Lanka see Ceylon

Straits Settlements

Penang (qv) was ceded to the East India Company in 1786, and Province Wellesley was acquired by the company in 1800. Malacca (qv) was captured from the Dutch in 1795 and returned to them in 1818. It was ceded to Britain in 1824, when the Dutch also recognized Singapore (qv), which Britain had occupied since 1819, as British. In 1826 Singapore, Malacca and Penang (including Province Wellesley), called the Straits Settlements, were separated from India and became a Crown colony with its own governor and nominated executive and legislative councils. The Cocos or Keeling Islands joined them in 1886 (having been proclaimed a British possession in 1857 and placed under the governor of Ceylon (qv) in 1878), Christmas Island in 1900, and Labuan (qv) in 1907.

The Straits Settlements were under Japanese occupation from 1942 to 1945 and British military administration from 1945 to 1946 (see WO 203). In 1946 the Straits Settlements were dissolved. Malacca and Penang then joined the Malayan Union (qv); Singapore, the Cocos Islands and Christmas Island united to form the colony of Singapore, and Labuan joined the colony of North Borneo (qv).

After the transfer of the Straits Settlements to the Colonial Office in 1867 a greater interest was taken in the Malay peninsula. In the last quarter of the nineteenth century and the early twentieth century British residents and advisers appointed to the Malay states were responsible to the governor of the Straits Settlements. Correspondence concerning them is included in CO 273 (see below). After 1920 there is a separate class for the Federated Malay States (qv).

See also under British Malaya, Federation of Malaya, Far East/South-East Asia.

Straits Settlements: Original Correspondence (CO 273) 1838 to 1946, 680 volumes, files

Straits Settlements: Register of Correspondence (CO 426) 1867 to 1945, 42 volumes

Straits Settlements: Register of Out-letters (CO 486) 1873 to 1926, 17 volumes

Straits Settlements: Entry Books (CO 425) 1867 to 1873, 8 volumes

Straits Settlements: Acts (CO 274) 1867 to 1949, 23 volumes

Straits Settlements: Sessional Papers (CO 275) 1855 to 1940, 155 volumes

Straits Settlements: Government Gazettes (CO 276) 1867 to 1942, 161 volumes

Straits Settlements: Miscellanea (CO 277) 1867 to 1939, 91 volumes

See also:

General Registers (CO 326) 1623 to 1849, 358 volumes

Colonies General: Supplementary Original Correspondence (CO 537) 1759 to 1955, 7862 volumes, files

Sungei Ujong
In 1874 a British resident was appointed to Sungei Ujong by request. In 1895 it became part of the modern Negri Sembilan (qv).

Sungei Ujong: Sessional Papers (CO 474) 1883 to 1893, 1 volume

Sungei Ujong: Government Gazettes (CO 475) 1893, 1 volume

Trengganu
Formerly under Siamese suzerainty, Trengganu became a British protected state in 1909 by agreement with Siam and received a British adviser. An advisory state council was established in 1911. Trengganu was under Japanese occupation from 1942 to 1945 and British military administration from 1945 to 1946 (see WO 203), when it joined the Malayan Union (qv).
See Federated Malay States.

Trengganu: Sessional Papers (CO 840) 1910 to 1940, 2 volumes

Trengganu: Government Gazettes (CO 909) 1939 to 1975, 20 volumes

Unfederated Malay States
British advisers appointed to the Malay states of Kelantan (qv) (1903), Kedah and Perlis (qv) (1909) and Johore (qv) (1910), were responsible to the governor of the Straits Settlements (qv). These states refused to join the Federation of Malay States, formed in 1896, and continued to be independent Malay monarchies. However, the advisers came under the direction of the secretary to the high commissioner of the Federated Malay States, the post of high commissioner being held by the governor of the Straits Settlements.
Correspondence concerning the unfederated states was filed under the Straits Settlements (qv), and in consequence there are no separate classes of original correspondence for the individual states, although there are classes of printed documents. From 1920 there is a separate class for Federated Malay States Original Correspondence (CO 717) which also includes correspondence relating to the unfederated states. The unfederated states were under Japanese occupation from 1942 to 1945 and British military administration from 1945 to 1946 (see WO 203). In 1946 all five states joined the short-lived Malayan Union and in 1948 the new Federation of Malaya.

See Straits Settlements for correspondence before 1920, and thereafter Federated Malay States. See also British Malaya, Federation of Malaya, Malayan Union, Malaysia, Straits Settlements, Far East/South-East Asia and the individual states.

Wei-Hai-Wei

Wei-Hai-Wei was leased to Britain by China in 1898 for use as a naval harbour. Administration was first undertaken by the senior naval officer and in 1899 it was transferred to a military and civil commissioner appointed by the War Office. In 1901 the War Office handed over control to the Colonial Office, and a civil commissioner was appointed in 1902. In 1930 Wei-Hai-Wei was restored to China in accordance with the terms of the lease. The civil commissioner's files in CO 873 were taken over by the Colonial Office on the relinquishing of the territory.

See also under Far East/South-East Asia.

Wei-Hai-Wei: Original Correspondence (CO 521) 1898 to 1933, 86 volumes, files

Wei-Hai-Wei: Register of Correspondence (CO 770) 1898 to 1931, 4 volumes

Wei-Hai-Wei: Register of Out-letters (CO 771) 1901 to 1926, 4 volumes

Wei-Hai-Wei: Acts (CO 841) 1903 to 1930, 1 volume

Wei-Hai-Wei: Government Gazettes (CO 744) 1908 to 1930, 3 volumes

Wei-Hai-Wei: Commissioner's Files (CO 873) 1899 to 1930, 779 files, etc

ATLANTIC

Ascension

Britain took control of Ascension in 1815 and until 1922 it was under Admiralty administration. In 1922 control was transferred to the Colonial Office and the island was made a dependency of St. Helena (qv), receiving a resident magistrate. For later correspondence see St. Helena.

Ascension: Original Correspondence (CO 749) 1922 to 1923, 1 volume

Ascension: Register of Correspondence (CO 823) 1922 to 1923, 1 volume

Bermuda see under CARIBBEAN AND WEST INDIES

Falkland Islands and Dependencies

The Falkland Islands were simultaneously settled by British (at Port Egmont) and French colonists in 1764. In 1767 the French sold their claim to Spain and in 1770 Spain expelled the British from Port Egmont, which was restored to Britain in 1771 but abandoned in 1774. In 1833 Britain finally took possession of the islands, whose dependencies are South Georgia, annexed by Captain Cook in 1775; South Sandwich, annexed by Cook in 1775; South Shetlands, annexed in 1819; South Orkney, annexed in 1821; and Graham Land, annexed in 1832. In 1962 the part of the Falkland Islands Dependencies lying south of latitude 60 degrees South became a separate British dependency – the British Antarctic Territory. This includes the South Orkney and South Shetland islands.

In 1841 a lieutenant-governor was appointed, who took over in 1842 from the naval officer who had been in charge of the islands. His title was changed to governor in 1843 when the islands were given nominated executive and legislative councils. A new constitution was introduced in 1949 and universal adult suffrage was established. Six of the eight members of the legislative council had now to be elected, and the executive council had to include two members elected by the legislative council.

Because of the territorial claim to the islands by the Argentine government, papers relating to the Falkland Islands and the dependencies will also be found in Foreign Office records, and in those of other departments. Many of the records are closed for extended periods.

After 1951 records about the Falklands will be found in several regional classes. See section 11.3–4.

Falkland Islands: Original Correspondence (CO 78) 1831 to 1951, 269 volumes, files

Falkland Islands: Register of Correspondence (CO 339) 1849 to 1951, 24 volumes

Falkland Islands: Register of Out-letters (CO 500) 1865 to 1926, 8 volumes

Falkland Islands: Entry Books (CO 399) 1832 to 1870, 7 volumes

Falkland Islands: Acts (CO 79) 1846 to 1965, 9 volumes

Falkland Islands: Sessional Papers (CO 80) 1845 to 1965, 23 volumes, files

Falkland Islands: Government Gazettes (CO 458) 1891 to 1965, 40 volumes

Falkland Islands: Miscellanea (CO 81) 1846 to 1944, 99 volumes

See also:

General Registers (CO 326) 1623 to 1849, 358 volumes

Index to Correspondence (CO 714) 1795 to 1874, 171 volumes

Colonies General: Supplementary Original Correspondence (CO 537) 1759 to 1955, 7862 volumes, files

Falkland Islands, St Helena and Tristan da Cunha: Original Correspondence (CO 1024) 1951 to 1960, 277 files

St Helena and Dependencies

St Helena was annexed by the Dutch in 1633 but only occupied by them from 1645 to 1651, when the English East India Company occupied it. The Dutch captured it in 1665 but were driven out, events which were repeated in 1673, when the East India Company was granted a charter to govern the island. In 1834 the company surrendered the government to the Crown.

St Helena has had a governor, assisted by an executive council, since 1673. Until 1834 he was appointed by the company, except for the period of Napoleon Bonaparte's imprisonment there (1815 to 1821) when, as after 1834, he was nominated by the Crown. A nominated advisory council was added during the Second World War. With constitutional changes in 1956 and 1963 an elective element was introduced in both the executive council and the advisory council. In 1967 a new constitution provided for a legislative council with an elected majority, and an executive council whose council committees had to have a majority of members from the legislative council. The committees were charged with executive powers and general oversight of departments of government.

Ascension (qv) has been a dependency of St Helena since 1922 and Tristan da Cunha since 1938.

For correspondence before 1805 see War Office class In-letters (WO 1). See chapter 11.3–4 to determine the regional classes in which correspondence for St Helena can be found.

St Helena: Original Correspondence (CO 247) 1805 to 1951, 261 volumes, files

St Helena: Register of Correspondence (CO 366) 1849 to 1951, 20 volumes

St Helena: Register of Out-letters (CO 491) 1872 to 1926, 5 volumes

St Helena: Entry Books (CO 248) 1815 to 1872, 18 volumes

St Helena: Acts (CO 249) 1837 to 1969, 10 volumes

St Helena: Sessional Papers (CO 250) 1836 to 1965, 24 volumes, files

St Helena: Government Gazettes (CO 251) 1845 to 1965, 11 volumes

St Helena: Miscellanea (CO 252) 1836 to 1941, 106 volumes

See also:

General Registers (CO 326) 1623 to 1849, 358 volumes

Index to Correspondence (CO 714) 1795 to 1874, 171 volumes

Colonies General: Supplementary Original Correspondence (CO 537) 1759 to 1955, 7862 volumes, files

Falkland Islands, St Helena and Tristan da Cunha: Original Correspondence (CO 1024) 1951 to 1960, 277 files

Tristan da Cunha see St Helena

AUSTRALIA AND NEW ZEALAND

Australia General
A federal council of Australasia was established in 1885 with power to legislate on

matters of common interest to the colonies in this region. South Australia (qv), Western Australia (qv), Fiji (qv under Western Pacific), Queensland (qv), Tasmania (qv) and Victoria (qv) participated. From 1890 a succession of conventions was held among the colonies in Australia, the outcome of which was the creation in 1901 of the Commonwealth of Australia (qv). Apart from CO 11 the classes below relate to these federal projects.

Australia: Original Correspondence (CO 418) 1889 to 1922, 226 volumes

Australia: Register of Correspondence (CO 557) 1889 to 1900, 1 volume

Australia: Memoranda (CO 11) 1842 to 1858, 1 volume

Australia: Acts (CO 12) 1886 to 1897, 1 volume

Australia: Sessional Papers (CO 433) 1886 to 1899, 8 volumes

High Commission and Consular Archives, Australia: Correspondence (DO 126) 1932 to 1954, 18 files

Confidential Print: Dominions (Australian) (DO 115) 1928 to 1936, 3 volumes

Australia and New Zealand

The correspondence from and about Australia and New Zealand (qv) presents special features. The registers for the separate Australian colonies, now states, and for New Zealand cease in 1900 on Australian federation, as does the Australian General Series (CO 557) (see above) which is devoted to correspondence about the colonies collectively. The registers below are succeeded by two separate series, each running until 1922: New Zealand (CO 361), which is a resumption of the old New Zealand series, and Commonwealth of Australia (CO 706). The registers, so far as they concern Australia, include despatches from the governors of the states as well as from the governor-general.

Australia and New Zealand: Register of Correspondence (CO 644) 1901 to 1908, 4 volumes

Australia and New Zealand: Register of Out-letters (CO 645) 1901 to 1908, 3 volumes

Auckland Islands

The Auckland Islands were visited by Captain Biscoe in 1806 and granted by Britain to Messrs Enderby as a whaling station, but they were abandoned in 1852, and subsequently administered by New Zealand. CO 394 covers papers now in a volume of New Zealand correspondence (CO 209/134).

Auckland Island: Entry Book (CO 394) 1950–1953, 1 volume

See also:

Index to Correspondence (CO 714) 1795 to 1874, 171 volumes

Commonwealth of Australia

The Commonwealth of Australia was constituted in 1901 by a federation of the colonies, thereafter states, of New South Wales (qv), Victoria (qv), South Australia (qv), Queensland (qv), Tasmania (qv), and Western Australia (qv). Since then the governor-general, acting for the sovereign, an elective senate and an elective house of representatives have formed the legislature, and the governor-general and executive council have constituted the executive. Each state has retained its own constitution, and records relating to them will be found under their separate heads. For original correspondence after 1922 and confidential print after 1936 see Dominions General under GENERAL.

Commonwealth of Australia: Register of Correspondence (CO 706) 1909 to 1922, 9 volumes

Commonwealth of Australia: Register of Out-letters (CO 707) 1909 to 1922, 7 volumes

Commonwealth of Australia: Acts (CO 558) 1901 to 1925, 23 volumes

Commonwealth of Australia: Acts (DO 15) 1926 to 1966, 66 volumes

Commonwealth of Australia: Sessional Papers (CO 562) 1901 to 1925, 88 volumes

Commonwealth of Australia: Sessional Papers (DO 79) 1926 to 1966, 126 volumes

Commonwealth of Australia: Government Gazettes (CO 559) 1901 to 1925, 36 volumes

Commonwealth of Australia: Government Gazettes (DO 16) 1926 to 1987, 282 volumes

Commonwealth of Australia: Public Service Lists (CO 561) 1902 to 1925, 21 volumes

Commonwealth of Australia: Public Service Lists (DO 18) 1926 to 1927, 2 volumes

Commonwealth of Australia: Miscellanea (CO 560) 1903 to 1925, 28 volumes

Commonwealth of Australia: Miscellanea (DO 17) 1925 to 1950, 39 volumes

Confidential Print: Australia (CO 881) 1833 to 1923, 15 volumes

Confidential Print: Dominions (Australian) (DO 115) 1928 to 1936, 3 volumes

High Commission and Consular Archives, Australia: Correspondence (DO 126) 1932 to 1954, 18 files

See also:

Dominions: Original Correspondence (CO 532) 1907 to 1925, 223 volumes

Dominions Office and Commonwealth Relations Office: Original Correspondence (DO 35) 1926 to 1961, 7158 volumes, files

Dominions: Supplementary Original Correspondence (DO 117) 1926 to 1929, 189 files

Index to Correspondence (CO 714) 1795 to 1874, 171 volumes

Colonies General: Supplementary Original Correspondence (CO 537) 1759 to 1955, 7862 volumes, files

New South Wales

New South Wales was first settled in 1788. In 1901 it became an original state of the Commonwealth of Australia (qv).

A governor was appointed in 1788, a nominated legislative council was established in 1823 and an executive council in 1825. The legislative council was established in 1823 and an executive council in 1825. The legislative council was made partly elective in 1842, but in 1856, when responsible government was introduced, it was replaced by a nominated legislative council and an elective house of assembly. In 1934 the legislative council was made elective.

Originally New South Wales administered much of eastern Australia. Tasmania (qv) was separated in 1825, Victoria (qv) in 1851 and Queensland (qv) in 1859. New Zealand (qv) was also under New South Wales until 1841.

After the Napoleonic Wars the British government appointed a number of commissions of inquiry. One was entrusted to a single commissioner, J T Bigge, who was sent to New South Wales in 1819. His correspondence, which presumably he brought home, forms part of the New South Wales Original Correspondence (CO 201/141).

Microfilm copies of records of the superintendent of convicts in New South Wales which were sent to London are held in class CO 207. The originals, formerly in this class, were returned to the government of New South Wales in 1973. See also the Home Office record classes HO 10 and HO 11.

New South Wales: Original Correspondence (CO 201) 1783 to 1900, 629 volumes

New South Wales: Register of Correspondence (CO 360) 1849 to 1900, 16 volumes

New South Wales: Register of Out-letters (CO 369) 1873 to 1900, 4 volumes

New South Wales: Entry Books (CO 202) 1786 to 1873, 78 volumes

New South Wales: Acts (CO 203) 1829 to 1925, 85 volumes

New South Wales: Acts (DO 44) 1926 to 1966, 71 volumes

New South Wales: Sessional Papers (CO 204) 1825 to 1925, 621 volumes

New South Wales: Sessional Papers (DO 45) 1925 to 1965, 219 volumes

New South Wales: Government Gazettes (CO 205) 1832 to 1925, 309 volumes

New South Wales: Government Gazettes (DO 46) 1926 to 1980, 206 volumes

New South Wales: Miscellanea (CO 206) 1803 to 1925, 187 volumes

New South Wales: Miscellanea (DO 47) 1925 to 1951, 27 volumes

New South Wales: Public Service Lists (CO 580) 1895 to 1916, 21 volumes

New South Wales: Entry Books relating to Convicts (CO 207) 1788 to 1868, 11 reels

See also:

General Registers (CO 326) 1623 to 1849, 358 volumes

Index to Correspondence (CO 714) 1795 to 1874, 171 volumes

New Zealand

New Zealand was settled from 1814 but was under the jurisdiction of New South Wales (qv) until 1841. In 1840 the local leaders ceded sovereignty over North Island to the British Crown, which in the same year proclaimed its sovereignty over South Island by right of settlement. In 1841 the islands became a separate colony and from 1841 to 1850 they were under the New Zealand Company (qv).

From 1833 to 1840 New Zealand had a British resident and thereafter a governor. Nominated executive and legislative councils were set up in 1841. In 1852 an elective house of representatives was added, although the new legislature did not meet until 1854. Responsible government was established in 1856. In 1907 New Zealand obtained dominion status under a governor-general.

Registers for 1901 to 1908 are under Australia and New Zealand (qv). See also under Auckland Islands. See Dominions General under GENERAL.

New Zealand: Original Correspondence (CO 209) 1830 to 1922, 313 volumes

New Zealand: Register of Correspondence (CO 361) 1849 to 1922, 21 volumes

New Zealand: Register of Out-letters (CO 365) 1873 to 1922, 9 volumes

New Zealand: Entry Books (CO 406) 1837 to 1872, 28 volumes

New Zealand: Acts (CO 210) 1841 to 1925, 43 volumes

New Zealand: Acts (DO 48) 1926 to 1947, 14 volumes

New Zealand: Sessional Papers (CO 211) 1841 to 1925, 347 volumes

New Zealand: Sessional Papers (DO 49) 1926 to 1965, 195 volumes

New Zealand: Government Gazettes (CO 212) 1841 to 1925, 115 volumes

New Zealand: Government Gazettes (DO 50) 1926 to 1980, 165 volumes

New Zealand: Miscellanea (CO 213) 1840 to 1925, 107 volumes

New Zealand: Miscellanea (DO 51) 1925 to 1951, 51 volumes

New Zealand: Public Service Lists (CO 719) 1916 to 1920, 2 volumes

High Commission and Consular Archives, New Zealand: Correspondence (DO 128) see *Current Guide* Part I: 805/5/1

See also:

Dominions: Original Correspondence (CO 532) 1907 to 1925, 335 volumes

Dominions Office and Commonwealth Relations Office: Original Correspondence (DO 35) 1926 to 1961, 7158 volumes, files

Dominions: Supplementary Original Correspondence (DO 117) 1926 to 1929, 189 files

General Registers (CO 326) 1623 to 1849, 358 volumes

Index to Correspondence (CO 714) 1795 to 1874, 171 volumes

Colonies General: Supplementary Original Correspondence (CO 537) 1759 to 1955, 7862 volumes, files

New Zealand Company
The New Zealand Company was a chartered company which was formed as a joint stock company in 1839 and incorporated in 1841. It was empowered to buy, sell, settle and cultivate lands in New Zealand (qv) and advance money on the security of such lands for promoting their cultivation. It did not prove a satisfactory agency for colonizing New Zealand and was induced to surrender its charters in 1850. It was finally dissolved in 1858. After the surrender, the records were handed over to the Colonial Office. They now form the class CO 208, which consists of in-letters and out-letters, registers, minute books, and accounts and registers of emigrants and land transfers.

New Zealand Company: Original Correspondence, etc (CO 208) 1837 to1861, 309 volumes, etc

See also:

General Registers (CO 326) 1623 to 1849, 358 volumes

Norfolk Island
Norfolk Island: Government Gazettes (DO 135) 1956 to 1960, 1 volume

North Australia
In the 1840s it was proposed that the northern part of New South Wales (qv) should be established as a separate colony for convicts and called North Australia. It was established by charter and a governor was appointed, but in 1846 the charter and the governor's letters patent were revoked.

North Australia: Entry Books (CO 395) 1846, 2 volumes

Northern Territory
Australia, Northern Territory: Government Gazettes (DO 108) 1948 to 1969, 8 volumes

Queensland
Queensland was first settled in 1824 from New South Wales (qv). It was separated

from New South Wales in 1859, and in 1901 it became an original state of the Commonwealth of Australia (qv).

When it became a separate colony in 1859, Queensland was given responsible government under a governor, the legislature consisting of a nominated legislative council and an elective legislative assembly. The legislative council was abolished in 1922.

Queensland: Original Correspondence (CO 234) 1859 to 1900, 71 volumes

Queensland: Register of Correspondence (CO 424) 1859 to 1900, 8 volumes

Queensland: Register of Out-letters (CO 450) 1873 to 1900, 2 volumes

Queensland: Entry Books (CO 423) 1859 to 1873, 4 volumes

Queensland: Acts (CO 235) 1860 to 1924, 32 volumes

Queensland: Acts (DO 60) 1925 to 1966, 62 volumes

Queensland: Sessional Papers (CO 236) 1860 to 1925, 288 volumes

Queensland: Sessional Papers (DO 61) 1926 to 1965, 105 volumes

Queensland: Government Gazettes (CO 237) 1859 to 1925, 125 volumes

Queensland: Government Gazettes (DO 62) 1926 to 1980, 269 volumes

Queensland: Miscellanea (CO 238) 1859 to 1920, 62 volumes

Queensland: Miscellanea (DO 103) 1925 to 1950, 19 volumes

See also:

Index to Correspondence (CO 714) 1795 to 1874, 171 volumes

South Australia

South Australia was established as a colony in 1836 under a charter granted to the South Australian Association, but in 1841 the charter was suspended. South Australia then became a Crown colony. In 1901 it became an original state of the Commonwealth of Australia (qv).

In 1842 nominated executive and legislative councils were established under a governor. The legislative council was made elective in 1850. In 1856, when responsible government was introduced, an elective house of assembly was added.

South Australia: Original Correspondence (CO 13) 1831 to 1900, 155 volumes

South Australia: Register of Correspondence (CO 331) 1849 to 1900, 12 volumes

South Australia: Register of Out-letters (CO 514) 1873 to 1900, 2 volumes

South Australia: Entry Books (CO 396) 1834 to 1873, 16 volumes

South Australia: Acts (CO 14) 1842 to 1925, 28 volumes

South Australia: Acts (DO 80) 1926 to 1965, 19 volumes

South Australia: Sessional Papers (CO 15) 1836 to 1925, 226 volumes

South Australia: Sessional Papers (DO 19) 1857 to 1966, 77 volumes

South Australia: Government Gazettes (CO 16) 1839 to 1925, 135 volumes

South Australia: Government Gazettes (DO 20) 1926 to 1980, 135 volumes

South Australia: Public Service Lists (CO 695) 1918 to 1920, 3 volumes

South Australia: Miscellanea (CO 17) 1836 to 1925, 101 volumes

South Australia: Miscellanea (DO 21) 1925 to 1950, 17 volumes

See also:

Index to Correspondence (CO 714) 1795 to 1874, 171 volumes

General Registers (CO 326) 1623 to 1849, 358 volumes

Tasmania

Britain took possession of Tasmania in 1803 and from then until 1825, when it became a separate colony, it was a dependency of New South Wales (qv). It was called Van Diemen's Land until 1853.

In 1825 Tasmania received its own governor and nominated executive and legislative councils. The legislative council was made elective in 1850, and in 1856, when responsible government was introduced, an elective house of assembly was added.

See also under Australia.

Tasmania: Original Correspondence (CO 280) 1824 to 1900, 403 volumes

Tasmania: Register of Correspondence (CO 370) 1849 to 1900, 13 volumes

Tasmania: Register of Out-letters (CO 371) 1873 to 1900, 2 volumes

Tasmania: Entry Books (CO 408) 1825 to 1872, 46 volumes

Tasmania: Acts (CO 281) 1830 to 1924, 35 volumes

Tasmania: Acts (DO 68) 1925 to 1965, 24 volumes

Tasmania: Sessional Papers (CO 282) 1825 to 1925, 204 volumes

Tasmania: Sessional Papers (DO 69) 1925 to 1965, 71 volumes

Tasmania: Government Gazettes (CO 283) 1816 to 1925, 143 volumes

Tasmania: Government Gazettes (DO 70) 1926 to 1980, 118 volumes

Tasmania: Miscellanea (CO 284) 1822 to 1925, 146 volumes

Tasmania: Miscellanea (DO 71) 1925 to 1950, 15 volumes

See also:

General Registers (CO 326) 1623 to 1849, 358 volumes

Index to Correspondence (CO 714) 1795 to 1874, 171 volumes

Victoria
Colonists from New South Wales (qv) established settlements at Victoria, which did not survive, in 1803 and 1825. In 1834 Victoria was colonized from Van Diemen's Land (Tasmania, qv). It was, however, administered from New South Wales (qv) until 1851, when it was separated and named Victoria. In 1901 it became an original state of the Commonwealth of Australia (qv).

In 1851 Victoria was given a governor, executive council and elective legislative council. An elective legislative assembly was added in 1855 when responsible government was introduced.

Victoria: Original Correspondence (CO 309) 1851 to 1900, 150 volumes

Victoria: Register of Correspondence (CO 374) 1852 to 1900, 14 volumes

Victoria: Register of Out-letters (CO 513) 1873 to 1900, 4 volumes

Victoria: Entry Books (CO 411) 1851 to 1872, 13 volumes

Victoria: Acts (CO 310) 1851 to 1925, 89 volumes

Victoria: Acts (DO 74) 1926 to 1964, 74 volumes

Victoria: Sessional Papers (CO 311) 1851 to 1925, 312 volumes

Victoria: Sessional Papers (DO 75) 1926 to 1966, 92 volumes

Victoria: Government Gazettes (CO 312) 1851 to 1925, 183 volumes

Victoria: Government Gazettes (DO 76) 1926 to 1980, 170 volumes

Victoria: Miscellanea (CO 313) 1838 to 1916, 96 volumes

Victoria: Public Service Lists (CO 479) 1892 to 1910, 19 volumes

See also:

General Registers (CO 326) 1623 to 1849, 358 volumes

Index to Correspondence (CO 714) 1795 to 1874, 171 volumes

Western Australia
Western Australia was first settled, by convicts, in 1826. In 1829 a lieutenant-governor was appointed and a free settlement was established. In 1901 the colony became an original state of the Commonwealth of Australia (qv). Nominated executive and legislative councils were established in 1832. In 1870 representative government was set up, with an executive council and a partially elective legislative council. Responsible government was granted in 1890, since when the legislature has consisted of two elective houses – legislative council and legislative assembly.

Western Australia: Original Correspondence (CO 18) 1828 to 1900, 228 volumes

Western Australia: Register of Correspondence (CO 332) 1849 to 1900, 14 volumes

Western Australia: Register of Out-letters (CO 353) 1873 to 1900, 3 volumes

Western Australia: Entry Books (CO 397) 1828 to 1873, 29 volumes

Western Australia: Acts (CO 19) 1844 to 1925, 31 volumes

Western Australia: Acts (DO 22) 1926 to 1966, 39 volumes

Western Australia: Sessional Papers (CO 20) 1832 to 1925, 78 volumes

Western Australia: Sessional Papers (DO 23) 1926 to 1965, 100 volumes

Western Australia: Public Service Lists (CO 563) 1909 to 1914, 6 volumes

Western Australia: Government Gazettes (CO 21) 1836 to 1925, 74 volumes

Western Australia: Government Gazettes (DO 24) 1926 to 1989, 243 volumes

Western Australia: Miscellanea (CO 22) 1833 to 1918, 95 volumes

Western Australia: Miscellanea (DO 98) 1925 to 1951, 10 volumes

See also:

Index to Correspondence (CO 714) 1795 to 1874, 171 volumes

General Registers (CO 326) 1623 to 1849, 358 volumes

CARIBBEAN AND WEST INDIES

West Indies

Up to 1825 the original correspondence class CO 318 contains despatches, but they are mainly of a military character. After that year, and until more recent times, the class consists mainly of domestic correspondence within the British government about the West Indies. From 1843 to 1873 a section of the correspondence is devoted to 'the immigration of indentured labourers', a subject which is eventually resumed in Immigration (CO 571). The class also contains correspondence with the commissioners appointed in 1822 to enquire into the administration of civil and criminal justice in the West Indies, and with the commissioners, first reporting in 1825, appointed to consider the state of Africans confiscated by the Crown under the anti-slave trade acts and thereafter apprenticed or otherwise living in the West Indies.

A royal commission was established in 1854 to investigate those landed estates in the West Indies whose owners had overburdened them with mortgages. The commission was dissolved in 1886 and its records and the correspondence resulting from its findings form the class CO 441.

The Imperial Department of Agriculture was established in 1898, with headquarters in Barbados, for research and experiment in tropical crops, especially sugar cane. In 1922 it was amalgamated with the Imperial College of Tropical Agriculture in Trinidad, which had been incorporated in the previous year.

The West India Royal Commission, appointed under the chairmanship of Lord Moyne in 1938, investigated social and economic conditions and related matters in Barbados, British Honduras, Jamaica, the Leeward Islands, Trinidad and Tobago and the Windward Islands and related matters. The records are in CO 950.

The commission's findings resulted in the appointment of the West Indies Development and Welfare Organization, which was set up under a comptroller for development and welfare. After the Second World War it continued to collaborate with local governments in working out long-term social reform programmes and development and welfare schemes for which United Kingdom grants were recommended. The comptroller also served as British co-chairman of the Caribbean Commission, established by the United States and the United Kingdom and joined by the French and Netherlands Governments in 1945 to strengthen economic and social co-operation and avoid duplication of research. With the creation of the Federation of the West Indies (qv) in January 1958 the Development and Welfare Organization's functions were largely assumed by the federal government, and in March 1958 the organization ceased to exist.

See also under America and West Indies and the individual territories in the region.

West Indies: Original Correspondence (CO 318) 1624 to 1951, 515 files, volumes

West Indies: Register of Correspondence (CO 375) 1849 to 1951, 30 volumes

West Indies: Register of Out-letters (CO 509) 1872 to 1926, 5 volumes

West Indies: Entry Books (CO 319) 1699 to 1872, 56 volumes

West Indies: Miscellanea (CO 320) 1820 to 1840, 10 volumes

Imperial Department of Agriculture (CO 617) 1899 to 1923, 18 volumes

West Indian Incumbered Estates Commission (CO 441) 1770 to 1893, 25 boxes

West India Royal Commission (1938 to 1939) (CO 950) 1938 to 1939, 961 volumes, files

West Indies, United States Bases: Original Correspondence (CO 971) 1941 to 1951, 163 boxes, files

West Indies, United States Bases: Register of Correspondence (CO 972) 1940 to 1951, 3 volumes

West Indian Department: Original Correspondence (CO 1031) 1948 to 1965, 2965 files

Confidential Print: West Indies (CO 884) 1833 to 1961, 38 volumes

British West Indies: Governor's Office: Registered Files (CO 1043) 1939 to 1959, 1 file

See also:

Colonial Papers General Series (CO 1) 1574 to 1757, 69 volumes

Immigration: Original Correspondence (CO 571) 1913 to 1920, 7 volumes

Immigration: Register of Correspondence (CO 780) 1913 to 1920, 1 volume

Emigration: Original Correspondence (CO 384) 1817 to 1896, 193 volumes

Emigration: Register of Correspondence (CO 428) 1850 to 1896, 14 volumes

Emigration: Register of Out-letters (CO 485) 1872 to 1903, 9 volumes

Emigration: Entry Books (CO 385) 1814 to 1871, 30 volumes

Land and Emigration Commission, etc (CO 386) 1833 to 1894, 194 volumes

Colonies General: Supplementary Original Correspondence (CO 537) 1759 to 1955, 7862 volumes, files

America and West Indies

This artificial class was formed in a large-scale reorganization of Colonial Office records undertaken in the Public Record Office in the early 1900s. It includes the original correspondence and entry books of the Board of Trade and the secretary of state, together with acts, sessional papers and miscellanea arranged under the following sub-divisions: Carolina (Propriety), North Carolina, South Carolina, Connecticut, East Florida, West Florida, Georgia, Maryland, Massachusetts, New England, New Hampshire, New Jersey, New York, Pennsylvannia, Rhode Island, Vermont, Virginia and Proprieties. The last comprises the Bahamas, Carolina, Connecticut, Maryland, East and West New Jersey, Pennsylvania and Rhode Island.

For further records see under West Indies and the individual West Indian colonies.

America and West Indies: Original Correspondence, etc (CO 5) 1606 to 1822, 1450 volumes, bundles

See also:

Colonial Papers General Series (CO 1) 1574 to 1757, 69 volumes

Antigua and Montserrat

Antigua and Montserrat were settled by the English from St Christopher (qv) in 1632. Antigua was captured by the French in 1666 and Montserrat in 1667, but both were restored to Britain by the Treaty of Breda in 1667. Montserrat was again captured by France in 1782 but restored to Britain in 1783.

Both were part of the general government of the Caribbean Islands until 1671, when they were made part of the new government of the Leeward Islands (qv). When this broke up in 1816, Antigua and Montserrat jointly formed a separate governmental unit, but in 1833 they were reunited with the other Leeward Islands under a governor-in-chief and in 1871 the federal legislature was reconstituted.

Antigua had a governor, nominated legislative council and elective house of assembly by 1644, a nominated executive council and administrative committee being added later. In 1867 a new constitution was substituted, consisting of governor, nominated executive council and a partly elective legislative council. In 1898 the legislative council became non-elective by its own decision, but in 1936 it again became partly elective.

By 1668 Montserrat had a nominated legislative council and an elective assembly under a governor. In 1861 this constitution was abolished by the local legislature and was succeeded by a president, nominated executive council and partly elective legislative assembly. In 1866 the legislative assembly was abolished, being replaced in 1867 by a nominated legislative council, which was made partly elective in 1936.

The Leeward Islands Federation, established in 1871, was dissolved in 1956 when Antigua and Montserrat became colonies in their own right. When the Federation of the West Indies was created in 1958, Antigua and Montserrat entered as separate units. The federation was dissolved in 1962, and Antigua and Montserrat were then again separately administered. Constitutional changes, including a system of ministerial government, were subsequently introduced in both territories. In 1967 Antigua ceased to be a dependent territory, assuming the status of an associated state with Britain, and in November 1981 it became a fully independent state within the Commonwealth. Montserrat, however, remained a dependent territory.

Correspondence from both territories, among others, is registered collectively in the Leeward Islands registers (CO 354). Documents relating to Montserrat alone will be found under Montserrat. Reference should also be made to Leeward Islands for correspondence about both territories. The first volume of acts, covering the years 1668 to 1706, relates also to Nevis (qv).

See also under Montserrat and West Indies.

Antigua and Montserrat: Original Correspondence (CO 7) 1702 to 1872, 144 volumes

Antigua and Montserrat: Entry Books (CO 393) 1816 to 1872, 15 volumes

Antigua: Acts (CO 8) 1668 to 1967, 43 volumes

Antigua: Sessional Papers (CO 9) 1704 to 1966, 81 volumes

Antigua and Montserrat: Miscellanea (CO 10) 1666 to 1887, 71 volumes

Antigua: Government Gazettes (CO 1049) 1967 to 1989, 23 volumes

See also:

Index to Correspondence (CO 714) 1795 to 1874, 171 volumes

General Registers (CO 326) 1623 to 1849, 358 volumes

Colonies General: Supplementary Original Correspondence (CO 537) 1759 to 1955, 7862 volumes, files

Bahamas

English settlements were established on New Providence from 1629 and Eleuthera from 1646. The islands were granted to successive proprietors by Charles I in 1629, Parliament in 1649 and Charles II in 1670. They surrendered to the American colonial forces in 1776 and were captured by Spain in 1782, but the British recaptured them and retained them by the peace of 1783. The Turks and Caicos Islands (qv) were annexed to the Bahamas in 1799 and separated in 1848.

Before 1670 the settlers had organized a constitution, including an elective house of assembly, and selected a governor. The governor's appointment was confirmed by the lords proprietors of Carolina, to whom the Bahamas were granted in 1670, and a parliament was established with an elective lower house and nominated upper house. With a few breaks because of hostile attack, this constitution survived until 1717, when the islands were resumed by the Crown and placed under a governor. An elective house of assembly was introduced in 1729 under the governor with an executive council. A nominated legislative council was added in 1841.

Changes in the constitution were introduced over the years and the extension of the franchise to all adults was completed by 1962. In 1964 a ministerial system of government was established under a new constitution. This led in 1969 to full internal self-government, and on 10 July 1973 the Bahamas became an independent state within the Commonwealth.

See also under West Indies.

Bahamas: Original Correspondence (CO 23) 1696 to 1951, 899 volumes, files

Bahamas: Register of Correspondence (CO 333) 1850 to 1951, 25 volumes

Bahamas: Register of Out-letters (CO 508) 1872 to 1926, 9 volumes

Bahamas: Entry Books (CO 24) 1717 to 1872, 34 volumes

Bahamas: Acts (CO 25) 1729 to 1973, 53 volumes

Bahamas: Sessional Papers (CO 26) 1721 to 1965, 184 volumes

Bahamas: Government Gazettes (CO 564) 1894 to 1965, 32 volumes

Bahamas: Miscellanea (CO 27) 1721 to 1941, 139 volumes

See also:

General Registers (CO 326) 1623 to 1849, 358 volumes

Index to Correspondence (CO 714) 1795 to 1874, 171 volumes

Colonies General: Supplementary Original Correspondence (CO 537) 1759 to 1955, 7862 volumes, files

Barbados

Barbados was annexed by Britain in 1625 and settled by 1627. The island has one of the oldest constitutions in the Commonwealth. The office of governor and a legislative council were established as early as 1627 and a house of assembly was formally constituted in 1639.

A distinctive feature of the constitutional development of Barbados was that it progressed and was regulated by convention rather than by formal legislation. An executive council created in 1876 became, in 1881, the nucleus of an executive committee; some of whose functions developed through the years into forms of ministerial government. A widening of the franchise in 1944, the emergence of a political party system and modified ministerial government in 1946, followed by universal adult suffrage in 1951, led to virtual self-goverment by 1957. This status was formally achieved in 1961.

Barbados had been a member of the Federation of the West Indies (qv), which was set up in 1958 but dissolved in 1962. In August 1965 the Barbados government announced its intention to seek separate independence. Barbados became an independent state within the Commonwealth on 30 November 1966.

From 1833 to 1885 Barbados correspondence is registered under Windward Islands.

See also under West Indies.

Barbados: Original Correspondence (CO 28) 1689 to 1951, 343 volumes, etc

Barbados: Register of Correspondence (CO 565) 1886 to 1948, 15 volumes

Barbados: Register of Out-letters (CO 501) 1872 to 1926, 8 volumes

Barbados: Entry Books (CO 29) 1627 to 1872, 41 volumes

Barbados: Acts (CO 30) 1643 to 1966, 62 volumes

Barbados: Sessional Papers (CO 31) 1660 to 1965, 156 volumes

Barbados: Government Gazettes (CO 32) 1867 to 1975, 191 volumes

Barbados: Miscellanea (CO 33) 1678 to 1947, 156 volumes, etc

See also:

General Registers (CO 326) 1623 to 1849, 358 volumes

Index to Correspondence (CO 714) 1795 to 1874, 171 volumes

Colonies General: Supplementary Original Correspondence (CO 537) 1759 to 1955, 7862 volumes, files

Bay Islands

The Bay Islands, occupied by Britain in 1839, were annexed and constituted a colony in 1852 with a governor representing the governor of Jamaica (qv), and an elective assembly. The islands were ceded to the Republic of Honduras in 1859.

Bay Islands correspondence between 1852 and 1854 is registered in Jamaica registers (CO 351) and then, until 1861, in the British Honduras registers (CO 348).

Bay Islands: Original Correspondence (CO 34) 1852 to 1861, 10 volumes

Bay Islands: Acts (CO 35) 1852 to 1859, 1 volume

Bay Islands: Miscellanea (CO 36) 1855 to 1859, 5 volumes

See also:

Index to Correspondence (CO 714) 1795 to 1874, 171 volumes

Belize see British Honduras

Bermuda

In 1612 the charter of the Virginia Company was extended to include the Bermuda islands and a party of settlers arrived from England. In 1684 the charter, which had been taken over by the Bermuda Company of London, was annulled and the colony passed to the Crown.

After 1620 the colony had a governor, a nominated executive council and an elective house of assembly (which makes it the oldest legislative body in the Commonwealth outside the British Isles). The executive council also acted as a legislative council until 1888, when a separate legislative council was created and given non-official members. Universal adult suffrage was established by 1966 and a new constitution in 1968 introduced a wide measure of internal self-government. Among amendments made to the constitution in 1973 was the establishment of a governor's council to deal with the governor's reserve powers of external affairs, defence and internal security. The cabinet, formerly the executive council, was henceforth to be presided over by the premier.

See also under West Indies.

Bermuda: Original Correspondence (CO 37) 1689 to 1951, 303 volumes

Bermuda: Register of Correspondence (CO 334) 1850 to 1951, 22 volumes

Bermuda: Register of Out-letters (CO 499) 1872 to 1925, 6 volumes

Bermuda: Entry Books (CO 38) 1615 to 1872, 38 volumes

Bermuda: Acts (CO 39) 1690 to 1965, 73 volumes

Bermuda: Sessional Papers (CO 40) 1687 to 1965, 166 volumes

Bermuda: Government Gazettes (CO 647) 1902 to 1965, 20 volumes

Bermuda: Miscellanea (CO 41) 1715 to 1950, 144 volumes

See also:

General Registers (CO 326) 1623 to 1849, 358 volumes

Index to Correspondence (CO 714) 1795 to 1874, 171 volumes

Colonies General Supplementary Original Correspondence (CO 537) 1759 to 1955, 7862 volumes, files

British Guiana (Guyana)

The Dutch West India Company occupied Berbice, Demerara and Essequibo from 1621, Demerara and Essequibo being united in 1784. The territories were captured by Britain in 1796, restored to the Dutch in 1802, recaptured in 1803 and formally ceded to Britain in 1814. All three were united in 1831 as British Guiana.

In 1803, the existing Dutch constitution was retained by the British. Each unit (Berbice and the united Demerara and Essequibo) had a partly elective court of policy as the legislature and a partly elective combined court for financial matters under a governor. After 1831 there was only one court of policy and one combined court for all three territories. In 1891 an executive council was added. In 1928 the court of policy and combined court were abolished and replaced by a partly elective legislative coucil. Following the recommendations of the British Guiana Constitutional Commission 1950 to 1951, a new constitution with adult suffrage, two chamber legislature and a ministerial system was introduced in 1953 and a general election held. Later in 1953 the constitution was suspended. A succession of constitutional changes were introduced after 1956 and on 26 May 1966 the country became independent under the name of Guyana. It became a republic within the Commonwealth on 23 February 1970.

A part of the records of the Dutch West India Company relating to the administration of Essequibo, Demerara and Berbice between 1686 and 1792 is to be found in the Miscellanea (CO 116) class listed below. They were surrendered to Britain by the Netherlands in 1819 on the grounds that they would be needed for the effective administration of those territories. The remainder of the accumulation is in the Rijksarchief at The Hague.

See also under West Indies.

British Guiana: Original Correspondence (CO 111) 1781 to 1951, 825 volumes, etc

British Guiana: Register of Correspondence (CO 345) 1850 to 1951, 39 volumes

British Guiana: Register of Out-letters (CO 502) 1872 to 1926, 10 volumes

British Guiana: Entry Books (CO 112) 1797 to 1872, 42 volumes

British Guiana: Acts (CO 113) 1837 to 1965, 32 volumes

British Guiana: Sessional Papers (CO 114) 1805 to 1965, 304 volumes, files

British Guiana and Guyana: Government Gazettes (CO 115) 1838 to 1975, 322 volumes

British Guiana: Miscellanea (CO 116) 1681 to 1943, 312 volumes

British Guiana: Sugar Industry Commission (Venn Commission, 1948 to 1949) (CO 946) 1948 to 1949, 4 pieces

British Guiana: Constitutional Commission (CO 951) 1950 to 1951, 70 files

British Guiana: Constitutional Commission (1954) (CO 891) 1954, 10 volumes

Commission of Inquiry into Disturbances in British Guiana in February 1962 (CO 887) 1962, 13 volumes, etc

See also:

General Registers (CO 326) 1623 to 1849, 358 volumes

Index to Correspondence (CO 714) 1795 to 1874, 171 volumes

Colonies General: Supplementary Original Correspondence (CO 537) 1759 to 1955, 7862 volumes, files

British Honduras (Belize)

British Honduras was settled by Britain from 1638, and was under the nominal superintendence of Jamaica (qv) until its final separation in 1884.

From the early years of settlement local magistrates were elected annually to discharge executive and judicial functions, while legislative power gradually came into the hands of a co-optive public meeting. These arrangements were officially recognized in 1765. In 1786 a British superintendent was appointed under the governor of Jamaica and the elected magistrates were abolished. In 1790 the superintendent was withdrawn, and elected magistrates were restored. When superintendents were restored in 1797 the magistrates were retained. A nominated executive council was established in 1840, and in 1853 the public meeting was replaced by a partly elective legislative assembly. In 1862 British Honduras was declared a colony and the superintendent was replaced by a lieutenant-governor, although still under the governor of Jamaica. In 1870 the legislative assembly was abolished and a nominated legislative council was set up. At its separation from Jamaica in 1884 the colony was given its own governor. In 1935 the legislative council was made partly elective. Under a new constitution in 1954 the legislative council was replaced by a legislative assembly with an elected majority, and universal adult was suffrage established. Ministerial government was introduced in 1961 and internal self-government attained in 1964. On 1 June 1973 the name of the territory was changed officially to Belize.

In March 1981 Britain and Guatemala signed an agreement providing the basis for a full negotiated settlement which would terminate Guatemala's claim to Belize and assure Belize's future security. Subsequent negotiations ended without agreement on a formal treaty.

The British Honduras Registers of Correspondence (CO 348) also include correspondence relating to the Bay Islands (1854 to 1861) and the Turks and Caicos Islands (1855 to 1867).

Belize became an independent state within the Commonwealth on 21 September 1981.

See also under West Indies.

British Honduras: Original Correspondence (CO 123) 1744 to 1951, 409 volumes, files

British Honduras: Register of Correspondence (CO 348) 1855 to 1951, 27 volumes

British Honduras: Register of Out-letters (CO 503) 1872 to 1926, 9 volumes

British Honduras: Entry Books (CO 124) 1630 to 1872, 15 volumes

British Honduras (Belize): Acts (CO 125) 1855 to 1977, 25 volumes

British Honduras: Sessional Papers (CO 126) 1848 to 1965, 83 volumes, file

British Honduras and Belize: Government Gazettes (CO 127) 1861 to 1975, 94 volumes

British Honduras: Miscellanea (CO 128) 1807 to 1943, 117 volumes

See also:

General Registers (CO 326) 1623 to 1849, 358 volumes

Index to Correspondence (CO 714) 1795 to 1874, 171 volumes

Colonies General: Supplementary Original Correspondence (CO 537) 1759 to 1955, 7862 volumes, files

British Virgin Islands

The English expelled the Dutch from some of the Virgin Islands in 1666 and from Tortola in 1672, and thereafter the islands were included in the government of the Leeward Islands (qv). When this broke up in 1816, the Virgin Islands, St Christopher (qv) and Nevis (qv) formed a separate governmental unit, but in 1833 they were reunited with the other Leeward Islands under a governor-in-chief, and in 1871 the federal legislature was reconstituted.

In 1773 the Virgin Islands were given a civil government, with an elective council, nominated legislative council and elective assembly. In 1854 the two legislative bodies were replaced by a partly elective legislative council, which became non-elective in 1867. In 1902 it abolished itself, and legislative powers for the islands were vested in the governor of the Leeward Islands. In 1950 representative government was reintroduced with a partly elective legislative council. In 1954 the legislative council was given an elected majority and universal adult suffrage was introduced. When the Leeward Islands were defederated in July 1956 the British Virgin Islands were established as a separate colony. The islands continued to be administered by the governor of the Leeward Islands until January 1960 when the office was abolished and the administrator (later governor) of the British Virgin Islands became directly responsible to the Colonial Office. In 1967 a new constitution introduced ministerial government. An amended constitution in 1977 gave wider responsibilities to ministers and increased the number of elected members in the legislative council.

St Croix and St Thomas are dealt with separately. See also under West Indies.

Virgin Islands: Original Correspondence (CO 314) 1711 to 1872, 24 volumes, etc

Virgin Islands: Acts (CO 315) 1774 to 1965, 17 volumes

Virgin Islands: Sessional Papers (CO 316) 1773 to 1965, 22 volumes

Virgin Islands: Miscellanea (CO 317) 1784 to 1896, 67 volumes

See also:

General Registers (CO 326) 1623 to 1849, 358 volumes

Index to Correspondence (CO 714) 1795 to 1874, 171 volumes

Caicos Islands see Turks and Caicos Islands

Cayman Islands

The Cayman Islands were ceded to Britain by Spain in 1670 and settled by British colonists from Jamaica (qv) in 1734. From then until 1959 they were a dependency of Jamaica and under its legislature, but in 1832 a partly elective legislative assembly was established locally. A new constitution was introduced in 1959 and elections held under universal adult suffrage. The islands, no longer dependencies of Jamaica, became a unit territory within the Federation of the West Indies (qv). With the dissolution of the federation in 1962, the Cayman Islands became a Crown colony under a new constitution. A revised constitution was introduced in 1972 which increased the elective element in the executive council and the legislative assembly and assigned departmental responsibilities to members of the council.

For correspondence up to 1959 see under West Indies.

Cayman Islands: Acts (CO 650) 1898 to 1966, 8 volumes

Cayman Islands: Sessional Papers (CO 857) 1908 to 1965, 7 volumes

Cayman Islands: Government Gazettes (CO 1019) 1956 to 1965, 7 volumes

Cayman Islands: Miscellanea (CO 651) 1912 to 1947, 35 volumes

Curaçao

Curaçao was occupied in 1597 by the Spaniards and captured in 1634 by the Dutch. During the years from 1800 to 1802 and 1807 to 1814 it was in British hands after being captured, but was then restored to the Dutch. Further records relating to Curaçao for the period 1800 to 1814 will be found among the War Office records.

Curaçao: Entry Books (CO 66) 1800 to 1816, 4 volumes

Dominica

Dominica was granted with other islands in the Caribbean to the earl of Carlisle by Charles I in 1627, but was settled first by the French in 1632. It was captured by Britain in 1761 and ceded to her in 1763. France recaptured it in 1778, but it was restored to Britain in 1783. It was made part of the Windward Islands Federation (qv) in 1763, became a separate colony in 1771, was put under the governor-in-chief of the Leeward Islands (qv) in 1833 and under the islands' new federal legislature in 1871, but rejoined the Windward Islands Federation in 1940.

Dominica was given its own governor in 1771, and in 1775 an elective house of assembly was established under a governor and nominated executive council. From 1832 the last also acted as the legislative council. In 1865 the constitution was changed to governor, nominated executive council and partly elective legislative assembly. In 1898 the legislative assembly abolished itself and was replaced by a nominated legislative council, which was made partly elective in 1924. On the dissolution of the Windwards group as an administrative unit in 1956, a ministerial system was introduced in Dominica followed by a new constitution in 1960. Between 1958 and 1962 Dominica was a member of the Federation of the West Indies. In March 1967 Dominica attained full internal self-government and assumed a status of association with Britain. On 3 November 1978 the island became an independent republic under the name of Commonwealth of Dominica.

See also under Leeward Islands, Windward Islands and West Indies.

Dominica: Original Correspondence (CO 71) 1730 to 1872, 144 volumes

Dominica: Entry Books (CO 72) 1770 to 1872, 18 volumes

Dominica: Acts (CO 73) 1768 to 1965, 32 volumes

Dominica: Sessional Papers (CO 74) 1767 to 1965, 57 volumes, files

Dominica: Government Gazettes (CO 75) 1865 to 1975, 57 volumes

Dominica: Miscellanea (CO 76) 1763 to 1940, 78 volumes

See also:

General Registers (CO 326) 1623 to 1849, 358 volumes

Index to Correspondence (CO 714) 1795 to 1874, 171 volumes

Colonies General: Supplementary Original Correspondence (CO 537) 1759 to 1955, 7862 volumes, files

Federation of the West Indies

The federation came into being in January 1958. It comprised the territories of Barbados, Jamaica (including the Cayman Islands and the Turks and Caicos Islands), the Leeward Islands (Antigua, Montserrat and St Christopher-Nevis-Anguilla), Trinidad and Tobago, and the Windward Islands (Grenada, Dominica, St Lucia and St Vincent). It did not include British Guiana, British Honduras or the Virgin Islands. The federation came to an end in 1962 with the decision of Jamaica to withdraw.

Agreement was reached at a conference in London in May 1962 on the formation of a new West Indies Federation of eight members: Barbados, the Leeward Islands and the Windward Islands, with the federal capital in Barbados. Trinidad and Tobago decided not to participate in the new federation. This federal arrangement was abandoned in 1966, and in January 1967 it was announced that the islands of Antigua, Dominica, Grenada, St Christopher-Nevis-Anguilla and St Lucia were to become states in association with Britain.

Britain's powers and responsibilities were limited to defence and external affairs. The office of the British government representive was at St Lucia. St Vincent became an associated state in 1969. Correspondence regarding the federation is in the main West Indies regional and territorial original correspondence classes.

Federation of the West Indies: Government Gazettes (DO 136) 1958 to 1961, 6 volumes

Federation of the West Indies: Acts (DO 139) 1958 to 1962, 2 volumes

Grenada

Grenada was temporarily settled by the English in 1609 and became French in 1650. It was captured by Britain in 1762 and ceded to her by France in 1763. Captured by France in 1779, it was restored to Britain in 1783 and reoccupied by Britain in 1784. In 1763 it became part of the Windward Islands government (qv) until all the other territories were separated, and it rejoined the new federation in 1833.

In 1766 a nominated legislative council, with executive and legislative functions, and an elective house of assembly were created under the governor. From 1856 to 1859 an executive council replaced the legislative council which was then restored. In 1875 the council and assembly were replaced by an executive committee and a partially elective legislative assembly. The legislative assembly was abolished at its own request in 1876, and a nominated legislative council was set up in 1877, which became partially elective in 1924. In 1956 a ministerial system of government came into force, and when the post of governor of the Windward Islands was abolished in 1960 a new constitution was introduced. Grenada was a member of the Federation of the West Indies (qv) between 1958 and 1962.

On 3 March 1967 the territory became self-governing in all internal affairs and assumed a status of association with Britain. Grenada became a fully independent state within the Commonwealth on 7 February 1974.

For original correspondence after 1874 see under Windward Islands. See also West Indies.

Grenada: Original Correspondence (CO 101) 1747 to 1873, 135 volumes, etc

Grenada: Register of Out-letters (CO 504) 1872 to 1882, 3 volumes

Grenada: Entry Books (CO 102) 1763 to 1872, 25 volumes

Grenada: Acts (CO 103) 1766 to 1965, 36 volumes

Grenada: Sessional Papers (CO 104) 1766 to 1965, 75 volumes

Grenada: Government Gazettes (CO 105) 1834 to 1975, 75 volumes

Grenada: Miscellanea (CO 106) 1764 to 1938, 132 volumes, etc

See also:

General Registers (CO 326) 1623 to 1849, 358 volumes

Index to Correspondence (CO 714) 1795 to 1874, 171 volumes

Colonies General: Supplementary Original Correspondence (CO 537) 1759 to 1955, 7862 volumes, files

Grenadines see St Vincent

Guadeloupe

Guadeloupe was colonized by the French in 1635, conquered by Britain in 1759 and restored to the French in 1763, It was captured by Britain in 1794, recaptured by France in 1795, recaptured by Britain in 1810, ceded to Sweden in 1813 and by her to France in 1814; Britain finally evacuated the island in 1816. The surviving records include entry books and miscellanea.

Guadeloupe: Original Correspondence, etc (CO 110) 1758 to 1816, 25 volumes

See also:

General Registers (CO 326) 1623 to 1849, 358 volumes

Guyana see British Guiana

Havana
Havana, founded in 1514 by Spain, was captured by Britain in 1762 but restored to Spain in 1763. The following class includes matters relating to the Havana expedition.

Havana: Original Correspondence (CO 117) 1762 to 1763, 2 volumes

Jamaica
Jamaica, settled by Spaniards and frequently raided by the English from 1596, was occupied by Britain in 1655 and recognized as British by Spain in 1670. From 1657 it had a governor and from 1661 a mainly elective coucil. A new constitution in 1662 comprised a governor with a nominated legislative council and an elective house of assembly. In 1853 a nominated privy council and executive committee were added. A new constitution in 1866 saw the abolition of the house of assembly, the legislature consisting of a nominated legislative council only, which was made partly elective in 1884. In 1944 a new constitution provided a governor, a nominated privy council, a partly official executive council with a majority elected by and responsible to the house of representatives, and a legislature consisting of a nominated legislative council and an elective house of representatives. In 1953 a new constitution provided for the appointment of a chief minister and seven other ministers, all drawn from the house of representatives. Thereafter the ministers exercised wide responsibility for the internal affairs of the island. Amendments to the constitution in 1957 and 1959 gave Jamaica full internal self-government. From 1958 to 1962 Jamaica was a member of the Federation of the West Indies, which broke up after Jamaica withdrew to seek independence alone. Jamaica became a fully independent state and a member of the Commonwealth on 6 August 1962.

For brief periods the Jamaica registers cover Bay Islands (qv), British Honduras (qv) and Turks and Caicos Islands (qv) correspondence. The Cayman Islands (qv) were administered from Jamaica up to 1959.

See also under West Indies.

Jamaica: Original Correspondence (CO 137) 1689 to 1951, 906 volumes, files, etc

Jamaica: Register of Correspondence (CO 351) 1850 to 1951, 42 volumes

Jamaica: Register of Out-letters (CO 494) 1872 to 1926, 12 volumes

Jamaica: Entry Books (CO 138) 1661 to 1872, 83 volumes

Jamaica: Acts (CO 139) 1662 to 1962, 133 volumes, etc

Jamaica: Sessional Papers (CO 140) 1661 to 1965, 369 volumes, etc

Jamaica: Government Gazettes (CO 141) 1794 to 1968, 156 volumes

Jamaica: Miscellanea (CO 142) 1658 to 1945, 155 volumes

See also:

General Registers (CO 326) 1623 to 1849, 358 volumes

Index to Correspondence (CO 714) 1795 to 1874, 171 volumes

Colonies General: Supplementary Original Correspondence (CO 537) 1759 to 1955, 7862 volumes, files

Leeward Islands

Until 1671 the Leeward Islands were part of the general government of Montserrat (qv), the Virgin Islands (qv) and Nevis (qv) under a governor-in-chief. From 1671 a federal legislature gradually grew up and in 1690 it was formalized for the five territories, consisting of a nominated legislative council and an elective assembly. It was little used and did not meet after 1798, although it was never formally abolished. In 1816 the old Leeward Islands administration broke into two, Antigua (qv) and Montserrat forming one division and St Christopher (qv), Nevis and the Virgin Islands the other. In 1833 they were reunited under one governor-in-chief and Dominica (qv) was added. In 1871 the federal colony of the Leeward Islands was constituted with a governor, executive council and a central legislative council, partly nominated and partly elected from the local legislatures. Dominica was transferred to the Windward Islands (qv) in 1940. The history of the presidencies of the federation, which retained their own institutions throughout, is under their separate heads. The Leeward Islands Federation was dissolved in 1956 and separate colonies were established under one governor. In 1960 the post of governor of the Leeward Islands was abolished.

The correspondence from and about Antigua, Dominica, Montserrat, Nevis, St Christopher and the Virgin Islands is registered collectively from 1850 in the Leeward Islands Register of Correspondence (CO 354).

See also under West Indies.

Leeward Islands: Original Correspondence (CO 152) 1689 to 1951, 547 volumes, files

Leeward Islands: Register of Correspondence (CO 354) 1850 to 1951, 44 volumes

Leeward Islands: Register of Out-letters (CO 507) 1872 to 1926, 11 volumes

Leeward Islands: Entry Books (CO 153) 1670 to 1816, 34 volumes

Leeward Islands: Acts (CO 154) 1644 to 1956, 17 volumes

Leeward Islands: Sessional Papers (CO 155) 1680 to 1956, 29 volumes, file

Leeward Islands: Government Gazettes (CO 156) 1872 to 1965, 60 volumes

Leeward Islands: Miscellanea (CO 157) 1683 to 1945, 57 volumes

See also:

General Registers (CO 326) 1623 to 1849, 358 volumes

Index to Correspondence (CO 714) 1795 to 1874, 171 volumes

Colonies General: Supplementary Original Correspondence (CO 537) 1759 to 1955, 7862 volumes, files

Martinique

Martinique has been French since 1635, except from 1762 to 1763 and again from 1794 until 1815 when it was in British hands after being captured. During the second period it retained its old institutions but was given a British governor with executive powers, aided by a consultative council. The following records include entry books and shipping returns. Some correspondence relating to the island will be found in the War Office class In-letters (WO 1).

Martinique: Original Correspondence, etc (CO 166) 1693 to 1815, 7 volumes

See also:

General Registers (CO 326) 1623 to 1849, 358 volumes

Montserrat

For details see Antigua and Montserrat. See also under West Indies.

Montserrat: Original Correspondence (CO 175) 1726 to 1872, 21 volumes, etc

Montserrat: Acts (CO 176) 1668 to 1960, 24 volumes

Montserrat: Sessional Papers (CO 177) 1704 to 1965, 44 volumes, file

Montserrat: Miscellanea (CO 178) 1829 to 1887, 57 volumes

Nevis

Nevis was colonized by the English from St Christopher (qv) in 1628. It was part of the general government of the Caribbean Islands until 1671, when they were made part of the new government of the Leeward Islands (qv). When this broke up in 1816 Nevis, St Christopher and the Virgin Islands (qv) formed a separate governmental unit, but in 1833 they were reunited with the other Leewards Islands under a governor-in-chief and in 1871 the federal legislature was reconstituted.

By 1671 Nevis had a nominated legislative council and an elective house of assembly under a governor. An executive council and an administrative committee were added later. In 1866 the legislative council and assembly were replaced by a partly elective legislative assembly, which was abolished in 1877 and replaced by a nominated legislative council. In 1882 Nevis joined with St Christopher and Anguilla to form one presidency with a single executive council and a single nominated legislative council. In 1936 the legislative council became partly elective. Universal adult suffrage was introduced in 1952. On the dissolution of the Leeward Islands Federation in 1956, St Christopher-Nevis-Anguilla became a separate colony with the capital in St Christopher. In 1956 a ministerial system was introduced and in 1960 a chief minister was appointed. From 1958 to 1962 the colony was a member state of the Federation of the West Indies (qv). On 27 February 1967 St Christopher-Nevis-Anguilla became an associated state with Britain. In 1971 Britain assumed direct administrative responsibility for Anguilla and in 1980 Anguilla was formally separated from St Christopher and Nevis.

Some Acts of 1668 to 1706 will be found with those of Antigua (qv). See also under West Indies.

Nevis: Original Correspondence (CO 184) 1703 to 1872, 20 volumes, etc

Nevis: Acts (CO 185) 1664 to 1882, 15 volumes

Nevis: Sessional Papers (CO 186) 1721 to 1882, 22 volumes, etc

Nevis: Miscellanea (CO 187) 1704 to 1882, 56 volumes

See also:

General Registers (CO 326) 1623 to 1849, 358 volumes

Index to Correspondence (CO 714) 1795 to 1874, 171 volumes

St Christopher (St Kitts)

St Christopher was first settled by the English in 1623. In 1625 French settlers arrived and the island was divided between the two nations. The French portion was captured by Britain in 1702 and formally ceded to her in 1713. Recaptured by France in 1782, it was restored to Britain in 1783. It was part of the general government of the Caribbean Islands until 1671, when it was made part of the new government of the Leeward Islands (qv). When this broke up in 1816 St Christopher, Nevis and the Virgin Islands formed a separate governmental unit, but in 1833 they were reunited with the other Leeward Islands under a governor-in-chief, and in 1871 the federal legislative was reconstituted.

By 1671 St Christopher had a nominated legislative council and an elective house of assembly under a governor, an executive council being added later and an administrative committee in 1858. The last was abolished in 1866, when the legislative council and assembly were replaced by a partly elective legislative assembly. This assembly abolished itself in 1878 and was replaced by a nominated legislative council. In 1882 St Christopher, Anguilla and Nevis (qv) were united to form one presidency with a single executive council and a single nominated legislative council. In 1936 the legislative council became partly elective. Universal adult suffrage was introduced in 1952. On the dissolution of the Federation of the Leeward Islands in 1956, St Christopher-Nevis-Anguilla became a separate colony with its capital in St Christopher. In 1956 a ministerial system was introduced and in 1960 a chief minister was appointed. From 1958 to 1962 the colony was a member state of the short-lived Federation of the West Indies. On 27 February 1967, St Christopher-Nevis-Anguilla became an associated state with Britain. Following disturbances in Anguilla in 1971, Britain assumed direct administrative responsibility for the island; and in 1980 Anguilla formally separated from St Christopher and Nevis, which remained an associated state with Britain.

The greater part of the following records are from after 1816, when the government included Nevis, Anguilla, Tortola and the Virgin Islands.
See also under Leeward Islands and West Indies.

St Christopher (St Kitts), Nevis and Anguilla: Original Correspondence (CO 239) 1702 to 1872, 126 volumes

St Christopher: Entry Books (CO 407) 1816 to 1872, 15 volumes

St Christopher (St Kitts), Nevis and Anguilla: Acts (CO 240) 1672 to 1972, 37 volumes

St Christopher (St Kitts), Nevis and Anguilla: Sessional Papers (CO 241) 1704 to 1960, 69 volumes, files

St Christopher (St Kitts), Nevis and Anguilla: Government Gazettes (CO 242) 1879 to 1989, 53 volumes

St Christopher (St Kitts), Nevis and Anguilla: Miscellanea (CO 243) 1704 to 1887, 75 volumes

See also:

General Registers (CO 326) 1623 to 1849, 358 volumes

Index to Correspondence (CO 714) 1795 to 1874, 171 volumes

St Croix
St Croix (or Santa Cruz), one of the Virgin Islands (qv), was jointly occupied by the British and Dutch in 1625. About 1645 the Dutch were ousted by the British, who were shortly after expelled by the Spaniards. In 1650 a French settlement was established and in 1651 the island became French. In 1653 Louis XIV gave it to the knights of Malta, and in 1733 Denmark purchased it. From 1801 to 1802, and again from 1808 to 1815, it was in British hands after being captured. In 1917 the United States of America acquired it from the Danes.
See also British Virgin Islands.
Original Correspondence will be found in the War Office class In-letters (WO 1). The following records include public accounts.

St Croix: Entry Books of Correspondence (CO 244) 1808 to 1815, 10 volumes

St Eustatius
St Eustatius was occupied by the Dutch in 1632. The British, from Jamaica (qv), captured it in 1665, but in 1666 were driven out by the French and it was restored to the Dutch. It was again captured by the British in 1672, but recaptured by the Dutch in 1673. In 1781 the British recaptured it, but later in the year the French captured it for the Dutch. It was taken by France in 1795 and was in British hands from 1801 to 1802 and from 1810 to 1815, as a result of capture, before being restored to the Dutch.

St Eustatius: Original Correspondence (CO 246) 1779 to 1783, 1 bundle

St Kitts see St Christopher

St Lucia

St Lucia was temporarily settled by the English in 1605 and claimed by France in 1635. In 1638 it was settled by the English from Bermuda and St Christopher, but they were driven off in 1641, and it was granted by France to the French West India Company in 1642. It was occupied by the English from St Christopher from 1664 to 1667 and then restored to France, being reannexed to the French Crown in 1674 and made dependent upon Martinique. After 1713 its possession was disputed for some years between Britain and France. Declared neutral in 1723, it was reoccupied by France in 1743, again declared neutral in 1748, defended by France in 1756, occupied by Britain in 1762, restored to France in 1763 and occupied by her until 1778, when it was captured by Britain. It was restored to France in 1783, recaptured by Britain in 1794, recaptured by France in 1795, again captured by Britain in 1797, restored again to France in 1802, and finally captured by Britain in 1803 and ceded to her in 1814. In 1838 it was incorporated within the Windward Islands government (qv).

Until 1800 the island was under the governor and the courts of justice, of which the counseil supérieur was invested with some executive and administrative functions. In 1816 a privy council was established and in 1832 nominated executive and legislative councils. In 1856 the office of lieutenant-governor was abolished and replaced by that of administrator, and in 1924 the legislative council became partly elective. In 1956 the government of the Windward Islands was abolished and four separate colonies, including St Lucia, were established under one governor. In 1960 the post of governor of the Windward Islands was abolished and a new constitution was introduced in each of the territories, providing for a large measure of internal self-government. On 1 March 1967 St Lucia assumed the status of an associated state with Britain and on 22 February 1979 became a fully independent member state of the Commonwealth.

Correspondence after 1873 will be found with the Windward Islands
Original Correspondence (CO 321).

St Lucia: Original Correspondence (CO 253) 1709 to 1873, 150 volumes, etc

St Lucia: Register of Correspondence (CO 367) 1850 to 1881, 5 volumes

St Lucia: Register of Out-letters (CO 505) 1872 to 1882, 3 volumes

St Lucia: Entry Books (CO 254) 1794 to 1872, 19 volumes

St Lucia: Acts (CO 255) 1818 to 1965, 25 volumes

St Lucia: Sessional Papers (CO 256) 1820 to 1965, 66 volumes, files

St Lucia: Government Gazettes (CO 257) 1857 to 1975, 125 volumes

St Lucia: Miscellanea (CO 258) 1722 to 1940, 136 volumes

See also:

General Registers (CO 326) 1623 to 1849, 358 volumes

Index to Correspondence (CO 714) 1795 to 1874, 171 volumes

St Thomas

St Thomas, one of the Virgin Islands, was captured by Britain in 1663, was recognized as British in 1667, but never properly settled, and became Danish in 1671. It was in British hands after being captured in 1801 and from 1807 to 1815 when it was restored to Denmark, from whom the United States of America acquired it in 1917. The following records include shipping returns and accounts of the Danish and Dutch loan commissioners. The accounts of the commissioners for liquidating the Danish and Dutch loans for St Thomas and St John are in the War Office class In-letters (WO 1).
See also under British Virgin Islands.

St Thomas: Entry Books of Correspondence, etc (CO 259) 1808 to 1815, 6 volumes, etc

St Vincent (St Vincent and the Grenadines)

St Vincent was granted to a proprietor by Charles I in 1627. With French agreement it was declared neutral in 1660, but in 1672 it was granted to a proprietor by Charles II although not settled. Later there were some French settlements, with disputes between Britain and France until it was again declared neutral in 1748. It was captured by Britain in 1762, ceded to her in 1763 and thereafter settled. Captured by France in 1779, it was restored to Britain in 1783. From 1763 until 1776, and again from 1833, it was within the Windward Islands government (qv).

In 1763 St Vincent had a governor, a nominated legislative council, which also acted as a privy council, and an elective assembly. In 1856 an executive council was formed from these two bodies and an administrative committee, similarly formed, was added in 1859 but discontinued in 1864. In 1868 the bicameral legislature was replaced by a partly elective legislative assembly, the executive council being retained. The legislative assembly was replaced in 1877 by a nominated legislative council, which was made partly elective in 1924. In 1956 the Windward Islands grouping was dissolved and four separate colonies, including St Vincent, were established under one governor. In each colony elected members were given a majority in the executive council and elected ministers took office for the first time. From 1958 to 1962 St Vincent was a member of the Federation of the West Indies. In 1960 the post of governor of the Windward Islands was abolished and a new constitution was introduced in each territory. On 27 October 1969 St Vincent attained full internal self-government and became an associated state with Britain. The territory of St Vincent, which includes the islands which make up the Northern Grenadines, became an independent member state of the Commonwealth on 27 October 1979 under the name of St Vincent and the Grenadines.

Correspondence after 1873 will be found with the Windward Islands Original Correspondence (CO 321). See also under West Indies.

St Vincent: Original Correspondence (CO 260) 1668 to 1873, 118 volumes, etc

St Vincent: Register of Out-letters (CO 506) 1872 to 1882, 3 volumes

St Vincent: Entry Books (CO 261) 1776 to 1872, 24 volumes

St Vincent: Acts (CO 262) 1768 to 1969, 37 volumes

St Vincent: Sessional Papers (CO 263) 1769 to 1965, 92 volumes, files

St Vincent: Government Gazettes (CO 264) 1831 to 1975, 82 volumes

St Vincent: Miscellanea (CO 265) 1763 to 1941, 121 volumes

See also:

General Registers (CO 326) 1623 to 1849, 358 volumes

Index to Correspondence (CO 714) 1795 to 1874, 171 volumes

Santo Domingo

Santo Domingo was occupied by a mixed company of French and English from St Christopher shortly after 1630. It was ceded to France in 1697, invaded by Britain in 1793, captured by Toussaint l'Ouverture in 1798, evacuated by France in 1803, occupied by Spain from 1806 to 1821, joined Haiti in 1822, and became an independent republic in 1844.

From 1793 to 1798 Santo Domingo had a British governor with executive powers, aided by a consultative council. The following records include entry books, accounts and miscellanea. Other records relating to Santo Domingo will be found in the classes WO 1 and T 81 (Santo Domingo Claims Committee, 1794–1812).

Santo Domingo: Original Correspondence, etc (CO 245) 1693 to 1805, 10 volumes, etc

Surinam

Surinam was settled by the English in 1630 but they left in 1645. In 1662 Charles II assigned it to Lord Willoughby and Lawrence Hyde, but in 1667 it was ceded to the Netherlands by the Treaty of Breda. Britain captured it in 1799, returned it to the Batavian Republic by the Treaty of Amiens in 1802, reconquered it in 1804 and finally restored it to the Netherlands in 1816. The following records include entry books and miscellanea.

Surinam: Original Correspondence, etc (CO 278) 1667 to 1832, 28 volumes

See also:

General Registers (CO 326) 1623 to 1849, 358 volumes

Tobago

The English first attempted to colonize Tobago in 1628, the Dutch in 1632, and the Courlanders in 1642. In 1654 the Courlanders effected a compromise with the Dutch, who in 1658 overpowered them and took possession of the whole island. In 1666 the English captured Tobago but surrendered it to the French in the same year. The Dutch regained it by the treaty of Breda in 1667, were expelled by the English in 1672, returned later, were driven out by the French in 1677, regained it by treaty in 1678, but abandoned it shortly after. The island was declared neutral in 1748, captured by Britain in 1762 and ceded to her in 1763, restored to France in 1783, captured by Britain again in 1803 and finally ceded to her in 1814. It was within the Windward Islands government (qv) from 1763 to 1783, and from 1833 until 1889, when it was annexed to Trinidad (qv).

Tobago was under a governor or lieutenant-governor from 1764 until 1880, when he was replaced by an administrator until 1892. A nominated legislative council and an elective house of assembly were established in 1768, restored in 1793 after the French rule and retained under the French governors of 1802 to 1803. A privy council and executive council were added in 1855. In 1874 the legislative council and assembly were replaced by a partly elective legislative assembly, which was replaced by a nominated legislative council in 1877. Tobago lost its separate institutions in 1889.

Tobago: Original Correspondence (CO 285) 1700 to 1873, 91 volumes, etc

Tobago: Register of Out-letters (CO 498) 1872 to 1882, 3 volumes

Tobago: Entry Books (CO 286) 1793 to 1872, 11 volumes

Tobago: Acts (CO 287) 1768 to 1898, 15 volumes

Tobago: Sessional Papers (CO 288) 1768 to 1898, 30 volumes

Tobago: Government Gazettes (CO 289) 1872 to 1898, 7 volumes

Tobago: Miscellanea (CO 290) 1766 to 1892, 73 volumes

See also:

General Registers (CO 326) 1623 to 1849, 358 volumes

Index to Correspondence (CO 714) 1795 to 1874, 171 volumes

Colonies General: Supplementary Original Correspondence (CO 537) 1759 to 1955, 7862 volumes, files

Trinidad

In 1797 Trinidad was captured from the Spanish by Britain, to whom it was formally ceded in 1802. Tobago (qv) was united with Trinidad in 1889 and the colony was thereafter known as Trinidad and Tobago.

Before 1831 the British governors had full executive and legislative powers, assisted by a nominated advisory council, which was replaced in 1831 by an executive and a nominated legislative council. The latter was made partly elective in 1924. The

1924 constitution was amended in 1928, 1941, 1942 and 1945 providing for a steady increase in the number of elected members to the council. The 1945 amending order brought in universal adult suffrage. In 1950 a new constitution, subsequently amended in 1956 and 1959, provided for a unicameral legislature with an elected majority; an executive council with a majority of members elected by the legislative council; and a ministerial system, which by 1959 became a cabinet of nine ministers presided over by a chief minister. A new constitution introduced in 1961 provided for full internal self-government with a bicameral legislature consisting of a nominated senate and an elected house of representatives. From 1958 to 1962 Trinidad and Tobago was a member state of the Federation of the West Indies. On 31 August 1962 Trinidad and Tobago became a fully independent member state within the Commonwealth and in 1976 assumed the status of a republic.

Correspondence relating to Trinidad from 1797 to 1801 will also be found in the War Office class In-letters (WO 1). See also West Indies.

Trinidad: Original Correspondence (CO 295) 1783 to 1951, 656 volumes, files

Trinidad: Register of Correspondence (CO 372) 1850 to 1951, 35 volumes

Trinidad: Register of Out-letters (CO 497) 1872 to 1926, 11 volumes

Trinidad: Entry Books (CO 296) 1797 to 1872, 31 volumes

Trinidad: Acts (CO 297) 1832 to 1960, 42 volumes

Trinidad and Tobago: Sessional Papers (CO 298) 1803 to 1965, 221 volumes

Trinidad and Tobago: Government Gazettes (CO 299) 1833 to 1975, 193 volumes

Trinidad: Miscellanea (CO 300) 1804 to 1945, 156 volumes, etc

See also:

General Registers (CO 326) 1623 to 1849, 358 volumes

Index to Correspondence (CO 714) 1795 to 1874, 171 volumes

Colonies General: Supplementary Original Correspondence (CO 537) 1759 to 1955, 7862 volumes

Trinidad and Tobago see Tobago, Trinidad

Turks and Caicos Islands

The Turks Islands were occupied by English from Bermuda from 1678, and the Caicos Islands were settled by loyalists from America after the War of Independence. They were both formally annexed to and administered from the Bahamas (qv) in 1799, when they were given representation in the Bahamas Assembly. In 1848 they were made a separate presidency, with a president, executive council and partly elective legislative council, but under the governor of Jamaica. In 1874 they became a dependency of Jamaica (qv) whence they were administered, but were given their own nominated legislative board under a commissioner. In 1959 the Turks and

Caicos Islands became a unit territory within the Federation of the West Indies. At the same time they were given a new constitution which provided for a partly elective executive council, and a legislative assembly with a majority of members elected under universal adult suffrage. It also provided for the appointment of an administrator with the powers formerly exercised by the governor through the commissioner. With the dissolution of the federaton, the island became a Crown colony. From 1965 the governor of the Bahamas was also the governor of the Turks and Caicos Islands, until 1973 when the Islands were given their own resident governor. In 1976 a new constitution introduced a ministerial system of government and a large measure of internal self-government was achieved.

See also under Bahamas.

Turks and Caicos Islands: Original Correspondence (CO 301) 1848 to 1882, 66 volumes

Turks and Caicos Islands: Register of Correspondence (CO 495) 1868 to 1882, 1 volume

Turks and Caicos Islands: Register of Out-letters (CO 496) 1872 to 1881, 2 volumes

Turks and Caicos Islands: Entry Books (CO 409) 1849 to 1872, 5 volumes

Turks and Caicos Islands: Acts (CO 302) 1849 to 1965, 13 volumes

Turks and Caicos Islands: Sessional Papers (CO 303) 1849 to 1965, 16 volumes

Turks and Caicos Islands: Government Gazettes (CO 681) 1907 to 1965, 13 volumes

Turks and Caicos Islands: Miscellanea (CO 304) 1852 to 1947, 95 volumes

See also:

General Register (CO 326) 1623 to 1849, 358 volumes

Index to Correspondence (CO 714) 1795 to 1874, 171 volumes

Windward Islands
In 1763 Grenada (qv), St Vincent (qv), Dominica (qv) and Tobago (qv) were united under a single government, called the government of the Southern Caribbee Islands. Dominica was separated in 1771, St Vincent in 1776, and Tobago on its cession to France in 1783. In 1833 Grenada, St Vincent, Tobago and Barbados (qv) were united under a single government, called the government of the Windward Islands, with a governor-in-chief, although the individual islands kept their own institutions, each under a lieutenant-governor or administrator. St Lucia (qv) was added in 1838, Barbados was separated in 1885, Tobago was separated and attached to Trinidad (qv) in 1889, and Dominica was added from the Leeward Islands (qv) in 1940. In 1956 the government of the Windward Islands was dissolved and four separate colonies (Grenada, St Vincent, St Lucia and Dominica) were established under one governor. The post of governor of the Windward Islands was abolished in 1960 and a new constitution was introduced in each territory.

See also under West Indies.

Windward Islands: Original Correspondence (CO 321) 1874 to 1951, 444 volumes, files

Windward Islands: Register of Correspondence (CO 376) 1850 to 1951, 42 volumes

Windward Islands: Register of Out-letters (CO 377) 1883 to 1926, 8 volumes

See also:

General Registers (CO 326) 1623 to 1849, 358 volumes

Index to Correspondence (CO 714) 1795 to 1874, 171 volumes

Colonies General: Supplementary Original Correspondence (CO 537) 1759 to 1955, 7862 volumes, files

EUROPE

Heligoland

Heligoland, an island in the North Sea off the coast of Germany, was captured from the Danes in 1807 and formally ceded to Britain in 1814. It retained its Frisian constitution under a British governor until 1864 when it was given nominated executive and legislative councils and an elective assembly called a combined court. In 1868 this constitution was withdrawn and all legislative and executive authority was vested in the governor advised by an executive council. Heligoland was ceded to Germany in 1890 in exchange for German claims in East Africa.

Heligoland: Original Correspondence (CO 118) 1807 to 1894, 62 volumes

Heligoland: Register of Correspondence (CO 346) 1850 to 1910, 6 volumes

Heligoland: Register of Out-letters (CO 347) 1874 to 1910, 2 volumes

Heligoland: Entry Books (CO 119) 1807 to 1877, 7 volumes

Heligoland: Acts (CO 120) 1883 to 1889, 1 volume

Heligoland: Sessional Papers (CO 121) 1881 to 1890, 1 volume

Heligoland: Miscellanea (CO 122) 1834 to 1890, 36 volumes

See also:

Index to Correspondence (CO 714) 1795 to 1874, 171 volumes

General Registers (CO 326) 1623 to 1849, 358 volumes

Colonies General: Supplementary Original Correspondence (CO 537) 1759 to 1955, 7862 volumes, files

Ireland

Ireland was never treated as a colony, for between the Act of Union of 1800 and the Anglo-Irish Treaty of 1921 it was an integral part of the United Kingdom. The lord lieutenant and the chief secretary of Ireland were members of the United Kingdom administration and conducted their official business from Dublin Castle. The Irish Office in London was a mere liaison point for them and did not act in relation to them in anything like the same way as the Colonial Office did in relation to a colonial governor.

When the Irish Free State (qv) government was formed in 1922 the bulk of the chief secretary's records were transferred to that government and remain in Dublin. The Dublin Castle records in class CO 904 below relate mainly to the measures planned or taken to combat the efforts of the nationalist organizations to secure independence. The Irish Office Records (CO 903) left behind in London are of a minor character.

The Irish Grants Committee, records in CO 762, was created in 1923 to replace the Irish Distress Committee formed the previous year. It was charged to recommend what grants or loans should be made to refugees from Ireland, and what advances should be made under the Criminal and Malicious Injuries Acts of the Irish Free State. It ceased to sit in 1926. The correspondence and records of claims made to the Compensation (Ireland) Commission are held separately in CO 905.

Reports of criminal and political activities in Ireland, including accounts of the United Irish League and Sinn Fein, were printed over a period for restricted circulation to ministers and government departments. These reports are held in the Confidential Print class CO 903.

The classes listed below have been formed from material previously held in several superseded classes.

Ireland Criminal Injuries – Irish Grants Committee Files and Minutes (CO 762) 1922 to 1930, 212 boxes, volumes

Ireland: Confidential Print (CO 903) 1885 to 1919, 19 volumes, etc

Ireland: Dublin Castle Records (CO 904) 1795 to 1926, 216 boxes, etc

Ireland: Claims for Compensation Registers, Indexes, etc (CO 905) 1922 to 1930, 22 volumes, etc

Irish Office Records (CO 906) 1796 to 1924, 31 volumes, etc

See also:

General Registers (CO 326) 1623 to 1849, 358 volumes

Irish Free State

The transfer of British power in Ireland to the provisional government of the Irish Free State was effected, after a prolonged period of disorders, by the Irish Free State (Agreement) Act 1922. Until then it was mainly administered by the lord lieutenant and the chief secretary, who were members of the United Kingdom administration. When power was transferred to the Free State government, the Department of the

Chief Secretary to the Lord Lieutenant was abolished, and the Irish Office became jointly responsible to the Home Office for the affairs of Northern Ireland and to the Colonial Office for the affairs of the Irish Free State. The Irish Office, or the Irish Branch as it had by then become, was in turn abolished in 1924.

The Free State constitution, enacted in Ireland in 1922, made provision for a legislature consisting of a chamber of deputies and a senate and a governor-general as the king's representative. The governor-generalship was reduced in status in 1932 and the senate abolished in 1936. A new constitution was enacted in 1937 which abolished the governor-generalship and the Free State. Thereafter the state was commonly known as Eire in official circles in Britain. The governor-general was replaced by a president. The senate was restored, and by the Republic of Ireland Act 1948 the British government formally recognized that Eire, or the Republic of Ireland as it now came to be known, had ceased to be part of His Majesty's dominions. With the passing of the act the formal association of the Republic with the Commonwealth was severed. The title of UK representative to Ireland was changed to ambassador in 1950, but the post continued to be responsible to the Commonwealth Relations Office.

The Free State (later Eire/Republic of Ireland) was treated by the Colonial Office and Dominions Office as a dominion. See also under Ireland.

Irish Free State: Original Correspondence (CO 739) 1922 to 1924, 27 volumes

Irish Free State: Register of Correspondence (CO 783) 1922 to 1924, 4 volumes

Irish Free State: Register of Out-letters (CO 784) 1922 to 1923, 2 volumes

Irish Free State: Dublin Gazettes (CO 785) 1923 to 1925, 5 volumes

Irish Free State and Republic of Ireland: Government Gazettes (DO 37) 1926 to 1975, 84 volumes

Irish Free State and Republic of Ireland: Sessional Papers (DO 99) 1922 to 1965, 47 volumes

Irish Free State and Republic of Ireland: Miscellanea (DO 100) 1925 to 1952, 10 volumes

Irish Office Records (CO 906) 1796 to 1924, 31 volumes, etc

United Kingdom Representatives to Eire: Archives, Correspondence (DO 130) 1939 to 1955, 123 files

See also:

Dominions Office and Commonwealth Relations Office: Original Correspondence (DO 35) 1926 to 1961, 7158 volumes, files

INDIAN OCEAN

British Indian Ocean Territory

The British Indian Ocean Territory was established by an order in council in 1965 and included islands formerly administered by Mauritius and the Seychelles. After the independence of both, the territory was redefined in 1976 as comprising only the islands of the Chagos Archipelago.

British Indian Ocean Territory: Acts (DO 151) 1965 to 1981, 1 volume

Mauritius

Mauritius was first settled by the Dutch in 1598, abandoned by them in 1710 and occupied by the French in 1715. In 1721 to 1722 it was placed under the administration of the French East India Company and its name changed to Isle de France. In 1767 it was transferred to the French Crown. It was conquered by the British in 1810. The former name of Mauritius was then restored and with its dependencies, including Rodrigues, it was ceded to Britain in 1814 by the Treaty of Paris.

From 1810 to 1903 Mauritius and Seychelles (qv) were administered as a single British colony. In 1814 sole authority was vested in the governor, resident in Mauritius, but in 1825 a nominated council of government was set up to advise him. This council was replaced in 1832 by an executive council and a nominated legislative council which became partly elective by 1885. Seychelles, which had by stages been given its own administration, became a separate colony in 1903. In 1947 a new constitution for Mauritius introduced a wide measure of enfranchisement. In 1957 a speaker was appointed to preside in the legislative council and a ministerial system was introduced. Constitutional development proceeded rapidly thereafter and, following the report of the Banwell Commission on the constitution and a conference held in London, full internal self-government was established by 1967. On 12 March 1968 Mauritius became an independent state within the Commonwealth.

After the close of the Napoleonic Wars, the government appointed a number of commissions of enquiry into colonial territories. The so-called Commissioners of Eastern Inquiry visited Mauritius in 1826 to 1828 and Ceylon in 1828 to 1830. Their records relating to Mauritius are held in CO 415 with copies of some reports in CO 167. The class CO 167 also includes Seychelles correspondence from 1887 to 1903. Seychelles correspondence for the same period is registered in CO 356, which also covers the Kuria Muria Islands (qv) correspondence.

See also under Western Pacific and Far East/South-East Asia.

Mauritius: Original Correspondence (CO 167) 1778 to 1951, 959 volumes

Mauritius: Registers of Correspondence (CO 356) 1850 to 1950, 42 volumes

Mauritius: Register of Out-letters (CO 490) 1873 to 1926, 13 volumes

Mauritius: Entry Books (CO 168) 1810 to 1872, 63 volumes

Seychelles: Government Gazettes (CO 470) 1889 to 1976, 59 volumes

Seychelles: Miscellanea (CO 471) 1899 to 1939, 41 volumes

See also:

Colonies General: Supplementary Original Correspondence (CO 537) 1759 to 1955, 7862 volumes, files

Zanzibar see under AFRICA: EAST

MEDITERRANEAN

Mediterranean

In 1801 the War Department and the Colonial Department were united under a single secretary of state, and when a separate secretary of state for war was appointed in 1854 a division of the papers of the former joint office was attempted. The complete separation, however, did not prove possible. The class CO 173 contains despatches from Mediterranean naval commanders Nelson (1803 to 1804) and Collingwood (1808); entry books of letters relating to the occupation of Toulon (1793) and to military affairs; précis of letters from Tangier, Algiers, Tunis, Tripoli, Gibraltar and Malta; and civil, military, ecclesiastical and commercial returns from Gibraltar, Malta and the Ionian Islands. Further despatches of 1805 from Nelson are in CO 537/151.

Mediterranean: Despatches and Entry Books (CO 173) 1793 to 1828, 6 volumes, etc

Mediterranean: Original Correspondence (CO 926) 1936 to 1966, 1127 volumes

Confidential Print Mediterranean (CO 883) 1844 to 1936, 10 volumes

See also:

General Registers (CO 326) 1623 to 1849, 358 volumes

Colonies General: Supplementary Original Correspondence (CO 537) 1759 to 1955, 7862 volumes, files

Corsica

Held for a long time by the Genoese, Corsica finally became French in 1769. In 1794 it was occupied by Britain, but it was evacuated and retaken by France in 1796. Britain retook it in 1814, but it was restored to France in 1815.

The following records are précis of despatches from Sir Gilbert Elliott, the civil administrator.

Corsica: Entry Books (CO 65) 1794 to 1796, 2 volumes

Cyprus

Held by Venice from 1489 until it was incorporated into the Ottoman Empire by conquest in 1570 to 1571, Cyprus was handed over to Britain by Turkey for administrative purposes in 1878. At the outbreak of war with Turkey in 1914 Cyprus was annexed to the British Crown. The annexation was recognized by Greece and Turkey under the Treaty of Lausanne and in 1925 Cyprus became a Crown colony. The movement among the Greek population of the island for the union of Cyprus with Greece (Enosis) was a constant feature of local political life during British rule. It continued up to and after independence in 1960.

A legislative council, with a permanent official majority, was set up in 1878 and was made partly elective in 1882. In 1907 an executive council was added. In 1931 the constitution was suspended and legislative power was vested in the governor. An advisory council was set up in 1933. Opposition by the Greek Cypriot community to the introduction of self-governing institutions rather than constitutional union with Greece led to the declaration of a state of emergency in April 1955. The emergency ended in February 1959 on the signing of the Zurich and London Agreements regarding the establishing of the Cyprus Republic, to which the Greek and Turkish governments were parties. Cyprus became an independent republic on 16 August 1960 and a member of the Commonwealth on 13 March 1961. Under the London Agreement, Britain retained sovereign rights in two areas of the island to ensure their effective use as military bases.

Some of the records listed below for the years 1878 to 1880 are records of the Foreign Office.

See also under Mediterranean.

Cyprus: Original Correspondence (CO 67) 1878 to 1951, 373 volumes, files

Cyprus: Register of Correspondence (CO 512) 1878 to 1951, 33 volumes

Cyprus: Register of Out-letters (CO 516) 1878 to 1926, 7 volumes

Cyprus: Acts (CO 68) 1878 to 1960, 16 volumes

Cyprus: Sessional Papers (CO 69) 1878 to 1965, 80 volumes, file

Cyprus: Government Gazettes (CO 70) 1878 to 1965, 59 volumes

Cyprus: Miscellanea (CO 456) 1878 to 1946, 68 volumes

See also:

Colonies General: Supplementary Original Correspondence (CO 97) 1759 to 1955, 7862 volumes, files

Gibraltar

Gibraltar was captured from Spain in 1704 and formally ceded to Britain by the Treaty of Utrecht in 1713. It withstood a combined French and Spanish force during the Great Siege of 1779 to 1783. Work began in 1894 to convert Gibraltar into a naval base. Legislative and executive authority was vested in the governor until 1922, when an executive council was appointed. In 1940 the entire civilian population (16,700) was evacuated to Britain. They returned between 1944 and 1951.

In 1950 a legislative council was set up and a form of ministerial government was introduced in 1959. In a referendum held in 1967 the people voted overwhelmingly to retain the link with Britain rather than change to Spanish sovereignty. A new constitution in 1969 replaced the legislative council (and the city council) with the house of assembly and formalised the delegation of executive responsibility for certain domestic matters of ministers. In 1978 Britain and Spain established working groups of officials to examine practical matters of mutual interest concerning Gibraltar.

See also under Mediterranean.

Gibraltar: Original Correspondence (CO 91) 1705 to 1951, 545 volumes, files

Gibraltar: Register of Correspondence (CO 342) 1850 to 1951, 34 volumes

Gibraltar: Register of Out-letters (CO 517) 1872 to 1926, 8 volumes

Gibraltar: Entry Books (CO 92) 1794 to 1872, 33 volumes

Gibraltar: Acts (CO 93) 1832 to 1965, 16 volumes

Gibraltar: Sessional Papers (CO 832) 1909 to 1965, 17 volumes, file

Gibraltar: Government Gazettes (CO 94) 1839 to 1965, 182 volumes

Gibraltar: Miscellanea (CO 95) 1704 to 1947, 130 volumes

See also:

General Registers (CO 326) 1623 to 1849, 358 volumes

Index to Correspondence (CO 714) 1795 to 1874, 171 volumes

Colonies General: Supplementary Original Correspondence (CO 537) 1759 to 1955, 7862 volumes, files

Ionian Islands

The Ionian Islands (Corfu, Paxos, Levkas, Ithaca, Kefallinia, Zakinthos and Kithira) were held by Venice from 1388 to 1797, when they were captured by France. In 1799 they were taken by Russia and in 1800 made a Russo-Turkish protectorate. The Treaty of Tilsit of 1807 restored them to France, but they were occupied by the British in 1809 to 1810 and made a British protectorate in 1814. A civil commissioner was appointed for the islands in 1813 and high commissioners from 1815 to 1864. From 1817 onwards the legislature consisted of a senate and a partly elective house of assembly. In 1864 Britain ceded the islands to Greece.

The original correspondence includes the local records of the islands which were sent to Britain when the protectorate over the islands was surrendered to Greece in 1864. The class (CO 136) also includes entry books, sessional papers and government gazettes.

The Order of St Michael and St George, created for Malta and the Ionian Islands, and the relevant records, are described under Malta.

See also under Mediterranean.

Ionian Islands: Original Correspondence, etc (CO 136) 1802 to 1873, 1433 volumes, etc

Ionian Islands: Register of Correspondence (CO 350) 1849 to 1910, 6 volumes

See also:

Honours: Register of Correspondence (CO 728) 1859 to 1940, 21 volumes

Confidential Print: Africa (CO 879) 1848 to 1961, 190 volumes

General Registers (CO 326) 1623 to 1849, 358 volumes

Index to Correspondence (CO 714) 1795 to 1874, 171 volumes

Colonies General: Supplementary Original Correspondence (CO 537) 1759 to 1955, 7862 volumes, files

Malta

Malta was ceded by Rome to the Knights of St John of Jerusalem in 1530 and captured from them by France in 1798. It was surrendered to Britain in 1800 and was ceded to her in 1814. From 1801 Malta had a British civil commissioner, who was replaced in 1813 by a governor. In 1835 a nominated council of government was established to advise the governor. In 1849 the council was made partly elective and given legislative powers. In 1881 an executive council was constituted and the constitution was slightly modified in 1887, 1898 and 1903. In 1921 responsible government was introduced and the council of government was replaced by a bicameral legislature consisting of a partly elective senate and an elective legislative assembly.

Between 1950 and 1958 a number of meetings were held between the British government and the main Maltese political parties about the future form of constitutional development for the island. Among the options considered was integration with Britain, with Maltese representation in the British parliament. However, agreement did not prove possible and the constitution had to be suspended in 1958 and direct rule instituted. In 1959 an interim constitution was introduced with executive authority vested in the governor who was advised by a nominated executive council which included non-official members. As a result of the report of the Malta Constitutional Commission, 1960, a new constitution giving the country internal self-government was put into operation in March 1962. Following the Malta Independence Conference held in London during July and August 1963 and subsequent discussions that year and in 1964, Malta attained independence and became a member state of the Commonwealth on 21 September 1964. In December 1974 Malta became a republic.

The order of St Michael and St George was created in 1818 for the indigenous inhabitants of Malta and the Ionian Islands and for other British subjects holding high position there or in the British naval forces serving in the Mediterranean. It was extended in 1868 to all colonies, and from 1879 persons connected with the conduct of foreign affairs were admitted. After 1930 the Honours register includes the Order of St Michael and St George correspondence.

See also under Mediterranean.

Malta: Original Correspondence (CO 158) 1801 to 1951, 590 volumes, files

Malta: Register of Correspondence (CO 355) 1850 to 1951, 40 volumes

Malta: Register of Out-letters (CO 518) 1872 to 1926, 9 volumes

Malta: Entry Books (CO 159) 1799 to 1872, 32 volumes

Malta: Acts (CO 160) 1839 to 1962, 23 volumes

Malta: Sessional Papers (CO 161) 1835 to 1965, 155 volumes

Malta: Government Gazettes (CO 162) 1818 to 1975, 199 volumes

Malta: Miscellanea (CO 163) 1816 to 1938, 157 volumes, files

Malta: Royal Commission (1912) (CO 945) 1911 to 1912, 86 files

See also:

Order of St Michael and St George: Original Correspondence (CO 447) 1836 to 1932, 129 volumes

Order of St Michael and St George (Dominions): Original Correspondence (DO 89) 1927 to 1928, 1 volume

Order of St Michael and St George: Register of Correspondence (CO 845) 1869 to 1930, 5 volumes

Order of St Michael and St George: Entry Books and Register of Out-letters (CO 734) 1838 to 1934, 7 volumes

Order of St Michael and St George: Original Warrants and Letters Patent (CO 844) 1852 to 1899, 8 volumes

Honours: Register of Correspondence (CO 728) 1859 to 1940, 21 volumes

General Registers (CO 326) 1623 to 1849, 358 volumes

Index to Correspondence (CO 714) 1795 to 1874, 171 volumes

Colonies General: Supplementary Original Correspondence (CO 537) 1759 to 1955, 7862 volumes, files

Minorca

Britain captured Minorca, one of the Balearic Islands, from Spain in 1708 and it was ceded by Spain in 1713 by the Treaty of Utrecht. Captured by France in 1756, it was restored to Britain in 1763. Again captured by France and Spain in 1782, it was ceded to Spain in 1783, was reoccupied by Britain in 1798 and finally restored to Spain by the Treaty of Amiens in 1802. While it was in British hands legislative and executive authority was vested in the governor.

Minorca: Original Correspondence and Entry Books (CO 174) 1711 to 1802, 21 volumes, etc

MIDDLE EAST

Middle East

At the end of the First World War the League of Nations allocated to Britain mandates in Palestine (qv), Iraq (qv) and Transjordan (qv). For the first time the Colonial Office began to receive correspondence dealing with Middle East matters generally in addition to material relative to the mandated territories. This led to the creation of a separate Middle East Department, later Division, in the Colonial Office which devoted a great deal of attention to Palestine in particular. The mandate in Iraq came to an end in 1932 and the Foreign Office took over responsibility for British relations.

In July 1941 a minister of state for the Middle East was appointed with headquarters at Cairo, seat of the Middle East Supply Centre. His sphere included, among other areas in the large region, Palestine and Transjordan, British Somaliland, Cyprus and Aden. His office was linked to the Cabinet Office rather than to the Colonial Office.

The mandate in Transjordan came to an end in 1946, and in Palestine in 1948. At that time the Colonial Middle East Division was abolished.

See also under Arabia.

Middle East: Original Correspondence (CO 732) 1921 to 1949, 89 volumes

Middle East: Register of Correspondence (CO 788) 1921 to 1944, 15 volumes

Middle East: Register of Out-Letters (CO 789) 1921 to 1926, 2 volumes

Confidential Print: Middle East (CO 935) 1920 to 1956, 25 volumes

See also:

Colonies General: Supplementary Original Correspondence (CO 537) 1759 to 1955, 7862 volumes, files

Aden, Aden Protectorate, Protectorate of South Arabia (South Yemen)

The Aden peninsula was occupied by the East India Company in 1839 by treaty with the sultan of Lahej. Little Aden was purchased by Britain in 1868 and Perim Island, first occupied by France in 1738 and temporarily by Britain in 1799, was finally occupied by Britain in 1857. Although Aden was part of British India until 1937, from 1921 the Colonial Office assumed some responsibility for arrangements; in 1937 the whole administration of Aden, which then became a colony, was transferred to the Colonial Office.

Between 1839 and 1914 rulers whose territories adjoined Aden Colony made protective treaty arrangements with the British. These territories formed the Aden Protectorate, known later as the Protectorate of South Arabia. The protectorate was never directly administered by the United Kingdom but from 1921 relations with the constituent states were conducted by the secretary of state for the colonies. The Colonial Office records before 1937 mainly concern the protectorate.

In 1959 a number of the protectorate states formed the Federation of Arab Emirates of the South, later called the Federation of South Arabia. In 1963 Aden Colony joined the federation but remained a colony until 1967. On independence in 1968, the Federation became the People's Republic of Southern Yemen, now the People's Democratic Republic of South Yemen.

See also under Middle East.

Aden: Original Correspondence (CO 725) 1921 to 1951, 106 volumes

Aden: Register of Correspondence (CO 773) 1921 to 1951, 19 volumes, files

Aden: Register of Out-letters (CO 774) 1921 to 1926, 1 volume

Aden: Acts (CO 858) 1937 to 1967, 10 volumes

Aden: Sessional Papers (CO 846) 1924 to 1966, 31 volumes

Aden: Government Gazettes (CO 853) 1932 to 1967, 41 volumes

Aden: Miscellanea (CO 817) 1926 to 1950, 29 volumes

See also:

Central Africa and Aden: Original Correspondence (CO 1015) 1950 to 1961, 2146 files

Central Africa: Registers of Correspondence (CO 1014) 1950, 1 volume

Colonies General: Supplementary Original Correspondence (CO 537) 1759 to 1955, 7862 volumes, files

Arabia

Questions of policy concerning Britain's relations with the Arab areas within British spheres of influence were transferred from the Foreign Office and the India Office to the Colonial Office in 1921. The classes named below comprise despatches between the secretary of state for the colonies and the political resident in the Persian Gulf and similar agents of more restricted responsibility, and associated domestic correspondence.

See also under Middle East.

Arabia: Original Correspondence (CO 727) 1921 to 1926, 14 volumes

Arabia: Register of Correspondence (CO 775) 1921 to 1926, 2 volumes

Arabia: Register of Out-letters (CO 776) 1921 to 1926, 1 volume

Iraq

Iraq, formerly Mesopotamia, came under British control as a result of the military operations of 1914 to 1918. Although Turkey did not formally renounce sovereignty until 1923, Britain was selected as mandatory in 1920, and the terms of the mandate were approved by the League of Nations in 1922. An Arab government was established in 1921 under an elected king, Sharif Faisal, advised by a British high commissioner. The first Iraq parliament opened in 1925. The British mandate in Iraq

came to an end in 1932 and thereafter British relations were conducted by the Foreign Office. British military presence continued under treaty until 1955.
See also under Middle East.

Iraq: Original Correspondence (CO 730) 1921 to 1932, 178 volumes

Iraq: Register of Correspondence (CO 781) 1921 to 1932, 17 volumes

Iraq: Register of Out-letters (CO 782) 1921 to 1926, 5 volumes

Iraq: Sessional Papers (CO 696) 1917 to 1931, 7 volumes

Iraq: Government Gazettes (CO 813) 1921 to 1932, 5 volumes

Iraq: Civil Commissioner's Staff Lists (CO 731) 1919 to 1920, 1 volume

See also:

Colonies General: Supplementary Original Correspondence (CO 537) 1759 to 1955, 7862 volumes, files

Jordan see Transjordan

Kuria Muria Islands

The five Kuria Muria islands were ceded to British in 1854 by the sultan of Oman for the purpose of a cable station. They were administered from Aden (qv) until 1963 when the administration was carried out through the political resident in the Persian Gulf, though legislative powers remained with the authorities in Aden. In 1967 the islands were returned to the Sultanate of Oman.

The correspondence in CO 143 below is registered in the Mauritius registers in CO 356.

Kuria Muria Islands: Original Correspondence (CO 143) 1857 to 1858, 1 volume

Palestine

A Turkish province after 1516, Palestine was conquered by Britain in 1917 to 1918 and in 1920 was granted as a mandated territory to Britain by the League of Nations, with effect from 1923. It was under British military government until 1920, when a high commissioner was appointed. In 1922 a constitution was promulgated and nominated executive and advisory councils were set up to advise the high commissioner, who also served as commander-in-chief. The mandate in Palestine was the most important of Britain's Middle East responsibilities and its business from 1921 onwards occupied a disproportionate amount of time. It was frequently argued, to no avail, that Palestine was an inappropriate responsibility for the Colonial Office and that either the Foreign Office should take charge or a special secretary of state should be appointed. In September 1947 it was announced that Britain wished to surrender the mandate. When Britain withdrew from Palestine in May 1948 the greater part of the territory became the state of Israel and most of the rest was amalgamated with

Transjordan to become Jordan. Although the Foreign Office then took charge of British relations with those states, it was later found necessary to create a small Palestine section in the General Department of the Colonial Office.
See also under Middle East.

Palestine: Original Correspondence (CO 733) 1921 to 1949, 495 volumes, files

Palestine: Registers of Correspondence (CO 793) 1921 to 1948, 49 volumes

Palestine: Register of Out-letters (CO 794) 1921 to 1925, 4 volumes

Palestine: Custodian of Enemy Property: Registered Files (CO 1044) 1939 to 1952, 6 files, volumes

Palestine: Acts (CO 765) 1921 to 1945, 10 volumes

Palestine: Sessional Papers (CO 814) 1921 to 1948, 41 volumes

Palestine: Government Gazettes (CO 742) 1919 to 1948, 26 volumes

Palestine: Miscellanea (CO 821) 1926 to 1945, 20 volumes

See also:

Colonies General: Supplementary Original Correspondence (CO 537) 1759 to 1955, 7862 volumes, files

South Yemen see Aden

Transjordan (Jordan)
Captured by British troops from the Ottoman Empire in 1917 to 1918, Transjordan was under British military administration until 1920 when it was assigned to Britain as a mandated territory. The mandate did not take effect until 1923, during which time Transjordan was administered jointly with Palestine under a British resident acting on the instruction of the high commissioner. Administration was under the amir, under whom a mainly elective legislative council was established in 1929. The mandate was terminated in 1946, and Transjordan became the independent state of Jordan. The Foreign Office assumed responsibility for British relations with Jordan.
See also under Middle East.

Transjordan: Original Correspondence (CO 831) 1928 to 1946, 61 files

Transjordan: Register of Correspondence (CO 870) 1928 to 1948, 7 volumes

See also:

Various Private Collections (CO 959) 1869 to 1922, 5 pieces

NORTH AMERICA

British North America
The earlier part of the original correspondence class (CO 6) concerns the boundary between British North America and the United States (1816 to 1840), and the North West Expedition (1819 to 1850). The later part consists of domestic correspondence (1857 to 1868) concerning the North American colonies collectively. The Emigration Registers (CO 327) were fused with the General Registers (CO 328) from 1863 to 1868; the confederation of Canada (qv) was formed in 1867. See also Emigration Departments in chapter 13.1.

British North America: Original Correspondence (CO 6) 1816 to 1868, 43 volumes

British North America: Emigration Registers (CO 327) 1850 to 1863, 2 volumes

British North America: General Registers (CO 328) 1850 to 1868, 4 volumes

British North America: Registers of Out-letters (CO 329) 1872 to 1880, 2 volumes

Confidential Print: North America (CO 880) 1839 to 1914, 32 volumes

See also:

General Registers (CO 326) 1623 to 1849, 358 volumes

Index to Correspondence (CO 714) 1795 to 1874, 171 volumes

Colonies General: Supplementary Original Correspondence (CO 537) 1759 to 1955, 7862 volumes, files

Emigration: Original Correspondence (CO 384) 1817 to 1896, 193 volumes

Emigration: Register of Correspondence (CO 428) 1850 to 1896, 14 volumes

Emigration: Register of Out-letters (CO 485) 1872 to 1903, 9 volumes

Emigration: Entry Books (CO 385) 1814 to 1871, 30 volumes

Land and Emigration Commission, etc (CO 386) 1833 to 1894, 194 volumes

Alberta
For details see under Canada.

Alberta: Sessional Papers (CO 643) 1906 to 1909, 1 volume.

Alberta: Sessional Papers (DO 95) 1937 to 1965, 36 volumes

Alberta: Government Gazettes (CO 556) 1905 to 1924, 15 volumes

Alberta: Government Gazettes (DO 14) 1925 to 1980, 144 volumes

America and West Indies see under CARIBBEAN AND WEST INDIES

British Columbia

British Columbia is an amalgamation of four colonial jurisdictions. Vancouver Island, granted to the Hudson's Bay Company, became a Crown colony in 1849. In 1852 the Queen Charlotte Islands were made a dependency of Vancouver Island. As a result of the large migration to the region on the discovery of gold on the Fraser and Thompson Rivers in 1858, the crown colony of British Columbia was constituted comprising roughly the southern half of its present mainland area. In 1862 the northern half of the area, including part of the present Yukon Territory, was established as the Territory of Stikine. In 1863 the Queen Charlotte Islands, British Columbia and the Stikine Territory were united under the name of British Columbia. In 1866 this colony of British Columbia and Vancouver Island were united under the former name, and in 1871 the composite colony of British Columbia became a province of Canada.

The government of British Columbia consists of a lieutenant-governor, an executive council and a legislative assembly, which, in 1871, replaced the former partly elective legislative council.

For records from 1871 to 1922 see also under Canada. After 1922 see Dominions General under GENERAL.

British Columbia: Original Correspondence (CO 60) 1858 to 1871, 44 volumes

British Columbia: Register of Correspondence (CO 338) 1858 to 1871, 3 volumes

British Columbia: Entry Books (CO 398) 1858 to 1871, 7 volumes

British Columbia: Acts (CO 61) 1858 to 1887, 10 volumes

British Columbia: Sessional Papers (CO 62) 1864 to 1925, 121 volumes

British Columbia: Sessional Papers (DO 33) 1926 to 1965, 127 volumes

British Columbia: Government Gazettes (CO 63) 1863 to 1925, 101 volumes

British Columbia: Government Gazettes (DO 34) 1926 to 1975, 167 volumes

British Columbia: Miscellanea (CO 64) 1860 to 1870, 11 volumes

See also:

Index to Correspondence (CO 714) 1795 to 1874, 171 volumes

Canada

French Canada, of which the first settlement was planted at Quebec in 1608, was conquered by Britain during the Seven Years' War and ceded to her in 1763. From 1763 until 1774 there was a military administration under a governor, but in 1774 a nominated council was established for executive and legislative functions. By the Canada Act of 1791 Canada was divided into two provinces, Upper Canada (now Ontario) and Lower Canada (now Quebec). An executive council, a nominated legislative council and an elective house of assembly were established in each province. In 1838 the constitution of Lower Canada was suspended, but by an act of 1840 the two provinces were reunited with a single executive council, nominated legislative council and elective house of assembly. Responsible government was established in 1842, and in 1856 the legislative council was made partly elective.

In 1867 the British North America Act united the Provinces of Ontario, Quebec, New Brunswick and Nova Scotia as the Dominion of Canada. Other provinces were added later: Manitoba in 1870, British Columbia in 1871, Prince Edward Island in 1873, Alberta and Saskatchewan in 1905 and Newfoundland in 1949. Since 1867 the federal constitution has consisted of a governor-general, elective council, nominated senate and elective house of commons, with responsible government. Quebec and Ontario have had a lieutenant-governor, executive council and elective legislative assembly, Quebec having a nominated legislative council also.

Acadia – now comprising roughly Nova Scotia, New Brunswick and part of the State of Maine – was colonized by the French in 1598. It remained French until 1713, except that from 1621 to 1632 there was a Scottish colony called Nova Scotia on Cape Breton Island and part of the mainland near by, and in 1654 Acadia was captured by the English and held until 1667. In 1713 Acadia was finally ceded to Britain, except that the French retained Cape Breton until 1758. The old name of Nova Scotia was resumed for the ceded territory. From 1749 there were executive and nominated legislative councils and in 1758 an elective assembly was added. In 1784 Cape Breton and New Brunswick were formed into separate colonies, the former being reunited with Nova Scotia in 1819. In 1786 Cape Breton and New Brunswick were given executive and nominated legislative councils and New Brunswick a legislative assembly also. Nova Scotia was given responsible government in 1848 and New Brunswick in 1854. Both became original provinces of the Dominion of Canada in 1867, retaining their old constitutions. New Brunswick abolished its legislative council in 1892 and Nova Scotia in 1926.

Vancouver Island was granted to the Hudson's Bay Company (qv) and made a colony in 1849. It obtained an executive council in 1851 and elective legislative assembly in 1856. British Columbia was settled from Vancouver Island and made a colony in 1858. It obtained an executive council in 1859 and a partly elective legislative council in 1864. In 1866 the two colonies were united under the name British Columbia with an executive council and a partly elective legislative council. In 1871 British Columbia entered the Dominion of Canada and provision was made for responsible government in the new province and the replacement of the legislative council by an elective legislative assembly.

Prince Edward Island, first settled by the French, was taken from them in 1758 and ceded to Britain in 1763, when it was annexed to Nova Scotia. It became a separate colony in 1769, and was given an executive council, elective legislative council and elective assembly in 1773. Responsible government was established in 1851 and the colony became a province of the Dominion of Canada in 1873, retaining its old constitution. The two provincial legislatures merged into an elective legislative assembly in 1893.

The Province of Manitoba became part of the Dominion of Canada in 1870, with a provincial executive council, nominated legislative council and elective assembly. The legislative council was abolished in 1876. Manitoba had previously formed part of Rupert's Land, the land granted by Charles II to Prince Rupert in 1670. The remainder of Rupert's Land and the North-West Territory, which had belonged to the Hudson's Bay Company (qv) until sold to Canada in 1869, were formed into the North-West Territories in 1876 under a lieutenant-governor and executive council, which became partly elective in 1885 and was replaced by an elective legislative assembly in 1888. Responsible government was introduced in 1897, when the executive council was reconstituted. In 1905 the southern portion of the territories was detached and joined the dominion as the Provinces of Alberta and Saskatchewan, each receiving a provincial constitution consisting of an executive council and an elective legislative assembly. The remainder of the North-West Territories was placed under a commissioner and a nominated legislative council, which later became partly elective.

Newfoundland, obliged to give up its powers of self-government in 1934 because of the impact of the world depression, voted to join Canada in 1948. Together with its dependency of Labrador, it became Canada's tenth province a year later. The inclusion of Newfoundland fulfilled the original design of the Canadian Confederation. In 1964 the name of the province was changed to Newfoundland and Labrador.

Although all legal and other restrictions imposed on the Canadian parliament by the British North America Act 1867 had been removed over the years, the restriction on the power to amend its own constitution remained. Not until 1982 did an agreement between the federal and all provincial governments enable them to introduce amending legislation to effect the final patriation of the Canadian constitution.

For Original Correspondence for Canada after 1922 see Dominions General under GENERAL. For other material about Canada see under British North America.

Canada: Original Correspondence (CO 42) 1700 to 1922, 1045 volumes

Canada: Register of Correspondence (CO 335) 1850 to 1922, 31 volumes

Canada: Register of Out-letters (CO 340) 1872 to 1922, 14 volumes

Canada: Entry Books (CO 43) 1763 to 1873, 158 volumes

Canada: Acts (CO 44) 1764 to 1925, 219 volumes

Canada: Acts, Orders in Council (DO 27) 1926 to 1942, 16 volumes

Canada: Sessional Papers (CO 45) 1764 to 1925, 1428 volumes

Canada: Sessional Papers (DO 28) 1926 to 1966, 337 volumes

Canada: Government Gazettes (CO 46) 1825 to 1925, 172 volumes

Canada: Government Gazettes (DO 29) 1926 to 1978, 272 volumes

Canada: Civil Service List (CO 569) 1887 to 1910, 6 volumes

Canada: Miscellanea (CO 47) 1764 to 1925, 213 volumes

Canada: Miscellanea (DO 30) 1926 to 1946, 38 volumes

High Commission and Consular Archives, Canada: Correspondence (DO 127) 1928 to 1955, 120 files

See also:

General Register (CO 326) 1623 to 1849, 358 volumes

Index to Correspondence (CO 714) 1795 to 1874, 171 volumes

Colonies General: Supplementary Original Correspondence (CO 537) 1759 to 1955, 7862 volumes, files

Aylmer Papers (CO 387) 1830 to 1837, 11 volumes

Cape Breton see under Canada and Nova Scotia and Cape Breton

Hudson's Bay

All the lands draining into Hudson's Bay, which Henry Hudson had explored in 1610, were assigned to the Hudson's Bay Company on its creation by royal charter in 1670. France recognised British sovereignty in 1713. In 1821 the company amalgamated with the North-West Company, which had been formed after 1763 to exploit the North-West Territories not covered by the 1670 charter. In 1869 the Hudson's Bay Company sold its territorial rights to Canada (qv).

Hudson's Bay: Original Correspondence (CO 134) 1675 to 1759, 3 volumes

Hudson's Bay: Entry Books (CO 135) 1670 to 1789, 4 volumes

Manitoba

Manitoba was formed from the territory, including the Red River Colony which was part of Rupert's Land, granted to the Hudson's Bay Company when it received a royal charter in 1670. It became a province of the Canadian Federation on 15 July 1870. At first the province extended over only a small area south of Lake Winnipeg but in 1912 it was increased to its present size of 251,000 square miles.

For correspondence relating to Manitoba see under Canada.

Manitoba: Acts (CO 164) 1867 to 1886, 6 volumes

Manitoba: Sessional Papers (CO 165) 1875 to 1924, 39 volumes

Manitoba: Sessional Papers (DO 96) 1938 to 1965, 64 volumes

Manitoba: Government Gazettes (CO 577) 1905 to 1925, 21 volumes

Manitoba: Government Gazettes (DO 38) 1926 to 1975, 83 volumes

New Brunswick

New Brunswick was part of the old French Province of Acadia and was ceded to Britain in 1713. It was first colonized by British subjects from New England in 1761, and in 1783 it received a large body of loyalists from the thirteen colonies. In 1784 it was separated from Nova Scotia, of which it had been part, and given a separate governor and assembly. In 1854 responsible government was established and in 1867 New Brunswick became an original province of the Dominion of Canada.

See also under Canada.

New Brunswick: Original Correspondence (CO 188) 1784 to 1876, 206 volumes

New Brunswick: Register of Correspondence (CO 358) 1850 to 1867, 4 volumes

New Brunswick: Entry Books (CO 189) 1769 to 1867, 21 volumes

New Brunswick: Acts (CO 190) 1786 to 1897, 26 volumes

New Brunswick: Sessional Papers (CO 191) 1786 to 1924, 156 volumes

New Brunswick: Sessional Papers (DO 137) 1956 to 1965, 19 volumes

New Brunswick: Government Gazettes (CO 192) 1842 to 1923, 26 volumes

New Brunswick: Government Gazettes (DO 43) 1924 to 1968, 18 volumes

See also:

General Registers (CO 326) 1623 to 1849, 358 volumes

Index to Correspondence (CO 714) 1795 to 1874, 171 volumes

Newfoundland

Newfoundland was incorporated into the realm of England in 1583, but not effectively colonized until well into the next century, when English and French settlers arrived. In 1713 British sovereignty was finally acknowledged. A nominated council was appointed in 1825, and replaced in 1832 by an executive council, nominated legislative council and elective assembly. Responsible government was granted in 1855, and the island came to be treated as a dominion.

In a referendum held in 1948 to resolve the constitutional issue a majority voted in favour of confederation with Canada rather than for responsible government and independence. Newfoundland, accordingly, joined Canada on 31 March 1949. In 1964 the name of the province was changed to Newfoundland and Labrador.

See also Dominions General under GENERAL.

Newfoundland: Original Correspondence (CO 194) 1696 to 1922, 303 volumes

Newfoundland: Register of Correspondence (CO 359) 1850 to 1922, 16 volumes

Newfoundland: Register of Out-letters (CO 363) 1868 to 1922, 8 volumes

British North America: Registers of Out-letters (CO 329) 1872 to 1880, 3 volumes

Newfoundland: Entry Books (CO 195) 1623 to 1867, 23 volumes

Newfoundland: Acts (CO 196) 1833 to 1925, 18 volumes

Newfoundland: Acts (DO 84) 1926 to 1948, 7 volumes

Newfoundland: Sessional Papers (CO 197) 1825 to 1925, 194 volumes

Newfoundland: Sessional Papers (DO 41) 1924 to 1963, 49 volumes

Newfoundland: Government Gazettes (CO 198) 1944 to 1923, 13 volumes

Newfoundland: Government Gazettes (DO 42) 1924 to 1968, 17 volumes

Newfoundland: Miscellanea (CO 199) to 1903, 98 volumes

See also:

General Registers (CO 326) 1623 to 1849, 358 volumes

Index to Correspondence (CO 714) 1795 to 1874, 171 volumes

Colonies General: Supplementary Original Correspondence (CO 537) 1759 to 1985, 7862 volumes, files

North-West Territories
For details see under Canada.

North-West Territories: Acts (CO 214) 1878 to 1881, 1 volume

North-West Territories: Sessional Papers (CO 215) 1877 to 1904, 4 volumes

North-West Territories: Government Gazettes (CO 216) 1883 to 1905, 4 volumes

Nova Scotia and Cape Breton
For details see under Canada.

Nova Scotia and Cape Breton: Original Correspondence (CO 217) 1710 to 1867, 242 volumes, etc

Nova Scotia and Cape Breton: Register of Correspondence (CO 362) 1850 to 1867, 5 volumes

Nova Scotia and Cape Breton: Entry Books (CO 218) 1710 to 1867, 37 volumes

Nova Scotia and Cape Breton: Acts (CO 219) 1749 to 1899, 81 volumes

Nova Scotia and Cape Breton: Sessional Papers (CO 220) 1725 to 1923, 206 volumes

Nova Scotia: Sessional Papers (DO 124) 1954 to 1965, 19 volumes

Nova Scotia and Cape Breton: Government Gazettes (CO 593) 1905 to 1925, 17 volumes

Nova Scotia: Government Gazettes (DO 52) 1926 to 1975, 74 volumes

Nova Scotia and Cape Breton: Miscellanea (CO 221) 1730 to 1866, 76 volumes

See also:

General Register (CO 326) 1623 to 1849, 358 volumes

Index to Correspondence (CO 714) 1759 to 1874, 171 volumes

Ontario
For details see under Canada.

Ontario: Acts (CO 222) 1867 to 1886, 18 volumes
Ontario: Sessional Papers (CO 223) 1867 to 1925, 507 volumes
Ontario: Sessional Papers (DO 53) 1926 to 1965, 129 volumes
Ontario: Government Gazettes (CO 595) 1905 to 1925, 34 volumes
Ontario: Government Gazettes (DO 54) 1926 to 1978, 161 volumes

Prince Edward Island
For details see under Canada.

Prince Edward Island: Original Correspondence (CO 226) 1769 to 1873, 111 volumes
Prince Edward Island: Register of Correspondence (CO 364) 1850 to 1873, 5 volumes
Prince Edward Island: Entry Books (CO 227) 1769 to 1872, 12 volumes
Prince Edward Island: Acts (CO 228) 1770 to 1888, 31 volumes
Prince Edward Island: Sessional Papers (CO 229) 1770 to 1925, 131 volumes
Prince Edward Island: Sessional Papers (DO 58) 1926 to 1965, 43 volumes
Prince Edward Island: Government Gazettes (CO 230) 1832 to 1925, 20 volumes
Prince Edward Island: Government Gazettes (DO 87) 1926 to 1968, 16 volumes
Prince Edward Island: Miscellanea (CO 231) 1807 to 1871, 54 volumes

See also:
General Registers (CO 326) 1623 to 1849, 358 volumes
Index to Correspondence (CO 714) 1795 to 1874, 171 volumes

Quebec
For details see under Canada.

Quebec: Acts (CO 232) 1867 to 1883, 13 volumes
Quebec: Sessional Papers (CO 233) 1867 to 1924, 248 volumes
Quebec: Sessional Papers (DO 94) 1920 to 1965, 37 volumes
Quebec: Government Gazettes (CO 602) 1905 to 1925, 41 volumes
Quebec: Goverment Gazettes (DO 59) 1926 to 1973, 186 volumes

Saskatchewan
For details see under Canada.

Saskatchewan: Sessional Papers (CO 606) 1906 to 1921, 9 volumes

Saskatchewan: Sessional Papers (DO 90) 1923 to 1965, 37 volumes

Saskatchewan: Government Gazettes (CO 605) 1905 to 1925, 19 volumes

Saskatchewan: Government Gazettes (DO 66) 1926 to 1966, 42 volumes

Vancouver Island
For details (and correspondence after 1867) see under British Columbia and Canada.

Vancouver Island despatches before 1853 are registered in the British North America registers (CO 328).

Vancouver Island: Original Correspondence (CO 305) 1846 to 1867, 30 volumes

Vancouver Island: Register of Correspondence (CO 373) 1853 to 1867, 2 volumes

Vancouver Island: Entry Books (CO 410) 1849 to 1867, 2 volumes

Vancouver Island: Acts (CO 306) 1853 to 1866, 1 volume

Vancouver Island: Sessional Papers (CO 307) 1860 to 1866, 2 volumes

Vancouver Island: Government Gazettes (CO 308) 1864 to 1866, 1 volume

Vancouver Island: Miscellanea (CO 478) 1863 to 1865, 3 volumes

See also:

Index to Correspondence (CO 714) 1795 to 1874, 171 volumes

WESTERN PACIFIC

Western Pacific High Commission
The office of high commissioner in, over and for the Western Pacific islands was created in 1877. Its jurisdiction extended over all the islands not within the limit of the colonies of Fiji, Queensland, New South Wales or New Zealand and not within the jurisdiction of any other colonial power. These included the Gilbert and Ellice Islands Colony, British Solomon Islands Protectorate, Tonga, New Hebrides Condominium and Pitcairn Islands. With the constitutional advances made in each of the territories and the appointment of separate governors, the jurisdiction of the high commissioner diminished and in 1976 the post was abolished.

As the high commissioner was the sole channel of communication, with this group of territories there are no separate classes of original correspondence, although there are territorial classes of printed documents. The records listed below relate to the Western Pacific territories in general, or to more than one territory, and in certain periods to Hong Kong, Ceylon, St Helena, Tristan da Cunha, Mauritius, Seychelles, the Falkland Islands and the Antarctic.

The regulations in CO 665 had the force of law, and the class is the equivalent of one of acts or ordinances.

See also under Fiji. There is also relevant material in the section on Far East/South-East Asia.

Western Pacific: Original Correspondence (CO 225) 1878 to 1951, 375 volumes, files

Western Pacific: Register of Correspondence (CO 492) 1878 to 1951, 29 volumes

Western Pacific: Register of Out-letters (CO 493) 1879 to 1926, 7 volumes

Western Pacific: Government Gazettes (CO 692) 1914 to 1971, 30 volumes

Western Pacific: King's Regulations (CO 655) 1879 to 1934, 2 volumes

Hong Kong and Pacific Department: Original Correspondence (CO 1023) 1946 to 1955, 242 files

Pacific Department: Original Correspondence (CO 1036) 1952 to 1967, 575 files

Confidential Print: Western Pacific (CO 934) 1914 to 1960, 8 volumes

See also:

Dominions: Original Correspondence (CO 532) 1907 to 1925, 335 volumes

Colonies General: Supplementary Original Correspondence (CO 537) 1759 to 1955, 7862 volumes, files

British New Guinea (Papua)

In 1883 that part of New Guinea not claimed by the Netherlands was annexed by Queensland. In 1884 a British protectorate was proclaimed and a special commissioner appointed. In 1888 it was annexed to the British Crown. In 1901 it was assigned to the Commonwealth of Australia for five years and in 1906 it was proclaimed a territory of the Commonwealth under the name of Papua. From 1945 to 1946 Papua was united with former German territory of New Guinea (qv) as a single territory under the name of Papua New Guinea (qv).

From 1888 Papua was governed by an administrator assisted by nominated executive and legislative councils. These councils were retained after 1906 until civil administration gave way to military control in 1942. Civil administration of Papua New Guinea was progressively restored from 1945. A new legislative council for the territory of Papua New Guinea was established in November 1951. It had a small elective element at first but this was greatly increased in subsequent years. In 1963 the legislative council was replaced by a house of assembly with a majority of elected members. A ministerial system was introduced in 1968 and the administrator's council became the executive council. Formal self-government was attained in December 1973 and Papua New Guinea became a fully independent state within the Commonwealth of 16 September 1975.

For other records relating to British New Guinea, the former German colony of New Guinea and the new state of Papua New Guinea see under Australia and Western Pacific.

British New Guinea (Papua): Original Correspondence (CO) 1884 to 1900, 15 volumes

British New Guinea (Papua): Register of Correspondence (CO 578) 1884 to 1900, 2 volumes

British New Guinea (Papua): Register of Out-letters (CO 579) 1884 to 1900, 1 volume

British New Guinea (Papua): Acts (CO 200) 1888 to 1906, 2 volumes

British New Guinea (Papua): Sessional Papers (CO 436) 1888 to 1925, 7 volumes

Papua: Sessional Papers (DO 97) 1910 to 1941, 3 volumes

British New Guinea (Papua): Government Gazettes (CO 453) 1888 to 1921, 4 volumes

Papua: Government Gazettes (DO 86) 1922 to 1949, 2 volumes

British Solomon Islands Protectorate

The southern Solomon Islands were declared a British Protectorate in 1893 and the others were added in 1898 to 1900. In 1900 several islands in the northern group were transferred under convention from Germany. Those not transferred by Germany in 1900 were administered by Australia under the mandate for New Guinea (qv). From 1893 until 1974 the islands were under the high commissioner, but a nominated advisory council was established in 1921.

The Japanese occupied the central Solomon Islands in 1942. During the extended hostilities large numbers of allied servicemen were based on the islands with the consequent disruption of the normal life of the population.

In 1952 the headquarters of the High Commission for the Western Pacific was moved from Fiji to Honiara, the capital of the Solomon Islands, and the high commissioner took over responsibility for the direct administration of the protectorate from the acting resident commissioner. Local councils (later called provincial assemblies) were established from 1952 in the large islands. In 1960 a new constitution provided for a nominated legislative council and an executive council and in 1967 the legislative council was made partly elective. In 1974 a new constitution established the separate office of the governor of the Solomon Islands Protectorate and the office of the high commissioner for the Western Pacific was accordingly redesigned. The constitution introduced a new legislative assembly and a council of ministers. In 1975 the official name of the protectorate was changed to Solomon Islands though its protectorate status remained unchanged. On 2 January 1976 the Solomon Islands attained internal self-government and on 7 July 1978 became a fully independent state within the Commonwealth.

See also under Western Pacific High Commission.

British Solomon Islands Protectorate: Acts (CO 907) 1935 to 1965, 9 volumes

British Solomon Islands Protectorate: Sessional Papers (CO 856) 1921 to 1965, 13 volumes

British Solomon Islands Protectorate: Miscellanea (CO 723) 1920 to 1942, 22 volumes

Fiji

Fiji was ceded to Britain on 10 October 1874, after a previous offer of cession had been refused. In 1879 immigration of indentured labourers from India was authorized.

From 1875 there was a governor with nominated executive and legislative councils; the legislative council became partly elective in 1904. A local government system first established in 1876 was known as the Fijian administration. It was based on indigenous institutions and had jurisdiction over all Fijian affairs. At the apex was the council of chiefs and the executive control was through the Fijian Affairs Board. In 1952 the governor's office was separated from that of the high commissioner for the Western Pacific with which post it had been joined since 1877. In 1963 a new constitution provided for an expanded legislature and an enlarged franchise. Universal adult suffrage was introduced in 1966 leading to an elected majority in the legislative council and in 1967 to a ministerial system of government. Following a constitutional conference held in London in April and May 1970, Fiji became an independent state within the Commonwealth on 10 October 1970, the 96th anniversary of the deed of cession. It left the Commonwealth in 1987.

Fiji correspondence before 1860 and in the period 1864 to 1872 is registered in the New South Wales (qv) and Victoria (qv) registers (CO 374). For the period before 1860 see the note in CO 419/2.

See also under Western Pacific High Commission. There is also relevant material in the section on Far East/South-East Asia.

Fiji: Original Correspondence (CO 83) 1860 to 1951, 261 volumes

Fiji: Register of Correspondence (CO 419) 1860 to 1951, 26 volumes

Fiji: Register of Out-letters (CO 515) 1873 to 1926, 9 volumes

Fiji: Entry Book (CO 400) 1859 to 1862, 1 volume

Fiji: Acts (CO 84) 1875 to 1965, 22 volumes

Fiji: Sessional Papers (CO 85) 1875 to 1965, 79 volumes

Fiji: Government Gazettes (CO 86) 1874 to 1975, 71 volumes

Fiji: Miscellanea (Co 459) 1874 to 1940, 66 volumes

See also:

Dominions: Original Correspondence (CO 532) 1907 to 1925, 335 volumes

Index to Correspondence (CO 714) 1795 to 1874, 171 volumes

Colonies General: Supplementary Original Correspondence (CO 537) 1759 to 1955, 7862 volumes, files

Fiji: South Pacific Office: Original Correspondence (CO 1009) 1947 to 1970, 816 files

Gilbert and Ellice Islands (Tuvalu, Kiribati)
The islands were brought under the jurisdiction of the high commissioner for the Western Pacific (qv) in 1877, under whom they became a British protectorate in 1892 and a colony in 1916, having been formally annexed at the request of local rulers in

1915. A British resident had been appointed in 1893. A new constitution introduced in 1941 recognized the representative island councils, existing since at least 1917 for local administrative and judicial purposes, which were supervised by district commissioners.

In 1939 two of the Phoenix Islands were placed under joint British and American control, following a United States claim to sovereignty. From 1942 to 1943 the Gilbert and Ellice Islands were occupied by the Japanese. Ocean Island was occupied until 1945.

Major constitutional advance began in 1963 when an advisory council and an executive council were established. Further constitutional changes were made in 1967 and 1970, and in 1971 the colony withdrew from the high commissioner's jurisdiction except for some judicial matters. In 1972 a governor was appointed and in 1974 ministerial government was introduced. On 1 October 1975 the Ellice Islands separated by agreement from the territory to form a separate dependency called Tuvalu (now independent). The Gilbert Islands became an independent republic within the Commonwealth on 12 July 1979 under the name Kiribati.

See also under Western Pacific High Commission.

Gilbert and Ellice Islands: Acts (CO 826) 1916 to 1965, 9 volumes

Gilbert and Ellice Islands: Sessional Papers (CO 860) 1922 to 1965, 6 volumes

Gilbert and Ellice Islands: Government Gazettes (CO 1051) 1968 to 1974, 5 volumes

Gilbert and Ellice Islands: Miscellanea (CO 833) 1930 to 1941, 11 volumes

Kiribati see Gilbert and Ellice Islands

Nauru

Nauru was annexed by Germany in 1888 and surrendered to Australian forces in 1914. At Australia's request it was administered by the high commissioner for the Western Pacific (qv) from then until 1921. A mandate to administer the island was conferred upon Britain by the League of Nations in 1920. The government of the United Kingdom, the Commonwealth of Australia and New Zealand agreed that it should be governed by Australia (qv), which from that time appointed the administator, in whom executive and legislative powers were vested. Nauru was occupied by the Japanese from 1942 to 1945. The first elections in the island took place in 1951 for the local government council, whose role was mainly advisory. From 1951 to 1964 discussion of Nauru's future centred on the possibility of resettling the island's population on another island whose economy would not be clouded by the eventual exhaustion of its phosphate deposits as was threatening Nauru. However, agreement was then reached over the transfer of the assets of the British Phosphate Commissioners to Nauru. The constitutional development of the island went ahead from 1965 with the establishment of the Nauru Legislative Council. Nauru became an independent republic within the Commonwealth on 31 January 1968.

Nauru: Government Gazettes (DO 83) 1926 to 1965, 15 volumes

See also:

British Phosphate Commissioners (DO 140) 1873 to 1983, 853 files, maps, photographs, etc

New Guinea (former German territory)

New Guinea was declared a German protectorate in 1884. From 1885 until 1899 it was controlled by the German New Guinea Company and then placed under the Imperial German government. It was captured by Australian forces in 1914 and in 1920 the League of Nations issued a mandate giving full powers to Australia. New Guinea was occupied by the Japanese in 1942, but had been partly recaptured by 1945. In 1945 to 1946 it was united with British New Guinea (Papua) (qv) as a single territory of the Commonwealth of Australia.

From 1914 until 1921 New Guinea was under military administration. In 1921 legislative authority was vested in the governor-general of Australia in council. In 1932 nominated executive and legislative councils were set up. In 1942 civil administration gave way to military control.

See also British New Guinea (Papua).

New Guinea (Former German Territory): Government Gazettes (CO 667) 1914 to 1925, 2 volumes

New Guinea and Papua New Guinea: Government Gazettes (DO 85) 1926 to 1975, 37 volumes

New Hebrides (Vanuatu)

In 1877 the islands were put under the jurisdiction of the high commissioner for the Western Pacific (qv) through whom all communications were channelled. In 1887 a joint Anglo-French naval commission was established for the protection of their nationals and in 1902 British and French resident commissioners were appointed. They were continued after 1906 when an Anglo-French condominium was proclaimed and three administrations were created – the British national, the French national and the condominium. A protocol, drawn up in London in 1914 to replace the Convention of 1906, was ratified in 1922. A representative assembly, which was partly elective and which replaced the former advisory council, first met in June 1975. A government of national unity was formed in December 1978 whose major task was to draw up an independence constitution acceptable to all the people of the New Hebrides. A constitutional committee was formed, assisted by advisers from Britain and France, and a constitutional conference was held in September 1979.

The new constitution was formally adopted by the British and French governments in an exchange of notes signed in Paris on 23 October 1979. Despite an attempt by dissidents in the island of Santo to break away from the rest of the New Hebrides, the country, renamed Vanuatu, became an independent republic within the Commonwealth on 30 January 1980.

New Hebrides: Sessional Papers (CO 983) 1934 to 1965, 2 volumes

New Hebrides: Government Gazettes (CO 829) 1927 to 1969, 5 volumes

New Hebrides: Miscellanea (CO 718) 1920 to 1923, 4 volumes

New Hebrides: Joint Regulations (CO 914) 1907 to 1923, 1 volume

Papua New Guinea

Papua New Guinea was formed in 1945 to 1946 when British New Guinea (qv), known since 1906 as Papua, was united with the former German colony of New Guinea (qv) as a single territory of the Commonwealth of Australia.

Military control of the territory was progressively withdrawn from 1946 and the civil administration restored. A new legislative council was established in November 1951, the elective element of which was greatly increased in subsequent years. In 1963 the legislative council was replaced by a house of assembly with a majority of elected members. A ministerial system was introduced in 1968 and the administrator's council became the executive council. Formal self-government was attained in December 1973 and Papua New Guinea became a fully independent state within the Commonwealth on 16 September 1975.

New Guinea and Papua New Guinea: Government Gazettes (DO 85) 1926 to 1975, 37 volumes

New Guinea (Former German Territory): Government Gazettes (CO 667) 1914 to 1925, 2 volumes

Solomon Islands see British Solomon Islands Protectorate

Tonga

Tonga became a British protected state in 1900. In 1875 King George Tupou I granted a constitution of an hereditary monarch, a privy council and cabinet, and a mainly elective legislative assembly. Tonga was under the jurisdiction of the high commissioner for the Western Pacific (qv) until 1952 when the responsibility was transferred to the governor of Fiji (qv). In 1959 a new treaty of friendship was ratified which continued British protection but provided for shared conduct of some external relations. In 1965 the British commissioner and consul became responsible directly to the secretary of state for the colonies and ceased to be subordinate to the governor of Fiji. In 1968 a revised treaty of friendship provided for the government of Tonga to have full responsibility for internal affairs and a greater degree of responsibility for external relations. On 4 June 1970 the Kingdom of Tonga became a fully independent member state of the Commonwealth.

See also under Western Pacific High Commission.

Tonga: Sessional Papers (CO 861) 1914 to 1965, 10 volumes

Tonga: Government Gazettes (CO 676) 1905 to 1975, 21 volumes

Tuvalu see Gilbert and Ellice Islands

Vanuatu see New Hebrides

Western Samoa
Formerly administered by New Zealand, Western Samoa became, on 1 January 1962, the first fully independent Polynesian state. It was treated as a member of the Commonwealth until its formal admission on 28 August 1970.

Western Samoa: Government Gazettes (DO 107) 1920 to 1973, 5 volumes

Western Samoa: Miscellanea (DO 113) 1916 to 1950, 1 volume

11.3 Alphabetical list of territories showing the geographical departments responsible for their affairs, 1861 to 1965

This list, arranged by the administrative names used by the Colonial Office, indicates the departments responsible for each territory down to the last full year that it was under the Colonial Office. Territories are not listed for years during which they were treated as dependencies of other territories.

The information has been taken from the *Colonial Office List*, which was not published during the Second World War. It was the practice to issue these lists in the year printed on the spine, but in fact they were normally prepared during the previous year, to which they relate most accurately. For consistency the dates here reflect the dates on the spines.

ADEN Middle East (1921–1928); Ceylon and Mediterranean (1929–1931); Middle East (1932–1945); Central African and Aden (1948–1959); Gulf of Aden and General (1960–1961); East African (1962); Aden and Social Service (1963); Aden (1964–1966)

ANTARCTICA Mediterranean (1949–1955); West African (1956); West Indian (1957); West African (1958); Pacific and Indian Ocean (1959–1964); Atlantic (1965–1966)

ANTIGUA West Indian (1862–1888); Number 1 (1889–1897); West Indian (1898–1966)

ASCENSION West Indian (1929–1931); Pacific and Mediterranean (1932–1936); West African (1938–1943); see also St Helena

ASHANTI West African (1906–1908); West African and Mediterranean (1909–1917); Gold Coast and Mediterranean (1918–1928); West African (1929–1945)

AUSTRALIA Australian and Eastern (1862–1867); North American and Australian (1868–1872); North American, Australian, African and Mediterranean (1873–1874); North American and Australian (1875–1888); Number 2 (1889–1897); North American and Australasian (1898–1907); Dominions Division (1908–1925)

BAHAMAS West Indian (1868–1888); Number 1 (1889–1897); West Indian (1898); North American and Australasian (1899–1906); West Indian (1907–1966)

BARBADOS West Indian (1862–1888); Number 1 (1889–1897); West Indian (1898–1966)

BASUTOLAND Number 4 (1889–1897); South African (1898–1907); Southern Africa (1962–1966)

BECHUANALAND African and Cyprus (1886–1888); Number 4 (1889–1897); South African (1898–1907); Southern Africa (1962–1966)

BERMUDA Australian and Eastern (1862–1864); North American (1865–1871); West Indian (1872–1888); Number 1 (1889–1897); North American and Australasian (1898–1906); West Indian (1907–1966)

BRITISH CAMEROONS Nigeria (1922–1928); West African (1929–1945); West African (1961)

BRITISH COLUMBIA North American (1862–1867); Eastern (1868–1871)

BRITISH GUIANA West Indian (1862–1888); Number 1 (1889–1897); West Indian (1898–1966)

BRITISH HONDURAS West Indian (1862–1888); Number 1 (1889–1897); West Indian (1898); North American and Australasian (1899–1905); West Indian (1906–1966)

BRITISH KAFFRARIA Mediterranean (1862–1867); African and Mediterranean (1868–1872); North American, Australian, African and Mediterranean (1873–1874); see also Cape Colony

BRUNEI Eastern (1908–1919); Far Eastern (1920–1931); Eastern (1932–1948); South-East Asia (1949–1954); Far Eastern (1955–1963)

CAICOS ISLANDS Number 1 (1889–1897)

CANADA North American (1862–1872); North American, Australian, African and Mediterranean (1873–1874); North American and Australian (1875–1888); Number 2 (1889–1897); North American and Australasian (1898–1907); Dominions Division (1908–1925)

CAPE COLONY Number 4 (1889–1897); South African (1898–1907); Dominions Division (1906–1925)

CAPE OF GOOD HOPE Mediterranean (1862–1867); African and Mediterranean (1868–1872); North American, Australian, African and Mediterranean (1873–1874); African and Mediterranean (1875–1887); African and Cyprus (1888); Number 4 (1889–1897); South African (1898–1907); Dominions Division (1908–1911)

CEYLON Australian and Eastern (1862–1867); Eastern (1868–1872); West Indian and Eastern (1873–1879); Eastern (1880–1888); Number 4 (1889–1896); Number 5 (1897); Eastern (1898–1919); Ceylon and Mauritius (1920–1928); Ceylon and Mediterranean (1929–1931); Eastern (1932–1943); Ceylon and Pacific (1944–1947)

CYPRUS African and Mediterranean (1881–1887); African and Cyprus (1888); Number 4 (1889–1891); No 2 (1892–1897); North American and Australasian (1898–1907); East African and Mediterranean (1908); West African and Mediterranean (1909–1917); Gold Coast and Mediterranean (1918–1927); Ceylon and Mediterranean (1928–1931); Pacific and Mediterranean (1932–1943); Mediterranean (1944–1960)

DOMINICA West Indian (1862–1879)

FALKLAND ISLANDS North American (1862–1867); African and Mediterranean (1868–1872); West Indian (1873–1874); African and Mediterranean (1875); West Indian (1876–1879); Eastern (1880); West Indian (1881–1888); Number 1 (1889–1897); North American and Australasian (1898); South African (1899); North American and Australasian (1900–1907); West Indian (1908–1931); Pacific and Mediterranean (1932–1943); Mediterranean (1944–1955); West African (1956); West Indian (1957); West African (1958); Pacific and Indian Ocean (1959–1966)

FIJI North American and Australian (1875–1888); Number 2 (1889–1907); Dominions Division (1908–1925); Ceylon and Mauritius (1926–1928); Far Eastern (1929–1931); Pacific and Mediterranean (1932–1943); Ceylon and Pacific (1944–1947); Hong Kong and Pacific (1948–1954); Pacific (1955–1966)

GAMBIA Mediterranean (1862–1867); African and Mediterranean (1868–1872); North American, Australian, African and Mediterranean (1873–1874); African and Mediterranean (1875–1888); Number 3 (1889–1898); West African (1899–1908); West African and Mediterranean (1909–1917); Gold Coast and Mediterranean (1918–1928); West African (1929–1961); Mediterranean (1962–1964)

GIBRALTAR Australian and Eastern (1862–1864); North American, Australian, African and Mediterranean (1873–1874); African and Mediterranean (1875–1887); Eastern (1888); Number 2 (1889–1897); North American (1898–1907); East African and Mediterranean (1908); West African and Mediterranean (1909–1917); Gold Coast and Mediterranean (1918–1928); Ceylon and Mediterranean (1929–1931); Pacific and Mediterranean (1932–1943); Mediterranean (1944–1962); Mediterranean and Atlantic (1963–1964); Atlantic (1965–1966)

GOLD COAST Mediterranean (1862–1867); African and Mediterranean (1868–1872), North American, Australian, African and Mediterranean (1873–1874); African and Mediterranean (1875–1887); African and Cyprus (1888); Number 3 (1889–1898); West African (1899–1908); West African and Mediterranean (1909–1917); Gold Coast and Mediterranean (1918–1928); West African (1929–1957)

GRENADA West Indian (1862–1879)

GRIQUALAND African and Mediterranean (1875–1880)

HELIGOLAND Mediterranean (1862–1867); African and Mediterranean (1868–1872); West Indian and Eastern (1873–1874); African and Mediterranean (1875); West Indian (1876–1879); Eastern (1880); West Indian (1881–1888); Number 1 (1889–1891)

HONG KONG Australian and Eastern (1862–1867); Eastern (1868–1872); West Indian (1873–1879); Eastern (1880–1888); Number 4 (1889–1896); Number 5 (1897); Eastern (1898–1919); Far Eastern (1920–1947); Hong Kong and Pacific (1948–1954); Far Eastern (1955–1963); Defence, Intelligence and Hong Kong (1964–1965); Hong Kong and West Indian 'C' (1966)

IONIAN ISLANDS Mediterranean (1862–1864)

IRAQ Middle East (1921–1932)

IRISH FREE STATE Dominions Division (1924–1925)

JAMAICA West Indian (1862–1888); Number 1 (1889–1897); West Indian (1898–1966)

KENYA East African and Mediterranean (1907–1908); East African (1909–1962)

LABUAN Australian and Eastern (1862–1867); Eastern (1868–1872); West Indian and Eastern (1873–1879); Eastern (1880–1888); Number 4 (1889–1896); Number 5 (1897); Eastern (1898–1908)

LAGOS Mediterranean (1863–1867); see Sierra Leone (1867–1874) and Gold Coast (1875–1886); African and Mediterranean (1886–1888); Number 3 (1889–1898); West African (1899–1908)

LEEWARD ISLANDS West Indian (1880–1888); Number 1 (1889–1897); West Indian (1898–1966)

MALACCA Australian and Eastern (1867); Eastern (1868–1872); West Indian (1873–1879); Eastern (1880–1888); Number 4 (1889–1896); Number 5 (1897); Eastern (1898–1945)

MALAY STATES Number 4 (1893–1896); Number 5 (1897); Eastern (1898–1919); Far Eastern (1920–1931); Eastern (1932–1948); South-East Asia (1949–1954); Far Eastern (1955–1962)

MALTA Mediterranean (1862–1867); African and Mediterranean (1868–1872); North American, Australian, African and Mediterranean (1873–1874); African and Mediterranean (1874–1886); Eastern (1888); Number 3 (1889–1898); South African (1899); West African (1900–1905); North American and Australasian (1906); Mediterranean (1906–1964)

MARION ISLANDS West Indian (1925–1931); Pacific and Mediterranean (1932–1943); see also Canada

MAURITIUS West Indian (1862–1867); Eastern (1868–1872); West Indian (1873–1879); Eastern (1880–1888); Number 3 (1889–1896); Number 5 (1897); Eastern (1898–1919); Ceylon and Mauritius (1920–1928); Far Eastern (1929–1931); Eastern (1932–1943); Ceylon and Pacific (1944–1947); Hong Kong and Pacific (1948–1954); Pacific (1955–1966)

MONTSERRAT West Indian (1862–1879)

NATAL Mediterranean (1862–1867); African and Mediterranean (1868–1872); North American, Australian, African and Mediterranean (1873–1874); African and Mediterranean (1875–1888); Number 4 (1889–1897); South African (1898–1907)

NEW BRUNSWICK North American (1862–1867)

NEWFOUNDLAND North American (1862–1872); North American, Australian, African and Mediterranean (1873–1874); North American and Australian (1875–1888); Number 2 (1889–1897); North American and Australasian (1898–1907); Dominions Division (1908–1925)

NEW GUINEA North American and Australian (1887–1888); Number 2 (1889–1897); North American and Australasian (1898–1907)

NEW SOUTH WALES Australian and Eastern (1862–1867); North American and Australian (1868–1872); North American, Australian, African and Mediterranean (1873–1874); North American and Australian (1875–1888); Number 2 (1889–1897); North American and Australasian (1898–1907)

NEW ZEALAND Australian and Eastern (1862–1867); North American and Australian (1868–1872); North American, Australian, African and Mediterranean (1873–1874); North American and Australian (1875–1888); Number 2 (1889–1897); North American and Australasian (1898–1907); Dominions Division (1908–1925)

NIGERIA West African (1899–1908); Nigeria (1909–1928); West African (1929–1960)

NORTH BORNEO (SABAH) Number 4 (1893–1896); Number 5 (1897); Eastern (1898–1919); Far Eastern (1920–1931); Eastern (1932–1948); South-East Asia (1949–1954); Far Eastern (1955–1963)

NORTHERN RHODESIA South African (1899–1907); Dominions Division (1908–1923); Tanganyika and Somaliland (1924–1939); Tanganyika (1940–1943); Central African and Aden (1948–1962); [Central African Office (1963–1964)]

NOVA SCOTIA North American (1862–1867)

NYASALAND East African and Mediterranean (1908); East African (1909–1928); Tanganyika and Somaliland (1920–1945); East and Central African (1946–1947); Central African and Aden (1948–1962); [Central African Office (1963–1964)]

ORANGE RIVER South African (1903–1907); Dominions Division (1908–1911)

PALESTINE Middle Eastern (1921–1948)

PENANG Australian and Eastern (1867); Eastern (1868–1872); West Indian and Eastern (1873–1879); Eastern (1880–1888); Number 4 (1889–1896); Number 5 (1897); Eastern (1898–1919); Far Eastern (1920–1931); Eastern (1932–1945)

PRINCE EDWARD ISLAND North American (1862–1872); North American, Australian, African and Mediterranean (1873–1874); West Indian (1925–1931); Pacific and Mediterranean (1932–1943)

QUEENSLAND Australian and Eastern (1862–1867); North American and Australian (1868–1872); North American, Australian, African and Mediterranean (1873–1874); North American and Australian (1875–1888); Number 2 (1889–1897); North American and Australasian (1898–1907)

ST HELENA Mediterranean (1862–1867); African and Mediterranean (1868–1872); North American, Australian, African and Mediterranean (1873–1874); African and Mediterranean (1875–1889); Number 3 (1889–1898); South African (1899–1907); West Indian (1908–1919); Ceylon and Mauritius (1920–1928); West Indian (1929–1931); Pacific and Mediterranean (1932–1937); West African (1938–1943); Ceylon and Pacific (1944–1947); Hong Kong and Pacific (1948–1954); Pacific (1955); West African (1956); West Indian (1957); West African (1958–1960); Mediterranean (1962); Mediterranean and Atlantic (1963–1964); Atlantic (1965–1966)

ST KITTS West Indian (1862–1879)

ST LUCIA West Indian (1862–1879)

St Vincent West Indian (1862–1879)

Sarawak Eastern (1908–1919); Far Eastern (1920–1931); Eastern (1932–1948); South-East Asia (1949–1954); Far Eastern (1955–1963)

Seychelles Eastern (1868–1872); West Indian and Eastern (1873–1879); Eastern (1880–1888); Number 3 (1889–1896); No 5 (1897); Eastern (1898–1919); Ceylon and Mauritius (1920–1928); Far Eastern (1929–1943); Ceylon and Pacific (1944–1947); Hong Kong and Pacific (1948–1954); Pacific (1955–1958); Pacific and Indian Ocean (1959–1966)

Sierra Leone Mediterranean (1862–1867); African and Mediterranean (1868–1872); North American, Australian, African and Mediterranean (1873–1874); African and Mediterranean (1875–1887); African and Cyprus (1888); Number 3 (1889–1898); West African (1899–1908); West African and Mediterranean (1909–1917); Gold Coast and Mediterranean (1918–1928); West African (1929–1962)

Singapore Australian and Eastern (1867); Eastern (1868–1872); West Indian and Eastern (1873–1879); Eastern (1880–1888); Number 4 (1889–1896); Number 5 (1897); Eastern (1898–1919); Far Eastern (1920–1931); Eastern (1932–1948); South-East Asia (1949–1954); Far East (1955–1963)

Somaliland East African and Mediterranean (1908); East African (1909–1919); Tanganyika and Somaliland (1920–1940); Tanganyika (1941–1943); Central African and Aden (1948–1959); East African (1960)

Straits Settlements Eastern (1868–1872); West Indian and Eastern (1873–1879); Eastern (1880–1888); Number 4 (1889–1896); Number 5 (1897); Eastern (1898–1919); Far Eastern (1920–1931); Eastern (1932–1945)

Southern Rhodesia South African (1899–1907); Dominions Division (1908–1925)

Swaziland Southern Africa (1962–1966)

Tanganyika Tanganyika and Somaliland (1920–1940); Tanganyika (1941–1943); East African (1944–1961)

Tasmania Australian and Eastern (1862–1867); North American and Australian (1868–1872); North American, Australian, African and Mediterranean (1873–1874); North American (1875–1888); Number 2 (1889–1897); North American and Australasian (1898–1906)

Tobago West Indian (1862–1879)

Togoland Gold Coast and Mediterranean (1922–1928); West African (1929–1945)

Tonga See Western Pacific; Pacific (1956–1958); Pacific and Indian Ocean (1959–1966)

Transjordan Middle East Department (1929–1947)

Transvaal African and Mediterranean (1878–1885); South African (1903–1907)

Trinidad West Indian (1862–1888); Number 1 (1889–1897); West Indian (1898–1962)

TRISTAN DA CUNHA West Indian (1929–1931); Pacific and Mediterranean (1932–1937); West Africa (1938–1943); see also St Helena

TURKS ISLANDS West Indian (1862–1888); Number 1 (1889–1897); West Indian (1898–1945)

UGANDA East African and Mediterranean (1908); East African (1909–1945); East and Central Africa (1946–1947); East Africa (1948–1963)

VANCOUVER ISLAND North American (1862–1867)

VICTORIA Australian and Eastern (1862–1867); North American and Australian (1868–1872); North American, Australian, African and Mediterranean (1873–1874); North American and Australian (1875–1888); Number 2 (1889–1897); North American and Australasian (1898–1907)

VIRGIN ISLANDS West Indian (1862–1879)

WEI-HAI-WEI Eastern (1905–1919); Far Eastern (1920–1930)

WESTERN PACIFIC North American and Australian (1879–1888), Number 2 (1889–1907); Dominions Division (1908–1925); Ceylon and Mauritius (1926–1928); Far Eastern (1929–1931); Pacific and Mediterranean (1932–1943); Ceylon and Pacific (1944–1947); Hong Kong and Pacific (1948–1954); Pacific (1955–1958); Pacific and Indian Ocean (1959–1966)

WINDWARD ISLANDS West Indian (1880–1888); Number 1 (1889–1897); West Indian (1898–1966)

ZANZIBAR East African (1915–1921; 1922–1946); East and Central African (1946–1963)

ZULULAND African and Mediterranean (1887–1888); Number 4 (1889–1897)

11.4 Breakdown of geographical department business, 1861 to 1965

This list traces the development of geographical departmental organization. With the list in 11.3 it will enable the reader to determine the way in which the Colonial Office handled geographical business at any given time. It may also be used in conjunction with chapter 7.3 to trace the territories for which an assistant secretary was responsible. It is particularly important for the period after 1951 when the Colonial Office arranged correspondence in series for each department. Chapter 15.4.1 provides a list of departmental filing codes for these departments.

For convenience, the departments are arranged under broad regional groupings. However, departments were often responsible for territories from more than one region, and cross-references are provided. The countries for which each department was responsible are initially listed fully and thereafter an indication is only given when a territory was added (+) or removed (–). When there was a major change the territories have been listed again.

For consistency, the dates given are those indicated on the spines of the annual volumes of the *Colonial Office List*. However, the printed *Lists* were normally prepared during the previous year, to which the dates refer most accurately. The printed *Lists* did not appear during the Second World War, causing a gap in the information.

Contents:
AFRICA, EAST AND CENTRAL:
  East African and Mediterranean Department (1908)
  East African Department (1909–1942)
  Tanganyika and Somaliland Department (1920–1940)
  Tanganyika Department (1941–1943)
  Central African Department (1943–1945)
  East African Department (1943–1945)
  East and Central African Department (1945–1947)
  East African Department (1948–1963)
  Central African and Aden Department (1948–1959)
  Central African Department (1960–1962)

AFRICA, SOUTH:
  Mediterranean Department (1862–1867)
  African and Mediterranean Department (1868–1872)
  North American, Australian, African and Mediterranean Department (1873–1874)
  African and Mediterranean Department (1875–1887)
  African and Cyprus Department (1888)
  Department Number 4 (1889–1896)
  South African Department (1898–1904)
  South African/South African Protectorates Department (1905–1907)
  Dominions Division (1908–1925)
  Southern Africa Department (1962–1966)

AFRICA, WEST:
  Mediterranean Department (1862–1867)
  African and Mediterranean Department (1868–1872)
  North American, Australian, African and Mediterranean Department (1873–1874)
  African and Mediterranean Department (1875–1887)
  African and Cyprus Department (1888)
  Department Number 3 (1889–1896)
  West African Department (1897–1908)
  West African and Mediterranean Department (1909–1917)
  Gold Coast and Mediterranean Department (1918–1927)
  Niger Department (1909–1919)
  Nigeria Department (1920–1928)
  West African Department (1929–1961)

AFRICA, GENERAL:
  African Studies Branch (1948–1962)

CARIBBEAN:
  West Indian Department (1862–1872)
  West Indian and Eastern Department (1873–1879)

West Indian Department (1880–1888)
Department Number 1 (1889–1897)
West Indian Department (1898–1965)
West Indian and Hong Kong Department (1966)

MEDITERRANEAN AND ATLANTIC:
Mediterranean Department (1821–1867)
African and Mediterranean Department (1868–1872)
North American, Australian, African and Mediterranean Department (1873–1874)
African and Mediterranean Department (1875–1887)
African and Cyprus Department (1888)
Department Number 4 (1889–1896)
South African/South African Protectorates Department (1897–1906)
East African and Mediterranean Department (1908)
West African and Mediterranean Department (1909–1917)
Gold Coast and Mediterranean Department (1918–1927)
Ceylon and Mediterranean Department (1928–1931)
Pacific and Mediterranean Department (1932–1943)
Mediterranean Department (1944–1962)
Mediterranean and Atlantic Department (1963–1964)
Atlantic Department (1965–1966)

MIDDLE EAST:
Middle East Division (1921–1925)
Middle East Department (1926–1947)
Central African and Aden Department (1948–1959)
Aden Department (1964–1965)

NORTH AMERICA AND AUSTRALIA:
North American Department (1862–1867)
Australian and Eastern Department (1862–1867)
North American and Australian Department (1868–1872)
North American, Australian, African and Mediterranean Department (1873–1874)
North American and Australian Department (1875–1888)
Department Number 2 (1889–1897)
North American and Australasian Department (1898–1907)
Dominions Division (1908–1925)

PACIFIC:
North American and Australian Department (1875–1888)
Department Number 2 (1889–1907)
Dominions Division (1908–1925)
Ceylon and Mauritius Department (1926–1928)
Far Eastern (1929–1931)
Pacific and Mediterranean Department (1932–1943)
Ceylon and Pacific Department (1944–1948)
Hong Kong and Pacific Department (1949–1954)
Pacific Department (1955–1958)
Pacific and Indian Ocean Department (1959–1966)

SOUTH AND SOUTH-EAST ASIA:
  Australian and Eastern Department (1862–1867)
  Eastern Department (1868–1872)
  West Indian and Eastern Department (1873–1979)
  Eastern Department (1880–1888)
  Department Number 4 (1889–1899)
  Department Number 5 (1897)
  Eastern Department (1898–1919)
  Far Eastern Department (1920–1931)
  Ceylon and Mauritius Department (1920–1928)
  Ceylon and Mediterranean Department (1928–1931)
  Eastern Department (1932–1948)
  Ceylon and Pacific Department (1944–1948)
  South-East Asia Department (1949–1962)
  West Indian and Hong Kong Department (1966)

AFRICA, EAST AND CENTRAL

East African and Mediterranean Department
1908 Nyasaland, East Africa Protectorate, Uganda, Somaliland Protectorate, Gibraltar, Malta, Cyprus

East African Department
1909–1913 Somaliland, Uganda, British East Africa, Nyasaland

1914–1919 as above + Zanzibar

1920 as above – Somaliland and Nyasaland

1921 Uganda, Kenya, Zanzibar, Nyasaland

1922–1942 Uganda, Kenya, Zanzibar

Tanganyika and Somaliland Department
1920–1923 Tanganyika Territory, Somaliland, Nyasaland

1924–1940 as above + Northern Rhodesia

Tanganyika Department
1941–1943 as above

Central African Department
1943–1945 Northern Rhodesia, Nyasaland

East African Department
1943–1945 Uganda, Kenya, Zanzibar

East and Central African Department
1945–1947 Uganda, Somaliland, Kenya, Tanganyika, Zanzibar, Rhodesia, Nyasaland

East African Department
1948–1950 Kenya, Tanganyika, Uganda, Zanzibar, East Africa, Zanzibar, flora and fauna

1951 East Africa, Kenya, Tanganyika, Uganda, Zanzibar, tsetse and trypanosomiasis, game preservation, community development, recognition of missionary societies

1952–1954 as above – community development

1955 East Africa, Kenya, Tanganyika, Uganda, Zanzibar, East and Central African transport, Overseas Food Corporation, missionary societies

1956–1958 as above – Overseas Food Corporation, Central African transport

1959–1961 as above + relations with Ethopia and Somalia; – East African transport, missionary societies

1962 Uganda, Kenya, East African defence and security, higher education

1963 Kenya, Uganda, East African defence and security, higher education, Zanzibar, East African Common Services Organization

Central African and Aden Department
1948–1958 Aden, Northern Rhodesia, Nyasaland, British Somaliland

1959 as above + Aden Protectorate, Middle East subjects

Then see Aden and Social Services Department in chapter 12.3.

Central African Department
1960–1962 Northern Rhodesia, Nyasaland

AFRICA, SOUTH

Mediterranean Department
1862–1867 see under Mediterranean

African and Mediterranean Department
1868–1872 Malta, Gambia, Sierra Leone, Gold Coast, Lagos, Cape of Good Hope, British Kaffraria, Natal, Heligoland, Gibraltar, Falkland Islands, St Helena

North American, Australian, African and Mediterranean Department
1873–1874 see under North America and Australia

African and Mediterranean Department
1875 Sierra Leone, Gambia, Gold Coast, Cape of Good Hope, Griqualand West, Natal, St Helena, Malta, Gibraltar, Heligoland, Falkland Islands

1876–1877 as above – Heligoland and Falkland Islands

1878–1880 as above + Transvaal

1881 as above + Cyprus; – Griqualand West

1882–1885 Cape of Good Hope, Natal, Transvaal, St Helena, Sierra Leone, Gambia, Gold Coast, Lagos, Malta, Gibraltar, Cyprus

1886 as above + Bechuanaland; – Transvaal

1887 as above + Zululand

African and Cyprus Department
1888 Cape of Good Hope, Natal, Zululand, Bechuanaland, St Helena, Sierra Leone, Gambia, Gold Coast, Lagos, Cyprus

Department Number 4
1889–1891 Ceylon, Hong Kong, Labuan, Cyprus, Straits Settlements, Cape, Natal, Zululand, Bechuanaland, Basutoland, South Africa High Commission, Borneo

1892 as above – Cyprus

1893–1896 as above + Malay States

South African Department
1898 as above – Zululand

1899 Cape of Good Hope, Natal, South Africa High Commission, Rhodesia, Bechuanaland Protectorate, Basutoland, Malta, St Helena, Falkland Islands

1900–1902 as above – Malta, Falkland Islands

1903–1904 Cape of Good Hope, South Africa High Commission, Transvaal, Orange River Colony, Rhodesia, Bechuanaland, Basutoland, Natal, St Helena

South African/South African Protectorates Department
1905–1907 Cape Colony, Basutoland, Natal, Transvaal, Orange River Colony, Bechuanaland, Southern Rhodesia, NW Rhodesia (Barotseland), British Central Africa Protectorate, NE Rhodesia, St Helena

Dominions Division
1908–1924 Canada, Australia, Australian states, New Zealand, Cape of Good Hope, Natal, Newfoundland, Transvaal, Orange River Colony, Fiji, Western Pacific, Basutoland, Bechuanaland, Swaziland, Rhodesia

1924–1925 as above + Irish Free State; – Rhodesia; + Southern Rhodesia

Southern Africa Department
1962–1966 Basutoland, Bechuanaland, Swaziland

AFRICA, WEST

Mediterranean Department
1862–1867 see under Mediterranean and Atlantic

African and Mediterranean Department
1868–1872 see under Africa, South

North American, Australian, African and Mediterranean Department
1873–1874 see under North America and Australia

African and Mediterranean Department
1875–1887 see under Africa, South

African and Cyprus Department
1888 see under Africa, South

Department Number 3
1889–1896 Gambia, Gold Coast, Lagos, Mauritius, Sierra Leone, St Helena, Malta

1897–1898 as above – Mauritius

West African Department
1899 West African colonies and protectorates

1900–1901 as above + Malta

1902–1905 Northern and Southern Nigeria, Lagos, Gold Coast, Sierra Leone, Gambia and Malta

1906–1907 as above + Ashanti, Northern Territories of Gold Coast, – Malta

1908 as above – Lagos

West African and Mediterranean Department
1909–1917 Gambia, Sierra Leone, Gold Coast, Ashanti, Northern Territories of Gold Coast, Gibraltar, Malta, Cyprus

Gold Coast and Mediterranean Department
1918–1919 as above

1922–1927 as above + Togoland

Niger Department
1909–1919 Southern and Northern Nigeria

Nigeria Department
1920–1921 Nigeria

1922–1928 Nigeria, British sphere of Cameroons

West African Department

1929–1937 Gambia, Sierra Leone, Gold Coast, Ashanti, Northern Territories of Gold Coast, British Togoland, Nigeria, British Cameroons

1938–1943 as above + St Helena, Ascension, Tristan da Cunha

1944 as above − St Helena (with Ascension and Tristan da Cunha)

1946–1951 Gambia, Gold Coast, Nigeria, Sierra Leone, West African Council, general West African questions

1952 as above + West African Inter-Territorial Conference; − West African Council

1953 as above + Secretariat and Conference

1954 Nigeria, Gold Coast, Sierra Leone

1955 as above + regional matters (except tsetse and research) affecting those territories

1956 as above + Falkland Islands and Antarctic, St Helena, Tristan da Cunha

1957 as above − Falkland Islands and Antarctic, St Helena, Tristan da Cunha

1958 Nigeria, Gambia, Sierra Leone, West African regional matters, Falkland Islands and Antarctic, St Helena and Tristan da Cunha

1959–1960 as above − Falkland Islands and Antarctic

1961 as above + Cameroons; − Nigeria

AFRICA, GENERAL

African Studies Branch

1948–1953 African local administration; land tenure; native law and courts; sociological research in relation to administrative problems; *Journal of African Administration*; secretariat for Land, Law, and Local Government Panels

1954 above + provides secretariat for Summer Conference; − secretariat for Land panel

1955 African local administration; land tenure; native law and courts; *Journal of African Administration*; secretariat for Law and Local Government Panels and for Summer Conference; information on current administrative problems

1956–1962 as above + sociological research

CARIBBEAN

West Indian Department
1862–1866 Jamaica, British Honduras, Turks Islands, British Guiana, Barbados, Bahamas, Trinidad, St Vincent, Grenada, Tobago, St Lucia, Antigua, Montserrat, St Kitts, Nevis, Virgin Islands, Dominica, Mauritius

1867 as above – Dominica

1868–1872 as above + Dominica; – Mauritius

West Indian and Eastern Department
1873–1874 as above + Bermuda, Ceylon, Hong Kong, Labuan, Straits Settlements, Mauritius, Seychelles, Heligoland, Falkland Islands

1875 as above – Heligoland, Falkland Islands

1876–1879 as above + Heligoland, Falkland Islands

West Indian Department
1880 Jamaica, Turks Islands, British Honduras, British Guiana, Trinidad, Windward Islands, Leeward Islands, Bahamas, Bermuda

1881–1888 as above + Falkland Islands, Heligoland

Department Number 1
1889–1891 as above + Caicos Islands

1892–1897 as above – Heligoland

West Indian Department
1898 Jamaica, Turks Islands, British Honduras, British Guiana, Bahamas, Trinidad, Tobago, Barbados, Windward Islands, Leeward Islands

1899–1905 Jamaica, Turks Islands, British Guiana, Trinidad, Barbados, Windward Islands, Leeward Islands

1906 as above + British Honduras, Bahamas

1907 as above + Bermuda

1908–1918 as above + Falkland Islands, St Helena

1919–1924 as above – St Helena

1925–1928 as above + Prince Edward and Marion Islands

1929–1931 Jamaica, Turks Islands, British Honduras, British Guiana, Bahamas, Bermuda, Trinidad, Barbados, Windward Islands, Leeward Islands, Falkland Islands, Prince Edward and Marion Islands, St Helena, Ascension, Tristan da Cunha

1932–1945 Jamaica, Turks Islands, British Honduras, British Guiana, Bahamas, Bermuda, Trinidad, Barbados, Windward Islands, Leeward Islands

1946–1948 Jamaica, Bahamas, Windward Islands, Leeward Islands, Trinidad, British Honduras, Bermuda, British Guiana, Barbados, Comptroller of Development and Welfare, Caribbean Commission, United States air bases, University College for the West Indies

1949–1950 Jamaica, Leeward Islands, Barbados, Bahamas, Bermuda, Trinidad, Windward Islands, British Guiana, British Honduras, United States bases, defence and security, closer association, Caribbean Commission, development and welfare organization, University College, regional economy, financial, labour and communications questions, international relations

1951–1954 Jamaica, Leeward Islands, Trinidad, Windward Islands, Barbados, British Guiana, British Honduras, Bermuda, Bahamas, defence and security, University College, United States bases, closer association, Caribbean Commission, development and welfare organization, regional economic questions except research, international relations except US bases, regional social services questions, ancient monuments and records

1955 as above + West Indian communities and labour abroad

1956 as above − defence and security

1957 as above + British Caribbean Federation, Falkland Islands, Antarctic, St Helena, Tristan da Cunha; − closer association

1958 Barbados, Jamaica, Leeward Islands, Trinidad, Windward Islands, United States bases, West Indian communities and labour abroad, East Indians, regional questions, Bahamas, Bermuda, British Guiana, British Honduras, West Indies Federation, Caribbean Committee, development and welfare organization, University College, international relations except US bases, ancient monuments and records

1959 West Indies federal affairs, Barbados, Jamaica, Leeward Islands, Trinidad, Windward Islands, Bahamas, Bermuda, British Guiana, British Honduras, United States bases, regional Caribbean questions, Caribbean Commission, University College, Imperial College of Tropical Agriculture, international relations except US bases, ancient monuments and records, West Indian communities and labour abroad, East Indians

1960 as above − international relations except US bases

1961 as above − Imperial College of Tropical Agriculture

1962 as above − East Indians

1963 West Indies (dissolution of the Federation, Interim Committee, common services, Federation of Barbados and the Leeward and Windward Islands), Barbados, Leeward Islands, Windward Islands, Bahamas, Bermuda, British Guiana, British Honduras, US bases, regional Caribbean subjects, Caribbean Organization, ancient monuments and records, West Indian communities and labour abroad

1964–1965 West Indies (dissolution of the Federation, the Interim Committee, common services, Federation of Barbados and the Leeward and Windward

Islands), Barbados, Leeward Islands, Windward Islands, Bahamas, Bermuda, British Guiana, British Honduras, Caribbean Organization, ancient monuments and records, West Indian communities and labour abroad

West Indian and Hong Kong Department
1966 as above + Hong Kong, Turks and Caicos Islands, − Caribbean Organization

MEDITERRANEAN AND ATLANTIC
The Atlantic territories were handled by many different departments at different times and are included in this section when they were grouped with the Mediterranean territories. Otherwise refer to 11.3.

Mediterranean Department
1862 Ionian Islands, Malta, Gambia, Sierra Leone, Gold Coast, St Helena, Cape of Good Hope, British Kaffraria, Natal, Heligoland

1863–1864 as above + Lagos

1863–1867 as above − Ionian Islands

African and Mediterranean Department
1868–1872 see under Africa, South

North American, Australian, African and Mediterranean Department
1873–1874 see under North America and Australia

African and Mediterranean Department
1875–1887 see under Africa, South

African and Cyprus Department
1888 see under Africa, South

Department Number 4
1889–1896 see under Africa, South

South African/South African Protectorates Department
1897–1906 see under Africa, South

East African and Mediterranean Department
1908 see under Africa, East and Central

West African and Mediterranean Department
1909–1917 see under Africa, West

Gold Coast and Mediterranean Department
1918–1919 see under Africa, West

1922–1927 as above + Togoland

Ceylon and Mediterranean Department
1928–1931 Ceylon, Aden, Cyprus, Malta, Gibraltar

Pacific and Mediterranean Department
1932–1943 see under Pacific

Mediterranean Department
1944–1948 Gibraltar, Malta, Cyprus, Falkland Islands, Falkland Islands Dependency Survey

1949–1952 as above + Antarctic matters, Falkland Island Dependencies

1953–1955 as above − Falkland Island Dependencies

1956–1958 Gibraltar, Malta, Cyprus

1959–1960 Cyprus, Gibraltar, Malta

1961 as above − Cyprus

1962 Gibraltar, Malta, Gambia, St Helena, Ascension, Tristan da Cunha

Mediterranean and Atlantic Department
1963–1964 as above

Atlantic Department
1965 Falkland Islands, Antarctic, Gibraltar, Gambia, St Helena, Ascension, Tristan da Cunha, ILO, application of international labour conventions in colonies, international trade union organizations, general questions of labour legislation

1966 as above − Gambia

MIDDLE EAST

Middle East Division
1921–1925 Mesopotamia (Iraq), Palestine, Aden and Arab areas under British influence

Middle East Department
1926–1928 Palestine, Aden, Arab areas under British influence

1929–1931 Palestine, Iraq, Transjordan and Arab areas under British influence

1932 as above + Aden

1933–1947 as above − Iraq

Central African and Aden Department
1948–1959 see East and Central Africa

Aden Department
1964–1965 Aden, Federation of South Arabia, Protectorate of South Arabia, Middle East affairs

NORTH AMERICA AND AUSTRALIA

North American Department
1862–1864 Canada, Nova Scotia, New Brunswick, Prince Edward Island, Newfoundland, Vancouver Island, British Columbia, Falkland Islands

1865–1867 as above + Bermuda

Australian and Eastern Department
1862–1864 New South Wales, Queensland, Victoria, Tasmania, South Australia, Western Australia, New Zealand, Ceylon, Hong Kong, Labuan, Bermuda, Gibraltar

1865–1866 as above – Bermuda, Gibraltar

1867 as above + Straits Settlements

North American and Australian Department
1868–1871 Canada, Prince Edward Island, Newfoundland, New South Wales, Queensland, Victoria, Tasmania, South Australia, Western Australia, New Zealand, Bermuda

1872 as above – Western Australia, Bermuda

North American, Australian, African and Mediterranean Department
1873–1874 Canada, Prince Edward Island, Newfoundland, New South Wales, Queensland, Victoria, Tasmania, South Australia, Western Australia, New Zealand, Malta, Gambia, Sierra Leone, Gold Coast, Lagos, Cape of Good Hope, British Kaffraria, Natal, Gibraltar, St Helena

North American and Australian Department
1875–1879 Canada, Newfoundland, New South Wales, Queensland, Victoria, Tasmania, South Australia, Western Australia, New Zealand, Fiji

1880–1886 as above + Western Pacific High Commission

1887–1888 as above + New Guinea

Department Number 2
1889–1891 as above + Gibraltar

1892–1896 as above + Cyprus

North American and Australasian Department
1897 as above

1898 Canada, Newfoundland, New South Wales, Victoria, South Australia, Western Australia, Queensland, Tasmania, New Zealand, Fiji, British New Guinea, Western Pacific High Commission, Cyprus, Gibraltar, Bermuda, Falkland Islands

1899 as above + Bahamas, British Honduras; − Falkland Islands

1900–1905 as above + Falkland Islands

1906–1907 Canada, Newfoundland, New South Wales, Victoria, South Australia, Western Australia, Queensland, Tasmania, New Zealand, Fiji, British New Guinea, Western Pacific High Commission, Cyprus, Gibraltar, Falkland Islands, Bahamas, British Honduras, Commonwealth of Australia, Malta

Dominions Division
1908–1925 See under Africa, South

PACIFIC

North American and Australian Department
1875–1888 see under North America and Australia

Department Number 2
1889–1907 see under North America and Australia

Dominions Division
1908–1925 see under Africa, South

Ceylon and Mauritius Department
1926–1928 see under South and South-East Asia

Far Eastern
1929–1931 see under South and South-East Asia

Pacific and Mediterranean Department
1932–1937 Fiji, Western Pacific High Commission, Falkland Islands, St Helena, Ascension, Tristan da Cunha, Gibraltar, Malta, Cyprus

1938–1943 as above − St Helena, Ascension, Tristan da Cunha

Ceylon and Pacific Department
1944–1948 Ceylon, Fiji, Western Pacific, Mauritius, Seychelles, St Helena

Hong Kong and Pacific Department
1949–1953 Hong Kong, Mauritius, Seychelles, St Helena, Fiji, Western Pacific High Commission Territories, South Pacific Commission

1954 as above + Tristan da Cunha

Pacific Department
1955 Mauritius, Seychelles, St Helena, Tristan da Cunha, Fiji, Western Pacific, South Pacific Commission, American bases in Pacific dependencies

1956 as above + Pitcairn and Tonga; – St Helena, Tristan da Cunha, American bases

1957–1958 Fiji, Pitcairn, Tonga, Western Pacific, South Pacific Commission, Mauritius, Seychelles

Pacific and Indian Ocean Department
1959–1964 Fiji, Pitcairn, Tonga, Western Pacific, South Pacific Commission, Mauritius, Seychelles, Western Pacific High Commission Territories, Falkland Islands, Antarctic

1965–1966 as above – Falkland Islands, Antarctic

SOUTH AND SOUTH-EAST ASIA

Australian and Eastern Department
1862–1867 see under North America and Australia

Eastern Department
1868–1871 Ceylon, Hong Kong, Labuan, Straits Settlements, Mauritius, Seychelles, British Columbia

1872 as above + Western Australia; – British Columbia

West Indian and Eastern Department
1873–1879 see under Caribbean

Eastern Department
1880 Ceylon, Hong Kong, Labuan, Straits Settlements, Mauritius, Seychelles, Falkland Islands, Heligoland

1881 as above – Heligoland, Falkland Islands

1882–1887 Ceylon, Hong Kong, Labuan, Straits Settlements, Mauritius, Seychelles

1888 as above + Gibraltar, Malta

Department Number 4
1889–1899 see under Africa, South

Department Number 5
1897 Ceylon, Mauritius, Hong Kong, Labuan, Borneo, Straits Settlements, Malay States

Eastern Department
1898–1903 as above + Seychelles

1904 as above + Wei-Hai-Wei

1905–1906 as above − Borneo

1907 as above − Labuan

1908 as above + business connected with the Protected States of Brunei, Sarawak, North Borneo

1909 Ceylon, Mauritius, Hong Kong, Straits Settlements, Malay States, Seychelles, Wei-Hai-Wei, business connected with the Protected States of Brunei, Sarawak, North Borneo

1910–1919 as above − Brunei

Far Eastern Department
1920–1928 Hong Kong, Wei-Hai-Wei, Straits Settlements, Malay States, business connected with Protected States of Sarawak and North Borneo

1929–1930 as above + Mauritius, Seychelles, Fiji, Western Pacific High Commission

1931 as above − Wei-Hai-Wei

Ceylon and Mauritius Department
1920–1925 Ceylon, Mauritius, Seychelles, St Helena

1926–1928 Ceylon, Mauritius, Seychelles, St Helena, Fiji, Western Pacific, Tristan da Cunha

Ceylon and Mediterranean Department
1928–1931 see under Mediterranean and Atlantic

Eastern Department
1932–1945 Hong Kong, Straits Settlements, Malay States, Mauritius, Seychelles, Ceylon, business connected with Protected States of Sarawak and North Borneo

1946–1947 general Eastern and Malayan politics, constitutional and economic questions, co-ordination between service and civil authorities, Hong Kong, Brunei, Sarawak, North Borneo

1948 Federation of Malaya, Singapore, Sarawak, North Borneo, Brunei, Commissioner General in South-East Asia

Ceylon and Pacific Department
1944–1948 see under Pacific

South-East Asia Department

1949–1954 as Eastern Department above

1955 as above + Hong Kong, Colombo Plan, claims arising from the war

1956–1957 as above – Colombo Plan

1958 as above + Colombo Plan

1959–1962 Hong Kong, residual matters relating to the Federation of Malaya, Singapore, Sarawak, North Borneo, Brunei, Commissioner General in South-East Asia

See also Defence, Intelligence and Hong Kong Department in chapter 12.3.

West Indian and Hong Kong Department

1966 see under West Indies

CHAPTER 12

Colonial Office Subject Departments and their Records

Although most Colonial Office business was handled by the geographical departments, following the reorganization of the Colonial Office in the late 1920s subject departments were established to take a broader view of developmental questions. In 1934 the General Department became the General Division and was split into two departments, General and Economic, which were gradually expanded to deal with the growing range of subjects handled by the office. Whenever the importance of a subject or an increasing load of business merited the appointment of an assistant secretary a new department was created. As the departments developed there were numerous splits, mergers and reallocations of responsibility.

The subject departments became increasingly important during and after the Second World War, and their records became more substantial in volume than those of the geographical departments. Subject department files may relate to a question generally, but sometimes they concern a specific region or territory.

After 1951 the papers of each subject department form a record class. Although class numbers have not been allocated for records post 1959, forthcoming classes can be determined by using the line chart in 12.1, the breakdown of subject department business in 12.3 and the list of Colonial Office departmental filing codes in chapter 15.4.1. After the transfer of the subject departments to the Department of Technical Co-operation the records will be found in the OD classes. See chapter 5.9.

Contents
12.1 Line chart of subject department development (see page 313)

12.2 List of subject department record classes with historical notes, 1934 to 1965

12.3 Breakdown of subject department business, 1934 to 1966

12.2 List of Colonial Office subject department record classes with historical notes, 1934 to 1965

This list, arranged alphabetically by department, provides brief departmental histories and summarises the relevant classes; the departments' responsibilites are listed in detail in chapter 12.3. Secret correspondence removed from these classes is found in the class of Supplementary Correspondence (CO 537) except for the period 1926 to 1945 when it is integrated with the relevant correspondence. The letters qv are used to direct the reader's attention to other parts of this list.

Contents:
Commercial Relations Department
Commercial Treaties Branch
Communications Department
Constitutional Planning Department
Defence Department
Economic Departments/Division
Economic General Department
Economic Intelligence and Planning Department
Economic Relations Department
Finance Department
French Relations Department
General Department/Division
Information Department
Intelligence and Security, and Police Departments
International Relations Department
Legal Department/Division
Marketing Department
Prisoners of War and Civilian Internees Department
Production and Marketing Departments
Public Relations Department
Research Department
Social Services Department
Statistics Department
Supplies Department
Welfare and Students Departments

Commercial Relations Department
The commercial relations functions of the Commercial Relations and Supplies Department (qv) were hived off in 1948 as a separate department, which was renamed Economic Relations (qv).

Commercial Treaties Branch
The Commercial Treaties Branch, originally part of the Economic Relations
(continued on page 314)

12.1 Line chart of subject department development

See also:

Colonies General: Original Correspondence (CO 323) 1689 to 1952, 1931 volumes and files

Niger and West Africa Frontier Force: Original Correspondence (CO 445) 1898 to 1926, 69 volumes

King's African Rifles: Original Correspondence (CO 534) 1905 to 1926, 63 volumes

Military: Original Correspondence (CO 820) 1927 to 1951, 77 volumes and files

Economic Departments/Division

Preparations for the Ottawa Conference in 1932 required technical work from a special economic section in the General Department which became the Economic Department in 1934. The General Department then became the General Division (qv), with two departments, General and Economic. The Economic Department dealt with the marketing and development of colonial products and with trade relations, including tariff matters; its head became a member of the Colonial Empire Marketing Board. At the outbreak of war in 1939 a new assistant under-secretary was appointed to look after economic affairs. The same year a financial adviser was appointed to deal with taxation, exchange control, war loans and war damage. The post developed into the Finance Department (qv) in 1942.

In 1943 the Economic Department itself was divided into Supplies and Production Departments (qv) which co-ordinated colonial requirements, production and distribution. The Supplies Department was represented in Washington by the British Colonial Supply Mission, which was charged with maintaining the flow of civil supplies from North America to the colonies. A separate Research Department (qv) was created in 1945 and a Marketing Department (qv) in 1946.

A major reorganization took place in 1947–1948. The Production and Marketing Departments were combined; Commercial Relations was separated from Supplies and renamed Economic Relations; and two new departments were added, Statistics, and Economic Intelligence and Planning. The latter was almost immediately renamed Economic General and dealt with economic research and planning. At the same time four economic liaison officers were appointed to assess local economic conditions and convey their impressions to London. Their number was reduced to one in 1950 and the position was discontinued in 1951.

By 1949 all the economic departments had been drawn together in an Economic Intelligence and Manning Division, accounting for one third of the administrative establishment of the Colonial Office, which oversaw colonial economic planning. In 1952 a Commercial Treaties Branch took over the work of the Economic Relations Department. In 1961 some of the division's functions were transferred to the Department of Technical Co-operation. The division was then reorganized and reduced to three departments: Economic General, Economic Relations, and Finance. In 1963 the Social Services Department (qv) was merged with the Economic General Department to form the Services Department, which absorbed the Economic Relations Department. It was renamed Economic General in 1965, and the same year a separate Communications Department was re-established within the division. The remaining departments became part of the Commonwealth Office in 1966.

The main class of Economic correspondence (CO 852; see chapter 15.3) covers the papers of most of the economic departments to 1951 and the papers of the Economic General Department thereafter. See also under individual departments: Commercial Treaties, Communications, Finance, Production and Marketing, Research, Statistics, Supplies.

Original Correspondence (CO 852) 1935 to 1963, 1739 boxes and files

Registers of Correspondence (CO 920) 1935 to 1952, 266 volumes

Economic General Department
The Economic General Department, created in 1948 when the Economic Intelligence and Planning Department (qv) was renamed, dealt with economic planning and research. It operated as two departments 'A' and 'B' between 1957 and 1960. In 1963 it merged with the Social Services Department to form the Services Department, and in 1964 it absorbed the Economic Relations Department and became the Economic General Department. It became the Economic Department in 1966 and was absorbed by the Commonwealth Office.

Economic: Original Correspondence (CO 852) 1935 to 1963, 1739 boxes and files

Registers of Correspondence (CO 920) 1935 to 1952, 266 volumes

Economic Intelligence and Planning Department
The department was created in 1948 when the economic departments underwent a major reorganization. It was almost immediately renamed Economic General (qv).

Economic Relations Department
When the economic departments underwent a major reorganization in 1948, the commercial relations functions were hived off from the Commercial Relations and Supplies Department (qv) and established as the Economic Relations Departments 'A' and 'B'. In 1951 Department 'B' became the Commercial Treaties Branch, which took over the remaining functions of the Economic Relations Department the following year. In 1961 when the Economic Division was reorganized the Economic Relations Department reappeared, but it was absorbed by the Economic General Department in 1964.

See Economic Departments for earlier correspondence.

Commercial Treaties Branch: Original Correspondence (CO 1016) 1951 to 1956, 115 files

Finance Department
A financial adviser was appointed in the Economic Department in 1939 to deal with taxation, exchange control, war loans and war damage. The post was converted to a Finance Department in 1942. It was called the Finance and Development Depart-

ment in 1944 and the Finance and Economic Department in 1945 before resuming its original name in 1946. It handled all important questions of post-war investment from colonial development funds. The department existed until 1966 when it was absorbed by the Commonwealth Office.

See Economic Departments for earlier correspondence.

Original Correspondence (CO 1025) 1951 to 1960, 126 files

French Relations Department

The fall of France in 1940 led to the creation of a temporary French Relations Department which handled all questions arising from the division of the former French colonial empire between the Vichy administration and the Free French. The papers of this department, which was closely associated with the Cabinet Committee on French Resistance, were never registered separately and are to be found in a large number of sub-files of the General Department (CO 323) and then in the Defence Department (CO 968) under 13076 and 13093. These files are registered in the General Secret Register (CO 694).

General Department/Division

In 1934 the General Department became the General Division and was split into two departments, General and Economic (qv). The General Department handled defence, international relations, mandates, labour, education, public health, communications and currency. In 1939 a Social Services Department (qv) was added. By 1940 the division also included a separate Defence Department (qv) and by 1943 a Communications Department (qv). The distribution of General Division work to these departments meant that by 1944 it had technically ceased to exist.

In 1944 the Defence and General Departments merged, but in 1945 the Defence Department was temporarily discontinued and all its staff were absorbed by the General Department which handled defence subjects. The Defence and General Department re-emerged in 1948 but was split into two departments again in 1955. In 1959 the General Department took on responsibility for Aden and became the Gulf of Aden and General Department. In 1961 it merged with the International Relations Department to become the International Relations and General Department.

See under Chief Clerk's and General Departments in chapter 13.1 for an account of the evolution of the General Department to 1932. See also chapter 11.2.

Original Correspondence (CO 323) 1689 to 1952, 1931 volumes and files (CO 1032) 1950 to 1960, 209 files

General Department Register of Correspondence (CO 378) 1852 to 1952, 218 volumes

Information Department

A Public Relations Department (qv) was established in the Colonial Office at the end of 1942. Its name was changed to the Information Department in 1946. It was concerned with publicity about the colonies in Britain and abroad through publications, broadcasting and the supply of information to the press. It was absorbed by the Commonwealth Office in 1966.

Original Correspondence (CO 875) 1940 to 1952, 75 files (CO 1027) 1952 to 1959, 352 files

Registers of Correspondence (CO 978) 1841 to 1952, 49 volumes

Intelligence and Security, and Police Departments

A political intelligence section was considered in 1948 and discussed again in 1953, but intelligence, security and police continued to be handled by the Defence and General Department until 1955 when two new departments were formed to handle these subjects. The Intelligence and Security Department provided guidance to colonial governments and liaised with security intelligence bodies in the UK; the Police Department dealt with general colonial questions. The two departments merged in 1959 to become Intelligence, Police and Security. In 1961 this department merged with Defence to become the Defence, Intelligence and Security Department.

Intelligence and Security Department: Original Correspondence (CO 1035)

Police Department: Original Correspondence (CO 1037) 1953 to 1959, 140 files

International Relations Department

In 1944 a separate International Relations Department was set up with responsibility for work resulting from participation by and on behalf of the territories in the activities of the many international bodies created during and after the war. It co-ordinated work in connection with the UN Trusteeship Council and was particularly concerned with the ILO, UNESCO and the FAO on colonial matters. From 1950 to 1952 it was divided into Departments 'A' and 'B'. In 1961 it merged with the General Department to become the International Relations and General Department, which was absorbed by the Commonwealth Office in 1966.

Original Correspondence (CO 936) 1944 to 1961, 597 boxes and files

Registers of Correspondence (CO 989) 1946 to 1951, 14 volumes

Legal Department/Division

Although there had been a Legal Adviser since the reorganization of the Colonial Office in 1866–1867, Legal Department was not created until 1949. It was treated as a division from 1951, and from this date a separate series of registered files was maintained.

The department's responsibilities encompassed a number of subjects formerly handled by the General Department and it dealt with all legal matters affecting the colonies in general in such areas as matrimonial and family law, constitutional and procedural matters, questions of nationality and naturalization, qualifications and appointment of lawyers and administration, as well as with a few particular cases of importance. It was absorbed by the Commonwealth Office in 1966.

Supplies Department

The Supplies Department was created in 1943 when the Economic Department was divided. It co-ordinated colonial requirements and distribution and was represented in Washington by the British Colonies Supply Mission. It was renamed the Commercial Relations and Supplies Department in 1945 and reverted to its original name in 1948 when Commercial Relations was hived off and renamed Economic Relations. It again became the Commercial Relations and Supplies Department in 1954, the year in which it was terminated.

See Economic Departments for earlier correspondence.

Original Correspondence (CO 1033) 1951 to 1956, 22 files

Welfare and Students Departments

A Welfare Section was set up in the Social Services Department in 1941 to look after the interests of colonial people in Britain, particularly students. Their growing numbers led to the creation of a separate Welfare Department to look after their interests in 1943. It was responsible for the administration of their clubs and hostels and for race questions generally in the United Kingdom. In 1951 it was renamed the Students Department and in 1956 the Students Branch. In 1961 it was transferred to the Department of Technical Co-operation.

Original Correspondence (CO 876) 1942 to 1952, 276 files (CO 1028) 1953 to 1960, 86 files

Registers of Correspondence (CO 977) 1942 to 1952, 22 files

Selected Personal Files (CO 981) 1941 to 1974, 139 files

12.3 Breakdown of subject department business, 1934 to 1960

This list traces the development of Colonial Office subject department organization from the establishment of the General Division in 1934. With the list in 12 it will enable the reader to determine the way in which the Colonial Office handled subject department business at any given time. It may also be used, in conjunction with chapter 7.3, to trace the subjects for which an assistant secretary was responsible. It is particularly important for the period after 1951 when the Colonial Office arranged correspondence in series for each department. Chapter 15.4.1 provides a list of departmental filing codes for these departments.

The information provided is arranged alphabetically by the name of the department or group of related departments. Each department's responsibilities are initially listed fully and thereafter an indication is given when a subject has been added (+) or removed (–). When there was a major change the subjects are listed again.

For consistency, the dates given are those indicated on the spines of the *Colonial Office List*. However, the printed lists were normally prepared during the previous year, to which the dates refer most accurately. The printed lists did not appear during the war, causing a gap in the information, but in some cases it has been possible to indicate a department's wartime responsibilities. In these cases the commencing date reflects the date of the department's establishment.

Contents:

Commercial Treaties Branch (1952–1954)

Communications Department (1944–1966)

Constitutional Planning Department (1966)

Defence Departments:
  Defence Department (1956–1961)
  Defence, Intelligence and Security Department (1962–1963)
  Defence, Intelligence and Hong Kong Department (1964–1965)
  Defence and Intelligence Department (1966)

Economic General Departments:
  Economic Intelligence and Planning Department (1949)
  Economic General Department (1949–1963)
  Economic General and Social Services Department (1964)
  Economic General Department (1965)
  Economic Department (1966)

Economic Relations Department (1949–1964)

Finance Department (1946–1966)

General Division/General Departments:
  General Division (1935–1940)
  General Department (1946–1948)
  Defence and General Department (1949–1955)
  General Department (1956–1959)
  Gulf of Aden and General Department (1960–1961)

Information Department (1947–1966)

Intelligence, Security and Police Departments:
  Intelligence and Security Department (1956–1958)
  Police Department (1956–1958)
  Intelligence, Police and Security Department (1959–1961)

International Relations Departments:
  International Relations Department (1944–1961)
  International Relations and General Department (1962–1966)

Legal Division (1950–1966)

Prisoners of War Department (1943–1948)

Production and Marketing Departments:
  Production Department (1943–1947)
  Marketing Department (1947)
  Production and Marketing Department (1947–1951)

Public Relations Department (1942–1947)

Research Department (1946–1961)

Social Services Departments:
  Social Services Department (1946–1962)
  Aden and Social Services Department (1963)

Statistics Department (1949–1960)

Supplies Departments:
  Supplies Department (1944–1945)
  Commercial Relations and Supplies Department (1946–1948)
  Supplies Department (1949–1954)
  Commercial Relations and Supplies Department (1955)

Welfare and Students Departments:
  Welfare Department (1944–1951)
  Students Department (1952–1961)

Abbreviations used in the list:

BBC	British Broadcasting Corporation
COI	Central Office of Information
CTCA	Commission for Technical Co-operation in Africa
ECA	Economic Commission for Africa (UNO)
ECAFE	Economic Commission for Asia and the Far East
ECE	Economic Commission for Europe
ECLA	Economic Commission for Latin America
ECOSOC	Economic and Social Council (UNO)
ECSC	European Coal and Steel Community
EEC	European Economic Community
EFTA	European Free Trade Association
ERP	European Recovery Programme
EURATOM	European Atomic Energy Authority
FAMA	Foundation for Mutual Assistance in Africa (South of the Sahara)
FAO	Food and Agriculture Organization (UNO)
GATT	General Agreement on Tariffs and Trade
IBRD	International Bank for Reconstruction and Development
ICTA	Imperial College of Tropical Agriculture
IDA	International Development Association (UNO)

IFC	International Finance Corporation
ILO	International Labour Organization
IMF	International Monetary Fund
ITA	Independent Television Authority
ITU	International Telecommunications Union
OEEC/OECD	Organization for European Economic Co-operation
UN	United Nations
UNESCO	United Nations Educational, Scientific and Cultural Organization
UNICEF	United Nations International Children's Emergency Fund
UNO	United Nations Organization
UNRRA	United Nations Relief and Rehabilitation Administration
UPU	Universal Postal Union
WHO	World Health Organization
WMO	World Meteorological Organization

COMMERCIAL TREATIES BRANCH

1952	see Economic Relations Department
1953–1954	commercial relations and treaties, GATT, colonial customs and excise questions

Then see Economic General Department.

COMMUNICATIONS DEPARTMENT

1944	civil aviation, telecommunications, postal matters (excluding stamp issues), mails, road transport, legislation, priority passages
1944–1947	civil aviation, meteorology, telecommunications, postal matters (excluding stamp issues), mails, shipping and ports, general questions relating to inland transport, and general communications questions
1948	as above – merchant shipping questions
1949	civil aviation, meteorology, telecommunications, postal matters (excluding stamp issues), mails, shipping and ports, general questions relating to inland transport and general communications questions
1950–1953	as above + stamp issues
1954	as above + surface transport; – inland transport
1955	as above – general questions relating to communications
1956–1958	as above – meteorology

1959	as above + meteorological questions
1960–1961	civil aviation, meteorological questions, telecommunications, postal matters, stamp issues, mails, shipping and ports, inland transport
1962–1965	the department was transferred to the Department of Technical Co-operation in 1961 but re-established within the Economic Division of the Colonial Office in 1965
1966	civil aviation, meteorology and WMO, telecommunications, postal matters including stamps, shipping and ports, roads and road transport, motor insurance, railways, general communications questions, UPU, ITU, Commonwealth Telecommunications Board, Inter-governmental Maritime Consultative Organization, tourism

CONSTITUTIONAL PLANNING DEPARTMENT

1966	general questions regarding future policy, co-ordination of constitutional developments, including related aspects of national legislative programme

DEFENCE DEPARTMENTS

See General Division for defence between 1940–1954 and Intelligence Departments for intelligence before 1961.

Defence Department

1956–1957	colonial defence policy, colonial forces, military duties in aid of civil power, military aviation in the colonies, visits of HM ships and foreign warships to colonial ports
1958	as above + military flights over colonies, colonial military legislation, Overseas Defence Committee, censorship; – military aviation, visits of HM ships to colonial ports
1959–1960	as above + war and military pensions policy; – military duties in aid of civil power
1961	as above + visiting forces, war histories, nuclear test control; – visits of warships

Defence, Intelligence and Security Department

1962–1963	intelligence and security matters in colonial territories, colonial police questions, civil defence, emergency powers, liaison with security and intelligence bodies in UK, general liaison with military authorities on colonial intelligence, colonial defence, colonial forces, military flights over colonies, visiting forces, colonial military legislation, military lands, Overseas Defence Committee, censorship, war histories, disarmament

Defence, Intelligence and Hong Kong Department
1964–1965   as above + security aspects of immigration and travel control, liaison with Chiefs of Staff and Joint Planning Staff, Hong Kong; – civil defence, liaison with security and intelligence bodies in UK, disarmament

Defence and Intelligence Department
1966   as above – Hong Kong

ECONOMIC GENERAL DEPARTMENTS

Economic Intelligence and Planning Department
1949   no information available

Economic General Department
1949   economic research and surveys, colonial development planning, co-ordination inside the Economic Division, relations with central planning staff

1950   as above + general economic planning, liaison with Colonial Development Corporation, hydro-electric development, co-operation; – colonial development planning

1951   economic research and surveys, general economic planning, co-ordination inside the Economic Division, liaison with Colonial Development Corporation, industrial development, co-operation

1952   as above – co-operation

1953   co-ordination within the Economic Division, general development plans and policy, Commonwealth economic relations, economic relations with the USA, OEEC, economic matters connected with the Council of Europe, UNO, ECOSOC and UN, regional commissions (ECAFE, etc), international technical assistance, relations with Colonial Development Corporation, industrial development, economic intelligence and research including preparation of Economic Survey of Colonial Territories

1954   as above + reviews of economic trends and progress

1955   as above + general questions on colonial development; general development plans and policy

1956–1957   co-ordination within Economic Division, general questions on colonial development, economic survey of colonial territories, Commonwealth Economic Committee, US aid, UN technical assistance, technical co-operation under Colombo Plan, IBRD economic surveys, Import-Export Bank, statutory development corporations, International Finance Corporation, OEEC, economic aspects of ECOSOC, ECAFE and

Council of Europe, foreign investment, economic intelligence and analysis, reviews of economic trends and progress, nuclear energy, commercial relations and treaties, bilateral trade agreements, GATT, customs and excise questions, supplies to colonies, import licensing, exchange control

1958 Department A: as above

Department B: co-ordination of work in Economic Division on the European Community and Free Trade Area

1959 Department A: as above + IMF; – Economic Survey of Colonial Territories, statutory development corporations, commercial relations and treaties, bilateral trade agreements; – GATT, customs and excise, import licensing

Department B: as above + GATT, import licensing, commercial relations, commercial treaties, bilateral trade agreements, customs and excise questions

1960 Department A: as above + FAMA, Commonwealth Consultative Council

Department B: as above

1961 Department A: as above + export credits

Department B: as above – import licensing

1962 general questions on statutory corporations, Colonial Development Corporation, Commonwealth Development Finance Company, general questions of industrial development, International Finance Corporation (other than subscriptions), Commonwealth Economic Committee and Consultative Council, export credits, OEEC/OECD, economic aspects of ECOSOC, ECAFE, ECA, ECLA and Council of Europe, general questions on monopolies and restrictive trade practices, Development Assistance Group, capital aid from Commonwealth and foreign countries, International Development Association, general agricultural, veterinary and marketing questions, fibres (including cotton), rubber, gums, spices, tobacco, agricultural commodities including sugar, coffee, cocoa, tea, cereals, fruit and vegetables, oilseeds and vegetable oils, animal products, Inter-African Phyto-Sanitary Commission, CTCA Soils and Animal Health Bureaux, foreign investment, economic intelligence and analysis, reviews of economic trends and progress, supplies to colonies, exchange control, IMF, IBRD, economic surveys

1963 general matters requiring co-ordination in Economic Division; general questions on development, Colonial Development Corporation, general questions of industrial development, Commonwealth Economic Consultative Council, Commonwealth Economic Committee, OECD, economic aspects (other than technical assistance) of ECOSOC, ECAFE, ECA, ECLA and Council of Europe, general questions on monopolies and restrictive trade practices, Development Assistance Committee, capital from Commonwealth and foreign countries, International Development Association, liaison with Export Credits Guarantee Department, central questions concerning the marketing of colonial agricultural exports, production and marketing matters affecting the commodities sugar, cocoa, coffee, tea, citrus and other fruits, cotton, sisal and other fibres, rubber, oilseeds and vegetable oils, essential oils, spices, tobacco, wines and spirits, rice and other cereals, hides and skins and other animal products, pyrethrum and other insecticides, international and Commonwealth sugar agreements, International Coffee Agreement and coffee study group, import licensing (into UK), general questions on foreign investment, economic advice and assistance, capital issues control, exchange control, IMF, IBRD and other economic surveys, international wheat agreement

Economic General and Social Services Department
1964   as above + international commodity policy, international commodity agreements and study groups, Commonwealth Economic Committee, strategic materials controls, wheat, FAO (colonial membership), IFC, IDA (subscription), labour administration and legislation, ILO, trade unions and industrial relations, international trade union organizations, workmen's compensation, social security, application of international labour conventions in the colonies; – liaison with Export Credits Guarantee Department, rubber, international and Commonwealth sugar agreements, international coffee agreements and coffee study group, import licensing, general questions concerning marketing of colonial agricultural exports, international wheat agreement

Economic General Department
1965   as above + World Power Conference, European economic questions, GATT, commercial relations and commercial treaties, colonial customs and excise questions, import licensing, Commonwealth preference, marketing of manufactured products, UN Conference on trade and development, EFTA, EEC, ECSC, EURATOM; – labour administration and legislation, ILO, trade unions and industrial relations, international trade union organizations, workmen's compensation, social security, application of international labour conventions in the colonies

Economic Department
1966   general economic relations and commercial treaties, general matters requiring co-ordination in Economic Division, external economic policy, Committee on Export Policy, export promotion, UK import restrictions, cotton textiles, industrial development in colonial territories, marketing of colonial manufactured products, EEC and EFTA, Commonwealth Prime Ministers and Trade Ministers Meeting, Commonwealth Consultative Council, Commonwealth Economic Committee, Commonwealth preference, commercial policy, GATT, UN Com-

mission on Trade and Development, general commodity policy questions (including those arising in the Committee on Trade and Development, UN Commission on Trade and Development and FAO), sugar, bananas and other individual commodities, FAO (colonial membership), strategic raw materials, World Power Conference, British Phosphate Commission, colonial customs and import licensing, statistics, US and other investment guarantees, economic aspects of ECOSOC, ECE, ECAFE, ECLA and ECA; general questions on foreign investment; economic advice and assistance, IBRD and other economic surveys, capital issues control, exchange control, IMF, IBRD, IFC, IDA (subscriptions)

ECONOMIC RELATIONS DEPARTMENT

1949 commercial relations and treaties, GATT, international trade organizations, customs and excise questions, property claims under peace treaties and property agreements with allied governments, ERP, economic aspects of Western Union, Customs Union Study Group, liaison in economic matters with western European and other colonial powers, economic activities of United Nations and other international organizations

1950 Department A: colonial aspects of ERP and OEEC, colonial economic questions arising in connection with the Council of Europe, liaison in economic matters with other European colonial powers, colonial aspects of economic activities of United Nations and associated economic agencies, certain aspects of United States foreign economic policy

Department B: commercial relations and treaties, GATT, international trade organizations, customs and excise questions, property claims under peace treaties and property agreements with allied governments

1951 Department A: as above – colonial economic questions arising in connection with the Council of Europe

Department B: as above – international trade organizations

1952 Economic Relations: as Department A above

Commercial Treaties Branch: as Department B above

1953–1961 see Economic Relations Department in chapter 12.2

1962 co-ordination of work in Economic Division on the European Economic Community and Free Trade Area, GATT, commercial relations, commercial treaties, bilateral trade agreements, colonial customs and excise questions, import licensing, Commonwealth preference, marketing of manufactured products

1963 as above + European Common Market questions: – co-ordination of work in Economic Division, bilateral trade

FINANCE DEPARTMENT

1946–1947   general financial questions, income tax, banking, loans, currency policy, price stabilization, insurance legislation, savings banks

1948   general financial questions, banking, loans, price stabilization, insurance legislation, currency, taxation, colonial estimates, colonial development and welfare, examination of development plans and applications for assistance

1949   as above + financial liquidation of former Palestine Government; – examination of development plans and applications for assistance

1950–1952   as above – financial liquidation of former Palestine Government

1953   control of votes of Parliament administered by Colonial Office, general financial questions, currency and banking, loans, taxation, colonial estimates, price stabilization, insurance legislation, colonial development and welfare, property claims under peace treaties and under property and financial agreements with other governments

1954   as above – price stabilization

1955   as above – colonial development and welfare

1956–1957   as above + ex-enemy property and property claims under peace treaties; – property claims under peace treaties

1958   as above + development and welfare schemes

1959–1962   as above + remanet Palestine services

1963–1964   as above + Exchequer loans

1965   as above – development and welfare schemes, Exchequer loans

1966   control of votes of Parliament administered by Colonial Office, general financial questions, currency and banking, loans, taxation, colonial estimates, insurance, general policy on Overseas Aid Development Assistance Committee, IDA, aid from Commonwealth and foreign countries, IBRD loans, ex-enemy property and property claims under peace treaties, remanet Palestine services

GENERAL DIVISION – GENERAL DEPARTMENTS

General Division

1935–1938   General Department: general questions relating to the colonies except those connected with economic matters and personnel. Subjects covered included defence, finance, international and inter-imperial

---

1964   as above + European economic questions; – European Common Market questions

relations (other than commercial relations), mandates, League of Nations matters, merchant shipping, labour, medical and public health matters, education, aviation, surveys, films, liquor traffic, legal and judicial matters, postal, telegraph and wireless matters, railway and transport developments

Economic Department: questions relating to economic matters in the colonial empire or in individual dependencies, including tariff matters and commercial relations with other parts of the empire and foreign countries

1939   General Department: as above – labour, medical, public health matters, education

Economic Department: as above

Social Services Department: questions relating to labour conditions, nutrition, public health, education, housing, etc

1940   General Department: general questions relating to colonies except those classed as defence, economic, personnel or social services. Subjects covered included international and inter-imperial relations (other than commercial relations), mandates, League of Nations matters, legal and judicial matters, postal matters, enemy property, agricultural and veterinary matters, flags, badges and ceremonial matters, extradition, industrial property, colonial reports

Defence Department: general defence questions including censorship, aviation, broadcasting, cables and wireless, aliens, nationality and naturalization, passports, consular matters, immigration and emigration, deportation, extradition, surveys and liaison with Ministry of Information

Colonial Development and Social Services Department: as for Social Services Department above + colonial development advisory committee work

1941–1945   no information available

General Department
1946–1948   General subjects: legal and judicial, constitutional and legal instruments, nationality and naturalization, patents, designs and trade marks, colonial arms, flags, seals, legalization of documents, consular matters, immigration and emigration, colonial regulations (except financial regulations), race questions, dangerous drugs

Defence subjects: naval, military and air operations, military aviation, defence security, war crimes, displaced persons, demobilization and rehabilitation, acquisition of land for defence purposes

Defence and General Department
1949   Defence subjects: security and defence of the colonies, both civil and military, Overseas Defence Committee, colonial defence schemes,

policy in regard to colonial local forces and the utilization of colonial manpower in the imperial forces, colonial contributions toward Commonwealth defence, military aviation in the colonies, instructions for guidance of colonial police, defence security, detention and deportation, war crimes, censorship, intelligence, demobilization

General subjects: legal and judicial matters and constitutional and legal instruments in conjunction with the legal advisers, ecclesiastical questions, war personnel injuries, nationality and naturalization, adoption of children, maintenance orders, territorial waters, visits of HM and foreign war ships to colonial ports, colonial arms, flags, seals, use of royal emblems, ceremonial matters, immigration and emigration, passports and visas, empire settlement, colonial stamp issues, dangerous drugs, war memorials, displaced persons and refugees, and other miscellaneous subjects of a general nature not falling appropriately into any other department

1950–1951 General subjects: passports and visas, immigration and emigration, empire settlement, colonial stamp issues, dangerous drugs, war memorials, consular matters, Imperial War Graves Commission, colonial regulations, other miscellaneous subjects of a general nature that do not appropriately fall to any other department

Defence subjects: as above + displaced persons and refugees, missionary societies, visits of HM and foreign war ships to colonial ports, − demobilization

1952 General subjects: as above + war service and medals, war pensions; − colonial stamp issues

Defence subjects: as above − missionary societies

1953 General subjects: as above − war crimes

Defence subjects: as above + colonial constitutions

1954 General subjects: colonial constitutions, consular matters, immigration and emigration, war graves, dangerous drugs, unallocated miscellaneous subjects, war memorials

Defence subjects: colonial defence policy, colonial police policy, Finance of colonial forces, colonial defence contributions, military aviation in the colonies, colonial forces, military lands in the colonies, civil defence, defence security, detention and deportation policy, censorship, intelligence, emergency legislation

1955 General subjects: as above

Defence subjects: as above + passports, etc

Then see under Defence Department.

General Department
1956 Colonial constitutions, consular matters, immigration and emigration,

war graves, memorials, ceremonial, precedence, dangerous drugs, passports, miscellaneous, unallocated subjects

1957　as above + policy on immigration from colonial territories

1958　as above; co-ordination of legislative programme, war pensions, flags, Commonwealth Parliamentary Association; − immigration and emigration

1959　as above + official committee on colonial policy, war service enquiries

Gulf of Aden and General Department

1960　as above + Aden and Aden Protectorate; Middle East subjects, Somaliland Protectorate, arms

1961　as above; privileges in UK, consecration of bishops, − ceremonial, precedence, Somaliland Protectorate

Then see International Relations Department.

INFORMATION DEPARTMENT

1947　publicity about the colonies in UK and other countries by broadcasting, photographs, film exhibitions, publications, press releases

1948　News Branch (A): public relations, liaison with press, Reference Section

Publications Branch (B): publications, colonial annual reports

Information Services Branch (C): supply of information about Britain and the Commonwealth to the colonies, supply of information about the colonies to the UK and foreign countries, organization of the regional information offices, broadcasting

1949　News Branch (A): as above

Publications Branch (B): as above

Information and Services Branch (C): as above + British Council; − regional information services

1950　Administration Branch (A): supply of information about the Commonwealth and Britain to the colonies, supply of information about the colonies to the UK and foreign countries, broadcasting, British Council, annual reports, preparation of booklets, picture sets and film strips, Reference Section

News Branch (B): public relations, technical advice on all press matters including press legislation

1951　Administrative Branch (A): as above + parliamentary liaison: − reference section

Press Branch (B): as for News Branch above

1953   General Branch (A): as Administrative Branch above

Press Section (B): As News Branch above

1954   Information: as General Branch above

Press Section: as above – press legislation

1955   Information: as General Branch above

Press Section: as above

1955–1956 Information: supply of information about the Commonwealth and Britain to the colonies, supply of information about the colonies to the UK and foreign countries, broadcasting, British Council, annual reports, preparation of booklets, picture sets and film strips, training courses in information work, parliamentary liaison

Press Section: public relations, technical advice on all press matters including press legislation

Information Offices: Gold Coast, Nigeria, Trinidad

1957   Information: as above

Press Section: as above

Information Offices: as above – Gold Coast

1958   Information: as above

Press Section: as above

Information Offices: Nigeria, Trinidad, Jamaica, Tanganyika, Singapore

1959   Information: as above + television, press legislation

Press Section: as above

Information Offices: Nigeria (Lagos; Northern Region, Kaduna; Western Region, Ibadan; Eastern Region, Enugu), Uganda, Trinidad, Jamaica, Tanganyika, Singapore

1960   Information: supply of information about the Commonwealth and Britain to the colonies, supply of information about the colonies to the UK and foreign countries, broadcasting, British Council, annual reports, preparation of booklets, picture sets and film strips, training courses in information work, parliamentary liaison, television, press legislation, UK information offices in the colonies, Corona library

Press Section: public relations, liaison with COI, BBC and ITA programme companies, news services

Information Offices: Nigeria (as above), Uganda, Trinidad, Jamaica, Tanganyika, Singapore, Kenya

1961   Information: as above

COLONIAL OFFICE SUBJECT DEPARTMENTS

Press Section: as above

Information Offices: as above – Nigeria

1962 Information: as above

Press Section: as above

Information Offices: as above + British Guiana, Zanzibar, Malta; – Uganda

1963 Information: as above

Press Section: as above

Information Offices: as above – Trinidad, Jamaica, Uganda

1965 Information: British information services in the colonies, supply of information about Britain and the Commonwealth to the colonies, supply of information about the colonies to the UK, Commonwealth and foreign countries, presentation in the Commonwealth and foreign countries of British colonial policy, broadcasting and television, British Council, colonial annual reports, parliamentary liaison, press legislation, Corona library

Press Section: press relations, liaison with COI, BBC and ITA programme companies, news services

Information Offices; British Guiana, Malta

1965 Information: as above

Press Section: as above

Information Offices: British Guiana, Mauritius

1966 Information: as above + films, British books export scheme

Press Section: as above

Information Offices: as above

INTELLIGENCE, SECURITY AND POLICE DEPARTMENTS

Intelligence and Security Department

1956–1957 general guidance for colonial governments in handling of liaison with security and intelligence bodies in UK, protective security (except in Colonial Office)

1958 intelligence from colonial territories, intelligence organizations in colonial territories, liaison with security and intelligence bodies in UK, protective security (except Colonial Office)

Police Department

1956   general colonial police questions, including relations between police and administration, problems affecting police forces in constitutionally advanced territories, civil defence

1957   as above + liaison with Home Office on police matters

1958   colonial police questions, civil defence, liaison with Home Office on police matters, emergency regulations

Intelligence, Police and Security Department

1959–1960   intelligence organizations and security training in colonial territories, colonial police questions, civil defence, liaison with Home Office on police matters, emergency regulations, liaison with security and intelligence bodies in UK, protective security (except in Colonial Office), general liaison with military authorities

1961   as above – liaison with Home Office on police matters, protective security

Then see Defence, Intelligence and Security Department under Defence Departments.

INTERNATIONAL RELATIONS DEPARTMENTS

International Relations Department

1944   no information available

1946–1947   UNO, League of Nations, mandates and peace treaties, treaties and conventions, international aspects of colonial policy, affairs in foreign countries, UNRRA, general questions

1948   international aspects of colonial policy, United Nations matters, including the trusteeship system, liaison with the French and Belgian colonial ministries, peace treaties and connected subjects

1949   as above + arrangements for international colonial co-operation, colonial representation in international organizations

1950   international aspects of colonial policy and United Nations matters:

Department A: United Nations, trusteeship and information from non-self-governing territories, international co-operation on colonial questions, correspondence with colonial attaché Washington and counsellor (colonial affairs) UK delegation to UN, supply of political intelligence to governors

Department B: Questions relating to ECOSOC and its commissioners, UNICEF, specialist agencies, colonial accession articles in international agreements, colonial representation in international organizations, colonial aspects of general Commonwealth policy

1951–1952   Department A: as above – supply of political intelligence to governors

Department B: as above + general international and Commonwealth Relations, International Children's Endowment Fund, diplomatic privileges and immunities for international organizations, human rights (United Nations and Council of Europe)

1953–1954   United Nations, trusteeship and information from non-self-governing territories, international colonial co-operation including liaison in Africa, questions relating to the colonial attaché Washington and counsellor (colonial affairs) UK delegation to UN, general international and Commonwealth relations, political questions relating to ECOSOC and its commissions and to the specialist agencies, colonial accessions articles in international agreements, colonial representation in international organizations, diplomatic privileges and immunities for international organizations, human rights (United Nations and Council of Europe)

1955–1956   as above + regional economic commissions for Asia and Latin America; – information from non-self-governing territories

1957–1958   as above

1959   as above + Colonial Office representation in UK Mission, New York, territorial waters; – liaison in Africa, questions relating to counsellor (colonial affairs) UK delegation to UN

1960   United Nations, trusteeship, international colonial co-operation, general international and Commonwealth relations, colonial accession articles in international agreements, colonial representation in international organizations, diplomatic privileges and immunities for international organizations, Commission on Human Rights, Colonial Office representation in UK Mission New York, territorial waters, political aspects of work of functional commissions, the specialist agencies and regional economic commissions for Africa, Asia and Latin America, colonial attaché Washington, political questions relating to ECOSOC and its commissions

1961   United Nations, trusteeship, international colonial co-operation, colonial attaché Washington and Colonial Office representation in UK Mission New York, general international and Commonwealth relations questions, political aspects of work of functional commissions, the specialist agencies and regional economic commissions for Africa, Asia and Latin America, colonial accession articles in international agreements, colonial representation in international organizations, Commission on Human Rights, territorial waters, etc

International Relations and General Department
1962   United Nations, trusteeship, international colonial co-operation, colonial attaché Washington and Colonial Office representation in UK Mission New York, general international and Commonwealth relations

questions, commissions on human rights and status of women, political aspects of work of other functional commissions, the specialized agencies and regional economic commissions for Africa, Asia and Latin America, colonial territorial application articles in international agreements, colonial representation in international organizations, privileges and immunities for international organizations, law of the sea including territorial waters, Court of Justice, colonial constitutions, Official Committee on Colonial Policy, legislative programme, consular matters, privileges in the UK, war graves, war pensions and war service enquiries, consecration of bishops, passports and visas, colonial immigration into UK, colour questions in the colonies, arms, and flags, etc, Commonwealth Parliamentary Association, dangerous drugs, honours, campaign awards

1963   as above + General Assembly (Fourth Committee matters), Steering Committee on International Organizations, appointments and privileges of foreign consuls and Commonwealth trade commissioners in colonies, capital punishment policy, precedence, ceremonial; – international colonial co-operation, Court of Justice

1964–1965   As above + courses in parliamentary procedure; – associate membership in international organizations

1966   United Nations general policy on colonial questions except for new constitutional patterns, General Assembly (Fourth Committee matters), liaison on colonial questions with UK mission to the United Nations New York, co-ordination of future policy for smaller territories, ECOSOC (except economic subjects); general international and Commonwealth relations questions including questions relating to the Commonwealth Secretariat and Commonwealth Foundation, Commonwealth commissioners in colonial territories, commissions on human rights and status of women, political aspects of work of other functional commissions, specialist agencies and regional economic commissions for Africa, Asia and Latin America, Steering Committee on International Organizations, Commonwealth Parliamentary Association and courses in parliamentary procedure, political aspects of arrangements for dealing with fugitive offenders, colonial territorial applications, articles in international agreements, privileges and immunities for international organizations, law of the sea including territorial waters, appointments and privileges of foreign consuls and Commonwealth trade commissioners in colonies, privileges of colonial representatives in the UK, treatment of offenders (including capital and corporal punishment policy), general liaison with Ministry of Overseas Development on educational, medical, social and staff questions, dangerous drugs, war graves, war pensions and war services enquiries, consecration of bishops, passports and visas, colonial immigration into the UK, arms and flags, honours, campaign awards, precedence, ceremonial

LEGAL DIVISION
1950–1966

PRISONERS OF WAR DEPARTMENT
1943–1948   matters relating to enemy alien prisoners of war

PRODUCTION AND MARKETING DEPARTMENTS

Production Department
1943–1947   commodity production policy, primary and secondary industries, electric and water power schemes, co-operation, land tenure, agricultural credit, locust control, West African Produce Control Board

Marketing Department
1947   marketing organization, bulk sales to government departments or agencies, international commodity schemes, rehabilitation of industries in Malaya

Production and Marketing Department
1948   Department A (Agriculture): production and marketing of agricultural and livestock resources of the colonies, general agricultural and veterinary questions, co-operation, irrigation and water supplies

Department B (other subjects): production and marketing of metals and minerals, fishery and forestry resources of the colonies, locust questions, development of secondary industries, hydro-electric power

1949   Department A: as above – water supplies

Department B: as above + production and marketing of petroleum and fibres (including cotton), questions relating to insecticides and the Imperial Institute, and geological surveys

1950   Department A: as above – co-operation

Department B: as above + production and marketing of rubber, gums, tobacco, oilseeds, paint oils, essential oils and insecticides; – questions relating to insecticides, locusts and the Imperial Institute

1951   Department A: general agricultural and marketing policy, irrigation, land settlement, production and marketing of certain agricultural commodities including sugar, cocoa, coffee, tea, wines and spirits, fruit and vegetables, cereals and rice, seeds, spices, meat and dairy products, hides and skins, ICTA

Department B: production and marketing of metals and minerals, fishery and forest resources of the colonies, petroleum and fibres including cotton, geological surveys, production and marketing of rubber, gums, tobacco, oilseeds, paint oils, essential oils and insecticides

1952 Department A: as above + FAO matters, co-operation

Department B: as above

1953 Department A: as above + general agriculture, veterinary and marketing policy; – land settlement, tea, wines and spirits

Department B: mining policy, mineral royalties and mining taxation, geological surveys, metals and minerals, petroleum, fibres (including cotton), rubber, gums, tobacco, essential oils, sponges and loofahs, production of insecticides, fisheries, forestry and timber, economic measures to deter aggression

1954–1955 Department A: as above – irrigation

Department B: as above

1956–1957 Department A: general agriculture, veterinary and marketing questions, agricultural commodities including sugar, cocoa, coffee, cereals, fruit, vegetables, oilseeds, vegetable oils, animal products, ICTA, FAO matters, co-operation, drainage and irrigation

Department B: as above + mineral policy; – essential oils

1958 Department A: as above

Department B: mining policy, royalties and taxation, mining legislation, geological surveys, metals and minerals, petroleum, fibres (including cotton), rubber, gums, tobacco, sponges, production of insecticides, forestry and timber and economic measures to deter aggression

1959 Department A: as above + forestry and timber; production of insecticides, fibres (including cotton), rubber, gums, tobacco, sponges and Sino-Soviet trade control

Department B: mining policy, mineral royalties and mining taxation, geological surveys, metals and minerals, petroleum, mining legislation, general questions on statutory development corporations, Colonial Development Corporation, liaison with Barclays Overseas Development Corporation and Commonwealth Development Finance Company

1960 Department A: general agriculture, veterinary and marketing questions, agricultural mechanization, forestry and timber, production of insecticides, fibres including cotton, rubber, gums, spices, tobacco, agricultural commodities including sugar, cocoa, coffee, tea, cereals, fruit and vegetables, oilseeds and vegetable oils, animal products, FAO, co-operation, drainage and irrigation, Sino-Soviet trade controls, Inter-African Phyto-Sanitary Commission

Department B: mining policies, royalties, taxation, mining legislation, geological surveys, metals and minerals, petroleum, general questions on statutory development corporations, Colonial Development Corporation, liaison with Barclays Overseas Development Corporation and Commonwealth Development Finance Company

1961　　Department A: as above + CCTA Soils and Epizootic Bureaux

Department B: as above − minerals

PUBLIC RELATIONS DEPARTMENT

1942–1947　Publicity about colonies in UK and other countries, publications, broadcasting and supply of information to the press

RESEARCH DEPARTMENT

1946–1947　Colonial research fellowships, archaeology and ethnology, housing and road research, social science, colonial products, agricultural and medical research, geodetic and topographical surveys, geological survey, demography

1948　　as above + animal health and forestry research, fisheries, census and statistics

1949–1950　agriculture, animal health and forestry research, insecticides, medical research, social science research, colonial products research, geodetic and topographical surveys, building and road research

1951　　as above + anti-locust research, Commonwealth Agricultural Bureaux

1952　　as above + veterinary research; − animal health

1953　　as above + pest control, economic research projects; − geodetic and topographical surveys, road research

1954　　agriculture and forestry research, insecticides, medical research, social science research, colonial products research, building, anti-locust research, fungicides and herbicides research, veterinary research, pest control, economic research projects, housing research

1955　　as above + Commonwealth Agricultural Bureaux, archaeological research, game preservation, tsetse and trypanosomiasis

1956–1957　as above + road research

1958　　as above + fisheries

1959　　as above + Colonial Products Council and Tropical Products Institute

1960　　as above + Colonial Products Council; − regional and inter-territorial research, Overseas Research Council

1960–1961　agricultural, veterinary and forestry research, insecticides, fungicides, herbicides and pest control research, medical research, social science and economic research projects, Overseas Research Council, Tropical

Products Institute, building and housing research, road research, Commonwealth Agricultural Bureaux, archaeological research, tsetse and trypanosomiasis research, fisheries research, regional and inter-territorial research

SOCIAL SERVICES DEPARTMENTS
See General Division for Social Services 1939–1945.

Social Services Department

1946–1947 labour legislation, trade unions, workmen's compensation, public health, education, social hygiene, social welfare, penal administration, nutrition

1948 Department A: social welfare, medicine and public health, nutrition, British Council, penal administration, social hygiene

Department B: labour questions, education, social insurance, trade unions, workmen's compensation, ILO, UNESCO

1949 Department A: education, social welfare, UNESCO, penal administration

Department B: labour questions, social insurance, trade unions, workmen's compensation, ILO, medicine and public health, nutrition, social hygiene

1950–1952 Department A: as above + community development

Department B: as above

1953 Department A: as above

Department B: labour administration and legislation, industrial relations, social insurance, workmen's compensation, ILO, medical administration and public health, WHO, UNICEF, nutrition, housing and town planning

1954 Department A: education, social welfare and development, UNESCO, treatment of offenders, libraries

Department B: as above

1955–1956 Department A: as above + UN Social Commission

Department B: as above

1958 Department A: education, libraries and museums, social welfare and development, UNESCO, UN Social Commission, treatment of offenders

Department B: labour administration and legislation, ILO, trade unions and industrial relations, workmen's compensation, social security, medical administration and public health, WHO, UNICEF, nutrition, housing and town planning

1959–1961   Department A: as above

Department B: as above + UN Children's Fund, colour questions in the colonies; – UNICEF

1962   labour administration and legislation, ILO, trade unions and industrial relations, workmen's compensation, social security, application of international labour conventions in the colonies

Aden and Social Services Department
1963   Aden Colony and Protectorate, Federation of South Arabia, southern Arabian Affairs, Middle East (official) Committee, labour administration and legislation, ILO, trade unions and industrial relations, workmen's compensation, social security, application of international labour conventions in the colonies

Then see Economic General Department; see also Middle East, Aden Department in chapter 11.3.

STATISTICS DEPARTMENT
1949–1960

SUPPLIES DEPARTMENTS

Supplies Department
1944–1945   no details

Commercial Relations and Supplies Department
1946–1947   supplies to colonies, shipping freights, enemy property, reparations, commercial relations and treaties, import licensing, customs and excise, exchange control

1948   as above + merchant shipping questions

Supplies Department
1949–1954   supplies to colonies, import licensing, exchange control

Commercial Relations and Supplies Department
1955   commercial relations and treaties, bilateral trade agreements, GATT, customs and excise questions, supplies to colonies, import licensing, exchange control

WELFARE AND STUDENTS DEPARTMENT

Welfare Department
1944–1949   administration of hostels and clubs, race questions in UK, liaison with

voluntary associations, further education and vocational training in UK, seamen's welfare, repatriation, identity and nationality of colonials in UK, colonial students in UK

1950–1951   as above – administration of hostels and clubs

Then see General Division and Social Services Departments.

Students Department

1952   as above

1953   as above + liaison with non-student welfare; – seamen's welfare

1954   colonial students in UK, arrangements for finance, studies and welfare, welfare of colonials in UK other than students, colour questions in UK

1955–1960   as above + colour discrimination in UK; – colour questions in UK

1959–1961   as above + employment of colonials in the UK other than students

CHAPTER 13

Colonial Office Internal Services and other Departments and their Records

Although most Colonial and War Department and Colonial Office business was handled by geographical departments from the early part of the nineteenth century, not all business could be fitted into a territorial framework and quite a number of matters affected the colonies collectively. These were handled at first by the chief clerk. By 1869 his office had evolved into the General Department. Gradually many of its responsibilities were devolved to a range of other administrative and special departments described below. In the twentieth century they developed a more elaborate bureaucracy to support the geographical and subject departments described in chapters 11 and 12.

List of internal services and other department record classes with historical notes

This list, arranged alphabetically by department, provides brief departmental histories and summarizes the relevant classes. Secret correspondence removed from these classes is found in the class of Supplementary Correspondence (CO 537) except for the period 1926 to 1945 when it is integrated in the relevant correspondence series.

Contents:
Internal Services Departments:

Accounts and Financial Departments
Chief Clerk's and General Departments
Establishment Department
Personnel Divisions

Other Departments:

Emigration Departments
Overseas Settlement Department

INTERNAL SERVICES DEPARTMENTS

Accounts and Financial Departments

Financial work was originally handled by the chief clerk. In 1869 the Accounts Branch, set up in pursuance of the Exchequer and Audit Act 1866, was brought under him. By 1874 it was a distinct body, no longer under his control, and had been renamed the Financial Department. The General and Financial Departments were fused in 1896 as the General and Financial Department under the chief clerk and dealt with major financial questions. It was renamed the General Department in 1901. A second Financial Department, set up in 1896, was concerned with accounting and became the Accounts Department in 1898; it continued until 1952 when its functions were divided between the Economic General and Finance Departments. Its files were not registered in a separate series after 1925.

Original Correspondence (CO 431) 1868 to 1925, 152 volumes

Register of Correspondence (CO 622) 1868 to 1921, 18 volumes

Entry Books and Register of Out-letters (CO 621) 1868 to 1908, 19 volumes

Miscellanea (CO 701) 1794 to 1913, 28 volumes

Chief Clerk's and General Departments

The chief clerk, first appointed in 1795, was originally simply the most senior among the clerks. He had various general duties, including all the financial work. His office was temporarily abolished between 1833 and 1839, but it achieved departmental status between 1843 and 1849. The chief clerk was still performing some of the general business of the Colonial Office in the 1860s. When the Accounts Branch was established in 1869 it was placed under his superintendence, but by 1874 it had become independent as the Financial Department.

In 1870 a separate General Department was set up with responsibility for general and miscellaneous questions, including defence. Its head was given charge of the copying department, library and registry. To this department other business was gradually transferred: governors' pensions, naval cadetships, uniforms, the drafting of formal instruments, establishment matters, the scrutiny of parliamentary notices, and circular despatches. The chief clerk remained responsible for honours, including the order of St Michael and St George, the management of the secret service fund and the internal arrangements of the office. In 1894 the General Department was merged with the Emigration Department. When the latter was abolished in 1896, the General Department was merged with the Financial Department as the General and Financial Department under the chief clerk. Renamed the General Department in 1901, it had a wide range of miscellaneous functions. From 1906 to 1907 it was briefly called the Chief Clerk's Department. In 1907 the General Department was reconstituted and charged with various matters common to all Crown colonies formerly dealt with by the Chief Clerk's Department.

The office of chief clerk was abolished in 1917 but the General Department continued. In 1928 it was split into two as a first step toward handling questions relating to a number of territories on a subject basis. One side dealt mainly with personnel questions and the other with the rest of the subjects which had customarily belonged to the General Department. In 1930 a Personnel Division was created and all personnel work was taken away from the General Department. See Personnel Divisions below.

See under General Department/Division in chapter 12.2 for an account of the evolution of the General Department after 1930. For a list of relevant classes see under Colonies General in chapter 11.2.

Establishment Department

An establishment officer was appointed in the Colonial Office, as in other large government departments, in 1922. The post became part of the joint establishment after the creation of the Dominions Office in 1925. Until 1930 it came under the General Department and thereafter was placed in the Colonial Service Department of the Personnel Division. By 1939 the Colonial Service Department contained an Establishment Branch, and by 1945 a separate Establishment Department had been set up. When the joint establishment broke up in 1947 a separate establishment officer was appointed to the Commonwealth Relations Office. In 1948 this separate establishment evolved into an Establishment and Organization Department. This was absorbed by the Commonwealth Office in 1966.

Original Correspondence (CO 866) 1922 to 1956, 108 boxes and files

Registers of Correspondence (CO 867) 1922 to 1951, 21 volumes

Establishment Miscellanea (CO 878) 1794 to 1965, 34 volumes

Personnel Divisions

The secretary of state for the colonies originally exercised a very wide patronage. As autonomy grew in the colonies with responsible government, he naturally appointed personnel to fewer and fewer offices in these. However, when the tropical empire was enlarged at the end of the nineteenth century, there was again need for him to fill large numbers of posts. Most of this patronage work was managed by his assistant private secretaries, but in 1910 a special assistant private secretary was appointed to concern himself mainly with patronage. In 1928, as a first step towards developing a subject side to the Colonial Office, the General Department was split into two branches, one of which dealt mainly with personnel questions. The other handled the rest of the subjects which had customarily belonged to the General Department.

In 1930 it was considered that some sort of uniform direction should be exercised over the various colonial services and so a separate Personnel Division was created in the Colonial Office. It comprised an Appointments Department, concerned with recruitment and training, and a Colonial Service Department, concerned with discipline, promotions and transfers, conditions of employment and pensions. The establishment officer was a member of the latter, and a separate Establishment Branch had been formed by 1939.

The division grew during the war, and although it embraced the same departments as before, each of them was separated into 'A' and 'B' departments. Toward the end of the war the division experienced major changes due to the great increase in recruitment to the colonial services and the revival of the system of regular reporting for promotions. By 1944 a separate department had been created to deal with demobilization and recruitment from the armed forces. In 1945 the division was renamed the Colonial Service Division, and at the same time an Establishment Department was set up. In 1949, following a Treasury O & M report on Colonial Office organization, the whole division was given a new shape. Its title was changed to Overseas Service Division in 1954. It was transferred to the new Department of Technical Co-operation in 1961 with the exception of the Honours Department and the Rajah of Sarawak Fund.

The Patronage original correspondence class (CO 429) has its own registers (CO 430) for the period 1867–1870. Directions were then given that applications for general employment should be entered in the 'General Miscellaneous' registers (CO 432), but these were discontinued the same year and it is not clear what happened to such applications. Letters applying for specific employment were registered in colony registers. Patronage original correspondence was resumed in 1881, but a separate set of Patronage registers (CO 430) did not start again until 1887. Between 1881 and 1886 the Colonies General Registers (CO 378) are the key to the class.

The class Governors' Pensions (CO 449) owes its origin to the Governors' Pensions Act 1865, to the negotiations that led up to it and to subsequent amending legislation. From 1825 until 1931 it seems to have been absorbed into Colonies General Original Correspondence (CO 323). After that it forms part of the Personnel Original Correspondence (CO 850). Up to 1932 it is registered in the Colonies General Registers.

Patronage Original Correspondence (CO 429) 1867 to 1919, 131 volumes

Patronage Register of Correspondence (CO 430) 1867 to 1918, 20 volumes

Governors' Pensions Original Correspondence (CO 449) 1863 to 1925, 10 volumes

Appointments Original Correspondence (CO 877) 1920 to 1952, 59 files

Appointments Register of Correspondence (CO 918) 1920 to 1952, 36 volumes

Personnel Original Correspondence (CO 850) 1932 to 1952, 268 boxes and files

Personnel Register of Correspondence (CO 919) 1932 to 1952, 47 volumes

Colonial Service Division and Overseas Service Division Original Correspondence (CO 1017) 1948 to 1962, 542 files

Training Registers of Correspondence (CO 1011) 1948 to 1952, 9 volumes

OTHER DEPARTMENTS

Emigration Departments/Overseas Settlement Department

A Colonial Land and Emigration Commission was created in 1840 to undertake the duties of two earlier and overlapping authorities which were both under the supervision of the secretary of state. These were the Colonization Commissioners for

South Australia, established under an act of 1834, and the Agent General for Emigration, appointed in 1837. The new commission dealt with land grants, the outward movement of settlers, the administration of the Passenger Acts 1855 and 1863 and, from 1846 to 1859, the scrutiny of colonial legislation. In 1855 it became the Emigration Commission. In 1873 the administration of the Passenger Acts was transferred to the Board of Trade. The commission's powers were gradually given up to the larger colonies as they obtained self-government, and after 1873 it was responsible only for controlling the importation of Indian labour into sugar-producing colonies. It was abolished in 1878.

On the dissolution of the commission in 1878, an Emigration Department was set up within the Colonial Office. In 1894 it was merged with the General Department and it was abolished altogether in 1896. Meanwhile in 1886 an Emigrants' Information Office had been established to provide impartial information about emigration. While under Colonial Office supervision, it had a voluntary committee of management.

Following the First World War the government began to exercise closer supervision over emigration. The voluntary committee was replaced in 1918 by the Government Emigration Committee, which was renamed the Oversea Settlement Committee the following year. The committee operated as a sub-department of the Colonial Office, with responsibility for the movements of British subjects wishing to settle overseas. After 1925 it came under the Dominions Office. In 1935 it ceased to operate as a separate entity and was replaced by the Oversea Settlement Board, which was responsible for advising the secretary of state for the Dominions on migration policy. Its activities were suspended during the Second World War, which it did not survive. Minutes of the committee are in DO 35/665–670 and of the board in DO 35/666 and DO 114/89–90.

Also in 1919, the Emigrants' Information Office became the Overseas Settlement Department, a branch of the Dominions Division, and after 1925 it was a branch of the Dominions Office. Until its dissolution in 1936 it advised the government on settlement within the Empire and the administration of the Empire Settlement Act 1922.

Until 1857, CO 384 consists of domestic letters alone. The series then ceases and is not resumed until 1872. From 1874 despatches are to be found as well as letters. Up to 1875, CO 428 appears to concern the West Indies only. Letters about emigration to North America are registered separately (see under North America in chapter 11.2).

Emigration:
Original Correspondence (CO 384) 1817 to 1896, 193 volumes

Register of Correspondence (CO 428) 1850 to 1896, 14 columns

Entry Books (CO 385) 1814 to 1871, 30 volumes

Register of Out-letters (CO 485) 1872 to 1903, 9 volumes

Original Correspondence and Entry Books of the Agent General for Emigration, the South Australian Commissioners and the Land and Emigration Commission (CO 386) 1833 to 1894, 194 volumes

Overseas Settlement:
Original Correspondence (CO 721) 1918 to 1925, 118 volumes

(DO 57) 1926 to 1936, 189 boxes

Register of Correspondence (CO 791) 1918 to 1926, 10 volumes

(DO 5) 1927 to 1936, 12 volumes

Daily Register of Correspondence (CO 792) 1919 to 1927, 4 volumes

(DO 6) 1928 to 1929, 3 volumes

CHAPTER 14

Dominions Office and Commonwealth Relations Office Departments and their Records

At the time of the establishment of the Dominions Office there were four departments organized on a functional basis; their number grew to five in 1935 and six in 1939. Staff lists were not published during the Second World War or in the post-war years, but when they resumed in 1952 there were eighteen departments in the Commonwealth Relations Office. These departments expanded steadily during the 1950s and early 1960s as responsibility for business relating to the newly independent Commonwealth countries was transferred from the Colonial Office to the Commonwealth Relations Office.

During the 1950s the principle of organization was still predominately functional but the actual distribution of the departments within the divisions was very much less clear-cut. The Political Division, for instance, was really a miscellaneous one. The one geographical division, Africa and General, also contained functional departments, and when responsibility for Ghana and Malaya was transferred to the office in 1957 new Ghana and Malaya departments were established within the Political Division. By the early 1960s it was becoming clear that, while suited to the old pattern of close relations with a small number of Commonwealth countries, the office organization was no longer conducive to administrative efficiency. By 1962 it was more coherent. The Political Division now comprised Constitutional and General Departments, while the Africa Division had three departments for the particular African regions. By 1966 the increased number of departments was divided between four geographical and four subject divisions.

Most of the records for the Dominions Office and the Commonwealth Relations Office are in one class (DO 35) which is described in chapters 5.1.2 and 11.2 (under Dominions General). DO 35 is also of increasing significance for each of the Colonial Office territories in the period prior to its independence. The Dominions Office, in the case of Ceylon, and the Commonwealth Relations Office after 1947, monitored local political developments closely. In a number of cases such as Ghana, Nigeria, Tanganyika or the Federation of the West Indies, the Commonwealth Relations Office appointed advisers (often designated as advisers on external affairs or on Commonwealth and external affairs) who provided the office with detailed information on local developments, sometimes including the activities of the governor.

The lists which follow have been compiled from a list provided by J M Lee, covering 1925–1939, and thereafter from the *Commonwealth Relations Office List*. It was the practice to issue the annual printed lists in the year indicated on the spine, but in fact they were normally prepared during the previous year. For consistency the dates here reflect the dates on the spines, but readers should be aware that the dates refer most accurately to the preceding year.

Contents:

14.1 Breakdown of Dominions Office departmental business

14.2 Breakdown of Commonwealth Relations Office departmental business

14.1 Breakdown of Dominions Office departmental business

Department A

1925–1930   foreign affairs, defence, consular and passport questions, telecommunications, censorship, prisoners of war, prize, honours, ceremonial, Nauru

1931–1933   legal, diplomatic and consular, ceremonial matters, passports and representations, defence and disarmament, imperial conference

1934   imperial conferences and constitutional matters, defence, arbitration and disarmament, nationality and passports; ceremonial; shipping policy, Irish Free State

1935   constitutional matters, ceremonial matters, nationality and passports, Irish Free State, defence, establishments

1936–1937   Imperial Conference and coronation arrangements, constitutional matters, nationality and passports, civil aviation, establishments

1938–1939   constitutional and nationality questions, Ireland, ceremonial and honours, civil aviation and establishments

Department B

1925–1930   Canada, Newfoundland, Irish Free State, economic, naturalization, merchant shipping

1931–1932   League of Nations, league and non-league multilateral treaties, bilateral treaties, Arctic and Antarctic, territorial waters, Nauru, codes and cyphers

1933   India, codes and cyphers, aviation, communications, conferences, matters concerning League of Nations

1934   foreign affairs, League of Nations and treaties (except arbitration) including international economic questions, aviation

1935   aviation, defence, foreign affairs, League of Nations and treaties (except commercial treaties and agreements)

1936–1937   defence (including disarmament and relevant treaties), foreign affairs, League of Nations, non-league conventions, Arctic and Antarctic

1938–1939   defence, imperial communications, broadcasting, bilateral non-League of Nations conventions, Arctic and Antarctic

Department C
1925–1930   Australia, New Zealand, South Africa, Commonwealth territories, settlement overseas, Asiatic questions.

1931–1932   economic matters including conferences and conventions, communications, aviation, Empire Marketing Board (except establishment), Imperial Conference economic

1933   trade missions to dominions or foreign countries, Imperial Economic Office, Imperial Shipping Office, Empire Marketing Board (except establishment), Imperial Conference economic

1934   economic questions of an inter-imperial character, establishment, Newfoundland

1935   economic questions (including commercial treaties and agreements), establishments

1936–1937   imperial economic relations, international questions of an economic character including commercial treaties, shipping

1938–1939   international questions of an economic kind, imperial economic relations, intra-imperial trade agreements, shipping

Department D
1931–1932   establishments, South Africa and territories, Irish Free State, Canada and Newfoundland

1933   establishments, Australia and New Zealand, South Africa and territories, Irish Free State, Canada and Newfoundland

1934   affairs relating individually to Canada, Australia, New Zealand, South Africa, Southern Rhodesia, cable and wireless, education, South Africa High Commission territories

1935–1937   Newfoundland, Basutoland, Bechuanaland Protectorate and Swaziland, Southern Rhodesia

1938–1939   Newfoundland, British Phosphate Commission, Southern Rhodesia, High Commission Territories in South Africa

Department E
1935–1939   migration, work relating to dominions not otherwise allocated

Department F
1939   major diplomatic questions relating to war preparations

The only information available for the period 1940–1946 is as follows. During the war the boundaries of the departments altered frequently and new quasi-departments were added. In 1940 Department C split into C1 and C2. These departments were temporarily amalgamated in 1946 and 1947, and in 1947 Department C2 became the Supply Department. By 1946 an Information Department had been established. It took on business relating to publicity and war propaganda which had formerly been handled by the Empire Division of the Ministry of Information.

14.2 Breakdown of Commonwealth Relations Office departmental business

The departments are arranged alphabetically, with the divisions indicated in brackets. The subjects for which a department was responsible are listed fully in the first instance and thereafter an indication is given only when a subject was added (+) or removed (–). When there was a major change the subjects are listed again in full.

Contents:
Accountant-General's Department (1953–1964)

Africa Departments:
    Central African and Territories Department (1953–1960)

    Central Africa Department (1961–1962)

    East and General Africa Department (1963)

    UN and General Africa Department (1964)

    East Africa Economic Department (1965)

    Development Policy and West and East Africa Economic Department (1966)

    East Africa Department (1964)

    East Africa Political Department (1965–1966)

    Malawi and Central Africa Economic Department (1965)

    Zambia Department (1965)

    Malawi and Zambia Department (1966)

    Southern Rhodesia Department (1965)

    Rhodesia Department (1966)

    Southern Africa Department (1960–1961)

    Ghana Department (1958–1960)

    West and General Africa Department (1961–1962)

    Nigeria Department (1961–1962)

    West Africa Department (1963–1964)

    West and General African Department (1965)

    Development and Financial Policy and West Africa Economic Department (1965)

    West and General African Political Department (1966)

    Africa Economic Department (1963–1964)

Atlantic Department (1964–1965)

Communications Department (1953–1965)

Constitutional Departments:
Constitutional Department (1953–1964)

Constitutional and Protocol Department (1965)

Commonwealth Policy and Planning Department (1966)

Defence Departments:
Defence Department (1953–1959)

Defence and Western Department (1959–1960)

Defence Department (1961–1966)

Defence Supplies Department (1964–1965)

Principal Staff Officers' Department (1955–1960)

Development Departments:
Development Department (1953–1955)

Colombo Plan Department (1956–1960)

Technical Assistance Department (1961)

Economic Departments:
Trade Department (1953–1955)

Economic Relations I Department (1956–1964)

Western Economic Department (1965–1966)

Economic Relations II Department (1956–1964)

Asia Economic Department (1965–1966)

Economic Policy Department (1956–1963)

Commercial Policy Department (1964–1965)

Economic General Department (1966)

Common Market Department (1963)

Oversea Finance Department (1953–1955)

Commodities Department (1953–1955)

Financial Policy Department (1964)

Irish Trade Negotiations Unit (1965)

Far Eastern Departments:
Far Eastern Department (1953–1957)

South Asia and Far Eastern Department (1958–1960)

Far East and Pacific Department (1961–1966)

Joint Malaysia/Indonesia Department (1966)

Malaya Department (1958–1960)

General Departments:
General Department (1953–1956, 1961–1962)

Migration and General Department (1957–1960)

Nationality and General Department (1963–1965)

General and Migration Department (1966)

Nationality and Consular Department (1966)

Information Departments and Sections:
Publicity Policy Section (1953–1955)

British Information Services Section (1953–1956)

News and Information Section (1953–1956)

Administration and Publicity Policy Section (1956)

Records and Research Section (1956)

Public Relations Section (1957–1958)

Information Overseas Section (1957–1958)

Cultural Relations Section (1957–1958, 1962–1966)

Administration Section (1957–1958)

Press and Public Relations Section (1959–1960)

Information Services Department (1959–1966)

Information Policy and Cultural Relations Section (1959–1960)

Information Policy Department (1961–1965)

News Department (1961–1966)

Education Department (1961)

Joint Information Policy and Guidance Department (1966)

Joint Administration Department (1966)

Joint Research Department (1966)

Mediterranean Departments:
Malta Department (1965)

Mediterranean Department (1965–1966)

Middle East Departments:
Middle East Department (1958–1960)

Western and Middle East Department (1961–1964)

United Nations, Western and Middle East Department (1965–1966)

Political Affairs Departments (1953, 1965)

Protocol Departments:
Protocol Department (1955–1956)

Protocol and Nationality Department (1956–1958)

Joint Protocol Department (1966)

Services Department (1953–1955)

South Asian Departments:
South Asian Department (1953)

South Asian and Middle East Department (1955–1957)

South Asia Department (1961–1965)

United Nations Departments:
Western and United Nations Department (1953–1958)

United Nations Department (1959–1963)

West Indies Department (1963–1964)

Western Departments (1953–1966)

Abbreviations used in the list

ANZAM	Australia, New Zealand and Malaya
ANZUS	Australian, New Zealand and US Defence Pact, Pacific Security Treaty
BB&S	Basutoland, Bechuanaland Protectorate and Swaziland
BBC	British Broadcasting Corporation
BIS	British Information Service
CDC	Commonwealth Development Corporation
CDFC	Commonwealth Development Finance Company
CD and W	Colonial Development and Welfare
CELU	Commonwealth Education Liaison Unit
CENTO	Central Treaty Organization (Baghdad Pact until 1959)
CICT	International Film and Television Council (Conseil international du cinema et de la television)
COI	Central Office of Information
COS	Chiefs of Staff Secretariat
CTB	Commonwealth Telecommunications Board
CTCA	Commission for Technical Co-operation in Africa
DAC	Development Assistance Committee
DTC	Department of Technical Co-operation
EACSO	East African Common Services Organization

ECA	Economic Commission for Africa
ECAFE	Economic Commission for Asia and the Far East
ECOSOC	Economic and Social Council (UNO)
ECSC	European Coal and Steel Community
EDC	European Defence Community
EEC	European Economic Community
EFTA	European Free Trade Association
EPC	European Political Community
ELDO	European Launcher Development Organization
ESRO	European Space Research Organization
EURATOM	European Atomic Energy Community
FAMA	Foundation for Mutual Assistance in Africa (South of the Sahara)
FAO	Food and Agriculture Organization
FBI	Federation of British Industry
FO	Foreign Office
GATT	General Agreement on Tariffs and Trade
HMOCS	Her (or His) Majesty's Overseas Civil Service
HMSO	Her (or His) Majesty's Stationery Office
IBRD	International Bank for Reconstruction and Development
ICAO	International Civil Aviation Organization
IDA	International Development Association
IDC	Imperial Defence College
IFC	International Finance Corporation
ILO	International Labour Organization
ITA	Independent Television Authority
ITU	International Telecommunications Union
ITV	Independent Television
LPS	Lord Privy Seal
MP	Member of Parliament
NATO	North Atlantic Treaty Organization
OAU	Organization of African Unity
ODM	Office of Defence Mobilization (USA)
ODM	Overseas Development Ministry
OECD	Organization for Economic Co-operation and Development
OEEC	Organization for European Economic Co-operation
SCAAP	Special Commonwealth African Assistance Plan
SEATO	South-East Asia Treaty Organization (also South East Asia Collective Defence Treaty Organization established in 1955)
SUNFED	Special United Nations Fund for Economic Development
TCS	Technical Co-operation Scheme
UAR	United Arab Republic
UKHC	United Kingdom High Commission
UN	United Nations
UNESCO	United Nations Educational, Scientific and Cultural Organization
UNO	United Nations Organization
UPU	Universal Postal Union
USA	United States of America
USSR	Union of Soviet Socialist Republics

VSO	Voluntary Service Overseas
WEU	Western European Union
WHO	World Health Organization
WMO	World Meteorological Organization

ACCOUNTANT-GENERAL'S DEPARTMENTS

Accountant-General's Department Branch I (Establishments and Organization Division)

1953　　Section A: salaries, wages, income tax, etc, home salaries, oversea salaries and outfit allowances, weekly paid staff, estimates, accounts and oversea settlement, treasury control (S Africa HC Territories), cemeteries expenditure in India and Pakistan, office expenses, special missions, conferences, Colombo Plan and miscellaneous payments

　　　　Section B: representation in India and Pakistan and in other Commonwealth countries, development and welfare (Basutoland, Bechuanaland Protectorate and Swaziland), Commonwealth Agricultural Bureaux, Commonwealth Economic Committee

1954　　no information available

1955　　as above; – home salaries, oversea salaries and outfit allowances, weekly paid staff

Branches I and II were then merged.

Accountant-General's Department Branch II (Finance and General Division)

1953　　pensions section (pensions of British officers of Indian and Burma forces and their families), compensation for Indian tax, accounts and estimates section, general section (Indian Government claims, leave pay, Indian Army, Burma civilians)

1954　　no information available

1955　　as above + Burma pensions and pensions paid overseas, pensions increase, service and family pensions

Accountant-General's Department Branch II (Establishments and Organization Division

1956　　pension funds, family pension funds (awards and fund accounts), vote accounts and estimates, outstanding balances, statistics, oversea settlement, colonial development and welfare, accounting (pension payments), Treasury control (High Commission Territories), repatriation recoveries, accounts work for Commonwealth Agricultural Bureaux and Commonwealth Economic Committee, miscellaneous payments, missions and conferences, office expenses, travelling expenses of pensioners, miscellaneous payments (Commonwealth services), Technical Co-operation Scheme expenditure, salaries, wages, income tax, oversea establishments, except UK-based salaries, India, Pakistan, other Commonwealth countries, award of pensions, commutations (civil and military), administration of disability cases, award of pension increases, issue of pensions (India), issue of pensions (Burma), colonial paymasters' claims, compensation for Indian and Burma tax, Indian and Burma accounting, residual Indian and Burma inter-governmental claims, compensation to Indian civil and defence services, residual passage claims, record of service, medals

1957	as above
1958	as above + diplomatic mail, telegrams and telephones, supplies for overseas posts, payments relating to Malaya, Ghana and foreign office posts, TCS experts and equipment and trainees, salaries, etc, Ghana, Malaya, Australia, South Africa, Ceylon, Canada, New Zealand, Federation of Rhodesia and Nyasaland, and Republic of Ireland
1959	family pensions funds (awards and fund accounts), payments relating to overseas posts, payments from CRO vote, information (operational) expenditure, Commonwealth conferences, claims from foreign office posts, tours and conferences, travelling claims, diplomatic mail, telegrams and telephones, miscellaneous claims, salaries, wages, income tax, overseas salaries, outfit allowances, audit of accounts, overseas establishments (estimates, provision of funds, recoveries from other departments), India, Pakistan, Ghana, Malaya, Canada, New Zealand, Federation of Rhodesia and Nyasaland, Republic of Ireland, Australia, South Africa, Ceylon, payments from Commonwealth services vote and overseas settlement vote, compensation for premature termination of employment (India and Burma services), passages on premature retirement (Indian government employees), overseas settlement, special payments from pensions vote, payments for Commonwealth services vote, vote accounts and estimates, outstanding balances, statistics, colonial development and welfare, Treasury control (High Commission Territories), residual Indian and Burma inter-governmental accounting, accounts for Commonwealth Agricultural Bureaux and Commonwealth Economic Committee, repatriation recoveries, Technical Co-operation Scheme expenditure, commutations (civil and military), administration of disability cases, award of pension increases, compensation for Indian, Pakistan and Burma tax, colonial paymasters' claims, medical claims
1960	as above
1961	as above + travelling and miscellaneous payments including information expenditure, relating to posts in Nigeria and Cyprus, weekly paid staff, audit of accounts of overseas establishments, recoveries from other departments, estimates, provision of funds, etc for Nigeria, accounts work for Commonwealth Education Liaison Unit, payment in

connection with educational co-operation in the Commonwealth, technical assistance expenditure

1962 as above + short visits overseas by home staff, travelling and miscellaneous payments including information expenditure relating to Irish Republic, library payments, audit of accounts of overseas establishments, recoveries from other departments, provision of funds for Sierra Leone, purchase tax, colonial development, corporation loans, exchequer loans – audit of accounts of oversea establishments, recoveries from other departments, provision of funds for South Africa

1963 co-ordination of estimates, Commonwealth grants and loans, Maldive Islands expenditure, contributions to Commonwealth organizations, royal visits, development and welfare payments, Colonial Development Corporation loans, exchequer loans, recoveries of loans, Burma account, vote account, statistics, Treasury control, award of India, Burma, etc pensions, award of pension increases, commutations (civil and military), administration of disability cases, Indian family pensions funds and pension issues, family pension funds, issue of pensions (including Nigeria pensions on behalf of DTC), compensation for India, Pakistan and Burma tax, colonial and other paymasters' claims, pensioners' travelling and medical expenses, audit of accounts of overseas establishments, recoveries from other departments, provision of funds, etc for posts in Canada, Africa and the West Indies, (Canada, Ghana, Jamaica, Trinidad, Rhodesia, Nyasaland, Tanganyika, Uganda, Nigeria, Sierra Leone), audit of accounts of overseas establishments, recoveries from other government departments, provisions of funds, etc, for posts in other Commonwealth countries (India, Pakistan, Australia, New Zealand, Irish Republic, Ceylon, Malaya, Cyprus), residual Indian claims, salaries, wages, income tax, overseas salaries, outfit allowances for staff in Canada, Africa and West Indies and in other Commonwealth countries, home salaries and wages of weekly paid staff, miscellaneous administrative payments, short visits overseas by home staff, expenses for Commonwealth conferences, governors, etc, travelling and miscellaneous payments relating to posts in Canada, Africa, and West Indies, travelling in UK, diplomatic mail, entertainment fund, travelling and miscellaneous payments relating to other Commonwealth countries, library expenses, telegrams and telephones, rail warrants, miscellaneous office expenses, military assistance, oversea settlement, compensation passages on premature retirement, purchase tax, pension appeal tribunal (Irish Republic), grant to Irish Republic (transferred officers), Cyprus and Malaya police units, repatriation recoveries, accounts work for Commonwealth Agricultural Bureaux, Commonwealth Economic Committee and Commonwealth Education Liaison Unit

1964 as above; – Treasury control + clearance of suspense items

AFRICA DEPARTMENTS

Central African and Territories Department (Finance and General Division)

1953   Central African Federation, Southern Rhodesia, Basutoland, the Bechuanaland Protectorate, Swaziland

1954   no information available

1955   Rhodesia and Nyasaland Federation, federal legislation, African Affairs Board, federal/territorial relations, higher education and Rhodesia University, external affairs of the Federation, federal economic and development plan, Southern Rhodesia, Basutoland, Bechuanaland Protectorate and Swaziland: general policy and administration, estimates, economic development and CD and W assistance, personnel and establishments

1956   as above + University of Nyasaland, Federal Public Service, immigration legislation, liaison with Economic Division on Federal and Southern Rhodesian questions

Central African and Territories Department (Africa and General Division)

1957   internal affairs of the Federation of Rhodesia and Nyasaland (including African Affairs Board), federal/territorial relations, higher education (including University of Rhodesia and Nyasaland), Federal Public Service, legislation relating to the above subjects including immigration legislation, external affairs of the Federation, liaison with Economic Division on Federal and Southern Rhodesian questions, Southern Rhodesian matters in general, legislation relating to above subjects, Basutoland, Bechaunaland Protectorate and Swaziland: general policy and administration, personnel and establishment, estimates, economic development and CD and W assistance

1958   Federation of Rhodesia and Nyasaland, Southern Rhodesia, Basutoland, Bechuanaland Protectorate and Swaziland, general policy and administration, personnel and establishments, estimates, economic development and CD and W assistance
1959 as above

1960   Federation of Rhodesia and Nyasaland, Southern Rhodesia

Central Africa Department (Africa Division)

1961   Federation of Rhodesia and Nyasaland: constitutional and internal affairs, Northern Rhodesia and Nyasaland affairs, constitutional affairs, Southern Rhodesia affairs, external affairs, legislation

1962   as above; – legislation + technical assistance and CD and W visits, arrangements for Federal Review Conference

Then see East and General Africa Department.

East and General Africa Department (Africa and Political Division 1963 Only)

1963 North Africa, foreign territories in East, Central and South Africa, political developments in the Federation of Rhodesia and Nyasaland and the High Commission Territories, Tanganyika, Uganda, Kenya, Zanzibar, East African services

United Nations and General Africa Department (division not indicated)

1964 political questions: matters concerning the constitution and organization of the UN, Security Council and the political and budgetary committees of the General Assembly, questions concerning UN interest in non-self-governing territories, Committee of Twenty Four, Trusteeship Council and Trusteeship Committee of the General Assembly, economic, social and legal questions, economic and social committees of the General Assembly, ECOSOC and associated commissions, International Court of Justice, specialist agencies (except otherwise allocated) including ILO, WHO and FAO, Antarctica, commonwealth liaison procedure, distribution of FO prints and telegrams, South Africa, political affairs of foreign countries and dependencies in Southern, Equatorial and Northern Africa in the UN context and as they affect Commonwealth relations, except as otherwise allocated, general Africa questions, political and constitutional developments in the High Commission Territories, the Rhodesias and Nyasaland, UN aspects, and political and constitutional developments, as they affect Commonwealth relations

See the East Africa Economic Department, East Africa Political Department, Malawi and Central Africa Economic Department, Southern Rhodesia Department, West and General African Department and Zambia Department for the continuation of these subjects.

East Africa Economic Department (East Africa Division)

1965 Tanganyika and Zanzibar, Uganda, Kenya, EACSO, coffee

Development Policy and West and East Africa Economic Department (East and West Africa Division)

1966 development policy, OECD (Development Assistance Committee), IBRD, IDA, IFC, CDC (general policy), CDFC implications of export credit policy upon development policy, ECA, economic and financial aspects of OAU, SCAAP economic relations with Ghana, Nigeria, Sierra Leone, The Gambia, Kenya, Uganda, Tanzania and EACSO, Kenya land questions, coffee, cocoa and oil seeds, Commonwealth gifts scheme

See also East Africa Political Department (1965–1966). Before 1965 see: Central African and Territories Department (1953–1960), Central Africa Department (1961–

1962), East and General Africa Department (1963), UN and General Africa Department (1964).

East Africa Department (division not indicated)
1964   Tanganyika and Uganda and their relations with neighbouring foreign countries, Kenya and Zanzibar and their relations with neighbouring foreign countries, East African Federation, political aspects of East African defence arrangements, EACSO (political questions)

East Africa Political Department (East Africa Division)
1965   general political questions including inter-territorial matters

East Africa Political Department (East and West Africa Division)
1966   political relations with Tanzania, Uganda, and Kenya, political aspects of EACSO, Horn of Africa, Portuguese territories in Africa, relations with Mauritius insofar as they affect Commonwealth relations

See also East Africa Economic Department (1965), Development Policy and West and East Africa Economic Department (1966). Before 1965 see Central African and Territories Department (1953–1960), Central Africa Department (1961–1962), East and General Africa Department (1963), UN and General Africa Department (1964).

Malawi and Central Africa Economic Department (Central Africa Division)
1965   constitutional, political and external affairs, financial and economic matters

Zambia Department (Central Africa Division)
1965   political, constitutional and external affairs

Malawi and Zambia Department (Central Africa Division)
1966   political relations with Malawi and Zambia, including finance and defence aid

Before 1965 see Central African Territories Department (1953–1960), Central Africa Department (1961–1962), East and General Africa Department (1963), UN and General Africa Department (1964).

Southern Rhodesia Department (Central Africa Division)
1965   political, constitutional and external affairs

Rhodesia Department (Central Africa Division)
1966   Rhodesia: political, constitutional and external affairs, financial and economic questions, general Central African financial and economic work, including post-dissolution questions

Before 1965 see Central African and Territories Department (1953–1960), Central

Africa Department (1961–1962), East and General Africa Department (1963), UN and General Africa Department (1963).

Southern Africa Department (Africa and General Division)
1960   Basutoland, Bechuanaland Protectorate and Swaziland, political, personnel and establishments, estimates, economic development and CD and W assistance, Union of South Africa: internal political affairs

Southern Africa Department (Africa Division)
1961   as above + defence

Ghana Department (Political Division)
1958   Topics related to Ghana: external relations, internal political affairs and residual questions from transfer of power, economic relations, Volta River Project, international trade in cocoa

1959   as above + training and other questions relating to individuals, constitutional development and internal political affairs in Nigeria

1960   as above + CTCA (excluding economic aspects); – residual questions from transfer of power

Then see Africa Division: West and General Africa Department.

West and General Africa Department (Africa Division)
1961   Ghana: external relations, internal political affairs, Pan-Africanism, CTCA, North Africa, Sudan, Horn of Africa, foreign territories and Central Africa, Ghana: economic and financial questions, Volta River Project, international trade in cocoa

1962   Ghana and foreign states in West Africa, political affairs, economic affairs, cocoa, CTCA, West Africa Research Office, foreign states and territories in North, East and Central Africa

Nigeria Department (Africa Division)
1961   general political questions, external relations, matters relating to and resulting from the transfer of power, the Cameroons, matters arising from the UK/Nigeria defence agreement, training, secondments, transfer of service personnel, economic and financial questions

1962   as above; – external relations, matters relating to and resulting from the transfer of power + liaison with Department of Technical Cooperation on residual HMOCS matters, Nigeria ministerial visitors, Sierra Leone: general and political questions, economic and financial questions

West Africa Department (Africa and Political Division, 1963. Division not stated in 1964)
1963–1964   Ghana: general political questions, external relations, political affairs

insofar as they affect Commonwealth relations of Guinea, Mali, Senegal, Ivory Coast, Togo, Dahomey, Upper Volta, Nigeria, Sierra Leone, general political questions and external relations, political affairs insofar as they affect Commonwealth relations of Republic of Cameroon, Niger and Liberia, Spanish and Portuguese territories in West Africa, co-ordination of programmes for ministerial visits from West Africa

West and General African Department (Africa Division)
1965   Ghana, Nigeria, Sierra Leone, General African questions

See also Development and Financial Policy and West African Economic Department (1965), and West and General Political Department (1966).

Development and Financial Policy and West Africa Economic Department (Aid Division)
1965   Ghana, Nigeria, Sierra Leone, general development, financial export credit and technical co-operation matters, Economic Commission for Africa and CTCA, gold, cocoa and oilseeds

Then see West and General African Political Department (1966).

West and General African Political Department (East and West Africa Division)
1966   Political relations with Ghana, Nigeria, Sierra Leone and The Gambia, general African questions including Congo and OAU, political affairs of foreign countries and dependencies in West, Equatorial and Northern Africa, African visitors' unit

Africa Economic Department (Africa and Political Division, 1963. Division not indicated in 1964)
1963–1964   Ghana and Sierra Leone: economic and financial questions, Volta River Project, international trade in cocoa, Nigeria: economic and financial questions, Economic Commission for Africa, CTCA, East Africa: economic and financial questions, international trade in coffee

Then see Development and Financial Policy and West Africa Economic Department (1964), East Africa Economic Department (1964), Malawi and Central Africa Economic Department (1964), Development Policy and West and East Africa Economic Department (1965), Rhodesia Department (1965).

ATLANTIC DEPARTMENT

Atlantic Department (Aid Division)
1964   Canada, USA, Caribbean

Atlantic Department (Asia and Atlantic Division)
1965   Political relations with Canada, political and economic relations with Jamaica, Trinidad, Tobago, CRO aspects of the following: relations with USA and British and foreign territories in Central and South America and the Caribbean, University of the West Indies, international trade in sugar, bananas, citrus fruits

COMMUNICATIONS DEPARTMENT

Communications Department (Finance and General Division)
1953   civil aviation, postal communications, telecommunications, shipping, migration

1954   no information available

Communications Department (Political Division)
1955   civil aviation, telecommunications, postal communications, CRO list, migration, communism in Commonwealth countries, labour and trade union affairs in Commonwealth countries, international trade union organizations

1956   as above + libraries, Indian records section

1957   as above + India Office building; – migration

Communications Department (Establishments and Organization Division)
1958–1960   as above

1961   civil aviation, postal communications, telecommunications, India Office building, CRO list, CRO library, India Office library, India Office records, communism, labour and trade union affairs

1962   as above + ICAO, UPU, Commonwealth Telecommunications Board and ITU, World Meteorological Organization

1963   as above + peaceful uses of outer space, satellite communications, ELDO, ESRO

1964   as above + information research

Communications Department (Trade Division)
1965   peaceful uses of outer space, ITU and satellite telecommunications, CTB, ICAO and civil aviation matters, UPU and postal matters, WMO

Communications Department (Mediterranean, South Asia and Defence Division)
communism, labour and trade union affairs

CONSTITUTIONAL DEPARTMENTS

Constitutional Department (Constitutional and Political Division)

1953 general Commonwealth constitutional questions, including coronation questions, constitutional affairs in Commonwealth countries, questions relating to the Irish Republic not dealt with by other departments, honours, decorations and medals (civil and military), including Korea operational and non-operational awards, foreign orders, investitures, title 'Excellency' and 'Honourable', ceremonial matters (civil and military), precedence, flags, arms and badges (civil and military), constitutional instruments, matters relating to royal family (eg petitions to queen, loyal messages, royal patronage, state portrait, requests for autographs, procedure for dealing with communications between Commonwealth countries and the queen, royal visits to other Commonwealth countries), governors and governors-general (constitutional and ceremonial questions, uniforms, royal instructions, commissions of appointment, dormant commission), channels of communication between UK and other Commonwealth governments, war histories, nationality and citizenship legislation, nationality and naturalization questions, registration of births, deaths and marriages abroad, passport and visa questions

1954 no information available

Constitutional Department (Political Division)

1955 as above + internal political (except labour and trade union) affairs of Commonwealth countries (except Federation of Rhodesia and Nyasaland) and Irish Republic, residuary questions relating to former Indian States (except Kashmir and Junagadh), printing and distribution of despatches and fortnightly summaries from all overseas posts, speech from the throne, emergency legislation, colonial affairs, Commonwealth representation in the colonies, constitutional development in dependent territories of other Commonwealth countries, Commission for Technical Co-operation in Africa, enquiries and requests for certificates, registration procedure in India and Pakistan; – honours, decorations and medals, foreign orders, investitures, titles, ceremonial matters, precedence, flags, arms, badges, constitutional instruments, governors and governors-general, channels of communication between UK and other Commonwealth governments, war histories, naturalization questions

1956 as above + labour and trade union affairs, immigration and emigration restrictions within the Commonwealth

1956 as above; – labour and trade union affairs, nationality and citizenship, passport and visa questions, immigration and emigration restrictions within the Commonwealth, births, deaths and marriages in Commonwealth countries, general enquiries and requests for certificates, registration procedure in India and Pakistan

1958	general Commonwealth constitutional questions, constitutional questions affecting the Crown, constitutional affairs, internal political affairs in Canada, Australia, New Zealand, South Africa (excluding labour and trade union affairs), constitutional and political questions affecting the Irish Republic, residuary questions relating to former Indian States (except Kashmir and Junagadh), speech from the throne, legislative programme, Commission for Technical Co-operation in Africa, printing and distribution of despatches and fortnightly summaries from all overseas posts, constitutional development and internal political affairs, Nigeria, Cyprus, Federation of the West Indies, other colonial affairs, Commonwealth representation in colonies, constitutional developments in dependent territories of other Commonwealth countries
1959	as above + matters affecting Australian states, colonial constitutional development (general policy), honours, decorations, medals, titles, honorary degrees, freedom of cities, matters relating to the royal family, anthems, arms, badges, flags, military alliances, precedence, seals, toasts, uniforms, commissions for governors-general, governors and high commissioner, BB&S, letters patent, royal instructions to governors, formal instruments of accreditation for UK ambassador, Dublin and certain UK high commissioners, royal charters, royal warrants, nationality legislation and policy, problems of Indian and Pakistan immigration into UK, immigration and emigration restrictions within the Commonwealth, visa questions, stateless persons, travel documents, seamen's certificates, registration of births, deaths and marriages in India, Pakistan, Ceylon and Ghana, deportation, passport and nationality cases, passport policy and practice in Commonwealth countries
1960	colonial constitutional developments – questions of general policy, Cyprus, West Indian affairs, other colonial affairs, Commonwealth representation in colonies, dependent territories of other Commonwealth countries, general Commonwealth constitutional questions, constitutional questions affecting the Crown, royal visits, speech from the throne, legislative programme, constitutional and political questions affecting the Irish Republic, internal political affairs of Australia and New Zealand, matters affecting the Australian states, planning unit, printing and distribution of despatches and fortnightly summaries from all overseas posts, cataloguing of CRO briefs, honours, decorations and medals, titles, honorary degrees, freedom of cities, matters relating to royal family, anthems, arms, badges, flags, military alliances, precedence, seals, toasts, uniforms, commissions for governors-general, governors and high commissioner, BB&S, letters patent, royal instructions to governors, formal instruments of accreditation for UK ambassador, Dublin, and certain UK high commissioners, royal charters, royal warrants, nationality legislation and policy: immigration of British subjects into the UK, immigration and emigration restrictions within the Commonwealth, visa questions, stateless

persons, travel documents, seamen's certificates, registration of births, deaths and marriages in India, Pakistan, Ceylon, Ghana, deportation, passport and nationality cases, passport policy and practice in Commonwealth countries

1961   as above + Commonwealth evolution, future of the smaller colonial territories, dependent territories of other Commonwealth governments, meetings of Commonwealth prime ministers, Sierra Leone, registration of treaties, formalities in respect of intra-Commonwealth agreements; – nationality legislation and policy, immigration of British subjects into the UK, immigration and emigration restrictions within the Commonwealth, visa questions, stateless persons, travel documents, seamen's certificates, registration of births, deaths and marriages in India, Pakistan, Ceylon, Ghana, deportation, passport and nationality cases, passport policy and practice in Commonwealth countries

1962   as above + letters of credence; – Sierra Leone, future of the smaller colonial territories, commissions for Basutoland, Bechuanaland Protectorate and Swaziland

Constitutional Department (Africa and Political Division)

1963   as above + South Africa: residual constitutional questions: constitutional developments in colonies (other than those dealt with in territorial departments), diplomatic and consular immunities and privileges (other than matters allocated to Administrations Department); – Commonwealth evolution, colonial constitutional developments (general policy), West Indies Federation

1964   as above + Commonwealth visits, Commonwealth co-operation, registration of treaties with the United Nations; – registration of treaties

Constitutional and Protocol Department (Western, Constitutional and General Division)

1965   general Commonwealth constitutional questions, meetings of Commonwealth prime ministers, royal visits, diplomatic and consular immunities, registration of treaties with UN, formalities, honours, anthems, commissions

Then see Commonwealth Policy and Planning Department.

Commonwealth Policy and Planning Department (Defence and Commonwealth Policy Division)

1966   Commonwealth prime ministers' meetings and the Commonwealth Secretariat, policy and constitutional questions affecting the Commonwealth as a whole, future of colonial territories, matters affecting the royal family, legislative programme, registration of treaties with UNO, documentation for certain diplomatic and consular appointments, planning

DEFENCE DEPARTMENTS

Defence Department (Foreign Affairs Division)

1953   India and Pakistan (defence co-operation, supply and munitions, employment of UK personnel), exchange of classified military information, visiting forces legislation, coronation – military details, war book questions, attendance of representatives from other Commonwealth countries at UK courses, civil defence, recruitment questions, defence co-operation with Australia, New Zealand, South Africa, Ceylon and Southern Rhodesia, Middle East defence questions, supply and munitions (excluding India and Pakistan), Oversea Defence Committee subjects (except war books), defence co-operation with Canada, defence aspects of Brussels and North Atlantic treaties, atomic energy, defence science, liaison with Ministry of Defence and COS Secretariat

1954   no information available

1955   defence co-operation with Commonwealth countries, UK defence programme, defence programmes of Commonwealth countries, supply of defence equipment, long-range weapons, atomic energy, maintenance of war books, policy questions connected with war books, services legislation, drafting of war legislation, service allowances

1956   arms and equipment programmes of UK and other Commonwealth countries, supply of arms and equipment, bases and installations, secondment of personnel to defence establishments, long-range weapons, atomic energy and nuclear weapons (development), war books, services legislation, war legislation, conditions of service of British service personnel on loan to Commonwealth governments, nomination schemes for cadetships at Dartmouth, Sandhurst and Cranwell and for the RAF apprenticeships, matters relating to personnel of the late Indian defence services, including civilians employed under the former Defence and War Departments of the Government of India, miscellaneous

1957   as above + maintenance and administration of facilities

1958   atomic energy, long-range and nuclear weapons, supply of arms and equipment, arms and equipment programmes, war books, war legislation, safety of British subjects overseas in wartime, services legislation, visiting forces legislation, matters of policy relating to personnel of the late Indian defence services, including civilians employed under the former Defence and War Departments of the Government of India, secondments and loans to and from other Commonwealth countries on defence matters, civil defence

1959   as above; – political aspects, outer space

Defence and Western Department (Foreign Affairs Division)

1959   as above + Canada, USA, foreign affairs questions relating to Western and Southern Europe, USSR and Eastern Europe, Western organizations, political aspects, disarmament, outer space, summit talks

Defence Department (Foreign Affairs Division)

1961   as above + exchange of classified military information, co-ordination in the CRO of defence matters affecting the Commonwealth, defence policy questions affecting individual Commonwealth countries, not otherwise allocated, subjects concerning Ministry of Defence, service departments, chiefs of staff, secretarial and joint planning staff, not otherwise allocated, global strategy, UK bases in other Commonwealth countries, training of Commonwealth service personnel in UK, liaison with Joint Intelligence Organization, service liaison staffs and advisers, service exercises (including NATO, CENTO, SEATO), visits of service personnel and units, service aircraft movements and air trooping, defence statistics; – Canada, USA, foreign affairs questions relating to Western and Southern Europe, USSR and Eastern Europe, Western organizations, political aspects, disarmament, summit talks

1962   as above + conditions of service for secondments, liaison with Ministry of Defence and COS Secretariat

1963   as above + nuclear tests (other than suspension of nuclear tests), military aspects of outer space, staff college, IDC courses, attendance of Commonwealth personnel at NATO, CENTO and SEATO exercises

1964   Co-ordination in the Commonwealth Relations Office of matters relating to military operations and planning, liaison with Joint Planning Organization, defence policy questions not otherwise allocated, financial policy on training of Commonwealth service personnel in Britain, service exercises, defence aspects of constitutional developments not otherwise allocated, liaison with Joint Intelligence Organization, exchange of classified military information, service aircraft movements and air trooping (including Gurkha air trooping), visits of British service personnel units to Commonwealth countries, service liaison staffs and advisers, general policy on secondment of British personnel to other Commonwealth forces, training of Commonwealth service personnel in Britain – other than financial policy, Commonwealth applications for service with British forces, liaison with Ministry of Defence and chiefs of staff

See also Defence Supplies Department (1964–1965).

Defence Department (Mediterranean, South Asia and Defence Division)

1965   Commonwealth defence matters

Defence Department (Defence and Commonwealth Policy Division)

1966   Commonwealth defence matters, military aid, training and equipment, war books and war legislation

Defence Supplies Department (division not indicated)

1964   supply of arms and equipment, long-range nuclear weapons, nuclear tests other than suspension of testing, military aspects of outer space, war books, war legislation, emergency communications and control point in CRO, civil defence (films, publications, training courses), services legislation, visiting forces legislation, status of forces agreements, customs concessions for forces personnel, technical advice on conditions of service personnel seconded or loaned to other Commonwealth forces, co-ordination of planning of safety of British subjects overseas in time of emergency, matters of policy relating to personnel of the late India defence services, including civilians employed under former Defence and War Departments of the Government of India

Defence Supplies Department (Mediterranean, South Asia and Defence Division)

1965   supply of arms and equipment, nuclear weapons, war books

Then see Defence Department.

Principal Staff Officers' Department (Foreign Affairs Division)

1954   no information available

1955   general defence co-ordination with CRO, liaison with Ministry of Defence and service departments, liaison with COS secretariat, liaison with directors of plans, global strategy, naval visits and flights by service aircraft between Commonwealth countries, visits by service officers to Commonwealth countries, liaison with intelligence co-ordination staff, exchange of classified military information, civil defence, appointments and reports from service advisers in Commonwealth countries, service training courses, attendance of Commonwealth officers at combined exercises, liaison with Minister of Defence

1956   as above + liaison with Joint Planning Organization, nuclear weapons (effects), defence policy questions affecting individual Commonwealth countries, defence statistics, air trooping, service liaison staffs and advisers, secondment of service personnel to and from Commonwealth defence forces; – liaison with directors of plans, appointments of and reports from service advisers in Commonwealth countries

1957   as above + UK bases in other Commonwealth countries (general policy), visits of RAF units

1958   as above + service exercises (including NATO, ANZAM, SEATO and Baghdad Pact exercises), training of Commonwealth service personnel in UK (including nominations for cadetships); – nuclear weapons (effects), attendance at training courses and combined exercises, secondment of service personnel to and from Commonwealth defence forces

1959   as above

1960   as above

Then see Defence Department.

DEVELOPMENT DEPARTMENTS

Development Department (Economic Division)
1953   sterling area development (Australia, New Zealand, South Africa, Irish Republic, India, Pakistan, Ceylon), capital goods, iron, steel, tinplate, cement, oil, Technical Co-operation Scheme, provision of equipment, Colombo Plan, United Nations papers on under-developed territories, UN technical assistance – training cases and experts, policy questions and training facilities, experts and consultants, technical personnel committee

1954   no information available

1955   sterling area development, UN papers on development, Colombo Plan, Technical Co-operation Scheme – policy, UN technical assistance questions, provision of services of consultants, equipment and training facilities under Technical Co-operation Scheme, recruitment of experts under Technical Co-operation Scheme

Then see Colombo Plan Department.

Colombo Plan Department (Economic Division)
Before 1956 see Development Department.

1956   Colombo Plan policy, Technical Co-operation Scheme policy, UN technical assistance, recruitment of experts and consultants, provision of equipment, training facilities in UK

1957–1958   as above + economic aspects of SEATO and Baghdad Pact

1959–1960   as above + Ghana technical assistance policy: consultants, FAMA, UN special fund, Technical Co-operation Scheme: Ghana

Then see Technical Assistance Department.

Technical Assistance Department (Economic Division)
1961   Colombo Plan policy, Technical Co-operation Scheme policy, Ghana technical assistance policy, consultants, UN technical assistance, economic aspects of SEATO and CENTO, FAMA, UN special fund, Canadian technical assistance, Nigerian technical assistance, technical co-operation schemes, Colombo Plan, Ghana, Nigeria, CENTO, FAMA, recruitment of experts, provision of equipment, training facilities in UK, medical, steel, scientific advisory staff

Then see Economic Relations Departments I and II. See also individual territory departments, Africa Economic Departments (1963–1964), Development and Financial Policy and West Africa Economic Department (1965), Development Policy and West and East Africa Economic Department (1966). The last two are under Africa Departments.

ECONOMIC DEPARTMENTS

Trade Department (Economic Division)

1953   tariffs and preferences, GATT, customs unions, commercial treaties and agreements, Commonwealth Economic Committee, Overseas Negotiations Committee, coal, trade affecting Canada, Irish Republic and Commonwealth countries, protection of UK commercial interests, OEEC, EEC and ECAFE, Commonwealth Liaison Committee

1954   no information available

1955   as above + UK–Canada Continuing Committee; shipping questions – insurance, Athlone fellowship and FBI scholarships, Japanese economic questions, ECSC (economic aspects), joint secretaries, Commonwealth Liaison Committee; – customs unions, trade affecting Canada, Commonwealth Economic Committee, coal

Then see Economic Relations Departments I and II, Economic Policy Department.

Economic Relations I Department (Economic Division)

1956–1957   international trade in meat, dairy products, fruit, sugar, wool, British Phosphate commissioners, financing Commonwealth forces in the Far East, capital issues general policy, economies of and economic relations with Australia, New Zealand, Irish Republic, Canada, South Africa, Federation of Rhodesia and Nyasaland, international trade in wheat, tobacco, fish, newsprint, timber, chemicals, copper, lead, gold, UK–Canada Continuing Committee, Athlone fellowships, FBI scholarships

1958   as above + repayment of cost of United States logistic support for Commonwealth forces in Korea, economic relations between Canada and the West Indies; – financing of Commonwealth forces in the Far East

1959–1961   as above + international trade in aluminium

1962   as above + economies of and relations with Cyprus; – economies of and economic relations with South Africa

1963   as above; – repayment of cost of United States logistic support for Commonwealth forces in Korea, capital issues general policy, economic relations between Canada and the West Indies, UK–Canada Continuing Committee
For 1962 see Common Market Department.

1964 British agricultural policy, economies of and economic relations with Australia, New Zealand, Irish Republic, Canada, Cyprus, Federation of Rhodesia and Nyasaland, international trade in wool, meat, dairy products, grains, Athlone fellowships, FBI scholarships, British Phosphate Commission

Then see Western Economic Department.

Western Economic Department (Trade Division)

1965 as above in Economic Relations I Department; – Federation of Rhodesia and Nyasaland

1966 as above; – Cyprus, Irish Republic

Economic Relations II Department (Economic Division)

1956–1957 economy of and economic relations with India, Pakistan, Ceylon, loans to and financial agreements with India, Pakistan, Ceylon, taxation questions in India, Pakistan, Ceylon, SUNFED, international trade in rice, oilseeds and oils, tea, coffee, hides and skins, jute, cotton, rubber

1958 as above + loans to and financial agreements with Ghana, Malaya, taxation questions in Ghana, Malaya, ECAFE

1959 as above + international trade in tin, Soviet economic policy overseas

1960 economy of and economic relations with India, Pakistan, Ceylon, Soviet economic policy overseas, international trade in cotton, rice, oilseeds and vegetable oils, coffee, hides and skins, ECAFE, loans to and financial agreements with India, Pakistan, Ceylon, double taxation question in India, Pakistan, Ceylon, international trade in tin, tea, rubber, jute

1961 as above + economy of and economic relations with Malaya, loans to and financial agreements with Malaya; – double taxation question in India, Pakistan, Ceylon

1962 as above + Colombo Plan policy and general liaison with Department of Technical Co-operation and vegetable oils, coffee, hides, skins; – international trade in cotton, oilseeds, vegetable oils, coffee, hides, skins

1963 economy of and economic relations with India, Ceylon, Pakistan, Malaya, economic questions arising out of the proposals for Malaysia, international trade in tin, tea, rubber, jute, technical co-operation policy, liaison with Department of Technical Co-operation, Colombo Plan policy, ECAFE, international trade in cotton, rice, hides, skins, Soviet economic policy overseas

1964 as above + economy of and economic relations with Malaysia, UN Freedom from Hunger Campaign (general policy), international trade in cotton textiles; – economy of and economic relations with Malaya, technical co-operation policy, liaison with Department of Technical

Co-operation, economic questions arising out of the proposals for Malaysia, Soviet economic policy overseas

Then see Asia Economic Department (1965–1966).

Asia Economic Department (Aid Division)

1965　　India, Pakistan, Ceylon, Malaysia, Colombo Plan, ECAFE, UN Freedom from Hunger Campaign, tin, rubber, jute, rice, tea, cotton, cotton textiles, hides and skins

Asia Economic Department (Asia and Atlantic Division)

1966　　as above + economic relations with Singapore, Brunei, remittance problems; – UN Freedom from Hunger Campaign

Economic Policy Department (Economic Division)

1956　　meetings of Commonwealth finance and economic ministers, collective approach, sterling area balance of payments, general expenditure questions, general development finance questions, Commonwealth Development Finance Company, European Payments Union, International Monetary Fund, International Bank, IFC, American aid general policy, exchange control, overseas trade and payments negotiations, commercial debts, GATT, OEEC, Economic Commission for Europe, international commodity policy, Food and Agriculture Organization, European Coal and Steel Community, commodity defence planning, strategic exports, commercial treaties, Commonwealth Economic Committee, shipping, Commonwealth Liaison Committee

1957　　as above + international trade in petroleum

1958　　as above + European Customs Union and free trade area, accountants, weights and measures, registration of companies, shipping

1959　　EEC and free trade area, GATT, OEEC, ECSC, Economic Commission for Europe, UK financial and development policies: sterling, balance of payments: UK and sterling area, IMF, IBRD, IFC, Commonwealth Development Finance Company, Colonial Development Corporation, exchange control, overseas trade and payments negotiations, commercial debts, international commodity policy, FAO, commodity defence planning, commercial treaties, shipping, international trade in petroleum, exhibitions and trade fairs, accountants, weights and measures, registration of companies, copyright, Commonwealth Economic Committee, American aid: general policy, strategic controls, meetings of Commonwealth finance and economic ministers, statistical section, Commonwealth Liaison Committee

1960　　as above + economic commission for Africa; – European customs union, collective approach, general development finance questions, European payments union, International Bank

1961　　as above + International Development Association; – meetings of Commonwealth finance and economic ministers

1962　　　　as above + export credits (general questions)

1963　　　　overseas trade and payments negotiations, commercial debts, international commodity policy, GATT, commodity defence planning, commercial treaties, international trade in petroleum, registration of companies, copyright, strategic controls, OECD (except DAC), meeting of Commonwealth Economic Consultative Council, Commonwealth Economic Committee and Commonwealth Liaison Committee, exchange control, shipping, British financial development and aid policies, sterling area, balance of payments, British and sterling area, US aid: general policy, OECD, Development Assistance Committee, export credits (general questions), IMF, International Bank for Reconstruction and Development, International Development Association, Commonwealth Development Finance Company, Colonial Development Corporation, statistical section
Then see Commercial Policy Department (1964–1965).

Commercial Policy Department (division not indicated)

1964　　　　Commonwealth trade (general aspects), Commonwealth Economic Consultative Council Meetings (other than finance ministers and balance of payments meeting), Commonwealth Economic Committee, Commonwealth Liaison Committee, GATT, United Nations Trade and Development Conference, commodity policy (general aspects including CICT), FAO (economic aspects), EFTA, European communities, OECD (other than financial and development aspects), commercial relations with foreign countries, Soviet external economic policy, East-West trade and strategic controls, international trade in petroleum, shipping, registration of companies, copyright

Commercial Policy Department (Trade Division)

1965　　　　Commonwealth trade (general), Commonwealth economic committees, GATT, UN Trade and Development conference, FAO, EFTA, OECD, commercial relations with foreign countries, petroleum, shipping, registration of companies, copyright, atomic energy – peaceful uses

See Economic General Department in 1966.

Economic General Department (Trade Division)

1966　　　　general questions on trade and economics in the Commonwealth, European economic communities, European Free Trade Association, OECD, GATT, FAO, IMF, sterling area, balance of payments, shipping, registration of companies, double taxation, copyright, peaceful uses of atomic energy, UN Trade and Development Conference, East-West trade and strategic controls, international trade in petroleum

Common Market Department (Economic Division)

1963　　　　India, Pakistan, Ceylon, Ghana, Malaya, Nigeria, Sierra Leone, Tanganyika, Jamaica, Trinidad, Rhodesia and Nyasaland, Canada, Australia, New Zealand, Cyprus, Irish Republic, EURATOM, European Coal and Steel Community, general

See also Economic Relations I Department in 1963.

Oversea Finance Department (Economic Division)

1953 financial questions relating to Australia, Canada, New Zealand, South Africa, Irish Republic, India, Pakistan, Ceylon, defence finance, general sterling area and balance of payments questions, capital issues, exchange control, IMF and International Bank, double taxation, currency, Japanese economic questions, statistical section

1954 no information available

1955 as above; – Japanese economic questions, statistical section

Then see Economic Relations Departments I and II, Economic Policy Department, Common Market Department (1963).

Commodities Department (Economic Division)

1953 food, individual food commodities, food gifts, FAO, strategic exports, RIP working party: NATO commodity problems, rubber commodity policy, International Materials Conference, non-ferrous metals and minerals, sulphur, chemicals and fertilizers, cotton, jute, newsprint, timber, wool, tobacco

1954 no information available

1955 food, FAO, tobacco, commodity policy, Colombo Plan policy, industrial raw materials, control of strategic materials, commodity defence problems and planning, Commonwealth Economic Committee

Then see Economic Policy Department (1956–1963), Economic Relations Departments I and II (1956–1964), Commercial Policy Department (1964–1965), Western Economic Department (1965–1966), Economic General Department (1966).

Financial Policy Department (division not indicated)

1964 meetings of Commonwealth finance ministers, development and aid policies, OECD (Development Assistance Committee), IBRD, IDA, CDC, CDFC, IMF, financial policy, gold, OECD (financial matters), export credits (general questions), technical co-operation policy, statistical section: sterling area balance of payments

Irish Trade Negotiations Unit (Economic Division)

1965 economic relations with the Irish republic

FAR EASTERN DEPARTMENTS

Far Eastern Department (Foreign Affairs Division)

1953　　foreign political affairs as they affect Commonwealth relations in the Far East, South-East Asia and Pacific Islands, Burma, Malaya, Thailand, Indo-China, Indonesia, Hong Kong, Pacific Pact, New Guinea, New Hebrides, Borneo, South Pacific Commission, Japan, China, Korea, Formosa, Philippines

1954　　no information available

1955　　as above + defence questions as they affect Commonwealth relations in the Far East, South-East Asia and Pacific Islands, Pacific defence including defence of Hong Kong, South-East Asia defence, ANZUS – Pacific Pact, Malaya

1956　　as above + Commonwealth forces in Korea

1957　　as above + Australia, New Zealand, ANZAM, ANZUS, South-East Asia Collective Defence Treaty, Malaya and Singapore (external defence questions)

South Asia and Far Eastern Department (Foreign Affairs Division)

1958　　political affairs, including connected defence questions, insofar as they affect Commonwealth relations in South Asia and the Far East (excluding Malaya and Singapore), Australia, New Zealand (excluding internal political affairs), ANZAM, ANZUS, South-East Asia defence, Philippines, Siam, Indo-China (excluding South-East Asia defences), India, Gurkha recruitment, Nepal, Bhutan, Sikkim, Tibet, Sinkiang, Portuguese territories in India, Ceylon, Maldive Islands, Burma, Indonesia, New Guinea, China, Hong Kong, Japan, Korea, Formosa, Pacific Islands, South Pacific Commission, Pakistan, political relations between India and Pakistan, Kashmir, Afghanistan, Gwadur, Himalayan expeditions

1959　　as above; – Gwadur

1960　　as above; – Maldive Islands, Gwadur, Himalayan expeditions

Then see South Asia Department, Far East and Pacific Department.

Far East and Pacific Department (Foreign Affairs Division)

1961　　External policies of and UK relations with Australia and New Zealand, political affairs (including connected defence questions) insofar as they affect Commonwealth relations of China (other than relations with India and Pakistan), Hong Kong, Japan, Korea, Formosa, Philippines, Indonesia, New Guinea, Thailand, Pacific Islands, South Pacific Commission, ANZAM, ANZUS, SEATO, Federation of Malaya, internal political affairs, Malayan defence questions, Malaya-Singapore relations, British Borneo territories, HM overseas civil services in Malaya: training, secondment, transfers and miscellaneous questions

1962 as above + political affairs insofar as they affect Commonwealth relations of Vietnam, Cambodia, Laos, British aid to expansion of Federation of Malaya's armed forces, external policy of Federation of Malaya, matters arising from UK/Malayan Defence Agreement, political affairs (including defence questions) of Singapore, proposal for Greater Malaysia; – economic aspects of SEATO, Malayan defence questions, Malaya-Singapore relations

1963 as above + North Borneo, Sarawak, Brunei; – HMOCS in Malaya

1963 as above; – Singapore, North Borneo, Sarawak, Brunei

Far East and Pacific Department (Far East and West Africa Division)
1965 Australia, New Zealand, Malaysia, Brunei, defence and other regional organizations, political affairs of other Far East territories insofar as they affect Commonwealth relations, ANZAM, ANZUS and SEATO

Far East and Pacific Department (Far East and Mediterranean Division)
1966 as above + political relations with Ceylon, Singapore, Maldive Islands; – economic aspects of SEATO

Joint Malaysia/Indonesia Department (division not indicated)
1966 questions arising from Indonesia's policy of 'confrontation' against Malaysia

Malaya Department (Political Division)
1958 general political questions, external relations, matters relating to and resulting from transfer of power, economic and financial questions, defence questions, UK-Malaya Defence Agreement, SEATO and ANZAM matters affecting Malaya, Commonwealth strategic reserve, Singapore, Christmas Island (Indian Ocean), colonial constitutional development (questions of general policy)

1959 as above + recruitment, appointments and transfers, other miscellaneous questions, aid to expansion of federation armed forces; – colonial constitutional development (general policy)

1960 as above + training, secondments, transfers, pensions, British Borneo Territories; – Commonwealth strategic reserve, Christmas Island

Then see Far East and Pacific Department.

GENERAL DEPARTMENTS

General Department (Constitutional and Political Division)

1953 — cemeteries, children (employment), claims (war injury, property and compensation), deportations, ecclesiastical, estates, extradition, Imperial War Graves Commission, judgements, legalization of documents: letters of request, locusts, lunatics, maintenance orders, matrimonial cases, miscellaneous enquiries (including questions of UK citizens in Commonwealth countries and British subjects in foreign countries), national service acts, nurses, pensions, library, records, etc, social security, stowaways, teachers, wartime evacuees, census, charitable funds under control of UK high commissioners, colonial appointments, Commission for Technical Co-operation in Africa, Commonwealth Agricultural Bureaux, CRO reference list, Commonwealth publications, Commonwealth students, companies registration, conferences, congresses and conventions (not otherwise allocated), consular appointments, consular conventions and instructions, copyright, diplomatic and consular appointments of other Commonwealth countries, diplomatic and social list, exhibitions, fisheries and whaling, flora and fauna, further education grants, gifts, matters arising on appointment of secretary of state, medical reciprocity, messages, non-official bodies interested in the Commonwealth, patents and designs, position of UK professions in Commonwealth countries, prisoners of war in Korea, surveys, trade marks, visits

1954 — no information available

General Department (Political Division)

1955 — As above; – library, records, colonial appointments, CTCA, CRO reference list, visits, consular appointments, consular conventions and instructions, diplomatic and social list, diplomatic and consular appointments of other Commonwealth countries, further education grants, prisoners in Korea + property acquisition acts, India and Pakistan, animal diseases, British Empire Games, colonial service recruitment, hydrography, Imperial Institute, veterinary reciprocity, natural disasters, police and fire services, private bills, seamen, territorial waters, weights and measures

1956 — matrimonial cases and maintenance orders, education, teachers, Commonwealth students, educational grants, child employment, letters to UK ministers (not otherwise allocated), UK citizens in Commonwealth countries, British subjects in foreign countries, census, claims (war injury, property, compensation), wartime evacuees, legalization of documents, letters of request, judgements, private bills, property acquisition acts for India and Pakistan, ecclesiastical matters, estates, national service acts, social insurance and security, social services, pensions, appeals for financial assistance, deportations and fugitive offenders, extradition, lunatics, stowaways, cemeteries, Imperial War Graves Commission, Maldive Islands, conferences, congresses and conventions (not otherwise allocated), tours (not otherwise allocated), arts, crafts, antiquities, institutes, societies, clubs, exhibitions, British Empire Games and Olympic Games, youth organizations, scientific bodies, Commonwealth Agricultural Bureaux, flora and fauna, forestry, veterinary services, animal diseases, locusts, surveys, hydrography, territorial waters, fisheries and whaling, weights and measures, inventions, medical and nursing services, diseases, police and fire services, seamen, position of UK professions in Commonwealth countries, non-official bodies interested in the Commonwealth, employment (other than teachers), copyright, registration of companies, Commonwealth publications, natural disasters, accidents, patronage, gifts, colonial service recruitment, colonial welfare and development scholars, colonial students in Commonwealth countries, Indian civil services: questions arising out of the winding up of the secretary of state's service in India and Burma, pensions questions arising out of the superannuation

Migration and General Department (Africa and General Division)

1957 Indian and Burma civil services, compensation, pensions, and other matters arising from winding up of secretary of state's services, other pensions, matrimonial cases and maintenance orders, census, claims (war injury, property, compensation), wartime evacuees, legalization of documents, letters of request, judgements, private bills, property acquisition acts – India and Pakistan, ecclesiastical matters, estates, social insurance and security, social services, appeals for financial assistance, cemeteries, Imperial War Graves Commission, patronage and gifts, national service acts, fugitive offenders, extradition, lunatics and stowaways, letters to UK ministers not otherwise allocated, UK citizens in other Commonwealth countries, British subjects in foreign countries, repatriation of UK citizens (excluding adjustment of cost), arts, crafts, and antiquities, public appeals, scientific bodies, Commonwealth Agricultural Bureaux, flora and fauna, forestry, medical, nursing and veterinary services, quarantine, diseases, locusts, police, prison and fire services, surveys, hydrography, territorial waters, fisheries and whaling, inventions, Commonwealth publications (acts, bills, gazettes), natural disasters, accidents, employment (other than teachers), position of UK professions in Commonwealth countries (except accountants), seamen, overseas service recruitment, migration

1958 as above + scientific and technical conferences and conventions, child employment, reception of distressed UK citizens, residual passage claims, British Indian records of service and medals; – wartime evacuees, aviation accidents

1959–1960 as above; – Commonwealth publications (acts, bills, gazettes), births, deaths and marriages in Commonwealth countries, requests for certificates.

General Department (Political Division)

1961   emigration of citizens of UK and colonies to Commonwealth countries, immigration of British subjects into the UK, law of the sea, fisheries and whaling, Commonwealth trust, relations with scientific research and technical bodies, recognition of UK professional qualifications, public health matters, locust control, police, prison and fire services, overseas service recruitment, patent rights, natural disasters, matrimonial cases and maintenance orders, child employment, census, letters of request, judgements, appeals for financial assistance, lunatics, repatriation (excluding adjustment of cost) and reception in UK of distressed UK citizens, nationality legislation and policy, deportation policy, visa and entry permit requirements within Commonwealth, consular instructions, travel documents (including those for seamen and stateless persons), registration of births, deaths and marriages by UKHC's in India, Pakistan, Ceylon and Ghana, deportation cases, passport and nationality cases, passport practice in Commonwealth countries, compensation claims of quasi-consular nature, including examination of property acquisition acts, deaths and injuries, legalization of documents, ecclesiastical matters, social insurance and social services, cemeteries and memorials in India and Pakistan, Imperial War Graves Commission, ministerial patronage and gifts between governments, national service, fugitive offenders, stowaways, Indian army records of service and medals, requests for certificates of births, deaths and marriages in Commonwealth countries

1962   as above + promotion of Commonwealth co-operation in scientific and professional fields, Commonwealth Agricultural Bureaux, residual work relating to former Indian ecclesiastical establishment, Commonwealth War Graves Commission, treatment in Britain of citizens of other Commonwealth countries, registration as citizens of the UK and colonies; – relations with scientific research and technical bodies, overseas service recruitment, patent rights, lunatics, Imperial War Graves Commission, national service, stowaways

Nationality and General Department (West Indies and General Division)

1963   as above + stowaways, Oversea Migration Board, animal health; – locust control, consular instructions, natural disasters, residual work relating to former Indian ecclesiastical establishment

Nationality and General Department (division not indicated)

1964   as above + British Commonwealth Scientific Committee and working party, pensions, compensation of officers of former overseas civil and military services, cases of deportation from Commonwealth countries; – promotion of Commonwealth co-operation in scientific and professional fields

Nationality and General Department (Western, Constitutional and General Division)

1965   citizenship policy, immigration, emigration, natural disasters, matrimonial cases and maintenance orders, Fugitive Offenders Act, Indian Army records, pensions, etc, India, Pakistan, Ceylon, Burma, passport and nationality cases, general matters concerning Commonwealth countries and Irish Republic

Then see General and Migration Department, Nationality and Consular Department. See also Irish Trade Negotiations Unit (1965) under Economic Departments.

General and Migration Department (General Division)

1966   migration, law of the sea, fisheries, co-operation on scientific matters with Commonwealth governments, authentication of documents, independence and other commemoration gifts, natural disasters in the Commonwealth, reciprocal enforcement of judgements, CRO Year Book, access to records, India Office building, CRO library, India Office library, India Office records, miscellaneous questions not covered by any other department

General and Migration Department (Trade Division)

1966   civil aviation, peaceful uses of outer space, satellite, Commonwealth postal communications and UPU, Commonwealth telecommunications, world communications, Meteorological Organization

Nationality and Consular Department (General Division)

1966   policy questions on Diplomatic Privileges Act 1964, Vienna consular convention, privileges of Commonwealth Organizations, nationality and citizenship legislation, honours and awards, protocol subjects not dealt with by the Joint Protocol Department (questions of policy and Commonwealth interest), consular protection of UK citizens, matrimonial cases and maintenance orders, Fugitive Offenders Act, Indian army records, pensions residual questions not dealt with by the ODM, wills, property, social insurance and services, Commonwealth War Graves Commission, expeditions (other than Himalayan), passport and nationality cases, visas, repatriation and deportation cases, registration of births, deaths and marriages

INFORMATION DEPARTMENTS AND SECTIONS

Information Department (Finance and General Division)

1953   Publicity Policy Section: administrative policy, publicity relating to foreign affairs, publicity on Commonwealth affairs in the UK, British Council policy and estimates, cultural relations with Commonwealth countries, liaison with PROs at Commonwealth houses, and with societies and organizations

British Information Services Section: selection and supply of publicity material to information posts in Commonwealth countries, liaison with heads of divisions at Central Office of Information, London press service, 'Commonwealth Survey', feature articles, visual material (other than films), reference material, official publications, books and pamphlets, films

News and Information Section: liaison with UK, Commonwealth and foreign press and the BBC, press cuttings section – records and research, supply of background material to departments, biographical notes on Commonwealth personalities and visitors

1954 no information available

1955 Publicity policy: as above

British Information Services Section: as above

News and Information: as above; – biographical notes of Commonwealth personalities and visitors

1956 Administration and Publicity Policy Section: as above in Publicity Policy

British Information Services Section: as above; – London press service, 'Commonwealth Survey'

News and Information Section: as above; – press cuttings section – records and research, supply of background material to departments, + London press service of COI and 'Commonwealth Survey'

Records and Research Section: supply of background material to departments

Information and Cultural Relations Department (Africa and General Division)

1957 Public Relations Section: publicity, liaison with UK, Commonwealth and foreign press, the BBC and ITA and with public relations officers, London press service of COI and 'Commonwealth Survey', material for speeches, press cuttings, publicity relating to foreign affairs

Information Overseas Section: supply of material to oversea posts, lecturers (Canada), exhibitions overseas (not otherwise allocated), miscellaneous enquiries from the BIS posts, feature articles, visual material (other than films), reference material, official publications, books and pamphlets, films and TV material

Cultural Relations Section: British Council, Commonwealth Parliamentary Association, cultural relations with other Commonwealth countries, liaison with universities, educational matters (including teacher exchanges, students, youth organizations, CD and W scholars, etc), British Empire Games and Olympic Games, Commonwealth, etc, societies in the UK, Imperial Institute

Administration Section: policy, administration, estimates, conferences, etc in Commonwealth countries (not otherwise allocated), visits and tours (not otherwise allocated)

1958 Public Relations Section: as above

Information Overseas Section: as above

Cultural Relations Section: as above + cultural and educational conferences

Administration Section: as above; – conferences, etc in Commonwealth countries

Information and Cultural Relations Department (Information and Cultural Relations Division)

1959–1960 Press and Public Relations Section: liaison with UK, Commonwealth and foreign press, liaison with policy departments of CRO, London press service of COI, 'Commonwealth Survey', special publicity arrangements (eg Commonwealth Ministers' meetings, ministerial visits to Commonwealth, etc), broadcasting, liaison with news services of BBC and ITA, preparation of speeches, press cuttings section, publicity relating to foreign affairs

Information Services Section: supply of all material to overseas posts, liaison with FO on intels and guidance telegrams, feature articles, visual material (other than films), preparation of Commonwealth Today, publications, books and pamphlets, magazines, including distribution of Commonwealth Today, exhibitions (not otherwise allocated), Colombo Plan publicity, miscellaneous enquiries, films and TV

Information Policy and Cultural Relations Section: information policy and administration, estimates, cultural relations with other Commonwealth countries, British Council, UNESCO, students and student welfare, visits and tours, supply of films, radio and other technical equipment to overseas posts, Commonwealth societies, Commonwealth Institute, youth organizations, sporting events (Olympic and Commonwealth games), Commonwealth Parliamentary Association and inter-parliamentary unions, general cultural conferences, Commonwealth weeks, lecture tours (overseas), Commonwealth Education Conference, educational co-operation with other Commonwealth countries, liaison with universities, Commonwealth educational conferences, teacher exchanges, Commonwealth touring exhibition

Information Policy Department (Information Division)

1961 as above in Information Policy and Cultural Relations Section students and student welfare, Commonwealth education conference, educational co-operation with other Commonwealth countries, liaison with universities, teacher exchanges

Information Services Department (Information Division)
1961 content of COI material, special Commonwealth projects, Commonwealth Today, liaison with FO on intels and guidance telegrams, supervision of TV and film production, assistance with production, acquisition of films and supply of films to posts, publications, references, exhibitions, Colombo Plan publicity section, exhibitions and trade fairs overseas, Colombo Plan publicity, general supervision of distribution, distribution of all books, magazines, pamphlets, white papers, etc., miscellaneous enquiries, supervision of radio tapes, production of visual material and press articles, radio tapes, feature articles

News Department (Information Division)
1961 as above in Press and Public Relations; – press cuttings section

Education Department (Information Division)
1961 educational co-operation with other Commonwealth countries, liaison with universities, Commonwealth educational conference, teacher exchanges, students and student welfare

Then see Cultural Relations Department.

Information Policy Department (Information Division)
1962 policy questions, British Council, external broadcasting (other than news liaison), publicity for the Commonwealth in Britain, Commonwealth Institute, UNESCO (other than education), administration of estimates, youth organizations, sporting events (Olympic and Commonwealth Games), Commonwealth Parliamentary Assocation, Inter-Parliamentary Union, training and refresher courses for information staff, low-priced book scheme, supply of equipment to information posts overseas, sponsored visits to Britain, speaker tours overseas, Commonwealth weeks and Commonwealth touring exhibition

Information Services Department (Information Division)
1962 Colombo Plan publicity, exhibitions and trade fairs overseas, posters, display and film strips, supervision of press articles (including Commonwealth commentary), press photographs, mats and stereos, cartoons and maps, supervision of production and distribution of publications, calendars, general liaison on intel and guidance telegrams and with CRO departments on information services, supervision of preparation and distribution of reference booklets and pamphlets, including factels, white papers, etc, commercial newspapers and magazines, miscellaneous enquiries, films and TV production vernacular versions and TV acquisitions, film acquisitions, feature films, festivals, catalogues, new films, supervision of distribution of films and radio tapes, theatrical distribution, miscellaneous enquiries for films and rights, withdrawal of films, radio tapes

News Department (Information Division)
1962   as above

Cultural Relations Department (Information Division)
1962   Educational co-operation with other Commonwealth countries, liaison with universities, Commonwealth educational conferences, teacher exchanges, students and student welfare

Information Policy Department (Information Division)
1963   as above + liaison with British Council on policy and finance, Commonwealth societies, visits by MPs to Commonwealth countries; – British Council, publicity for the Commonwealth in Britain, Commonwealth Institute, UNESCO, Commonwealth weeks and Commonwealth touring exhibition

Information Services Department (Information Division)
1963   as above + picture sets, book presentations, general liaison with COI, reporting, etc; – supervision of distribution of films and radio tapes, theatrical distribution, miscellaneous enquiries for films and rights, withdrawal of films

Cultural Relations Department (Information Division)
1963   policy questions related to educational co-operation in the Commonwealth, scholarship and fellowship plan, Commonwealth education conferences, cultural relations in the Commonwealth, liaison with British Council on education, teaching of English in Commonwealth countries, student welfare and the arts, UNESCO, Commonwealth publicity in Britain, Commonwealth Institute, Commonwealth Information Centre (Marlborough House)

News Department (Information Division)
1963   Liaison with British, Commonwealth and foreign press, liaison with policy departments of CRO and London press services of COI, special publicity arrangements (eg Commonwealth ministers' meetings, ministerial visits to Commonwealth, press at Marlborough House), press conferences and briefings, arrangements for British journalists to visit Commonwealth countries, analyses of British press reactions to events in the Commonwealth, and Commonwealth press reactions to events in Britain, liaison with High Commissions on news matters, liaison with home and overseas services of BBC, ITV and other radio and TV organizations, preparation of speeches, press cuttings, publicity relating to foreign affairs

Information Policy Department (division not indicated)
1964   general policy questions, overseas information ceiling, external broadcasting, Commonwealth societies, British information services administration and estimates co-ordination, supply of equipment to in-

formation offices, information training and refresher courses, Commonwealth Parliamentary Association, Inter-Parliamentary Union

Information Services Department (division not indicated)
1964   magazines official and commercial, supplements, newspapers, COI booklets and pamphlets, COI reference material, HMSO publications, film publications, supply of commercially published books, LPS feature articles, illustrated material for overseas posts, low-priced books, exhibitions and Colombo Plan publicity, picture sets, posters, wall sheets and maps, sponsored visitors to Britain, speakers, tours overseas, visits by MPs to other Commonwealth countries, co-ordination of special exercises and requests from posts, miscellaneous requests from posts, TV services and productions, conventional and feature films and acquisitions, radio services

News Department (division not indicated)
1964   liaison with the British, Commonwealth and foreign press, liaison with press officers at Commonwealth houses, policy questions relating to the COI London press service, intel and guidance telegrams, liaison with the home and overseas services of BBC, ITV and other radio and TV organizations, press cuttings

Cultural Relations Department (division not indicated)
1964   as above; – teaching English in Commonwealth countries, student welfare and the arts + sporting events, youth organizations

Information Policy Department (Information Division)
1965   as above; – overseas information ceiling, supply of equipment to information offices, information training and refresher courses + equipment and training

Information Services Department (Information Division)
1965   magazines, supplements, newspapers, reference material, low-priced books, exhibitions and Colombo Plan publicity, sponsored visitors to Britain, speakers' tours overseas, visits by MPs to other Commonwealth countries, films, radio and TV services

Cultural Relations Department (Information Division)
1965   Commonwealth educational co-operation, UNESCO, educational conferences, CELU, scholarship commission, OSWEP, liaison with DTC and VSO, trusts and foundations, British Council, Commonwealth sporting events, Commonwealth publicity in Britain, Commonwealth Institute, cultural and artistic matters, youth organizations, Commonwealth Information Centre (Marlborough House)

News Department (Information Division)
1965   liaison with press, radio and TV

Information Policy and Guidance Department: Joint Department (Information Division)
1966   liaison with political departments, preparation of guidance, relations with agencies concerned with news dissemination

Information Administration Department: Joint Department (Information Division)
1966   control of information estimates and expenditure, information co-ordination and deployment of resources, information training

Information Services Department (Information Division)
1966   publications, exhibitions, sponsored visitors, use of films, radio and TV by Information Services, COI reference material

News Department (Information Division)
1966   as above

Cultural Relations Department (Information Division)
1966   as above; – liaison with DTC + liaison with ODM, book schemes

Joint Research Department (division not indicated)
1966   preparation of research papers and factual memoranda

MEDITERRANEAN DEPARTMENTS

Mediterranean Department (Mediterranean, South Asia and Defence Division)
1965   Cyprus

Malta Department (Mediterranean, South Asia and Defence Division)
1965   Malta

Mediterranean Department (Far East and Mediterranean Division)
1966   Political and economic relations with Cyprus and Malta, and with Gibraltar insofar as they affect Commonwealth relations

MIDDLE EAST DEPARTMENTS

Middle East Department (Foreign Affairs Division)
Before 1958 see South Asian and Middle East Department.

1958   political affairs (including connected defence questions, insofar as they affect Commonwealth relations in the Middle East and North Africa),

Middle East countries (excluding Turkey, but including Egypt and Sudan), Suez Canal, Baghdad Pact (excluding economic aspects), Persian Gulf (including consular property), North Africa

1959   as above

1960   as above + Iran, Iraq, Arabia, Lebanon, Jordan, Maldive Islands, United Arab Republic (Egypt and Syria), Israel, Horn of Africa

Western and Middle East Department (Foreign Affairs Division)

For Western subjects before 1961 see Defence and Western Department (1960), Western and UN Department (1953–1958).

1961   Canada: external relations, internal political affairs, western organizations: political aspects, political affairs, including connected defence questions, insofar as they affect Commonwealth relations of USA, Central and South America and Western and Southern Europe, USSR and satellites, Yugoslavia, Finland, East-West negotiations, UAR (Egypt and Syria), Israel, Iraq, Arabia and Persian Gulf, Lebanon, Jordan, disarmament, suspension of nuclear tests, atomic energy, peaceful uses

1962   as above + Berlin, Iran

1963   as above + NATO, WEU, Council of Europe; – USSR and satellites, Yugoslavia, Finland

1964   as above; – Central and South America

United Nations, Western and Middle East Department (Western Constitutional and General Division)

For UN subjects before 1965 see UN and General Africa Department (1964), UN Department (1959–1962), Western and UN Department (1953–1958).

1965   NATO, WEU, Council for Europe, East/West relations, Irish Republic, Antarctica, Aden and Middle East, disarmament, UN and specialist agencies: political, social and legal matters

UN, Western and Middle East Department (General Division)

1966   United Nations and the specialist agencies, Middle East and South Arabian affairs (including defence), disarmament, East-West relations, Western Organizations, Commonwealth liaison procedure, relations with Irish Republic

POLITICAL AFFAIRS DEPARTMENTS

Political Affairs Department (Constitutional and Political Division)

1953   internal political affairs, including labour and trade union affairs (Canada, Australia, Union of South Africa, New Zealand, Ceylon, India,

Pakistan), international trade union organizations, residuary questions relating to former Indian princely states (except Kashmir and Junagadh)

1954 no information available

Then see Foreign Affairs Division Departments. For Labour and Trade Union Affairs see Communications Department (1965).

Political Affairs Department (Defence and Commonwealth Policy Division)

1965 political affairs, liaison with Joint Intelligence Organization, information research, labour and trade union affairs

PROTOCOL DEPARTMENTS

Before 1955 see Constitutional Department (1953).

Protocol Department (Political Division)

1955 liaison with Commonwealth high commissioners in London with special reference to matters of ceremonial, privilege, etc, diplomatic privileges, diplomatic immunity, consular conventions, foreign service instructions, general arrangements for government hospitality, Commonwealth Parliamentary Association, formalities in connection with appointment of high commissioners in London, matters arising out of appointments of secretary of state, visits, messages of congratulations, condolence, and valediction, other than to CRO staff, public ceremonies, national days, letters of credence for Commonwealth diplomatic representatives in foreign countries, consular commissions and exequaturs, full powers and ratification, registration with UN of agreements with other Commonwealth countries and the Irish Republic, formal aspects of representations of other Commonwealth governments in other countries, CRO reference list, biographical notes of Commonwealth personalities and visitors, governors-general and governors, honours, decorations, medals, foreign decorations, titles, honorary degrees, freedom of cities, matters relating to royal family, including royal visits, loyal messages, gifts, patronage and royal bounty, audiences of the queen, petitions to the queen, court mourning, anthems, arms, badges, flags, military alliances, precedence, seals, toasts, uniforms, commissions for governors-general, governors and high commissioners, BB&S, letters patent, royal instruction to governors, royal charters, royal warrants

1956 as above + FO list of representatives of foreign states and Commonwealth countries

Then see Protocol and Nationality Department.

Protocol and Nationality Department (Political Division)

1956   as in Protocol Department above + nationality legislation and related matters, passport and citizenship, immigration and emigration restrictions within the Commonwealth, visa questions and stateless persons, travel documents, births, deaths and marriages in Commonwealth countries, general enquiries and requests for certificates, registration procedure in India, Pakistan and Ceylon, deportations, formal instruments of accreditation for UK ambassador, Dublin and for UK high commissioner, New Delhi, title 'royal', use of royal names and emblems, autographs; – Commonwealth Parliamentary Association

1958   as above + visits of high commissioners to the UK, messages of congratulation, condolence, valediction in relation to the High Commission territories, formal instruments of accreditation for certain UK high commissioners, registration procedure in Ghana, seamen's certificates; – formal instruments of accreditation for UK high commissioner in New Delhi

Then see Constitutional Department (1959–1964), General Department (1961–1964), Constitutional and Protocol Department (1965, under Constitutional Departments), Nationality and General Department (1965), Nationality and Consular Department (1966), Joint Protocol Department (1966).

Joint Protocol Department (division not indicated)

1966   privileges and immunities of foreign and Commonwealth missions and international organizations, diplomatic and consular appointments, diplomatic lists, issue of identity cards, honours, decorations and awards

SERVICES DEPARTMENT

Services Department (Finance and General Division)

1953   winding up of the secretary of state's services in India and Burma

1954   no information available

1955   as above

SOUTH ASIAN DEPARTMENTS

South Asian Department (Foreign Affairs Division)

1953   Kashmir, political relations between India and Pakistan, foreign policy in India, Pakistan, Ceylon, French and Portuguese possessions in India, Afghanistan and North West frontier, diplomatic and consular property, Persian Gulf, Kamaran and the pilgrimage, Aden, Sinkiang,

Nepal, Tibet and Bhutan, Indians, Pakistanis and Ceylon overseas (except South Africa), Himalayan expeditions

1954 no information available

South Asian and Middle East Department (Foreign Affairs Division)

1955 as above + Gurkha recruitment, Sikkim, Middle East regional defence, treaties with Jordan, Iraq and Libya, defence negotiations with Egypt, Suez Canal, foreign policies of Middle East countries (including Abyssinia but excluding Turkey), Sudan; − Pakistanis, Indians and Ceylon overseas (except South Africa), Kamaran and the pilgrimage

1956 as above + Gwadur

1957 as above + Baghdad Pact (excluding economical aspects); − Middle East regional defence, treaties with Iraq, Sudan

Then see South Asia and Far Eastern Deparment, Middle East Department.

South Asia Department (Foreigh Affairs Division)

1961 politics and policies of and UK relations with India (including Bhutan and Sikkim) and Pakistan, political relations between India and Pakistan, Kashmir, Portuguese territories in India, relations of India and Pakistan with China and Tibet, Afghanistan, CENTO, Indo-China, Burma, Nepal, Gurkha recruitment, consular property in Persian Gulf, politics and policies of and UK relations with Ceylon, Maldive Islands and Indo-China.

1962 as above + consular property in Iran and Afghanistan

1963 as above; − policies of and UK relations with Maldive Islands and Indo-China + internal political affairs of Maldive Islands

1963 external relations with India and Pakistan, Indo-Pakistan relations (including Kashmir), internal political affairs of India and Pakistan, CENTO, Nepal, Gurkha recruitment, Bhutan and Sikkim, biographical material (India and Pakistan), external relations of Ceylon, internal political affairs of Ceylon, biographical material (Ceylon), Maldive Islands

South Asia Department (Mediterranean, South Asia and Defence Division)

1964 India, Pakistan, Ceylon, CENTO, Gurkha recruitment, Afghanistan, Bhutan and Sikkim, Maldive Islands

South Asia Department (Asia and Atlantic Division)

1965 as above; − Ceylon, Maldive Islands + Burma, Nepal

UNITED NATIONS DEPARTMENTS

Western and United Nations Department (Foreign Affairs Division)

1953　　Commonwealth liaison procedure on foreign affairs, distribution of FO print, intels and telegrams, foreign affairs (USA, Middle East and North Africa, registration of treaties, Disarmament Commission), foreign affairs (Europe and Soviet Union, North Atlantic Treaty Organization (political), European Defence Community, Council of Europe, European Political Community), United Nations (general assembly and Security Council, Economic and Social Council, Trusteeship Council, non-self-governing territories, South African racial relations, South West Africa, Indians in South Africa, in UN context, International Court of Justice, World Health Organization, UNESCO, International Labour Organization, refugee questions), foreign affairs (Central and South America, Arctic and Antarctic)

1954　　no information available

1955　　as above + charter revision, UNESCO, USSR and satellites, foreign affairs: Southern Europe and Balkans (including Turkey), North Africa (except Libya, Egypt, Sudan), Polar Committee, Western and Northern Europe; – distribution of FO print, intels and telegrams, foreign affairs of Middle East, Soviet Union, registration of treaties, non-self-governing territories

1956　　as above + general foreign policy of Union of South Africa, World Health Organization, general foreign policy of Canada and Irish Republic, Cyprus (external), WEU; – arctic, EDC, EPC, Polar Committee

1957　　foreign political affairs, including connected defence questions, as they affect Commonwealth relations in Europe, North and South America, South Africa, and in the United Nations, general UN political questions (including South Africa questions), the Irish Republic, Union of South Africa, general UN economic and social questions, International Court of Justice, foreign affairs relating to Western and Northern Europe, USSR and satellites, Antarctica, North Africa (except Libya, Egypt, Sudan), Canada, NATO (political questions), disarmament, WEU, Council of Europe, foreign affairs questions relating to USA, Central and South America, Southern Europe, Cyprus (external), Commonwealth liaison procedure

1958　　as above

Then see United Nations Department and Defence and Western Department under Defence Departments.

United Nations Department (Foreign Affairs Division)

1959　　general UN questions, International Court of Justice, Union of South

Africa (foreign political questions), non-British territories in Southern Africa, Irish Republic (foreign political questions), Central and South America, Antarctic, Commonwealth liaison procedure, ECOSOC, Trusteeship Council, ILO, WHO

1960   general UN questions, International Court of Justice, ECOSOC (general, political and social questions), human rights, status of women and narcotic drugs commissions, ILO, WHO, Union of South Africa (foreign political questions), Irish Republic (foreign political questions), Trusteeship Council, non-British territories in Southern Africa, Central and South America, Antarctica, Commonwealth liaison procedure

1961   as above; – Antarctica, Central and South America, International Court of Justice, Trusteeship Council, non-British territories in Southern Africa, + UN trusteeship questions

1962   political questions: matters concerning the constitution and organization of the UN, proceedings of the Security Council and the Political and Budgetary Committees of the General Assembly, South West Africa legal questions, proceedings of the Legal Committee of the General Assembly, International Court of Justice, foreign political questions of Irish Republic and the Republic of South Africa, questions concerning the interest of UN in non-self-governing territories, proceedings of the Trusteeship Committee of the General Assembly including South West Africa, Trusteeship Council, etc, economic and social questions, proceedings of the Economic and Social Committees of the General Assembly, ECOSOC and associated commissions, specialist agencies (except as otherwise allocated), in particular WHO and ILO, Antarctica, Commonwealth liaison procedure

1963   as above + distribution of documents

1964   see United Nations and General Africa Department under Africa Departments

1965–1966   see United Nations, Western and Middle East Department under Middle East Departments

WEST INDIES DEPARTMENT

West Indies Department (West Indies and General Division)

1963   Jamaica, Cayman Islands, Turks and Caicos Islands, British Honduras, Trinidad, Eastern Caribbean, British Guiana, Interim Commission

1964   Jamaica, University of the West Indies, economic questions affecting the region generally, international trade in bananas, citrus and sugar, Cuba, Haiti, Dominican Republic, Trinidad, British territories in the Eastern Caribbean, British Honduras, British Guiana, Regional Shipping Council, all foreign territories in Latin America and the Caribbean, Caribbean Organization

WESTERN DEPARTMENTS

Western Departments (Foreign Affairs Division)
1953–1958 see Western and United Nations Departments under UN Departments

1959–1960 see Defence and Western Department under Defence Departments

1960–1963 see Western and Middle East Department under Middle East Departments

1965–1966 see United Nations, Western and Middle East Department under Middle East Departments

CHAPTER 15

Registry Codes

Contents:

15.1 Abbreviations used in the registration of in-letters, 1849 to 1925

15.2 Allocation of Colonial Office file numbers, 1927 to 1951

15.3 Colonial Office Economic Original Correspondence (CO 852) file registration numbers, 1935 to 1951

15.4 Departmental filing codes

15.1 Abbreviations used in the registration of in-letters 1849 to 1925

In this period the references given in the 'former and other papers' column of the in-letter registers consist of the registration number, as shown in the daily register, and indicating the department of state, organization or individual concerned. The abbreviations should enable the searcher to set a particular paper in its context as described in chapter 4.3.2. The list that follows is incomplete.

Adm	Admiralty
AG	Agents-General
AM	Air Ministry
B of C & E	Board of Customs and Excise
BIR	Board of Inland Revenue
BO	Burma Office
BSAC	British South Africa Company
BT	Board of Trade
C or C'cl	Council
CA or CAgs	Crown Agents
CO	Colonial Office
DO	Dominions Office
DOT	Department of Overseas Trade
FO	Foreign Office
GG	Governor General
Gov	Governor
HCr	High Commissioner
HO	Home Office
H of C	House of Commons
H of L	House of Lords
IO	India Office
LO	Law Officers

M Agric	Ministry of Agriculture
MCA	Ministry of Civil Aviation
MI	Miscellaneous Institutions
MO	Miscellaneous Offices
Min A & F	Ministry of Agriculture and Fisheries
Min F & P or MFP	Ministry of Fuel and Power
Min Trans or M/T	Ministry of Transport
OAG	Officer administering the government
OSD	Overseas Settlement Department
Parl	Parliament
PO	Post Office
R Cr	Resident Commissioner
Treas, Trsy, Ty	Treasury
TWED	Trading with the Enemy Department
WCO	War Cabinet Offices
WO	War Office

15.2 Allocation of Colonial Office file numbers, 1927 to 1951

15.2.1 File registration numbers, 1927 to 1934
During this period the blocks of numbers allocated changed annually. See chapter 4.4.4.

REGISTRY CODES

	1927	1928	1929	1930	1931	1932	1933	1934
Nigeria	1–530	1–381	382–703	704–1022	1023–1310	1311–	1001–1400	21001–21400
West Africa	1–530	4001–4120	4121–4230	4231–4352	4353–4480	4481–	1401–1600	21401–21600
Gold Coast	4001–4690	6001–6294	6295–6563	6564–6816	6817–7133	7134–	1601–2000	21601–22000
Sierra Leone	4001–4690	9001–9205	9206–9367	9368–9531	9532–9722	9723–	2001–2300	22001–22300
Gambia	4001–4690	12001–12078	12079–12180	12181–12267	12268–12382	12383–	2301–2500	22301–22500
Military (WAFF & KAR)	8001–8208	13001–13226	13227–13417	13418–13579	13580–13757	13758–	2701–3000	22701–23000
Kenya	10001–10559	15001–15445	15501–15960	15961–16393	17001–17414	18001–	3001–3500	23001–23500
Uganda	14001–14396	20001–20203	20251–20475	20476–20676	21001–21187	22001–	3501–3800	23501–23800
Zanzibar	14001–14396	23001–23143	23151–23266	23267–23387	24001–24117	24501–	3801–4000	23801–24000
East Africa	17001–17235	25001–25184	25201–25380	25381–25562	26001–26165	27001–	4001–4200	24001–24200
Africa	—	—	—	—	—	28001–	4201–4300	24201–24300

	1927	1928	1929	1930	1931	1932	1933	1934
Tanganyika	18001–21112	29001–29288	29289–29603	29604–29898	30001–30269	31001–91650	5001–5300	25001–25300
Nyasaland	18001–21112	33001–33178	33179–33354	33355–33522	34001–34156	34157–98400	5301–5800	25301–25500
N Rhodesia	18001–21112	35001–35217	35218–35469	35470–35716	36001–36263	36264–98550	5501–5800	25501–25800
Somaliland	22001–22712	38001–38102	38103–38210	38211–38306	38501–38610	38611–98800	5801–6000	25801–26000
Mediterranean	22001–22712	39001–39508	39509–39932	39993–40366	41001–41458	—	—	—
General	25001–28000	50001–52000	60001–62000	70001–72000	80001–82000	90001–91650	10001–13000	30001–33000
Gibraltar	—	—	—	—	—	98301–98400	19401–19500	39401–39500
Malta	—	—	—	—	—	98401–98550	19501–19700	39501–39700
Cyprus	—	—	—	—	—	98551–98800	19701–20000	39701–40000
Personnel	—	—	—	—	—	91651–91900	9001–10000	29001–30000
Straits Settlements	28001–29000	52001–52300	62001–62300	72001–72300	82001–82300	92001–92250	13001–13300	33001–33300

REGISTRY CODES

	1927	1928	1929	1930	1931	1932	1933	1934
Malay States	29001–30000	52301–52600	62301–62600	72301–72600	82301–82600	92251–92500	13301–13600	33301–33600
Borneo and Sarawak	31701–31750	52601–52700	62601–62700	72601–72700	82601–82700	92501–92550	13601–13700	33601–33700
Hong Kong	30001–30800	52701–53000	62701–63000	72701–73000	82701–83000	92551–92850	13701–14000	33701–34000
Eastern	30801–31700	53001–53150	63001–63150	73001–73150	83001–83150	92851–92950	14001–14200	34001–34200
Wei-Hai-Wei	31751–31800	53151–53200	63151–63200	–	–	–	–	–
Ceylon	31801–32800	53201–53650	63201–63650	73201–73650	83201–83650	92951–93250	14201–14500	34201–34500
St Helena	34801–35000	53651–53800	63651–63800	73651–73800	83651–83800	93251–93350	19101–19200	39101–39200
Fiji	34301–34800	53801–54100	63801–64100	73801–74100	83801–84100	93351–93550	18401–18700	38401–38700
Western Pacific	33801–34300	54101–54500	64101–64500	74101–74500	84101–84500	93551–93900	18701–19100	38701–39100
Mauritius	32801–33500	54501–54900	64501–64900	74501–74900	84501–84900	93901–94150	14501–14900	34501–34900
Seychelles	33501–33800	54901–55000	64901–65000	74901–75000	84901–85000	94151–94250	14901–15000	34901–35000

REGISTRY CODES

	1927	1928	1929	1930	1931	1932	1933	1934
British Guiana	38201–39000	55001–55240	65001–65420	75001–75240	85001–85240	94251–94500	15001–15300	35001–35300
Barbados	37501–37700	55241–55300	65241–65300	75241–75300	85241–85300	94501–94650	15301–15500	35301–35500
British Honduras	37901–38200	55301–55450	65301–65450	75301–75450	85301–85450	94651–94800	15501–15700	35501–35700
Dominica	39901–40000	55451–55500	65451–65500	75451–75500	85451–85500	94801–94875	15701–15800	35701–35800
Leewards	39501–39900	55501–55700	65501–65700	75501–75700	85501–85700	94876–95050	15801–16000	35801–36000
Grenada	39001–39500	55701–55800	65701–65800	75701–75800	85701–85800	95051–95150	16001–16100	36001–36100
St Lucia	39001–39500	55801–55850	65801–65850	75801–75850	85801–85850	95151–95200	16101–16200	36101–36200
St Vincent	39001–39500	55851–55900	65851–65900	75851–75900	85851–85900	95201–95300	16201–16300	36201–36300
Bermuda	37701–35701	55901–56000	65901–66000	75901–76000	85901–86000	95301–95400	16301–16400	36301–36400
Jamaica	35701–36500	56001–56250	66001–66250	76001–76250	86001–86250	95401–95650	16401–16700	36401–36700
Bahamas	37301–37500	56251–56400	66251–66400	76251–76400	86251–86400	95651–95750	16701–16800	36701–36800

REGISTRY CODES

	1927	1928	1929	1930	1931	1932	1933	1934
Trinidad	36501–37300	56401–56600	66401–66600	76401–76600	86401–86600	95751–95950	16801–17000	36801–37000
West Indies	35201–35700	56601–56750	66601–66750	76601–76750	86601–86750	95951–96100	17001–17200	37001–37200
Falklands	35001–35200	56751–57000	66751–67000	76751–77000	86751–87000	96101–96300	19201–19400	39201–39400
Iraq	40001–44000	58001–59000	68001–69000	78001–79000	88001–89000	96301–97001	—	—
Palestine	44001–48000	57001–58000	68001–68000	77001–78000	87001–88000	97001–98800	17201–17700	37201–37700
Transjordan	44001–48000	59401–59550	69401–69550	79401–79550	89401–89550	97701–97850	17701–17900	37701–37900
Aden	48001–49000	59251–59400	69251–69400	79251–79400	89251–89400	97851–98000	17901–18100	37901–38100
Middle East	49901–50000	59001–59250	69001–69250	79001–79250	89001–89250	98001–98300	18101–18400	38101–38400
Establishment	60001–66084	99001–99400	99001–99400	99001–99400	99001–99400	99001–99400	8501–8700	28501–28700
Reparation Claims	55001–55138	99501–99590	99501–99590	99501–99590	99501–99590	—	—	—
Chief Clerk (and Honours)	50001–50350	47000–47467	47000–47489	48000–48419	49000–49308	49500–5000	8701–9000	28791–29000

2A

15.2.2 Subject file registration numbers, 1935 to 1951

During this period the blocks allocated largely remained consistent from year to year. The major exception was the Economic Original Correspondence which is covered in 15.3. See also chapter 4.4.5.

General	1001–10000	Economic Eastern	59001–59700
Defence & General	10001–11000	Brunei	59701–60000
Welfare, Students	11001–11500	British Guiana	60001–61500
Social Services	11501–13000	Leeward Islands	61501–63000
Defence	13001–15000	Grenada	63001–63750
Economic	15001–20000	St Lucia	63751–64250
*Economic Palestine	16550–16599	St Vincent	64251–65500
	19510–19599	Dominica	65151–65500
Personnel	20001–22000	Barbados	65501–66500
Communications	22001–25000	British Honduras	66501–67500
Telecommunications	24001–24000	Bermuda	67501–68000
International Relations	25001–26000	Bahamas	68001–68500
Honours	26001–27000	Jamaica	68501–70000
Appointments, Recruits,		Trinidad	70001–71000
Training	27001–28000	West Indies	71001–72000
Research	28001–29000	US Bases	72001–75000
Nigeria	30001–31000	Palestine	75001–77000
Gold Coast	31001–32000	Transjordan	77001–78000
Sierra Leone	32001–33000	Aden	78001–79000
Gambia	33001–33500	Middle East	79001–80000
West Africa	33501–34000	Fiji	85001–86000
Military Africa	34001–35000	Western Pacific	86001–87500
Military General	36001–37000	St Helena	87501–88000
St Helena	35001–35500	Falkland Islands	88001–88500
Kenya	38001–40000	Gibraltar	88501–89000
Uganda	40001–41000	Malta	89001–90000
Zanzibar	41001–42000	Cyprus	90001–91500
Tanganyika	42001–44000	Mediterranean	91501–92000
Central Africa	43001	Defence General	94001–96000
Nyasaland	44001–45000	Information	96001–97000
N Rhodesia	45001–46000	Economic Relations	97001–97250
Somaliland	46001–46500	Economic General	97251–97500
East Africa	46501–47000	British Council	97501–97600
Africa	47001–47200	**Legal 1950	97601–97850
Malay Straits	50001–51500	Prize Court 1951	97851–98000
Malay States	51501–53000	Special Care	98001–98600
N Borneo	53001–53500	Statistics	98201–98500
Hong Kong	53501–55000		
Eastern	55001–55500		
Ceylon	55501–57000		
Mauritius	57001–58000		
Seychelles	58001–58500	* After termination of mandate	
Sarawak	58501–59000	** Placed in Colonies General CO 323.	

15.3 Colonial Office Economic Original Correspondence (CO 852) file registration numbers, 1935 to 1951

This section covers the Economic Original Correspondence in CO 852; 15.3.1 provides a breakdown by principal subjects and 15.3.2 is a box list. There is a general description of the registration of economic papers in chapter 4.4.5. See the description of Economic Departments in chapter 12 to identify economic correspondence in other record classes.

From 1935 until 1939 all economic subjects, of which 'commodities' was by far the most important, took numbers in the 15000 block. The block continued to be used, but after 1940 the only new subject to be allocated numbers in it was 'economic provisions', in 1941. From 1940 onward the bigger subjects such as 'finance', 'statistics', 'agriculture', 'commodities', 'shipping', 'industrial development', 'supplies' and 'production and marketing', were allocated numbers in the 16000–19000 blocks as well, but they tended to continue using the 15000 numbers originally assigned alongside the new allocations until the introduction of the new registration system in 1951–1952.

As new subjects were introduced during and after the war they tended to take numbers exclusively in the 16000–19000 blocks. The 16000 block was introduced in 1939 for 'war trade' and was used regularly, though sparsely, from 1942, mainly for financial subjects. The 17000 block was introduced after the creation of the Supplies Department in 1943 and was used for 'food supplies'; from 1950 it was used for general supplies questions. Other blocks were used in other years for general supplies and for other aspects of the Supplies Department's work. The 18000 block, introduced in 1940 for 'commodities', was mainly allocated in 1944; it was predominantly identified with 'supplies' and 'statistics', although these subjects also took numbers from other blocks. The 19000 block was used far more than the others after 1943. Until then it was used only for 'supplies', but thereafter it was used for a variety of subjects. It was used for 'commodities' during 1943, the final year of this subject, and then for 'production/marketing' which took over as the predominant subject. The block was also identified with 'colonial development' from 1941 to 1948, and with questions of 'reconstruction' planning from 1943 to 1945.

Two other blocks were introduced. The 97000 block, associated with various subjects, was used from 1947. During the transition period to the new registration system in 1950–1951 nearly all new subjects took numbers in this block. The 59000 block was used for only one subject, 'eastern' supplies, products and requirements, from 1944 to 1946. Part of the block was used for Brunei.

15.3.1 CO 852: breakdown by principal subjects

This chart provides a starting point for using CO 852 but is not exhaustive for any particular subject as some files on the same subjects appear in miscellaneous groupings. Used in conjunction with the box list provided at 15.3.2, it should assist in locating files on given subjects and tracing cross references.

Agriculture (includes locust control). See also Soil erosion and Production and marketing (1949–1953).

| 1938–1939 | 15551–15609 | 1944–1946 | 15570–15804 |
| 1941–1943 | 15571–15643 | 1947–1949 | 19934–19936 |

Capital investment and issues control
1950–1952   97358

Certificates of origin
1938   15218

Colonial development. See also Economic, Finance/financial (1950–1953).

Colonial Development Fund/Colonial Development Advisory Committee
1937–1939   15279

Colonial welfare and development
1944–1949   19275–19298

Colonial Development Corporation
1947–1949   18706   1950–1952   97357

Development planning
1948   19331–19339

Committee on Colonial Development
1949   97304

Colonial expenditure
1939   15279–15298   1944–1946   16302–16411

Colonial Native Law Advisory Panel
1948   19302

Colonial Labour Advisory Committee
1948   19305

Colonial Primary Products Committee
1948–1949   19907

Colonial surveys
1944–1949   16600–16616   1950–1951   16601

Co-operation. See also Production and marketing.
1944–1949   19350–19357

Commercial conditions in the colonies

   1946–1949   15390–15481   1950–1951   97087

Commercial relations with foreign countries

   1935–1943   15300–15361   1947–1949   15300–15384

   1944–1949   15300–15400   1950–1952   97087–97090

Commodities (includes food and utilitarian crops, hides and skins, mineral deposits, fish, subjects affecting crops, West African Produce Control Board (1942–1943)). See also Production and marketing and Trade: war trade.

   1935–1939   15001–15090   1940   15001–15179

   1939   15613–15624   1942–1943   18000–18320

                                                                      19600–19902

Congo Basin treaties

   1950–1951   97082

Crown Agents

   1938   15298; 15536   1940   15477–15536

Currency. See also Finance/financial.

   1938–1946   15101–15200   1945–1946   15482–15504

Customs. See Tariffs, customs and excise.

Dependencies (includes economic survey of the empire). See also Economic: economic planning, programming, research and development.

   1935–1942   15201

East African Production and Supply Council

   1943   19097

Eastern

   1944–1946   59002–59754

Economic

   general

      1936   15218–15281

   Imperial Economic Committee and Imperial Shipping Committee

      1938   15287

Economic Advisory Council/Committee (includes Colonial Development and Welfare Act). See also Colonial development.

1938	15289	1944–1946	19250–19275
1943	19250		

economic dependencies

1940　　　　15085

economic provisions

1941–1943　　15244

economic planning, programming, research and development (includes Colonial Development and Welfare Act, Colonial Development Working Party, Colonial Economic and Development Council, Colonial Economic Research Committee, Committee on Colonial Development, Colonial Social Science Research Council, study of colonial economies). For other economic surveys see Colonial surveys and Dependencies.

1943　　　　19260–19502

1947–1949　　19260–19339

Commonwealth Economic Committee

1948	19340–19341	1948–1952	97281–97483
1950–1952	97330–97331		

economic relations (includes President Truman's Fourth Point, Colombo Plan, United Nations, UN General Assembly, UN Food and Agriculture Organization, General Agreement on Tariffs and Trade, Economic Commission for Asia and the Far East).

1950–1952　　97111–97181

Enemy (includes treatment of persons and property, trading). See also Trade: war trade.

1944–1946　　18202–18280　　　　1947–1953　　97055–97061

European Recovery Programme (includes OEEC, Economic Co-operation Act, US–UK Economic Co-operation Agreement)

1948	19315	1950–1952	97181–97260
1949	97001–97006		

Exhibitions

1938–1940　　15431–15447　　　　1948　　　　19315

REGISTRY CODES

Finance/financial (includes colonial loans, exchange rates, defence finance regulations, war loans, insurance, taxation, savings banks, colonial expenditure, price stabilization, price control, currency returns, banking, statistics, Colonial Development and Welfare Act (1950–1952)). See also Currency and Statistics.

1938–1940	15453–15550	1946–1949	15501–15566
1941–1943	15477–15569		15803–16510
	15700–16465	1947–1949	15103–15194
1944–1946	15536–15562	1950–1952	15104–16581
	15843–16500		19261–19309
	18872–19124		

Forestry

1935–1944   15401–15415

Imperial College of Petroleum Technology, Trinidad

1938   15293

Imperial Institute

1927–1943   15272–15274   1946–1947   15272

Imperial preferences. See also Tariffs, customs and excise.

1938–1940   15246–15252   1950–1952   97084

Imports and exports. See also Trade: war trade and Supplies.

textile import quotas

1935–1940   15213   1941–1942   15213–15270

import and export control. See also Supplies.

1941–1949   18495–18610

Industrial development. See also Reoccupation of British territories/reconstruction of industry.

1935–1940	15212	1941–1946	18650–18717
1938	15247	1950–1952	97260–19280
1941–1943	15212–15513		

Insurance. See War risk insurance and Finance/financial.

Investment of foreign capital in the colonies

1948–1949   19309

Land
1938   15291
1944–1951   16700–16708

League of Nations Committee
1938   15248

Marketing. See Production and marketing.

Merchandise marks
1938   15214

Mining legislation
1938–1946   15286

Miscellaneous
1937–1940   15221–15234   1944   19400

Nutrition
1936   15282

Peace treaties
1947–1950   18270   1950–1952   97052–97053

Planning
1943   19094

Price stabilization
1941–1943   18872–18895   1948   18889

Production and marketing (includes food and utilitarian crops). See also Commodities.

marketing board for colonial produce
1937   15263–15270

Colonial Empire Marketing Board
1938–1943   15263

production (includes locust control, geological surveys)
1944–1946   19600–19940   1947–1949   15597, 16601

REGISTRY CODES

marketing

| 1946 | 18000 | 1947 | 18015 |

production and marketing (includes, from about 1949, UN Food and Agriculture Organization, Imperial College of Tropical Agriculture, agriculture, veterinary, horticulture, Colonial Products Advisory Bureau)

| 1947–1949 | 18650–18667 | 1948–1950 | 18706–18719 |
| | 19350–19907 | 1947–1952 | 19600–19967 |

Public works and buildings

1944–1946   16651–16657

Reoccupation of British territories/reconstruction of industry (includes UNRRA). See also Eastern and Supplies.

1943–1945   19202–19233

Reparations

1945   19261

Savings

1944–1946   15953–15984

Shipping. See also Supplies and Trade: war trade.

1937–1939	15276–15278	1944–1946	18330–18430
1940	15276–15287	1946–1949	18455–18493
1941–1943	18330–18545		

Soil erosion. See also Agriculture.

1941–1943   15570

Statistics. See also Finance/financial.

| 1940 | 15235 | 1947–1951 | 18128–18187 |
| 1944–1946 | 18121–18128 | 1950–1952 | 18163–18197 |

Supplies (includes financial arrangements, development schemes, prices, UK and colonial requirements, Lord Hailey's committee on colonial post-war problems (1941), UK–US reciprocal aid, import policy, export licenses). See also Eastern, Imports and exports, Trade: war trade.

1942–1943   16857–17960   18630–18632

	18843–19086		18895–19097
1944–1946	18843	1947–1949	18202–18282
	19045–19082	1950–1952	16914–17693
1944–1949	16901–17555		18330–18879
1946–1949	16911–17755		

Tariffs, customs and excise. See also Imperial preferences.

1935–1943	15202–15211	1950–1952	97081–97082
1938	15241–15245		97100
1944–1949	15204–15271		

Taxation

1944	15855–15901

Trade

    trade commissioner, agents, etc.

1936–1942	15216	1951–1952	97086

    obstacles to international trade

1938	15294

    war trade (includes commodities, import-export, licenses, supplies, shipping)

1939	15609–16155	1940	18000–19026

    trade returns

1943	15201

    international trade negotiations

1947–1949	15305–15805	1950–1951	97085

Validity of contracts entered into before and during Japanese occupation

1947–1949	15488–15489

Veterinary policy. See also Production and marketing (1949–1952).

1947–1949	19927–19954

War Cabinet

1940	18888

REGISTRY CODES

War damage

1942–1946   16200–16237

War risk insurance

1941–1943   15540

World Power Conference

1938   15219

15.3.2   CO 852: box location list
year   box number   original
                           registration
                           number

1935	1–27	15001–15404		559–568	17000–17555
1936	28–65	15001–15410		569–583	18000–18997
1937	66–131	15001–15413		584–662	19037–19940
1938	132–190	15001–15609		663–671	59002–59754
1939	191–251	15001–15609	1947–1949	672–766	15103–15950
	251–270	16000–16155		766–790	16400–16996
	311–348	18000–18867		790–802	17005–17755
1940	271–310	15000–15628		803–851	18000–18889
	311–353	18000–18898		52–1018	19082–19954
	353	19026		1019–1054	97001–97483
1941–1943	354–406	15103–15984	1950–1951	1055–1075	15104–15950
	406–412	16200–16947		1075–1088	16163–16996
	412–430	17000–17960		1088–1126	17005–17963
	430–502	18000–18977		1126–1144	18163–18879
	502–533	19016–19902		1144–1236	19261–19967
1944–1946	534–552	15103–15984		1237–1360	97051–97432
	553–559	16200–16996			

15.4   Departmental filing codes

Under the reorganized registry systems established in 1951, filing codes were introduced in both the Colonial Office (see chapter 4.5.2) and the Commonwealth Relations Office (see chapter 5.5). The Commonwealth Relations Office records continued to form part of the single series of Dominions Office/CRO correspondence (now DO 35), but there was a separate series for each Colonial Office department. When new departments were set up, or when responsibility for countries or subjects was reallocated between departments, the codes changed. Exceptionally, the countries covered by the Mediterranean and Atlantic Department, formed in 1962, and the Atlantic Department, formed in 1964, kept the Mediterannean Department letter code (MED). The lists that follow include codes in use at any time during the periods specified and should enable readers to relate file references to the correct class.

15.4.1   Colonial Office, 1951 to 1965
ASB   African Studies Branch   CO 955

BBS	Southern Africa Department	CO 1048
BCD	Overseas Service Departments B,C,D	CO 1017
CAA	Central African and Aden Department	CO 1015
COM	Communications Department	CO 937
COR	Coronation Department	CO 1021
CSA	Colonial Service Division	CO 1017
CTB	Commercial Treaties Branch	CO 1016
DEF	Defence Department	CO 968
EAF	East African Department	CO 822
EGD	Economic General Department	CO 852
EOD	Establishment and Organization Department	CO 866
FED	Far Eastern Department	CO 1030
FIN	Finance Department	CO 1025
FST	Falkland Islands, St Helena and Tristan da Cunha Department	CO 1024
GEN	General Department	CO 1032
HKP	Hong Kong and Pacific Department	CO 1023
INF	Public Relations and Information Department	CO 875
INF	Information Department	CO 1027
IRD	International Relations Department	CO 936
ISD	Intelligence and Security Department	CO 1035
LEG	Legal Division	CO 1026
MED	Mediterranean Department	CO 926
OSA	Overseas Service Division	CO 1017
PAC	Pacific Department	CO 1036
PMD	Production and Marketing Departments	CO 1029
POL	Police Department	CO 1037
RES	Research Department	CO 927
SEA	South-East Asia Department	CO 1022
SSA	Social Service Department A	CO 859
SSB	Social Service Department B	CO 859
SSD	Social Services Department	CO 859
STA	Statistics Department	CO 1034
STU	Welfare and Students Department	CO 876
STU	Students Department	CO 1028
SUP	Commercial Relations and Supplies Department	CO 1033
TEL	Telegraph Branch	CO 1038
WAF	West African Department	CO 554
WIS	West Indian Departments	CO 1031

15.4.2 Commonwealth Relations Office, 1951 to 1966
The codes which follow were in use until 1 January 1964 when a new file cycle was begun. The series was distinguished from the 1951 to 1963 series by the addition of the figure '2' in front of the departmental code, viz 2ADM, 2AED, 2AG.

ADM	Administration Department
AED	Asia Economic Department
AG	Accountant General's Department

REGISTRY CODES

BBS	High Commission Territories
CA	Central Africa Department
CD	Commodities Department
CMD	Common Market Department
COM	Communications Department
CON	Constitutional Department
CPD/CPP	Commercial Policy Department
CRD	Cultural Relations Department
DEF	Defence Department
DEV	Development Department
EA	East Africa Department
EAG	East and General Africa Department
EC	Economic Division
ECA	Africa Economic Department
EGA	Eastern and General Africa Department
ED	Education Department
EP	Economic Policy Department
ERI	Economic Relations I Department
ERII	Economic Relations II Department
EST	Establishment Department
FD	Food and Development Department
FDP	Finance and Development Policy Department
FE	Far East and Pacific Department
GHA	Ghana Department
INF	Information and Cultural Relations Division Information
CUL	Cultural Relations
IPD	Information Policy Department
ISD	Information Services Department
INSP	Inspectorate
KYA	Kenya Department
LA	Latin America Department
MAL	Malaya Department
ME	Middle East Department
NAT	Nationality and General Department Nationality
GEN	General
MIG	Migration
NEW	News Department
NIG	Nigeria Department
OF	Overseas Finance Department
PA	Political Affairs Department
PAC	Far East and Pacific Department
PER	Personnel Department
PG	Communciations Department
PLA	Planning and Research Unit
PRO	Protocol Files
PSO	Political Staff Officers Department
RM	Raw Materials Department
SA	South/Southern Africa Department

SAI	Union of South Africa (Internal Political Affairs/Southern Africa Department)
SEA	South-East Asia Department
SR	Southern Rhodesia and Communications Department
TA	Technical Assistance Department
TB/TD	Telegraph Section
TR	Trade Department
UN	United Nations Department
WA	West Africa Department
WAE	West Africa Economic Department
WED	Western Economic Department
WES	Western and Middle East Department Western
ME	Middle East
WID	West Indies Department

15.4.3 Foreign Office, Commonwealth Office, Diplomatic Service Administration Office (political and functional departments), 1967 to 1968
The three offices used a common registry system, described in chapter 5.6, between January 1967 and October 1968 in preparation for their merger.

A	American Department
AD	Atomic Energy and Disarmament
AE	Asia Economic Department
AT	Aviation and Telecommunications Department
B	Arabian Department
BA	Aden Department
C	Central Department
CL	Library (CO)
CU	Cultural Relations Department (CO)
CR	Cultural Relations Department (FO)
D	South-East Asia Department
DD	Defence Department (CO)
DSR	Registrar's Branch
DSY	Communications Department
E	Eastern Department
EC	Common Market Department
EG	Economic General/Commonwealth Trade Department
EW	East West Department
F	Far Eastern
FP	Aid Department
FPC	Commonwealth Policy and Planning Department
FPE	Economists Branch
G	Atlantic Department
GL	General Department
GM	General and Migration Department
H	Far East and Pacific Department
HE	British Property in Egypt Department/Far East and Pacific (Economic) Department

REGISTRY CODES 419

HW	Hong Kong and West Indian 'C' Department
IA	Information Administration Department
IC	News Department (CO)
IG	Guidance Department
IN	News Department (FO)
IP	Information Policy and Guidance Department
IR	Information Research Department
IS	Information Services Department
IU	Information Advisory Unit
J	West and Central Africa Department
KL	Claims Department
K/KO	Consular Department
L	Library Department (FO)
LR	Research Department
LX	Legal Executive Branch
M	Middle East, Western and United Nations Department
ME	European Economic Organizations Department
N	Northern Department
NN	Nationality and Consular Department
NR	Zambia Department
NT	Nationality and Treaty Department
OD	Oil Department
PA	Political Affairs Department (CO)
P	East Africa (Political) Department
PE	East Africa (Economic) Department
PP	Commonwealth Policy and Planning Department
R	Western Department
RE	Rhodesia Economic Department
RP	Rhodesia Political Department
S	South Asia Department
S(E)	South Asia (Economic) Department
SA	Southern Africa Department
SR	Scientific Relations Department
Q	Pacific and Indian Ocean Department
T	West and General Africa Department
TC	Dependent Territories Constitution Division
TE	West and General Africa (Economic) Department
TP	Protocol and Conference Department
TY	Treaty and Nationality Department
U	Economic Relations Department
UG	International and General Department
UP	United Nations (Political) Department
US	United Nations (Economic and Social) Department
UW/WE	Western Economic Department
V	North and East Africa Department
W	Western Organizations and Co–ordination Department
WA	West Indian 'A' Department
WB	West Indian 'B' Department

WE/UW	Western Economic Department
Y	Gibraltar and South Atlantic Department/North and East Africa Department
ZD	Defence Department (FO)
ZP	Planning Staff
ZDS	Defence Supply Department

CHAPTER 16

Illustrations of Colonial Office Registry Procedures

Prior to 1926, documents arriving in the Colonial Office were registered separately; in due course they were bound in chronological sequence in annual volumes for each series. The procedures followed are described in chapter 4.3 and are illustrated in 16.1. From 1926 correspondence was kept on subject files; the procedures involved are described in chapter 4.4 and illustrated in 16.2.

16.1 Action taken on a letter received from the Treasury in 1901

The foundation of the paper illustrated in plates 1–4, which is now bound up in CO 323/468, ff 395–7, is a letter (plates 2–3) from the Treasury dated 6 September 1901. Its Treasury registration number, 14860/01, is typed at the top left-hand corner (the related Treasury file is in the Public Record Office under the reference T 1/9760/20552/01). The diagonal stroke in the left-hand margin shows that it originally contained an enclosure, namely a copy of the Natal Government Gazette of 25 June 1901. That gazette forms part of CO 182/32. On its arrival in the Colonial Office the letter was entered in the 'daily' register (CO 382/55) and stamped with the number which it bears in that register. This number, ͟ ͟65, appears at the top right-hand corner of the letter with the date of receipt and registration.

After it had been entered in the 'daily' register the letter was next entered in the 'Colonies General' register (CO 378/15). Into this the following details were posted: the date of registration, number, 'name' (ie from whom it came), date (sc of signature), 'colony', and 'subject' (in two columns). Also in the column in that register headed 'former and other papers' was entered the number of the letter to which it was a reply, namely Agts. 29572/01.

At the time of entry in the 'Colonies General' register the clerk inscribed the letter itself with certain references. The first of these was to the letter under reply. Although the number is typed into the letter, the clerk has, for clarity's sake, entered it in ink in the margin, and has prefixed the abbreviation 'Agts' to the number. This shows that the letter in question is grouped with the correspondence with agents or agents general for that year in CO 323/463, f 361. The other connections are to (i) a communication of 1 March, which, as is shown by the abbreviation 'Gov' and the word 'Victoria', is a despatch kept with the correspondence with the governor of Victoria for that year (CO 323/463, f 281); (ii) an earlier letter from the agent general, marked 'Agts' (CO 323/463, f 125); and (iii) an earlier letter from the Treasury itself, marked 'Treas.' which will be found on f 91 of the same volume (CO 323/468) as that which contains the letter of 6 September.

These connections having been inserted, the registry clerk placed a minute sheet (plate 1) on top of the letter. Since the letter would eventually be classed with the domestic correspondence of the Office and not with the despatches, the clerk chose a sheet on which the word 'Domestic' was printed and not the word 'Despatch'. In the panel at the top, in the centre, are stamped the words 'General' and 'Natal', showing that the letter had been registered in the 'Colonies General' register, and that it also had a bearing on Natal. It was not, however, registered in the Natal Colony register (CO 357/12). Below those words has been entered in ink the registration number, which, as has been shown, was taken from the 'daily' register and had already been entered on the original letter. The clerk has also filled in the point of origin of the letter, its date, and the last previous paper, as shown in the margin of the letter itself. He also copied from the 'Colonies General' register the 'subject', ie a very brief statement of the theme, and below that a rather fuller statement, also to be found, with a minor variation in wording, in the 'Colonies General' register, of the particular point made in the letter. It is to be imagined that he would then have placed the connected papers, as shown in the margin of the letter under reply, behind that letter, tied them all together, and sent them to the branch or 'department' of the Office which dealt with that class of correspondence.

The person who first received the file was Frederick Evans, an acting first class clerk. He, no doubt, received it on 7 September, the day of registration, but for the reason given in his minute, it was not 'sent forward' to his superior C P (later Sir Charles) Lucas, an assistant under-secretary, until 11 September. On that day Evans wrote a minute suggesting what should be done with the letter. Lucas agreed with Evans's submission, subject to one small amendment, and authorized 'action' on the same day by appending his initials and the words 'at once' at the foot of the minute sheet. He did not consider it necessary to send the paper to any higher official, or to the secretary of state, as he might have done if the subject had been of greater importance.

The action authorized was to send the agent general for Natal a copy of the Treasury letter. This was done under cover of a short letter from the Colonial Office. The drafting of this letter was entrusted to C H Niblett, a higher grade clerk of the second division, who wrote out the draft (plate 4) and forwarded it to Evans on the same day. Evans sent it on to Lucas, and Lucas approved its terms, with the small amendment shown, on 12 September. His approval is indicated by the letters 'fs' ['for signature'] against his name. The draftsman has inscribed the draft with (i) the Colonial Office reference, the number, the year, the class and the sender, (ii) the addressee's name, and (iii) a diagonal line surmounted by the words 'Treasury 6 Sept.' indicating what was to be copied for enclosure within it.

The paper next went to the copying branch so that the draft might be fair-copied. The letter was issued on 13 September and someone in that branch entered that date at the top of the draft. Someone has also indicated that the Treasury letter is to be copied by writing the word 'Copy' at the top of it, and this word has been crossed out to show that the direction has been complied with. Someone has also written Lucas's initials at the bottom to show that Lucas actually signed the letter. In the margin of the draft has also been inserted the registration number of the agent general's incoming letter. Who wrote this and when is uncertain.

Action in the 'Department' was thus completed, but the registry's work was not over, for the registry was bound to note in the daily register of out-letters (CO 668/1) the fact that an out-letter had been issued. The evidence for this is provided by the word 'indexed' written on the draft. The registry was also bound to enter, both in the 'How disposed of' column of the 'Colonies General' register and in the fourth panel in the left-hand column of the minute sheet, particulars of the action taken. The evidence that this has been done is presumably furnished by the word 'Regd' written on the minute sheet.

The letter to the agent general for Natal called for a reply. That it was duly received is shown by the inscription on the draft of the words 'Ansd' 32582.1'. That same number with the addition of the abbreviation 'Agts' is entered in the fourth and fifth panels in the left-hand column of the minute sheet. In the fifth panel headed 'Next subsequent Paper' is also entered a reference to a despatch from the Governor of Natal. Besides appearing in that panel the references have also been entered in the 'Former and Other Papers' column of the 'Colonies General' register. By working out the references it would be possible to establish what happened next.

The reference '1970' of f 395 is to an analytical index covering the period 1863–1908, then maintained in the General Department. The Figure '197' denotes the page on which the subject of this paper is indexed. Where, as in this case, the entries about one subject cover several pages of the index the pages subsequent to the first are lettered. The index has not been transferred to the Public Record Office. The figures 395–7 stamped at the top right-hand corners of the paper are foliation numbers of the volume added by the Public Record Office in recent times.

16.2 Action recorded in 1939 on the question of raising a further loan for Tanganyika

The file 42011/3/39 'East African Guaranteed Loan: Proposed Further Issues' (now in CO 691/170) covers two related issues. The first was handled immediately within the Tanganyika and Somaliland Department as described below. The second, a much more complex matter, was considered over a period of six months and most of the action was taken on a second, secret file, 42022/6/39, 'Permanency of Mandate: Assistance to Non-German Planters'.

On 20 December 1938 E R Surridge, the assistant chief secretary in Tanganyika, wrote to C A Grossmith, a principal in the Tanganyika and Somaliland Department, requesting a copy of a private letter dated 17 November 1931 from Sir Cecil Bottomley, assistant under secretary of state, to the governor of Tanganyika regarding Tanganyika loans (plate 9). As C E Lambert, assistant principal, noted in his minute of 18 January, the letter in question (13 on file 30250/A/31) was marked 'private and confidental' and presumably the governor did not consider that it should be placed on the Secretariat file. Lambert saw no objection to supplying a copy, and Grossmith concurred on 19 January. The same day, E B Boyd, assistant secretary in charge of the department, authorized an affirmative reply (plate 10), which was despatched under Grossmith's signature on 26 January with a copy of the letter requested. These actions are recorded on the register sheet for the file (plate 5) and in the minute sheets (plates 7–8); the file cover (plate 6) records the movement of the file within the office.

On 12 January, while Surridge's request was still under consideration, G R Sandford, the financial secretary in Tanganyika, wrote to E B Boyd regarding the possibility of raising a loan for Tanganyika for purposes not covered by the Palestine and East Africa Loan Act 1926 and the Colonial Development Act 1929. The letter was placed on a secret file 42022/6/38 'Permanency of Mandate: Assistance to Non-German Planters' (now in CO 691/160), with a typed extract on the open file (plate 11). A register sheet was opened for the secret file and was later bound with the sheets for the year, but it indicated only the file title and the file registration number; details of the contents of the file were recorded in a secret register which is under a fifty-year closure.

On 14 February Boyd wrote to E Hale, a principal assistant secretary in the Treasury, seeking his view on the question of a further loan for Tanganyika. The draft of Boyd's letter was placed on the secret file, with a carbon copy on the open file. Hale's reply of 10 March (Treasury S.43449) suggesting a reply to Sandford, was filed on the 1939 continuation of the secret file and a typescript copy was placed on the open file (see plate 5).

As Hale indicated, Sandford's letter raised financial and political considerations which made it difficult for the Colonial Office to reply immediately. Not only was the Treasury reluctant to extend its commitments in the way of guarantees, but a further loan for Tanganyika would involve asking Parliament to pass fresh legislation providing for a guarantee, and this would inevitably give rise to a debate on the future of the ex-German territories. With the rapidly changing situation in Europe it seemed possible that HMG might in fact be willing to make an open statement on its future intentions toward Tanganyika, and the question was reviewed by various Colonial Office officials at intervals over the next few months (see plate 12). By July, however, it was clear that there was unlikely to be any clarification of the international situation in the near future. A reply was then drafted to Sandford and despatched on 12 July under Boyd's signature (plates 13–14).

The plates which follow illustrate the successive phases of this action.

The Plates

395
DOMESTIC.

GENERAL
NATAL
Nº. 31365.

C.O
31365

Office or Individual.	(Subject.)
Treasury	Natal Stocks as Trust Investments.
1901	
6 Sept	
Last previous Paper.	Are prepared to add Natal Stocks to Statutory List as soon as certain formalities indicated are complied with.
Agts / 29572	

(Minutes.)

Mr. Lucas

I kept this over to see whether the ~~Australian~~ Cape mail brought copies of the Act. I understand that no copies have been received & that there is no gazette in the Library to show that the Act has received the Governor's Assent —

I think we had better tell the Agent General the substance of the Treasury reply & leave it to him to obtain which is required —

C.P.L. 11
at once

Copy to Agt. Genl. 13 Sept 1901
Arvd. 16 Sept. 1907 & agt. 32582

Send him a copy
CPL
11/9

W B & L

Next subsequent Paper.
Agts. 32582
+
Gov. 32239 / Natal (Natal Act).

Plate 1

Copy

TREASURY CHAMBERS,

C.O. 3136
Rec? & Regt 7 SEP 01
396

In the reply to this Letter the following Number should be quoted.

14860/01

6 September 1901

Sir,

I am directed by the Lords Commissioners of His Majesty's Treasury to acknowledge the receipt of Mr Cox's letter of the 30th ultimo (No.29572/01) transmitting by direction of the Secretary of State for the Colonies a copy of the Natal Government Gazette of the 25th June last and a copy of a letter from the Agent General for Natal respecting the proposed admission of the Stocks of that Colony to the list of Trustee Stocks under the Colonial Stock Act, 1900.

In returning the copy of the Gazette, as requested, I am to point out that the Natal Bill No.18 as printed therein, agrees in its enacting clauses with the draft which was accepted by Treasury Letter of the 20th March last, the only changes being unimportant amendments in the preamble. The Bill is stated to have passed the Natal Parliament, but it does not appear whether it has yet received the Governor's assent. My Lords are prepared to notify the admission of the Natal Stocks to the list as soon as the necessary formalities have been complied with, but two things are still required

(1) Unless authenticated copies of the Act have now been received, there should be a statement as in the case of Victoria (Colonial Office letter of 1st March 1901 No.7311) that the Governor has assented, and that His Majesty will not be advised to exercise His powers of disallowance

The Under Secretary of State
Colonial Office.

disallowance with respect to this Act

(2) An authenticated copy of the Minute of Council of which a telegraphic report was enclosed with the Colonial Office letter of March 20th (10321/01), should be furnished, as requested by This Board in Their letter of that date.

Agts. 10321:/
Treas. 10947:/

    I am,
        Sir,
            Your obedient servant,

S. Spring Rice

Treasury
31365/01 Sent
Indexed
397

DRAFT. The Agent General for Natal

13 September 1901.

Sir,

In reply to your letter of the 23rd ult. respecting the proposed admission of Natal Stocks to the list of Trustee Stocks under the Colonial Stock Act 1900. I am directed by Mr Secretary Chamberlain to transmit to you a copy of a letter from the Treasury indicating what is still required, before the desired notification can be made.

C.P.L.

MINUTE.

Mr. Hibbett 11 Sept 1901
Mr. Cox 11/9
Mr. Antrobus.
Mr. Cox.
Mr. Lucas. 12 f.
Mr. Graham.
Sir M. Ommanney.
Earl of Onslow.
Mr. Chamberlain.

2957/

Ansd. 32582.1

Treasury 6 Sept

Previous 1938.	SUBJECT East Africa Guaranteed Loan. Proposed Further Issue			No. 42011/3
Subsequent				
No.	SUBJECT.	FROM.	DATE.	ACTION.	ANSD. BY
1.	Requests a copy of No. 13 on 30250/A/21 to complete the Secretarial file.	A. Lunedge (S/o)	20·12·38.	2. To Lunedge (S/o) 13 on 30250/A/31 encls) 6. (1 thread) S/o - 26·1·39.	
2.	Enquires regarding the possibilities of raising a loan for purposes not covered by the Palestine & E.A. Loans Act and outside the scope of the Colonial Development Act. (Original on 42022/6/38 Secret)	Extract from a S/o letter from Mr. Sandford to Mr. Nyed	12·1·39.	4. To Halo (Treasury) S/o - corr. - 14·2·39. (Smfc on 42022/6/38 Secret)	S.
3.	Suggests a reply to Mr. Sandford regarding the possibility of raising a loan. (Original on 42022/6/39 Secret)	Treasury (S/o) S. 47449.	10·3·39.	Puty.	

Plate 5 (42011/3/39): Register sheet showing the receipt of communications, the action taken, and the location of related papers on the secret files. The tick at the top right corner of the sheet indicates that the file has been preserved.

| 42011/3 | **1939**
 C 0691/170
 TANGANYIKA | 42011/3 |

EAST AFRICA GUARANTEED LOAN

Proposed Further Issue

Previous

1938

Subsequent

R98
Mr Lambert 5/1
Mr Grossmith 19/1
Mr Boyd 19/1
Mr Lambert 19/1
R298 19/1
98 26/1

FILE A.

Plate 6 (42011/3/39): File cover showing the circulation ladder followed; the officials involved were all in the Tanganyika and Somaliland Department.

C.T.
Financial
(Loan).

1. R. Surridge (⅙). 20·12·38
Requests copy of No. 13 on 30250/A/31 to complete the Secretariat file.

The letter to which Mr. Surridge refers was marked "Private & Confidential" & I assume that in view of this the then Governor did not consider that it should be placed on the Secretariat file.

I do not see any objection to sending out a copy of the letter enclosure, but you may think that we should ask that it should not form part of the Secretariat's "open" records.

C. Lambert
18/1/39.

I see no objection, at this late date, to a copy of No 13 & enclosure on 30259/A/31, being lent out privately, for Confidential record.

A. J. Smith
19/1
T. I. K. Lloyd
19/1/39

2. To: Surridge. (W/C 13 on 30250/A/31 file) (1 encl.) 26.1.39
(& encls. 6) on same file.

Plates 7–8 (42011/3/39): Minute sheets recording the receipt of communications, the action taken and the comments by Tanganyika and Somaliland Department officials.

3. Extract from a s/o. letter from Mr. Sandford to Mr. Boyd dated 12·1·39.
Enquires regarding the possibilities of raising a loan for purposes not covered by the Palestine & E.A. Loans Act and outside the scope of the Colonial Development Act.
(Original on 42022/6/38 Secret)

4. To Hale (Treasury) - s/o - cons. - 14·2·39.
(Draft on 42022/6/38 Secret).

5. Treasury. S.43449. (Copy) — 10·3·39.
Gives suggested reply to Mr. Sandford regarding possibility of raising a loan.
(orig. on 42022/6/39 TT. Secret.)

Noted to BU.
with 42022/6/39.
TT Secret. on 3/4/39.
1/5/39 [initials]

Plates 7–8 (42011/3/39): Minute sheets recording the receipt of communications, the action taken and the comments by Tanganyika and Somaliland Department officials.

THE SECRETARIAT,
DAR ES SALAAM,
20 DECEMBER, 1938.

No. 20930/330.

My dear Grossmith –

In the last meeting of the Legislative Council one of our nominated members raised the question of Tanganyika floating a loan on its own security without recourse to the facilities provided by the Palestine and East African Guaranteed Loan Acts or other similar Acts, e.g. the Tanganyika and British Honduras Loans Act.

On examining the matter we find that there is a gap in our files in that there is no trace of Bottomley's private letter to the Governor dated the 17th November, 1931, which is referred to in the Secretary of State's confidential telegram No.3 of the 7th of January, 1932. If it could be arranged, we should be very grateful for a copy of this letter or at least to be given the gist of its contents.

May I add that we have no desire to float a non-guaranteed loan, and that the information is only required to complete our file.

Yours ever,

R. Surridge.

C. A. GROSSMITH, ESQUIRE,

Plate 9 (42011/3/39) Item one on the file, letter from R Surridge, assistant chief secretary in Tanganyika, to C A Grossmith, principal in the Tanganyika and Somaliland Department.

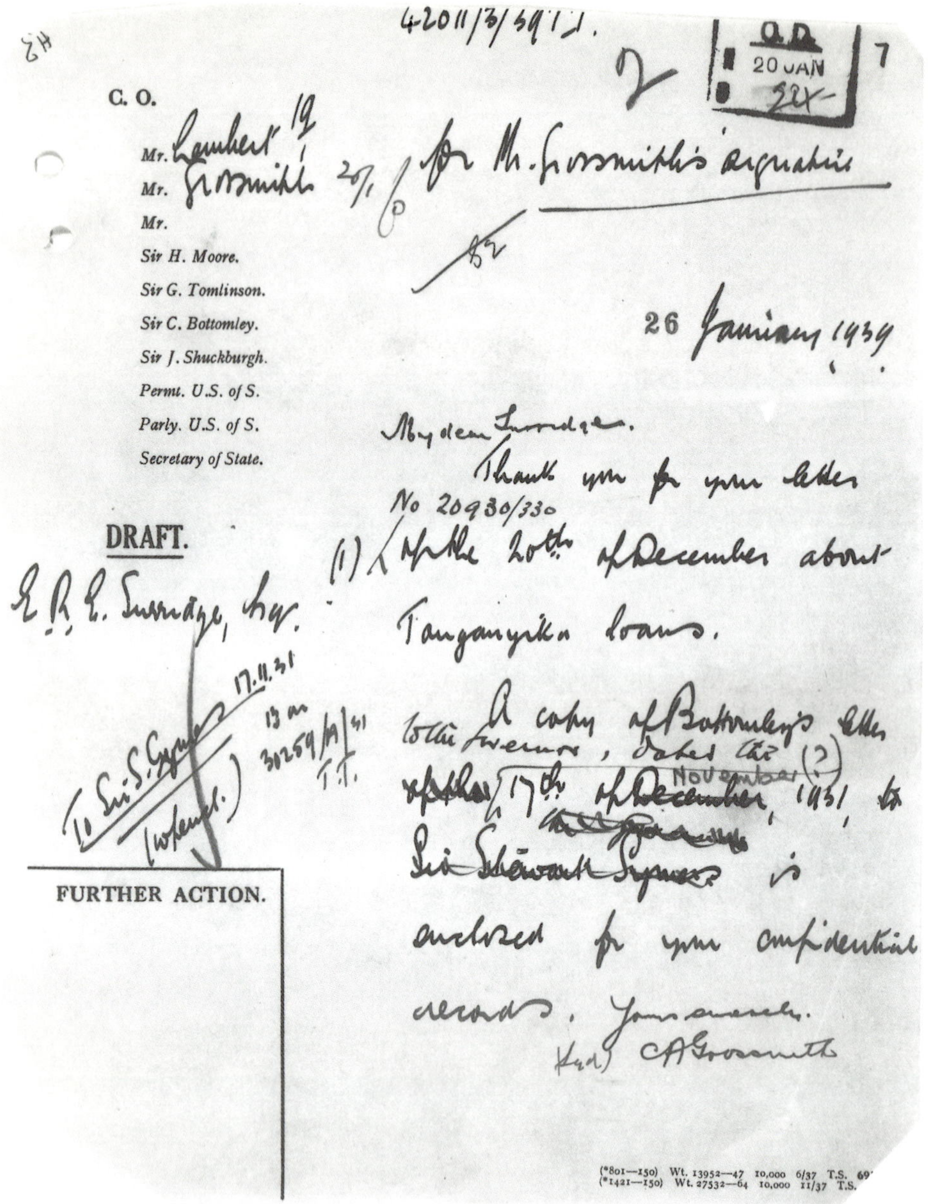

42011/3/39
20 JAN
7
C. O.
Mr. Lambert 19/1
Mr. Grossmith 20/1
Mr.
Sir H. Moore.
Sir G. Tomlinson.
Sir C. Bottomley.
Sir J. Shuckburgh.
Permt. U.S. of S.
Parly. U.S. of S.
Secretary of State.
For Mr. Grossmith's signature
26 January 1939.
DRAFT.
E. R. E. Surridge, Esq.
My dear Surridge,
Thank you for your letter No 20930/330 of the 20th of December about Tanganyika loans.
A copy of Bottomley's letter to the Governor, dated the 17th of November, 1931, is enclosed for your confidential records. Yours sincerely,
(Sgd) C A Grossmith
FURTHER ACTION.
(*801—150) Wt. 13952—47 10,000 6/37 T.S.
(*1421—150) Wt. 27532—64 10,000 11/37 T.S.

Plate 10 (42011/3/39): Item two on the file, draft of the reply from Grossmith to Surridge.

Plate 11 (42011/3/39): Item three on the file, extract of a letter from G R Sandford, financial secretary in Tanganyika, to E B Boyd, assistant secretary in charge of the Tanganyika and Somaliland Department, enquiring about the possibility of Tanganyika raising a further loan.

EXTRACT FROM LETTER FROM MR. SANDFORD TO MR. BOYD,
DATED 12th JANUARY, 1939.

x   x   x

As you are aware, from despatches which have gone to you, an organisation is being set up to consider development schemes on a wide basis and I hope that proposals will be submitted before long. It would be of great assistance in considering some of the proposals that are likely to be dealt with by this organisation if you could let me know, without prejudice of course, whether recent pronouncements relating to the Mandate have in any way affected the possibility of Tanganyika raising a loan for purposes not covered by the Palestine and East Africa Loans Act and lying outside the scope of the Colonial Development Act - see paragraph 3 of the Secretary of State's Confidential (2) despatch of the 12th of August, 1938. As a case in point the desire which has already been widely expressed to promote non-native enterprise and settlement leads directly to the suggestion that a Land and Agricultural Bank should be instituted, an institution which might not only be indispensable to further effective settlement and to the best results being obtained from past endeavour, but one which may prove to have considerable political justification also by opening out to sound German agricultural undertakings the possibility of finance on terms unrelated to the obligations which subsidisation by the German Government entails.

x   x   x

Plate 12 (42022/6/39): File cover showing the 'secret' classification and the circulation ladder. The officials concerned were from the Tanganyika and Somaliland, Economic and Colonial Development, and Social Services Departments; A J Dawe was the assistant under-secretary of state responsible for the Tanganyika and Somaliland Department.

42022/6/39.   CONFIDENTIAL   Colonial Office,
                                        Downing Street,
                                      12 July, 1939.

Dear Sandford,

   Your letter No.15782/64 of the 12th January has remained unanswered not because I had overlooked it but on account of the difficulty I find in sending you any satisfactory reply. I feel, however, that I cannot delay writing to you longer.

   As I am sure you realise, the question of the issue of a new loan for Tanganyika for purposes outside the scope of the Colonial Development Fund and the Palestine and East Africa Loan presents some knotty problems.

   One is the undesirability of adding to the number of loans requiring a British Government guarantee. Then there is the political difficulty arising from the present international situation. This aspect of the matter, you will remember, was touched on in the course of our discussions last autumn. In all essentials the position

G. R. SANDFORD, ESQ., C.M.G., O.B.E.

position remains the same today, and I am afraid I cannot give you any idea whether in existing circumstances the Government would be disposed to introduce a Bill into the House involving a new guarantee for Tanganyika.

Needless to say, we will continue to bear your problem in mind. You may care to have a word about it with Freeston, who is, I think you will find, fully aware of the various considerations involved. But, if the position now is that, in order to launch their new development programme, the Tanganyika Government require loan funds in excess of those available under their present borrowing powers, and the matter is like to become a live issue in the near future, perhaps it would be best if the Governor were to raise the question and let us have a despatch explaining how matters stand and what his requirements are likely to be.

Yours sincerely,

(signed) E. B. Boyd.

Plates 13–14 (42022/6/39) Item seven on the file, carbon copy of Boyd's reply to Sandford.

Index

Abbiss, Sir George, 100, 101
abbreviations, xiii–xv, 323–324, 357–359, 399–400
Aberdeen, 4th Earl of *see* Gordon, George Hamilton
Abrahams, Sir Sidney Solomon, 98–101
Abstracts on hygiene, 135
Abyssinia *see* Ethiopia
academic questions, 147
Acadia, 274, 276
access to records, 385
accidents, 383
Accountant-General's Department *see* Commonwealth Relations Office Departments
accountants, 377
accounts, 359
   audit of, 149, 360
Accounts Branch *see* Colonial Office, shared services with Dominions Office; Commonwealth Relations Office Departments; Dominions Office
Accounts Department *see* Commonwealth Relations Office Departments
Accounts and Financial Departments *see* Colonial Office Internal Services and other Departments; Commonwealth Relations Office Departments
Accra, 197
   resident minister at, 18, 196–197
Acheson, Andrew Basil, 78–80
acquisition of land for defence purposes, 331
acts *see* Colonial Office records
Adderley, Sir Charles Bowyer, 1st Baron Norton, 71
Addison, Christopher, 1st Viscount Addison, 86, 88
addresses, 31
Aden, Aden Protectorate, 10, 73, 81, 163, 170, 268–270, 287, 297, 304, 305, 317, 333, 343, 392, 394, 406
   Indian government, responsibility for, 268
   record classes, 170, 171, 269
Aden Department *see* Colonial Office Geographical Departments
Aden and Social Services Department *see* Colonial Office Subject Departments
Adler, Lt-Colonel W M, 107
Administration Branch/Department/Section *see* Colonial Office Subject Departments; Commonwealth Relations Office Departments
Administration and Publicity Policy Section *see* Commonwealth Relations Office Departments
administrative service, 15
administrative studies, 152
administrative training, 123, 146

Admiralty, 35
   administers Ascension, 223
   Board of, 5
adoption of children, 332
adult education, 124
adult literacy, 124
advertising, 156
advisory committees *indexed under key word of title*
advisory services, 124
aeronautical research, 120
Afghanistan, 380, 394, 395
Africa, 147, 154, 162, 169–170, 363, 406
   Colonial Office departments, 169
   Company of Merchants trading to, 53
   Company of Royal Adventurers of England trading with, 53
   Confidential Print series, 52, 170
   courts and native law, 117
   cultures, 146
   economic development, 149
   ethnology, 146
   funds for posts in, 361
   governments, 146
   health education, 134
   interest in, 152
   languages, 146, 154
   liaison in, 337
   libraries, 133
   local administration, 300
   maps, 68
   military papers, 44–45, 406
   new territories, 10
   peoples, 154
   Portuguese territories in, 364
   record classes, 47–48, 170
   region, 162, 169–170
   Regional Economic Commission for, 337, 338
   research, 146
   'scramble for', 5
   social institutions, social studies, 146
   sociology, 146
   see also Central Africa; Central and Southern Africa; East Africa; North Africa; South Africa; West Africa
Africa, Central *see* Central Africa; Central and Southern Africa
Africa Departments *see* Commonwealth Relations Office Departments
Africa, East *see* East Africa
Africa Economic Department *see* Commonwealth Relations Office Departments
Africa and General Division *see* Commonwealth Relations Office Departments
Africa, North *see* North Africa

Africa, South *see* South Africa; Southern Africa
Africa, West *see* West Africa
African administration, conferences on, 170
African Affairs, 152
African Affairs Board, 362
African Company, 198, 199
African and Cyprus Department *see* Colonial Office Geographical Departments
African Division *see* Colonial Office Geographical Departments
African Governors' Conference (1947), 20
African housing, standing committees on, 170
African Liquor Traffic Control Committee, 109, 112
African and Mediterranean Department *see* Colonial Office Geographical Departments
African Studies Association, 130, 131
African Studies Branch *see* Colonial Office Geographical Departments
African Survey, 14
African visitors unit, 366
Agent General for Emigration, 349
agents-general of self-governing territories, in London, 24, 39, 57, 143
agricultural adviser, 97–106
agricultural commodities, production and marketing, 339, 340
agricultural credit, 339
agricultural development, 137
Agricultural Economics, Bureau of, 136
Agricultural Engineering, National Institute of, colonial liaison officer, 104
agricultural implements, 152
agricultural industries, 157
agricultural interests, 117, 147
agricultural and livestock resources of the colonies, production and marketing, 339
agricultural mechanization, 115, 152, 340
agricultural policy, general, 339, 340
agricultural questions, general, 110, 339, 340
agricultural research, 113, 115, 136, 155, 320, 341
agricultural sciences, 157
agricultural and veterinary matters, 13, 15, 113, 327, 331, 339
agriculture, 146, 152, 155, 157
  entomological work, 139
  ministries of, 142
  trading in, 138
  tropical, 157
Agriculture, Animal Health, Forestry and Fisheries, Advisory Committee on, 110
Agriculture, Economic original correspondence, 407, 413
Agriculture, Fisheries and Food, Ministry of, specialized agencies transferred to Ministry of Overseas Development, 8
Agriculture and Fisheries, Board of, 119
Aid Department, 418
aid for Commonwealth and foreign countries, 330
Air Ministry Microgram Service, 49
air operations, 331
air services, 21, 26, 27
air transport, 120, 123
air trooping, 373

Alberta, 164, 272, 274, 275
  record classes, 272
Algiers, 263
aliens, 319, 331
Allan, W A, 100, 101
Allen, Harold Treadwell, 77, 78
Allen, M E, 90
Allied Headquarters, north-west Africa, minister resident, 17
Allies' Economic Mission in West Africa, Dakar, 18
Alport, Cuthbert James McCall, Baron Alport, 88
Alternative Uses for Colonial Produce, Committee on, 118
aluminium trade, 375
Amatongaland, 162, 171
  proclamations, 171
America *see* North America; United States of America
America, British North *see* British North America
America and West Indies
  maps, 68
  record class, 163, 164, 236, 272
American aid general policy, 377, 378
American Department, 418
American Historical Association Reports, 55
American loyalists, 276
  settle Caicos Islands, 256
American War of Independence, 4, 256
Amery, Julian, 72
Amery, Leopold Charles Maurice Stennett, 12, 13, 15, 16, 23, 71, 72, 86, 96
Amery, William Bankes, 87
Amherst, Jeffrey, Baron Amherst, papers, 54
Amiens, Treaty of, 4, 254, 267
Amman (Jordan), 151
ancient monuments and records, 302, 303
Anderson, G D, 91
Anderson, Sir John, 72
Anglo-Irish Treaty (1921), 25, 259
Anglo-Sierra Leonean Society, 130, 131
Angola, 185
Anguilla *see* St Christopher
Animal Breeding and Genetics, Bureau of, 136
animal diseases, 124, 139, 382, 383
animal health, 110, 114, 341, 384
  adviser, 97–106
  research, 115
Animal Health, Bureau of, 136
animal husbandry, 113
Animal Nutrition, Bureau of, 136
animal products, 136, 156, 327, 328, 340
Ankole, 194
annual reports *see* colonial annual reports
Antarctica, 74, 144, 154, 280, 287, 300, 302, 304, 307, 352, 363, 392, 396, 397
  bases, 144
anthems, 369, 370, 393
anthropology, 118
anti-locust research *see* locust control
Anti-Locust Research Centre, 8, 21, 126, 129, 131
Anti-Locust Research, Advisory Committee on, 131
Antigua, 136, 236–237, 245, 248, 287, 301
Antigua and Montserrat, 163, 236–237
  record classes, 237

INDEX

see also Leeward Islands; West Indies
Antrobus, Maurice Edward, 87, 89, 90
appeals for financial assistance, 382, 383
applications, Commonwealth, for service with British forces, 372
Applied Nutrition Unit, 130, 131
appointments, original correspondence, 348, 406
appointments and privileges of foreign consuls and trade commissioners in colonies, 338
Appointments Department see Colonial Office Internal Services and other Departments
Arabia, 163, 269, 392
   record classes, 269
   southern, affairs, 343
Arabia, South, Protectorate of, 163, 268–269, 305, 392
   Federation of see Federation of Arab Emirates of the South
Arabian Department, 418
arbitration, 352
arboricides, 117
archaeology, 132, 134, 172, 341, 342
Archer, Norman Ernest, 87, 89
Arctic, 352
   foreign affairs of, 396
Argentina, claim to the Falklands, 224
armed forces, 145
Armitage-Smith, J N, 84, 85
arms, coats of, 333, 338, 368, 369, 393
arms and equipment programmes, 371
   supply of, 371, 373
Arnold, Sydney, 1st Baron Arnold, 72
art, study of, 152, 154
arts, the, 151, 154, 389, 390
arts, crafts and antiquities, 383
Ascension, 76, 163, 223, 225, 287, 300, 301, 304, 306
   record classes, 223
Ashanti, 163, 197, 199, 200, 201, 287, 299
   Acts, 197
Ashley and Cooper families, Earls of Shaftesbury, papers, 54
Ashley, Evelyn, 71
Asia
   regional economic commissioners, 337, 338
   regions, 154, 206–223
   see also Central Asia; Far East; western Asia
Asia Economic Department see Commonwealth Relations Office Departments
Asian Review, 144
Asiatic questions, 353
Aspin, Norman, 91, 92
Assistant secretaries of state (departmental), 69, 77–86
Assistant secretaries of state for Commonwealth Affairs, 94
Assistant secretaries of state for Commonwealth Relations, 89–92
Assistant secretaries of state for Dominions Affairs, 87
Assistant under-secretaries of state for the colonies, 14, 15, 38, 50, 69, 73–77, 96
Assistant under-secretaries of state for Commonwealth Affairs, 93

Assistant under-secretaries of state for Commonwealth Relations, 89
Assistant under-secretaries of state for Dominions Affairs, 87
Association of British Malaya, 132
   see also British Association of Malaya
Association of Commonwealth Universities, 132, 140
Association of Universities of the British Commonwealth, 132
Astley, A, 103
astronomical questions, 118
Athlone fellowships, 375, 376
Atkinson, G A, 102, 104–106
Atlantic Department see Commonwealth Relations Office Departments
Atlantic region, 163, 223–225
atomic energy, 371
   peaceful uses, 378, 392
Atomic Energy and Disarmament, 418
attendance of Commonwealth officers at combined exercises, 373
attendance of Commonwealth representatives at UK defence courses, 371
Attlee, Clement Richard, 1st Earl Attlee, 54, 186
Auckland Islands, 163, 236
   record classes, 226
audiences of the queen, 393
Augusta, Dowager Princess of Wales, Botanic Garden of (Kew), 153
Austin, Thomas Aitken, 100, 101
Australasia, federal council of, 225
Australia (Commonwealth of Australia), 6, 10, 66, 226, 227–228, 231, 233, 281, 282, 284–287, 298, 306, 353, 360, 379, 380, 381
   appoints accredited representative in Ottawa (1940), 25
   British High Commission established, 25
   Canadian high commissioner appointed in, 25
   Cocos (Keeling) Islands and Christmas Island transferred to, 220
   confidential print, 60, 226, 227
   convict settlements, 5
   defence co-operation with, 371
   Dominions Office series of print, 60
   Dominions Office, deals with, 6
   economy of and economic relations with, 375, 376
   external policies of and UK relations with, 380
   federal projects, 225, 226
   financial questions relating to, 379
   forces capture German New Guinea, 285
   funds for posts in, 361
   governors-general, 57
   interest in South Pacific, 12
   internal political affairs, 369, 392
   liaison officer in London, 25
   London high commission office established, 24
   migrants to, 139
   Nauru administered from and surrendered to, 284
   question of autonomy, 5
   record classes, 226
   representative for migration, 25

sterling area development, 374
termite research, 155
trade commissioners, 25
war production in, 27
Australia and New Zealand
region, 63, 225–234
regional record classes, 226
Australia, New Zealand and Malaya (ANZAM), xiii, 357, 373, 380, 381
Australia, North *see* North Australia
Australia, South *see* South Australia
Australia, Western *see* Western Australia
Australian-British Trade Association, 129, 132
Australian and Eastern Department *see* Colonial Office Geographical Departments
Australian, New Zealand and United States Defence Pact, Pacific Security Treaty (ANZUS), xi, 357, 380, 381
authentication of documents, 385
autographs, 394
aviation, 58, 314, 352, 383
 special adviser on, 314
 subject registers, 58
 see also civil aviation; military aviation
Aviation and Telecommunications Department, 418
awards, 385, 394
Aylestone, Baron *see* Bowden, Herbert William
Aylmer, Matthew, Baron Aylmer, papers, 54, 276
Azania, 134

background material, 386
bacteriology, 146
badges, 331, 368, 369, 393
Baghdad Pact, 373, 374, 392, 395
Bahamas, 31, 157, 163, 236, 237–238, 256, 287, 301–303, 306, 406
 governor of, 257
 record classes, 238
 see also West Indies
Bakswana, 173
balance of payments, 377–379
Baldwin, T H, 99–106
Balearic Islands, 267
Balfour, Arthur James, 1st Earl of Balfour, 24, 25
Balfour Declaration (1926), 24, 57
Balkans, foreign affairs of, 396
Ball, J, 71
Bamangwato, 172
 chiefs Sekgoma and Khama III, 173
bananas, trade in, 329, 367, 397
Bank of England, 26
banking, 157, 330, 411
 representatives, 117
Banwell Commission (constitution of Mauritius (1965–1966)), 261, 262
Barbados, 136, 163, 235, 238–239, 245, 257, 288, 301–303, 406
 controller for colonial development and welfare at, 18
 record classes, 239
 see also West Indies; Windward Islands
Barbary Coast, 53
Barbary States, 33

Barclays Bank, 151
Barclays Overseas Development Corporation, 340, 341
Barltrop, Ernest William, 99–103
Barnes, W L Gorell *see* Gorell Barnes
Barotseland, 177, 298
bases and installations, 371
Bass, Harry Godfrey Mitchell, 90–92, 94
Basutoland (Lesotho), 6, 25, 162, 171–172, 181, 182, 288, 298, 362, 369, 370, 393
 dependent territory outside Union of South Africa, 25
 development and welfare in, 359, 362, 365
 matters dealt with by Dominions Office, 6, 25, 353
 record classes, 171–172
 South African customs union, 180
 see also South Africa High Commission
Batavian Republic, 173, 254
Bathurst, Henry, 3rd Earl of Bathurst, 4, 53, 70
Bathurst (Banjul), 198
Batterbee, Sir Harry Fagg (H F), 87
Battershill, Sir William Denis, 16, 72, 73
Baxter, George Herbert, 89
Bay Islands, 165, 239, 247
 record classes, 239
'beachcombers' (colonial service officers seconded to Colonial Office), 16
Beard, E H, 106
Bechuanaland Protectorate (Botswana), 6, 25, 162, 170, 172, 181, 182, 288, 298, 362, 365, 369, 370, 393
 dependent territory outside Union of South Africa, 25
 development and welfare in, 359, 362, 365
 matters dealt with by Dominions Office, 6, 25, 353
 record classes, 172
 South African customs union, 180
 see also British Bechuanaland; South Africa High Commission
Beckett, H, 77–81
Belcher, Ronald Harry, 89–91
Belgium, 193
 colonial ministry, 336
 forces, 193
 government, 146
 West African territories, 196
Belize, 163, 239, 242
 see also British Honduras
Bennett, John Sloman, 80–86, 94
Berbice, 55, 240, 241
 see also British Guiana
Berlin, 392
Bermuda, 10, 66, 163, 223, 240, 252, 257, 288, 301–303, 305, 306, 406
 record classes, 240
 see also West Indies
Bermuda Company of London, 240
Beswick, Frank, Baron Beswick, 72, 88, 93
Bhutan, 380, 395
bibliographical work, 146
bibliographies of literature on Commonwealth subjects, 153

INDEX

Bieneman, G A J, 99
Bigg, Wilfred Joseph, 79–83
Bigge, John Thomas, 228
bilateral trade agreements, 327, 329, 343
bilateral treaties, 352
bills, 383
Bingham, Col Sir George Charles Patrick, 6th Earl of Lucan, 88
biographical notes of Commonwealth personalities and visitors, 386, 393, 395
biological problems in forestry, 138
births, marriages and deaths, certificates of, 383, 384
Biscoe, Captain John, 226
Bishop, Major-General Sir (William Henry) Alexander, (Alec), (W H), 89
bishops, consecration of, 333, 338
Blackburne, Sir Kenneth William, 80, 81
Blaikley, Robert Marcel, 86, 94
Blaxter, Kenneth William, 79–82
blue books see Colonial Office records
Board of Commissioners of Currency, Malaya and British Borneo, 129, 132
Board of Control, 5
Board of Trade see Trade, Board of
Bonar Law, Andrew, 71
booklets, etc, 333, 334, 388
books, 124, 133, 386–391
  export scheme, 335
Borley, J O, 97, 98
Borneo, British North (Sabah) see British North Borneo
botanic adviser, 153
Botswana see Bechuanaland Protectorate
Bottomley, Arthur George, 86, 88, 93, 95
Bottomley, Sir James (Reginald Andrew), 91, 93
Bottomley, Sir (William) Cecil, 73, 77, 423
Bourdillon, Henry Townsend, 75, 76, 80–82
Bowden, Herbert William, Baron Aylestone, 93
Bowring, Theodore Louis, 104–106
Boyd, 1st Viscount see Lennox-Boyd, Alan Tindal
Boyd, Edmund Blaikie, 78, 79, 423, 424
Brabourne, 1st Baron see Knatchbull-Hugessen, Edward Hugessen
Braine, Sir Bernard (Richard), 88
Branney, L, 105, 106
Breda, Treaty of, 236, 254, 255
British Academy, 134
  Archaeological and Historical Advisory Committee for Overseas Co-operation, 130, 132
British agricultural policy, 376
British-American Parliamentary Group, 140
British Antarctic Survey, 130, 132, 154
British Antarctic Territory, 154, 224
British Association of Malaya, 129, 132, 155
British Bechuanaland, 162, 173, 181
  government gazettes, 173
British Borneo Territories, 381
British Broadcasting Corporation (BBC), xiii, 323, 334, 335, 357
  liaison with, 386, 387, 389
British Cameroons, 6, 163, 197–198, 202, 288, 299, 300, 365

record classes, 197–198
British Caribbean Association, 130, 133
British Caribbean Currency Board, 130, 133
British Central Africa Protectorate, 162, 173, 178, 191, 298
British colonial policy, presentation of, 335
British Colonial Supply Mission, Washington, 18, 63, 136, 315, 321
British Columbia, 10, 164, 273, 274, 288, 305, 307
  record classes, 273
British Commonwealth Ex-Services League, 133
British Commonwealth Forestry, Standing Committee on, 113
British Commonwealth League, 129, 133, 137
British Commonwealth Scientific Committee, 109, 113, 120, 141, 384
British Commonwealth Scientific Conference, Standing Committee for the, 113, 121
British Commonwealth Scientific Official Conference, 119–121, 141
British Commonwealth Union Ltd, 133
British Council, 119, 123–124, 129, 133, 140, 147, 333–335, 342, 386, 387, 390, 406
  liaison with, 389
  policy and estimates, 385
British Council of Churches, 149
British Defence Co-ordination Committee, Far East, 207
British Dominions Women's Citizens Union, 137
British East Africa, 296
British East African Company, 194
British East India Company (East India Company, English East India Company), 4, 5, 213, 221, 224, 225, 268
British Empire Ex-Services League, 129, 133
British Empire Forestry Conference (1923), 138
British Empire Games, 382, 383, 386
British Empire League, 138
British Empire Producers' Association, 138
British Empire Producers' Organization, 129, 133, 140
British Empire Union Ltd, 129, 133, 134
British financial enterprises, 148
British Guiana (Guyana), 136, 157, 158, 163, 240–241, 245, 288, 301–303, 397, 406
  Commision of Inquiry into Disturbances (1962), 241
  Constitutional Commission, 241
  Information Office, 335
  record classes, 241
  Sugar Industry Commission (Venn Commission), 241
  see also Berbice; Demerara; Essequibo
British high commissioners
  to Australia (1906), 25
  to Canada (1928), 25
  to New Zealand (1939), 25
  to South Africa (1930), 25
British Honduras (Belize), 155, 157, 163, 235, 241–243, 245, 247, 288, 301–303, 306, 397, 406
  governor of, 16
  record classes, 242–243
  see also Belize

British Imperial Council of Commerce, 129, 134, 144
British Indian Ocean Territory, 163, 261
    acts, 261
British industry and commerce, 149, 154
British Information Service (BIS), xiii, 335, 357
    administration and estimates co-ordination, 389
    posts, 386
British Information Services Section *see* Commonwealth Relations Office Departments
British Institute of History and Archaeology, 130, 134
British Institute of International and Comparative Law, 130, 134
British Kaffraria, 288, 297, 303, 305
British Leprosy Relief Association, 129, 134
British Library, Oriental and India Office Collections, 213, 218
British Malaya *see* Malaya
British Medical Association, 139
British Missionary Societies, Conference of, 149
British Museum, received colonial newspapers, 52
British Museum (Natural History), 155
British National Committee on Space Research, 121
British New Guinea (Papua), 164, 281–282, 285, 286, 305, 306
    record classes, 281–282
British-Nigeria Association, 130, 134
British North America, 164, 272
    colonies, 3, 4, 272
    forces take Bahamas, 237
    Land and Emigration Commission, 272
    question of autonomy, 5
    R J Wilmot Horton letter books, 54
    record classes, 35, 272
British North America Act (1867), 224, 275
British North Borneo (Sabah), 132, 163, 207, 208, 214–217, 219–221, 291, 297, 308, 309, 381, 406
    Commission of Inquiry into North Borneo and Sarawak regarding Malaysian Federation (Cobbold Commission, 1962), 217, 219, 220
    Commonwealth relations with, 380
    record classes, 217
British North Borneo Company, 207, 214, 217
    papers, 53, 217
British Phosphate Commission, 284, 329, 353, 375, 376
    records, 285
British Property in Egypt Department, 418
British Society for International Health Education, 130, 134
British Solomon Islands Protectorate, 164, 280, 282
    record classes, 282
    see also Western Pacific; Western Pacific High Commission
British Somaliland *see* Somaliland
British South Africa Company, 162, 173, 177, 180, 182
British subjects in foreign countries, 382, 383
    in wartime, 371

British Virgin Islands, 163, 243, 245, 248–251, 293, 301
    record classes, 243
    see also St Croix; St Thomas
British Women's Emigration Association, 158
broadcasting, 144, 314, 318, 319, 331, 333–335, 341, 352, 387–389
broadsides, 31
Bromley, Rear-Admiral Sir Arthur, 8th baronet, 99, 101
Brooke, Sir James, rajah of Sarawak, 219
Brown, Alan James, 91, 92
Brownrigg, General Sir Robert, papers, 54
Bruce, Victor Alexander, 9th Earl of Elgin and 13th Earl of Kincardine, 71
Brunei, 132, 163, 207–209, 216, 217, 219, 288, 308, 309, 381, 406, 407
    economic relations with, 377
    record classes, 209
Brussels treaty defence aspects, 371
Buchanan, Sir John (Cecil Rankin), 100–106
Buckingham and Chandos, 3rd Duke of *see* Grenville, Richard
Buganda, 194
building materials, 116
building matters, 150
bulk sales to government departments or agencies, 339
Buller, Sir Redvers Henry, papers, 54
Bulletin of Entomological Research, 139
Bunning, Arthur John Farrant, 99, 100
Bunyoro, 194
Bureau *indexed under key word of title*
Burma, 7, 143, 144, 207, 380, 385, 395
    accounting, 360
    business dealt with by Foreign Office, 7
    civil service, 383
    civilians, 359
    compensation for tax, 360, 361
    pensions, 359, 360
    residual inter-governmental claims, 360
    winding up of secretary of state's service in, 383, 391
Burma Office, abolished (1948), 7
Burns, Sir Alan Cuthbert, 16, 73
Burns constitution, Gold Coast, 200
bursaries, 133
Bushe, Sir (Henry) Grattan, 96–98
business communities, 144
business execution, courses for, 154
business questions, adviser on, 96, 98, 99
business visits, 149
businessmen, 150, 157
Butler, Richard Austen, 7, 175
Butters, H R, 80
Buxton, Sydney Charles, Earl Buxton, 71

Cabinet, 5
    committees *see individual committees indexed under key word*
    decision to review Colonial Office, 19
    Minister resident in North Africa, 18, 196–197
    secretary to, 25, 28
Cabinet Office, 6, 28

INDEX

cable and wireless, 121, 331, 353
cadetships, 371, 373
Cadogan, George Henry, 5th Earl Cadogan, 71
Caicos Islands, 163, 243, 288, 301
  see also Turks and Caicos Islands
Caine, Sir Sydney, 72, 74, 78, 79, 98
Cairo, 268
Calcutta, Colonial Government Emigration
    Agencies at, 136
Caldecote, 1st Viscount see Inskip, Thomas Walker
    Herbert
Calder, Sir John Alexander (J A), 78, 79
calendars of colonial state papers, 39, 65
Cambodia, Commonwealth relations with, 381
Cambridge
  conference of the Royal Agricultural Society of
    the Commonwealth, 152
  summer school for officers serving in Africa, 20
Cambridge History of the British Empire, xiii
Cambridge University, Tropical African Service
    course at, 15
Camden, 1st Marquess of see Pratt, John Jeffreys
Cameroon, Republic of, 197, 202, 366
Cameroons see British Cameroons; French
    Cameroons
campaign awards, 338
Campbell, Archibald, 83–85
Campbell, Sir John, 97, 98
Canada, 4, 6, 54, 66, 136, 164, 272–277, 288, 298,
    305, 306, 352, 353, 360, 371, 372, 379
  British High Commission established, 25
  defence co-operation with, 371
  economic relations, West Indies, 375
  economy of, 375, 376
  foreign policy of, 396
  funds for posts in, 361
  governors-general, 57
  high commissioners in dominions, 25
  high commissioners of dominions in Ottawa, 25
  interest in Caribbean, 12
  internal political affairs, 369, 392
  lecturers, 386
  London high commissioner's office, 24
  Lower Canada, 54, 273
  migrants to, 139
  outfit allowances for staff in, 361
  record classes, 56, 275–276
  relations with, 376
  technical assistance, 374
  trade affecting, 375
  Upper Canada, 273
  US ambassador in, 25
  war production in, 27
Canada Act (1791), 273
Canadian Blue Books, 52
Canberra, 132
Cape Breton, 164, 274, 276
Cape Coast Castle, 204
Cape Colony, Cape of Good Hope, 4, 162, 171,
    173–174, 176, 181, 186, 187, 288, 297, 298,
    303, 305
  Commissioners of Eastern Inquiry, 174
  record classes, 174–175
  see also South Africa

capital aid, 327, 328
capital goods, 374
capital investment, 138, 408
capital issues control, 328, 329, 408
capital issues general policy, 375, 379
capital punishment policy, 338
card indexes
  Colonial Office, 66
  Dominions Office, 58, 66
Cardwell, Edward, Viscount Cardwell, 70
  papers, 54
cargoes, 31
Caribbean, 366, 367, 398
Caribbean Commission (1946), 235, 302
Caribbean, Eastern, 397
Caribbean Organization, 302, 303, 398
Caribbean and West Indies region, 163, 234–258
Caribbee Islands, South, Government of the
    (1763), 257
Carlingford, Baron see Fortescue, Chichester
    Samuel
Carlisle, Earl of see Hay, James
Carnarvon, 4th Earl of see Herbert, Henry Howard
    Molyneux
Carolina
  Lords Proprietors of, 236, 238
  records sub-divisions, 236
Carstairs, Charles Young, 75, 76, 79–81
Carter, P L, 93
Carter, Sir (Richard Henry) Archibald, 89
Carter, William Stovold, 86, 94
cartographic techniques, 143
cartoons, 388
Castle, Barbara Anne, 95
Castlereagh, Viscount see Stewart, Robert
catalogues, 388
Catherine of Braganza, 196
Cavendish, Andrew Robert Buxton, 11th Duke of
    Devonshire, 71, 88
Cavendish, Edward William Spencer, Marquess of
    Hartington, 10th Duke of Devonshire, 72, 86
Cavendish, Victor Christian William, 9th Duke of
    Devonshire, 71
Cavendish, William Henry, 3rd Duke of Portland,
    70
Cayman Islands, 163, 243–245, 247, 397
  record classes, 244
  see also West Indies
cement, 374
cemeteries, 382, 383
  expenditure in India and Pakistan, 359, 384
censorship, 314, 331, 332, 352
census, 341, 382–384
Central Africa, 147, 162, 170–171, 363–365, 406
  Governors' Conferences, 17, 170
  record classes, 171
  transport, 297
Central African Archives, 182
Central African and Aden Departments see Colonial
    Office Geographical Departments
Central African Council, Standing, 170
Central African Department see Colonial Office
    Geographical Departments; Commonwealth
    Relations Office Departments

Central African Federation *see* Rhodesia and Nyasaland, Federation of
Central African Office (CAO), xiii, 7, 61, 175, 291
Central African and Territories Department *see* Commonwealth Relations Office Departments
Central and South America, 367, 392, 396, 397
Central and Southern Africa, region, 162, 170–189
Central Asia, 153
Central Department, 418
Central Office of Information (COI), xiii, 323, 357, 388
   British Empire Collection of Photographs, 67
   liaison with, 334, 335, 386, 389
   press services, 386, 387, 389, 390
   reference material, 390, 391
   see also Information, Ministry of
Central Opening Section *see* Colonial Office, shared services with Dominions Office; Dominions Office
central planning staff, relations with, 326
Central Treaty Organization (CENTO), xiii, 357, 372, 374, 395
Central Welfare Co-ordinating Committee, 109, 113
cereals, 327, 328, 339, 340
ceremonial, 57, 331–333, 338, 352, 368, 393
ceremonial and reception secretary, 99, 101
certificates, enquiries and requests for, 368, 383, 384, 394
certificates of origin, 408
Ceylon, 4, 7, 10, 135, 163, 200, 209–210, 280, 288, 298, 301, 304–308, 360, 385, 395, 406
   biographical material, 395
   Commissioners of Eastern Inquiry, 210, 261
   defence co-operation with, 371
   economy, loans, finance, taxation, 376–379
   foreign policy in, 394, 395
   funds for posts in, 361
   government records, 54, 210
   governor of, 221
   internal political affairs, 392, 395
   political relations with, 380, 395
   record classes, 210
   registration procedures, 35, 369, 370, 384
   self-governing member of Commonwealth, 209
   Special Commission on the Constitution, 210
   sterling area development, 374
   see also Sri Lanka
Ceylon and Mauritius Department *see* Colonial Office Geographical Departments
Ceylon and Mediterranean Department *see* Colonial Office Geographical Departments
Ceylon and Pacific Department *see* Colonial Office Geographical Departments
Ceylon Association in London, 128, 135
Chadwick, Gerald William St John, 89–91
Chagos Archipelago, 261
Chaka, 173
Chalmers, Lt-Colonel J D, 99
Chamberlain, Joseph, 71, 142, 181
chambers of commerce, 144, 145
Chandos, 1st Viscount *see* Lyttelton, Oliver
Channel Islands, 33

channels of communication, UK–Commonwealth, 368
charitable funds under control of UK high commissioners, 382
charitable grants, 134
Charles I, king of England, grants by, 237, 244, 253
Charles II, king of England, 196
   grants by, 237, 253, 254, 274
chartered companies, 53
Chartwell Trust papers *see* Churchill
chemical investigations, 139
chemicals, trade in, 375, 379
Chief Clerk's and General Departments *see* Colonial Office Internal Services and other Departments
chief medical officer *see* Colonial Office
chief nursing officer *see* Colonial Office
chief security officer *see* Colonial Office
chief statistician *see* Colonial Office
Chiefs of Staff, 326, 372
   Secretariat (COS), xiii, 357, 371–373
children
   employment, 382–384
   evacuation, 135
Children's Overseas Reception Board, 129, 135
China, 395
   cedes Hong Kong, 212
   Commonwealth relations with, 380
   lease and restoration of Wei-Hai-Wei, 223
   restoration of sovereignty in Hong Kong (1997), 212
Chinn, Wilfred Henry, 99–106
Christian councils, 157
Christian values, 146
Christmas Island, 163, 208, 215, 219–221, 381
   see also Straits Settlements
Christofas, K C, 86, 94
Church of Scotland mission, 178
Churchill, Sir Winston Leonard Spencer, 71
   Chartwell Trust papers, 54
circular despatches *see* Colonial Office records
citizenship policy, 385
citrus fruit, trade, 328, 367, 397
civil aviation, 120, 314, 324, 352, 366, 385
   adviser on, 96, 99
   standing committee on, 170
civil defence, 325, 326, 331, 332, 356, 371, 373
Civil Research, Committee of, 131
   Locust Sub-Committee, 131
civil returns, 263
Civil Service Commissioners, 15
civil services, 145
Civil Supplies Board, 189
Civil War, English, 1
claims
   compensation, 382–384
   property, 382, 383
   residual passage, 360, 383
   war inquiry, 382, 383
Claims Department, 419
Clarendon, 6th Earl of *see* Villiers, George Herbert Hyde
Clark, Sir (William) Arthur (Weir), 89, 93
Clauson, Sir Gerard Leslie Makins, (G L), 73–75, 78

INDEX

Clay, Sir Geoffrey Fletcher, (G F), 99–103
Cleary, Denis Mackrow, 89–91, 94
climatology, 143
Clinton, Henry Pelham Fiennes Pelham, 5th Duke of Newcastle, 70
Clinton-Thomas, Robert Anthony, 94
Clive, N D, 94
clubs, 383
Clutterbuck, Sir (Peter) Alexander, (P A), 87, 89
Clyde, Dr William McCallum, 96, 98, 99
coal, 375
Cobbold, Cameron Fomanteel, 1st Baron Cobbold, 216
  Cobbold Commission of Inquiry (Anglo-Malayan Commission, 1962), 216, 219, 220
cocoa, 327, 328, 339, 340, 363, 365, 366
  research, 115
Cocos (Keeling) Islands, 163, 210, 215, 220, 221
  see also Straits Settlements
Cockram, Ben, 90, 91
codes and cyphers, savingrams, 48–49, 352
Codrington, General Sir William John, papers, 54
coffee, 327, 328, 339, 340, 363, 366, 376
Cohen, Sir Andrew Benjamin, 74, 75, 79, 80, 95
Cole, A K, 79, 80
Cole, Sir David (Lee), (D L), 91
colleges
  development of, 111
  in UK, 151
Collier, Frank Simon, 100–103
Collingwood, Cuthbert, Baron Collingwood, 263
Colombo Plan, 309, 326, 359, 374, 376, 379, 387, 388, 390, 410
Colombo Plan Department see Commonwealth Relations Office Departments
Colonial Advisory Council of Agriculture and Animal Health, 109, 113, 114
Colonial Advisory Council of Agriculture, Animal Health and Forestry, 109, 114
  Soil sub-committee, 114
Colonial Advisory Medical Committee, 52, 114, 120
  Venereal Diseases sub-committee, 127
Colonial Advisory Medical and Sanitary Committee for Tropical Africa, 109, 114
colonial agents, 143
Colonial Agricultural, Animal Health and Forestry Research Committee, 109, 115
Colonial Agricultural Machinery Advisory Committee, 110, 115
colonial agricultural research, secretary for, 101–106
Colonial Agricultural Service, Committee on the organization of, 113
colonial agricultural services, 113, 157
colonial annual reports, 67, 162, 333, 335
colonial appointments, 164, 382
colonial arms, 331, 332
colonial attaché, Washington, and Counsellor (colonial affairs) UK delegation to UN, 336, 337
Colonial Audit Department, 149
Colonial Building Liaison Section, 135, 150
colonial building research liaison officer and housing adviser, 102, 104

Colonial Cinema, 135
Colonial Civil Service, 136
Colonial Colleges of Arts, Science and Technology, Advisory Committee on, 110, 111
Colonial Conferences, 145
colonial constitutions, 332, 338, 369, 370, 381
colonial contributions to Commonwealth defence, 332
Colonial Council (1670), 2
colonial defence, 314, 325, 331, 332
colonial development, 317, 361, 408
  planning, 326
Colonial Development Acts, 25
  1929, 14, 115, 320, 424
Colonial Development Advisory Committee, 109, 115, 116, 320, 331, 408
Colonial Development, Committee on, 408, 410
Colonial Development Corporation (CDC), 129, 135, 137, 156, 326, 340, 341, 361, 377–379, 408
Colonial Development Fund, 408
Colonial Development and Social Services Department see Colonial Office Subject Departments
colonial development and welfare (CD&W), xiii, 46, 111, 330, 357, 359, 360, 362, 365, 408
  research scheme, 155
  scholars, 386
Colonial Development and Welfare Acts, 7, 20, 118, 410
  1940, 115, 126, 135, 320
  1945, 17
  1950–1952, 411
Colonial Development and Welfare assistance, Africa, 362, 365
Colonial Development and Welfare Fund, 131, 150
Colonial Economic Advisory Committee, 109, 115
Colonial Economic and Development Council, 109, 115, 410
Colonial Economic Research Committee, 109, 115
colonial economies, 410
Colonial Empire Marketing Board, 129, 135, 169, 315, 412
colonial estimates, 330
  see also estimates
colonial expenditure, 408, 411
Colonial Film Unit, 129, 135
Colonial Fisheries Advisory Committee, 109, 115
colonial forces, 325, 332
Colonial Forest Resources Development Department, 129, 135
Colonial (Geodetic and Topographical) Surveys, director of, 99–106
Colonial Geological Surveys, 129, 135, 150
  director, 99–106
  Directorate, 99
Colonial Geology and Mineral Resources, Advisory Committee on, 110–112
Colonial Government Emigration Agencies at Calcutta, 128, 136
Colonial Housing Research Group, 100, 116
Colonial Housing and Town Planning Advisory Panel, 110, 116
Colonial Income Tax Office, 129, 136, 151

Colonial Insecticides Committee, 109, 116, 117
Colonial Insecticides, Fungicides and Herbicides Committee, 116, 117
Colonial Intelligence League, 158
Colonial Labour Advisory Committee, 109, 116, 408
Colonial Labour Committee, 109, 116
Colonial Land and Emigration Commission (1840), 128, 136, 348–349
Colonial Land Tenure Advisory Panel, 109, 116
colonial legislation, scrutiny of, 349
colonial loans, 143, 411
colonial local forces, 332
Colonial Local Government Advisory Panel, 110, 116
Colonial Land Tenure Advisory Panel, 109, 116
colonial medical research
  adviser on, 106
  director of, 101–105
Colonial Medical Research Committee, 109, 114, 116–117
  personnel sub-committee, 117
colonial military legislation, 325
Colonial Native Law Advisory Panel, 109, 117, 408
Colonial Office (CO)
  advisers, 12–15, 17–20, 96–107
  advisory bodies, 108–127
  advisory committees, 13, 14, 17–20
  advisory staff, 13–14, 17, 19–20
  chief clerk, 11, 33, 345, 346
  chief medical officer/adviser, 20, 96–106
  chief nursing officer, 99–106
  chief security officer, 102–107
  chief statistician, 99, 101, 320
  clerks, 11, 33, 38
    clerk for the parliamentary papers, 11
  Colonial Office List, 66, 69, 96
  control of Votes of Parliament administered by, 330
  Crown Colonies Division, 6
  Currency Committee, 109, 117
  departments *see* Colonial Office Geographical Departments; Colonial Office Subject Departments; Colonial Office Internal Services and other Departments
  development planning adviser, 18, 96, 99
  director of economic investigations, 20
  Dominions Division, 6, 57, 159, 167–169, 287–295, 298, 306
  economic liaison officers, 20
  educational adviser, 98–106, 147
  establishment officer, 12, 50, 347
  legal adviser, 13, 14, 96–107, 318, 332
  libraries, 11, 62, 63
  offices, Downing Street, Church House, Sanctuary Buildings, 11, 19, 28, 62
  officials, 69, 72–86
  Organization Committee (1948), 19, 46, 47
  post-war organization, 18–21
  records *see* Colonial Office records
  Registration Committee, 41, 43, 55
  related official and non-official organizations and institutions, 128–158
  representatives in UK Mission, New York, 337
  representatives on Consultative Committee on the Welfare of Colonial Students in the UK, 123–124
  Research Committee (1942), 14
  responsibilities transferred
    to Commonwealth Relations Office, 351
    to Ministry of Overseas Development, 7–8
  separate from Dominions Office (1925), 6, 11, 12, 23
  Summer Conference (1948), 119
  technical advisers, 13
  widening gap with Commonwealth Relations Office, 28
Colonial Office Geographical Departments, 14–21, 45, 47, 159–309
  (1822–1867)
  Eastern, 10
  Mediterranean and African, 10
  North American, 10, 48
  West Indies, 10
  (1867–1966)
  Aden Department, 76, 77, 85, 86, 287, 295, 305
  African and Cyprus Department, 288, 289, 292, 294, 295, 298, 299, 303
  African and Mediterranean Department, 288–295, 297–299, 303
  African Division, 20, 74, 75, 169
  African Studies Branch, 20, 21, 48, 75, 76, 81–85, 169–170, 294, 300, 415
    head of, 99–102, 104–106
    land tenure specialist, 104–106
    research officer, 105, 106
  Atlantic Department, 77, 85, 86, 287, 289, 291, 295, 304, 415
  Australian and Eastern Department, 287–293, 295, 296, 305, 307
  Central African and Aden Department, 46, 48, 75, 76, 81–83, 287, 291, 292, 294, 295, 297, 304, 416
  Central African Department, 74, 79, 294, 296, 297
  Ceylon and Mauritius Department, 73, 77, 288–293, 295, 296, 306, 308
  Ceylon and Mediterranean Department, 73, 77, 287–289, 295, 296, 304, 308
  Ceylon and Pacific Department, 74, 79, 80, 288–293, 295, 296, 306, 308
  Department No 1, 10, 287–290, 292, 293, 295, 301
  Department No 2, 10, 287–293, 295, 305, 306
  Department No 3, 10, 289–292, 294, 299
  Department No 4, 10, 288–296, 298, 303, 307
  Department No 5, 288–292, 296, 308
  East African and Mediterranean Department, 288–296, 303
  East African Department, 43, 46, 73–79, 81–85, 287, 290–294, 296, 247, 416
  East and Central African Department, 74, 80, 291, 293, 294, 297
  Eastern Department, 10, 17, 73, 74, 77–81, 159, 288–293, 296, 307, 308
  Falkland Islands, St Helena and Tristan da Cunha Department, 416
  Far Eastern Department, 43, 48, 73–77, 79, 80,

INDEX

83–85, 288–293, 295, 296, 306, 308, 416
Gold Coast and Mediterranean Department, 73, 77, 287–289, 292, 294, 295, 303
Hong Kong and Pacific Department, 48, 74, 75, 81, 82, 212, 289–293, 295, 307, 416
Hong Kong and West Indian 'C' Department, 86, 289
Mediterranean and Atlantic Department, 76, 85, 289, 291, 295, 304, 415
Mediterranean Department, 43, 73–76, 79–85, 287–292, 294, 295, 297, 299, 303, 304, 415, 416
Middle East Department, 10, 43, 73, 74, 77–80, 268, 287, 289, 291, 292, 295, 304
Middle East Division, 10, 295, 304
Niger Department, 294, 299
Nigeria Department, 73, 77, 288, 291, 294, 299
North America Department, 10, 159, 288–293, 295, 305
North American and Australasian Department, 10, 287–293, 295, 306
North American, Australian, African and Mediterranean Department, 287–295, 297, 299, 303, 305
North American and Australian Department, 10, 287–293, 295, 305, 306
Pacific Department, 75, 76, 83, 289–293, 295, 307, 416
Pacific and Indian Ocean Department, 76, 77, 84–86, 287, 289, 292, 293, 295, 307
Pacific and Mediterranean Department, 73, 77–79, 287–291, 293, 295, 304, 306
South African/South African Protectorates Department, 288–292, 294, 295, 298, 303
South-East Asia Department, 48, 74, 75, 81, 82, 288, 290–292, 296, 309, 416
Southern Africa Department, 76, 77, 85, 288, 292, 294, 298, 416
Tanganyika Department, 73, 79, 291, 292, 294, 296
Tanganyika and Somaliland Department, 73, 77, 78, 291, 292, 294, 296, 423
West African Department, 43, 73–84, 287–294, 299, 300, 416
West African and Mediterranean Department, 287–289, 292, 294, 295, 299, 303
West Indian Departments, 10, 43, 46, 48, 73–86, 159, 233, 235, 287–295, 301, 416
West Indian and Eastern Department, 288–292, 294, 296, 301, 307
West Indian and Hong Kong Department, 295, 296, 303, 309
Colonial Office internal organization (1795–1966)
formation, 5
impact of Second World War, 16–18
joint establishment with Dominions Office (1925–1947), 6
office structure (1795–1925), 10–11
post-war organization, 18–21
reorganization (1925–1939), 12–16
Colonial Office Internal Services and other Departments, 345–350
Accounts and Financial Departments, 11, 41, 43, 47, 346

Appointments Department, 15, 79, 80, 347
Chief Clerk's and General Departments, 11, 48, 164, 166, 346–347
Colonial Service Department, 73, 74, 79–82, 347
Colonial Service Division, 348, 416
Coronation Department, 75, 416
Economic Section, 46
Emigration Departments, 11, 346–349
Establishment Branch, 347
Establishment Department, 45, 46, 79, 80, 347, 348
Establishment and Organization Department, 81–86, 347, 416
Finance and Honours Department, 47
Financial Department, 47, 346
General Department, 11, 164–169, 346, 347, 349
General and Financial Department, 346
Honours Department, 43, 47, 348
Overseas Service Departments, B, C, D, 416
Overseas Services Division 21, 61, 75, 76, 82–85, 348, 416
Overseas Settlement Departments, 63, 165, 168, 169, 348–350
Personnel Divisions, 11, 13, 15, 16, 73, 77–79, 347–348
Colonial Office records
acts, 32, 39, 40, 52, 66, 162, 164–287 *passim*, 383
appointments original correspondence, 348
blue books of statistics, 39, 52–53, 162, 164–287 *passim*
circular despatches, 42, 48–49, 164, 346
circulating and minuting papers, 38–39
classification scheme (1951), 46–47
colonial statistical tables, 40
colonies general miscellanea, 40
colonies general registers, 40, 348
confidential print, other print, 51–52, 164–287 *passim*
destruction schedules, 62, 63
economic original correspondence file registration numbers, 45, 407–415
establishment correspondence and notices, 66–67
file system, 41–42
  allocation of file numbers, 400–405
  arrangement of files and registers, 42–43
  filing codes, 415–416
gazettes, 39, 52, 66, 164–287 *passim*
governors' correspondence, indexes, 40, 49
governors' pensions, original correspondence, 348
Honours correspondence, 406
lithographed forms (LFs), 37
minuting of letters, 36–39
original correspondence, 36–40, 65, 162, 164–287 *passim*
out-letter books, 33, 36
patronage original correspondence, 348
personnel original correspondence, 348
photographs, posters, maps, 67–68
précis books, 31–33
private office papers and private collections, 53–54

Prize Court cases, 40
record creation and record keeping, 30–55
registers, registrars, registration, registries, 11, 19, 33–36, 39, 41–48, 67, 162, 164–287 *passim*, 346, 415
registration of geographical and subject papers
  by geographical and subject departments, 45
  of in-letters, 34–36, 399–400
  of military and economic papers, 44–45
  of out-letters, 36, 37
  by region, 47–48
  impact of post-war investigations, 45–46
  sub-registries, 43–44, 46
registry codes, 399–420
registry procedures, 421–424
reorganization, 39–40
savingrams, saving telegrams, 48–49
secret and semi-official communications, 49–51, 162
sessional papers, 39, 52, 64, 66, 67, 162, 164–287 *passim*
subject code classification scheme, 46–47
subject registration numbers, 44, 406
supplementary correspondence, 40, 164–287 *passim*, 345
telegrams, 49, 162
training registers of correspondence, 348
United Kingdom Command Papers, 40
use of records
  access, 64
  custody and selection, 62–64
  reference, finding aids, 65–67
Colonial Office, shared services with Dominions Office
Accounts Branch, 11
Central Opening Section, 11
Colonial Office and Dominions Office Bulletin, 11
Colonial Office and Dominions Office List, 11
Library, 11, 62, 64, 418
Printing Branch/Department/Unit, 11, 51
Revision of Records Branch, 11
Telegraph Section, 11
Whitley Council, 11, 63
Colonial Office Subject Departments, 13–21, 45, 310–344
Aden and Social Services Department, 85, 287, 323, 343
Administration/ive Branch, 333
Colonial Development and Social Services Department, 73, 79, 320, 331
Colonies and Protectorates Division, 10
Commercial Relations Department, 311
Commercial Relations and Supplies Department, 74, 80, 311, 315, 321, 323, 343, 416
Commercial Treaties Branch, 75, 311, 315, 317, 322, 324, 416
  head of, 101, 102
Communications Department, 16, 21, 61, 74–77, 79–86, 314, 315, 317, 322, 324–325, 416
Constitutional Planning Department, 77, 86, 314, 322, 325
Defence Department, 16, 44, 73–76, 79, 80, 83–85, 314, 317, 322, 325, 416

Defence and General Department, 74, 75, 79, 314, 317, 318, 322, 331–332
Defence and Intelligence Department, 86, 314, 322, 326
Defence, Intelligence and Hong Kong Department, 85, 289, 314, 322, 326
Defence, Intelligence and Security Department, 76, 77, 85, 314, 318, 322, 325
Economic Department, 15, 16, 21, 45, 46, 73, 78, 79, 310, 315–317, 322, 328–329
Economic Departments/Division, 11, 21, 108, 315
Economic Division, 45, 314, 316, 326–329
Economic General Department, 74–77, 81–85, 314–316, 319, 320, 322, 326–328, 346, 416
Economic General and Social Services Department, 85, 322, 326, 328
Economic Intelligence and Manning Division, 315
Economic Intelligence and Planning Department (Economic General), 74, 315, 316, 322, 326
Economic Relations Department, 74, 75, 81, 82, 311, 312, 315, 316, 321, 322, 329–330
Enquiries and Casualties Branch, 319
Finance Department, 16, 21, 74–76, 80–86, 315, 316, 322, 330, 346, 416
Finance and Development Department, 316–317
Finance and Economic Department, 74, 79, 80, 317
French Relations Department, 16, 311, 317
General Department, 14, 43, 48, 50, 73–80, 83, 84, 164–169, 310, 314, 317–319, 322, 331–333, 345, 346, 416, 423
General Division, 164, 310, 314, 317, 321, 322, 330–331
Gulf of Aden and General Department, 76, 84, 85, 287, 317, 322, 333
Information Department, 21, 75–77, 80–86, 135, 317, 319, 322, 333–335, 416
Information Offices, 333–335
Information Services Branch, 233
Intelligence and Security Department, 75, 76, 83, 84, 318, 322, 335, 416
Intelligence, Police and Security Department, 76, 84, 318, 322, 336
International Relations Department, 74–76, 80–85, 317, 318, 322, 336–337, 416
International Relations and General Department, 76, 77, 85, 86, 317, 318, 322, 337–338
Legal Department, 14, 47, 318–319
Legal Division, 318–319, 322, 339, 416
Marketing Department, 16, 17, 74, 80, 315, 319, 322, 339
Military Branch, 191, 206
Military Section, 16, 43, 314
News Branch, 333
Police Department, 75, 76, 83, 84, 318, 319, 322, 336, 416
Press Branch, 333
Press Section, 334–335
Prisoners of War and Civilian Internees Department, 16, 319

INDEX 437

Prisoners of War Department, 74, 79, 80, 322, 339
Production Department, 16, 73, 74, 79, 80, 315, 319, 322, 339
Production and Marketing Department, 21, 74–76, 80–85, 315, 319, 322, 339–341, 416
Public Relations Department, 16, 73, 74, 79, 80, 317, 319–320, 323, 341
Public Relations and Information Department, 416
Publications Branch, 333
record classes, 310–311, 314–321
Research Department, 16, 21, 74, 80–85, 108, 315, 320, 323, 341–342, 416
Services Department, 315, 316
Social Service Department A, 21, 416
Social Service Department B, 21, 416
Social Services Department, 15, 16, 45, 74–76, 79–85, 108, 315, 316, 320, 323, 342–343, 416
Statistics Department, 74–76, 315, 320, 323, 343, 416
Students Department/Branch, 16, 21, 75, 76, 82–85, 321, 323, 344, 416
Supplies Department, 16, 73–75, 79–82, 315, 321, 323, 343, 407
Telegraph Branch, 416
Welfare Department, 16, 74, 75, 79–81, 321, 323, 343–344
Welfare and Students Departments, 321, 416
colonial paymasters' claims, 360, 361
Colonial Penal Administration Committee, 109, 112, 117
colonial pest infestation liaison officer, 102, 104–106
Colonial Pesticides Research Committee, 117
colonial police
 inspector general of, 101–107
 questions, 332, 336
 see also police
Colonial Policy, Official Committee on, 333, 338
colonial ports, 325
Colonial Primary Products Committee, 109, 117–118, 408
Colonial Products Advisory Bureau (Plant and Animal), 20, 129, 136, 156, 413
Colonial Products Council, 118, 156, 341
Colonial Products Laboratory, 118, 156
colonial products, marketing and development, 315, 319
colonial products research, 118, 341
 adviser on, 101
Colonial Products Research Council, 17, 109, 118, 156
colonial regulations, 332
colonial reports, 331
Colonial Research Committee, 109, 118, 126
Colonial Research Council, 118, 126–127
colonial research fellowships, 341
Colonial Road Research, Committee on, 110, 119
colonial road research liaison officer, 102
Colonial Road Research Section, 152
 Tropical Section, 119, 152
Colonial Secretary *see* Secretaries of State for the Colonies

Colonial Service, 15, 16, 71–79
 officers, training, 146
 recruitment, 382, 383
Colonial Service Department *see* Colonial Office Internal Services and other Departments
Colonial Service Division *see* Colonial Office Internal Services and other Departments
Colonial Services Appointments Board, 15
Colonial Services Committee, 14
Colonial Social Science Research Council, 109, 118, 320, 410
Colonial Social Welfare Advisory Committee, 109, 112, 118
Colonial Social Welfare Committee Penal (later Treatment of Offenders) Sub-Committee, 112
colonial stamp issues, 382
 see also stamp issues
Colonial Statistical Tables, 40
colonial students in Commonwealth countries, 383
 in UK, 110, 123, 124, 344
Colonial Supply Liaison, 129, 136
Colonial Survey Committee, 109, 118
Colonial Survey and Geophysical Committee, 118, 143
colonial surveys, 408
colonial territorial applications, 338
colonial universities, 146, 147
Colonial Universities Grants Advisory Committee, 109, 119, 147
Colonial Veterinary Committee, 109, 119
Colonial Veterinary Services Committee, 113
colonial welfare and development scholars, 383
colonials, identity, employment, nationality of, 344
 in UK, 344
Colonies General, classes, 108, 164–167
Colonies General, miscellanea, 40, 165, 166
Colonies General, original correspondence, 164–165
Colonies General supplementary, original correspondence, 162
Colonization Commissioners for South Australia, 348–349
colour questions, 338, 343
 in UK, 344
Command Papers, 40
commercial conditions in the colonies, 409
commercial debts, 377, 378
commercial development, 139
commercial education, 111, 124
commercial interests, 147
Commercial Policy Departments *see* Commonwealth Relations Office Departments
commercial relations, 311, 316, 324, 327–329, 331, 343, 378, 409
Commercial Relations Departments *see* Colonial Office Subject Departments
commercial returns, 263
commercial treaties, 324, 327–329, 343, 352, 353, 375, 377, 378
Commercial Treaties Branch *see* Colonial Office Subject Departments
Commission for Foreign Plantations, 1
Commission on Higher Education in the Colonies, 119, 147

Commission for Technical Co-operation in Africa (CTCA), xiii, 323, 357, 365, 366, 369, 382
   Soils and Animal Health Bureaux, 327, 341
   Soils and Epizootic Bureaux, 341
Commission in the United Kingdom of the Eastern Caribbean Governments, 130, 136
Commission on Virginia (1631), 1
commissioner-general for the United Kingdom in South-East Asia, 207–208, 217, 219, 308, 309
Commissioners of Eastern Inquiry (1821–1831), 33, 53, 210
   Mauritius, 261
commissions, 31, 32, 36, 39, 164, 165, 368–370
commissions for governors-general, governors and high commissioners, 393
commissions of inquiry, 40
Committees *indexed under key word of title*
commodities, 407, 409, 414
Commodities Department *see* Commonwealth Relations Office Departments
commodity defence planning, 377–379
commodity policy, general, 329, 378, 379
commodity production policy, 319, 339
Common Market Department *see* Commonwealth Relations Office Departments
Commonwealth Advisory Aeronautical Research Council, 109, 120
Commonwealth Agricultural Bureaux, 136, 140, 341, 342, 359–361, 382–384
Commonwealth air conversations, Canada (1944), 120
Commonwealth Air Transport Council, 109, 120
Commonwealth Charter (inconclusive), 12
Commonwealth Collections of Micro-Organisms, Committee of the, 109, 113, 119
Commonwealth commissioners in colonial territories, 338
Commonwealth Committee on Fuel Research, 110, 120–121
Commonwealth Committee on Mineral Processing, 110, 113, 121
Commonwealth Committee on Mineral Resources and Geology, 110, 113, 121
Commonwealth Communications Council, 121, 123
Commonwealth Conferences, 360, 361
Commonwealth constitutional questions, 368–370
Commonwealth Consultative Council, 328
Commonwealth Consultative Space Research Committee, 110, 121
Commonwealth co-operation, 370
   see also co-operation
Commonwealth co-operation in scientific and professional fields, 384
Commonwealth Council of Mining and Metallurgical Institutions, 110, 122
Commonwealth Countries League, 137
Commonwealth countries and the Irish Republic, 385, 392
Commonwealth defence matters, 332, 372
Commonwealth Development Act (1963), 137
Commonwealth Development Corporation (CDC), xiii, 137, 156, 327, 357, 363, 379
   see also Colonial Development Corporation

Commonwealth Development Finance Company (CDFC), xiii, 130, 137, 327, 340, 341, 357, 363, 377–379
Commonwealth development projects, 123
Commonwealth Economic Committee, 109, 122, 327, 328, 359–361, 375, 377–379, 410
Commonwealth economic committees, 378
Commonwealth Economic Conference 1953, 137
Commonwealth Economic Consultative Council, 110, 122, 377, 378
Commonwealth Economic Relations, 326
Commonwealth Education Conference, 122, 137, 140, 387–390
Commonwealth education funds, 119
Commonwealth Education Liaison Committee, 110, 122, 137
Commonwealth Education Liaison Unit (CELU), xiii, 122, 130, 137, 357, 360, 361, 390
Commonwealth and Empire Industries Association, 138
Commonwealth, European and Overseas Review, 142
Commonwealth evolution, 370
Commonwealth Fellowship, 138
Commonwealth finance and economic ministers' meetings, 122, 377
   finance ministers' meetings, 379
Commonwealth forces in the Far East, financing, 375
Commonwealth Forestry Association, 137–138
Commonwealth Forestry Institute, Oxford University, 138
Commonwealth Foundation, 123, 328
Commonwealth Games, 387, 388
Commonwealth geological liaison office, 121
Commonwealth geological survey, 121
Commonwealth gifts scheme, 363
Commonwealth grants and loans, 361
Commonwealth high commissioners in London, 139
   liaison, 393
Commonwealth Industries Association Ltd, 138
Commonwealth Information Centre (Marlborough House), 389, 390
Commonwealth Institute, 138–139, 147, 387–390
Commonwealth Institute of Entomology, 139
Commonwealth Journal, 153
Commonwealth League for Economic Co-operation, 130, 139
Commonwealth Liaison Committee, 110, 123, 375, 377, 378
Commonwealth liaison procedure, 363, 392, 396, 397
Commonwealth Medical Advisory Bureau, 130, 139
Commonwealth Medical Conference, 123
Commonwealth Migration Council Ltd, 130, 139
Commonwealth ministers' meetings, 387, 389
Commonwealth missions, 394
Commonwealth Mycological Institute, 140
Commonwealth of Australia *see* Australia
Commonwealth Office
   committees, 108
   Commonwealth Affairs officials, 93–94
   Departments and codes used jointly with

INDEX

Foreign Office and Diplomatic Service 1967–1968, 418–420
Dependent Territories Division, 8, 21
established (1966), 8, 28, 347
merger with Foreign Office (1968), 8, 28, 60
registration system, 60
Commonwealth Office Yearbooks, 66, 69, 108, 128
Commonwealth Organizations
 contributions to, 361
 privileges of, 385
Commonwealth Parliamentary Associations, 123, 140, 333, 338, 386–388, 393, 394
Commonwealth Policy and Planning Department, 418, 419
Commonwealth postal communications, 385
Commonwealth preference, 328, 329
Commonwealth Prime Ministers' and Trade Ministers' meetings, 28, 328, 370
Commonwealth Producers Organization, 140
Commonwealth projects, special, 388
Commonwealth publications, 382, 383
Commonwealth relations, general, 337
Commonwealth Relations Office (CRO)
 absorption of India Office, 7, 27–28
 advisers, 351
 advisory bodies, 108–127
 briefs, cataloguing of, 369
 confidential print, 59
 departments and records, 351–398
 file system, 59
 filing codes, 415–418
 liaison with Foreign Office, 8, 28, 387, 388
 library, 28, 367, 385
 merger with Colonial Office, 8, 21, 28, 47
 ministers, 88
 new name for Dominions Office, 7, 12, 27
 officials, 89–92
 organization, 28, 351
 records, and of predecessor, 56–61, 351
 reference list, 382, 393
 registers, registry, 59
 responsibilities, 7
 schedules for documents, 63
 Vote, payments from, 360
 Year Book, 385
Commonwealth Relations Office Departments
 Accountant-General's Department, 354, 359–361, 416
 Accounts Branch, 346
 Accounts Department, 346
 Accounts and Financial Departments, 346
 Administration Department, 91, 92, 370, 416
 Administration and Publicity Policy Section, 356, 386
 Administration Section, 356, 387
 Africa Departments, 354, 362–366
 Africa Economic Departments, 91, 92, 354, 366, 417
 Africa and General Division, 92, 351, 362
 Asia Economic Department, 92, 355, 377, 416
 Atlantic Department, 92, 354, 366–367
 British Information Services Section, 356, 386
 Central Africa Department, 91, 354, 362–363, 417

Central African and Territories Department, 89, 90, 354, 362
Colombo Plan Department, 90, 91, 355, 374
Commercial Policy Department, 92, 355, 378, 417
Commodities Department, 89, 90, 355, 379, 417
Common Market Department, 91, 355, 378–379, 417
Commonwealth Policy and Planning Department, 92, 355, 370
Communications Department, 63, 89–92, 355, 367, 417
Constitutional Departments, 89–92, 351, 355, 368–370, 417
Constitutional and Protocol Department, 92, 355, 370
Cultural Relations Department/Section, 91, 92, 356, 386–387, 389–391, 417
Defence Departments, 89–92, 355, 371–374, 417
Defence Supplies Department, 92, 355, 373
Defence and Western Department, 90, 91, 355, 371–372
Development Departments, 89, 90, 355, 374–375, 417
Development and Financial Policy and West Africa Economic Department, 354, 366
Development Policy and West and East Africa Economic Department, 92, 354, 363–364
East Africa Department, 91, 354, 364, 417
East Africa Economic Department, 92, 354, 363
East Africa Political Department, 92, 354, 364
East and General Africa Department, 91, 354, 363, 417
Eastern and General Africa Department, 417
Economic Departments, 355, 375–379
Economic Division, 362, 417
Economic General Department, 92, 355, 378
Economic Policy Department, 90, 91, 355, 377–378, 417
Economic Relations I Department, 90–92, 355, 375–376, 417
Economic Relations II Department, 90, 91, 355, 376–377, 417
Education Department, 91, 356, 391, 417
Establishment Department, 89–91, 417
Far East and Pacific Department, 91, 92, 355, 380–381, 417
Far Eastern Departments, 89, 90, 355–356, 380–381
Finance and Development Policy Department, 417
Finance and General Division, 359
Financial Policy Department, 91, 92, 355, 379
Food and Development Department, 417
General Departments, 89–91, 351, 356, 382–385
General and Migration Department, 92, 356, 385
Ghana Department, 90, 351, 354, 365, 417
Indian Records Section, 213
Information and Cultural Relations Department, 90, 91, 386–387
Information and Cultural Relations Division, 417
Information Departments and Sections, 89, 90, 356, 385–391

439

Information Overseas Section, 356, 386–387
Information Policy Department, 91, 92, 356, 387–390, 417
Information Policy and Cultural Relations Section, 356, 387
Information Services Department, 91, 92, 356, 388–391, 417
Information Services Section, 387
Inspectorate, 417
Irish Trade Negotiations Unit, 92, 355, 379
Joint Administration Department, 92, 356, 391
Joint Information Policy and Guidance Department, 92, 356, 391
Joint Malaysia/Indonesia Department, 92, 356, 381
Joint Protocol Department, 92, 357, 385, 394
Joint Research Department, 92, 356, 391
Kenya Department, 417
Latin America Department, 417
Malawi and Central Africa Economic Department, 92, 354, 364
Malawi and Zambia Department, 92, 354, 364
Malaya Department, 90, 91, 351, 356, 381, 417
Malta Department, 92, 356, 391
Mediterranean Department, 92, 356, 391
Middle East Departments, 90, 91, 356–357, 391–392, 417, 418
Migration and General Department, 90, 91, 356, 383
Nationality and Consular Department, 92, 356, 385
Nationality and General Department, 91, 92, 356, 384–385, 417
News Department, 91, 92, 356, 388–391, 417
News and Information Section, 356, 386
Nigeria Department, 91, 354, 365, 417
Oversea Finance Department, 89, 90, 355, 379, 417
Personnel Department, 91, 92, 417
Planning and Research Unit, 369, 417
Political Affairs Departments, 89, 92, 357, 392–393, 417
Political Division, 351
Political Staff Officers Department, 417
Press and Public Relations Section, 356, 387
Principal Staff Officers Department, 355, 373–374
Protocol Departments, 90, 357, 393–394, 417
Protocol and Nationality Department, 90, 357, 394
Public Relations Section, 356, 386–387
Publicity Policy Section, 356, 385–386
Raw Materials Department, 417
Records and Research Section, 356, 386
Rhodesia Department, 92, 354, 364–365
Services Department, 89, 90, 357, 394
South/Southern Africa Department, 354, 365, 417
South Asia Departments, 89, 91, 92, 357, 394–395
South Asia and Far Eastern Department, 90, 355, 380
South Asian and Middle East Department, 90, 357, 395

South-East Asia Department, 91, 418
Southern Africa Department, 91, 354, 365
Southern Rhodesia Department, 92, 354, 364
Southern Rhodesia and Communications Department, 418
Tanganyika and Somaliland Department, 423
Technical Assistance Department, 91, 355, 374–375, 418
Telegraph Section, 418
Trade Department, 89, 90, 355, 375, 418
United Nations Department, 90, 91, 357, 396–397, 418
United Nations, Western and Middle East Department, 92, 357, 392
United Nations and General Africa Department, 92, 354, 363
West Africa Department, 91, 92, 354, 365–366, 418
West Africa Economic Department, 92, 418
West and General Africa Department, 91, 92, 354, 365
West and General African Political Department, 354, 366
West Indies Departments, 91, 92, 357, 397–398, 418
Western Departments, 357, 398
Western Economic Department, 92, 355, 376, 418
Western and Middle East Department, 91, 92, 357, 392, 418
Western and United Nations Department, 89, 90, 357, 396
Zambia Department, 92, 354, 364
Commonwealth Relations Office List, 66, 69, 108, 128, 351, 367
Commonwealth Relations, Secretary of State for *see* Secretaries of State for Commonwealth Relations
Commonwealth representation in colonies, 368, 369
Commonwealth Scholarship Commission in the United Kingdom, 130, 140
Commonwealth Scholarship and Fellowship Plan, 137, 140
Commonwealth Scientific Committee, 113, 123
Commonwealth Scientific Liaison Offices, 113, 119, 129, 141
Commonwealth Secretariat, 8, 28, 122, 338, 370
  Education Division, 122
Commonwealth Shipping Committee, 109, 123
Commonwealth societies, 386, 387, 389
Commonwealth sporting events, 390
Commonwealth strategic reserve, 381
Commonwealth students, 382, 383
  see also welfare
Commonwealth sugar agreements, 148, 328
Commonwealth Survey, 386, 387
Commonwealth Teacher Training Bursary Scheme, 61
Commonwealth telecommunications, 385
Commonwealth Telecommunications Board (CTB), xiii, 110, 123, 325, 357, 367
Commonwealth Telecommunications Conference (1945), 123

Commonwealth Telegraphs Agreement (1948), 123
Commonwealth Today, 387, 388
Commonwealth touring exhibitions, 387–389
  see also exhibitions
Commonwealth trade, general, 145, 378
  and marketing, 122
Commonwealth trade commissioners, 338
Commonwealth Trade Department, 418
Commonwealth Trade and Economic Conference, Montreal (1958), 122
Commonwealth, tropical, 146
Commonwealth Trust, 384
Commonwealth Union of Trade, 138
Commonwealth Universities, Association of, 132, 140
Commonwealth visits, 370
  see also visits
Commonwealth War Graves Commission, 385
  see also war graves
Commonwealth weeks, 387–389
communications, 15, 317, 324, 325, 352, 353, 406
Communications Department *see* Colonial Office Subject Departments; Commonwealth Relations Office Departments
communism in Commonwealth countries, 367
community development, 112, 119, 141, 297, 342
  staff, 112
Community Development Bulletin, 141
Community Development Clearing House, 129, 141
commutations, 360, 361
companies, income tax, 151
Company of Merchants Trading to Africa, 53
compensation claims, 382–384
compensation for premature termination of employment, India and Burma, 360
Compensation (Ireland) Commission, 259
conditions of employment, 347
conditions of service, 15
  personnel on loan to Commonwealth countries, 371
Condon, Denis David, 94
conferences, 352, 359, 360, 382, 387
Conference of British Missionary Societies, 149
Conference of Engineering Institutions of the British Commonwealth, 129, 141
confidential print series *see* Colonial Office records
Congo, 366
Congo Basin treaties, 409
Congress, Library of, 55
congresses, 382
Connecticut, 31, 236
consecration of bishops, 333, 338
Conservative Commonwealth and Overseas Council, 130, 141–142
Conservative Overseas Bureau, 129, 141–142
Conservative Parliamentary Commonwealth Affairs Committee, 130, 142
Constitutional Departments *see* Commonwealth Relations Office Departments
constitutional developments, 314, 368–370, 372
constitutional and legal instruments, 331, 332, 368
constitutional matters, 352, 368–370
Constitutional Planning Department *see* Colonial Office Subject Departments
Constitutional and Protocol Department *see* Commonwealth Relations Office Departments
consular appointments, 382
consular commissions and exequaturs, 393
consular conventions, 382, 393
Consular Department, 419
consular instructions, 382, 384
consular matters, 331, 332, 338, 352
consular property, 395
consular protection of UK citizens, 385
consultants, 125, 374
conventions, 382, 383
convict settlements in the antipodes, 5
convicts, 228, 230, 233
Cook, Captain James, 224
Cook, Thomas Fotheringham, 72
co-operation, 126, 339, 340, 409
  adviser on, 99–106
  defence, 371
Co-operation in the Colonies, Advisory Committee on, 109, 111
Co-operation in the Colonies, Office Committee on, 109, 126
co-operative societies, 111
Co-operatives, Advisory Committee on, 110, 111
co-ordination inside the Economic Division, 326–328
co-ordination of defence matters, 372
co-ordination of legislative programme, 333
copper, trade, 375
copyright, 377, 378, 382, 383
Corfu, 265
Corona Club, 129, 142
Corona library, 334, 335
Coronation Department *see* Colonial Office Internal Services and other Departments
coronations, 352, 368
  military details, 371
corporal punishment, 338
corporation loans, 361
Corsica, 163, 263
  entry books, 263
Costar, Sir Norman (Edgar), (N E), 89–92
Costley-White, Cyril Grove, 89, 94
cotton, 327, 328, 339, 340, 376, 377, 379
cotton growing, 142
Cotton Research Corporation, 142
cotton textiles, 328, 376, 377
Council of Commonwealth Municipalities, 130, 142
Council for Education in the Commonwealth, 130, 142
Council of Europe, 326, 327, 329, 337, 392, 396
Council of Foreign Plantations, 2, 30
Council for Scientific and Industrial Research, 156
Council of State, standing committee on Trade and Foreign Affairs (1649–1652), 1
Council of Trade (1660), 2, 30
Council for Trade (1670), 2, 30
Council for Trade and Plantations (1672), 2, 30
countryside, 146
Courlanders, attempt to colonize Tobago, 255

Court of Justice, 338
court mourning, 393
courts, African, 117
Courtney, L H, 71
Cowell, Hubert Russell, 77, 78
Cox, Sir Christopher (William Machell), 14, 98–106
Cranborne, Viscount *see* Gascoyne-Cecil, Robert Arthur James, 5th Marquess of Salisbury
Cranwell, cadetships, 371
Crawley, Desmond John Chetwode, 90
Creasy, Sir Gerald Hallen, (G H), 73, 74, 78, 79
Creech Jones, Arthur, 71, 72
Creighton, J L, 101
Crewe-Milnes, Robert Offley Ashburton, Earl and Marquess of Crewe, 71
Crick, W F, papers, 54
Crimean War, 5
Croft, Sir William Dawson, 89
Crombie, George Edmond, 90
crop production, 152
crops, 409
Cross, B C H, 96, 99
Crosthwait, Timothy Leland, 91
Crown Agents for Oversea Governments and Administrations, 24, 142, 143, 151, 409
  see also Joint Agents General for the Crown Colonies
Crown Colony government, 5
Cruikshank, John Merrill, 99
Crutchley, Ernest Tristram, 87
Cuba, 185, 397
cultural activities, 156
cultural and artistic matters, 390
cultural conferences, 387
Cultural Relations Department/Section *see* Commonwealth Relations Office Departments; Foreign Office
cultural relations with Commonwealth countries, 133, 385–387, 389
cultural studies, 152
cultures, 146
Cumming-Bruce, F E H T, 89, 90
Cunliffe-Lister, Sir Philip, 1st Earl of Swinton, 71, 88
Curaçao, 163, 244
  entry books, 244
currency, 26, 117, 132, 133, 143, 151, 157, 244, 317, 330, 379, 409, 411
  hard currency, 20
Curson, Bernard Robert, 90, 92, 94
Customs, Board of, 5
customs and excise, 15, 324, 327–329, 343, 409, 414
  customs concessions, 373
  customs unions, 375
customs of the East, 152, 154
Customs Union Study Group, 329
Cyprus, 5, 73, 140, 163, 264, 268, 288, 296, 298, 304–306, 369, 371, 391, 406
  economy of, 376
  expenditure relating to posts, 360
  external affairs, 396
  foreign affairs of, 396
  funds for posts in, 361

  governor, Sir William Battershill, 16
  maps, 68
  police units, 361
  record classes, 264
  relations with, 391

Dahomey, 366
dairy products, trade, 339, 375, 376
Dairy Science, Bureau of, 136
Dairy Science and Technology, Bureau of, 136
Dakar, 18
Dale, Sir William (Leonard), (W L), 97–102
dangerous drugs, 331–333, 338
Darby, Lt-Colonel G, 101
Darnley, E R, 77
Dartmouth, 2nd Earl of *see* Legge, William
Dartmouth cadetships, 371
Davey, George, 90
David, Sir Edgeworth Beresford, (E B), 82
Davies, H E, 89–91
Davies, Kenneth Arthur, 106
Davis, Sir Charles Thomas, 86
Davis, T W, 80
Dawe, Sir Arthur James, (A J), 72–74, 78
De la Warr, 9th Earl *see* Sackville, Herbrand Edward Dundonald Brassey
De Worms, Baron Henry, later 1st Baron Pirbright, 71
deaths and injuries, 384
DeComarmond, J H, 100
decorations, 368, 369, 393, 394
  see also medals; honours
Deegan, Joseph William, 103–105
defence, 15, 24, 26, 28, 43, 314, 317, 330–332 346, 352, 406
  equipment, 371
  finance, 379
  finance regulations, 411
  of the Empire, 149
  organizations, 381
  policy, 145, 372, 373
  political aspects, 371, 372
  programmes, 371
  questions, 380, 391, 392
  science, 371
  security, 331, 332
  statistics, 372, 373
Defence Department *see* Colonial Office Subject Departments; Commonwealth Relations Office Departments; Foreign Office
Defence and Intelligence Departments *see* Colonial Office Subject Departments
Defence, Ministry of, 27, 371–373
Defence Supplies Department *see* Commonwealth Relations Office Departments
Defence and Western Department *see* Commonwealth Relations Office Departments
defoliants, 117
Delhi, 18
Demerara, 55, 240, 241
  see also British Guiana
demobilization and rehabilitation, 331

INDEX

demography, 146, 341
　adviser on, 96, 99
Denmark, 332
　acquires St Thomas, 253
　Heligoland captured from, 258
　in Gold Coast, 199
　loans for St Thomas and St John, 253
　purchases St Croix, 251
dental services, 125
Departmental Records, Committee on (Grigg Committee, 1954), 63–64
Departments *indexed under key word of title*
Departments 1, 2, 3, 4, 5 *see* Colonial Office Geographical Departments
Departments A, B, C, D, E, F *see* Dominions Office
dependencies, 409
Dependent Territories Constitution Division, 419
deportation, 314, 351, 352, 369, 370, 382, 384, 385, 394
Deputy permanent secretaries of overseas development, 95
Deputy under-secretaries of state for the colonies, 50, 72
Deputy under-secretaries of state for Commonwealth Affairs, 93
Deputy under-secretaries of state for Commonwealth Relations, 89
Deputy under-secretaries of state for Dominions Affairs, 86
Derby, Earls of *see* Stanley
Desecretization Committee, 50, 60, 63–64
designs, 331, 382
despatches, printing and distribution, 368, 369
detention and deportation, 332
development and aid policies, 379
Development Assistance Committee (DAC), xiii, 328, 357
Development Assistance Group, 327
Development Commission, 155
development corporations *see* statutory development corporations
Development Departments *see* Commonwealth Relations Office Departments
development finance, 377
development and planning, 319, 408
development planning adviser *see* Colonial Office
development plans, 330
development policy, 363
Development Policy Departments *see* Commonwealth Relations Office Departments
development programmes, 137
development projects, 156
development schemes, 413
development of secondary industries, 339
development and welfare
　payments, 361
　schemes, 235, 330
　see also colonial development and welfare
Devonshire, Dukes of *see* Cavendish
Dickson-Poynder, Sir John Poynder, Baron Islington, 72
Diggines, Christopher Ewart, 92, 94
Dindings, the, 208

diplomatic and consular appointments, 352, 370, 382, 394
diplomatic and consular immunities and privileges, 337, 338, 370, 393, 394
diplomatic and consular property, 394
diplomatic lists, 394
diplomatic mail, 360, 361
Diplomatic Privileges Act (1964), 385
diplomatic questions relating to war preparation, 353
Diplomatic Service Administration Office, 8, 60, 418–420
diplomatic and social list, 382, 393
Directorate of Colonial (Geodetic and Topographic) Surveys, 143
Directorate of Overseas Surveys, 21, 61, 129, 143
directors of plans, 323
disability cases, 360, 361
disarmament, 325, 326, 352, 372, 392, 396
Disarmament Commission, 396
discipline, 347
Discovery Committee, 14, 124, 125
diseases, 124, 138, 139, 383
displaced persons, 331, 332
display strips, 388
distribution of goods, standing committee on, 170
distribution of information, 388, 389
Dixey, Sir Frank, (F), 99–105
Dixon, Sir Charles William, 87, 89, 90
doctors, visiting UK, 139
Dodds-Parker, Sir (Arthur) Douglas, (A D), 88
Dominica, 136, 163, 244–245, 248, 257, 289, 301, 406
　record classes, 245
　see also Leeward Islands; West Indies; Windward Islands
Dominican Republic, 397
Dominions Correspondence series, 56, 168–169
Dominions, correspondence through high commissioners, 57
Dominions Division *see* Colonial Office
Dominions General, record class, 167–169
Dominions Office (DO)
　Accounts Branch, 11
　advisory bodies, 108–127
　becomes Commonwealth Relations Office (1947), 7, 12, 27
　Central Opening Section, 11
　confidential print, 60–61
　correspondence with dominions, 57
　created (1925), 6, 11, 23
　departmental business, breakdown, 352–354
　departments and records, 351–398
　Departments A, B, C, 23, 352
　Departments D, E, F, 353
　destruction schedules, 63
　file system, 56, 58
　functions, 24, 26, 27
　Information Department, 352
　involvement in Second World War exchange control, supply, productions, 27
　Library, 11
　officials, 86–87
　organization, 23, 24, 351

Overseas Settlement Department, 158, 349
printing policy, 60
Printing Unit, 11
private office papers, 53
registration, registry, 43, 56–58, 66
Revision of Records Branch, 11
secret correspondence, 60
shared services with Colonial Office, 6, 11, 347
single dominions correspondence series, 56–57, 66
subject files and sub-files, 58–59
Supply Department, 352
Telegraph Section, 11
Whitley Council, 11
Dominions Office and Colonial Office List, 66, 108, 128
Dorman, Sir Maurice Henry, (M H), 81
Douglas-Home, Sir Alexander Frederick, 14th Earl of Home, later Baron Home of the Hirsel, 88
Downie, Sir Harold Frederick, (H F), 78, 79
Downshire, 1st Marquess of *see* Hill, Wills
drainage *see* irrigation
drugs, 136
Drummond, John David, 17th Earl of Perth, 71
Dublin Castle, 259
Dudley, Sir Alan Alves, 95
Duff, Sir (Arthur) Anthony, (A A), 94
Dufferin and Ava, Marquess of *see* Hamilton-Temple-Blackwood, Basil Sheridan
Dugdale, John, 71
Duncan, Sir Harold Handasyde, (H H), 97, 98
Dundas, Henry, 1st Viscount Melville, 70
Dunk, George Montagu, 2nd Earl of Halifax, 3
Dunlop, Major-General Dermott, 101–107
Dunraven, Earl of *see* Quin, Windham Thames Wyndham
Dutch
annexe St Helena, 224
attempt to colonize Tobago, 255
capture Curaçao, 244
claim to New Guinea, 281
expelled from Virgin Islands, 243
Gold Coast settlements, 199
government, Caribbean Commission, 235
jointly occupy St Croix, 251
loans for St Thomas and St John, 253
Netherlands East Indies, 207
occupy Malacca, 215, 221
occupy St Eustatius, 251
settle Mauritius, 261
settlements in Ceylon, 209
Surinam ceded to, 254
suzerainty of Selangor, 220
Dutch East India Company, 173
Dutch Guiana, 4
Dutch West India Company, 240
records surrendered to UK, 55, 241
Dutton, James Macfarlane, 92

East Africa, 150, 163, 189, 297, 406
Civil Supplies Board, 189
Conference of Governors, 17, 189
defence arrangements, 364
defence and security, 297
economic and financial questions, 366
Economic and Fiscal Commission, 189
foreign territories in, 363, 365
history and archaeology, 134
record classes, 43, 47–48, 189
region, 163, 189–196
Royal Commission, 189
transport, 297
East Africa Council for Medical Research, 117
East Africa Economic Department *see* Commonwealth Relations Office Departments
East Africa High Commission, 181, 190
record classes, 190
East Africa Political Department *see* Commonwealth Relations Office Departments
East Africa Protectorate, 163, 190–191, 194, 195, 296
see also Kenya
East African Common Services Organization (EACSO), xiii, 189, 190, 297, 363, 364
East African Community, 189
East African Currency Board, 129, 143
East African Department *see* Colonial Office Geographical Departments; Commonwealth Relations Office Departments
East African Federation, 364
East African Inter-Territorial Languages Committee, 190
East African Literature Bureau, 190
East African and Mediterranean Department *see* Colonial Office Geographical Departments
East African Posts and Telegraphs, 190
East African Production and Supply Council, 189, 409
East African services, 363
East African Veterinary Research Organization, 190
East African War Supplies Board, 189
East and Central African Department *see* Colonial Office Geographical Departments
East and Central African transport, 297
East and General Africa Department *see* Commonwealth Relations Office Departments
East and West Africa, 41, 55
East India Association, 128, 143–144, 154
East India Company *see* British East India Company
East Indies papers, calendar, 65
East, Kenneth Arthur, 91, 92
East-West Department, 418
East-West relations, 392
East-West trade and strategic contols, 378
Eastern, Confidential Print series, 52
Eastern correspondence, 43, 47–48, 406, 409
Eastern Department *see* Colonial Office Geographical Departments
Eastern Group Supply Council, Delhi, 18
Eastwood, Christopher Gilbert, 74–77, 79, 80
ecclesiastical questions, 322, 382, 383
ecclesiastical returns, 263
ecology, 143
economic advice and assistance, 328, 329

Economic Advisory Council/Committee, 120, 410
  Committee on Locust Control, 131
economic affairs, 145
Economic Commission for Africa (ECA), xiii, 323, 327, 329, 358, 363, 366, 377
Economic Commission for Asia and the Far East (ECAFE), xiii, 323, 326, 327, 329, 358, 375–377, 410
Economic Commission for Europe (ECE), xiii, 323, 329, 377
Economic Commission for Latin America (ECLA), xiii, 323, 327, 329
economic consultation, 122
economic co-operation, 139, 235
Economic Co-operation, Committee on, 26
Economic Co-operative Acts, 410
Economic correspondence, 406–415
economic data, 139
Economic Departments, Division, Section see Colonial Office Subject Departments; Commonwealth Relations Office Departments
economic dependencies (correspondence), 410
economic development, 15, 115, 139, 142, 146, 149, 157
economic entomology, 139
economic and financial adviser, 97, 98
Economic General Departments see Colonial Office Subject Departments; Commonwealth Relations Office Departments
economic intelligence and analysis, 327
Economic Intelligence Departments see Colonial Office Subject Departments
economic liaison, 329
Economic Liaison Officers, 100, 101, 315
economic measures to deter aggression, 340
economic planning, programming, research and development, 17, 21, 315, 316, 326, 410
economic plants, 124
economic policy, 115
Economic Policy Department see Commonwealth Relations Office Departments
economic possibilities of empire, 157
economic problems, 123, 138
economic provisions, 407, 410
economic questions, 331, 352, 353
economic relations (correspondence), 406, 419
Economic Relations Department see Colonial Office Subject Departments; Commonwealth Relations Office Departments
economic research
  projects, 341
  regional institutes, 115
  and statistics, 115
  and surveys, 326
Economic and Social Council (United Nations Organization) (ECOSOC), xiv, 323, 326, 327, 329, 336–338, 358, 363, 397
economic studies, 152
Economic Survey of Colonial Territories, 326
Economic Survey of the Empire, 409
economic surveys, 329
economic trade and progress, 326, 327
Economic Warfare, Ministry of, 27

economics of tropical Commonwealth, 146
Economists Branch, 76, 418
Eden, Robert Anthony, (R A), 1st Earl of Avon, 86
Edmonds, Edward Reginald, 80–84
Edmonds, Robert Humphrey Gordon, 94
education, 122, 124, 133, 146, 153, 317, 320, 331, 342, 353, 382, 386
  adult education, 124
  higher education, 119, 123, 131, 147, 297, 362
  mass education, 119–120
Education in the Colonies, Advisory Committee on, 14, 111–112, 120
  Higher Education and Recruitment and Training of Women in the Education Service sub-committees, 111
Education, Consultative Panel on, 110, 124
Education Department see Commonwealth Relations Office Departments
Education, Minister of, 139, 148
Education and Science, Department of, specialized agencies, 8
Education in Tropical Areas, Department of, at the University of London Institute of Education, 141
educational adviser, 14, 98–106, 147
educational conferences, 387–390
educational co-operation with Commonwealth countries, 137, 361, 387–390
educational films, 135
educational grants, 382
educational problems, 142
educational projects, 157
educational questions, 111, 338
educationalists, 142
Egypt, 10, 33, 392, 395, 396
  captures Sudan, 192
  claim to Somaliland, 192
  relations through Foreign Office, 10
Ehrhardt, A, 96, 97
Eire see Irish Republic
electric and water power schemes, 339
electricity undertakings, 137
Eleuthera, 237
Elgin, Earl of see Bruce, Victor Alexander
Elliott, Sir Gilbert, 263
Ellis, Joseph Stanley, 91, 92
Ellis, Walter Devonshire, 77
Ellis, Wellbore, 1st Baron Mendip, 70
Emanuel, Aaron, 81–84
emergency communications, 373
emergency controls, 16
emergency legislation, 332, 368
emergency powers, 325
emergency regulations, 336
Emery, Eleanor Jean, 91, 92
Emigrants Commission, 128, 144
Emigrants Information Office, 63, 128, 144, 349
emigration, 126, 149, 272, 331–333, 384, 385
  registers, 35, 230
  restrictions, 368–370, 394
Emigration Commission, 349
Emigration Departments see Colonial Office Internal Services and other Departments
Emly, Baron see Monsell, William

Emmott, Alfred, 1st Baron Emmott, 72
Empire Air Mail Service, 27
Empire Cotton Growing Association, 129, 142, 144
Empire Forestry Association, 129, 137–138, 144
Empire Forestry Conference and Standing Committee on Empire Forestry, 109, 113, 124
Empire Industries Association, 129, 138, 144
Empire Marketing Board, 26, 126, 129, 144, 353
  posters, 67
  records, 63, 169
Empire Parliamentary Association, 129, 140, 144
empire settlement, 332
Empire Settlement Act (1922), 349
employment, 383
  prospects overseas, 158
  terms of, 115
Employment in the United Kingdom of Surplus Colonial Labour, Working Party on, 110, 127
Emrys-Evans, Paul Vychan, 86
Enderby, Samuel, Samuel and Charles, whalers, 226
enemy alien prisoners of war, 339
enemy (correspondence), 410
enemy property, 331, 343
engineering adviser, 102–106
engineering appointments adviser, 96, 104–106
engineering contracts, 143
engineering development, 137
Engineering Institutions of the British Commonwealth, Conference of, 129, 141
English Royal Show (1957), 152
English-Speaking Union, 158
English, teaching of, 133, 389, 390
Enosis (Greek Cypriot movement for union with Greece), 264
Enquiries and Casualties Branch *see* Colonial Office Subject Departments
entertainment fund, 361
Entomological Research Committee, 109, 124–125
entomology, 139
Entomology, Institute of (Trinidad), 136
entry books, 30, 32, 39, 40, 66, 162, 164–287 passim
Enugu (Nigeria), 334
equality, men and women, 137
Equatorial Africa, political affairs, 363, 366
equipment
  provision of, 374
  and training, 390
Essequibo, 55, 240, 241
Establishment Department *see* Colonial Office Internal Services and other Departments; Commonwealth Relations Office Departments
Establishment and Organization Department *see* Colonial Office Internal Services and other Departments
establishments, 346, 352, 353
estates, 382, 383
estimates, 359, 360, 387, 388
Estimates, Select Committee on (1959–1960), 7
Ethiopia (Abyssinia), 297, 395
ethnology, 146, 341

Europe, 258–260, 396
  defence, 396
  Eastern, 372
  foreign affairs, 386
  Southern, foreign affairs, 396
  Western and Northern, 396
  Western and Southern, 372, 392
  Whitehall's increasing involvement with (1950s), 28
European Atomic Energy Community (EURATOM), xiv, 323, 328, 379
European Coal and Steel Community (ECSC), xiv, 323, 328, 358, 375, 377, 379
European Common Market, 329, 330
European communities, 378
European Community and Free Trade Area, 327, 377, 378
European Customs Union, 377
European Defence Community (EDC), xiv, 358, 396
European Economic Community (EEC), xiv, 323, 328, 329, 358, 375, 377, 378
European economic questions, 328, 329
European Free Trade Area (EFTA), xiv, 323, 328, 329, 358
European international relations/colonial questions, 5
European Launcher Development Organization (ELDO), xiv, 358, 367
European Payments Union, 377
European Political Community (EPC), xiv, 358, 396
European Recovery Programme (ERP), 122, 323, 329, 410
European Space Research Organization (ESRO), xiv, 358, 367
evacuation of children to dominions, 135
Evans, Frederick, 422
Evans, Sir (Sydney) Harold, (S H), 82, 83
exchange of classified military information, 371–373
exchange control, 27, 315, 316, 327–329, 343, 377–379
exchange rates, 411
Exchequer and Audit Act (1866), 36, 346
Exchequer loans, 336, 361
executive councils, 39, 52, 64, 162
ex-enemy property, 330
exhibitions, 135, 139, 153, 382, 383, 386–388, 390, 391, 410
  and trade fairs, 377, 378
expeditions, 385
exploration, 14, 153, 170
Export Credits Guarantee Department, 328
Export Policy, Committee on, 328
exports, 132, 149
  export credits, 327, 363, 366, 378, 379
  export licences, 413
  export promotion, 132, 328
ex-servicemen's organizations, 133
extradition, 314, 333, 382, 383

Faber, Richard Stanley, 94
factels, 388

INDEX 447

Fairclough, Anthony John, 85, 86, 94
Faisal, Sharif, king of Iraq, 269
Falkland Islands and Dependencies, 76, 163, 223–224, 280, 289, 297, 298, 300–302, 304–307, 406
  record classes, 224
Falkland Islands, Committee for Research in the Dependencies of the, 109, 119, 125
Falkland Islands Dependencies, research sponsored by Discovery Committee, 14
Falkland Islands Dependencies Scientific Bureau, 130, 144
Falkland Islands Dependencies Scientific Committee, 124, 125, 154
Falkland Islands Dependencies Survey, 125, 130, 144, 304
Falkland Islands, St Helena and Tristan da Cunha Department *see* Colonial Office Geographical Departments
family pensions, 359–361
Far East/South-East Asia, 163
  Commonwealth relations in, 380, 381
  record classes, 48, 206–208
Far East, minister of state resident in, 17, 207
Far East and Pacific Departments *see* Commonwealth Relations Office Departments
Far Eastern Department *see* Colonial Office Geographical Departments; Commonwealth Relations Office Departments
Far Eastern Economic and Supplies Committee, 208
Far Eastern Reconstruction, record class, 48
farmers, young, 152
farming, 155
Farquharson, Sir James (Robbie), 106
feature articles, 386–388, 390
feature films, 388, 390
federal legislation, Africa, 362
Federal Public Service, 362
Federal Review Conference (1962), 362
federal/territorial relations, 362
Federated Malay States *see* Malay States, Federated
Federation of Arab Emirates of the South, later Federation of South Arabia, later the People's (Democratic) Republic of South Yemen, 343
Federation of British Industry (FBI), xiv, 138, 358
  scholarships, 375, 376
Federation of Commonwealth Chambers of Commerce, 144–145
Federation of Malaya *see* Malaya
Federation of Rhodesia and Nyasaland *see* Rhodesia and Nyasaland
Federation of the West Indies *see* West Indies
fellowships, 134
Ferguson, D S, 106
Fernando Po, 163, 198, 204
  record classes, 198
fertilizers, 379
festivals, 388
fibres, 327, 339, 340
Fiddes, Sir George Vandeleur, 72
Fiddian, A F, 77, 78
Figg, Sir Clifford, 98, 99

Fiji, 6, 7, 136, 164, 167, 206, 226, 280, 282–283, 286, 289, 298, 305–308, 406
  Fiji Constitutional Conference sound recordings, 283
  record classes, 283
  responsibility of Foreign Office, 7
  South Pacific Office original correspondence, 48, 283
Fijian Affairs Board, 283
film production, adviser on, 104–106
films, 133, 135, 331, 335, 373, 386–391
  exhibitions, 333
  film strips, 333, 334
finance, 15, 26, 319, 330
  of colonial forces, 332
  correspondence, 407, 411
Finance Department *see* Colonial Office Subject Departments
Finance and Development Department *see* Colonial Office Subject Departments
Finance and Development Policy Department *see* Commonwealth Relations Office Departments
Finance and Economic Department *see* Colonial Office Subject Departments
Finance and General Division *see* Commonwealth Relations Office Departments
Finance and Honours Department *see* Colonial Office Internal Services and other Departments
financial adviser, 79, 97, 98, 316
financial arrangements, 413
Financial Committee, Standing, 109, 127
Financial Department *see* Colonial Office Internal Services and other Departments
financial matters, 124
financial policy, 15, 379
Financial Policy Department *see* Commonwealth Relations Office Departments
fnancial problems, 123
financial questions, general, 127, 330
finding aids, 65–66
Finland, 392
fire services *see* police and fire services
First World War, 6
fish, trade, 375, 409
Fisher, Sir Nigel (Thomas Loveridge), (N), 72, 88
Fisher, Sir (Norman Fenwick) Warren: Warren Fisher Committee (interdepartmental Colonial Services Committee), 15
fisheries, 110, 115, 137, 340, 385
  adviser, 97–106
  research, 155, 341, 342
  resources, 339
  and whaling, 125, 226, 382
Fitzclarence, Sir Geoffrey William Richard Hugh, 5th Earl of Munster, 72, 194
flags, 331–333, 338, 368, 369, 393
flies, biting, 124
Flood, John Ernest William, 77, 78
flora and fauna, 297, 382, 383
  advice, 105, 106
floras, forest, 138
Florida, East and West, records sub-divisions, 236

Foggon, George, 104–106
food, 379
  commodities, 379, 409
  gifts, 379
  production, 113
  supplies, 207, 407
  technology, 131, 148
  utilitarian crops, 412
  wartime adviser on, 96, 98, 99
Food and Agriculture Organization (United Nations Organization) (FAO), xiv, 155, 318, 323, 328, 329, 340, 358, 363, 377–379, 410, 413
Food and Development Department *see* Commonwealth Relations Office Departments
Food, Ministry of, 27, 117
  minister of food, 150
foodstuffs, 27, 136, 138, 150
Ford Foundation, 149
Ford, Joseph Francis, 94
foreign affairs, liaison, etc, 352, 386, 387
Foreign Affairs Forum for Parliamentary Candidates (Conservative), 142
Foreign and Commonwealth Office merger (1968), 8, 28
foreign consuls, 338
foreign decorations, 393
foreign investment, 327, 328
Foreign Office (FO), xiv, 5, 24, 25, 28, 34, 64, 358
  Barbary Coast relations, 53
  Cultural Relations Department, 418
  Defence Department, 420
  departmental filing codes, 418–420
  dominions matters, 6
  Library Department, 419
  maps and plans, 68
  merger with Commonwealth Office, 60
  News Department, 419
  posts, claims from, 360
  prints and telegram distribution, 363, 396
  protectorates, 5
  registration system, 60
  responsibilities transferred to Ministry of Overseas Development, 8
  wartime telegrams and military reports, 27
foreign orders, 368
Foreign Plantations, Committee for, 2
Foreign Plantations, Council of, 2
foreign service officers, 146
foreign service orders, 393
forestry, 15, 113, 114, 137, 138, 155, 340, 383, 411
  adviser, 99–106
  correspondence, 411
  library, 138
  products, 135
  research, 115, 138, 341
  resources, 339
Forestry Bureau, 136
formal instruments
  accreditation for ambassadors, 394
  drafting of, 346
formalities, 370
Formosa, Commonwealth relations with, 380
Forster, William Edward, 71

Fortescue, Chichester Samuel, (C S), afterwards Parkinson-Fortescue, Baron Carlingford, 71
fortnightly summaries, printing and distribution, 368, 369
Foster, Sir John (Galway), (J G), 88
Foster, Robert Spence, 99
Foulger, Robert Edward, 101
Foundation for Mutual Assistance in Africa (South of the Sahara) (FAMA), xiv, 323, 327, 358, 374
foundations, 390
Fourah Bay College, Sierra Leone, 111
Fowler, Sir Robert (William Doughty), (R W), 89, 90
Foxlee, Richard William, 102
France
  acquires Grenada, 245
  acquires St Croix, 251
  aggression, West Africa, 206
  Anglo-French joint naval commission in New Hebrides, 285
  annexes Seychelles, 262
  besieges Gibraltar, 264
  captures Antigua and Montserrat, 236
  captures Ionian Islands, 265
  captures Malta, 266
  captures Minorca, 267
  cedes Gambia, 198
  claims Falklands, 223
  claims St Lucia, 252
  claims St Vincent, 253
  colonial ministry, liaison with, 336
  colonizes Acadia, 274, 276
  colonizes Guadeloupe, 246
  drives Britain out of St Eustatius, 251
  fall of (1940), 317
  government, member of the Caribbean Commission, 235
  government support for International African Institute, 146
  holds Martinique, 249
  in Canada, 273, 274
  influence in Togoland, 205
  jointly occupies Santo Domingo, 254
  mandate, Cameroons, 197
  occupies Corsica, 263
  occupies Mauritius, 261
  occupies Perim Island, 268
  possessions in India, 394
  recognizes British sovereignty in Hudson's Bay, 276
  settles Dominica, 244
  settles Newfoundland, 277
  settles part of St Christopher, 250
  settles Prince Edward Island, 274
  Tobago surrendered to, 255
  troops, 197, 205
  Vichy administration, 317
  war with, 4
  West African territories, 196
Fraser, Sir Hugh (Charles Patrick Joseph), 72
Fraser, James Duncan, 92
Fraser River, 273
Fraser, General Simon Joseph, 14th Baron Lovatt, 12, 86
Free Church of Scotland, mission, 178

INDEX

free enterprise, 138
Free French, 317
freedom of cities, 369, 393
Freeston, Sir (Leslie) Brian, 78
Freetown, 198
French Cameroons, 197
French East India Company, 261
French Relations Department *see* Colonial Office Subject Departments
French Resistance, Cabinet Committee on, 317
French West India Company, 252
Frisian constitution of Heligoland, 258
fruit, fruit trade, 327, 328, 329, 340, 375
  see also citrus
fuel research, 120, 121
fugitive offenders, 339, 382–384
Fugitive Offenders Act, 385
full powers, 393
functional commissions, political aspects of work, 337, 338
fungi, diseases caused by, 140
fungicides and herbicides research, 117, 341
Furse, Major Sir Ralph Dolignon, 12, 15, 77–80, 100
further education
  grants, 382
  and vocational training, 344

Gallagher, Francis George Kenna, 92, 94
Galsworthy, Sir Arthur (Norman), (A N), 72, 75, 76, 80–82, 93
Gambia, 5, 76, 125, 157, 163, 198–199, 204, 289, 297–300, 303–305, 363, 406
  record classes, 199
  relations with, 366
game preservation, 297, 341
Gandee, John Stephen, 91, 92
Garner, Sir Saville, (J J S), 89, 93
Garnett, Walter James, 89
Garrat, O V, 105, 106
Garson, Alexander Denis, 80–84
gas undertakings, 137
Gascoyne-Cecil, Robert Arthur James, Viscount Cranborne, 5th Marquess of Salisbury, 71, 86, 88
Gater, Sir George Henry, 72
gazettes *see* Colonial Office records
General Agreement on Tariffs and Trade (GATT), xiv, 323, 324, 327–329, 343, 358, 375, 377, 378, 410
General Departments/Division *see* Colonial Office Subject Departments; Commonwealth Relations Office Departments
General and Migration Department *see* Commonwealth Relations Office Departments
Genoese, held Corsica, 263
Gent, Sir (Gerard) Edward (James), (G E), 73, 74, 78, 79
geodetic and topographical surveys, 143, 341
geography, 157
  of empire, 157
geological adviser and director of Colonial/Overseas Geological Surveys, 99–106, 150

geological questions, 118
geological service, 15
geological surveys, 112, 121, 150, 320, 339–341, 412
geologist, principal, 99
geology, 143, 150
geomorphology, 143
geophysical questions, 118
George V, king of England, coronation, 140
George, Tupou I, king of Tonga, 286
Georgia, records sub-division, 236
Germain, George Sackville, 1st Viscount Sackville, 70
German New Guinea Company, 285
Germany, 182
  annexes Nauru, 284
  Cameroons, 197
  claims Uganda, 194
  claims Zanzibar, 195
  Gold Coast, 199
  Heligoland ceded to, 195, 258
  influence in Togoland, 205
  move into Rhineland, 26
  parts of former empire 'mandated' to Britain, 6, 184, 193, 205, 282, 285, 423–424
  South West Africa, 184
  Tanganyika, 193
  transfer of some Solomon Islands, 282
Ghana, 157, 163, 199, 200, 351, 360, 363, 365, 366, 378
  funds for posts in, 360, 361
  loans and financial agreements with, 376
  Kumasi College of Technology, 111
  registration procedures (births, marriages and deaths), 369, 370, 384, 394
  taxation questions, 376
  technical assistance policy, 374
  see also Gold Coast
Ghana Department *see* Commonwealth Relations Office Departments
Gibraltar, 4, 35, 163, 263–265, 289, 296–299, 304–307, 406
  maps, 68
  record classes, 265
  relations with, 391
Gibraltar and South Atlantic Department, 420
Gibson, J P, 89, 90
Gibson, Sir Leslie Bertram, 101
Gidden, Barry Owen Barton, 82, 84, 85
gifts, 382–385, 393
Gilbert and Ellice Islands, 164, 280, 283–284
  record classes, 284
  see also Kiribati; Tuvalu; Western Pacific; Western Pacific High Commission
Gladstone, William Ewart, 70, 71
Glendevon, 1st Baron *see* Hope, Lord John Adrian
Glenelg, Baron *see* Grant, Charles
global strategy, 372, 373
Glover, W E, 98
Goderich, Viscount *see* Robinson, Frederick John, later 1st Earl of Ripon
Gold Coast, 5, 125, 163, 197, 199–201, 204, 205, 289, 297–300, 303, 305, 406
  Commission of Inquiry into Disturbances

(Watson Commission), 200
   governor of, 16
   Information Office, 334
   record classes, 200
   see also Ghana
Gold Coast, Eastern Province of, 205
Gold Coast and Mediterranean Department see
   Colonial Office Geographical Departments
Gold Coast Northern Territories, 163, 199, 201,
   205, 299
gold
   discovery of, 273
   trade, 366, 375, 379
Golds, Anthony Arthur, 91, 92
Gordon, George Hamilton, 4th Earl of Aberdeen,
   70
Gordon-Smith, David Gerard, 101, 107
Gordon-Walker, Patrick Chrestien, 88
Goree, 204
Gorell Barnes, Sir William (Lethbridge), (W L), 72,
   74–76
Gorsuch, L H, 81
Goulburn, Henry, 4
government, 146
Government Emigration Committee, 109, 125, 349
government gazettes see Colonial Office records
government hospitality, 393
governors, 3, 15, 16, 30–32, 361, 368, 369, 393
   conferences, regional, 17
   pensions, 165, 346, 348
   royal instructions to, 393
governors-general, 24, 57, 368, 369, 393
   position of, 24
   see also governors
Governors' Pensions Act (1865), 348
Graham Land, 224
grains, trade in, 376
Grant, Charles, Baron Glenelg, 70
Grant Duff, Sir Mountstuart Elphinstone, 71
grants, 164
Granville, Earls see Leveson-Gower
grasshoppers, 131
Great Trek, 179, 186
Greece
   Ionian Islands ceded to, 54, 265
   recognizes British annexation of Cyprus, 264
Green, J F, 77, 78
Greene, H, 104–107
Greenhill, B J, 91, 92
Greenwood, Anthony, 71, 95
Grenada, 136, 163, 245–246, 259, 289, 301, 406
   record classes, 246
   see also West Indies; Windward Islands
Grenadines, 163, 246
   see also St Vincent
Grenville, Richard Plantagenet Campbell Temple
   Nugent Brydges Chandos, 3rd Duke of
   Buckingham and Chandos, 70
Grenville, William Wyndham, Baron Grenville, 70
Grey, Sir George, 70, 71
Grey, Henry George, Viscount Howick, later 3rd
   Earl Grey, 70, 71
Gribble, G R, 103, 107
Griffiths, James, 71

Grindle, Sir Gilbert Edmund Augustine, 73
Griqualand West, 162, 176, 289, 298
   record classes, 176
Grossmith, Caryll Archibald, 80, 81, 423
Grotius Society, 134
Guadeloupe, 163, 246–247
   record classes, 246–247
Guatemala, settlement of claim to Belize, 242
Guidance Department, 419
Guilford, 2nd Earl of see North, Frederick
Guinea, 366
Guinness, Walter Edward, 1st Baron Moyne, 71,
   235
Gulf of Aden and General Department see Colonial
   Office Subject Departments
gums, 327, 339, 340
Gurkha
   air trooping, 372
   recruitment, 380, 395
Guyana, 163, 241, 247
   see also British Guiana
Gwadur, 380, 395
Gwilliam, Miss F H , 99–106

Hacking, Douglas Hewitt, 1st Baron Hacking, 86
Hague, Rijksarchief at The, 55, 241
Hailey, William Malcolm, 1st Baron Hailey, 14,
   113, 116
   committee on colonial post-war problems, 413
   papers, 170
Haiti, 254, 397
Hale, E, 424
Halifax, 2nd Earl see Dunk, George Montagu
Hall, D W, 102, 104–106
Hall, G H, 71, 72
Hall, Harold Percival, 83–86, 93
Hamilton, Sir Robert William, 72
Hamilton, William Aitken Brown, 89, 93
Hamilton-Temple-Blackwood, Basil Sheridan,
   Marquess of Dufferin and Ava, 72
Hampshire, Sir (George) Peter, (G P), 89–91
Hampton, 1st Baron see Pakington, Sir John
   Somerset
Hankey, Sir Maurice Pascal Alers, 1st Baron
   Hankey, 6
Hankinson, Sir Walter Crossfield, (W C), 87
Harcourt, Lewis, 71
Harding, Sir (Alfred) John, (A J), 77
Harding, Sir Edward John, (E J), 86, 87
Harding, Hugh Alastair, 81–85
hardware, 27
Hare, John Hugh, 1st Viscount Blakenham, 71
Hare, William Francis, 5th Earl of Listowel, 71
Harlech, 4th Baron see Ormsby-Gore, William
   George Arthur
Harlow, Frederick James, 100–103
Harrison, Francis Anthony Kitchener, 90–92
Harrison, J A, 104–106
Hart, Dame Judith (Constance Mary), 93
Hart, W H, 99
Hartington, Marquess of see Cavendish, Edward
   William Spencer
Hastings, W G W, 99
Havana, 163, 247

INDEX

original correspondence, 247
Hawes, Sir Benjamin, (B), 71
Hay, James, Earl of Carlisle, granted Dominica (1627), 244
Hay, R W, 53, 72
Head, W G, 90
headmasters, 157
Heaf, Frederick Roland George, 104
health, 15, 153
  education, 134
Heddy, Brian Huleatt, 94
Heligoland, 4, 163, 195, 258, 289, 297, 298, 301, 303, 307
  maps, 68
  papers, 54–55
  record classes, 258
helminthiasis, 117
Helminthology, Bureau of, 136
Henderson, A, 88
Hennessey, Robert Samuel Fleming, 99
Hennings, John Dunn, 92
Herbert, Auberon Thomas, Baron Lucas, 72
Herbert, Henry Howard Molyneux, 4th Earl of Carnarvon, 49, 54, 70, 71
Herbert, Sir Robert George Wyndham, 72
Herbert, Sidney, 1st Baron Herbert of Lea, 70
herbicides *see* fungicides
Herklots, Geoffrey Alton Craig, 101
Hewins, William Albert Samuel, 72
Hibbert, J G, 80–82
Hickling, Charles Frederick, 99–106
Hicks-Beach, Sir Michael Edward, 1st Earl of Aldwyn, 70
hides and skins, trade, 136, 328, 339, 376, 377, 409
High Commission territories, 182, 417
high commissioners, 24, 57, 369, 393, 394
  as representative of British government, 24
  charitable funds under control of, 382
  in London in Second World War, 27
  liaison with, 389, 393
  review of records, 63
  system, 23–26
Higham, John Drew, 81–85
higher education *see* education
highway engineers, 152
Hill, Wills, Earl of Hillsborough, later 1st Marquess of Downshire, 70
Himalayan expeditions, 380, 385, 395
His/Her Majesty's Overseas Civil Service (HMOCS), xiv, 151, 358, 365
  in Malaya, 381
His/Her Majesty's Stationery Office (HMSO), 67, 358
  publications, 390
  sectional lists, 67
history, 154
  and administration, standing committee on, 118
  of colonial territories, 132
  of the East, 152
  of East Africa, 134
  of Pakistan, 151
  of tropical Commonwealth, 146
Hobart, Robert, 4th Earl of Buckinghamshire, 70

Holden, Angus William Eden, 3rd Baron Holden, 88
holiday visits, 149
Holland, David George, 94
Holland, Sir Henry Thurstan, 1st Viscount Knutsford, 70
Holmes, Sir Stephen Lewis, 87, 89
Holt, John, shipowner, 145
Home, 14th Earl of *see* Douglas-Home
Home Office, 4
  entry books including colonial correspondence, 32
  Factories division, 116
  liaison on police matters, 336
  Plantations Bureau, 4
  records, 66
Home Secretary, 40
Honduras, Republic of, 239
Hone, Major-General Sir (Herbert) Ralph, 103–106
Hong Kong, 5, 76, 163, 206, 207, 212, 280, 289, 301, 303, 305, 307–309, 326, 406
  Commonwealth relations with, 380
  record classes, 212
Hong Kong and Pacific Department *see* Colonial Office Geographical Departments
Hong Kong and West Indian 'C' Department *see* Colonial Office Geographical Departments
Honiara (Solomon Islands), 282
honorary degrees, 369, 393
honours, 57, 58, 167, 338, 346, 352, 368–370, 385, 393, 394, 406
  record classes, 167
Honours Department *see* Colonial Office Internal Services and other Departments
Hope, G W, 71
Hope, Lord John Adrian, 1st Baron Glendevon, 88
Hopkinson, Henry, 71
Hopkinson, J E, 101
Hopwood, Sir Francis J S, 72
Horn of Africa, 364, 365, 392
Hornby, Richard Phipps, 72, 88
horticulture, 413
Horticulture and Plantation Crops, Bureau of, 136
Horton, Sir Robert John Wilmot, 54
hospitality, 140, 158
hospitals, 157
hostels and clubs, administration of, 321, 343, 344
hotels, 137
Hotine, Brigadier Martin, 99–106
Houghton, H, 103–106
housing, 116, 137, 150, 153, 320, 331
  research, 341, 342
  and town planning, 342
Howard, F J, 79
Howick, Viscount *see* Grey, Henry George
Hudson, Henry, 276
Hudson, Rowland Skeffington, 81–85, 99–102, 104–106
Hudson's Bay, 164, 276
Hudson's Bay Company, 53, 273, 274, 276
  record classes, 39, 276
Hughes, C, 88
Hughes, John Turnbull, 91, 92
human diseases, 124, 139

Human Rights, Commission on, 337, 338
human rights (United Nations and Council of Europe), 337
Humphries, Lt-Colonel George James, 106
Hunt, Sir David (Wathen Stather), (D W S), 89, 90
Hunt, J J, 90, 91
Hunt, R C, 90, 91, 94
Huskisson, William, 54
Huxley, Gervas, 101
Hyde, Lawrence, Earl of Rochester, 254
hydro-electricity
  development, 326
  power, 339
hydrography, 382, 383
hydrology, 143
Hygiene and Tropical Diseases, Bureau of, 13, 129, 134–135

Ibadan (Nigeria), 334
Iberian peninsula, 33
Iddon, C, 89, 90
identity cards, 393
'Île de France' (Mauritius), 261
immigration, 234–236, 331–333, 369, 370, 385, 394
  of British subjects into UK, 369, 370, 384
  colonial, into UK, 333, 338
  of indentured labourers, 283
  legislation, 362
  record classes, 234–236, 262
  regulations, 158
  restrictions, 328, 368–370, 394
  for retirement, 149
immunity, 393, 394
Imperial Agricultural Bureau, 13, 129, 136, 139, 145
Imperial British East Africa Company, 190
Imperial Bureau of Entomology, 129, 131, 139, 145
Imperial Bureau of Mycology, 129, 140, 145
Imperial College of Petroleum Technology, Trinidad, 411
Imperial College of Tropical Agriculture (ICTA), xiv, 129, 145, 156–157, 234, 302, 323, 339, 340, 413
imperial communications, 352
Imperial Communications Advisory Committee, 26, 109, 121, 123, 125
Imperial Conferences, 6, 26, 128, 145, 165, 352, 353
  (c. 1907), 5–6, 145
  (1921), 6
  (1926), 23–24
  (1930), 24, 26
  Committee on Economic Co-operation (1930), 26
Imperial Defence, Committee of, 6, 25, 145
Imperial Defence College (IDC), xiv, 129, 145, 358, 372
Imperial Department of Agriculture, records, 234, 235
Imperial Economic Committee, 26, 109, 122, 125, 139, 409
Imperial Economic Conference, Ottawa
  (1923), 122
  (1932), 26
Imperial Economic Office, 353
imperial economic relations, 353
Imperial Forestry Institute, 129, 138, 145
Imperial Institute, 13, 118, 138–139, 339, 382, 386, 411
  Plant and Animal Products Department, 136, 156
  see also Commonwealth Institute
Imperial Institute of Entomology, 139, 145
Imperial Institute of the United Kingdom, the Colonies and India, 128–129, 138
  see also Imperial Institute
Imperial Mineral Resources Bureau, 138, 145
Imperial Mycological Institute, 140, 145
imperial preferences, 26, 138, 411
Imperial Service Order papers, 57, 167
Imperial Shipping Committee, 26, 109, 123, 125, 409
Imperial Shipping Office, 353
Imperial War Conferences (1917, 1918), 6, 123, 140
Imperial War Graves Commission, 332, 382–384
Imperial Wireless and Cable Conference (1928), 121
Import-Export Bank, 326
imports, 149
  and exports, controls, 411, 414
  licensing, 327–329, 343
  policy, 413
income tax, 330, 359–361
  commissioners, 151
Incorporated Liverpool School of Tropical Medicine, 129, 145–146
independence and commemoration gifts, 385
Independent Television (ITV), 358, 389
Independent Television Authority (ITA), xiv, 324, 334, 335, 358, 386, 387
India, 5, 7, 14, 24, 143, 144, 163, 213, 352, 360, 385, 395
  accounting, 360
  army, 359, 384, 385
  biographical material, 395
  cemeteries and memorials, 384
  cemeteries expenditure, 359
  civil services, 383
  Commonwealth relations with (1947), 7
  compensation for premature termination of employment, 359, 360
  compensation for tax, 359–361
  compensation to civil and defence services, 360
  defence services, personnel, 371, 373
  economy, loans, finance, taxation, 376–379
  foreign policy in, 394
  former ecclesiastical establishment, residual work, 384
  former princely states, residuary questions, 369, 393
  French possessions in, 394
  funds for posts in, 361
  immigration to Fiji, 283
  immigration to the UK, 369
Indian government claims, 359
Indians overseas, 395

internal political affairs, 380, 392, 395
medals, 383
passages on premature retirement, 360
pensions, 359–361, 385
political relations with Pakistan, 380, 394, 395
Portuguese territories in, 380, 394, 395
property acquisition acts, 382, 383
record classes, 213
records of service, 383
registration procedures (births, marriages, deaths), 368–370, 384, 394
relations with China and Tibet, 395
relations with UK, 395
representation, 359
residual inter-governmental claims, 360, 361
secretary of state's services, questions arising out of winding-up, 383, 394
sterling area development, 374
termite research, 155
UK high commissioner, formal instruments of accreditation, 394
see also British East India Company
India Office, 269
  abolished, 7, 27–28
  building, 28, 367, 385
  records, 63, 65
India Office Library and Records, 63, 213, 367, 385
Indian labour importation, 136, 349
Indian Ocean, region, 261–263
Indian Records Section see Commonwealth Relations Office Departments
Indian States, former, 368
Indo-China, 207, 380, 395
Indonesia, 381
  Commonwealth relations with, 380
industrial development, 139, 326–328
  correspondence, 407, 411
industrial enterprises, 137
industrial interests, 147
industrial problems, standing committee on, 170
industrial property, 331
industrial raw materials, 379
industrial relations, 328, 342, 343
industrial research, 113, 155
industrialists, 157
industries, primary and secondary, 339
information, 406
  supply of, 333–335
Information Administration Department, 419
Information Advisory Unit, 419
Information Departments see Colonial Office Subject Departments; Commonwealth Relations Office Departments; Dominions Office
Information, Ministry of, 27, 135
  Empire Division, 354
  liaison with, 331
  see also Central Office of Information
Information Offices, 334–335
information (operational) expenditure, 360, 391
information policy and administration, 387–389
Information Policy Departments see Commonwealth Relations Office Departments

Information Policy and Guidance Department, 419
information posts, 386
information research, 393
Information Research Department, 419
information services, adviser on, 101
Information Services Branch see Colonial Office Subject Departments
Information Services Department and Section see Commonwealth Relations Office Departments
Ingrams, William Arnold, 101, 102
inland transport, 324, 325
  adviser on, 99, 100
Inner London Education Authority, 151
insane correspondents, 36
  see also lunatics
insect pests, control of, 156
insecticides, 117, 136, 328, 339–341
insects, 124
Inskip, Sir Thomas Walker Hobart, 1st Viscount Caldecote, 86
Inspectorate see Commonwealth Relations Office Departments
Institute of Biological Control, 136
Institute of Civil Engineers, 141
Institute of Colonial/Commonwealth Studies, University of Oxford, 129, 146
Institute of Commonwealth Studies, University of London, 129–130, 146
Institute of Entomology, 136
Institute of Rural Life at Home and Overseas, 130, 146
institutes, 383
Institution of Electrical Engineers, 141
Institution of Mechanical Engineers, 141
instructions, 164
insurance, 330, 375, 411
  legislation, 330
intelligence, 332
  bodies in UK, 335, 336
  from colonial territories, 335
  organizations in colonial territories, 335, 336
  and security, 318, 325, 326
Intelligence and Security Departments see Colonial Office Subject Departments
intels, 387, 388, 390, 396
Inter-African Phyto-Sanitary Commission, 327, 340
Inter-departmental Committee on Locust Control, 131
Inter-departmental Committee on Research and Development in the Dependencies of the Falkland Islands, 125
Inter-governmental Maritime Consultative Organization, 325
Interim Commission, 397
inter-imperial relations, 330, 331
Inter-Imperial Relations Committee (Balfour Declaration), 23–24
inter-imperial trade, 123, 144
International African Institute, 129, 146
international agreements, 319, 338
  colonial territorial application articles in, 337, 338

International Alliance of Women for Suffrage and Equal Citizenship, Overseas Committee, 137
international aspects of colonial policy, 336
International Bank for Reconstruction and Development (IBRD), xiii, 122, 137, 323, 327–329, 363, 377–379
  economic survey, 326
  loans, 330
International Children's Endowment Fund, 337
International Civil Aviation Organization (ICAO), xiii, 358, 367
International Coffee Agreement and coffee study group, 328
international colonial co-operation, 336–338
international commodity agreements and study groups, 328
international commodity policy, 328, 377, 378
international commodity schemes, 339
International and Comparative Law Quarterly, 134, 154
International Court of Justice, 185, 363, 396, 397
International Development Association (IDA) (United Nations Organization), xiv, 323, 327–330, 358, 363, 377–379
international economic questions, 153, 352
International Film and Television Council (CICT), xiii, 357, 378
International Finance Corporation (IFC), xiv, 324, 327–329, 358, 363, 377
International and General Department, 419
international labour conventions, 304, 328, 343
International Labour Organization (ILO), xiv, 304, 318, 324, 328, 342, 343, 358, 363, 396, 397
International Materials Conference, 379
International Monetary Fund (IMF), xiv, 122, 324, 327–329, 377–379
international organizations
  associate membership in, 338
  colonial representation in, 336–338
  economic activities, 329
  privileges and immunities, 337, 338, 394
International Organizations, Steering Committee on, 338
international politics, 153
international relations, 15, 302, 317, 318, 330, 331, 337, 338, 406
International Relations Department *see* Colonial Office Subject Departments
International Relations and General Department *see* Colonial Office Subject Departments
international sugar agreements, 148, 328
international technical assistance, 326
International Telecommunications Union (ITU), xiv, 324, 325, 358, 367
international trade, 58
  negotiations, 414
  obstacles to, 414
  organizations, 329
international trade union organizations, 304, 328, 367, 393
international wheat agreement, 328
internees, 319
Inter-Parliamentary Union, 387, 388, 390
interregnum, 2

Inter-University Council for Higher Education in the Colonies (later Overseas), 119, 129, 146–147
intra-Commonwealth agreements, 370
intra-imperial trade agreements, 26, 353
inventions, 383
investitures, 368
investment
  of foreign capital in the colonies, 329, 411
  guarantees, 329
  promotion, 149
Ionian Islands, 4, 163, 263, 265–266, 289, 303
  local government records, 265
  maps, 68
  record classes, 54, 266
Iran, 392, 395
Iraq, 6, 163, 268–270, 289, 304, 392, 395
  mandated to Britain, 269
  record classes, 270
Ireland, 66, 163, 259
  London high commissioner's office, 25
  lord lieutenant and chief secretary of, 259
  record classes, 259
  see also Irish Free State; Irish Republic
Ireland, Northern, 260
Irish Distress Committee, 109, 125, 259
Irish Free State, 6–7, 163, 259–260, 290, 298, 352, 353
  correspondence, 57
  Criminal and Malicious Injuries Acts, 125, 259
  record classes, 260
Irish Free State (Agreement) Act (1922), 259
Irish Grants Committee, 125, 259
Irish Office, London, 259, 260
Irish Republic, Republic of Ireland (Eire), 6, 7, 260, 360, 379, 385, 392, 396
  British special representative, 25
  constitutional and political questions, 369
  dealt with by Dominions Office, 260, 352
  economic relations with, 375, 376, 379
  economy of, 375, 376
  financial questions, 379
  foreign affairs, 397
  foreign policy, 396
  funds for posts in, 361
  grant to, 361
  information expenditure, 361
  internal political affairs, 368
  pension appeal tribunal, 361
  relations with Commonwealth countries, 392
  sterling area development, 374
  trade affecting, 375
  UK ambassador, formal instruments of accreditation, 369
Irish Trade Negotiations Unit *see* Commonwealth Relations Office Departments
iron, 374
irrigation, 339, 340
  drainage, 340
  drainage/land drainage and irrigation, adviser on, 102, 104–106
  water supplies, 339
Islington, Baron *see* Dickson-Poynder, Sir John Poynder

INDEX

Ismay, General Sir Hastings Lionel, 1st Baron Ismay, 88
Israel, 270, 392
  see also Palestine
Italy, occupation of Somaliland, 192
Ithaca, 265
Ivory Coast, 366

Jack, H W, 99
Jamaica, 136, 163, 235, 242–245, 247–248, 251, 256, 290, 301, 302, 379, 397, 406
  distribution of industry in, 115
  funds for posts in, 361
  governor of, 239, 242, 247, 256
  Information Office, 334
  record classes, 247–248
  registration procedures, 35, 36, 46
  relations with, 367
  see also West Indies
Jamaica and the West Indies, standing committee on, 1
James Island, 198
James, Sir (John) Morrice (Cairns), (J M C), 89, 93
Jamieson, G W, 85
Japan, 414
  Commonwealth relations with, 380
  economic questions, 375, 379
  war with, 220
Japanese occupation
  of Brunei, 208
  of Gilbert and Ellice Islands, 284
  of Hong Kong, 212
  of Johore, 213
  of Kedah and Perlis, 214
  of Kelantan, 214
  of Labuan, 214
  of Malay States, 211, 222
  of Nauru, 284
  of Negri Sembilan, 216
  of New Guinea, 285
  of North Borneo, 217
  of Pahang, 218
  of Perak, 218
  of Sarawak, 219
  of Selangor, 220
  of Solomon Islands, 282
  of Straits Settlements, 221
  of Trengganu, 222
  of Unfederated Malay States, 222
Jasper, Robin Leslie Darlow, 90
Jeffries, Sir Charles Joseph, (C J), 72–74, 77, 78
Jelebu, 163, 213, 216
  record classes, 216
  see also Negri Sembilan; Sungei Ujong
Jenkins, Sir Leoline, 2
Jenkinson, Robert Banks, 2nd Earl of Liverpool, 70
Jerrom, T C, 84–86, 94
Johannesburg town council, 186, 187
Johnson, Sir William Clarence, (W C), 100, 101
Johnston, Sir John (Baines), (J B), 83, 90, 93
Johore, 163, 208, 211, 213, 218, 222
  record classes, 213
Joint Administration Department see Commonwealth Relations Office Departments
Joint Africa Board, 129, 147
Joint Agents General for the Crown Colonies, 128, 143, 147
  see also Crown Agents for Oversea Governments and Administrations
Joint Commonwealth Societies Council, 130, 147
Joint East Africa Board, 147
Joint East and Central African Board, 147
Joint Information Policy and Guidance Department see Commonwealth Relations Office Departments
Joint Intelligence Organization, 372, 392
Joint Malaysia/Indonesia Department see Commonwealth Relations Office Departments
Joint Planning Organization Staff, 326, 372, 373
Joint Protocol Department see Commonwealth Relations Office Departments
Joint Research Department see Commonwealth Relations Office Departments
joint secretaries, 375
Jones, John Cyril, 103–106
Jordan, 163, 270, 271, 392, 395
  see also Transjordan
Journal of African Administration, 170, 300
Joyce, Alec Houghton, 89
judgments, 382–385
Junagadh, 368, 369, 392
jurisprudence, 153
justice, administration of, 3
jute, trade, 376, 377, 379

Kaduna (Nigeria), 334
Kamaran, 394, 395
Kandyan Kingdom, 209
Kashmir, 368, 369, 380, 392, 394, 395
Kauntze, William Henry, 98
Kedah and Perlis, 163, 208, 211, 213–214, 222
  record classes, 214
Keeble, Thomas Whitfield, 91, 92
Keeling Islands see Cocos (Keeling) Islands
Keith, John Lucien, 79–83
Kefallinia, 265
Kelantan, 163, 208, 211, 214, 222
  record classes, 214
Kennedy, Francis, 82–84
Kenya (formerly East Africa Protectorate), 189–191, 290, 296, 297, 363, 406
  government of, 134
  governor of, 16
  Information Office, 334
  Kenya Coastal Strip Commission, 191
  Kenya Constituencies Delimitation Commission, 191
  Kenya Land Transfer, 191
  Kenya Northern Frontier District Commission, 191
  Kenya Regional Boundaries Commission, 191
  land questions, 363
  record classes, 191
  relations with, 363, 364
  Royal Technical College, 111
  Stamp Mission, transfer of land, 191

Kenya Department *see* Commonwealth Relations Office Departments
Khama, Sir Seretse M, 172
Killearn, 1st Baron *see* Lampson, Sir Miles Wedderburn
Kimber, Gurth, 90, 91
Kimberley, 1st Earl of *see* Wodehouse, John
King's African Rifles (KAR), xiv, 10, 16 163, 176, 191–192, 206, 314
  record classes, 191–192
Kingsley, Mary Henrietta, 152
Kiribati, 164, 283, 284
  see also Gilbert and Ellice Islands
Kirkness, Donald James, 85, 86
Kisch, John Marcus, 83–85, 92
Kitchener, Horatio Herbert, 1st Earl Kitchener of Khartoum, papers, 54
Kithira, 265
Knatchbull-Hugessen, Edward Hugessen, 1st Baron Brabourne, 71
Knutsford, 1st Viscount *see* Holland, Sir Henry Thurstan
Korea
  awards, 368
  Commonwealth forces in, 375, 380
  Commonwealth relations with, 380
  prisoners of war in, 382
  repayment of cost of US logistic support, 375
Kowloon peninsula, 212
Kuczynski, Professor Robert René, 96, 99
Kumasi College of Technology, Ghana, 111
Kuria Muria Islands, 163, 261, 270
  record classes, 270

Labouchere, Henry, Baron Taunton, 70, 71
labour, 15, 115, 317, 331
  administration and legislation, 328, 342, 343
  adviser, 98–106
  conditions, 320, 331
  legislation, 116, 304, 342
  questions, 320, 342
  and trade union affairs, 367, 368, 392, 393
Labour, Ministry of, 116, 158
  overseas aid, 7
Labrador, 275, 277
Labuan, 163, 208, 214–215, 217, 220, 221, 290, 298, 301, 305, 308
  record classes, 215
  see also British North Borneo; Straits Settlements
Lacey, Gerald, 102, 104
Lagos, 163, 199, 201, 202, 204, 205, 290, 297–299, 303, 305, 334
  record classes, 201
  see also Nigeria
Lahej, Sultan of, 268
Laithwaite, Sir (John) Gilbert, 89
Lake Nyasa, 178
Lake Victoria Fisheries Board, 190
Lamarque, W G, 92
Lamb, G P, 99
Lambert, Charles Ernest, 81–84, 423
Lampson, Sir Miles Wedderburn, 1st Baron Killearn, 207

Lancaster House Agreements (Zimbabwe), 184
land
  correspondence, 412
  grants, 349
  settlement, 339–340
  tenure, 116, 118, 300, 339
  tenure specialist, 104–106
  transfers, 230
Land and Emigration Commission, 348–349
  records, 272, 349
Land Panel, 170, 300
languages, 146, 151–154
Lansdowne, Marquesses of *see* Petty; Petty-Fitzmaurice
Laos, Commonwealth relations with, 381
Larmour, Sir Edward Noel, (E N), 90
Latin America
  foreign territories in, 398
  regional economic commission, 337, 338
Latin American Department *see* Commonwealth Relations Office Departments
Lausanne, Treaty of, 264
law
  African, 117, 154
  in the Commonwealth, 134
  of the sea, 338, 384, 385
  oriental, 154
  public international, 134
  standing committee on, 118
law officers' opinions and reports, 164
Law Panel, 170, 300
lead, trade, 375
League of the British Commonwealth and Empire, 147
League of the Empire, 129, 147, 149
League for the Exchange of Commonwealth Teachers, 147
League of Nations, 205, 331, 336, 352
  mandate system, 6, 7, 197, 200, 268–271, 284, 285
League of Nations Committee, 412
Lebanon, 392
lecture tours overseas, 387
Lee, Frederick, 71
Leeward Islands, 163, 235–237, 243–245, 248–250, 290, 301–303, 406
  governor of, 243, 244, 248
  record classes, 248–249
  see also Antigua; British Virgin Islands; Dominica; Montserrat; Nevis; St Christopher
Leeward Islands Federation, 237, 243, 244, 248–250
legal adviser *see* Colonial Office
Legal Department, Legal Division *see* Colonial Office Subject Departments
Legal Executive Branch, 419
legal matters, 352
  and judicial matters, 331, 332
legal service, 17
legal studies, 152
legalization of documents, 331, 382, 383
Legge, William, 2nd Earl of Dartmouth, 70
legislation, 3, 4, 154, 324
legislative councils, 39, 52, 64, 162

legislative programme, 333, 338, 369, 370
Lennox-Boyd, Alan Tindal, 1st Viscount Boyd of Merton, 71
leprosy research, 134
Leprosy Review, 134
Lesotho *see* Basutoland
Le Tocq, Eric George, 91, 94
letter books, 162
letters of credence, 370, 393
letters of request, 382–384
letters patent, 369, 393
letters to UK ministers, 382, 383
Leveson-Gower, Granville, 1st Earl Granville, papers, 54
Leveson-Gower, Granville, 2nd Earl Granville, 70
  papers, 54
Levkas, 265
Lewthwaite, Raymond, 101–106
Leyden, J L, 100, 101
liaison
  in Africa, 337
  with chiefs of staff and joint planning staff, 326
  with COS secretariat, 373
  with directors of plans, 373
  with intelligence co-ordination staff, 373
  with Ministry of Defence, etc, 371–373
  with press, 386, 387, 389, 390
  with PROs at Commonwealth houses, 385
  with societies and organizations, 385
  with universities, 386–389
  with voluntary associations, 343–344
Liberia, 366
libraries, 123, 342, 367, 382
  and museums, 342
  payments, 361
  services, 148
Library Association, Advisory Committee on Library Services in the Colonies, 130, 148
Library Department *see* Colonial Office, shared services with Dominions Office; Commonwealth Relations Office; Dominions Office; Foreign Office
Libya, 395, 396
Liesching, Sir Percivale, 87, 89
linguistics, 118, 146
Lintott, Sir Henry, (H J), 89
liquor traffic, 112, 331
Liston, James Malcolm, 106
Listowel, 5th Earl of *see* Hare, William Francis
literature, 151, 152, 154, 156
lithographed forms (LFs) *see* Colonial Office records
Littlejohn, later Littlejohn Cook, George Steveni, 94
Liverpool, 2nd Earl of *see* Jenkinson, Robert Banks
Liverpool School of Tropical Medicine *see* Incorporated Liverpool School of Tropical Medicine
livestock
  breeding, 152
  diseases, 119
living conditions overseas, 153, 158
Livingstone, David, 178, 180
Lloyd, George Ambrose, 1st Baron Lloyd, 71, 72

Lloyd, Sir Thomas Ingram Kynaston, (T I), 72, 74, 79
Lloyd Report, 19
loans, 330
local education authorities, 148
local government
  individual authorities, 142
  policy, 20, 116
Local Government Panel, 170, 300
locust control, 339, 382–384, 407, 412
  anti-locust research, 131, 341
  locust questions, 339
Loggin, George Nicholas, 96
London
  businessmen, 147
  centre for study in, 134
  conferences, lectures in, 146, 153
London Agreement (Cyprus), 264
London, City of, development capital requirements for dominions, 26
London press service, 386, 387, 389, 390
London School of Hygiene and Tropical Medicine, 129, 131, 148
  Department of Human Nutrition, 130, 148
London School of Tropical Medicine, 13, 129, 148
London, University of
  adviser to Overseas Students, 123
  Institute of Commonwealth Studies, 129–130, 146
  Institute of Education, Department of Education in Tropical Areas, 141
  School of Oriental and African Studies, 154
  teaching departments for the diploma in public health, 148
Long, Walter Hume,(W H), 1st Viscount, 71
long-range weapons, 371, 373
Longford, 7th Earl of *see* Pakenham, Francis Aungier
loofahs, 340
Lord Chancellor, 64
Lord, L, 99–103
Lord Privy Seal (LPS), xiv, 358
Lords Commissioners for promoting the Trade of our Kingdom, and for inspecting and improving our Plantations (Board of Trade, 1696) *see* Trade, Board of
Lovatt, 14th Baron *see* Fraser, General Simon Joseph
low-priced book scheme, 388, 390
Lowry Cole, Sir Galbraith, papers, 54
Lowther, James, 71
Loyalists *see* American Loyalists
Lucan, 6th Earl of *see* Bingham, Colonel Sir George Charles Patrick
Lucas, Baron *see* Herbert, Auberon Thomas
Lucas, Sir Charles Prestwood, (C P), 422
Luke, Sir Stephen (Elliott Vyvyan), (S E), 75, 79, 80
lunatics, 382–384
  see also insane correspondents
Lunn, William, 72, 86
Lusaka, 183
Lyttelton, Alfred, 71
Lyttelton, George William, 4th Baron Lyttelton, 71

Lyttelton, Oliver, Viscount Chandos, 71
Lytton, Sir Edward George Earle Lytton Bulwer, 1st Baron Lytton, 70

MacDonald, A M, 104
MacDonald, Malcolm John, 71, 86, 207
MacFarlane, Donald, 94
Machtig, Sir Eric Gustav, 86, 87, 89
Mackintosh, Sir Angus (MacKay), (A M), 82–85
Maclay, John Scott, 1st Viscount Muirshiel, 71
McLean, Sir William Hannah, 104–107
Maclennan, Sir Ian (Morrison Ross), (I M R), 89
Macleod, Iain Norman, 71
Macmillan, (Maurice) Harold, 1st Earl of Stockton, 72
McNeill, Major-General John Malcolm, 92, 94
McNulty, A B, 99, 100
McPetrie, Sir James (Carnegie), (J C), 99–107
Macpherson, Sir John Stuart, 72
Madras, 136
  presidency, 209
Maffey, Sir John Loader, 1st Baron Rugby, 72
magazines, 387, 388, 390
mails, 324, 325
  see also postal communications
Maine, 274
maintenance orders, 332, 382–385
Majendie, Major A E, 104, 105
Malacca (Melaka), 5, 163, 211, 215, 216, 218, 221, 290
  record classes, 215
  see also Straits Settlements
malaria, 46, 117
Malawi, 134, 162, 176, 364
  relations with, 364
  see also Nyasaland
Malawi and Central Africa Economic Department *see* Commonwealth Relations Office Departments
Malawi and Zambia Department *see* Commonwealth Relations Office Departments
Malay States, 290, 298, 308, 406
Malay States, Federated, 163, 208, 210–211, 215, 216, 218, 220–222
  exceptional colony registration arrangements, 35
  record classes, 211
  see also Negri Sembilan; Pahang; Perak; Selangor
Malay States, Unfederated, 163, 215, 222–223
  see also Johore; Kedah and Perlis; Kelantan
Malaya, 351, 360, 378
  'British Malaya', 163, 208
  civil servants at Tropical Affairs Service courses, 15
  Commonwealth relations with, 380
  Defence Agreement with UK, 381
  defence questions, 380, 381
  economy of and relations with, 381
  HM overseas civil services in, 381
  importance as dollar earner, 20
  loans to, financial agreements, 376
  payments for Foreign Office posts, 360, 361
  police units, 361
  political affairs, 380
  rehabilitation of industries in, 339
  relations with Singapore, 380–381
  taxation questions, 376
  see also Malay States, Federated; Malay States, Unfederated; Malaya, Federation of; Malaysia
Malaya, 132
Malaya and British Borneo, Board of Commissioners of Currency, 130, 132
Malaya Department *see* Commonwealth Relations Office Departments
Malaya, Federation of, 132, 163, 211–220, 222, 308, 309, 380, 381
  Federation of Malaya Constitutional Commission, 212
  record classes, 212
Malayan Bulletin, 132
Malayan Planning Unit, 17
Malayan Union, 163, 211, 213–216, 218, 220–222
  registers of correspondence, with Singapore, 48, 215
Malaysia, 66, 163, 211–219, 376, 377, 381
  Commission of Inquiry in North Borneo and Sarawak Regarding Malaysian Federation (1962), records, 216, 219
Malaysia, Federation of, 209
Malaysia-Singapore Commercial Association Inc, 130, 148
Maldive Islands, 209–210, 216, 382, 392, 395
  expenditure, 361
  internal political affairs, 395
  political relations with, 381, 395
Maldives, Republic of, 210
Mali, 366
Malta, 4, 163, 263, 266–267, 290, 296–299, 303, 304, 306, 307, 406
  Constitutional Commission (1960), 266
  Independence Conference (1963), 266
  Information Office, 335
  maps, 68
  Order of St Michael and St George, 55, 265–267
  officers at arms' records, 55
  record classes, 267
  relations with, 391
  Royal Commission (1912), 267
Malta Departments *see* Commonwealth Relations Office Departments
Malta, Knights of, given St Croix, 251
mandates, 6, 7, 317, 331, 336
  acquisition of ex-Turkish territories by, 6, 10, 268
  see also League of Nations
Manitoba, 164, 274, 276
  record classes, 276
manufacturing industries, 157
maps, 67–68, 143, 144, 388, 390
marine biological stations, 125
Marion Islands, 290, 301
maritime transport, 26, 123
marketing, 122, 144, 156, 327, 412, 413
marketing boards, 17, 412
Marketing Department *see* Colonial Office Subject Departments

marketing manufactured products, 329
marketing officers, 135
marketing organizations, 319, 339
marketing policy, 339, 340
marketing promotion, 149
Marlborough, 9th Duke of *see* Spencer-Churchill, Charles Richard John
Marlborough House *see* Commonwealth Information Centre
Marnham, John Ewart, 77, 81–85
Marshall, Robert Smith, 103–106
Martin, Sir John (Miller), 72, 74, 75
Martin, Victor Cecil, 91, 92, 94
Martinique, 163, 249, 252
  record classes, 249
Maryland, 31, 249
  records sub-division, 236
Mason, R W, 92
Mass Education (Community Development), Committee on, 110, 112, 119–120
Massachusetts, records sub-division, 236
master of the rolls, 53
Masterton-Smith, Sir James Edward, 72
Matabele, 171, 173
Mathieson, William Allan Cunningham, 81–85
matrimonial cases, 318, 382–385
mats and stereos, 388
Mau Mau rebellion, 190
Maudling, Reginald, 71
Mauritius, 4, 10, 163, 206, 261–262, 280, 290, 299, 301, 306–308, 406
  Chamber of Agriculture, 128, 148
  Commissioners of Eastern Inquiry, 261, 262
  Commission on the Constitution (Banwell Commission, 1965–1966), 261, 262
  Electoral Boundary Commission (1957), 262
  Information Office, 335
  record classes, 261–262
  relations with, 364
Mayall, A L, 92, 94
Mayle, Norman Leslie, 79–84
Maynard, Major A E, 106
Maynard, Major W A, 107
Mayne, J E, 104
Meade, Sir Robert Henry, 72
meat, trade, 339, 375, 376
medals, 332, 360, 368, 369, 393
medical administration (medicine) and public health, 331, 342
Medical Advisory Committee, 110, 125
medical advisory staff, 374
medical aid, 125
medical awards, 140
medical claims, 360
medical education, 125, 139
medical expenses, 361
medical interests, 117
medical organizations, 139
medical practitioners, 125, 146
medical profession of Great Britain, 125
medical questions, 114, 338
medical reciprocity, 382
medical research, 114, 116–117, 127, 155, 341
Medical Research Council, 116, 127, 155

Medical Research into the British Caribbean Territories, Standing Advisory Committee on, 117
Medical and Sanitary Committee for Tropical Africa, Advisory, 109, 112, 114
medical service, 12, 15, 383
medical services and equipment, ancillary, 125
medical staff, 125
medicine, technical assistance, 125
Mediterranean
  record classes, 48, 52, 163, 263, 406
  region, 263–267
  war in, 33
Mediterranean and African Department *see* Colonial Office Geographical Departments
Mediterranean and Atlantic Department *see* Colonial Office Geographical Departments
Mediterranean Departments *see* Colonial Office Geographical Departments; Commonwealth Relations Office Departments
Melaka *see* Malacca
Melville, 1st Viscount *see* Dundas, Henry
Melville, Sir Eugene, 75, 76, 80, 81
members of Parliament, 147, 157
  visits by, 389, 390
memorials, 384
Mendip, 1st Baron *see* Ellis, Wellbore
merchandise marks, 412
merchant shipping, 314, 324, 331, 343, 352
Merivale, H, 72
Mesopotamia *see* Iraq
messages, 382
  of condolence, 393, 394
  of congratulation, 393, 394
  of valediction, 393, 394
metals and minerals
  non-ferrous, 379
  production and marketing, 339–341
Metcalf, Maurice Rupert, 89, 90
Meteorological Organization, 385
meteorology, 118, 324, 325
Meyer, S C, 100
micro-organisms, 119
Middle East, 6, 163, 268, 297, 304, 333, 391–392, 406
  Confidential Print series, 52, 268
  defence, 371, 395
  foreign affairs, 396
  minister resident in, 17
  minister of state for, 268
  (Official) Committee, 343
  record classes, 47–48, 268
  region, 163, 268–271
  Supply Centre, 268
  termination of mandates in, 7, 268
Middle East Departments *see* Colonial Office Geographical Departments; Commonwealth Relations Office Departments
Middle East Division *see* Colonial Office Geographical Departments
Middle East, Western and United Nations Department, 419
migration, 138, 349, 353, 367, 383, 385, 417
  British migrants, 139

welfare of migrants, 136
Miles, Frank Stephen, 94
military aid, training and equipment, 372
military alliances, 369, 393
military aspects of outer space, 372
military assistance, 361
military aviation, 325, 331, 332
Military Branch, Military Section *see* Colonial Office Subject Departments
military correspondence, 43–45
military duties in aid of civil power, 325
military flights over colonies, 325
military information, classified, 371–373
military lands in the colonies, 332
military legislation, 325
military liaison officers, 10
military operations, 18, 44, 331, 372
military papers, registration, 164–165
military returns, 263
Military Secretariat, War Cabinet Office, 27
military staff officer, 104–107
Millard, Raymond Spencer, 104–106
millers, 148
Milner, Alfred, Viscount Milner, 71, 181
  papers, 54
minerals, 319, 409
  laboratory investigations, 150
  non-ferrous, 379
  policy, 340
  processing, 121
  resources, 112, 121, 122
  royalties, 340
mining
  congresses, 122
  development, 137, 150
  legislation, 150, 340, 412
  organizations, 150
  policy, 340
  representatives of, 157
  taxation, 340
ministerial visits to Commonwealth, 387, 389
Ministers of Overseas Development, 7, 95, 111, 124–127, 148, 150
Ministers of State for Colonial Affairs, 19, 71, 111, 112, 114–116, 118
Ministers of State for Commonwealth Affairs, 93
Ministers of State for Commonwealth Relations, 88, 125
ministers resident, 17
Ministry *indexed under key word of title*
Minorca, 163, 267
  record classes, 267
Miscellaneous Confidential Print, 52
Miscellaneous Expenditure, Select Committee on, 55
missionaries, 146
missionary societies, 297, 332
Molesworth, Sir William, 70
Monckton, Walter Turner, 1st Viscount Monckton, chairman of Commission on the Constitution of Rhodesia and Nyasaland, 175
monopolies and restrictive trade practices, 327, 328
Monsell, William, Baron Emly, 71

Monson, Sir (William Bonnar) Leslie, (W B), 75, 76, 79, 80, 93
Monteagle, 1st Baron *see* Spring-Rice, Thomas
Montgomery, Robert Eustace, 97
Montserrat, 136, 163, 236–237, 245, 248, 249, 290, 301
  record classes, 237, 249
  see also Leeward Islands; West Indies
Moore, Sir Henry Monck-Mason, 15, 73
Moreton, Sir John (Oscar), (J G), 91, 93
Morgan, Sir George Osborne, 1st baronet, 71
Morgan, James Conwy, 83–85, 91–93
Morley, Sir Alexander Francis, (A F), 89
Morrice, Humphrey Alan Walter, 104, 105
Morris, Nigel Godfrey, 104–107
Morris, Owen Humphrey, 83–85
Morris, William Alexander, 81–85
Morton, John Percival, 107
motor insurance, 325
Moyne, 1st Baron *see* Guinness, Walter Edward
Moynihan, Martin John, 90, 91
Muller, Walter Angus, 101–103
multilateral treaties, 352
munitions, 27, 371
Munster, 5th Earl of *see* Fitzclarence, Sir Geoffrey William Richard Hugh
Murray, Sir George, 70
  papers, 54
music, 151
Mycological Institute, 136
mycologists, 140
Mycology, Imperial Bureau of *see* Imperial Bureau of Mycology

Nairobi, 134, 143
Namibia, 163, 176, 185
  see also South West Africa
Napier, General Sir Charles James, papers, 54
Napoleon Bonaparte, 225
Napoleonic Wars, 4, 175, 210, 261
narcotic drugs commission, 397
Natal, 162, 176–177, 180, 187, 290, 297, 298, 303, 305, 412
  Agent-General for, 421–423
  Government Gazette, 421
  Governor of, 188, 423
  record classes, 177
National Co-operating Body for Libraries, 148
National Council for the Supply of Teachers Overseas, 130, 148–149
national days, 393
national service, 384
  acts, 382, 383
National Union of Manufacturers, 138
nationality and citizenship legislation and policy, and passports, 318, 331, 332, 352, 368–370, 384, 385, 394
Nationality and Consular Department *see* Commonwealth Relations Office Departments
Nationality and General Department *see* Commonwealth Relations Office Departments
Nationality and Treaty Department, 419

Native Education in the British Tropical Dependencies, Advisory Committee on, 109, 111, 112
Native Land Tenure in Africa, Committee on, 116
native law and courts, 117, 300
NATO *see* North Atlantic Treaty Organization
natural disasters, 382–384
natural resources, 139
naturalization, 47, 331, 332, 352, 368
Nauru, 6 164, 167, 284–285, 352
  administered from Australia, 6, 167
  administered by Dominions Division, 6, 167
  government gazettes, 284
  see also British Phosphate Commissioners
naval cadetships, 346
naval operations, 331
naval visits and flights by service aircraft between Commonwealth countries, 373
Neale, Kenneth James, 92, 94
Negri Sembilan, 210, 211, 216, 222
Negri Sembilan, Sungei Ujong and Jelebu, 163, 216
  record classes, 216
Nelson, Horatio, Viscount Nelson, 263
Nepal, 380, 395
Netherlands *see* Dutch
Nevis, 163, 243, 248–251, 301
  record classes, 250, 277
  see also Leeward Islands; St Christopher; West Indies
New Brunswick, 164, 274, 276–277, 290, 305
  record classes, 277
New England, 276
  records sub-division, 236
New Guinea, 164, 281, 285, 290
  Commonwealth relations with, 380
  government gazettes, 285
  see also British New Guinea (Papua)
New Hampshire, records sub-division, 236
New Hebrides (Vanuatu), 164, 280, 285–286, 380
  record classes, 285–286
New Jersey, 31
  records sub-division, 236
New Providence, 237
New South Wales, 4, 10, 163, 227–231, 233, 280, 291, 305, 306
  record classes, 228–229
  superintendent of convicts in, 54, 228
New Territories (Hong Kong), 212
New York, records sub-division, 236
New Zealand, 6, 10, 66, 140, 163, 226, 228–230, 280, 284, 287, 291, 298, 305, 306, 360, 379–381
  administers Samoa, 287
  Australia and New Zealand registers, 226
  British High Commission established, 25
  Canadian high commissioner appointed in, 25
  defence co-operation with, 371
  economy of, 375, 376
  external policies, 380
  financial questions, 379
  funds for posts in, 361
  interest (with Australia) in South Pacific, 12
  internal political affairs of, 369, 380, 392
  London high commissioner's office, 24

matters dealt with by Dominions Office, 6, 57, 353
  migrants to, 139
  Prime Minister's Office, 25
  question of autonomy, 5
  policies of and UK relations with, 380
  record classes, 229
  relations with, 380
  sterling area development, 374
New Zealand Company, 53, 163, 229, 230
  record classes, 230
New Zealand Society, 129, 149
Newbolt, (Arthur) Francis, 79–82
Newcastle, 5th Duke of *see* Clinton, Henry Pelham Fiennes Pelham
Newfoundland, 25, 164, 274, 275, 277–278, 290, 298, 305, 306, 352, 353
  correspondence, 40, 56, 58
  governor of, 57
  record classes, 277–278
  relinquishes dominion status (1933), 25
Newfoundland and Labrador, 275, 277
News Branch *see* Colonial Office Subject Departments
News Departments *see* Commonwealth Relations Office Departments
news dissemination, 391
news services, 334, 335, 387
newspapers, 31, 39, 52–53, 66, 162, 388, 390
newsprint, trade, 375, 379
Niblett, C H, 422
Niger Coast Protectorate, 16, 201–202, 205
  record classes, 202
Niger Department *see* Colonial Office Geographical Departments
Niger and West Africa Frontier Force *see* West Africa Frontier Force
Nigeria, 134, 157, 163, 197, 202–203, 205, 291, 299, 300, 351, 366, 378, 406
  Commission on Minority Groups (Willink Commission) files, 203
  Council of Ministers papers, 203
  economic relations with, 363
  external relations, 365
  funds for posts in, 360, 361
  general political questions, 365
  governor of, 197
  Information Offices, 334, 335
  internal political affairs, 365
  ministerial visitors, 365
  railways, 202–203
  record classes, 202–203
  relations with, 366
  UK/Nigeria Defence Agreement, 365
  see also Lagos; Nigeria, Northern; Nigeria, Southern
Nigeria Departments *see* Colonial Office Geographical Departments; Commonwealth Relations Office Departments
Nigeria, Northern, 163, 202, 203, 205, 299
  record classes, 203
  see also Nigeria
Nigeria, Southern, Protectorate of, 163, 201–203, 205, 299

contributes to Entomological Research Committee, 125
record classes, 205
see also Nigeria
Nigerian College of Arts, Science and Technology, 111
Nigerian technical assistance, 374
Noakes, Philip Reuben, 85, 86, 94
Noble, Commander Sir Allan (Herbert Percy), 88
Noel-Baker, Philip John, Baron Noel-Baker, 88
nomination schemes for cadetships, 371
non-ferrous metals and minerals, 379
non-self-governing territories, 336, 337, 386, 397
Norfolk Island, 4, 163, 230
government gazettes, 230
Normanby, 1st Marquess of see Phipps, Constantine Henry
Norris, Sir Eric (George), (E G), 93
North Africa, 163, 196, 363, 365
foreign affairs, 363, 366, 391, 392, 396
see also Tangier
North and East Africa Department, 419, 420
North America, 396
emigration to 349
region, 272–280
see also British North America
North American and Australasian Department see Colonial Office Geographical Departments
North American, Australian, African and Mediterranean Department see Colonial Office Geographical Departments
North American and Australian Department see Colonial Office Geographical Departments
North American Department see Colonial Office Geographical Departments
North Atlantic Treaty Organization (NATO), xiv, 358, 392, 396
commodity problems, 379
defence aspects, 371–373
North Australia, 163, 230
entry books, 230
North Borneo see British North Borneo (Sabah)
North, Frederick, Lord North, later 2nd Earl of Guilford, 70
Northcote, Henry Stafford, 1st Baron Northcote, papers, 54
North-Eastern Rhodesia, Northern Rhodesia see Rhodesia
Northern Department, 419
Northern Territory, 163, 230
government gazettes, 230
North-West Company, 276
North-West Expedition, 272
North-West Frontier, 394
North-West Territories, 164, 274–276, 278
record classes, 278
Nova Scotia, 274, 276, 291, 305
and Cape Breton, 164, 278
record classes, 278
nuclear energy, 327
nuclear tests, 325, 372, 373
suspension of, 392
nuclear weapons, 371, 373
Nuffield Foundation, 149

nurses, 382, 383
appointment, 150
training, 120
nursing homes, 151
nursing services, 125
nutrition, 120, 131, 148, 320, 331, 342, 412
correspondence, 412
liaison officers, 131
Nutrition in the Colonial Empire, Committee on, 109, 120
Nyasaland (Malawi), 7, 61, 162, 170, 175, 178–180, 183, 291, 296, 297, 406
funds for posts in, 361
record classes, 179
University of, 362
see also Rhodesia and Nyasaland
Nye, Sir Geoffrey (Walter), 99–106

O'Brien, Arthur John Rushton, 97, 98
ocean freights, 123
Ocean Island, 284
office expenses, 359
Office of Defence Mobilization (USA) (ODM), xiv, 358
Office of the Trade Representative for Seychelles, 130, 149
official publications, 386
Ogilvie, Miss S A, 99–106
Ogmore, 1st Baron see Rees-Williams, David Rees
oil and oilseeds, trade in, 136, 327, 328, 339, 340, 363, 366, 374, 376
Oil Department, 419
Oil Rivers Protectorate, 201
see also Niger Coast Protectorate
Old Calabar, 201
Olympic Games, 383, 386–388
Oman, Sultan of, 270
Ommanney, Sir Montagu Frederick, 72
Onslow, William Hillier, 4th Earl of Onslow, 71
Ontario, 164, 273, 274, 277–278
record classes, 279
open date for records, 64
Oram, Albert Edward, Baron Oram, 95
Orange Free State, 162, 179–182, 186
record classes, 179–180
Orange River, 291
Orange River Colony, 162, 179–180, 186, 187, 298
record classes, 180
see also Transvaal
Orde Browne, Major Sir Granville St John, 98, 99
papers, 4
Order of St Michael and St George, 54, 57, 265, 346
see also Malta
Orders in Council, 164
Ordnance, Board of, 5
ores
low grade, 121
laboratory investigations, 150
Organization of African Unity (OAU), xiv, 363, 366
Organization of a Colonial Agriculture Service, Committee on, 113
Organization for Economic Co-operation and Development (OECD), xiv, 358, 363, 378, 379
Development Assistance Committee, 363, 378, 379

INDEX 463

Organization for European Economic Co-operation (OEEC), xv, 324, 326, 327, 329, 358, 375, 377, 410
Oriental and India Office Collections, British Library, 63
oriental languages, 152–153
original correspondence *see* Colonial Office records
Ormerod, Richard Caton, 91
Ormsby-Gore, William George Arthur, 4th Baron Harlech, 71, 72
OSWEP, 390
Ottawa Agreements, 26
Ottawa, British high commissioner to (1928), 25
Ottawa Conference (1932), 315
Ottoman Bank, 151
Ottoman Empire
  conquers Cyprus, 264
  Transjordan captured from, 271
out-letter books *see* Colonial Office records
outer space
  military aspects, 371–373
  peaceful uses of, 367, 385
outfit allowances, 359, 360
outstanding balances, 359, 360
oversea establishments, 360, 361
Oversea Finance Department *see* Commonwealth Relations Office Departments
Oversea Mechanical Transport Council and Oversea Transport Directing Committee, 109, 126
Oversea Migration Board, 110, 126, 384
Oversea Service, 130, 149
oversea settlement, 353, 359, 360
Oversea Settlement Board, 129, 149, 349
Oversea Settlement Committee, 109, 126, 349
Overseas Aid Development Assistance Committee, 330
overseas appointments, 149
Overseas Audit Department, 129, 149
Overseas Audit Service, 149
overseas capital markets, 137
Overseas Club, 149
Overseas Club and Patriotic League, 129, 149
Overseas Colleges of Arts, Science and Technology, Council for, 111, 124
Overseas Defence Committee, 325, 331, 371
Overseas Development Institute Ltd, 130, 149–150
Overseas Development, Ministry of, 7–8, 61, 108, 119, 124, 131, 142, 143, 146, 147, 150–152, 155, 156, 358, 385
  liaison with, 338, 391
Overseas Division, Building Research Station, Department of Scientific and Industrial Research, 129, 135, 150
Overseas Food Corporation, 129, 150, 297
Overseas Geological Surveys, 150
  Principal, Mineral Resources Division, 106
Overseas Geology and Mineral Resources, 150
Overseas Geology and Mineral Resources, Advisory Committee, 112
overseas information ceiling, 389, 390
overseas information services adviser, 101, 102
Overseas Negotiations Committee, 375
Overseas Nursing Association, 129, 150–151
Overseas Pest Control Committee, 110, 126, 155

Overseas Research Council, 127–128, 341
Overseas Research, Privy Council Committee on, 127
Overseas Resources Development Acts
  1948, 150
  1959, 137
Overseas Service College, Farnham Castle, 130, 151
Overseas Service Departments *see* Colonial Office Internal Services and other Departments
overseas service recruitment, 383, 384
Overseas Services Division *see* Colonial Office Internal Services and other Departments
Overseas Services Resettlement Bureau, 21, 130, 151
Overseas Settlement Department *see* Colonial Office Internal Services and other Departments; Dominions Office
overseas students
  accommodation, 133
  adviser to, 123
  assistance to, 142
  training, 151
  unions, 123
Overseas Students Advisory Bureau, 130, 151
overseas studies, comparative, 146
Overseas Territories Income Tax Office, 129, 151
Overseas Territories Tax Office, 61
Overseas Trade, Department of, 25, 135, 138
  transfer of trade commissioners to, 25
overseas trade and payments registrations, 377, 378
overseas visitors, 146
Oxford University
  Commonwealth Forestry Institute, 138
  Institute of Colonial/Commonwealth Studies, 129, 146
  Queen Elizabeth House, 130, 151–152
  Tropical African Service course at, 15

Pacific Cable Board, 129, 151
Pacific defence, 380
Pacific Department *see* Colonial Office Geographical Departments
Pacific and Indian Ocean Department *see* Colonial Office Geographical Departments
Pacific Islands, 380
Pacific and Mediterranean Department *see* Colonial Office Geographical Departments
Pacific Pact, 380
Pahang, 163, 210, 211, 218
  record classes, 218
  see also Malay States, Federated
paint oils, 339, 340
Pakenham, Francis Aungier, 7th Earl of Longford, 71
Pakington, Sir John Somerset, 1st Baron Hampton, 70
Pakistan, 143–144, 151, 163, 218, 360, 385, 395
  biographical material, 395
  cemeteries expenditure, 359
  cemeteries and memorials in, 384
  Commonwealth Relations Office relations with, 7

compensation for tax, 360, 361
defence, 371
economy, loans, finance, taxation, 376–379
foreign policy, 394
funds for posts in, 361
immigration to UK, 369
internal political affairs, 380, 392, 393, 395
Pakistanis overseas, 395
political relations with India, 380, 394, 395
property acquisitions acts, 382, 383
record classes, 218
registration procedure (births, marriages, deaths), 368–370, 384, 394
relations with China and Tibet, 395
relations with UK, 395
representation in, 359
sterling area development, 374
Pakistan Society, 130, 151
Palestine, 6, 66, 163, 268, 270–271, 291, 304, 406
Currency Board, 129, 151
former government, 330
mandated to Britain, 6, 270
Palestine Custodian of Enemy Property registered files, 271
record classes, 271
remanet services, 330
see also Israel
Palestine, Anglo-American Committee of Inquiry on (1946), 54
Palestine and East Africa Loan Act (1926), 423–424
Palmer, William Waldegrave, 2nd Earl of Selborne, 71
pamphlets, 386–388, 390
Pan-Africanism, 365
Papua see British New Guinea
Papua New Guinea, 164, 281, 286
government gazettes, 286
Parasite Service, 136
parasitology, 146
Pares, Peter, 91
Paris Peace Conference (1919), 153
Paris, Treaty of (1814), 261
Parker, John, 86
Parkinson, Sir (Arthur Charles) Cosmo, (A C), 72, 73, 77, 86, 87
parliament, debates in, 147
parliamentary commission (for the colonies), 1
Parliamentary Commonwealth Affairs Committee, 141
parliamentary governments, 140
parliamentary liaison, 104–107, 333–335
parliamentary notices, scrutiny of, 346
parliamentary privileges, 140
parliamentary procedure, courses in, 338
parliamentary questions, 34, 41, 116
Parliamentary secretaries of Overseas Development, 93, 124
Parliamentary under-secretaries of state for the Colonies, 4, 14, 16, 38, 49, 53, 71–72, 111, 112, 114–118, 120, 124–127
Parliamentary under-secretaries of state for Commonwealth Affairs, 93
Parliamentary under-secretaries of state for Commonwealth Relations, 88, 126

Parliamentary under-secretaries of state for Commonwealth Relations and for the Colonies, 72
Parliamentary under-secretaries of state for Dominions Affairs, 86, 126
Parry, E, 100–106
Paskin, Sir (Jesse) John (J J), 74, 75, 79, 80
Passenger Acts (1855, 1863), 349
Passfield, 1st Baron see Webb, Sidney
passports, 331
applications, 164
and nationality cases, 331, 333, 352, 369, 370, 384, 385, 394
policy, 369, 370
practice, 384
and visas, 332, 338, 368
patents, 36, 382, 384
Patrick, Sir Paul Joseph, 89
Patriotic League of Britons Overseas, 149
patronage, 347, 383, 384
patronage original correspondence, 165, 348
Paxos, 265
peace treaties, 336, 412
Peck, Jasper Augustine, 99–107
Pedler, Sir Frederick (Johnson), (F J), 79, 80
Peel, Sir Frederick, (F), 79, 80
penal administration, 117, 320, 342
Penang, 5, 163, 208, 211, 213, 215, 218, 221, 291
government gazettes, 218
responsibility transferred to Colonial Office, 5
see also Straits Settlements
Pennsylvania, 31
records sub-division, 236
pension funds, 359
pensioners, income tax, 151
pensions, 15, 45, 133, 325, 347, 359–361, 381, 382, 383, 385
Perak, 163, 210, 211, 218, 220
record classes, 218
see also Malay States, Federated
Perim Island, 268
periodicals
circulation, 154
collection, 153
Perlis, 163, 211, 214, 219
record classes, 214, 219
see also Kedah and Perlis
Permanent secretaries of Overseas Development, 93
Permanent under-secretaries of state for the colonies, 4, 11, 19, 33, 50, 53, 54, 72, 127
Permanent under-secretaries of state for Commonwealth Affairs, 93
Permanent under-secretaries of state for Commonwealth Relations, 89
Permanent under-secretaries of state for Dominions Affairs, 86
Persian Gulf, 392, 394
political resident in, 269, 270
Personnel Department see Commonwealth Relations Office Departments
Personnel Divisions see Colonial Office Internal Services and other Departments
personnel and establishments (Africa), 362

personnel, medical, 117
Personnel original correspondence, 348, 406
personnel questions, 331
Perth, 17th Earl of *see* Drummond, John David
Pest Articles and News Summaries, 155
pest control, 126, 138, 155, 156, 341
pesticides, use and research, 127
Peters, William, 94
petitions, 31, 39, 164
　to the queen, 393
petroleum trade, 339–341, 377, 378
Petty, William, 1st Marquess of Lansdowne and Earl of Shelburne, 70
Petty-Fitzmaurice, George John Charles Mercer Nairne, 8th Marquess of Lansdowne, 71, 88
Phelps-Stokes Fund grant to Advisory Committee on Education in the Colonies, 14
Philippines, Commonwealth relations with, 380
Phipps, Constantine Henry, 1st Marquess of Normanby, 70
Phoenix Islands, 284
phosphate deposits, 284
photogrammetric techniques, 143
photographs, 67, 144, 383
Pickard, Sir Cyril (Stanley), (C S), 89, 90
picture sets, 334, 389, 390
Piper, R W, 85, 86, 94
Pirbright, 1st Baron *see* De Worms, Baron Henry
Pitcairn Islands, 280, 307
planning, 150, 370, 412
　correspondence, 412
　development schemes, 143
Planning and Research Unit *see* Commonwealth Relations Office Departments
Planning Staff, 420
Plant, D F, 87
plant and animal products, 136, 156
Plant Breeding and Genetics, Bueau of, 136
plant diseases, 140
plantation affairs, pre-restoration advisory bodies, 1–2, 30
plantations, 1–3
　West Africa, 157
planters, 148
Planters Association of Ceylon, 135
plants, 124, 138, 153
Plymouth, 2nd Earl of *see* Windsor-Clive, Ivor Miles
Polar Committee, 396
police, 318, 325, 336
police adviser, 100
Police Department *see* Colonial Office Subject Departments
police and fire services, 15, 382–384
Political Affairs Department *see* Commonwealth Relations Office Departments
Political Division *see* Commonwealth Relations Office Departments
political intelligence, supply of to governors, 336, 337
political parties, UK, 123–124, 133
Political Staff Officers' Department *see* Commonwealth Relations Office Departments

political studies, 152
politicians, 150
politics of tropical Commonwealth, 146
Pondoland, 181
Ponsonby, Arthur Augustus Harry, 1st Baron Ponsonby of Shulbrede (A), 86
Port Egmont, Falklands, 223
Portland, 3rd Duke of *see* Cavendish, William Henry
Portugal, the Portuguese, 173, 180, 196
　African territories, 182, 364
　Gold Coast, 199
　Indian territories, 380, 394, 395
　rule in Kedah, 213
　occupy Malacca, 215
　West Africa, 366
Post Office, 5
post-war planning, 27
post-war reconstruction, 16–18
Post-War Reconstruction in the Colonies/Post-War Problems, Committee on, 14
postal communications, 314, 367
　see also mails
postal matters, 15, 26, 324, 325, 331, 367
postgraduate medical education, 139
postgraduate students, 146, 148
postgraduate training in tropical agriculture, 157
posters, 67, 388, 390
Poynton, Sir (Arthur) Hilton, 72, 74, 79, 80
Poyser, Sir Kenneth Elliston, 98
Pratt, John Jeffreys, 2nd Earl and 1st Marquess of Camden, 70
precedence, 167, 333, 338, 368, 369, 393
précis books *see* Colonial Office records
preferences, 375
Prentice, Reginald Ernest, 95
President Truman's Fourth Point, 410
press
　archives, 153
　articles, 388
　conferences and briefings, 389
　cuttings, 386, 388–390
　legislation, 333–335
　liaison with, 333, 335, 386, 387, 389, 390
　London service *see* London press service
　matters, technical advice on, 333
　photographs, 388
　reactions, 389
　releases, 333
　supply of information to, 139, 318, 319, 341
Press Branch *see* Colonial Office Subject Departments
Press Section *see* Colonial Office Subject Departments
Pretoria
　British High Commissioner in, 25
　Town Council and Municipal Commission, 186, 187
preventive medicine, 125
Price, Sir (Charles) Roy, (C R), 87, 91, 92
price control, 411
price stabilization, 330, 411, 412
prices, 413
Pridie, Sir Eric Denholm, 100–103

primary producers, 140
primary and secondary industries, 339
prime ministers of dominions, 26
Prime Minister's Office, wartime contact with Dominions Office, 27
Prince Edward Island, 164, 274, 279, 291, 301, 305
  record classes, 279
Principal Staff Officers' Department *see* Commonwealth Relations Office Departments
Printing Branch/Department/Unit *see* Colonial Office, shared services with Dominions Office; Dominions Office
priority passages, 324
prison administration in the overseas dependent territories, adviser on, 105, 106
prison service, 383, 384
prisoners of war, 56, 319, 339, 352
  in Korea, 382
Prisoners of War Departments *see* Colonial Office Subject Departments
Pritchard, Sir Neil, (N), 89, 93
private bills, 382, 383
privileges, 393, 394
  of colonial representatives in UK, 333, 338
  diplomatic, 393
Privy Council, 1, 2, 32
Privy Council Committee of 1675 (the Lords of Trade), records 2, 3, 32
Privy Council Committee on Overseas Research, 127
prize, 352
Prize Court cases, 40, 167, 406
proclamations, 31, 52
Production Department *see* Colonial Office Subject Departments
production, improvement of methods of, 156
Production and Marketing, 13, 328, 407, 412–413
Production and Marketing Department *see* Colonial Office Subject Departments
Production, Ministry of, wartime involvement with Dominions Office, 27
professional education, 111
professional qualifications, 384
professional and technical services, 15
professorships, visiting, 140
Profumo, John Dennis, 72
promotions, 15, 347, 348
property, 385, 410
property acquisition acts, Indian and Pakistan, 382–384
property agreements with allied governments, 329, 330
property claims, 382, 383
  under peace treaties, 329, 330
Proprieties, 31, 236
protection of UK commercial interests, 375
protective security, 335, 336
Protector's Council, 1
protectorates, 5
protocol, 385
Protocol Departments *see* Commonwealth Relations Office Departments
Protocol files, 417

Protocol and Conference Department, 419
Protocol and Nationality Department *see* Commonwealth Relations Office Departments
Proud, Commander J C, 106
provision of equipment, 374
public appeals, 383
public ceremonies, 393
public health, 155, 317, 320, 331, 342, 384
  diploma in, 148
Public Offices, Committee of Inquiry into, 55
Public Record Office, xv, 62, 64, 65
  arranging Colonial Office records, 30, 39–40, 65
Public Record Office Act 1877, 62
Public Record Office Current Guide, 65
Public Records Acts
  1958, 63, 64
  1967, 64
public relations, 132, 333, 334
Public Relations Department *see* Colonial Office Subject Departments
Public Relations and Information Department *see* Colonial Office Subject Departments
public relations officers, 385, 386
Public Relations Section *see* Commonwealth Relations Office Departments
public works and buildings, correspondence, 413
publications, 124, 146, 153, 318, 319, 333, 341, 373, 387, 388, 390, 391
Publications Branch *see* Colonial Office Subject Departments
publicity, 135, 144, 149, 317, 319, 333, 341, 385–390
Publicity Policy Section *see* Commonwealth Relations Office Departments
purchase tax, 361
pyrethrum, 328

qualifications of lawyers, 318
quality improvement, 156
quarantine, 383
quasi-government organizations, 151
Quebec, 164, 273, 274, 279
  record classes, 279
Queen Charlotte Islands, 273
Queen Elizabeth House, Oxford, 130, 151–152
Queensland, 163, 226–228, 230–231, 280, 281, 291, 305, 306
  record classes, 231
Quin, Windham Thomas Wyndham, 4th Earl of Dunraven, 71

race questions in UK, 321, 331, 343
race relations, 133, 146
radio, 139, 389–391
  equipment, 387
  tapes, 388
  see also wireless
Rae, Sir Alexander (Montgomery) Wilson, (A M W), 99–105
rail warrants, 361
railway and transport developments, 331
railways, 325
Rajah of Sarawak Fund, 348

INDEX

Rankine, T A, 101
ratification, 393
raw materials, 27, 45, 138, 379
Raw Materials Department *see* Commonwealth Relations Office Departments
reception of distressed UK citizens, 383, 384
reciprocal, enforcement of judgments, 385
reconstruction, 16–18, 413
records, 382
   access to, 385
Records and Research Section *see* Commonwealth Relations Office Departments
recoveries
   from other departments, 360, 361
   of loans, 361
recreation, 153
recruitment
   director of, overseas service, 76
   of experts, 374
   questions, 371, 406
   of teachers, 148–149
   and training, 77–79, 115
Red River Colony, 276
Redpath, A W, 91
Reed, Adrian Harbottle, 91, 92, 94
Rees-Williams, David Rees, 1st Baron Ogmore, 72, 88
reference material, 386, 388, 390, 391
reference section, 333
refresher courses in information work, 388–390
refugees, 125, 332, 396
   from Ireland, 259
regional commissions, 326
regional councils for medical research, 117
Regional Economic Commissions for Africa, Asia and Latin America, 337, 338
regional information offices, 333
regional and inter-territorial research, 342, 342
Regional Shipping Council, 397–398
regionalism, 16
registers, registrars and registration, Colonial Office *see* Colonial Office records
Registrar's Branch, 418
registration as citizens of the UK and colonies, 384
registration of births, marriages and deaths, 368–370, 384, 385, 394
registration of companies, 377, 378, 382
registration of treaties with United Nations, 370, 396
registry codes *see* Colonial Office records
religion, 151, 154
remittance problems, 377
Reoccupation of British territories, correspondence, 413
Reparations, 343
   correspondence, 413
repatriation, 344, 385
   recoveries, 359, 361
   UK citizens, 383, 384
representations, 352
Republic of Ireland *see* Irish Republic
Republic of Ireland Act (1948), 260
Research Committee, 14, 320
Research Department *see* Colonial Office Subject Departments
research funds, 148
research institutes
   academic staffs, 146
   directors, 20
   records, 61, 406
research laboratories, 113
research organizations, 117, 150, 155
research papers, 391
research personnel, training, 118
research and planning, education, 124
research policy, 126
research projects, 146
research students, 153
resettlement, 151
residential club facilities, 153, 154
residual passage claims, 360, 383
Restoration, the, 2
Review of Applied Entomology, The, 139
Review of Applied Mycology, The, 140
Revision of Records Branch *see* Colonial Office, shared services with Dominions Office; Dominions Office
Revision of Records Committee, 63
Rhind, Donald, 102–106
Rhode Island, 31
   records sub-division, 236
Rhodesia, 162, 180, 297, 298, 364
   funds for posts in, 361
   sessional papers, 180
   see also Rhodesia, North-Eastern; Rhodesia, Northern; Rhodesia and Nyasaland, Federation of; Rhodesia, Southern
Rhodesia Department *see* Commonwealth Relations Office Departments
Rhodesia Economic Department, 419
Rhodesia, North-Eastern, 162, 177, 180, 298
Rhodesia, Northern (Zambia), 6, 7, 61, 162, 167, 170, 175, 177–178, 180, 182, 183, 291, 296, 297, 406
   record classes, 178
Rhodesia, Northern and Nyasaland, 362
Rhodesia and Nyasaland, Federation of (Central African Federation), 7, 61, 162, 170, 175–177, 179, 183, 360, 362, 368, 379
   economy of, 375, 376
   external affairs, 362
   internal affairs, 362
   Monckton Commission, 175
   political developments, 363
   record classes, 175
Rhodesia and Nyasaland Inter-Territorial Conference, Standing Advisory, 170
Rhodesia Political Department, 419
Rhodesia Railways, 170
Rhodesia, Southern (Zimbabwe), 6, 7, 61, 167, 168, 170, 175, 180, 182–184, 291, 298, 362, 364
   correspondence, 57
   dealt with by Commonwealth Relations Office, 7
   dealt with by Dominions Office, 6, 353
   defence co-operation with, 371
   governor of, 57
   London High Commission Office, 25
   record classes, 184

Rhodesia University, 362
rice, trade, 328, 339, 376, 377
Richards, F B, 92
RIP Working Party, 379
Ripon, 1st Earl of *see* Robinson, Frederick John
Ripon, 1st Marquess of *see* Robinson, George Frederick Samuel
Risley, Sir John Shuckburgh, 96, 97
road development projects, 152
road planning and construction, 152
road research, 119, 152, 341, 342
Road Research Board, 129, 152
Road Research Laboratory Colonial Section/Tropical Section, head of, 104–106
Road Research Organization, 119, 152
road transport, 314, 324, 325
Rob, John Vernon, 93
Roberts, Charles Stuart, 85, 86
Roberts, Frederick, Earl Roberts of Kandahar, papers, 54
Roberts-Wray, Sir Kenneth Owen, 97–105
Robertson, Patrick Allan Pearson, 83
Robertson, W A, 99–100
Robinson, Frederick John, Viscount Goderich, later 1st Earl of Ripon, 70
Robinson, George Frederick Samuel, 1st Marquess of Ripon, 70
Robinson, K E, 80
Robinson, S, 79, 80
Robison, Lionel McDowall, 99–102
Rochester, Earl of *see* Hyde, Lawrence
rock, laboratory investigations, 150
rocket and satellite vehicles, 121
Roddan, Gilbert McMickling, 99, 103–106
Rodrigues, 261
Rogers, Sir Frederic, 72
Rogers, Sir Philip, 75, 76, 80–82
Ross Institute of Tropical Hygiene, 148
Rowell, T R, 98
Royal Adventurers of England trading with Africa, Company of, 53
Royal African Company of England, 3, 53, 199
Royal African Society, 129, 152
Royal Agricultural Society of the Commonwealth, 130, 152
Royal Air Force (RAF), xv
  apprenticeships, 371
  units, visits of, 373
Royal Asiatic Society, 128, 152–153
Royal Botanic Gardens, Kew, 13, 128, 153
royal bounty, 393
Royal Central Asian Society, 129, 153
Royal Colonial Institute, 128, 153
royal commission to investigate landed estates in West Indies overburdened with mortgages (1854), 234
Royal Commission on the West Indies, 18, 116, 235
Royal Commonwealth Society, 153
  Commonwealth Library, 152, 153
  Information Bureau, 153
royal charters, 276
  grant of, 173, 231
  warrants, 369, 393
royal emblems, use of, 332

Royal Empire Society, 153
royal family, 368–370, 393
  autographs, 368
  gifts, 393
  loyal messages, 368, 393
  patronage, 368, 393
  speeches from the throne, 368, 369
  state portraits, 368
  visits, 368, 393
Royal Geographical Society, 68
royal instructions to governors, 368, 369
Royal India, Pakistan and Ceylon Society, 154
Royal Institute of International Affairs, 129, 153
royal names and emblems, use of, 394
Royal Niger Company, 202, 203, 205
Royal Overseas League, 129, 154
Royal Society
  Biological Secretary of, 155
  National Committee on Antarctic Research, 130, 154
Royal Society for India, Pakistan and Ceylon, 130, 154
Royal Technical College, Kenya, 111
Royal West Africa Frontier Force *see* West Africa Frontier Force
royalties and taxation, 340
Ruanda-Urundi, 193
rubber, 327, 328, 329, 340
  commodity policy, 379
  trade, 328, 376, 377
Rumbold, Sir (Horace) Algernon (Fraser), (H A F), 89
Rupert, Prince, grant to, 274
Rupert's Land, 274, 276
rural development, 157
rural life, 146
Rushford, Antony Redfern, 100, 101, 106, 107
Russell, Sir Alison, 98, 99
Russell, Lord John, 1st Earl Russell, 70
  papers, 54
Russia
  takes Ionian Islands, 265
  see also Union of Soviet Socialist Republics

Sabah, 163, 216–218, 220
  see also British North Borneo
Sabine, N J, 79, 80
Sackville, 1st Viscount *see* Germain, George Sackville
Sackville, Herbrand Edward Dundonald Brassey, 9th Earl De La Warr, 72
safety of British subjects overseas in emergency, war, 371, 373
St Aldwyn, 1st Earl *see* Hicks-Beach, Sir Michael Edward
St Andrew's Island, 198
St Christopher (St Kitts), 136, 163, 236, 243, 245, 248–252, 254, 291, 301
  record classes, 251
  see also Leeward Islands; Nevis; West Indies
St Christopher-Nevis-Anguilla, 245, 249–251
St Croix (Santa Cruz), 163, 251
  record classes, 251
  see also West Indies

INDEX

St Eustatius, 163, 251–252
  original correspondence, 252
  see also West Indies
St Helena, 4, 76, 290, 291, 297, 298, 300–308, 406
  and dependencies, 163, 224–225
  record classes, 225
St John, 253
St Kitts see St Christopher
St Lucia, 4, 136, 163, 245, 252–253, 257, 291, 301, 406
  record classes, 253
  see also West Indies; Windward Islands
St Michael and St George, Order of see Malta; Order of St Michael and St George
St Thomas, 163, 253
  entry books, 253
  see also West Indies
St Vincent, 136, 163, 245, 253–254, 257, 292, 301, 406
  and the Grenadines, 253
  record classes, 254
  see also West Indies; Windward Islands
salaries, home and overseas, 359–361
Salisbury, 5th Marquess of see Gascoyne-Cecil, Robert Arthur James
Salisbury, Southern Rhodesia, 183
Sandford, G R, 423, 424
Sandhurst, cadetships, 371
Sandys, Duncan, Baron Duncan-Sandys, 71, 88
sanitary questions, 114
Santa Cruz see St Croix
Santo, New Hebrides, 285
Santo Domingo, 163, 254
  Claims Committee, 254
  original correspondence, 254
Sarawak, 5, 132, 163, 207–209, 216, 217, 219–220, 292, 308, 309, 406
  Commission of Inquiry into North Borneo and Sarawak regarding Malaysian Federation (Cobbold Commission, 1962), 217, 219, 220
  Commonwealth relations with, 381
  Rajah of Sarawak Fund, papers, 219
  record classes, 219
Sarawak Association, 129, 154
Saskatchewan, 164, 274, 275, 279–280
  record classes, 279–280
satellite communications, 123, 367, 385
savingrams see Colonial Office records
savings banks, 330, 411
Savings, correspondence, 413
Scheme for the Interchange of Teachers, 147
scholars, 150
scholarships, 148
  for study abroad, 125
  for study in Britain, 133
  selection of candidates, 132, 140
  scholarship and fellowship plan, 389
  scholarship commission, 390
School of Oriental Studies, 129, 154
School of Oriental and African Studies see London, University of
schools
  lectures for use in, 157
  loan service for, 153

VSO help, 157
Schuster, Sir G, 97
science of the East, 152
scientific advisory staff, 374
scientific bodies, 320, 383, 384
scientific conventions, 383
scientific co-operation, 138
scientific developments, 141
scientific enquiries, 141
Scientific and Industrial Research, Department of, 155, 156
  Overseas Division, Building Research Station, later Colonial Building Liaison Section, later Tropical Division, 129, 150
scientific information, exchange, 141
scientific liaison offices, 141
scientific papers, reports, 144
scientific personnel, government, 115
Scientific Relations Department, 419
scientific research, 113
Scoones, Sir Geoffry Allen Percival, 89
Scott, Sir Davis (Aubrey), (D A), 90, 91
Scott, Sir Michael, (M), 94
Scott, Sir Robert, 207
Scott, T A, 91
'Scramble for Africa', 5
seals, 231, 332, 369, 393
seamen, 382–384
  certificates, 369, 370, 394
  welfare, 344
Searle, W F, 101
Second World War, 7, 43
  impact on Colonial Office, 16–17, 66
  impact on Dominions Office, 27, 58–59, 66
secret correspondence, 345
secret despatches, 162
secret and semi-official communications, Colonial Office, 49–51
secret service fund, 346
Secretaries of State, 2, 3, 30, 32, 40
Secretaries of State for the Colonies (1768–1794), 3, 4, 70
Secretaries of State for the Colonies (1854–1966), 5, 8, 14, 17, 21, 23, 37, 38, 40, 47, 49, 53, 54, 70–71, 96, 116, 127, 132, 133, 135, 136, 142, 145, 148–151, 157, 268, 269, 286
Secretaries of State for Commonwealth Affairs, 8, 93, 382
Secretaries of State for Commonwealth Relations, 7, 8, 21, 88, 147, 393
Secretaries of State for Dominions Affairs, 6, 7, 23, 26–27, 54, 86, 144
Secretaries of State for Foreign Affairs, 27, 207
Secretaries of State for War and the Colonies, 4, 40, 70
Secretary for Technical Co-operation, 7, 110, 111, 119, 124, 125
Secretary, Southern, 2, 3, 40
security bodies in UK, 335, 336
security and defence of the colonies, 331
security intelligence advisers, 104–107
security officer for overseas duties, 101
security training, 336
Sedgwick, Richard Romney, 89

seeds, 339
Seel, Sir George Frederick, (G F), 74, 79, 80
Seely, Colonel J E B, 71
Selangor, 163, 210, 211, 220
   record classes, 220
   see also Malay States, Federated
Selborne, Earl of see Palmer, William Waldegrave
Sellers, W, 104–106
Senegal, 199, 366
Senegambia, 163, 203
   Confederation, 199
   see also Gambia
service advisers in Commonwealth countries, 373
service aircraft movements and air trooping, 372, 373
service allowances, 371
service, conditions of, 371–373
service exercises, 372, 373
service liaison, staffs and advisers, 372, 373
service pensions, 359
service personnel, secondment to and from Commonwealth defence forces, 371–373
service, record of, 360
service recruitment, 383, 384
service training courses, 373
Services Department see Colonial Office Subject Departments; Commonwealth Relations Office Departments
services legislation, 371, 373
settlement overseas, 155, 349, 353, 359–361
Seven Years' War, 273
Sewell, Thomas Robert McKie, 94
Seychelles, 4, 163, 206, 261–263, 280, 292, 301, 306–308, 406
   Office of the Trade Representative for, 130, 149
   record classes, 262–263
Shaftesbury, Earls of see Ashley
Shakespeare, Sir Geoffrey Hithersay, (G), 86
Shannon, Godfrey Eccleston Boyd, 89, 93
Shaw, John Dennis, 92
Shaw-Lefevre, Sir John George, 71
Sheffield, A H, 84, 85
Shelburne, Earl of see Petty, William
Shepherd, Malcolm Newton, 2nd Baron Shepherd, 93
Shiels, Sir (Thomas) Drummond, 72
shipping, 21, 314, 353, 367, 375, 377, 378, 407, 413, 414
   see also merchant shipping
shipping controls, 18
shipping freights, 343
shipping policy, 352
shipping and ports, 324, 325
shipping returns, 162, 249, 253
ships, 125
   cargoes, 31
Shuckburgh, Sir John Evelyn, 72, 73
Siam see Thailand
Sidebotham, John Biddulph, 79–82
Sierra Leone, 4, 5, 131, 157, 163, 198, 199, 201, 204–205, 292, 297–300, 303, 305, 366, 370, 378, 406
   contribution to Entomological Research Committee, 125

   economic and financial questions, 365, 366
   economic relations with, 363
   Fourah Bay College, 111
   funds for, 361
   funds for posts in, 361
   general and political questions, 365
   governor of, 15
   record classes, 54, 204–205
   relations with, 366
   rice farming in, 115
Sierra Leone Company, 204
Sikkim, 380, 395
silvicultural problems, 138
Simmons, R J, 99–102
Simonsen, Sir John Lionel, 101
Simpson, S R, 104–106
Singapore, 5, 132, 148, 163, 207, 208, 214–217, 219–221, 292, 308, 309
   commissioner-general for the UK in South-East Asia at, 207
   deputy UK commissioner, 76
   economic relations with, 377
   fall of (1942), 207
   Information Office, 334
   minister of state for the Far East at, 207
   political relations with, 381
   Polytechnic, 111
   record classes, 220–221
   relations with Malaya, 380, 381
   responsibility of Colonial Office, 5
   see also Straits Settlements
Sinkiang, 380, 394
Sinn Fein, 259
Sino-Soviet trade control, 340
sisal, 328
slave trade, 5, 198, 234
slavery, 5
Smart, Archibald Guelph Holdsworth, 98
Smedley, Sir Harold, (H), 91, 92
Smele, William Samuel George, 92
Smith, D M, 84, 85
Smith, Lt-General Sir Harry G W, papers, 54
Smith, John, 98, 99
Smith, Maurice George, 84, 85
Smith, R V, 71
Smith, Trafford, 76, 77, 80–82, 93
Smith, William Jeffrey, 91
Snelling, Sir Arthur (Wendell), 89, 93
social affairs, 145
social co-operation, 235
social development, 115, 124 141, 146
   training, 124
Social Development, Consultative Panel for, 110, 124
Social Development in the Colonies, Advisory Committee on, 110, 112, 118
social hygiene, 342
social institutes, 146
social insurance, 342, 382–384
social life of empire, 157
social matters, 158
social questions, 338
social reform programmes, 235
social science, 146, 341

research in, 118
social security, 328, 342, 343, 382–384
Social Service Departments *see* Colonial Office Subject Departments
social services, 331, 382, 383, 406
  projects, 157
social studies, 152
social welfare, 17, 113, 118, 141, 157, 320, 342
  adviser on, 99–106
  and development, 342
  services, 112
social workers, 112, 118
societies, 147, 383
Society of Comparative Legislation and International Law, 129, 134, 154
Society for the Overseas Settlement of British Women, 158
sociology, 118, 146, 152
  sociological research, 300
soil conference, 114
soil erosion, 413
soil research, 115
Soil Science, Bureau of, 136
soil use in colonies, 114
Soils, Bureau of, 136
Solomon Islands *see* British Solomon Islands Protectorate
Somaliland, 163, 170, 191, 192, 268, 292, 296, 297, 406
  Protectorate, 296, 333
  record classes, 192
South Africa, 123, 162, 180–181, 360, 370, 396
  constabulary, 180, 181
  customs union, 180, 181
  intercontinental Council, 180, 181
  railways, 180, 181
  record classes, 181
  Secretary of State's Tour, 181
  war in (1870s), 5
  war in (Boer War, 1899–1902), 5
  see also South Africa, Union of
South Africa High Commission, 25, 57, 162, 180–183, 185, 298, 393
  commissions for high commissioner, 369
  correspondence, 57
  exceptional registration arrangements, 35
  governor of Cape Colony as high commissioner, 181
  record classes, 182–183
  territories, 6, 25, 58, 167, 168, 353, 359, 360, 363
  see also Basutoland; Bechuanaland Protectorate; Swaziland
South Africa, Republic of, 187
South Africa, Union of, 121, 162, 186–188
  appoints accredited representative in Ottawa, 25
  British high commissioner to (1930), 25
  Canadian high commission appointed in, 25
  defence co-operation with, 371
  economy of, 375
  financial questions, 379
  foreign affairs, 396, 397
  funds for, 361
  governors-general, 57
  handled by Dominions Office, 6, 57, 353
  high commissioner *see* South Africa High Commission
  Indians in, 396
  internal political affairs, 365, 369, 392, 418
  London high commission office established, 24
  mandated territory, 184–185
  racial relations, 396
  record classes, 56, 188
  separate Dominions Office series of confidential print, 60
  sterling area development, 374
  territorial ambitions, 12
South African Colonization Society, 158
South African/South African Protectorates Department *see* Colonial Office Geographical Departments
South African Republic *see* Transvaal
South America, economic development, 149
South Arabia, Federation of, 343
South Asia/Asian Departments *see* Commonwealth Relations Office Departments
South Asia (Economic) Department, 419
South Australia, 163, 226, 227, 231–232, 305, 306
  record classes, 231–232
South Australian Association, 231
South-East Asia *see* Far East
South-East Asia Collective Defence Treaty, 380
South-East Asia defence, 380
South-East Asia Department *see* Colonial Office Geographical Departments
South-East Asia Treaty Organization (SEATO), xv, 358
  Commonwealth relations with, 380
  economic aspects, 374, 381
  matters affecting Malaya, 381
  service exercises, 372
South Georgia, 125, 224
South Orkney, 224
South Pacific Air Transport Council, 120
South Pacific Commission, 307
  Commonwealth relations with, 380
South Sandwich, 224
South Shetlands, 224
South West Africa (Namibia), 162, 184–185, 396, 397
  record classes, 185
South Yemen, 163, 271
  see also Aden
Southern Africa Air Transport Council, 120
Southern Africa, 147, 155
  non-British territories in, 363, 397
Southern Africa Department *see* Colonial Office Geographical Departments; Commonwealth Relations Office Departments
Southern Africa Settlement Association, 129, 155
Southern Rhodesia *see* Rhodesia, Southern
Southern Rhodesia Departments *see* Commonwealth Relations Office Departments
Southgate, S J, 82
Soviet Union *see* Union of Soviet Socialist Republics
space research, 121

Spain
  captures Bahamas, 237
  cedes Cayman Islands to Britain, 243
  claim in Falklands, 223
  Fernando Po, 198
  founds Havana, 247
  Gibraltar captured from, 264
  Minorca captured from, 267
  Minorca ceded to, 267
  occupies Curaçao, 244
  occupies St Croix, 251
  occupies Santo Domingo, 254
  settles Jamaica, 247
  territories in Portuguese West Africa, 366
  Trinidad captured from, 255
special care, 406
Special Commonwealth African Assistance Plan (SCAAP), xv, 358, 363
special missions, 359
Special United Nations Fund for Economic Development (SUNFED), xv, 358, 376
specialist agencies, 336, 337
specimens, 144
speeches
  material for, 386, 387
  preparation of, 389
  speaker tours, 388, 390
Spencer-Churchill, Charles Richard John, 9th Duke of Marlborough, 71
spices, 327, 328, 339, 340
sponges, 340
sponsored visits, 388, 390, 391
sporting events, 387, 388, 390
Spring-Rice, Thomas, 1st Baron Monteagle, 70
Sri Lanka (formerly Ceylon), 163, 209, 221
Stacpoole, John Westworth, 86, 94
staff college, 372
staff questions, 338
stamp issues, 324, 325
  see also colonial stamp issues
Standing Central African Council, 170
Standing Conference for the Co-ordination of Scientific Research, 129, 155
Standing Committees *indexed under key word of title*
Stanhope, Edward, 70
Stanley, Edward Geoffrey, Lord Stanley, 14th Earl of Derby, 54, 70
Stanley, Edward Henry, 15th Earl of Derby, 70
Stanley, Edward Montague Cavendish, Lord Stanley, 86
Stanley, Frederick Arthur, 16th Earl of Derby, 70
Stanley, Henry Sydney Herbert Cloete, 92
Stanley, Oliver Frederick George, 71
Stanton, Sir (Ambrose) Thomas, 96, 97
State Paper Office, 30, 62
state papers domestic, 66
stateless persons, 369, 370, 384, 394
statistical section, 377–379
Statistical Summary of the Mineral Industry, 150
statistics, 115, 139, 329, 341, 359–361, 406, 407, 411, 413
  returns, 164
  see also Colonial Office records: blue books

Statistics Department *see* Colonial Office Subject Departments
status of forces agreements, 373
Statute of Westminster (1931), 24
statutory development corporations, 326, 327, 340, 341
steel, 374
steel advisory staff, 374
Steel-Maitland, Sir Arthur Herbert Drummond Ramsay, 72
Steering Committee on International Organizations, 338
Stephen, Sir James, 4, 38, 72
Stephenson, Sir John Everard, (J E), 86, 87, 89
sterling, 28, 377
sterling area, 27, 137, 138, 374, 377–379
Sterling Area Statistical Committee, 123
stereos, 388
Stevenson, Sir James, Baron Stevenson of Holmbury, 96
Stewart, Robert, Viscount Castlereagh, 70
Stikine, Territory of, 273
Stockdale, Sir Frank Arthur, 96–99
Stone, Bertram Gilchrist, 83
Stonehouse, John Thomson, 72
Storar, Leonore Elizabeth Therese, 92
stored products research, 115
stores and equipment, 143
Stourton, Sir Ivo (Herbert Evelyn Joseph), 102–107
stowaways, 382–384
Strachey, Sir Charles, 73
Straits Settlements, 5, 163, 221–222, 292, 298, 301, 305, 307, 308, 406
  governor of, 208, 211, 213, 214, 222
  record classes, 221–222
  responsibility of Colonial Office, 5
  see also Christmas Island; Cocos (Keeling) Islands; Labuan; Malacca; Penang; Singapore
Straits Settlements Association (1903), 129, 132, 155
strategic exports, 377, 379
strategic materials controls, 328, 329, 377–379
Stuart, C R, 99
students, 321, 344, 386–388, 406
  hospitality to, 144
  research students, 153
  welfare, 136, 387–389
Students Department *see* Colonial Office Subject Departments
study centre, 152
subject departments *see* Colonial Office
Sudan, 5, 163, 192–193, 365, 392, 395, 396
  government gazettes, 193
Suez Canal, 392, 395
sugar, 5, 327–329, 339, 340, 349, 367, 375, 397
  industry, 148
  sugar cane, 234
sugar agreements, international and Commonwealth, 148, 328
sulphur, 379
Summer Conference, secretariat for, 170, 300
summit talks, 372
Sungei Ujong, 163, 216, 222

record classes, 222
see also Jelebu; Negri Sembilan
supplementary correspondence *see* Colonial Office records
supplements, 390
supplies to colonies, 20, 327, 343
supplies, correspondence, 407, 413–414
Supplies Department *see* Colonial Office Subject Departments
supplies and food, 79
supplies for overseas posts, 360
supply of arms and equipment, 371, 373, 388–390
Supply Department *see* Dominions Office
supply and munitions, 371
Supply, Ministry of, 27
surface transport, 324
Surinam, 163, 254
  record classes, 254
Surridge, Brewster Joseph, 99–106
Surridge, Sir (Ernest) Rex (Edward), (E R), 423
Survey of International Affairs, 153
surveys, 118, 320, 326, 331, 382, 383
surveys adviser and Director of Colonial (Geodetic and Topographical) Surveys, 99–106
Swabey, F S, 104–106
Swaziland, 6, 25, 162, 181, 182, 185–186, 292, 298, 353, 362, 365, 369, 370, 393
  development and welfare in, 359, 362, 365
  record classes, 185–186
  see also South Africa High Commission
Sweaney, William Douglas, 83–85
Sweden, Guadeloupe ceded to, 246
Swinton, 1st Earl of *see* Cunliffe-Lister, Sir Philip
Sydney, Royal Agricultural Society of the Commonwealth conference at, 152
Sydney, 1st Viscount *see* Townshend, Thomas
Syers, Sir Cecil George Lewis, (C G L), 87, 89
Sykes, Edwin Leonard, 85, 89, 91, 92
Symon, Sir Alexander Colin Burlington, (A C B), 89
Syria, 392

Tait, Hugh Nimmo, 87
Tanganyika, 6, 163, 189, 193–195, 292, 296, 297, 351, 363, 364, 406
  funds for posts in, 361
  governor, 16, 193, 423
  Information Office, 334
  loans, 423–424
  mandated, 6, 193
  manpower problems in, 115
  record classes, 193
  see also Tanzania
Tanganyika Agricultural Corporation, 150
Tanganyika Department *see* Colonial Office Geographical Departments
Tanganyika and Somaliland Department *see* Colonial Office Geographical Departments; Commonwealth Relations Office Departments
Tangier, 163, 196, 263
  domestic records, 54, 196
  original correspondence and general registers, 196

Tanzania, 163, 193–195, 363, 364
  see also Tanganyika; Zanzibar
Tariff Reform League, 138
tariffs
  tariff matters, 132, 331
  and trade agreements, 315, 375, 414
Tasmania (Van Diemen's Land), 4, 10, 163, 226–228, 232–233, 292, 305, 306
  record classes, 232–233
taxation, 153, 315, 316, 330, 411, 414
  double taxation, 378, 379
  legislation, 151
taxonomic work, 155
Taylor, Sir Reginald William, 103
Taylor, Stephen James Lake, Baron Taylor of Harlow, 72, 88
tea, trade, 327, 328, 339, 340, 376, 377
teachers, 382
  associations/organizations, 147, 148
  exchange, 147, 386–389
  recruitment, 148, 149
  training, 124
teaching materials, 133
Tebbitt, Sir Donald (Claude), (D C), 94
technical assistance, 111, 116, 125, 362
  bodies, 384
  expenditure, 21, 361
  policy, 374
Technical Assistance Department *see* Commonwealth Relations Office Departments
technical co-operation, 124, 131, 138
  expenditure, 366
  policy, 376, 379
Technical Co-operation, Department of (DTC), xiii, 7, 61, 131, 132, 143, 151, 156, 357, 361
  becomes Ministry of Overseas Development, 7
  committees, 168
  Communications Department, 21, 61, 127
  liaison with, 21, 365, 376, 390, 391
  overseas aid departments of, combined, 7
  Overseas Division, 21
  records, 61
  registration system, 61
  transfer of Colonial Office departments to, 20, 21, 47, 170, 310, 314, 315, 319–321, 325, 348
  see also Secretary for Technical Co-operation
Technical Co-operation Scheme (TCS), xv, 358, 360, 374
technical education, 111, 124
  adviser, 105, 106
Technical Education and Training for Overseas Countries, Council for, 111, 124
technical information, exchange, 131
technical investigations, 139
technical personnel committee, 374
technical staff, 143
telecommunications, 21, 123, 314, 324, 325, 352, 367, 406
  liaison officer, 101
  see also satellite
telegrams 48, 49
  guidance, 387, 388, 390
  and telephones, 26, 360, 361, 396

Telegraph Branch *see* Colonial Office Subject
    Departments
telegraph matters, 331
    communications, 121
    services, 121
Telegraph Section *see* Colonial Office, shared
    services with Dominions Office;
    Commonwealth Relations Office
    Departments; Dominions Office
television, 133, 139, 334, 335, 386–391
    adviser on, 106
Tempany, Sir Harold Augustin, (Dr H A), 98, 99
Terengganu (Tregganu, Trengganu, Trenggnu,
    Trenggany), 163, 208, 211, 222
    record classes, 222
Termite Research Unit, 126, 130, 155
territorial waters, 332, 337, 338, 352, 382, 383
textile import quotas, 411
Thailand (Siam), 207, 380
    agreement about Trengganu, 222
    occupies Kedah, 213–214
    suzerain of Kelantan, 214
theatrical distribution, 388, 389
Thomas, Ambler Reginald, 75, 76, 80–82
Thomas, (Thomas) George, 93
Thomas, Ivor, later Bulmer-Thomas, 72
Thomas, James Henry, 71, 86
Thompson, John Kenneth, 82–84
Thompson, Sir Richard, (Hilton Marler), (R H), 1st
    baronet, 88
Thompson River, 273
Thomson, George Morgan, Baron Thomson of
    Monifieth, 93
Thomson, J B, 97
Thomson, John (Ian), 90
Tibet, 380, 395
Tilney, Sir John (Dudley Robert Tarleton), (J D),
    72, 88
Tilsit, Treaty of (1807), 265
timber, 137, 138, 340, 375, 379
tin, trade, 376, 377
tinplate, 374
titles, 369, 393
    'Excellency', 'Honourable', 368
    'Royal', 394
toasts, 369, 393
tobacco, trade, 327, 328, 339, 340, 375, 379
Tobago, 4, 163, 235, 255, 292, 301
    record classes, 255
    relations with, 367
    see also Trinidad; West Indies; Windward Islands
Togo, 366
Togoland, 6, 163, 201, 205–206, 257, 292, 299,
    300, 304
    mandated to Britain, 6, 200, 205
    record classes, 205–206
Tomlinson, Sir George John Frederick, 73
Tonga, 164, 280, 286, 292, 307
    record classes, 286
    see also Western Pacific High Commission
topographical mapping, surveying, 143
Toro, 194
Toronto, Royal Agricultural Society of the
    Commonwealth conference at, 152

Tortola, 243, 251
Toulon, occupation of (1793), 263
tourism, 136, 149, 325
tours, 360, 383, 387
Toussaint l'Ouverture, François Dominique, 254
town planning, 116
Townshend, Thomas, 1st Viscount Sydney, 70
trade agreements, 26
    bilateral, 327, 329, 343
Trade, Board of (1696–1782), 3–4, 25–27, 30
    acts and proceedings of colonial councils and
        legislation, in records, 32
    calendars, 31
    entry books, 30–32, 66, 236
    journals, 31
        transcript (1704–1782), 65
    letter books, 30
    'Naval office lists', 31
    president, 3, 4
Trade, Board of (1784–c. 1801), 32–33
    adviser to government, 4
Trade, Board of, 36–117
    administers Passenger Acts (1873), 349
    co-operation with Dominions Office, Second
        World War, 27
    shared care of Imperial Institute (1902), 138
    specialized agencies' responsibilities transferred
        to Ministry of Overseas Development, 8
Trade, Commission of (1625), 1
trade commissioners, 25, 338
    agents etc, 414
trade, correspondence, 414
Trade, Council of (1660), 2
Trade, Council for (1670), 2
Trade Department *see* Commonwealth Relations
    Office Departments
Trade and Development, Committee on, 329
trade marks, 331, 382
trade missions, 353
Trade and Navigation Committee (1657), 1
trade negotiations, international, 414
Trade and Plantations, Lords of (Privy Council
    Committee, 1675), 2, 3, 31
trade, preferential, 138
trade promotion, 136
trade, reciprocal, 140
trade returns, 414
trade unions, 342, 343
    and industrial relations, 328, 343
    see also labour
Trades Union Congress, 116
trading, 410
training, 406
    cases and experts, 374
    postgraduate training, 138
    undergraduate training, 138
    see also recruitment
training courses
    in civil defence, 373
    for the Colonial Service, adviser on, 100
    in information work, 334, 388, 389–391
training facilities, 110–111, 120, 124, 131, 374
Training of Nurses for the Colonies, Committee on
    the, 109, 120

INDEX

transactions of learned societies, collection, 153
transfers, 15, 347, 381
Transjordan (Jordan), 163, 268, 271, 292, 304, 406
    record classes, 271
Transkeian Territories, 162, 186
    sessional papers, 186
translations from oriental languages, 152–153
transport, 21
    development, 137
    mechanical, 126
    planners, 152
    problems, 152
    surface, 324
Transport, Ministry of, 152
transportation, 5
Transvaal, 162, 180–182, 185–187, 292, 298
    Municipality of Johannesburg, 186, 187
    Municipality of Pretoria, 186, 187
    record classes, 187
    Volksraad, 186
Transvaal and Orange River Colony, 162, 187
    registers, 187
travel
    arrangements, 158
    bureau, 154
    claims, 360
    documents, 369, 370, 384, 394
        see also passports; visas
    expenses, 359, 361
    payments, 360, 361
    in UK, 361
Treadwell, Charles James, 94
Treasury, 4, 25, 26, 28, 36, 115, 117, 421, 422, 424
    control, 359–361
    investigations and report on Colonial Office organization (1949), 19, 46, 59, 348
    Organization and Methods (O&M) Unit, xiv, 19, 46, 59
    responsibilities transferred to Ministry of Overseas Development, 8
    Second World War co-operation with Dominions Office, 27
treaties
    bilateral, 352
    and conventions, 168, 336, 352
    registration of, 370, 393
treatment of offenders, 112, 338, 342
Treatment of Offenders in the Colonies, Advisory Committee on, 110, 112
treatment of persons and property, 410
trees, identification of, 138
Trengganu *see* Terengganu
Trevelyan-Northcote Committee (Committee of Inquiry into Public Offices) (1848–1849), 34, 39
trials, 31
Trinidad, 4, 136, 163, 235, 245, 255–257, 292, 301, 302, 379, 397, 406
    funds for posts in, 361
    Information Office, 334, 335
    record classes, 256
    relations with, 367
    see also Tobago; West Indies
Trinidad and Tobago, 256

Tripoli, 263
Tristan da Cunha, 6, 7, 76, 163, 167, 225, 280, 293, 300–302, 304, 306–308
    responsibility of Foreign Office, 7
    see also St Helena
Tropical African Service courses at Oxford and Cambridge Universities, 15
Tropical African Service personal files model for reorganization of registration, 41, 42
Tropical Agricultural College Committee, 157
tropical agriculture, 143, 157
    adviser on, 18
Tropical Building Section Head and Housing Adviser, 105, 106
tropical crops research, 234
tropical diseases, 119, 134–135, 146
    research, 114
Tropical Diseases Bulletin, 135
tropical hygiene, 146, 148
tropical liaison officer, 106
tropical medicine, 146, 148
Tropical Medicine Research Board, 110, 114, 117, 127
Tropical Pesticides Research Committee, 110, 127
Tropical Pesticides Research Headquarters and Information Unit, 126, 130, 155–156
Tropical Pesticides Research Unit, 126
Tropical Products Institute, 8, 130, 155, 156, 341–342
Tropical Products Institute Advisory Committee, 156
Tropical Products Institute Steering Committee, 118, 156
Tropical Science, 156
tropical soils, adviser on, 104–107
Tropical Stored Products Centre, 126
trusteeship, 336, 337
Trusteeship Council *see* United Nations Organization
trusts, 390
Trypanosomiasis Panel, 127
trypanosomiasis, standing committee, 170
tsetse and trypanosomiasis, 127, 297, 341, 342
Tsetse Fly and Trypanosomiasis Committee, 109, 127
tuberculosis, consultant on, 104
Tunis, 263
Turkey
    administers Cyprus, 264
    empire, parts mandated to Britain, 6, 10
    foreign affairs, 392, 395, 396
    Jordan captured from 271
    Palestine captured from, 270
    sovereignty over Mesopotamia, 269
    see also Ottoman Empire
Turks Islands, 256, 293, 301
Turks and Caicos Islands, 163, 237, 245, 247, 256–257, 303, 397
    record classes, 257
    see also West Indies
Tuvalu, 164, 283, 284, 287
    see also Gilbert and Ellice Islands
Twist, Henry Aloysius, 90–92
typhus, 117

Udell, Miss F N, 99–106
Uganda, 156, 163, 189, 191, 194–195, 293, 296, 297, 363, 364, 406
   funds for posts in, 361
   Information Office, 334, 335
   record classes, 194–195
   relations with, 363, 364
Uganda Britain Society, 130, 156
Uganda Railway, 194, 195
Uganda Railway Publicity Office, 129, 156
UK-Canada Continuing Committee, 375
UK-Malaya Defence Agreement, 381
UK-Nigeria defence agreement, 365
UK-US reciprocal aid, 413
UNESCO *see* United Nations Educational, Scientific and Cultural Organization
Unfederated Malay States *see* Malay States
UNICEF *see* United Nations International Children in Emergency Fund
uniforms, 346, 368, 369, 393
Union of South Africa *see* South Africa, Union of
Union of Soviet Socialist Republics (USSR), 358, 392
   and Eastern Europe, defence matters, 372
   economic policy overseas, 376–378
   foreign affairs, 396
   and satellites, 392, 396
   Soviet section of Eastern European and Soviet registry, 60
   see also Russia
United Arab Republic (UAR), xv, 358, 392
United Irish League, 259
United Kingdom (UK)
   ambassador to Dublin, 394
   bases in Commonwealth countries, 372, 373
   citizens in Commonwealth countries, 382
   commissioner for South-East Asia, 217
   delegation to United Nations, 336, 337
   financial and development policies, 377
   High Commission (UKHC), xv, 358
      see also high commissioners
   member of Commonwealth Telecommunications Board, 123
   member of Imperial Communications Advisory Committee, 121
   mission, New York, 337, 338
   National Commission for UNESCO, 148
   prime minister, 145
   professions in Commonwealth countries, 382–384
United Nations Departments *see* Commonwealth Relations Office Departments
United Nations (Economic and Social) Department, 419
United Nations Educational, Scientific and Cultural Organization (UNESCO), xv, 120, 146, 318, 324, 342, 358, 387–390, 396
United Nations and General Africa Department *see* Commonwealth Relations Office Departments
United Nations International Children in Emergency Fund (UNICEF), xv, 324, 336, 342, 343
United Nations Organization (UNO), xv, 183, 324, 326, 336, 358, 410
   charter revision, 396
   Children's Fund, 343
   Commission on Trade and Development, 328, 329
   Committee of Twenty-Four, 363
   conference, San Francisco (1940s), 185
   Conference on trade and development (1965), 328, 378
   constitution and organization, 363, 397
   economic activities, 326, 329
   economic and social questions, 316
   Freedom from Hunger Campaign, 376, 377
   General Assembly, 185, 396
      economic and social committees, 363, 397
      Fourth Committee, 338
      Legal Committee, 397
      Political and Budgetary Committees, 363, 397
      Trusteeship Committee, 363, 397
   interest in non-self-governing territories, 363, 397
   papers on undeveloped territories, 374
   political questions, 396
   registration of agreements, Commonwealth Countries and Irish Republic, 393
   Social Commission, 342
   special fund, 374
   specialized agencies, 8, 363, 392, 397
   technical assistance, 326, 374
   Trusteeship Council, 318, 363, 396, 397
   trusteeship system, 197, 336, 337
   UK delegation to, 336, 337
   see also Economic and Social Council; Food and Agriculture Organization
United Nations (Political) Department, 419
United Nations Relief and Rehabilitation Administration (UNRRA), xv, 324, 336, 413
United States of America (USA), 66, 185, 358, 366
   acquires St Croix, 251
   acquires St Thomas, 253
   aid, US, 326, 378
   appoints ambassador to Ottawa (1928), 25
   bases, 406
      Pacific dependencies, 307
      West Indies, 235, 302
   boundary, 272
   claims to Phoenix Islands, 284
   defence matters, 371, 372
   economic relations with, 326
   foreign affairs, 396
   foreign economic policy, 329
   government member of Caribbean Commission, 235
   investment guarantees, 329
   Lend-Lease Act (1941), 136
   logistic support for Commonwealth forces in Korea, 375
   relations with, 367, 392
US-UK Economic Co-operation Agreement, 410
Universal Postal Union (UPU), xv, 324, 325, 358, 367, 385
universities
   home, 117, 119, 131, 132, 146, 147, 151
   liaison with, 132, 386–389

overseas, 119, 146, 147, 157
representatives of, 150
research in, 155
Universities Bureau of the British Empire, 129, 132, 156
Universities Mission to Central Africa (Anglican), 178
University Secondment, Committee for, 110, 119
UNO *see* United Nations Organization
UNRRA *see* United Nations Relief and Rehabilitation Administration
Upper Volta, 366
Utrecht, Treaty of (1713), 264, 267
Uvarov, Sir Boris (Petrovitch), 131

validity of contract before and after Japanese occupation (1947–1949), 414
Valueless Colonial Office Documents, Report of the Committee, 62–63, 68
Van Diemen's Land *see* Tasmania
Vancouver Island, 164, 273, 274, 280, 293, 305
record classes, 280
Vanuatu, 164, 285, 287
see also New Hebrides
vegetable oils, 327, 328, 340, 376
vegetables, 327, 339, 340
Venereal Disease Sub-committee of the Colonial Advisory Medical Committee, 109, 127
Venice
held Cyprus, 264
held Ionian Islands, 265
Vermont, records sub-division, 236
Vernon, James William, 82–85
Vernon, Roland Venables, 77, 78
Versailles, Treaty of (1919), 184
veterinary interests, 117
veterinary policy, 340, 413, 414
veterinary questions, 339, 340
see also agricultural and veterinary matters
veterinary reciprocity, 382
veterinary research, 13, 119, 341
veterinary science, 113
veterinary service, 12, 15, 388
vice-chancellors and principals of the universities of the UK, committee of, 132
Vichy administration, 317
Victoria, 163, 226–228, 233, 293, 305, 306, 421
record classes, 34, 233
Victoria, Queen, Jubilee: Imperial Institute, 138
Vienna consular convention, 385
Vietnam, Commonwealth relations with, 381
Vile, R J, 82–85
Villiers, George Herbert Hyde, 6th Earl of Clarendon, 86
Virgin Islands *see* British Virgin Islands; St Croix; St Thomas
Virginia Company, 240
Virginia, records sub-division, 236
visas, 368–370, 384, 385, 394
see also travel documents; passports
visiting forces, 325
legislation, 371
visits, 361, 382, 387, 388, 393
visits of warships, 325, 332

Visual Instruction Committee, 129, 157
visual material, 386–388
vocational training, 344
Volksraad, Transvaal, 186
Volta River Project, 365
voluntary agencies, co-operation with, 112
voluntary associations, liaison with, 343, 344
voluntary organizations, officials, 157
Voluntary Service Overseas (VSO), xv, 130, 157, 359
liaison with, 390
voyages, 153

wages, 359–361
see also salaries
Wakeley, Leonard John Dean, 91
Walker, Sir (Charles) Michael, (C M), 89, 90
Walker, Sir Hubert Edmund, 104
Walker, Robert, 92, 94
wall sheets, 390
Wallace, John Henry, 81
Wallace, Walter Ian James, 76, 77, 81–85
Walsh Atkins, Leonard Brian, 89, 93
Walvis Bay, 185
war aims, 16
war book questions, 371–373
War Cabinet, 27, 414
War and Colonial Department, 4–5, 32–33, 53
see also Secretaries of State for War and the Colonies
war crimes, 331, 332
war damage, 315, 316, 414
War Department, 40, 263
records, 40
war graves, 332, 333, 338
war histories, 325, 368
war injury claims, 382, 383
war legislation, 371–373
war loans, 315, 316, 411
war memorials, 332, 333
war and military pensions policy, 325
War Office, 36, 223
defence colonies records, Second World War, 44
Directorate of Civil Aviation, Malayan Planning Unit (1943), 17
secondment of military liaison officers concerned with West Africa Frontier Force, 10
war pensions, 332, 333, 338
war personal injuries, 332
war production and supply, 16
war risk insurance, 414
war service, 332, 333
enquiries, 333, 338
war trade correspondence, 407, 414
War Transport, Ministry of, 27
wartime evacuees, 382, 383
wartime food supplies, adviser on, 96, 98, 99
wartime trade, 18
Ward, William Ernest Frank, 99–103
warrants, 31, 36
stamps on, 165
Washington
British Colonial Supply Mission at, 18, 136, 315, 321

colonial attaché, 336, 337
minister resident at, 17
water power schemes, 339
water supplies, 339
water undertakings, 137
Watson Commission (Gold Coast) (1948), 200
Watson, Sir (Noel) Duncan, (N D), 81–85, 89
Watt, Ian Buchanan, 83–85, 92
Wearing, John Frederick, 94
Webb, Sir (Ambrose) Henry, 99
Webb, Sidney James, 1st Baron Passfield, 71, 86
Webber, Fernley Douglas, 81–85
Wei-Hai-Wei, 163, 206, 223, 293, 308
   record classes, 223
weights and measures, 377, 382, 383
welfare, 136, 344, 406
Welfare of Colonial Peoples in the United Kingdom, Advisory Committee on, 109, 112
Welfare of Colonial Students in the United Kingdom, Consultative Committee on, 110, 123–124
Welfare Department *see* Colonial Office Subject Departments
Welfare and Students Departments *see* Colonial Office Subject Departments
Wellesley Province, 213, 218, 221
West Africa, 163, 196–197, 300, 406
   acquisition of new territories, 5
   economic adviser for, 196, 197
   foreign states in, 365, 366
   ministerial visits from, 366
   record classes, 47–48, 196–197
   regions, 163, 196–200
   regional governors conferences in, 17, 196
   resident minister, 17, 196, 197
   Spanish and Portuguese territories in, 366
West Africa/African Departments *see* Colonial Office Geographical Departments; Commonwealth Relations Office Departments
West Africa Committee, 130, 157, 197
West Africa Frontier Force (WAFF), xv, 10, 16, 41, 43, 73, 163, 191, 206, 314
   record classes, 206
West Africa Research Office, 365
West African Council, 197, 300
West African Council for Medical Research, 117
West African Currency Board, 129, 157, 197
   files, 197
West African Governors' Conference, 196
West African Institute of Social and Economic Research, 115
West African Inter-Territorial Council/Conference, 197, 300
West African and Mediterranean Department *see* Colonial Office Geographical Departments
West African Produce Control Board, 17, 339, 409
West African Settlements, 198, 201, 204
West and Central Africa Department, 419
West and General Africa Departments *see* Commonwealth Relations Office Departments
West India Committee, 39, 128, 157
West Indian 'A' and 'B' Departments, 419

West Indian Club Ltd, 129, 158
West Indian Confidential Print series, 52, 235
West Indian Department *see* Colonial Office Geographical Departments
West Indian and Eastern Department *see* Colonial Office Geographical Departments
West Indian Encumbered Estates Commission, 234, 235
West Indian and Hong Kong Department *see* Colonial Office Geographical Departments
West Indian sugar, protective tariff on, 5
West Indies, 4, 5, 54, 125, 165, 234–236, 369, 406
   ancient monuments and records, 302, 303
   communities and labour abroad, 302, 303
   defence and security, 302
   Development and Welfare Organization, 18, 48, 235, 302
   economic questions, 397
   economic relations with Canada, 375
   funds for posts in, 361
   Imperial Department of Agriculture, 234, 235
   Interim Commission, 397
   international relations, 302
   Land and Emigration Commission, 236, 349
   United States bases, West Indies, 48, 235, 302
   see also Royal Commission on the West Indies; *and under individual islands*
West Indies Departments *see* Commonwealth Relations Office Departments
West Indies, Federation of the, 136, 163, 235, 237–239, 244–247, 250, 253, 256, 257, 302, 351, 369
   record classes, 245
West Indies, University of the, 302, 367, 397
   Faculty of Agriculture, 156
West New Jersey Society (chartered company), 53
western Asia, 153
Western Australia, 10, 163, 226, 227, 232–234, 305–307
   record classes, 234
Western Christian civilization, 149
Western civilization, impact on African societies, 146
Western Departments *see* Commonwealth Relations Office Departments
Western Economic Departments *see* Commonwealth Relations Office Departments
Western European colonial forces, economic liaison with, 329
Western European Union (WEU), xv, 358, 392, 396
Western and Middle East Department *see* Commonwealth Relations Office Departments
Western Organizations, 372, 392
Western Organizations and Co-ordination Department, 419
Western Pacific, 164, 280–287, 293, 298, 306, 307, 406
   record classes, 47–48
Western Pacific High Commission, 6, 7, 164, 167, 206, 280–286, 305–308
   Confidential Print series, 52, 281
   Dominions Division administration, 6

exceptional colonies registration arrangements, 35
record classes, 281
see also British Solomon Islands Protectorate; Gilbert and Ellice Islands; New Hebrides; Pitcairn Islands; Tonga
Western Samoa, 164, 287
record classes, 287
Western Union, economic aspects, 329
Western and United Nations Department see Commonwealth Relations Office Departments
whaling see fisheries
wheat trade, 328, 375
Whiskard, Sir Geoffrey Granville, (G G), 87
White, Mrs Eirene, 72
White Papers, 67, 388
Whitehead, George Sydney, 94
Whitley Council see Colonial Office, shared services with Dominions Office; Dominions Office
Whitley, S P, 86, 92
Whitlock, William Charles, 93
Whittle, R A, 80–93
Wiggins, William Denison Clare, 106
Willbourn, E S, 99
William III, king of England, 3
Williams, Douglas, 85, 86
Williams, F H, 102, 105, 106
Williams, John Basil, 74, 75, 79, 80
Williams, John Robert, 94
Williams, Owen Gwyn Revell, 77–80
Williamson, Thomas Broadwood, 81–85
Willink Commission (Commission on Minority Groups in Nigeria), 203
Willoughby, William, 6th Baron Willoughby of Parham, 254
wills, 385
Wilson, G M, 95
Wilson, Brigadier-General Sir Samuel Herbert, 12, 72
Windham, W, 70
Windsor-Clive, Ivor Miles, 2nd Earl of Plymouth, 72, 86
Windward Islands, 163, 235, 245, 248, 253, 255, 257–258, 293, 301–303
Federation, 244, 245, 252, 253, 257
governor of, 246, 252, 253, 257
record classes, 258
see also Barbados; Dominica; Grenada; St Lucia; St Vincent; Tobago
wines, spirits, 328, 339, 340
see also liquor traffic
Wingfield, Sir Edward, 72
Winnipeg, lake, 276
wireless matters, 331
see also cable and wireless

Wiseman, Robert Arthur, 87
Wodehouse, John, 1st Earl of Kimberley, 70
woman educational adviser, 103–106
women
commission on status of, 338, 397
equality with men, 137
organizations, 158
settlers, 158
Women Speakers for the Commonwealth, 130, 158
Women's Advisory Council on Indian Affairs, 158
Women's Corona Club, 158
Women's Corona Society, 129, 158
Women's Council, the, 129, 158
Bulletin, 158
Women's Migration and Overseas Appointments Society, 129, 158
Wood, Edmund Frederick Lindley, (E F L), 1st Earl of Halifax, 72
wool, trade, 375, 376, 379
workmen's compensation, 328, 342, 343
world communications, 385
World Health Organization (WHO), xv, 155, 324, 342, 358, 363, 396, 397
World Meteorological Organization (WMO), xv, 324, 325, 358, 367
World Power Conference, 328, 329, 414
World War II see Second World War
worm-related diseases see helminthiasis
Worthington, Edgar Barton, 105, 106

Yam Tuan of Sri Menati, in Negri Sembilan, 216
Yearbooks of the Commonwealth, 66
Yemen, South, Southern, 268–269
Young, Major Sir Hubert Winthrop, 77
youth clubs, 157
youth organizations, 383, 386–388, 390
youth services, 124
Yugoslavia, 392
Yukon Territory, 273

Zakinthos, 265
Zambia, 162, 188, 364
see also Rhodesia, Northern
Zambia Department see Commonwealth Relations Office Departments
Zanzibar, 163, 189, 192, 195–196, 263, 293, 296, 297, 363, 364, 406
Information Office, 335
record classes, 195–196
see also Tanzania
Zimbabwe, 162, 184, 188
national archives of, 182
see also Rhodesia, Southern
Zulu, Zululand, 162, 171, 173, 188–189, 293, 298
Chaka, 173
record classes, 188–189
Zurich Agreement on Cyprus, 264